AutoCAD 2025 3D For Beginners

Tutorial Books

For resource files, contact us at
Online.books999@gmail.com

Table of Contents

Introduction

Welcome to *AutoCAD 2025 3D For Beginners* book. This book is written to assist students, designers, and engineering professionals in designing 3D models. It covers the essential features and functionalities of AutoCAD using relevant tutorials and exercises.

Chapter 1: Getting Started with AutoCAD 3D

Introduction to AutoCAD

AutoCAD is a legendary software used to create 2D drawings and 3D Models. It enables you to convert 2D drawings into a 3D model rapidly. In addition to that, you can manipulate existing geometry easily. It makes it quick and simple for non-expert or casual CAD users to create new models and modify existing models.

System requirements

The following are system requirements for running AutoCAD smoothly on your system.

- 64-bit Microsoft® Windows® 11 and Windows 10 version 1809 or above.
- CPU Type:
    - Basic: 2.5 to 2.9 gigahertz (GHz)
    - Recommended: 3+ GHz processor (base), 4+ GHz (turbo)
- 8 GB of RAM (32 GB Recommended).
- Resolution 1920 x 1080 or higher recommended with True Color.
- Resolutions up to 3840 x 2160 supported on Windows 10, 64 bit systems (with capable display card) for High Resolution & 4K Displays.
- 10 GB of free space for installation.
- Google Chrome Browser.
- .NET Framework Version 8

Starting AutoCAD 2025

To start **AutoCAD 2025**, double-click the **AutoCAD 2025** icon on your Desktop (or) click **Start > All apps > AutoCAD 2025 > AutoCAD 2025**.

3D Modeling Workspaces in AutoCAD

In AutoCAD, there are separate workspaces created to work on 3D models. In these workspaces, the tools are organized into ribbon tabs, menus, toolbars, and palettes to perform a specific task in 3D Modeling. You can activate these workspaces by using the **Workspace** drop-down located on the **Quick Access Toolbar**, or by using the **Workspace Switching** menu on the status bar. You can also start an AutoCAD session directly in the 3D Modeling workspace using the **acad3D.dwt, acadiso3D.dwt, acad -Named Plot Styles3D**, or **acadISO-Named Plot Styles3D** templates.

*Tip: If the **Workspace** drop-down is not displayed at the top left corner, click the down arrow next to the Quick Access Toolbar. Next, select **Workspace** from the drop-down; the **Workspace** drop-down will be visible on the Quick Access Toolbar.*

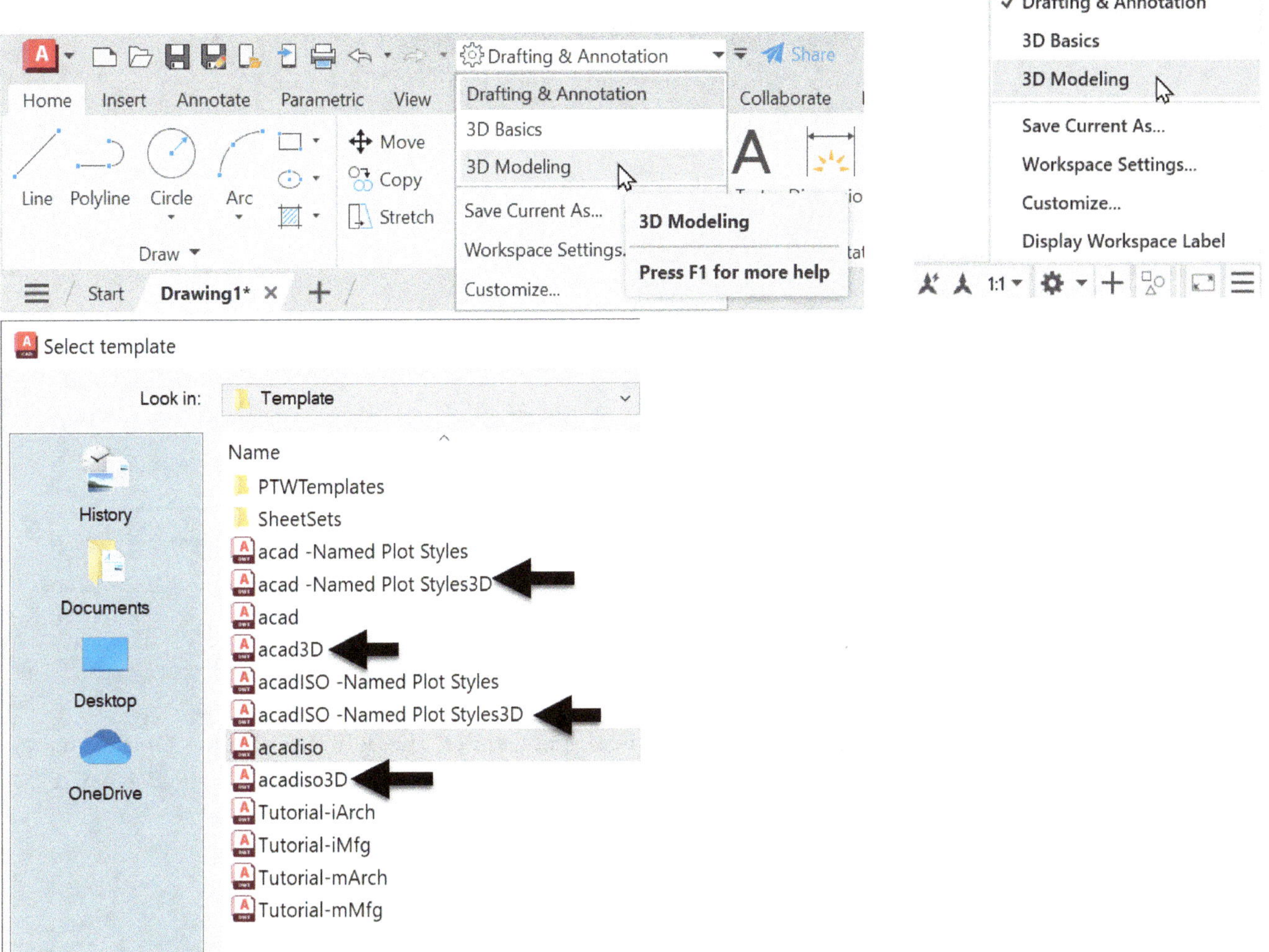

There are two workspaces of 3D Modeling: **3D Basics** and **3D Modeling**. The **3D Basics** workspace has commonly used tools, whereas the **3D Modeling** workspace includes all the tools required for creating 3D models.

The 3D Modeling Workspace

Activating the **3D Modeling** workspace either using the template or from the **Workspace** drop-down displays the screen as shown below. It contains the ribbon and tools related to 3D Modeling. By default, the **Home** tab is activated in the ribbon. From this tab, you can access the tools for creating and editing solids and meshes, modifying the model display, working with coordinate systems, sectioning 3D models, etc.

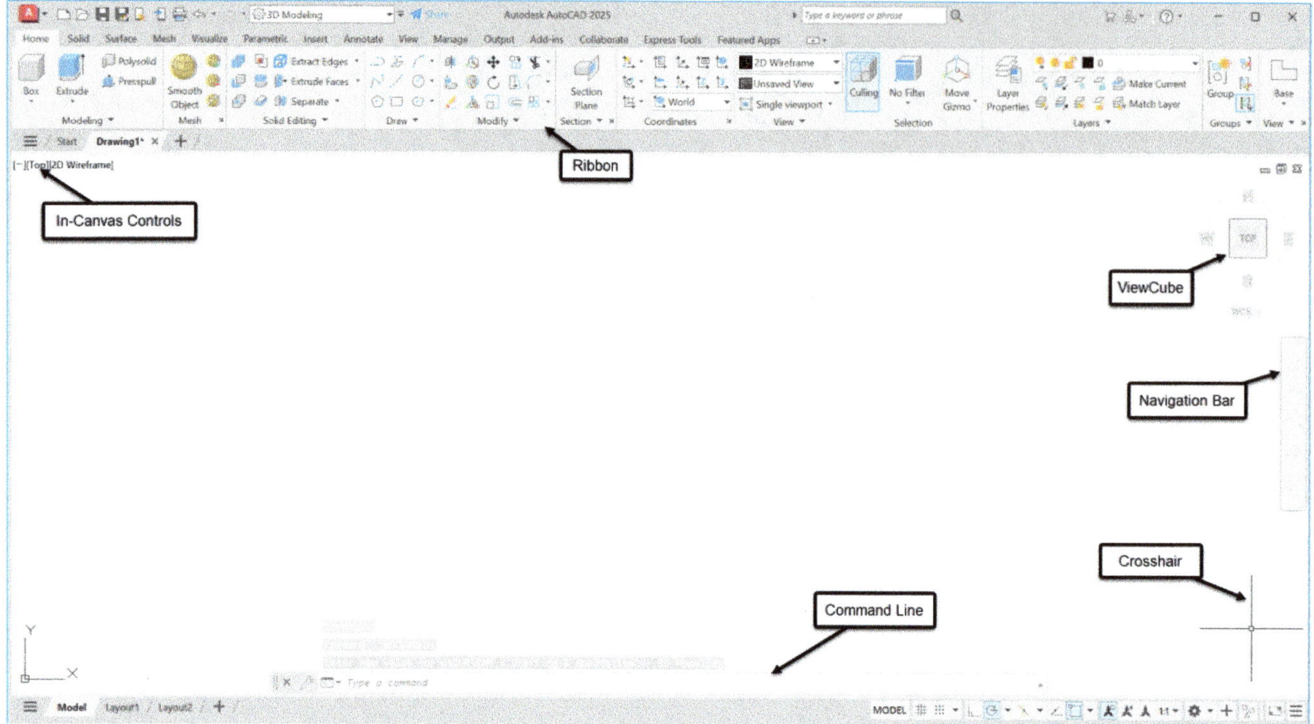

There are some additional tabs, such as **Solid**, **Surface**, **Mesh**, and **Render**. The **Solid** tab contains tools to create solid models; the **Surface** and **Mesh** tabs are used to create surface models and complex shapes; the **Visualize** tab is used for creating realistic images of solid and surface models.

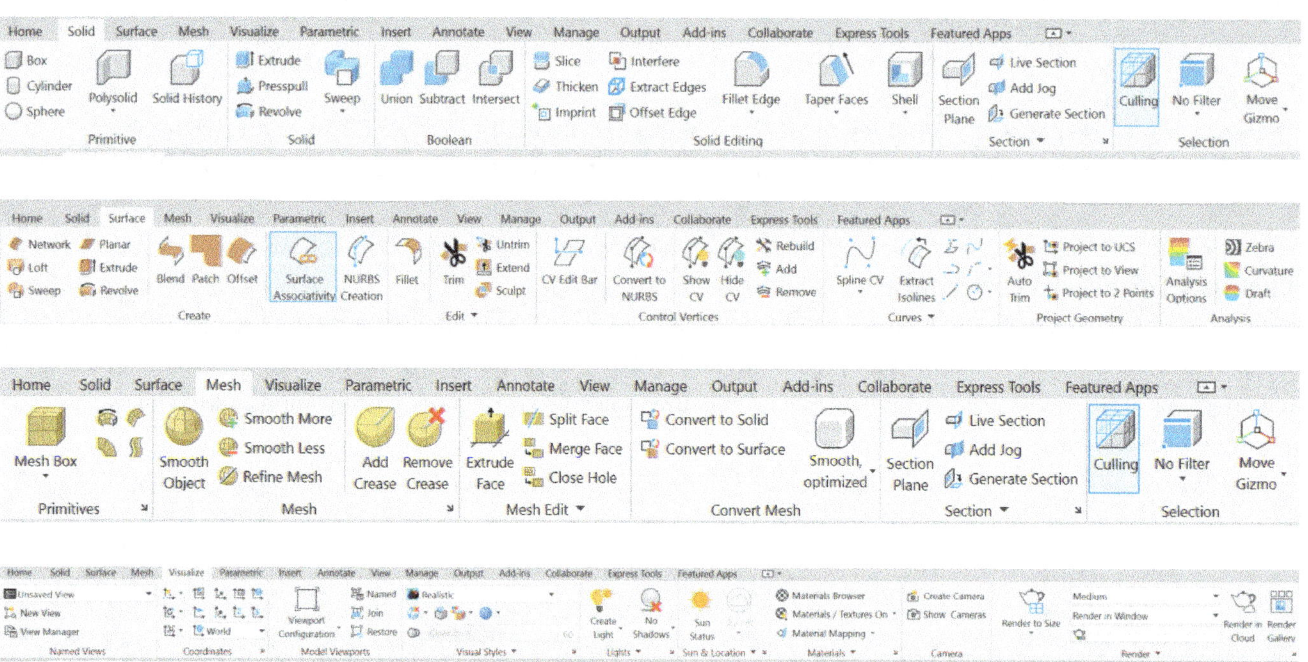

The **ViewCube** can be used to modify the view of the model quickly and easily. It is located at the top right corner of the graphics window. Using the ViewCube, you can switch between the standard and isometric views, rotate the model, switch to the **Home** view of the model, and create a new user coordinate system. You can also change the way the ViewCube functions by using the **ViewCube Settings** dialog. Right-click on the ViewCube, and then select the **ViewCube Settings** option; the **ViewCube Settings** dialog will be opened.

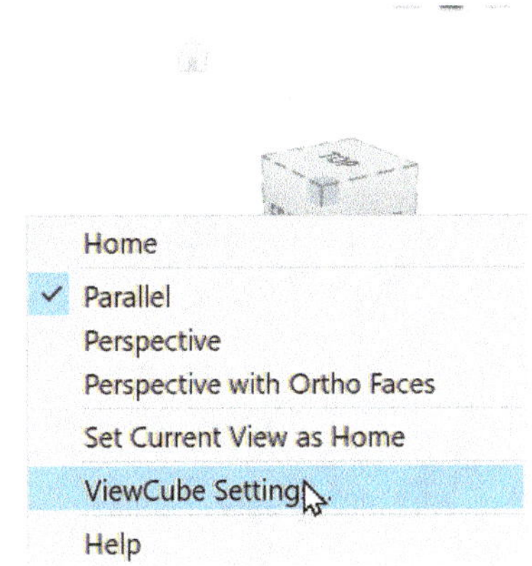

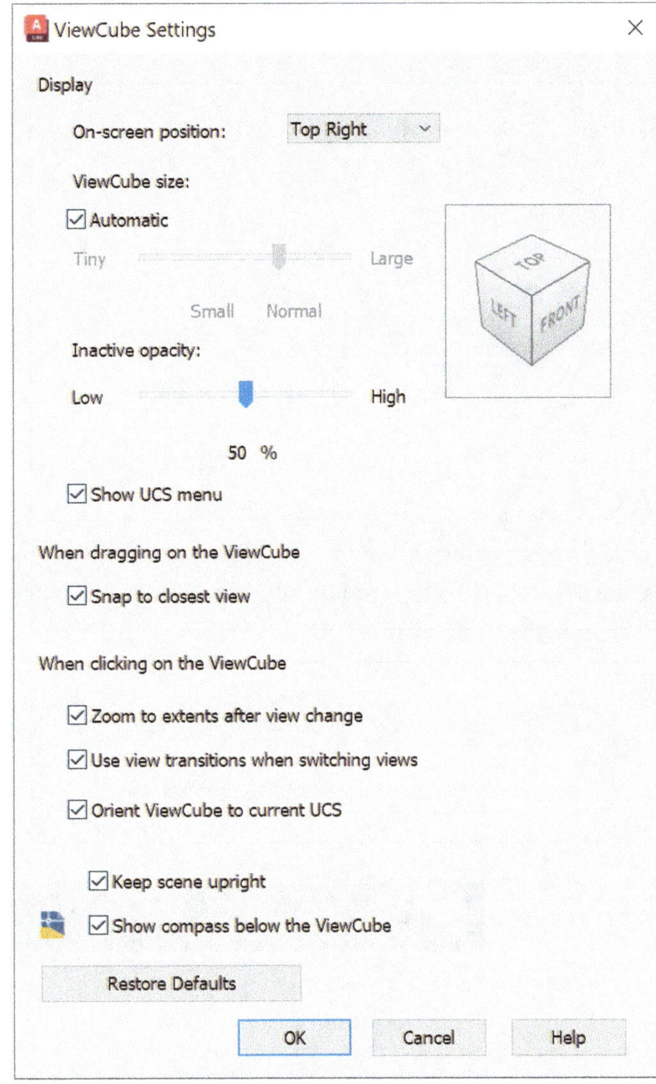

You can also modify the model view by using the In-canvas controls. In addition to that, you can also change the Visual Style of the model and control the display of other tools in the graphics window using the In-canvas controls.

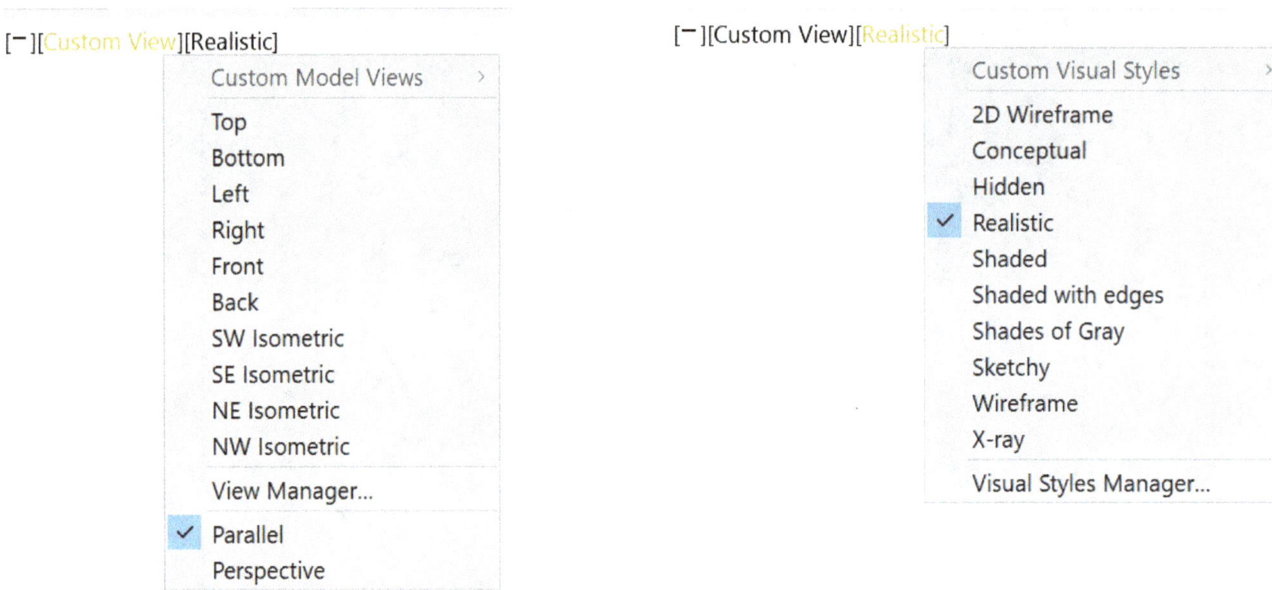

AutoCAD Help

Press F1 or type a keyword in the search bar located at the top right corner of the window to get help. On the **Autodesk AutoCAD 2025 –Help** window, click the **Find** option next to the topic; an animated arrow appears on the window showing the tool location.

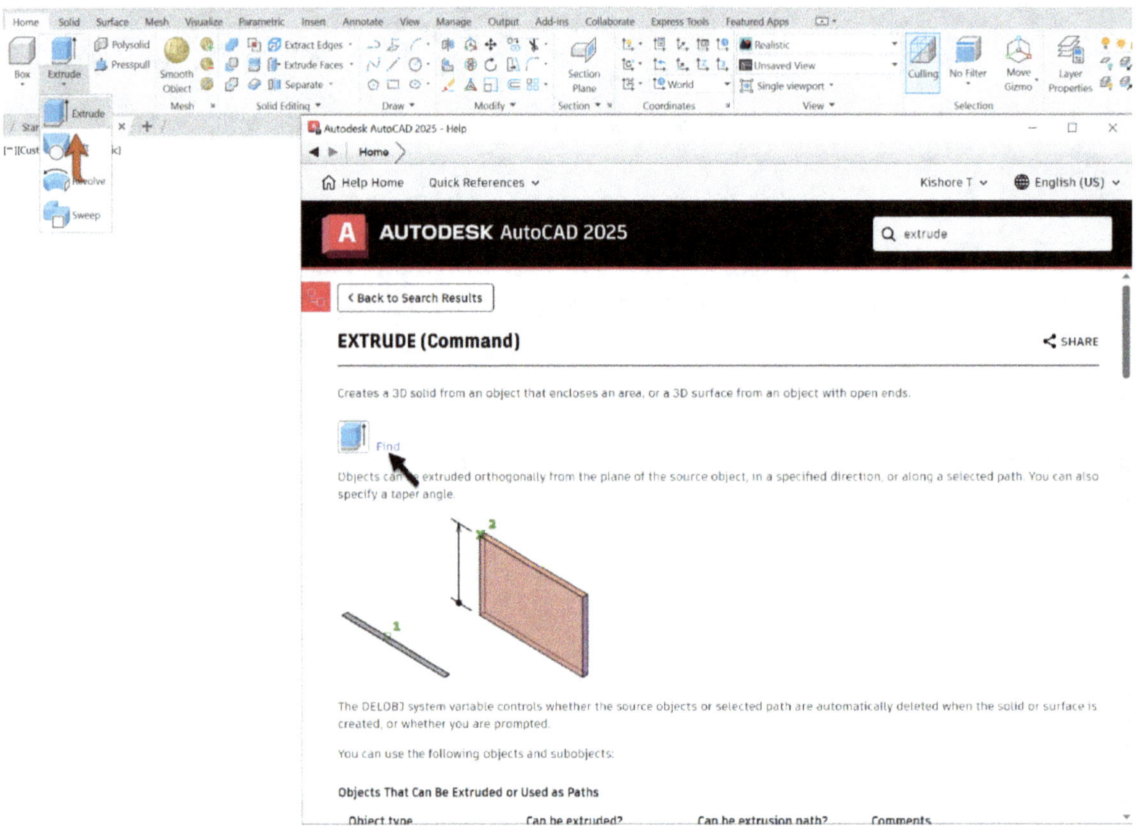

Chapter 2: Extrude and Revolve Features

This chapter covers the methods and commands to create extruded and revolved features. The topics covered in this chapter are:

- *Constructing Extruded features*
- *Constructing Revolved features*
- *Creating Polysolids*
- *Creating Boolean Operations*
- *Creating UCS*

Creating the Extruded Solid

Extrusion is the process of taking a two-dimensional profile and converting it into 3D by giving it some thickness. A simple example of this would be taking a circle and converting it into a cylinder. To create an Extruded solid, first, you need to have a 2D region. To create a closed region, first create a close drawingg using the drawing and editing tools available on the **Draw** and **Modify** panels of the **Home** ribbon tab. Next, expand the **Draw** panel and click the **Region** tool. Create a selection window across all the elements of the drawing, and then press ENTER.

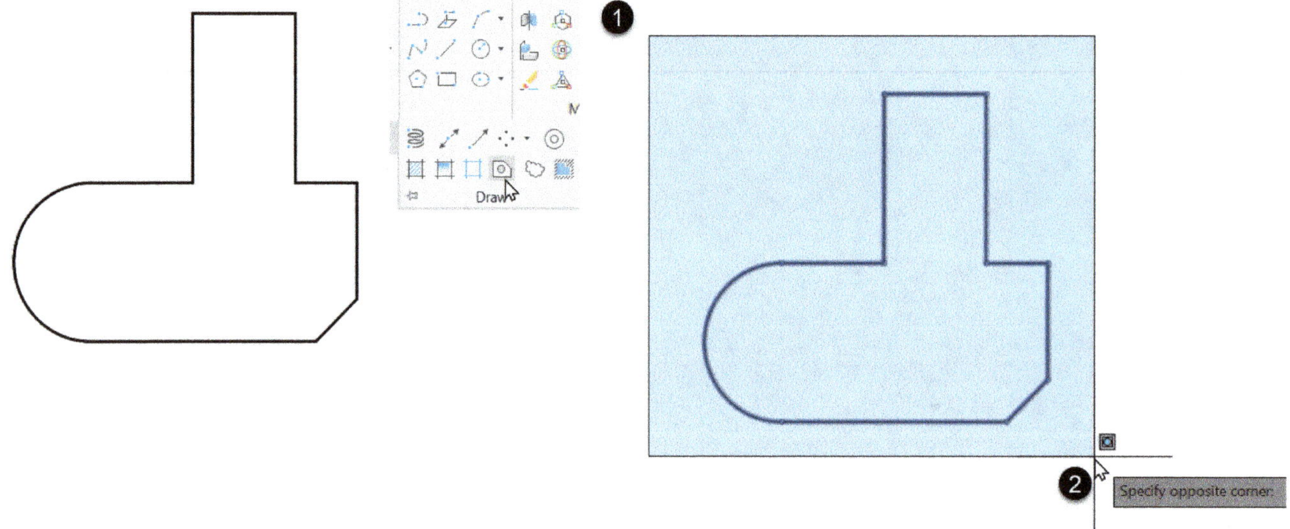

Activate the **Extrude** tool (on the ribbon, click **Home** tab > **Modeling** panel **> Extrude**). Click on the closed region and press ENTER. Next, move the pointer in the direction perpendicular to the closed region. Type-in the extrusion height and press ENTER.

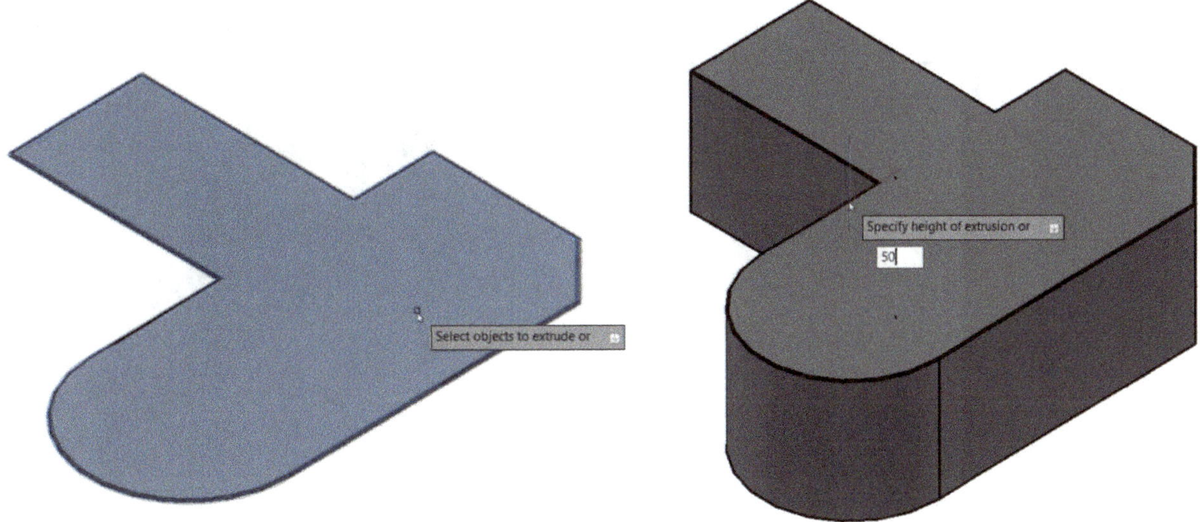

Direction

While creating an *Extruded* solid, AutoCAD adds material in the direction normal 2D region. If you want to manually define the direction in which the material will be added, then select the **Direction** option from the command line. Next, select two points from the graphics window.

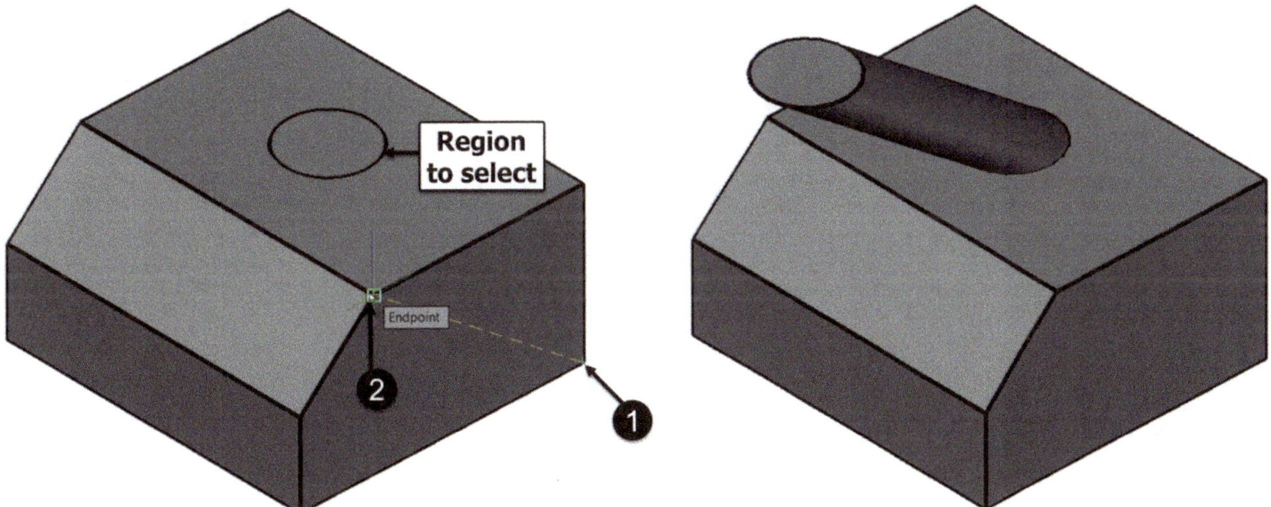

Path

The **Path** option allows you to extrude the region along a selected path. Activate the **Extrude** tool from the **Modeling** panel and select the region to be extruded. Next, press ENTER, select the **Path** option from the command line, and select the path from the graphics window; the region will be extruded along the selected path.

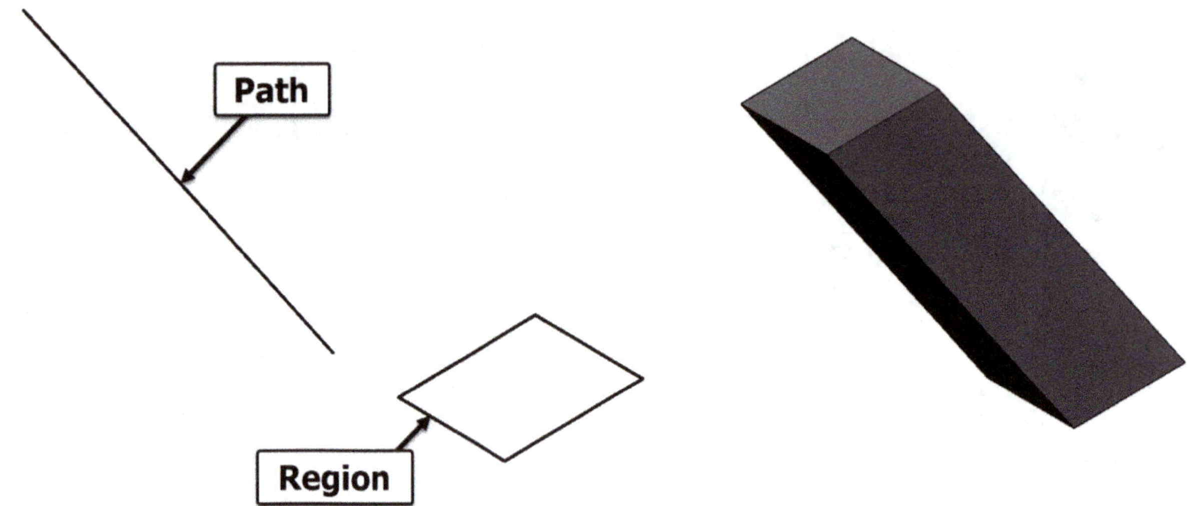

Taper angle

The **Taper angle** option will help you to apply a draft to the extrusion. Activate the **Extrude** tool from the **Modeling** panel and select the region to be extruded. Next, press ENTER and select the **Taper angle** option from the command line. Type the taper angle and press ENTER. Next, move the pointer upward or downward and click.

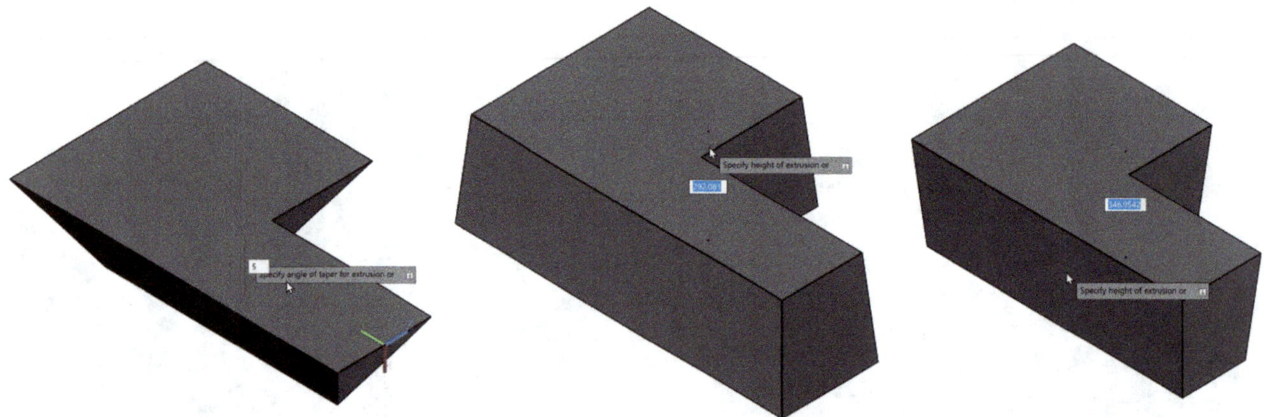

The Presspull tool

In AutoCAD, you can create multiple *Extrude* solids using a single drawing with internal loops in it. To do this, draw a sketch containing internal loops. Next, click **Home > Modeling** panel > **Presspull** on the ribbon. Click in the region of the sketch, as shown. Click and move the mouse pointer; the sketch extrudes. Click or type-in a value in the command line and press ENTER to specify the extrude height.

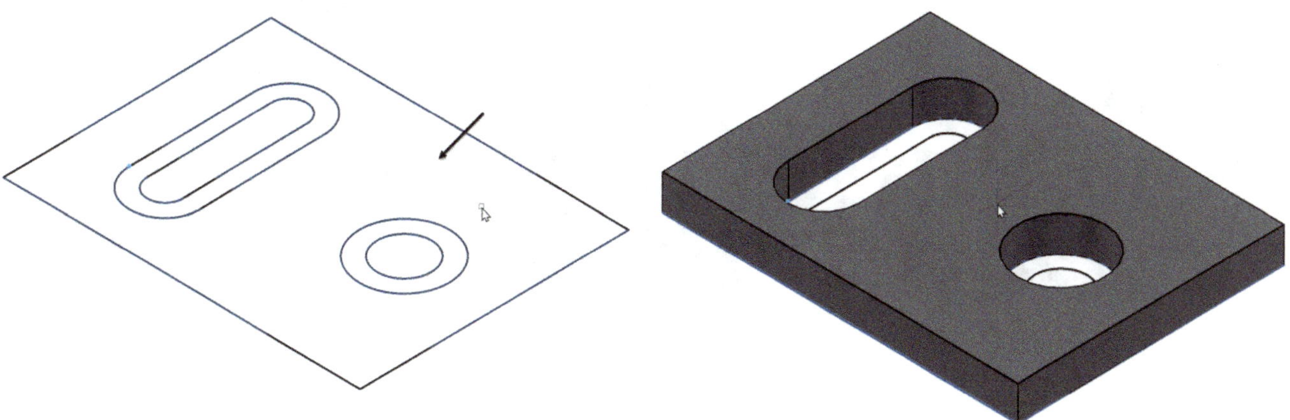

Click in the region, as shown. Next, move the pointer up to a height higher than the previous extrusion height.

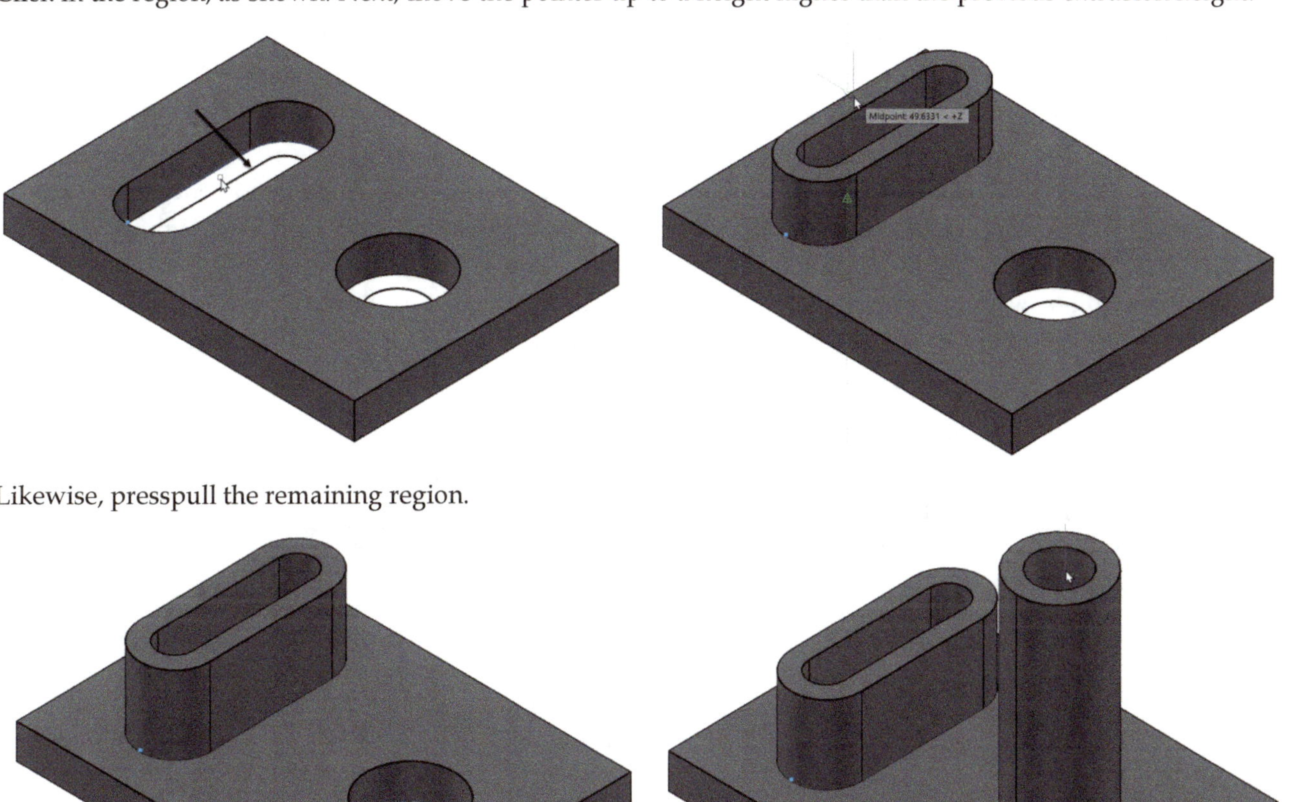

Likewise, presspull the remaining region.

Open Sketch Extrusion

AutoCAD helps you to add or remove material using an open sketch. It closes the profile by using the adjacent edges. Note that the endpoints of the sketch should touch the adjacent edges of the geometry. Activate the **Presspull** command, and then click inside the open profile. Move the pointer outside the existing geometry to add material to the existing geometry. Move the pointer in to the geometry to remove material from the existing geometry.

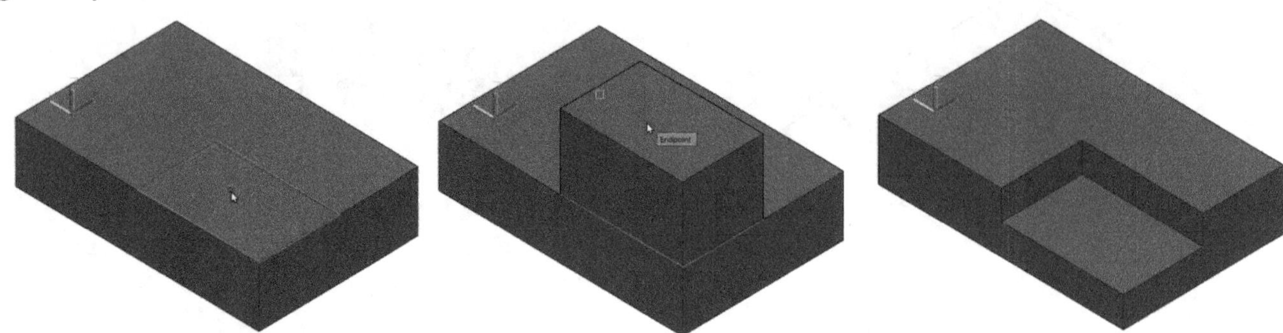

Polysolid

The **Polysolid** tool will help you to create a wall easily. On the ribbon, click **Home > Modeling > Polysolid** 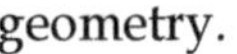 and select the **Height** option from the command line. Type-in the height value and press ENTER. Next, select the Width option from the command line, type-in the width value and press ENTER.

Click in the graphics window to specify the start point of the polysolid. Move the pointer and notice that a wall is attached to the pointer. You can turn ON the ORTHOMODE icon on the status bar to create a straight polysolid. Click to specify the end point of the polysolid; notice that another wall is attached to the pointer. Select the **Arc** option from the command line to switch to the arc mode. Move the pointer and click to create a curved wall tangent to the previous straight wall. Select the Line option from the command line to switch back to the line mode.

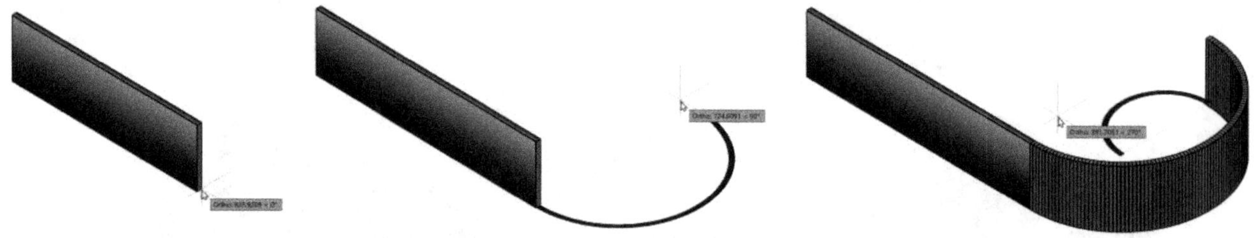

You can convert a drawing into a polysolid using the Object option. To do this, activate the **Polysolid** tool and select **Justify** option from the command line. Next, select anyone of the three options from the command line: Left, Center, or Right. The **Left** option creates the polysolid on the left side of the selected line, arc, spline, or polyline. The **Center** option creates the polysolid on both sides of the selected object. The **Right** option creates the polysolid on the right side of the selected object. After specifying the required justification option, select the **Object** option from the command line and select an object.

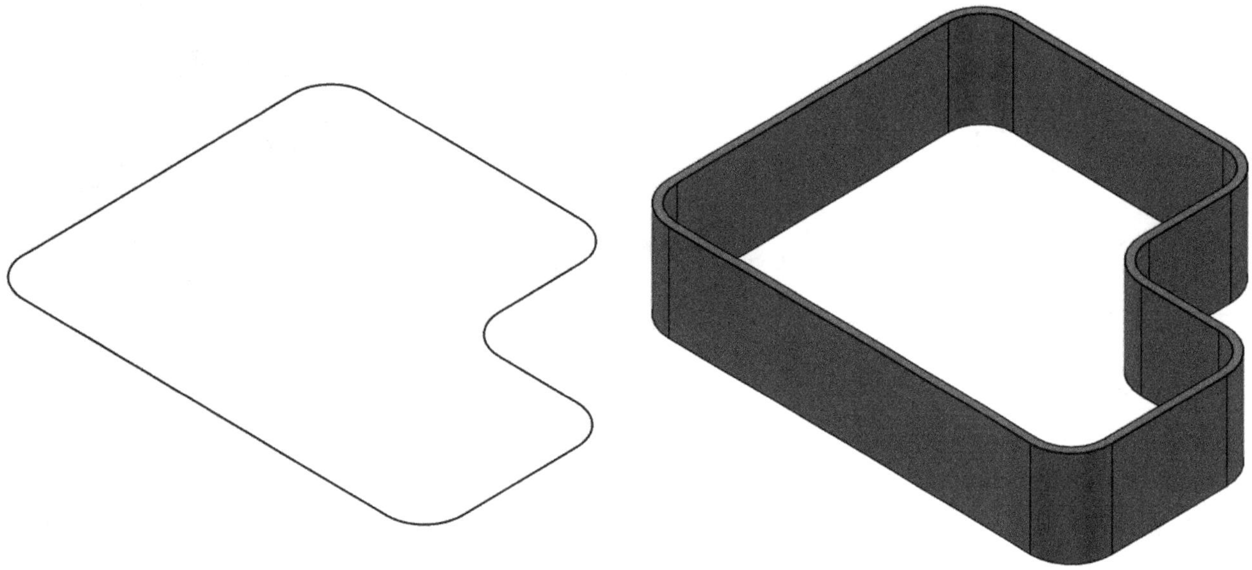

Creating the Revolved Solid

Revolving is the process of taking a two-dimensional profile and revolving it about a centerline to create a 3D geometry (axially symmetric shapes). While creating a sketch for the *Revolve* feature, it is important to think about the cross-sectional shape that will define the 3D geometry once it is revolved about an axis. For instance, the following geometry has a hole in the center. You can create it by subtracting a cylindrical solid from it. However, to make that hole a part of the *Revolved* solid, you need to draw the revolution axis at some distance from the profile.

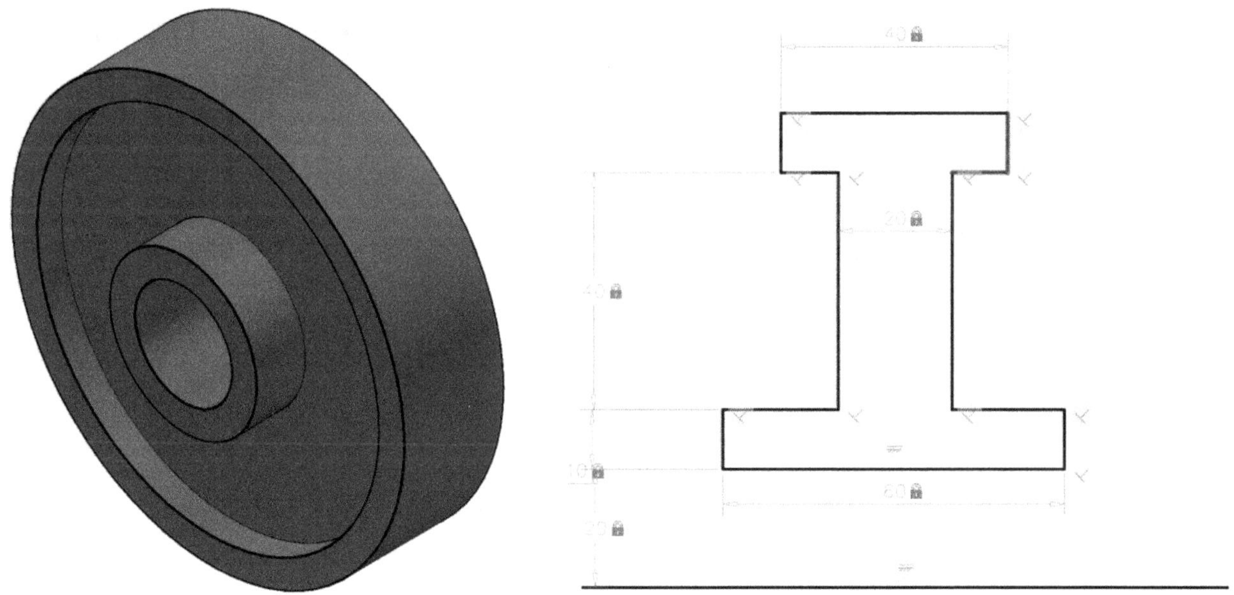

To create a *Revolved* solid, first, draw a revolve profile along with axis of revolution. Next, click **Home** tab > **Modeling panel > Solid** drop-down **> Revolve** on the ribbon. Select the revolved profile and press ENTER. Next, select the Object option from the command line and select the revolution axis. Type-in the revolution angle and press ENTER (or) simply press ENTER to create a full 360 degrees revolved solid.

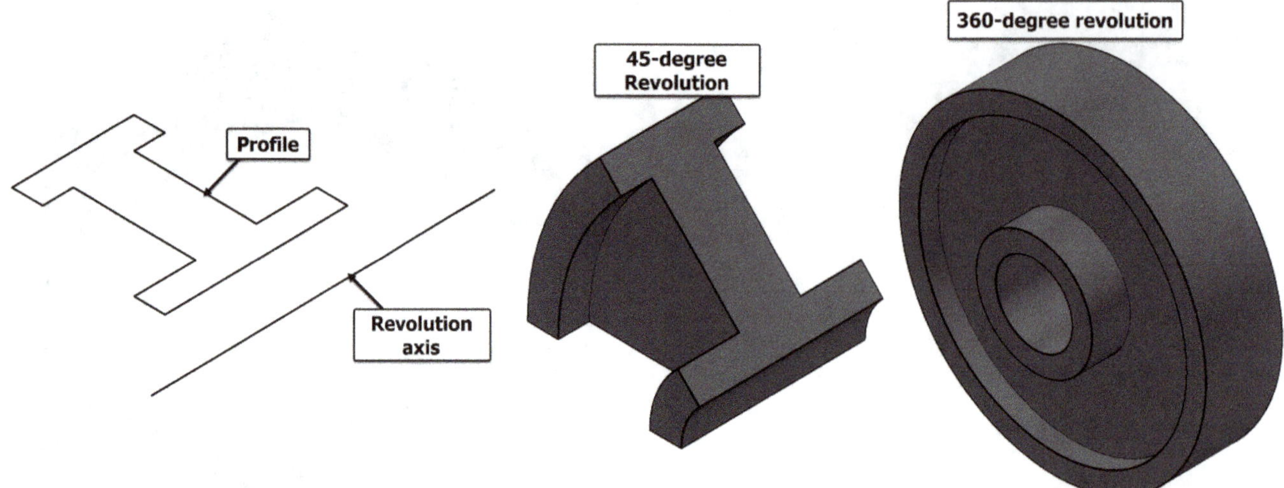

By default, the start point of the revolution is defined on the plane on which it is created. However, you can specify the start point from the which revolution will created. To do this, activate the Revolve tool and select the profile and press ENTER. Next, select the **Object** option from the command line and select the revolution axis. Select the **STart angle** option from command line, type an angle value and press ENTER. After specifying the start angle, type-in the angle of revolution and press ENTER.

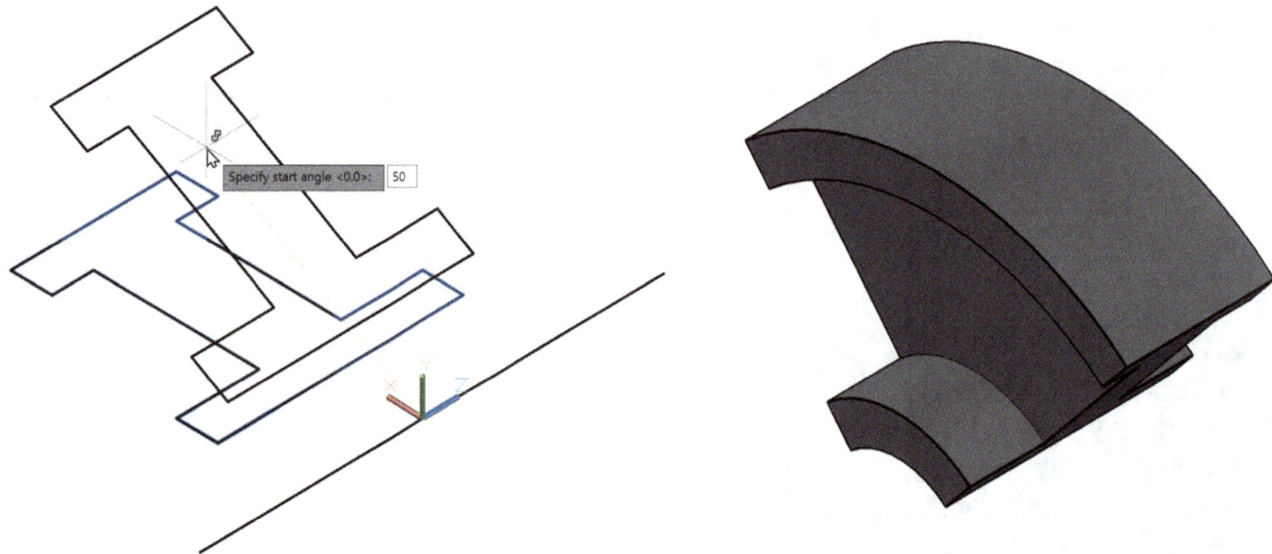

Creating Primitive Solids

You can create various primitive solids such as boxes, cylinders, spheres using the **Primitives** drop-down on the **Modeling** panel of the **Home** tab of the ribbon.

Box

On the ribbon, click **Home** tab > **Primitives** drop-down > **Box** . Next, click in the graphics window to specify the first corner of the box. Next, move the pointer and click to specify the opposite corner. Move the pointer upward or downward and click to specify the height of the box.

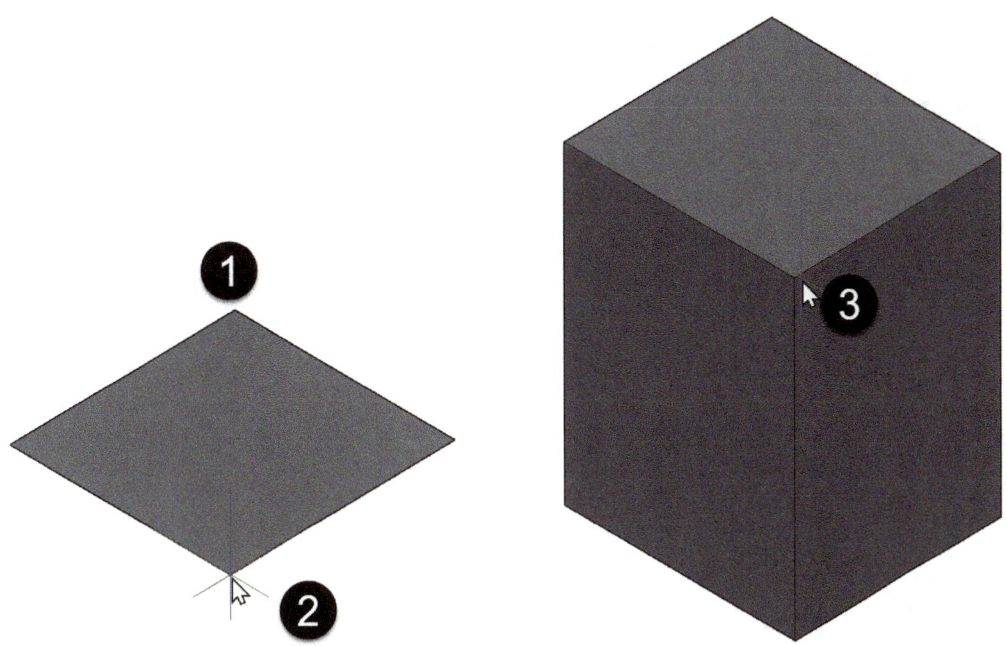

Create a Box by specifying the Center and corner points

Activate the Box tool and select the Center option from the command line. Next, click in the graphics window to specify the center point of the box. Move the pointer outward and click to specify the corner. Move the pointer in the perpendicular direction and click to specify the box height.

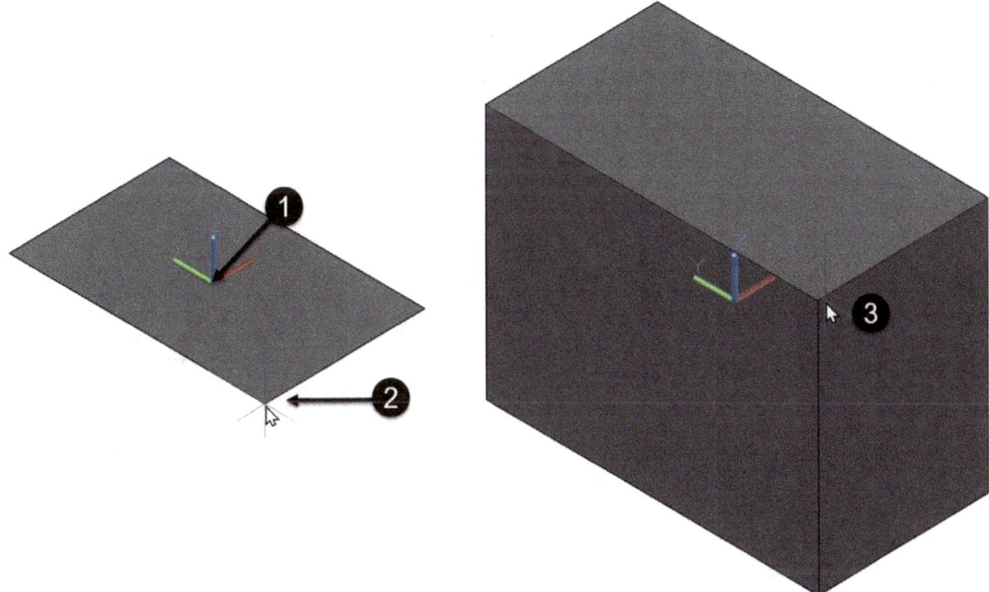

Create a Cube

Activate the Box tool and click to specify the first corner of the box. Next, select the Cube option from the command line. Move the pointer and click specify the length of one of the cube edges (or) type-in the length of the cube edge and press ENTER.

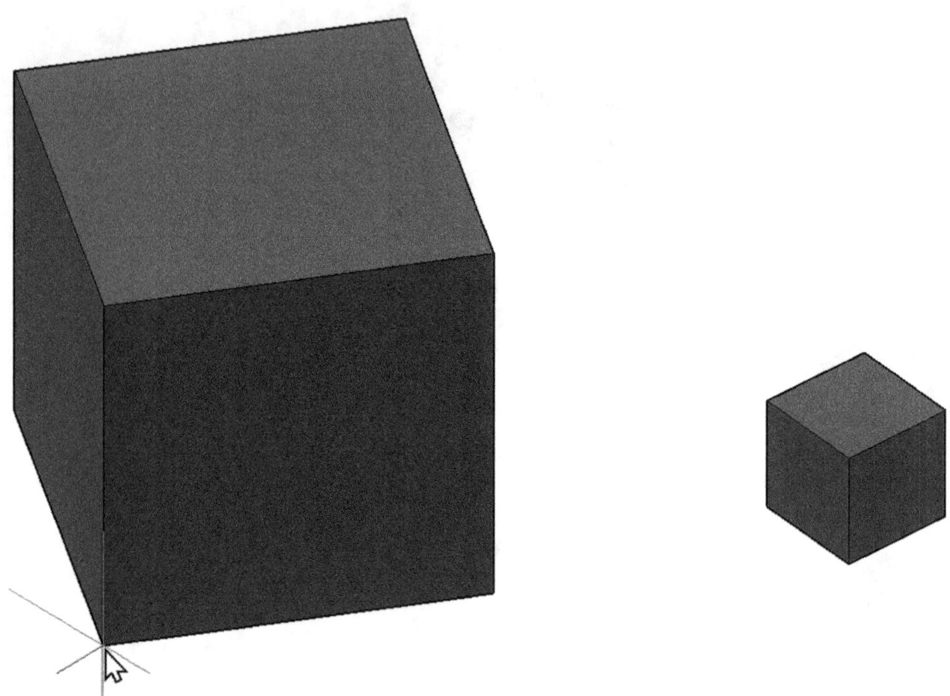

Create a Box by specifying its Length and Width

Activate the Box tool and click to specify the first corner of the box. Next, select the **Length** option from the command line and specify the length and it orientation. You specify the length and orientation using the Dynamic Input mode. Next, press ENTER and specify the width value, and then press ENTER. Type-in the height value or use the **2Point** option to specify the height of the command line. Select this option from the command line and select two points from the graphics window to specify the height of the box.

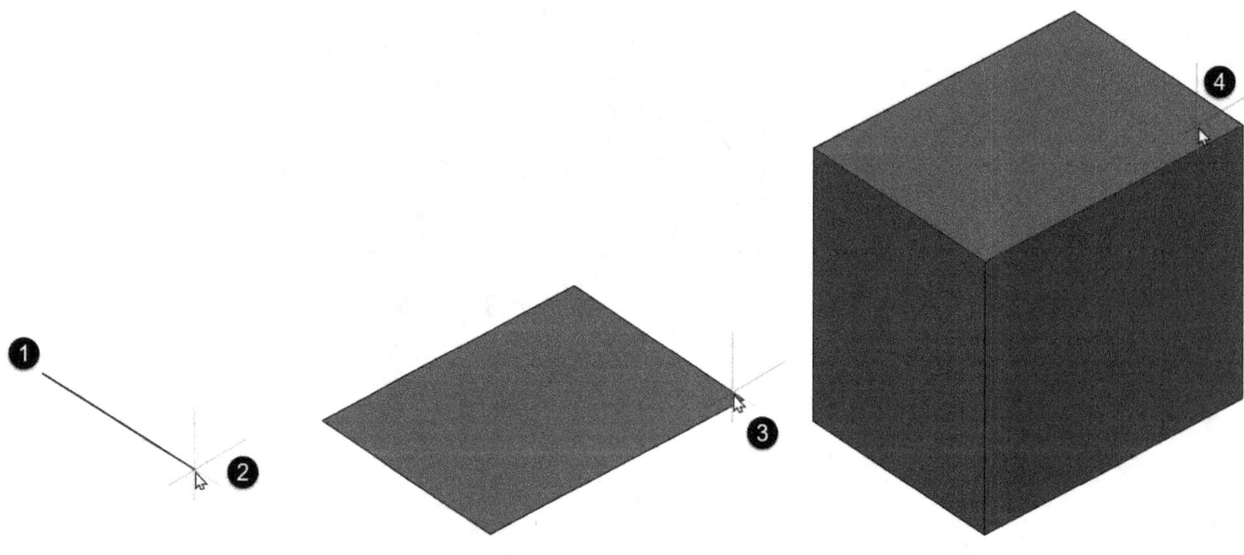

Cylinder

The **Cylinder** tool (On the ribbon, click **Home** tab > **Primitives** drop-down > **Cylinder**) allows you to create a cylinder by specifying its base and height. There are five options to specify the base of the cylinder: **Centerpoint**, **3P**, **2P**, **Ttr**, and **Elliptical**.

Centerpoint

Click in the graphics window to specify the centerpoint of the base. Next, move the pointer outward and click to specify the radius of the cylinder (or) type-in a value in the command line and press ENTER. You can also specify the diameter value of the cylinder instead of the radius by selecting the **Diameter** option from the command line.

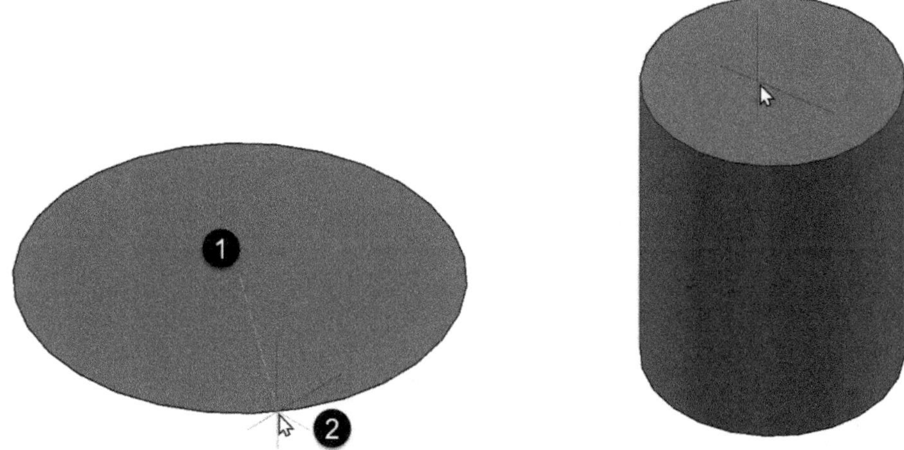

3P

Activate the Cylinder tool and select this option from the command line. Next, select the first, second, and third points of the cylindrical base.

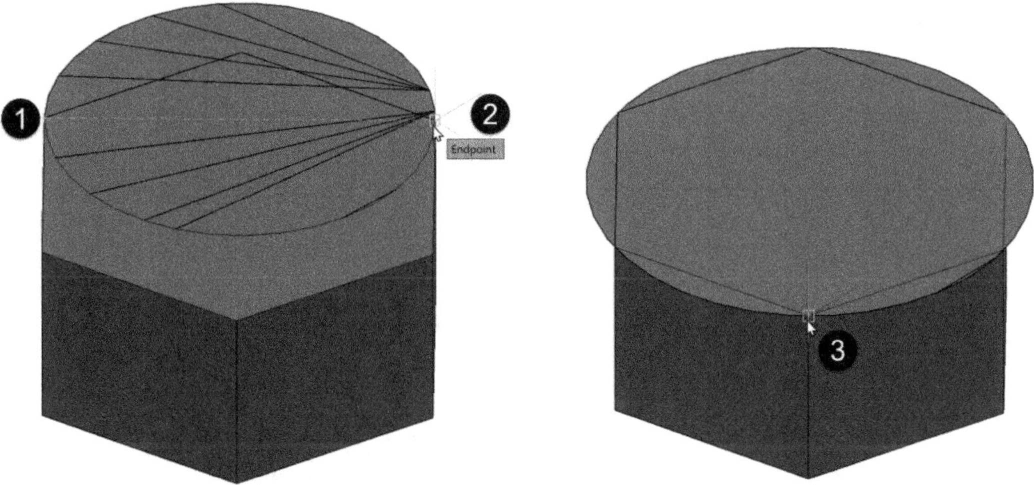

2P

Activate the **Cylinder** tool and select the **2P** option from the command line. Next, select the first and second points of the cylindrical base.

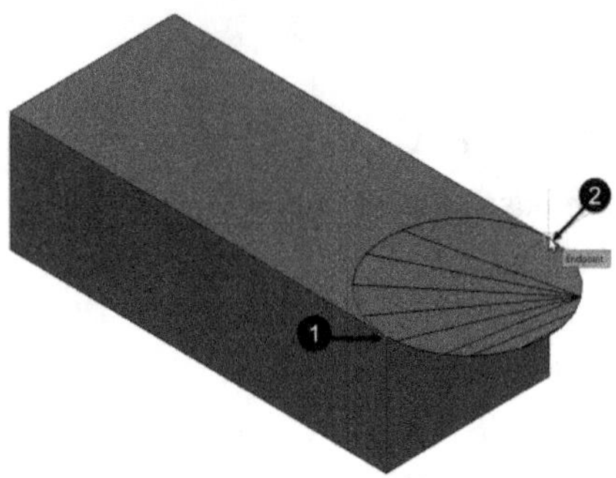

Ttr

Select the **Ttr** option from the command line. Next, select two edges from the existing geometry. Type-in the radius value and press ENTER.

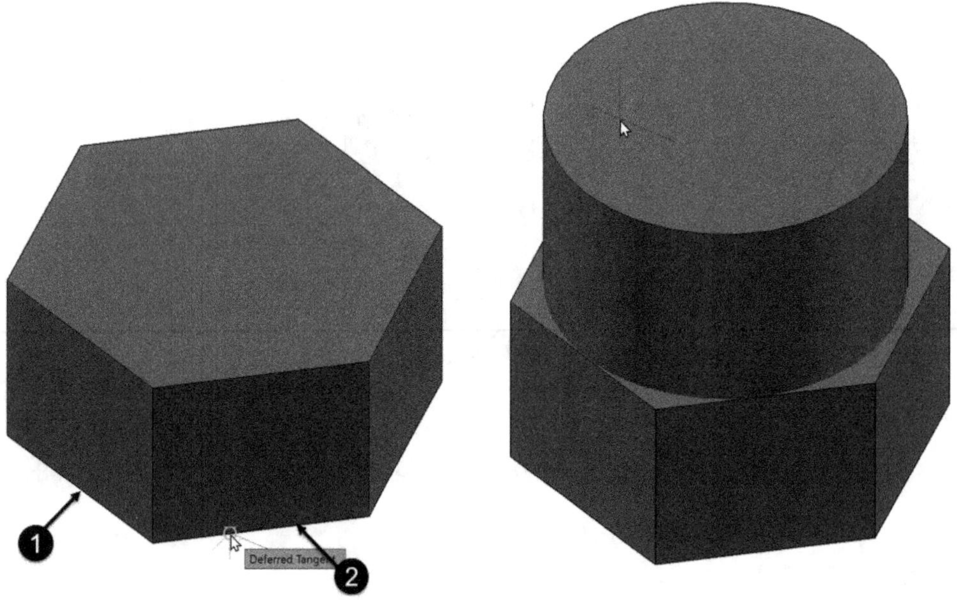

Elliptical

Select the **Elliptical** option from the command line. Click in the graphics window to specify the endpoint of the first axis of the ellipse. Next, move the pointer and click to specify the other endpoint of the ellipse. Specify the endpoint of the second axis of the ellipse.

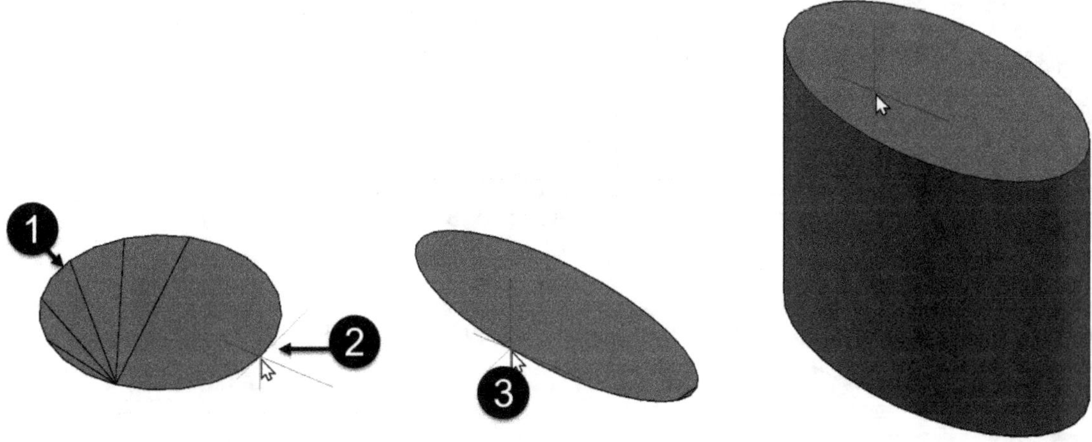

After specifying the base of the cylinder, you need to specify the cylinder. There are three ways to specify the height.

2Point

Select this option from the command line and select two points from the graphics window.

Axis endpoint

Select this option from the command line and specify the endpoint of the cylinder axis.

Cone

On the ribbon, click **Home** tab > **Primitives** drop-down > **Cone** , and then click in the graphics window to specify the center point of the base. Next, move the pointer outward and click to specify the cone radius. Move the pointer upward or downward and click to specify the cone height (or) type-in the cone height value and press ENTER.

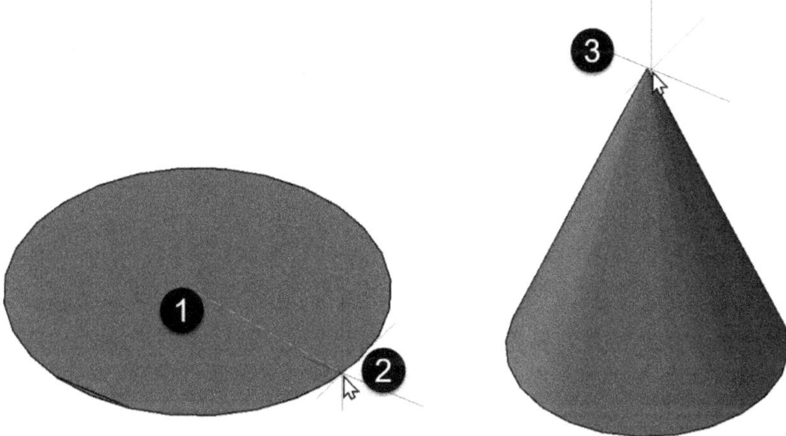

Top Radius

This option allows you to specify the top radius of the cone. Activate the Cone tool and specify the center and bottom radius of the cone. Next, select the Top radius option from the command line. Type-in the top radius value and press ENTER. Next, specify the cone height.

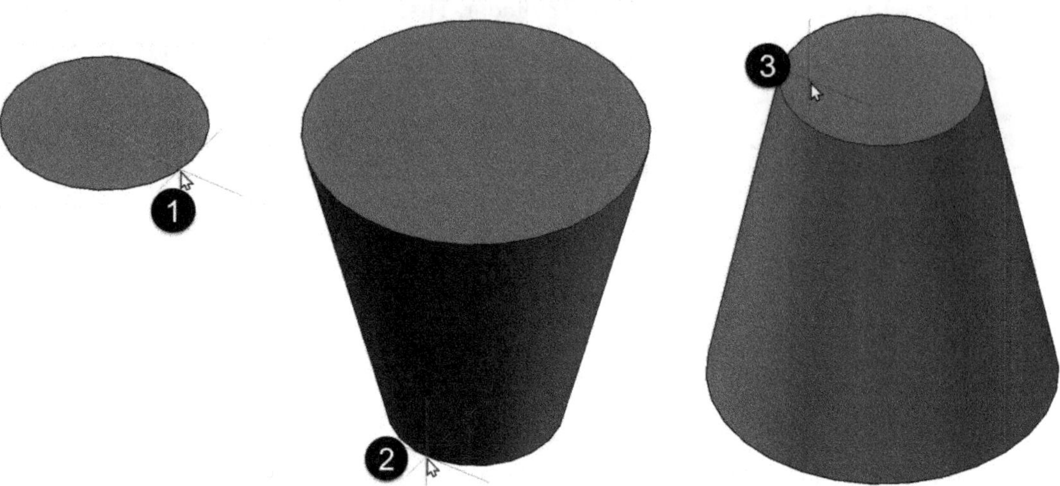

Sphere

On the ribbon, click **Home** tab > **Primitives** drop-down > **Sphere** 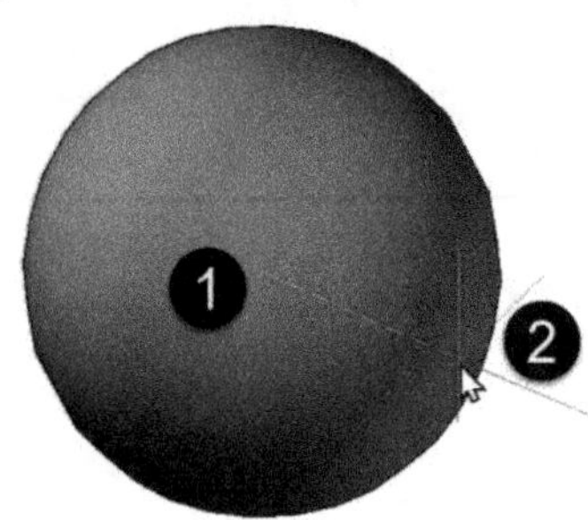, and then click in the graphics window to specify the center point of the sphere. Next, move the pointer outward and click to specify the radius of the sphere.

Pyramid

To create pyramid, you need to first specify its base by creating a polygon. To do this, click **Home** tab >

Primitives drop-down > **Pyramid** on the ribbon, and then select the Sides option from the command line. Specify the number of sides of the polygon and press ENTER. Next, specify the centerpoint of the polygon and move the pointer outward and click to specify the base radius of the polygon. You can also select the **Edge** option from the command line to specify the length of one of the sides of the polygon.

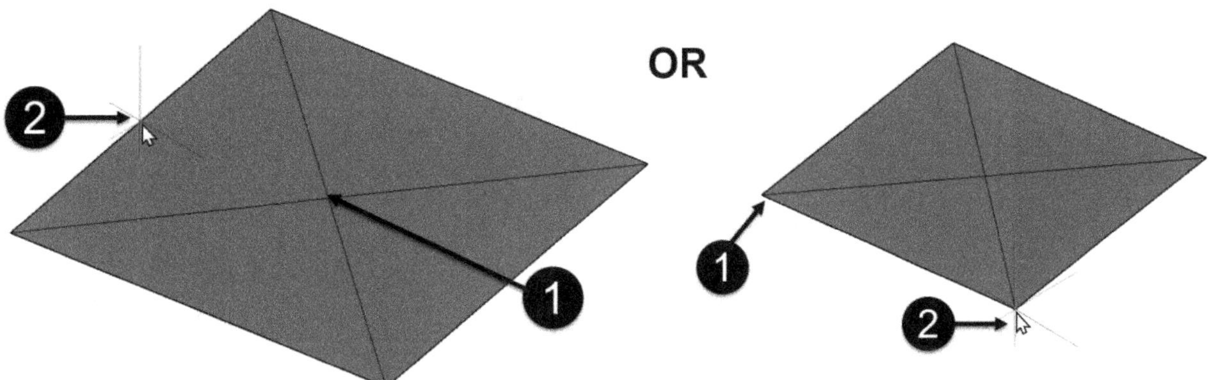

After specifying the base of the pyramid, move the pointer in the direction perpendicular to the base and click to specify the height (or) type-in height of the pyramid in the command line and press ENTER. You can also select the **Top radius** option to specify the top radius of the pyramid.

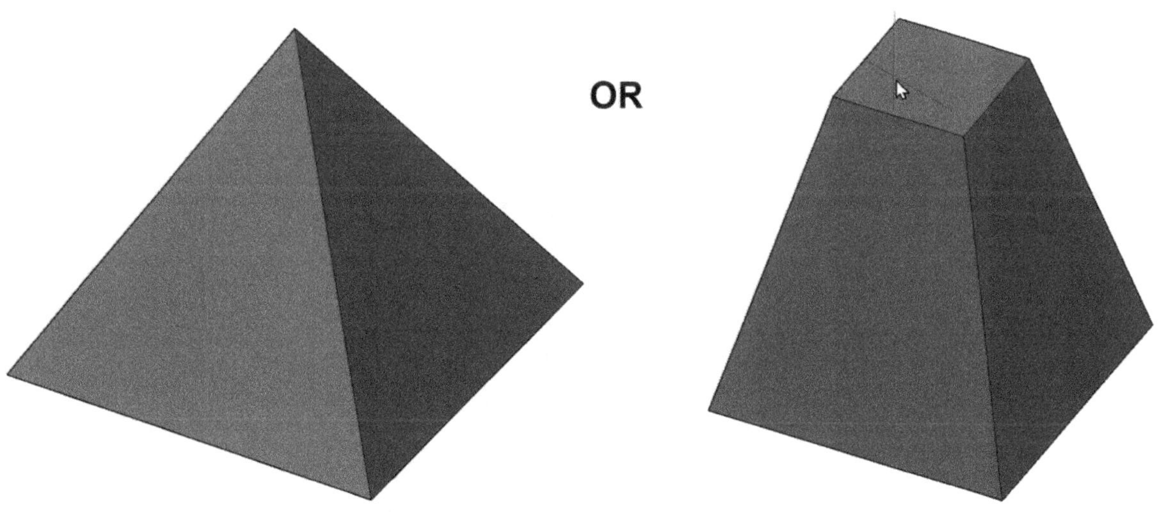

Wedge

On the ribbon, click **Home** tab > **Primitives** drop-down > **Wedge** . Next, click in the graphics window to specify the first corner of the wedge. Next, move the pointer and click to specify the opposite corner. Move the pointer upward or downward and click to specify the height of the wedge.

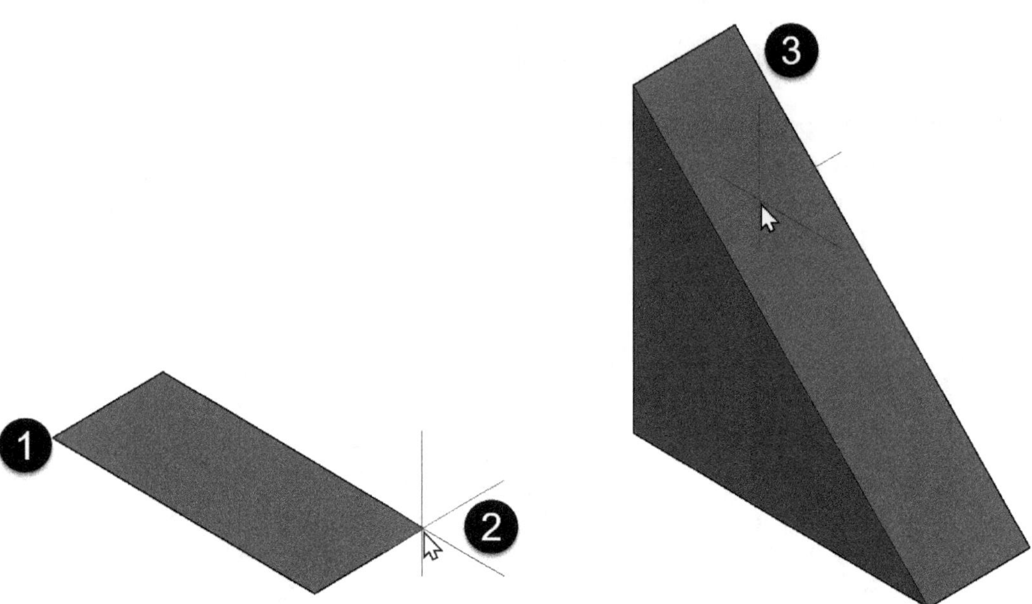

Torus

AutoCAD creates a torus by sweeping circle along a large circle. On the ribbon, click **Home** tab > **Primitives**

drop-down > **Torus** and specify the center point of the large circle. Next, move the pointer outward and click to specify the radius of the large circle (or) type-in the radius value in the command line and press ENTER.

Specify the tube radius (radius of the small circle) by moving the pointer and clicking (or) entering a value in the command line.

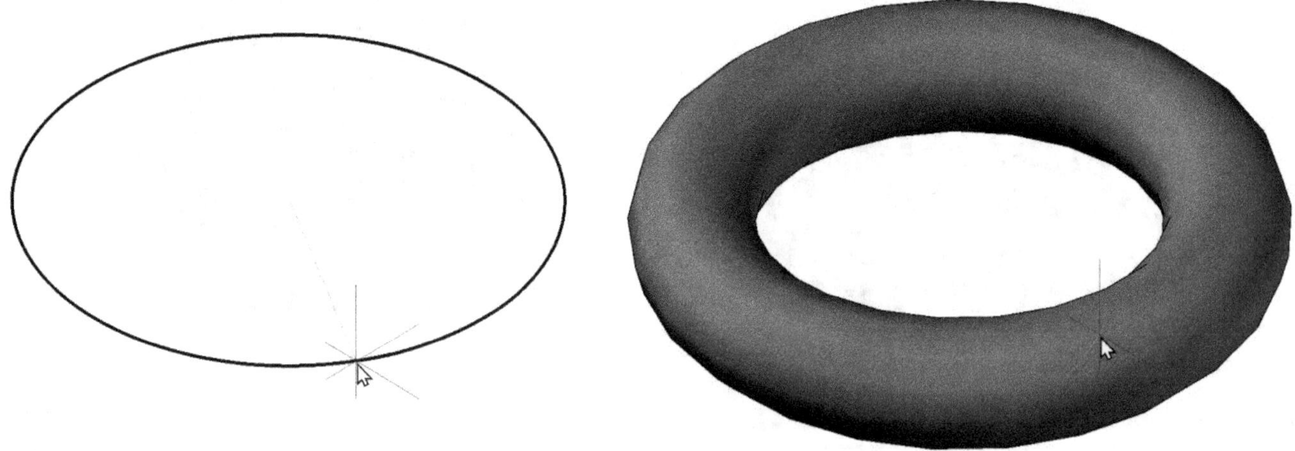

Boolean

The Boolean operations allow to add, subtract, or intersect solids from each other.

Union

The **Union** command is used to combine two solids into a single one. For example, you can add a sphere at the end face of the cylinder. To do this, first create a cylinder, as shown. Next, click **Home** tab > **Modeling** panel > **Primitives** drop-down > **Sphere** on the ribbon. Next, select the center point of the end face of the cylinder, as shown. Move the pointer outward and select the quadrant point of the circular edge, as shown. After creating the sphere, you can add it to the cylinder using the **Union** command.

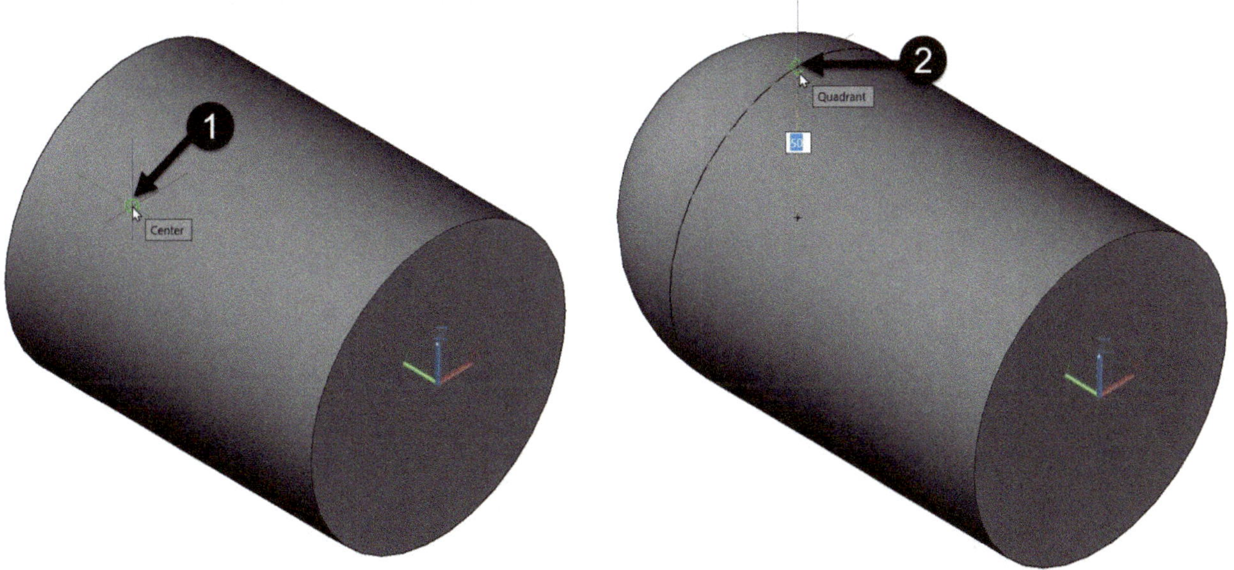

On the ribbon, click **Solid > Boolean > Union**. Next, select the cylinder and the sphere, and then press ENTER; the two solids are combined.

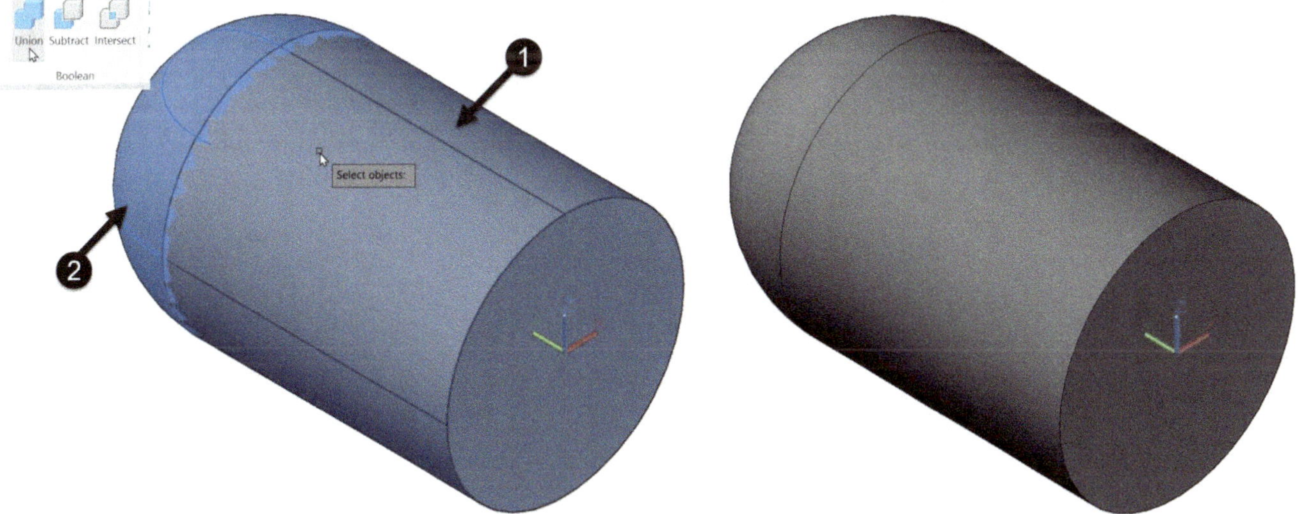

Subtract

This command performs the function of subtracting one solid body from another. For example, you can subtract a box from the body, as shown. To do this, click **Home** tab > **Modeling** panel > **Primitives** drop-down > **Box**. Next, select the quadrant point of the circular edge, as shown; the first corner of the box is defined. Next, move the pointer backward and click at the location outside the solid body. Move the pointer in the upward direction and click to create a box.

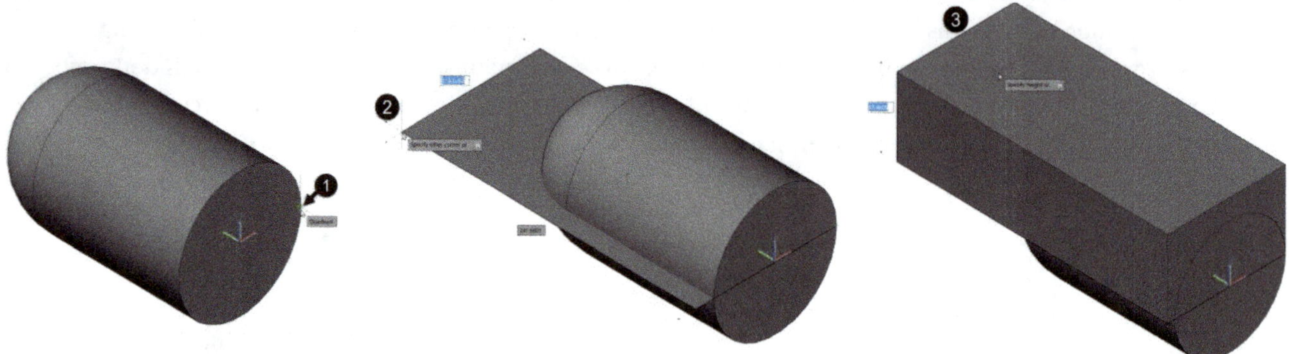

On the ribbon, click **Solid > Boolean > Subtract**. Next, select the main body and press ENTER. Select he box and press ENTER to subtract the box from the main body.

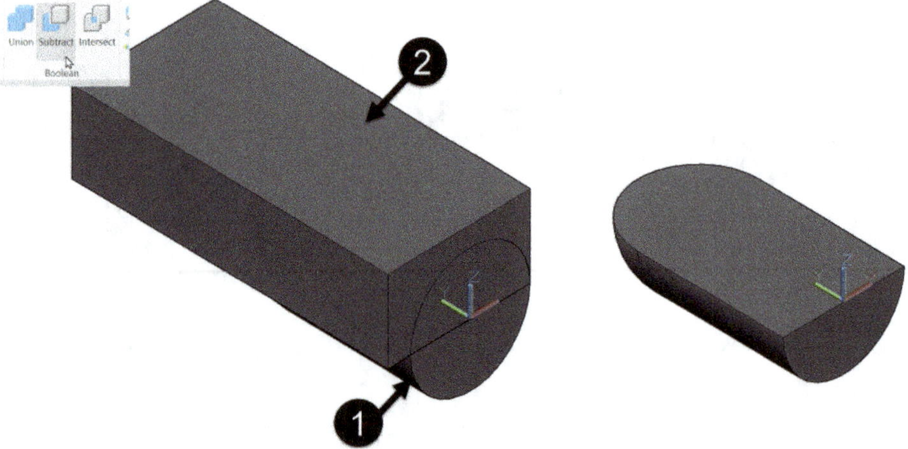

Intersect

By using the **Intersect** command, you can generate bodies defined by the intersecting volume of two bodies. On the ribbon, click **Solid > Boolean > Intersect**. Next, select the intersecting bodies. Press ENTER to see the resultant single solid body.

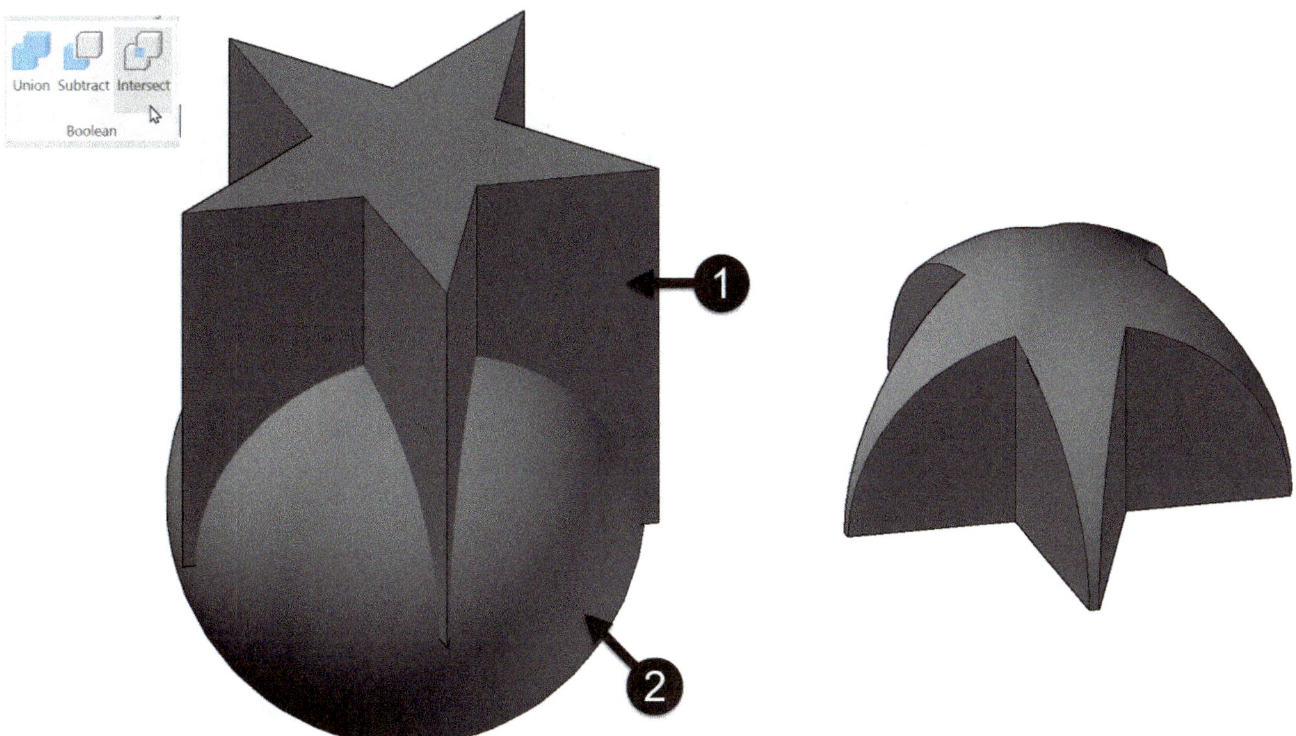

Creating the User Coordinate System

User Coordinate Systems assist you while creating 3D models. They are used to create construction planes on which you can add additional features to the model. Various methods to create User coordinate systems are discussed next.

The UCS command

On the status bar, click the **Customization** button and select **Dynamic UCS** from the menu. Also, select **3D Object Snap** from the menu. Next, deactivate the **Dynamic UCS** icon on the status bar. Click **Home > Coordinates > UCS** on the ribbon; the UCS is attached to the pointer.

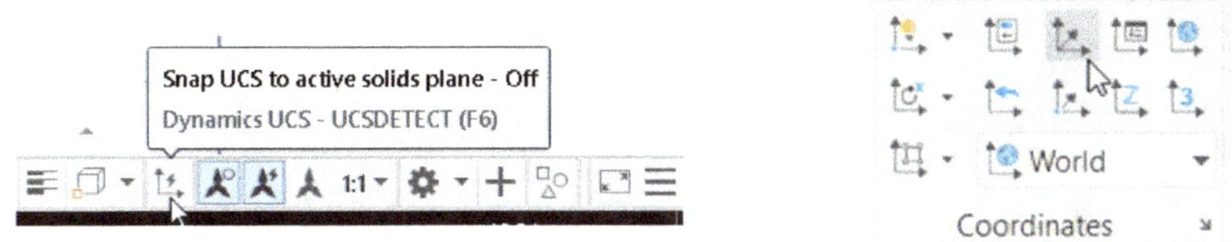

Activate the **3D Object Snap** icon on the status bar. Select the vertex point, as shown below. Press ENTER to accept the orientation of the UCS.

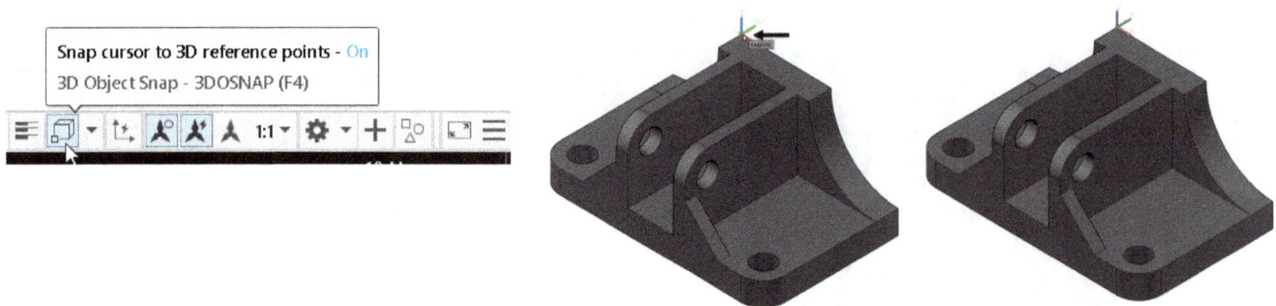

Creating UCS by selecting 3-points

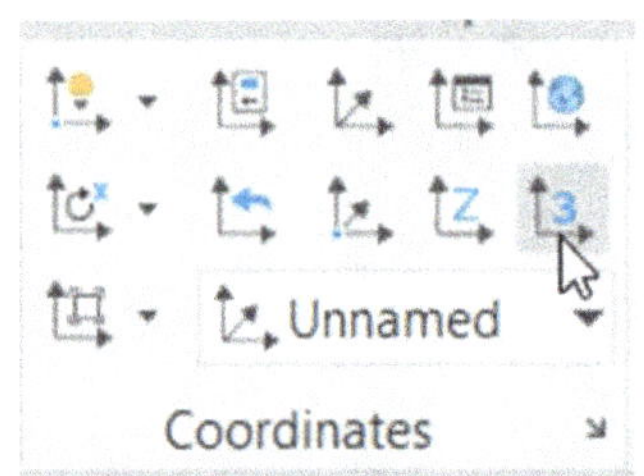

You can create a UCS by selecting three points. The first point will be the origin of the UCS, the second point will define the X-axis, and the third point defines the Y-axis. To do this, click **Home > Coordinates > 3 Point** on the ribbon. Select the lower endpoint of the wedge, as shown in the figure.

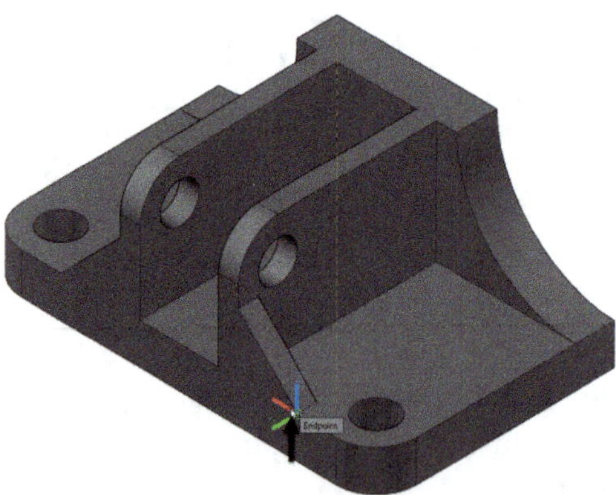

Move the pointer toward the right. Select the other endpoint of the bottom edge of the inclined face, as shown in the figure. Move the pointer along the diagonal edge of the wedge. Select the endpoint on the top edge, as shown. The UCS will be created and aligned to the inclined face of the wedge.

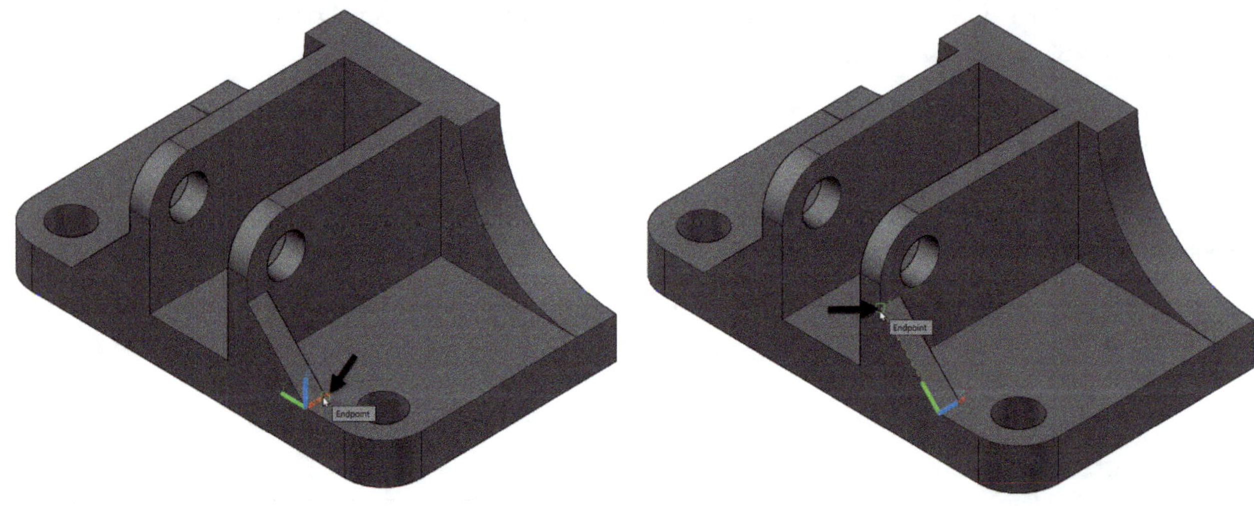

Returning to the previous position of the UCS

Click **Home > Coordinates > UCS, Previous** on the ribbon; the UCS will return to its previous position.

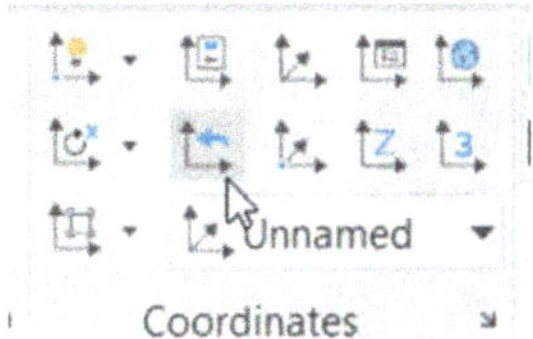

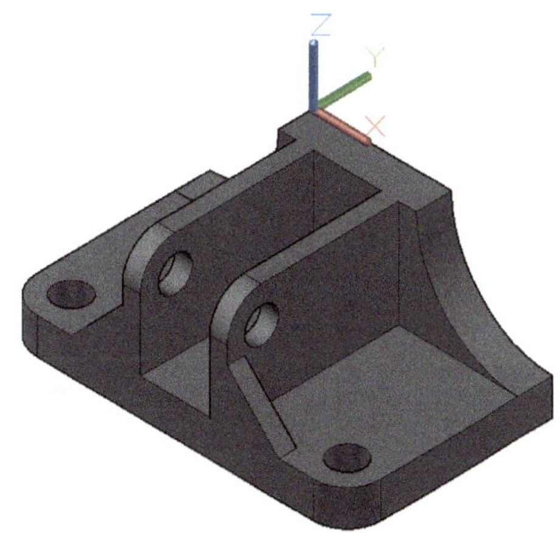

Creating a UCS by specifying its origin

Click **Home > Coordinates > Origin** 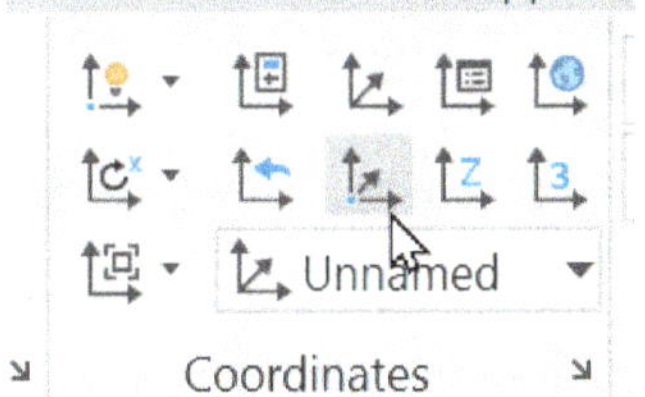 on the ribbon; the UCS will be attached to the pointer. Select the lower-left corner point of the model; the UCS will be placed at that point. Note that the orientation will not change.

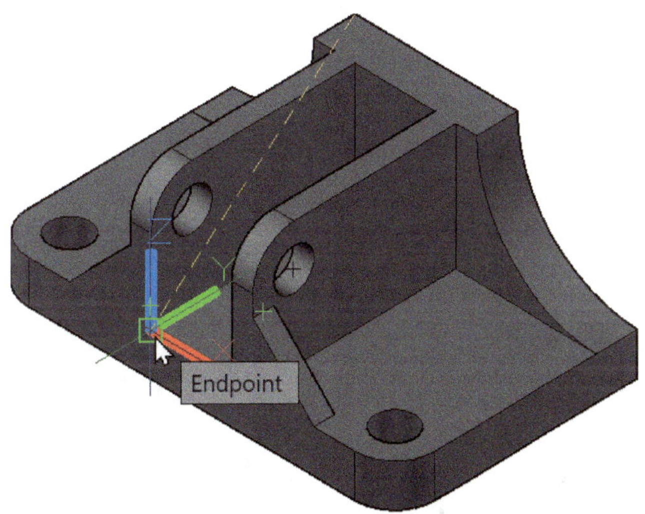

Rotating the UCS about X, Y, and Z axes

You can rotate a UCS about X, Y, or Z axes by using the drop-down available in the **Coordinates** panel. Select the **X** option from the drop-down. Also, a rubber band line originating from the Y axis is attached to the pointer. Rotate the pointer and pick a point to specify the rotation angle. You can also type in the rotation angle in the dynamic input or command line.

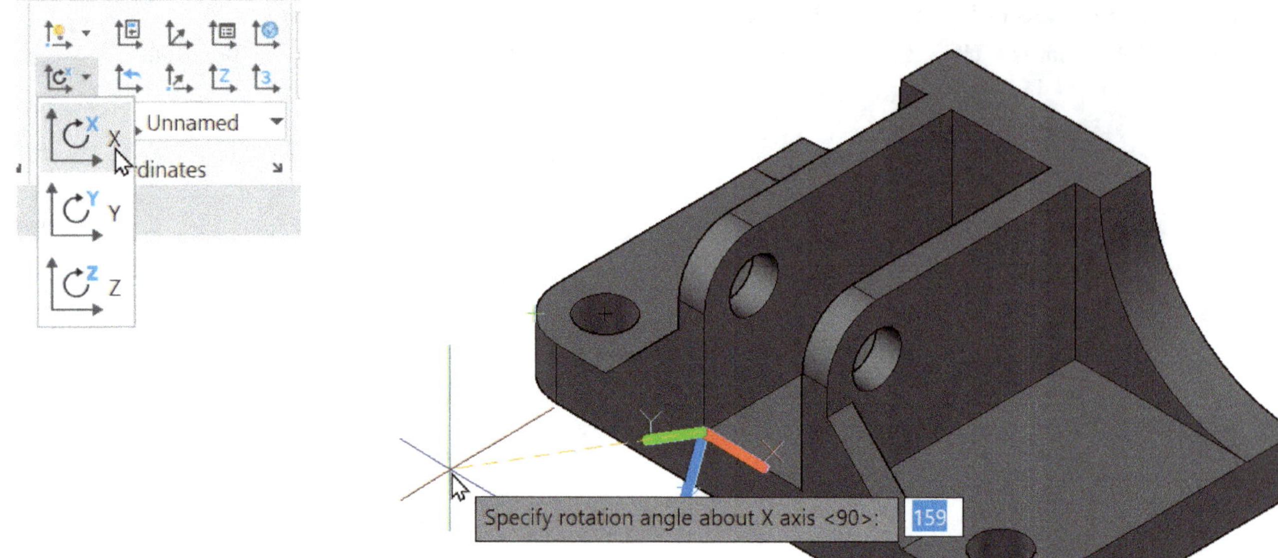

Similarly, you can rotate the UCS about the Y and Z axes using the respective options from the drop-down.

Creating the UCS by specifying the Z-axis

Using the **Z-Axis Vector** tool, you can create a UCS by specifying its Z-axis. Click **Home > Coordinates > Z-Axis Vector** on the ribbon. Select the corner point as the origin, as shown. Also, a rubber band line originating from the Z-axis is attached to the pointer. Now, as you move the pointer, you will notice that the Z-axis also moves. Move the pointer and select the left endpoint of the horizontal edge, as shown; the Z-axis will be aligned to the horizontal edge.

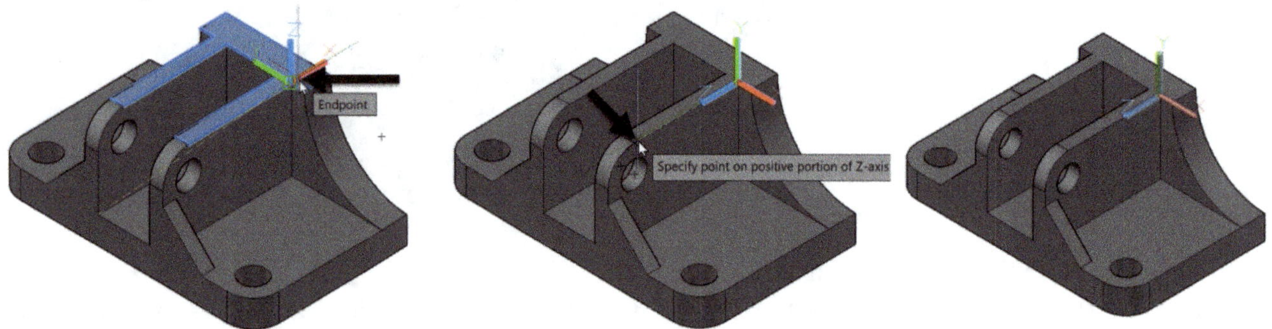

Creating UCS parallel to the screen

Using the **View** tool in the **Coordinates** panel, you can create a UCS which is parallel to the screen. Click **Home > Coordinates > View** on the ribbon; the XY plane of the UCS will become parallel to the screen. The UCS origin will not change. This tool is useful if you want to use the current view and add a title block or any other annotation.

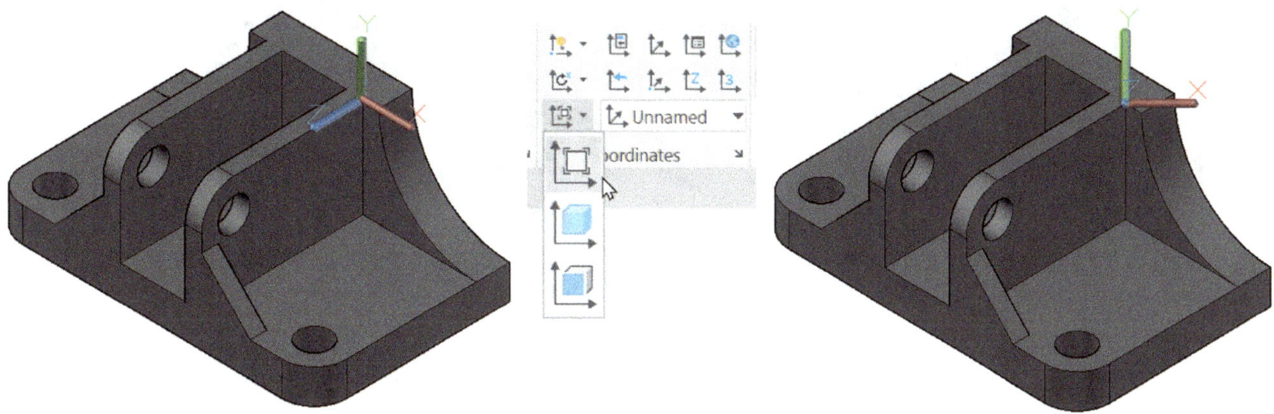

Creating UCS aligned to an object

You can create a UCS aligned to an object using the **Object** tool. The origin of the UCS will be aligned to the

nearest endpoint of the object. Click **Home > Coordinates > View > Object** on the ribbon. Select the cylindrical object from the model; the UCS will be aligned to it.

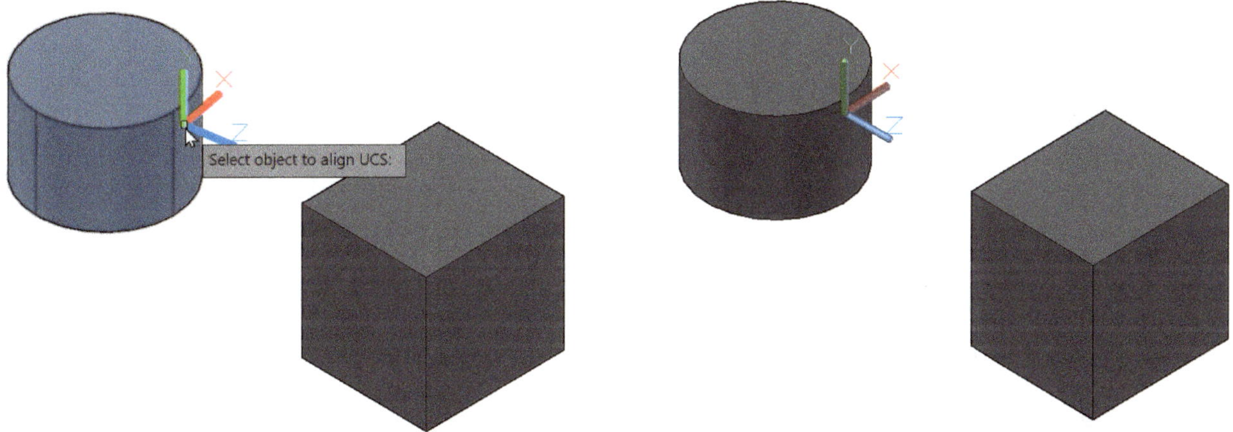

Creating UCS aligned to a face

You can align a UCS to a planar or curved face of a model using the **Face** tool. Click **Home > Coordinates >View**

drop-down **> Face** on the ribbon. Move the pointer over the faces of the model; you will notice that the UCS is displayed on the faces.

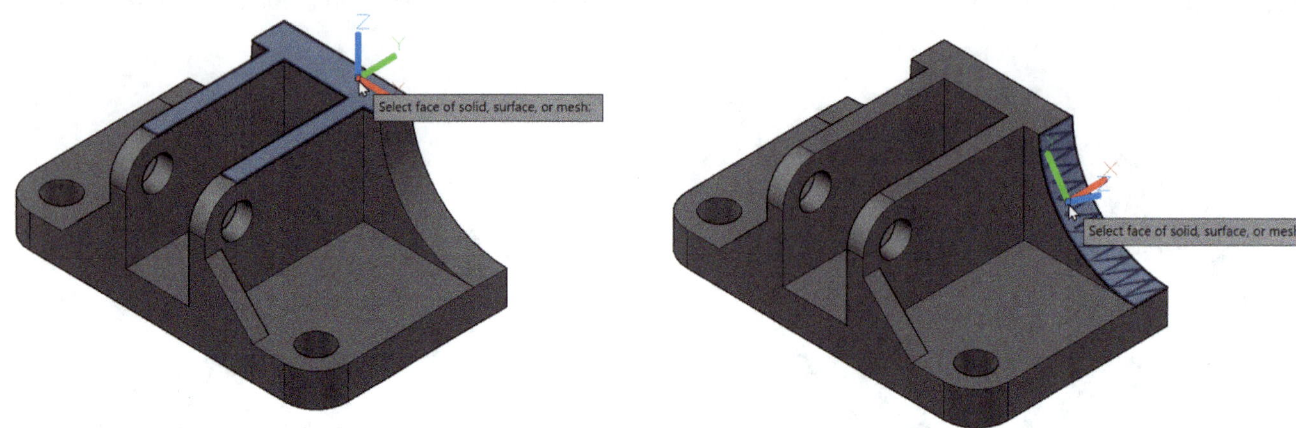

Select the horizontal face of the model; the message, "Enter an option [Next/Xflip/Yflip] <accept>:" appears in the command line. If you select the **Next** option, the adjacent face will be highlighted. The **Xflip** option is used to rotate the UCS 180 degrees about the X axis. The **Yflip** option is used to rotate the UCS 180 degrees about the Y axis. Press ENTER to accept; the UCS will be aligned to the selected face.

Using Dynamic User Coordinate System

In the previous section, you have learned to create various types of static user coordinate systems. They are active until you define another user coordinate system. You can also create dynamic user coordinate systems. A Dynamic User Coordinate System is a temporary UCS that appears automatically when you place your pointer over the face of a 3D solid object. Note that the Dynamic User Coordinate system appears only when you use tools that create objects directly (For example, drawing tools and primitive tools). To create a Dynamic UCS, you need to activate the **Dynamic UCS** option on the status bar.

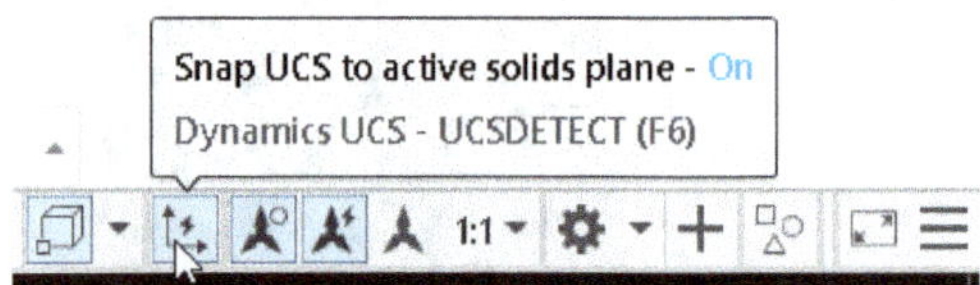

Click the **Cylinder** button on the **Modeling** panel. Ensure that the **Dynamic UCS** button is active on the status bar. Move the pointer over the faces of the model; they will be highlighted. Click on the horizontal face of the model and create the cylinder, as shown below.

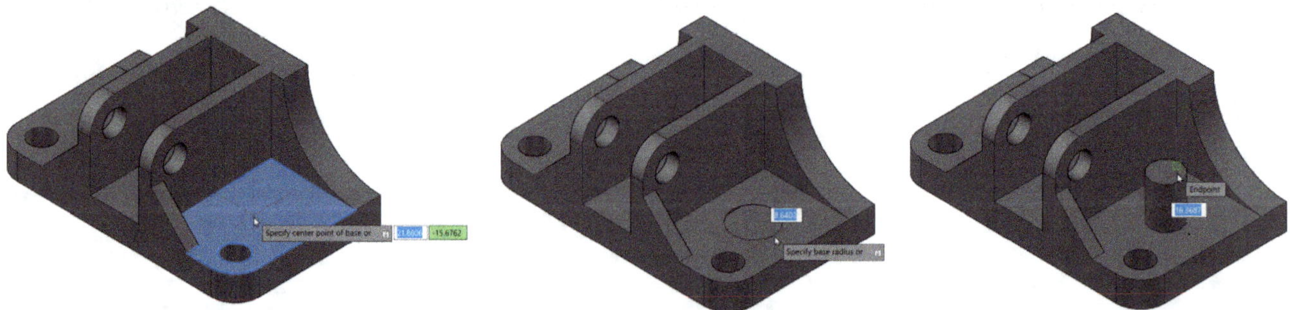

View commands

The model display in the graphics window can be changed using various view commands. Most of these commands are located on the **Navigation Bar**.

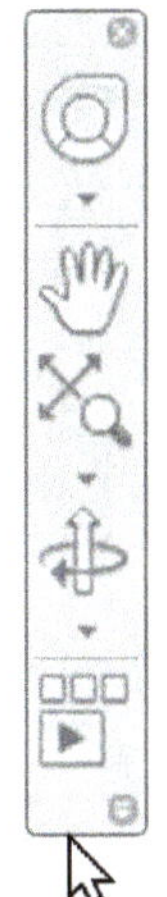

The following are some of the main view commands:

	Zoom Extents	The model will be fitted in the graphics window's current size to be visible completely.
	Zoom Window	Select this option and drag a rectangle. The contents inside the rectangle will be zoomed.
	Zoom Realtime	Select this option and press the left mouse button. Drag the mouse to vary the size of the objects accordingly.
	Zoom Object	This option fits the selected objects in the graphics window.
	Zoom Previous	This option displays the previous zoom view.
	Zoom All	This option helps you to view all the objects in the graphics window.
	Zoom Dynamic	This option helps you to zoom an object by creating a dynamic view box.
	Zoom Scale	This option helps you to zoom in or out by specifying the zoom scale.

	Zoom Center	This option helps you to zoom-in or out specifying the center and magnification value.
	Zoom In	This option helps you to zoom into the drawing by a scale factor of 2.
	Zoom out	This option helps you to zoom out off the drawing by a scale factor of 2.
	Pan	Select this option and press the left mouse button. Drag the pointer to move the model view on a plane parallel to the screen.
	Orbit	Select this option and press the left mouse button. Drag the pointer to rotate the model view.
	Navigation wheel	This wheel has various navigation options such as **Zoom, Pan, Orbit**, and **Rewind**. 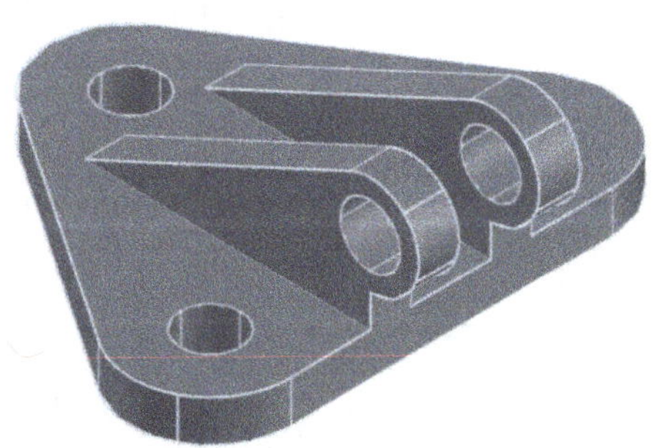

Visual Styles

The **Visual Styles** drop-down on the **View** panel of the **Home** ribbon tab allows you to change the model geometry's representation. These display styles are explained next.

	**Shaded with Edges**	This represents the model with shades along with visible edges.

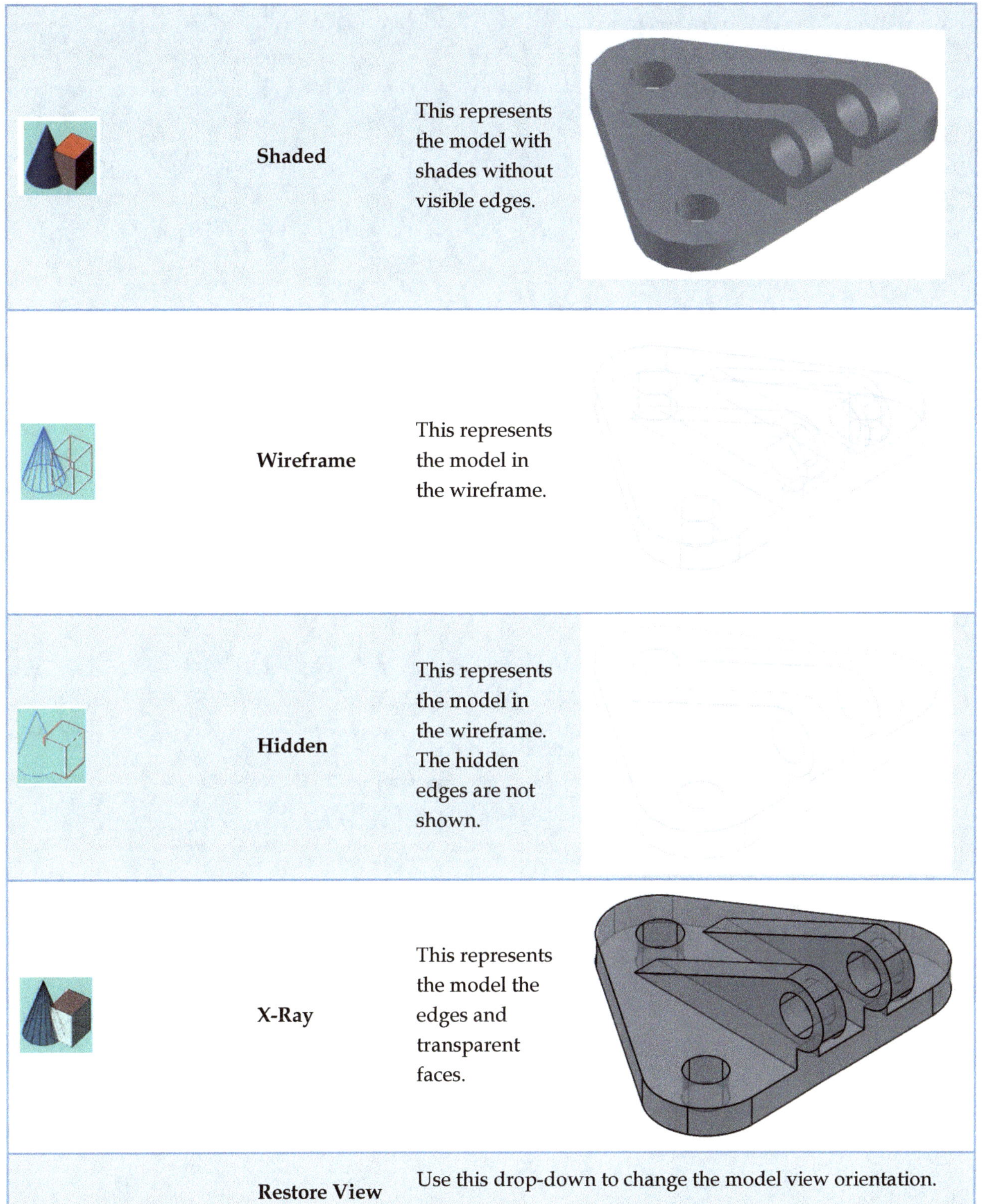

	Shaded	This represents the model with shades without visible edges.	
	Wireframe	This represents the model in the wireframe.	
	Hidden	This represents the model in the wireframe. The hidden edges are not shown.	
	X-Ray	This represents the model the edges and transparent faces.	
	Restore View	Use this drop-down to change the model view orientation.	

Tutorial 1 (Millimeters)

In this example, you create the part shown below.

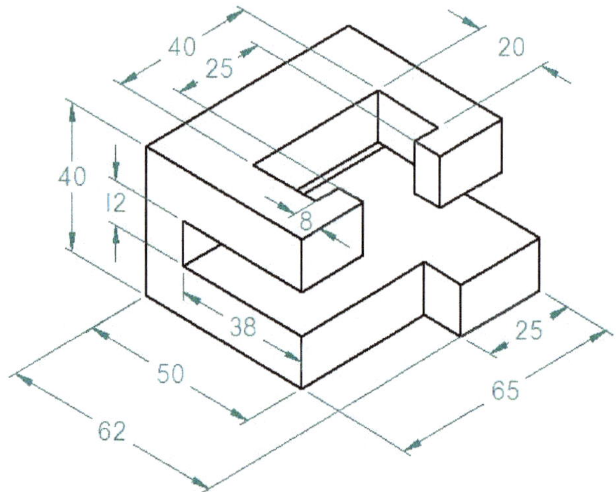

Creating a New File

1. Click the **AutoCAD 2025** icon on your desktop.
2. On the **Start** page, click **New** drop-down > **Browse Templates**.

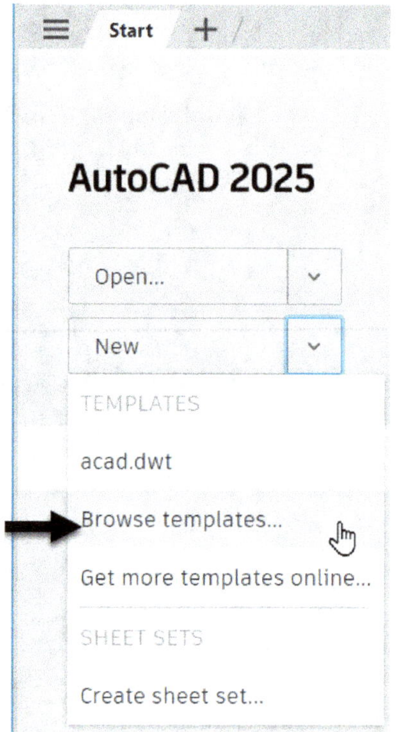

3. Select the **acadiso3D** template from the **Select Template** dialog and click **Open**.
4. On the status bar, click **Workspace Switching** drop-down > **3D Modeling**.
5. Deactivate the **GRIDMODE** icon on the status bar.

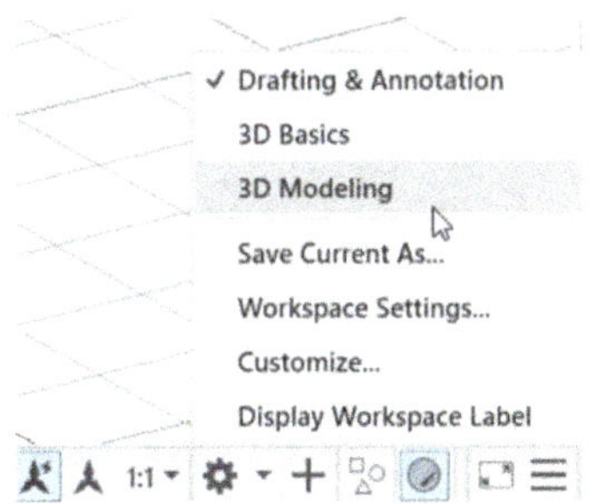

Creating a Box

1. On the ribbon, click **Home** tab > **Modeling** panel > **Primitive** drop-down > **Box**.

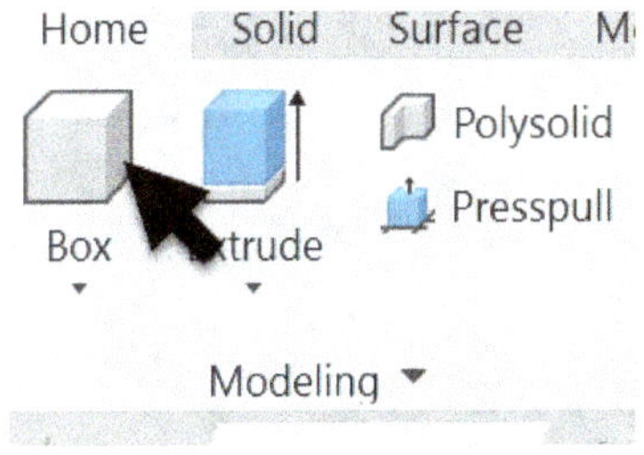

2. Type 0,0 in the command line and press ENTER. The first corner of the box is defined.
3. Type 50,65 in the command line and press ENTER. The second corner of the box is defined.
4. Move the pointer upward.
5. Type 40 in the command line and press ENTER. The height of the box is specified.
6. Click the **Zoom Extents** icon on the Navigation Bar to fit the box into the graphics window.

Creating the Cuts using the Subtract Boolean Operation

1. On the ribbon, click **Home** tab > **Modeling** panel > **Primitive** drop-down > **Box**.
2. Type 12,0,14 in the command line to specify the first corner of the box.
3. Press ENTER.
4. Select the **Length** option from the command line.
5. Click the ORTHOMODE icon on the status bar.
6. Move the pointer along the X direction, as shown.

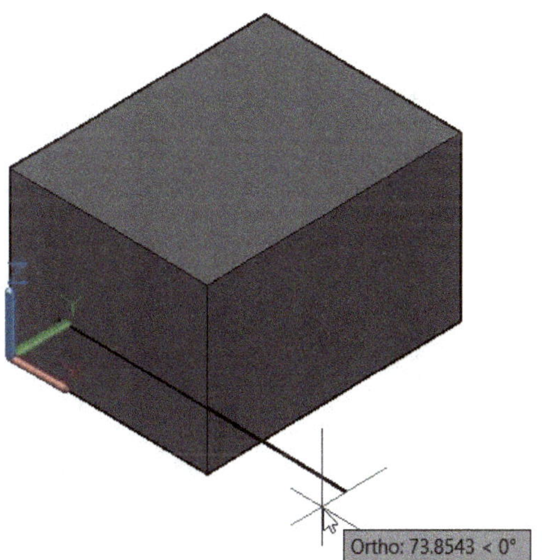

7. Type 38 and press ENTER.
8. Move the pointer along the Y direction, as shown.

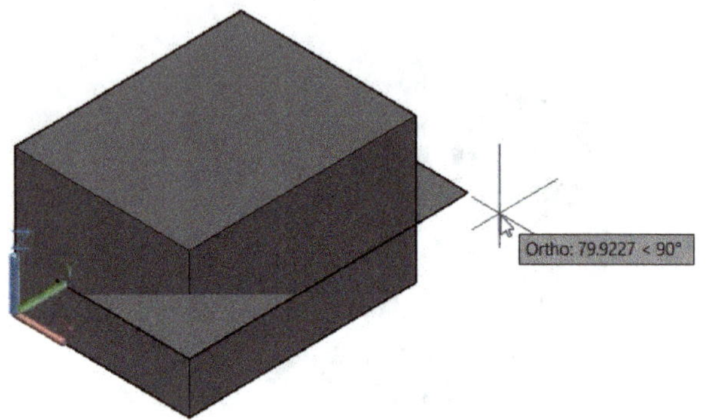

9. Type 65 and press ENTER.
10. Move the pointer **upward**.

11. Type 12 and press ENTER.
12. On the ribbon, click **Home** tab > **View** panel > **Visual Style** drop-down > **Shades of Gray**.

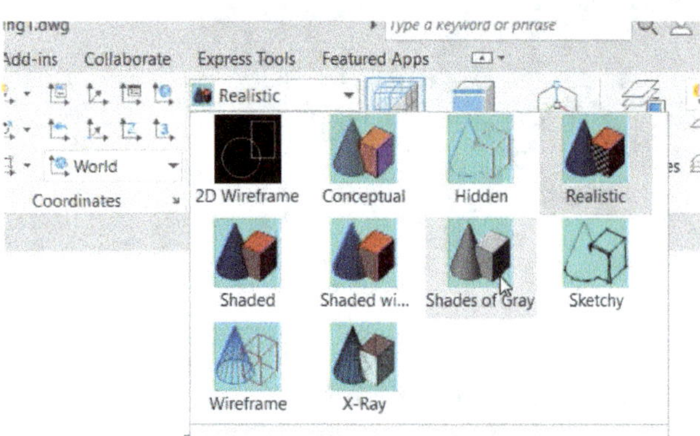

13. On the ribbon, click **Home** tab > **Solid Editing** panel > **Solid, Subtract**.

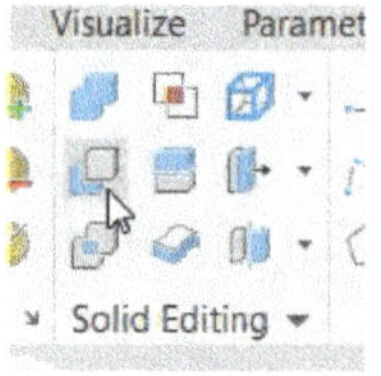

14. Select the large box and press ENTER.

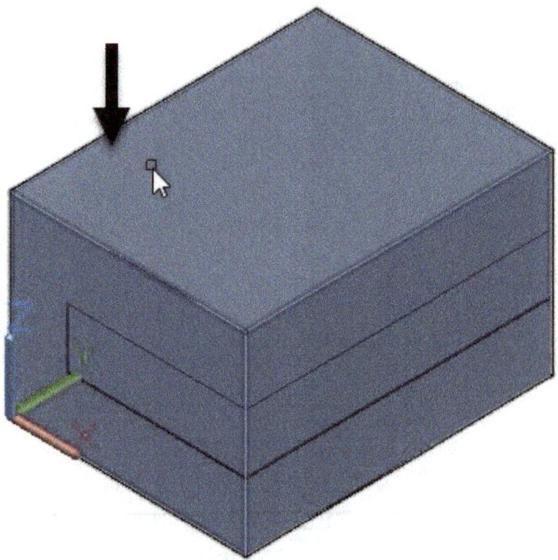

15. Select the small box and press ENTER.

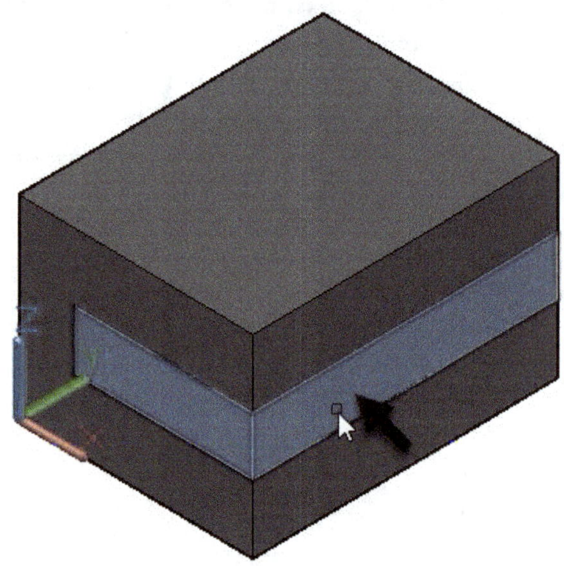

16. On the ribbon, click **Home** tab > **Modeling** panel > **Primitive** drop-down > **Box**.
17. Type 42,20,26 in the command line to specify the first corner of the box.
18. Select the **Length** option from the command line.

19. Click the ORTHOMODE icon on the status bar.
20. Move the pointer along the X direction, as shown.

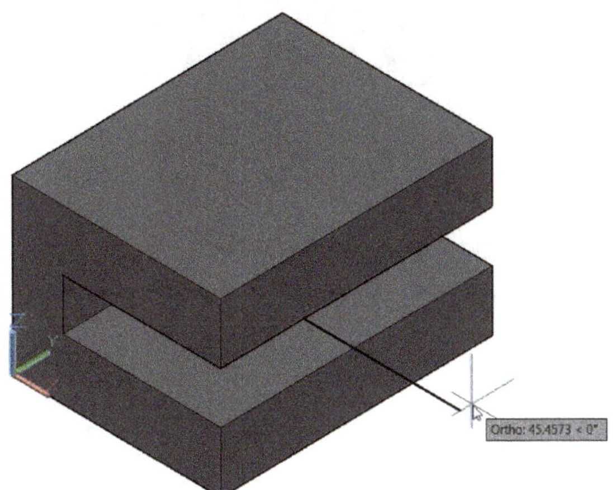

21. Type 8 and press ENTER.
22. Move the pointer along the Y direction, as shown.

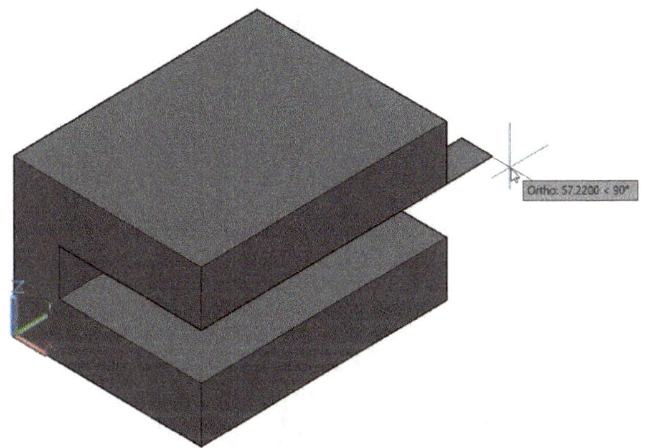

23. Type 25 and press ENTER.
24. Move the pointer upward.
25. Type 14 and press ENTER.

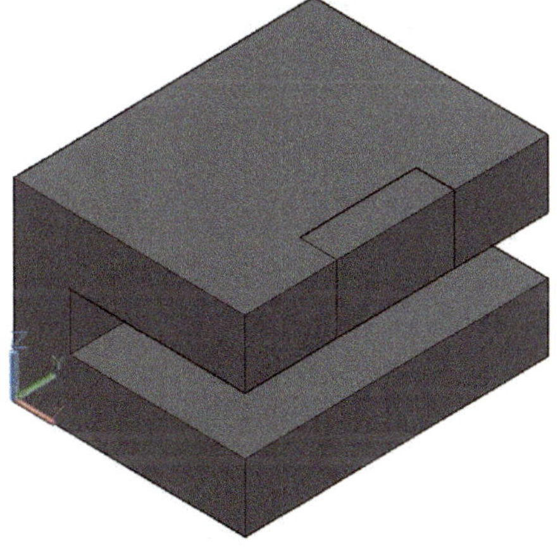

26. On the ribbon, click **Home** tab > **Modeling** panel > **Primitive** drop-down > **Box**.
27. Type 22,12.5,26 in the command line to specify the first corner of the box.
28. Select the **Length** option from the command line.
29. Click the ORTHOMODE icon on the status bar.
30. Move the pointer along the X direction, as shown.

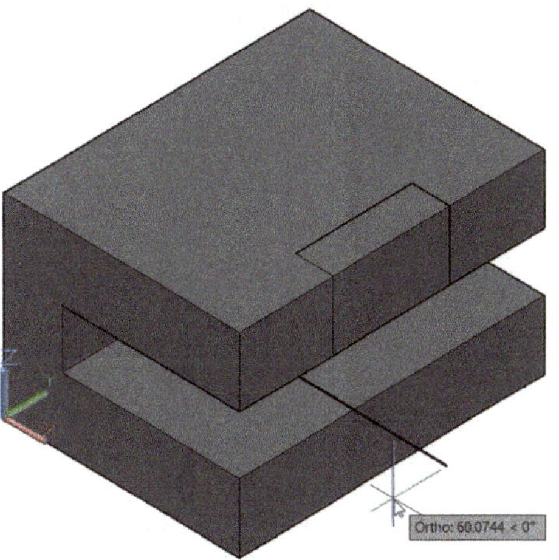

31. Type 20 and press ENTER.
32. Move the pointer along the Y direction, as shown.

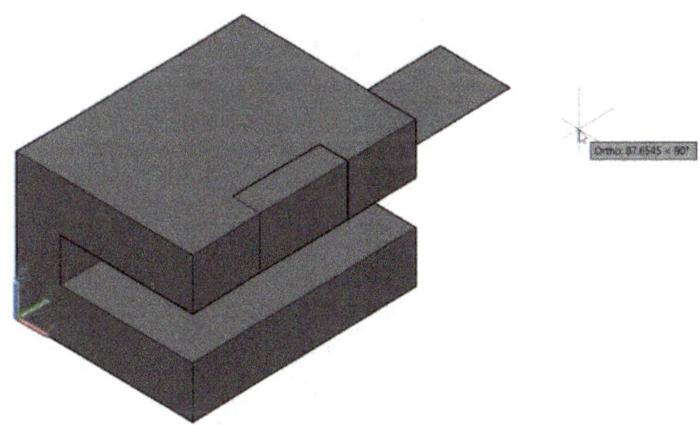

33. Type 40 and press ENTER.
34. Move the pointer upward.
35. Type 14 and press ENTER.

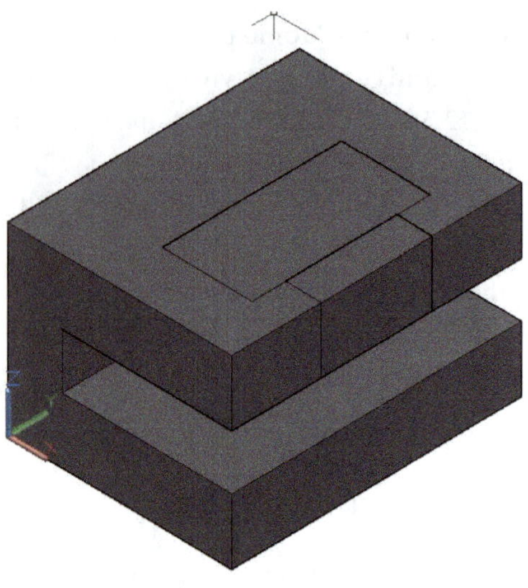

36. On the ribbon, click **Home** tab > **Solid Editing** panel > **Solid, Subtract**.
37. Select the main body and press ENTER.

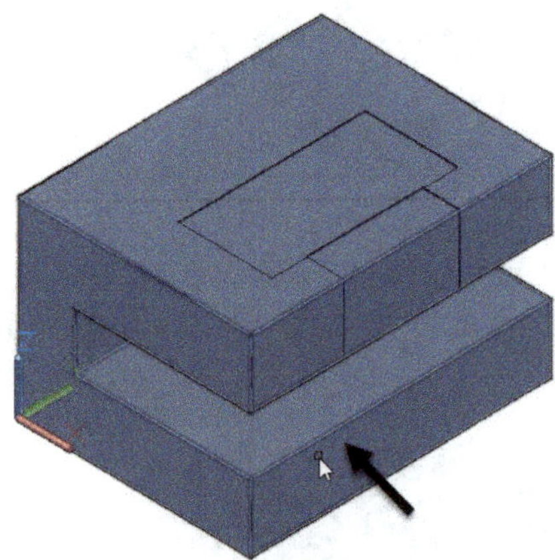

38. Select the two boxes and press ENTER.

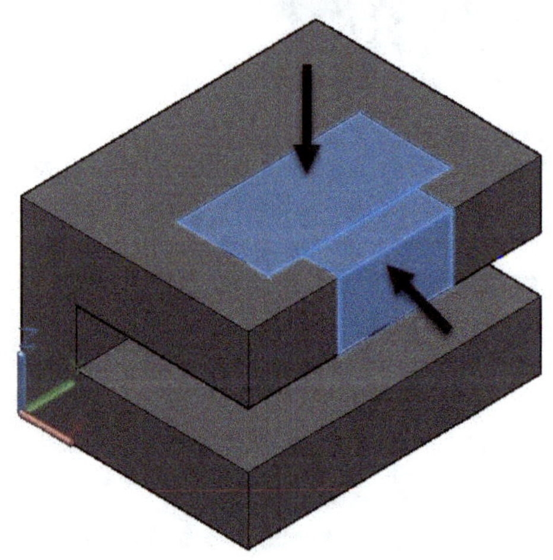

Adding a Solid using the Union Boolean Operation

1. On the ribbon, click **Home** tab > **Modeling** panel > **Primitive** drop-down > **Box**.
2. Type 50,40 in the command line and press ENTER. The first corner of the box is defined.
3. Type 62,65 in the command line and press ENTER. The second corner of the box is defined.
4. Move the pointer upward
5. Type 14 in the command line and press ENTER. The height of the box is specified.

6. On the ribbon, click **Home** tab > **Solid Editing** panel > **Solid, Union**.

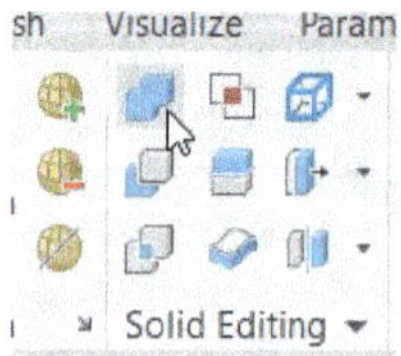

7. Select the main body.

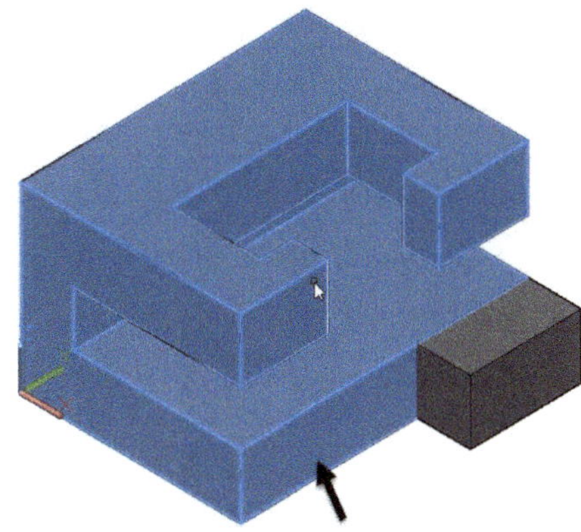

8.   Select the small box and press ENTER.

9.   Click the **Save**  icon on the Quick Access Toolbar.
10. Browse to a location on your computer.
11. Type **Ch2_tutorial1** in the **File name** box.
12. Click the **Save** button.
13. Close the file tab located above the graphics window.

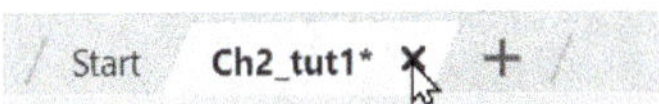

Tutorial 2 (Inches)

In this example, you create the part shown below.

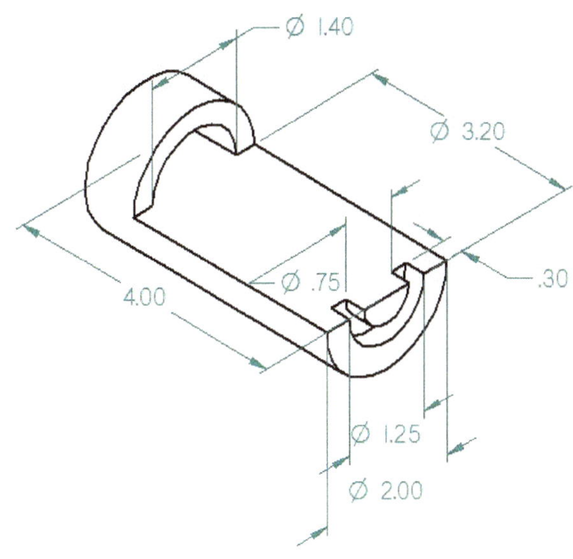

Creating a New File

1.   Click the **AutoCAD 2025** icon on your desktop.
2.   On the **Start** page, click **New** drop-down > **Browse templates**.
3.   Select **acad3D.dwt** and click **Open**.
4.   On the status bar, click **Workspace Switching** drop-down > **3D Modeling**.
5.   Deactivate the **GRIDMODE** icon on the status bar.

Creating a Revolved Solid

1.   On the ribbon, click **Home > Draw > Rectangle**.

2.   Type 0,0 in the command line and press ENTER. The first corner of the rectangle is defined.
3.   Select **Dimensions** from the command line.
4.   Type **4** in the command line and press ENTER. The length of the rectangle is defined.
5.   Type **1** in the command line and press ENTER. The width of the rectangle is defined.
6.   Move the pointer toward the left and click to create the rectangle.
7.   Click the **Zoom Extents** icon on the Navigation Bar to fit the rectangle in the graphics window.

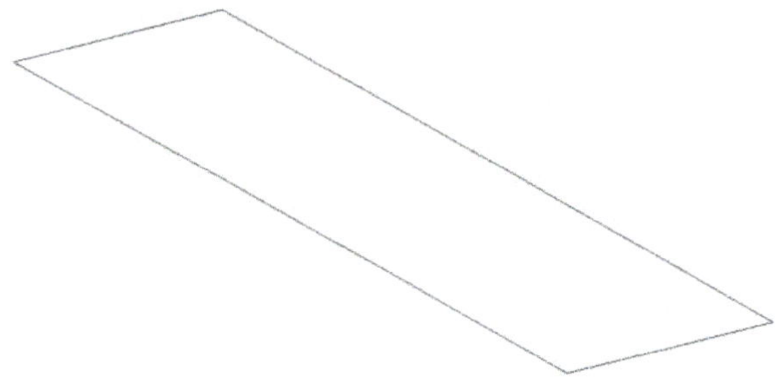

8. On the ribbon, click **Home > Modeling > Solids** drop-down > **Revolve**.

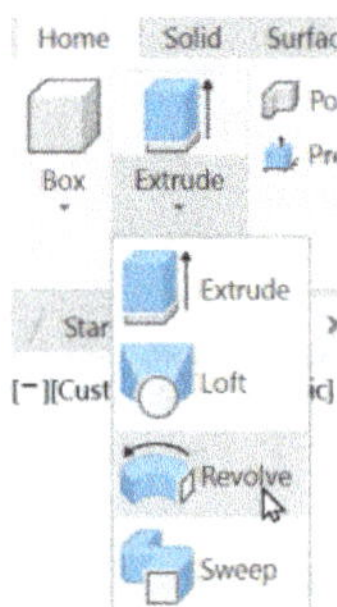

9. Select the rectangle and press ENTER.
10. Select the **X** option from the command line. The X-axis is used as the axis of revolution.
11. Type 180 in the command line and press ENTER. The angle of revolution is defined.

Creating a Cut feature

1. Activate the Dynamic UCS icon on the status bar.

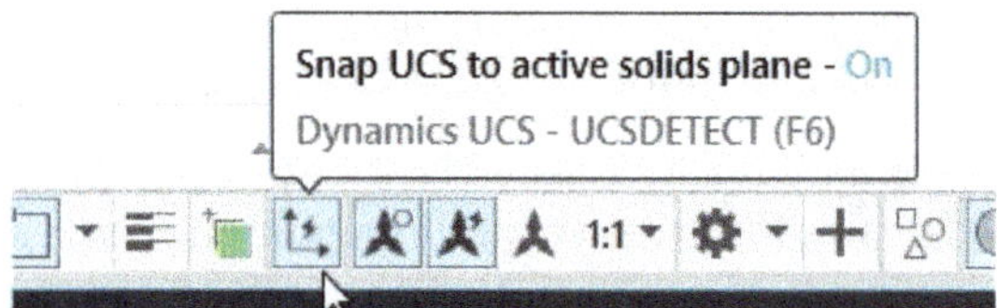

2. On the ribbon, click **Home > Draw > Circle** drop-down > **Circle, Diameter**.

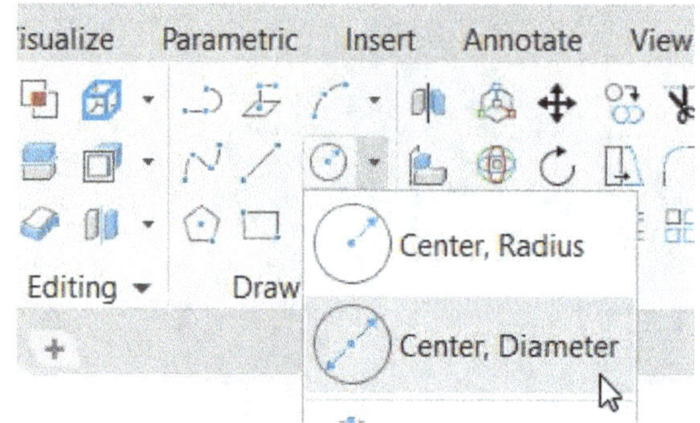

3. Place the pointer on the right face of the model; the face is highlighted.

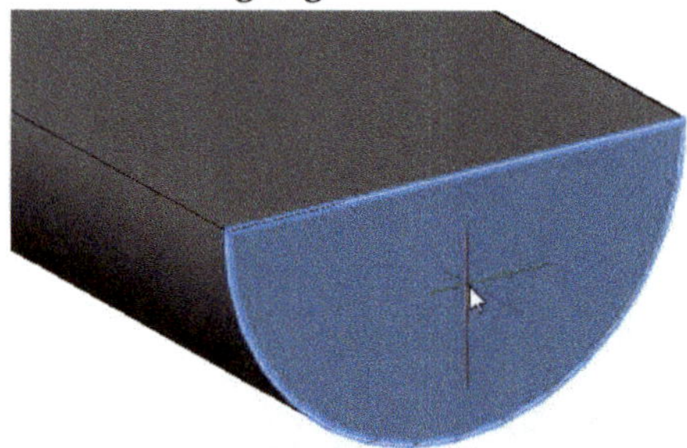

4. Click on the right face of the model.
5. Select the **Diameter** option from the command line.
6. Type 0.75 in the command line and press ENTER.

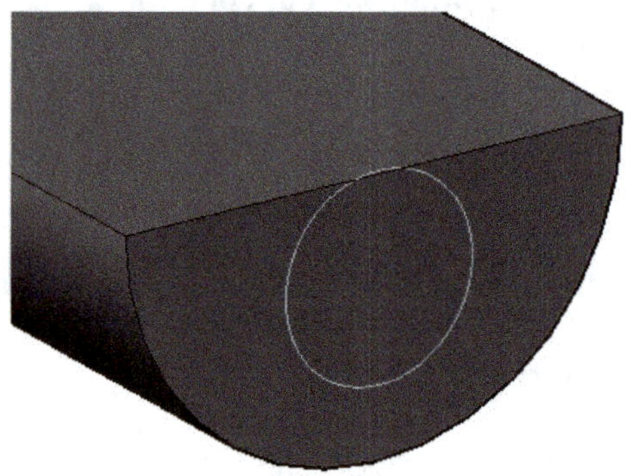

7. On the status bar, click the down arrow next to the **Object Snap** icon and select the **Center** and **Midpoint** options.
8. On the ribbon, click **Home > Draw > Circle** drop-down > **Circle, Diameter**.
9. Place the pointer on the right face of the model.
10. Click near the center point of the circle; the centerpoint of the circle is selected.

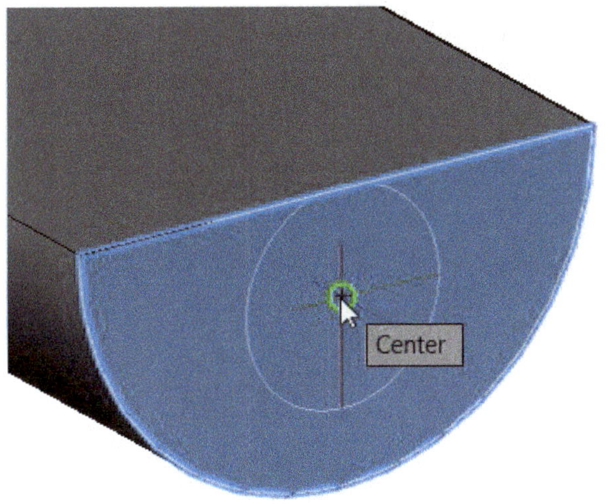

11. Type 1.25 in the command line and press ENTER.
12. Click on the two newly created circles; the Move gizmo is displayed at the centerpoint of the circles.
13. Click on the origin point of the Move gizmo.
14. Move the pointer upward and select the Midpoint of the horizontal edge.

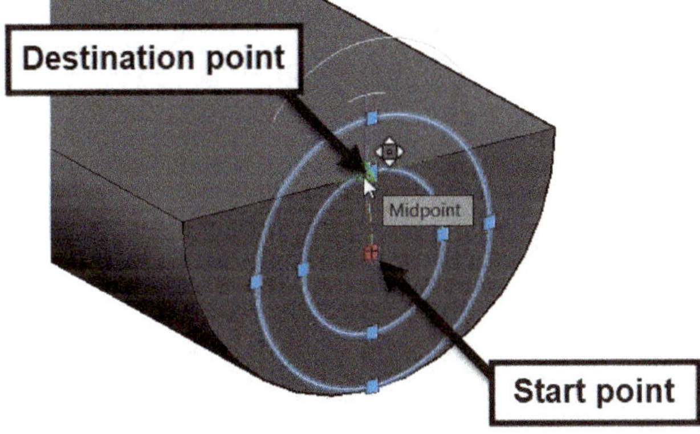

The circles are moved to the new location.

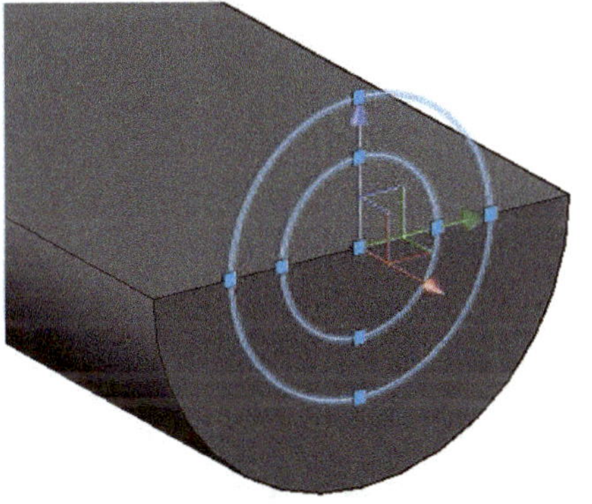

15. On the ribbon, click **Home > Modeling > Presspull** .
16. Click in the region between the two circles.

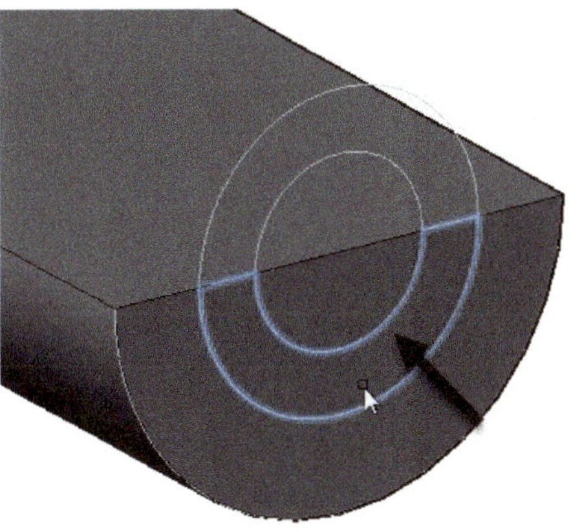

17. Type **-0.3** in the command line and press ENTER.

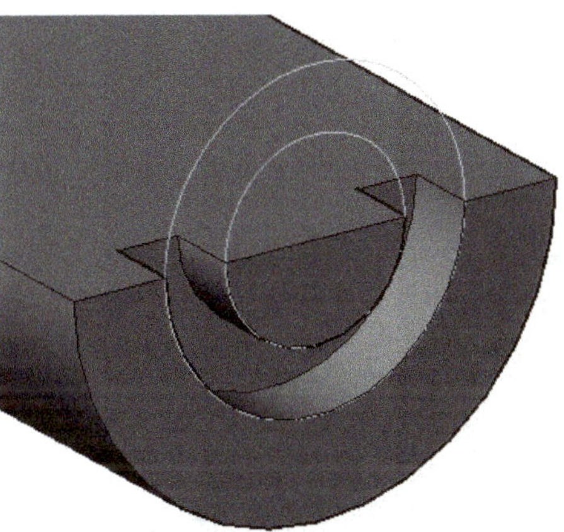

18. On the ribbon, click **Home > Draw > Rectangle**.
19. Select the left corner point of the model, as shown.

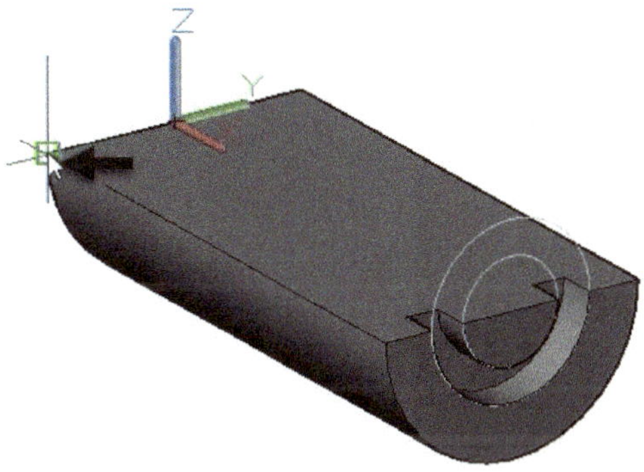

20. Select the **Dimensions** option from the command line.

21. Type 0.8 in the command line and press ENTER.
22. Type 0.3 in the command line and press ENTER.
23. Move the pointer toward the right and click to create the rectangle.

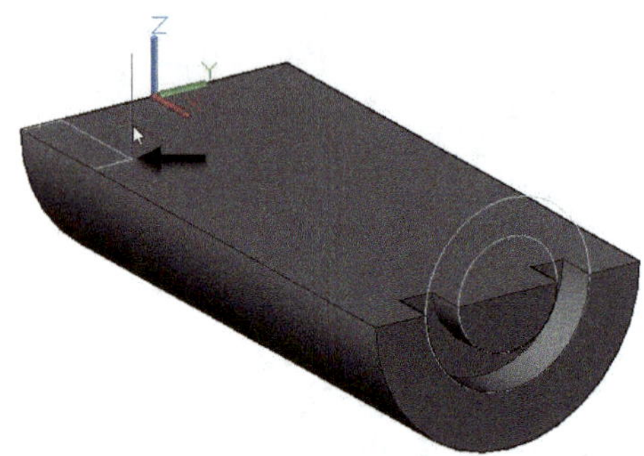

24. On the ribbon, click **Home > Modeling > Solid drop-down > Revolve**.
25. Select the rectangle and press ENTER.
26. Select the **X** option from the command line. The X-axis is selected as the axis of revolution.
27. Select the **Reverse** option from the command line. The revolution direction is reversed.
28. Type 180 in the command line and press ENTER.

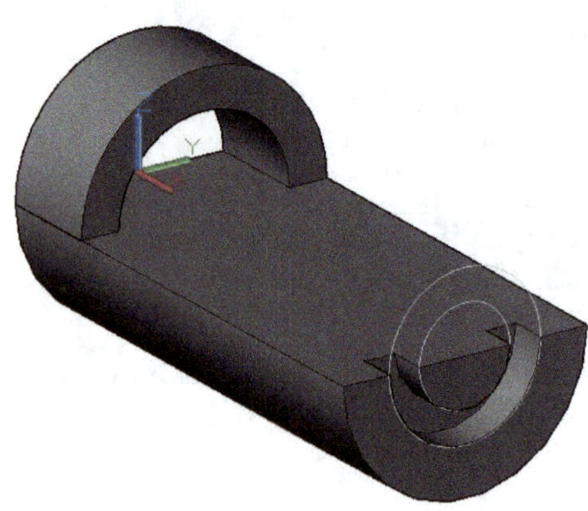

29. On the ribbon, click **Home** tab > **Solid Editing** panel > **Solid, Union**.
30. Select the main body.
31. Select the newly created revolved solid and press ENTER.

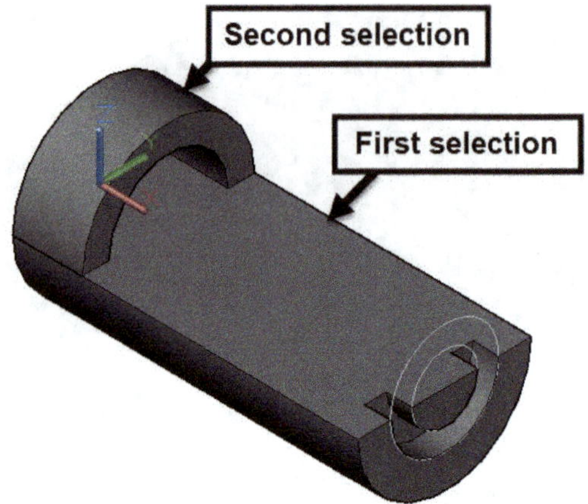

32. Select the two circles.

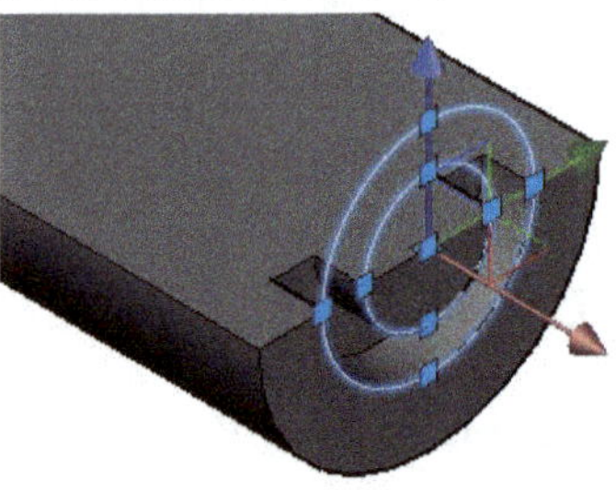

33. Right-click and select **Isolate > Hide Objects**.

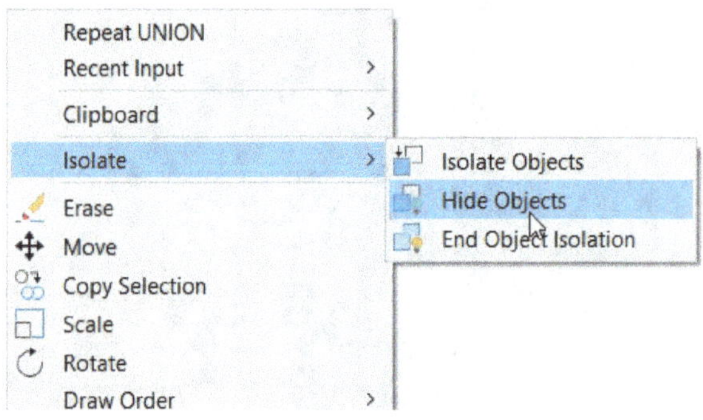

34. Click **Application Menu > Save**.
35. Browse to a location on your computer.
36. Type **Ch2_tutorial2** in the **File name** box.
37. Click the **Save** button.
38. Click **Application Menu > Close > Current Drawing**.

Exercises

Exercise 1

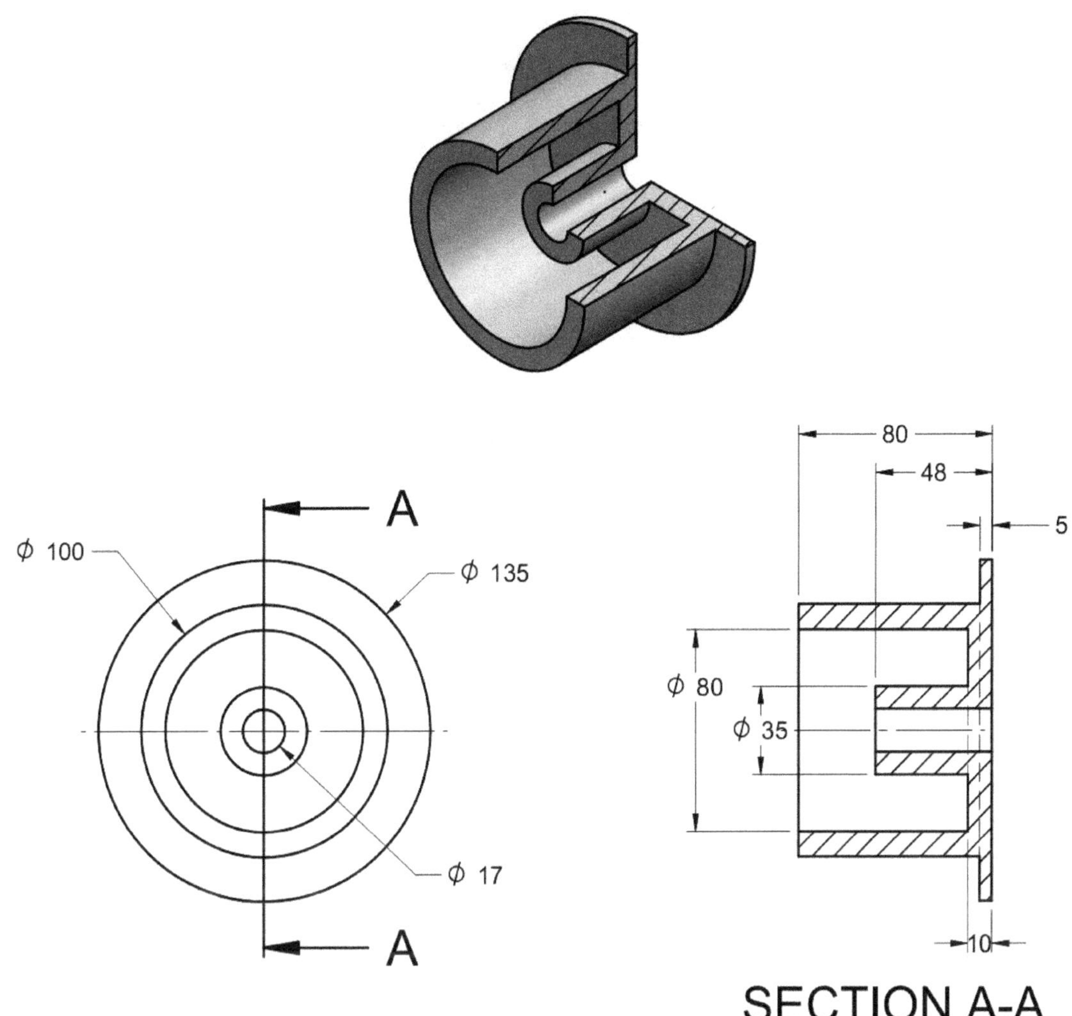

Exercise 2

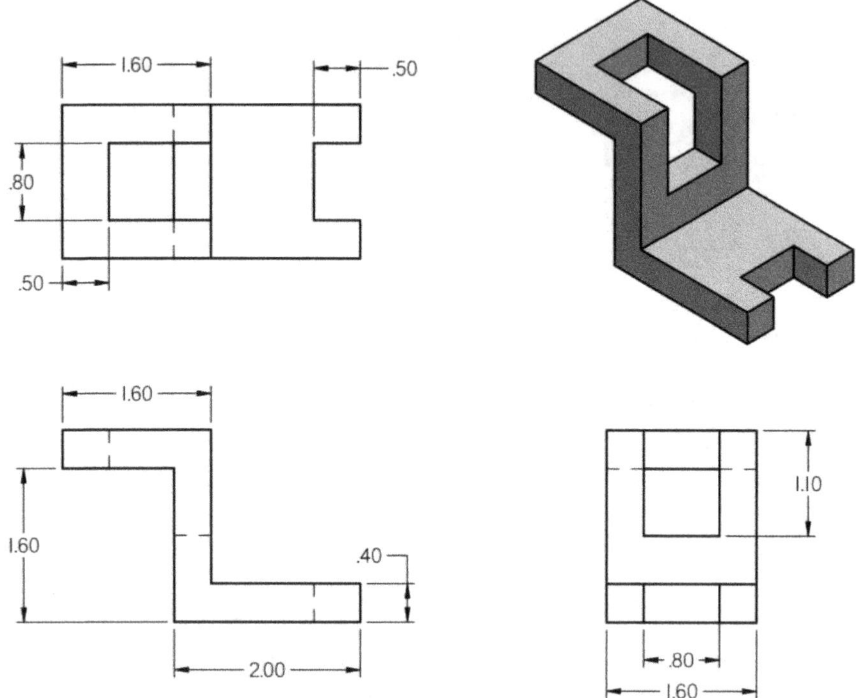

Exercise 3

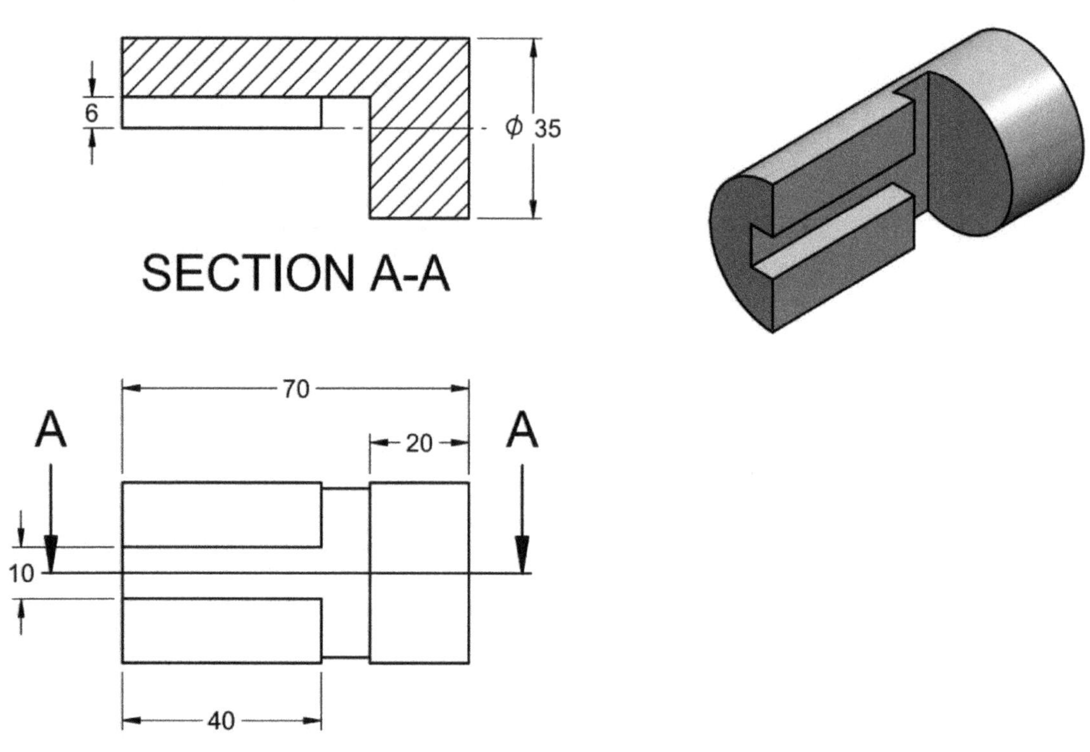

SECTION A-A

Chapter 3: Placed Features

Until now, all of the features that were covered in the previous chapter were based on 2D drawings. However, there are certain features in AutoCAD that do not require a drawings at all. You can just place them on your models. However, you must have some existing geometry to add these features. Unlike a 2D drawing based feature, you cannot use a placed feature for a model's first feature. For example, to create a *Fillet* feature, you must have an already existing edge. In this chapter, you will learn how to add a placed features to your design.

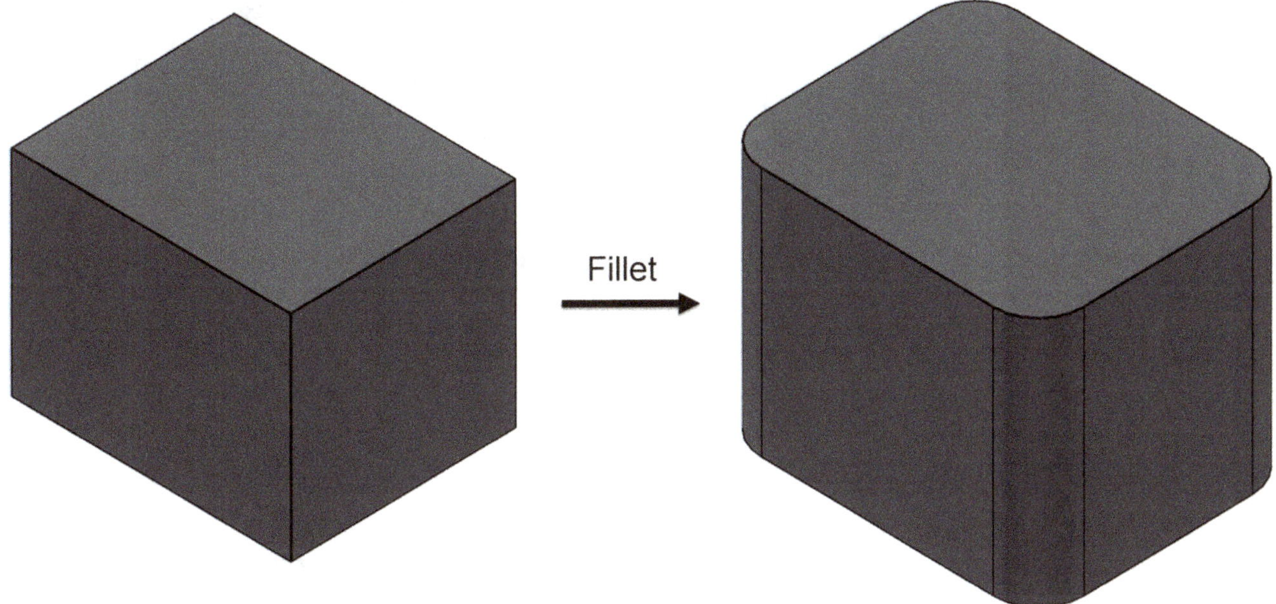

The topics covered in this chapter are:

- *Fillets*
- *Chamfers*
- *Drafts*
- *Shells*

Fillet Edge

This tool breaks the sharp edges of a model and blends them. You do not need a 2D drawing to create a fillet. All

you need to have is model edges. Click **Solid > Solid Editing > Fillet Edge** on the ribbon and select the edges to be filleted. You can select the edges located at the back of the model by rotating the model using the **Orbit** tool available on the Navigation Bar. However, you can also select the edges located on the back side of the model. To do this, you need to select **Home > View > Visual Styles > Wireframe** from the ribbon before activating the **Fillet Edge** tool.

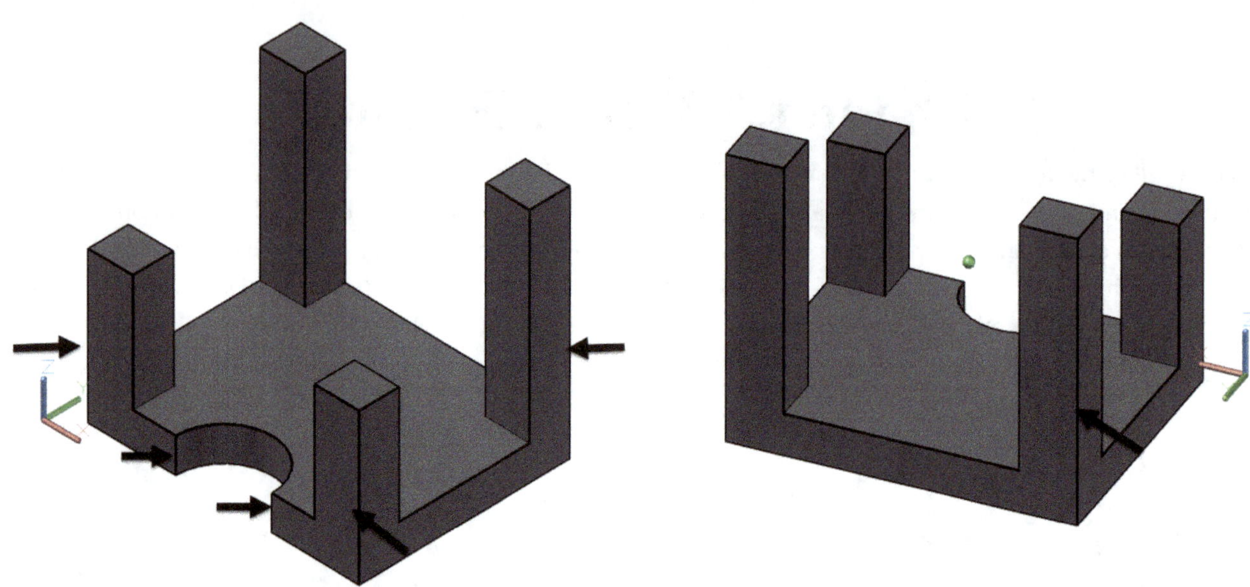

Select the **Radius** option from the command line and type-in the radius value in the command line, and then press ENTER. Again, press ENTER to fillet the edges.

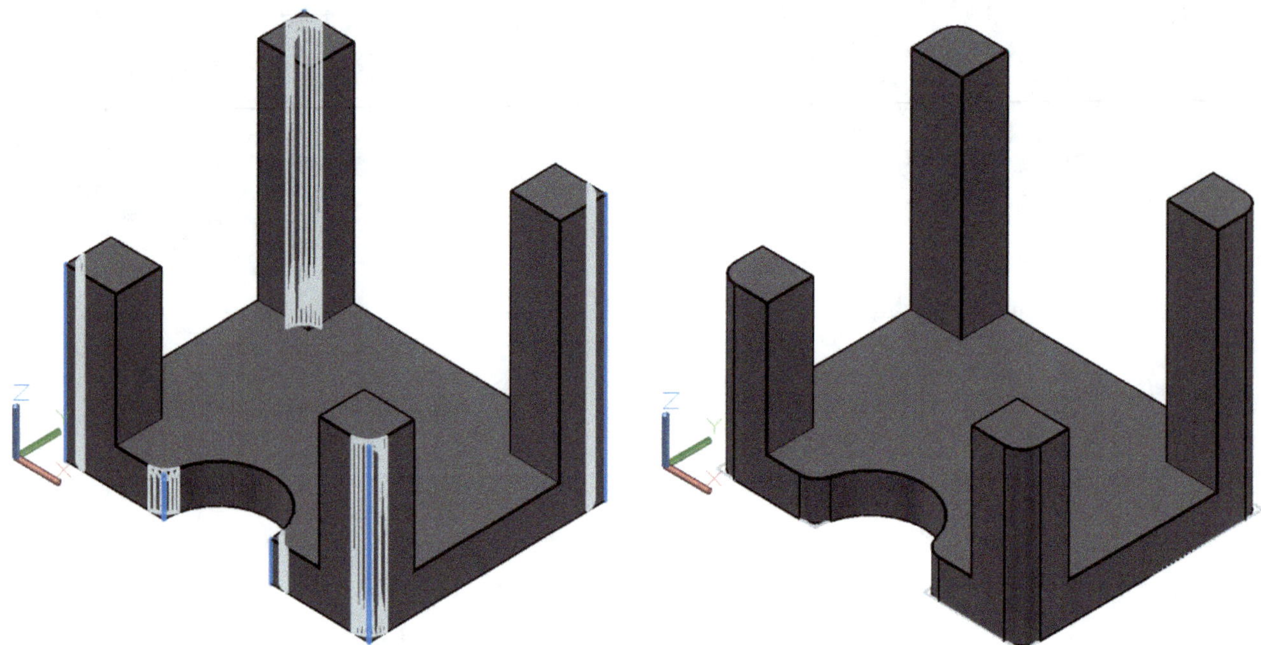

If you want to select all the edges tangentially connected, activate the **Fillet Edge** tool and select the **Chain** option from the command line. Next, select anyone of the tangently connected edges; all the connected edges are selected.

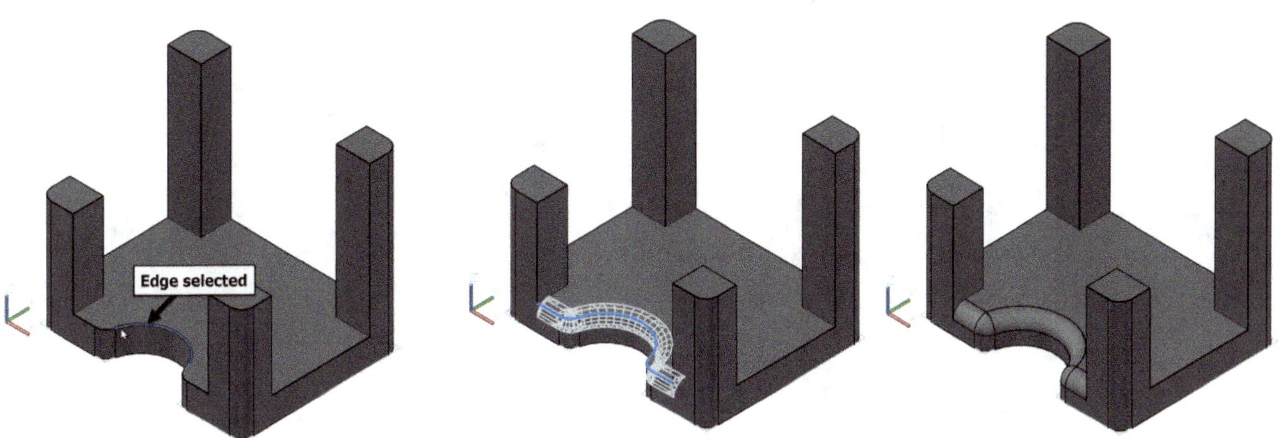

The **Loop** option allows you to select all the edges forming a closed loop. Activate the **Fillet Edge** tool and select the **Loop** option from the command line. Next, click on anyone of the edges of a face, as shown. All the edges of the face are highlighted in blue. Select the **Next** option from the command line to highlight the edges of the adjacent face. Select the **Accept** option to select the highlighted edges.

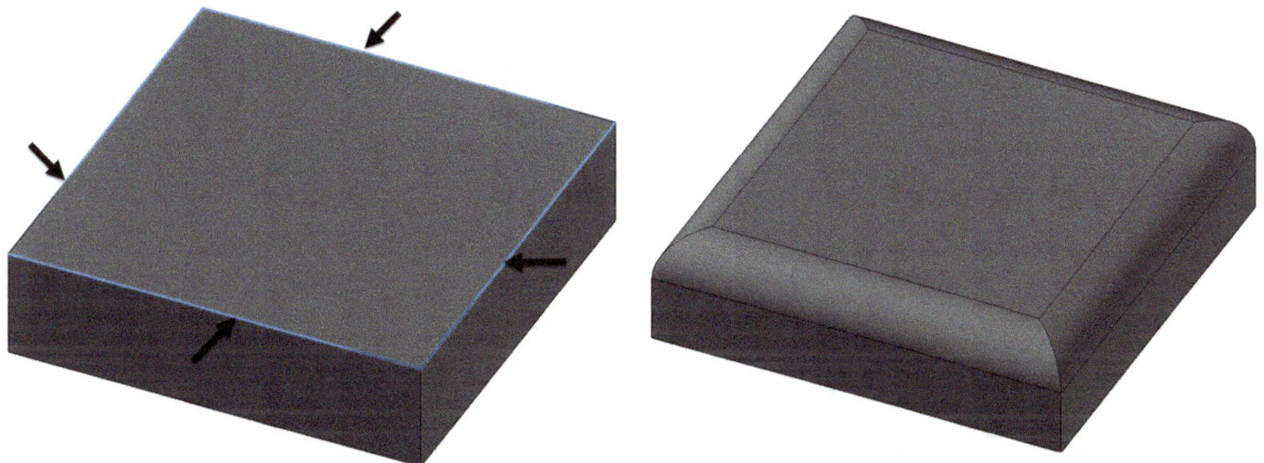

Chamfer Edge

The **Chamfer Edge** and **Fillet Edge** commands are commonly used to break sharp edges. The difference is that the **Chamfer Edge** command adds a bevel face to the model. A chamfer is also a placed feature. On the **Solid** tab of the ribbon, click **Solid Editing** panel > **Fillet Edge** drop-down > **Chamfer Edge** . Next, select the **Distance** option from the command line. Type-in the distance1 value in the command line and press ENTER. Next, type-in the Distance 2 value in the command line and press ENTER. Press ENTER twice to chamfer the edges of the model.

Taper Faces

When creating cast or plastic parts, you are often required to add a draft (taper) to them so that they can be molded easily. A draft is an angle or taper applied to the components' faces to be removed from a mold easily. The following illustration shows a molded part with and without the draft.

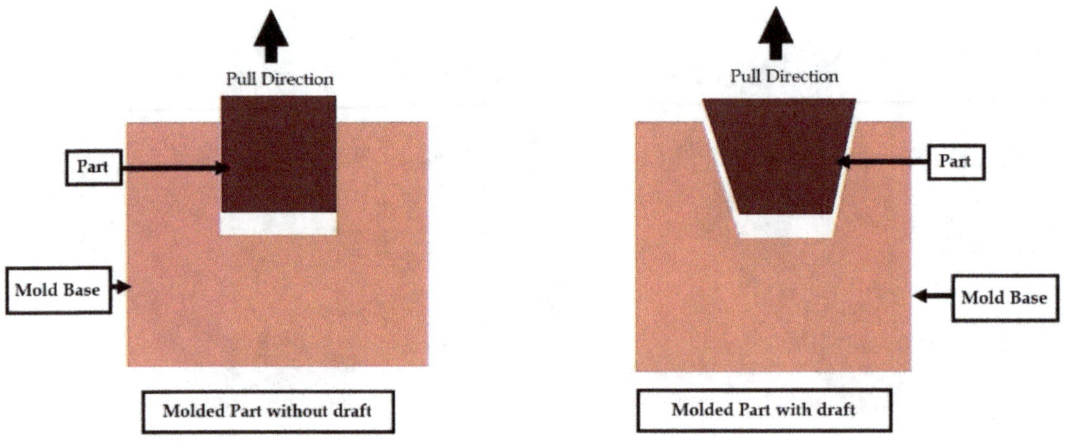

When creating *Extruded* features, you can predefine the taper angle. However, most of the time, it is easier to apply the taper after creating the features. On the **Solid** tab of the ribbon, click **Solid Editing > Solid Editing**

drop-down **> Taper Faces** . Next, select a flat face or faces to be tapered, and then press ENTER. Next, you need to specify the axis of the taper angle. To do this, click in the graphics window to specify the base point of the axis. Next, move the pointer vertically or horizontally, and then click. Next, type-in the taper angle and press ENTER. Select **eXit** from the command line.

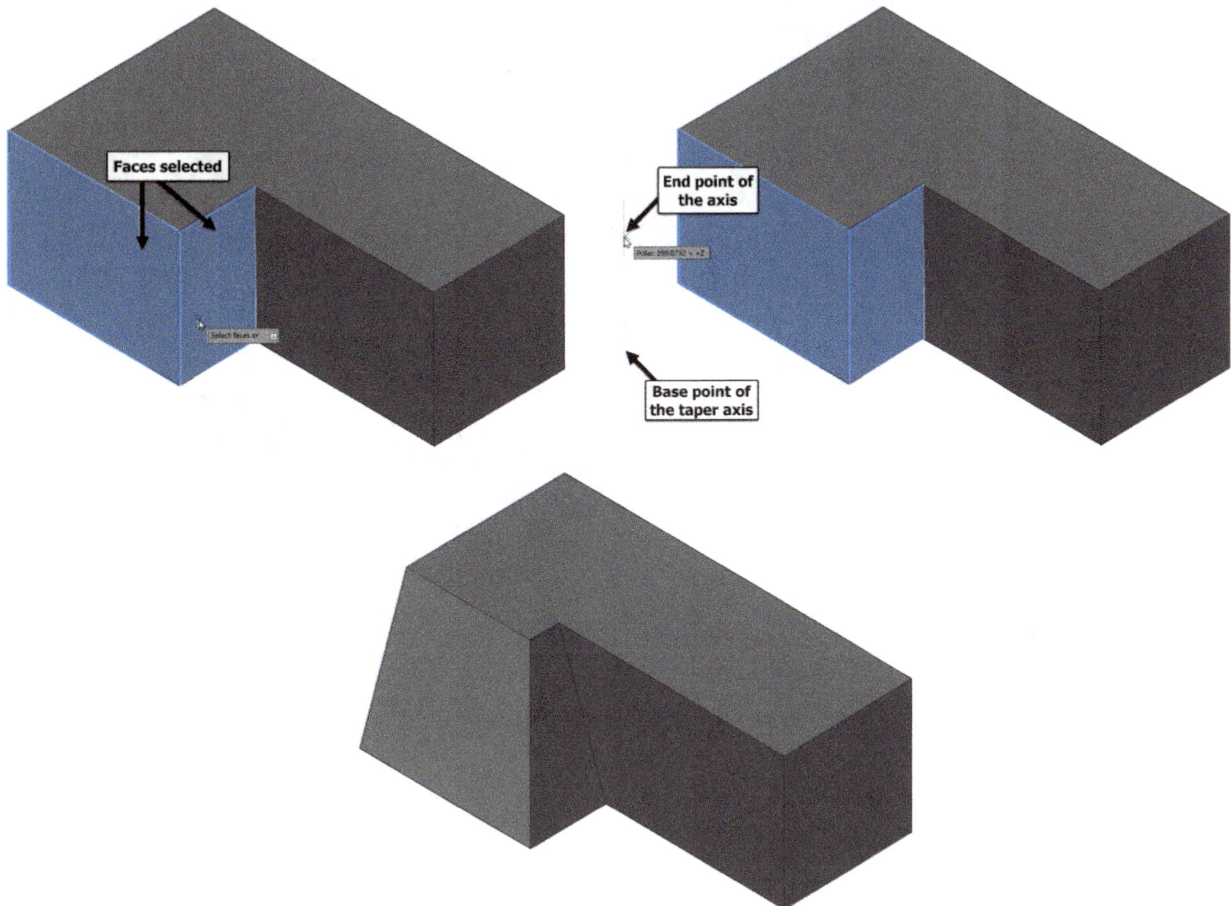

Shell

Shell is another useful feature that can be applied directly to a solid model. It allows you to take a solid geometry and make it hollow. This can be a powerful and time-saving technique when designing parts that call for thin walls such as bottles, tanks, and containers. This command is easy to use. First, create a solid body, and then click **Solids**

> Solid Editing panel **> Shell** on the ribbon. Next, select the solid body from graphics window and click on the faces to be removed. Press ENTER and type-in the thickness value of the shell. Next, press ENTER and select the **eXit** option from the command line.

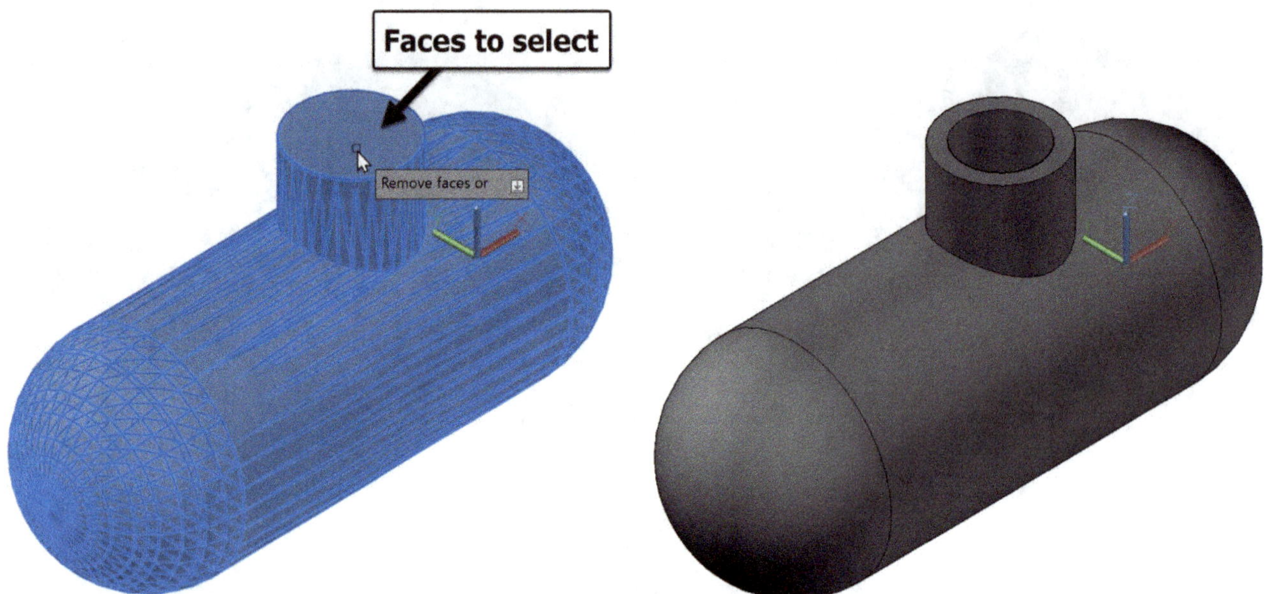

If you want to shell the solid body without removing any faces, activate the **Shell** command, select the solid body, and then press ENTER. Next, type-in the thickness value and press ENTER. Select **eXit** from the command line; this creates the shell without removing the faces. Change the **Visual Style** to **2D Wireframe** or **Wireframe** to view the shell.

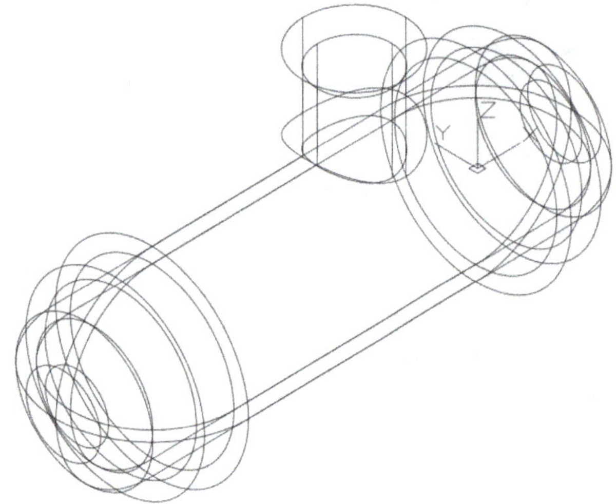

Tutorial 1 (Millimetres)

In this example, you create the part shown next.

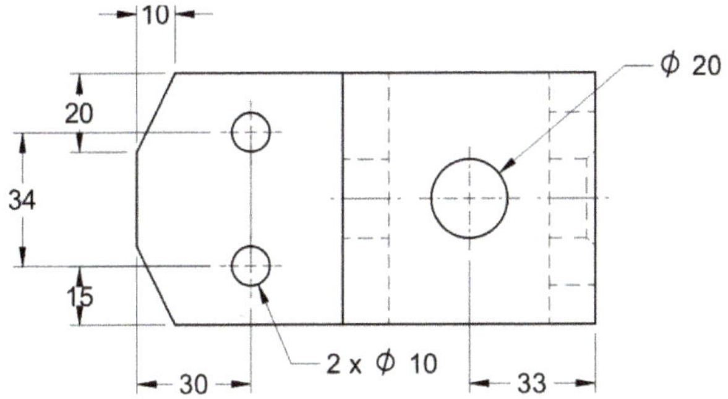

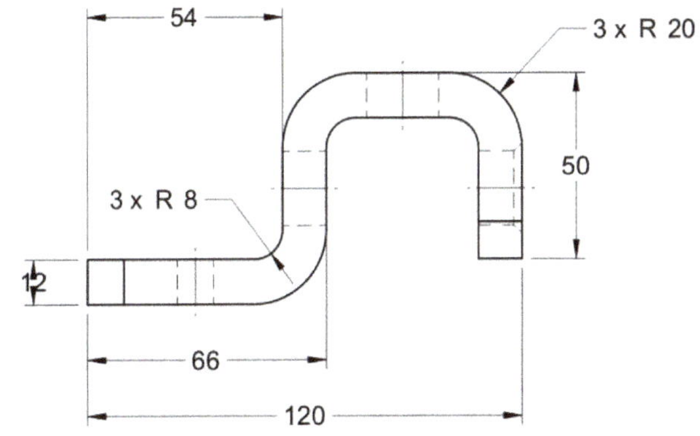

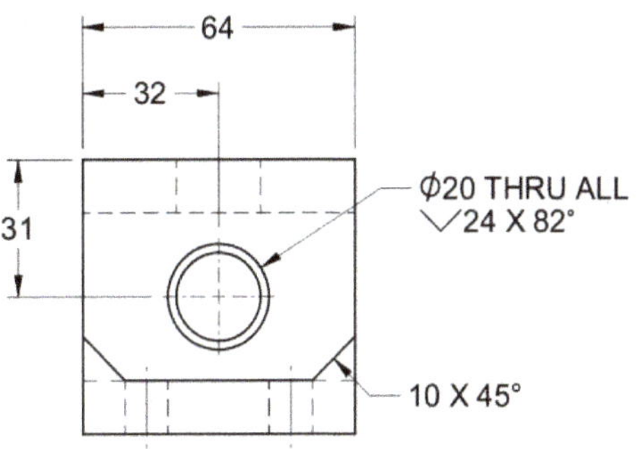

Creating a New File

1. Click the **AutoCAD 2025** icon on your desktop.
2. On the **Start** page, click **New** drop-down > **acadiso3D.dwt**.
3. Deactivate the **GRIDMODE** icon on the status bar.

Creating the Extruded Solid

1. On the ribbon, click **Home** tab > **View** panel > **View Manager** drop-down > **Front**. The view orientation is changed to Front. Also, the X and Y axis of the UCS is set to Front view.

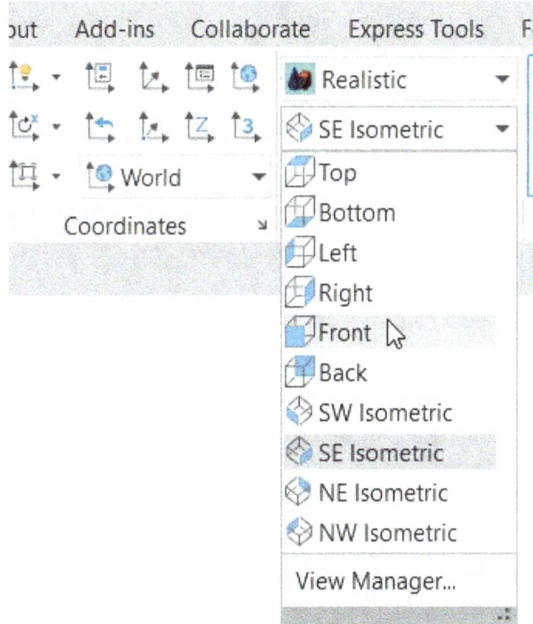

2. On the ribbon, click **Home** tab > **Draw** panel > **Polyline**.

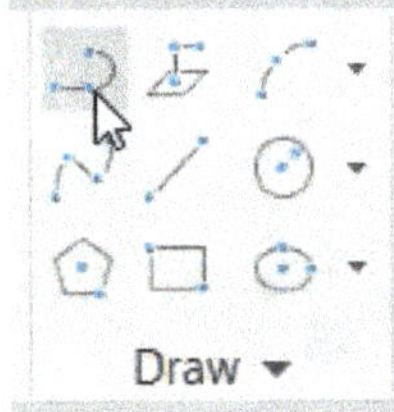

3. Type 0,0 in the command line and press ENTER.
4. Turn ON the Dynamic Input and ORTHOMODE icons on the status bar.
5. Move the pointer toward the right.
6. Type 66 and press ENTER.
7. Move the pointer upward.
8. Type 55 and press ENTER.
9. Move the pointer toward the right.
10. Type 42 and press ENTER.
11. Move the pointer downward.
12. Type 38 and press ENTER.
13. Press ESC.

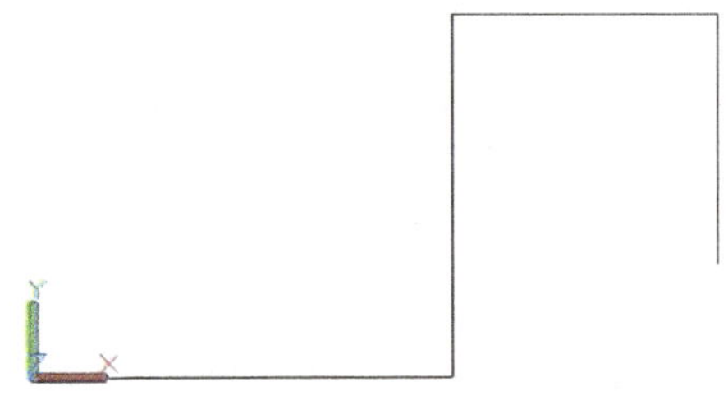

14. On the ribbon, click the **Home** tab > **Modify** panel > **Offset**.
15. Type 12 in the command line and press ENTER. The offset distance is defined.
16. Select the polyline from the graphics window.
17. Move the pointer upward and click.

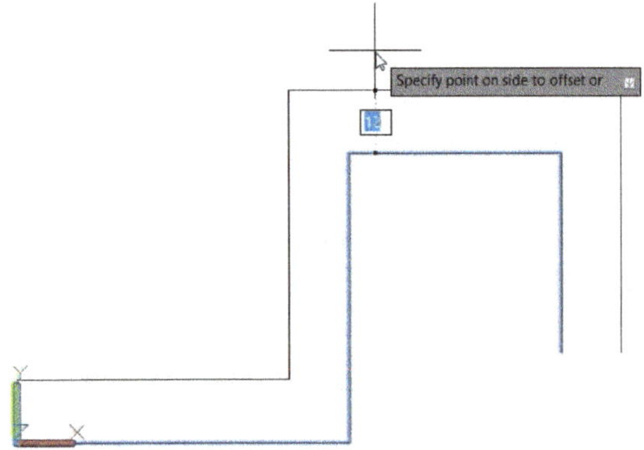

18. On the ribbon, click **Home** tab > **Draw** panel > **Line**.

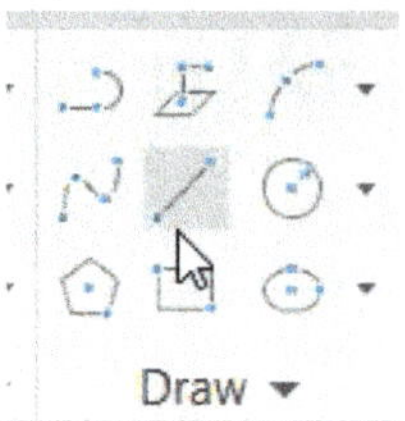

19. Select the right endpoints of the two polylines, as shown.

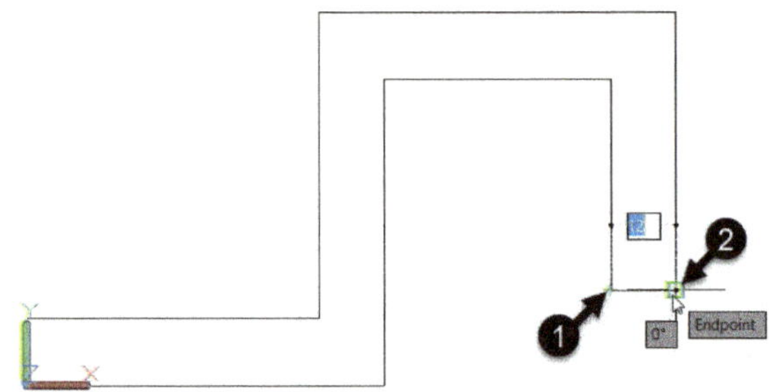

20. Press ESC.
21. On the ribbon, click **Home** tab > **Draw** panel > **Line**.
22. Select the left endpoints of the two polylines, as shown.

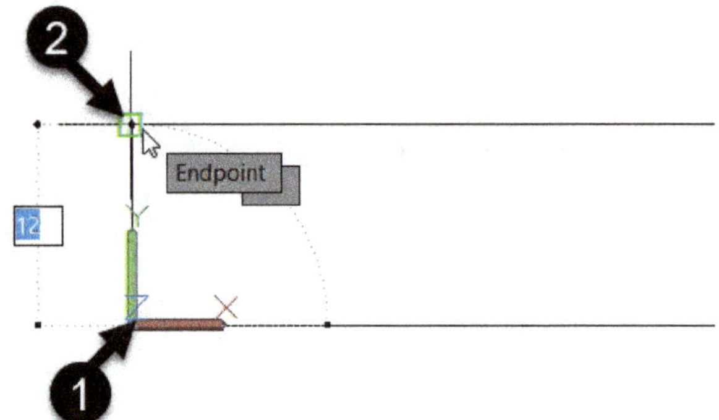

23. Press ESC.
24. On the **Home** tab of the ribbon, expand the **Draw** panel and click the **Region** icon.

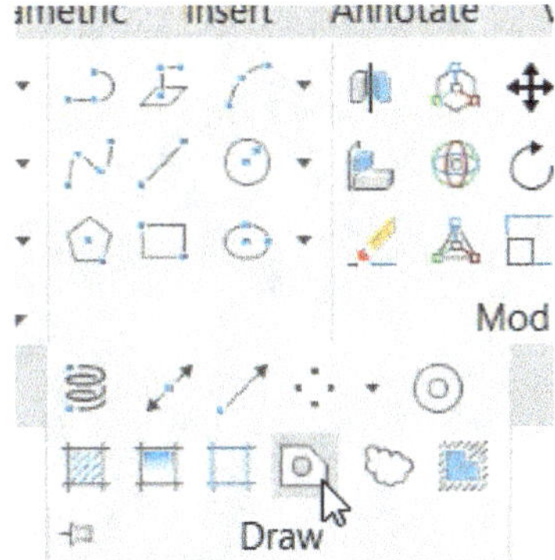

25. Create a selection window from left to right across all the elements of the drawing.

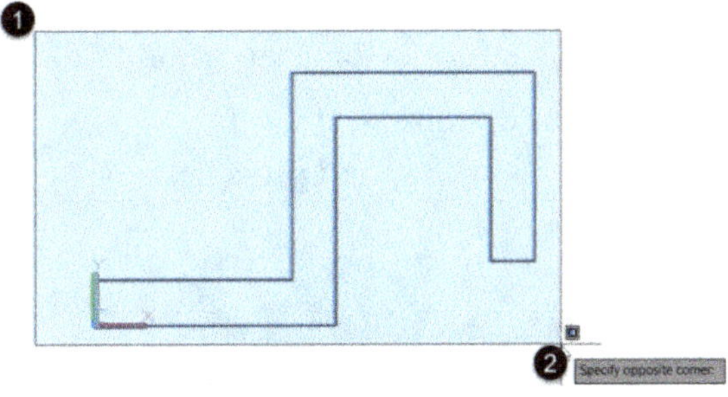

26. Press ENTER to convert all the 2D elements into a region.

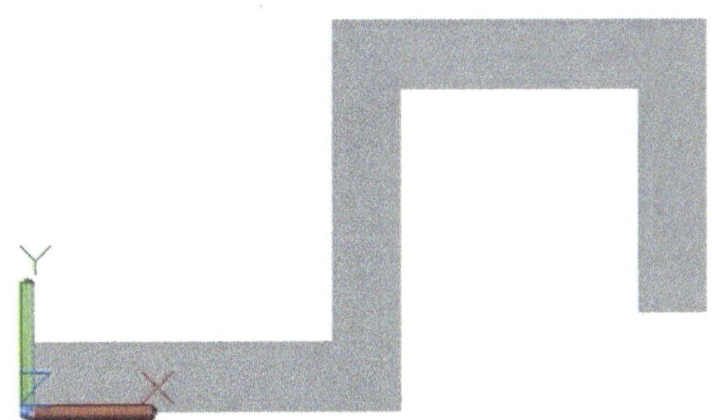

27. On the ribbon, click **Home** tab > **View** panel > **View Manager** drop-down > **SE Isometric**. The view orientation is changed to South East Isometric.

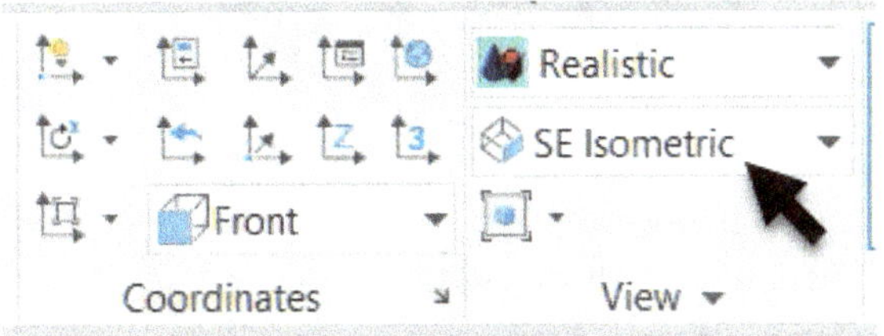

28. On the ribbon, click **Home** tab > **Modeling** panel > **Solids** drop-down > **Extrude**.
29. Click on the newly created region.
30. Press ENTER.
31. Move the pointer toward the right.
32. Type 64 and press ENTER.

Creating Holes

1. On the ribbon, click **Home** tab > **Coordinates** panel > **UCS**.

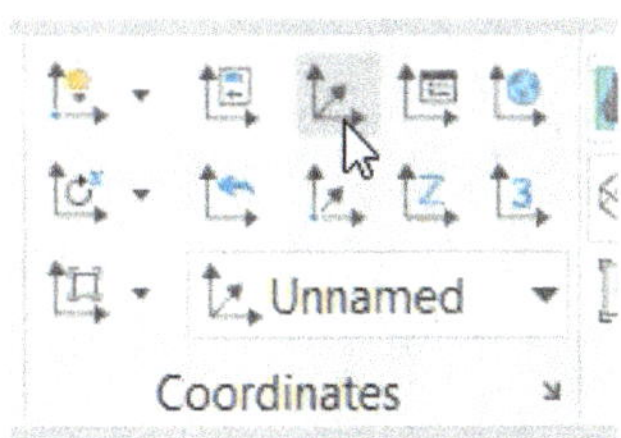

2. Select the lower-left corner of the right-side face to define the origin of the UCS.

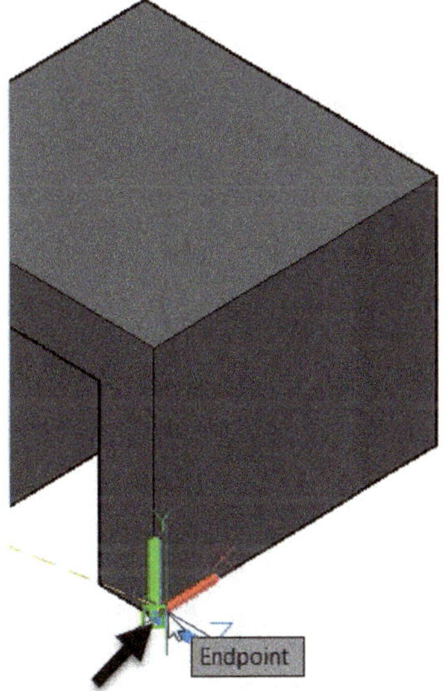

3. Move the pointer toward the right and select the lower right corner.

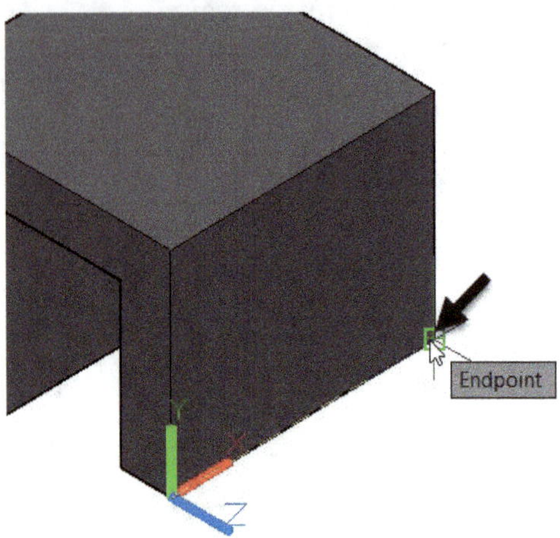

4. Move the pointer upward and select the top-left corner.

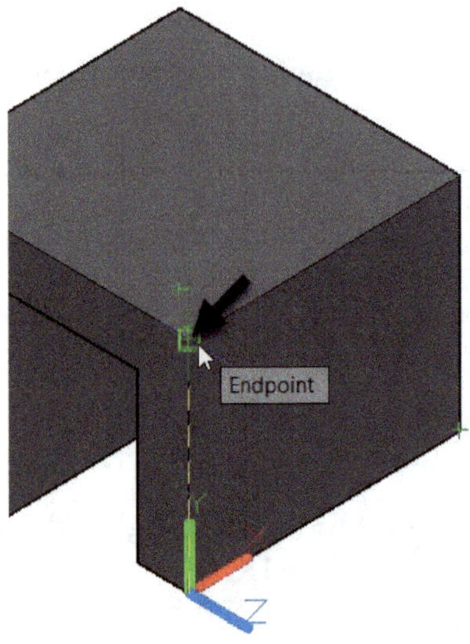

5. On the ribbon, click **Home** tab > **Modeling** panel > **Primitives** drop-down > **Cylinder**.
6. Type **32,19** in the command line and press ENTER. The centerpoint of the cylinder is defined.
7. Type **10** in the command line and press ENTER. The radius of the cylinder is defined.
8. Move the pointer toward the left and click to create the cylinder.

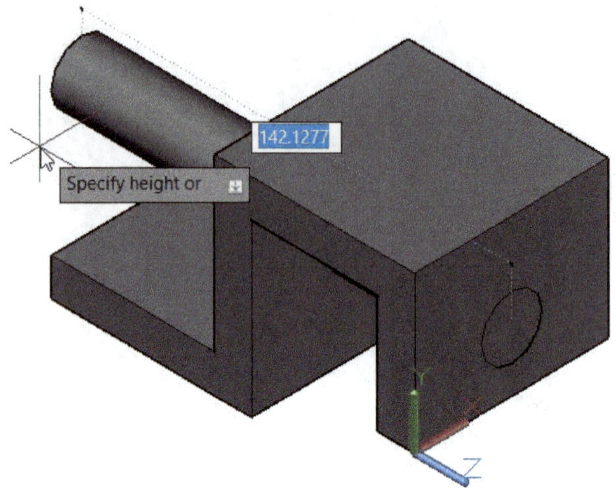

9. On the ribbon, click **Home** tab > **Solid Editing** panel > **Solid, Subtract** .
10. Select the main body and press ENTER.

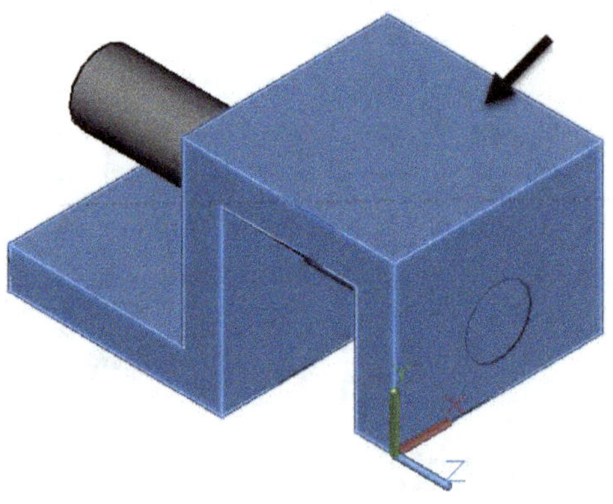

11. Select the cylinder and press ENTER. The cylinder is removed from the main body.

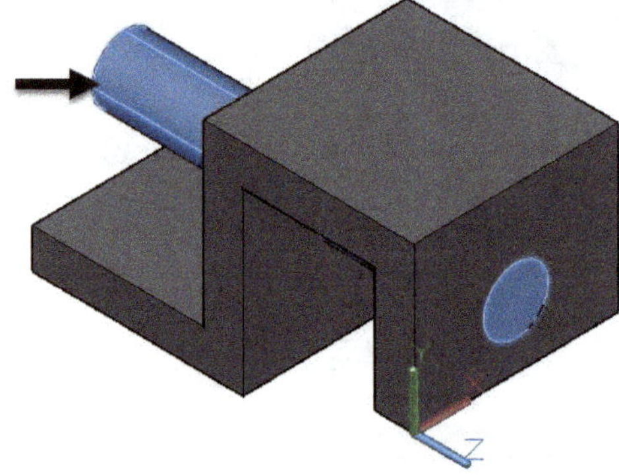

12. On the ribbon, click the **Solid** tab > **Solid Editing** panel > **Fillet Edge** drop-down > **Chamfer Edge**.

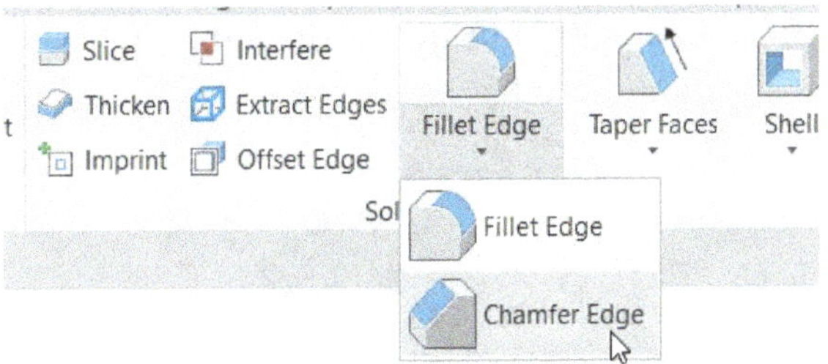

13. Select the circular edge of the hole.

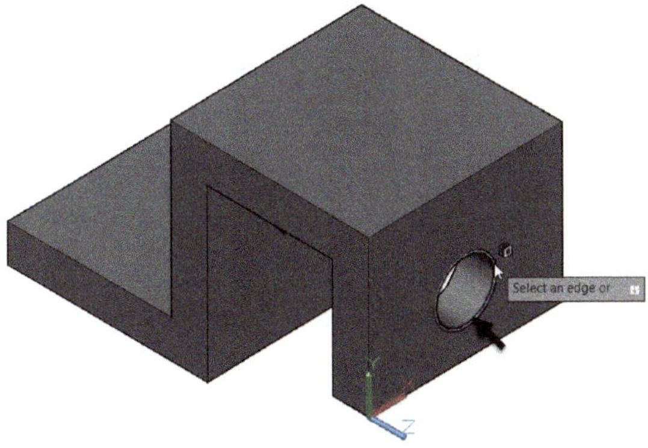

14. Select the **Distance** option from the command line.
15. Type **2** in the command line and press ENTER. Distance 1 is defined.
16. Type **1.5** in the command line and press ENTER. Distance 2 is defined.
17. Press ENTER twice to create the chamfer.

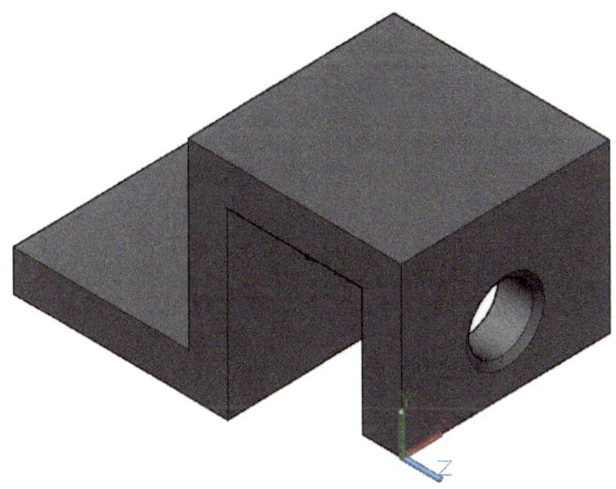

18. On the ribbon, click **Home** tab > **Coordinates** panel > **UCS** .
19. Select the top left corner of the right-side face to define the origin of the UCS.

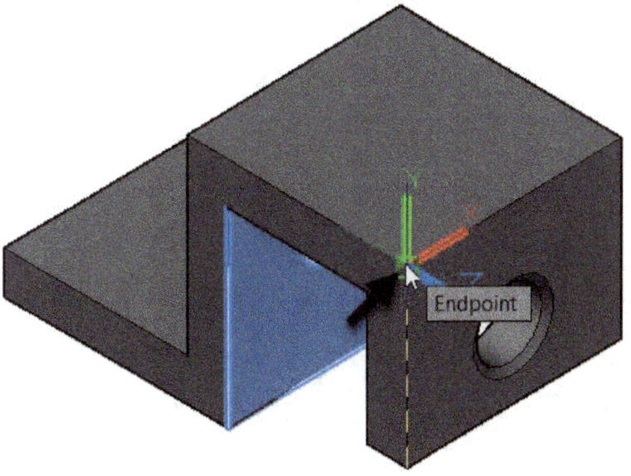

20. Move the pointer toward the right and select the top right corner of the right-side face.

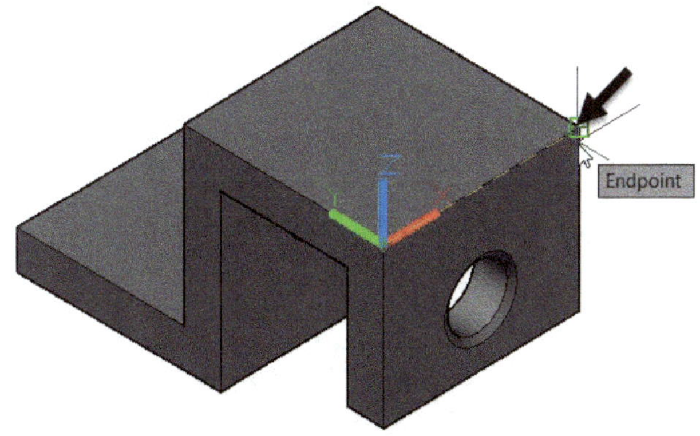

21. Move the pointer toward the left and select the corner of the top face, as shown.

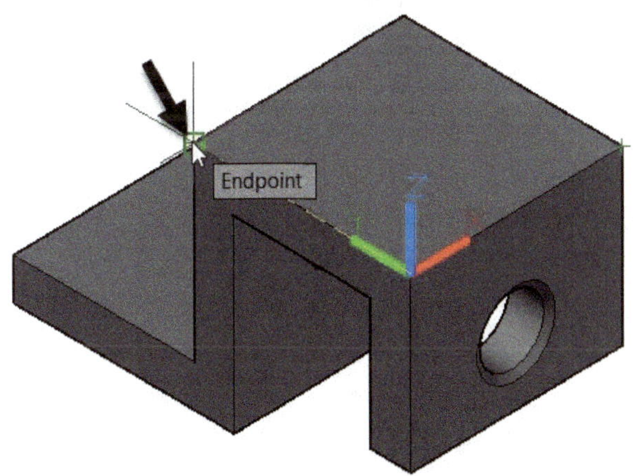

22. On the ribbon, click **Home** tab > **Modeling** panel > **Primitives** drop-down > **Cylinder**.
23. Type 32, 33 in the command line and press ENTER. The centerpoint of the cylinder is defined.
24. Type 10 in the command line and press ENTER to specify the radius of the cylinder.

25. Move the pointer downward and click to create the cylinder.

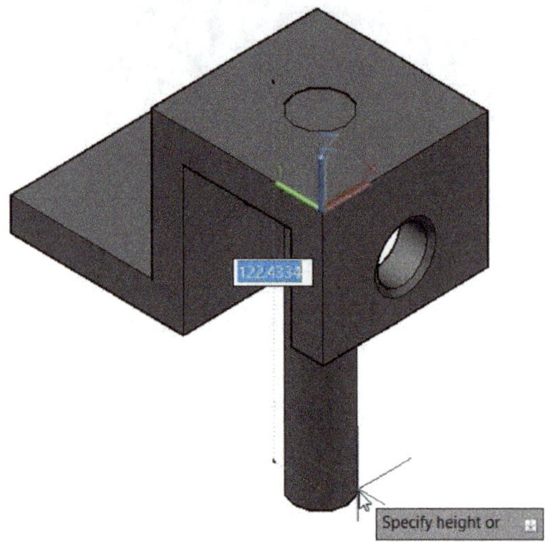

26. On the ribbon, click **Home** tab > **Coordinates** panel > **UCS** .

27. Select the front left corner of the flat face, as shown.

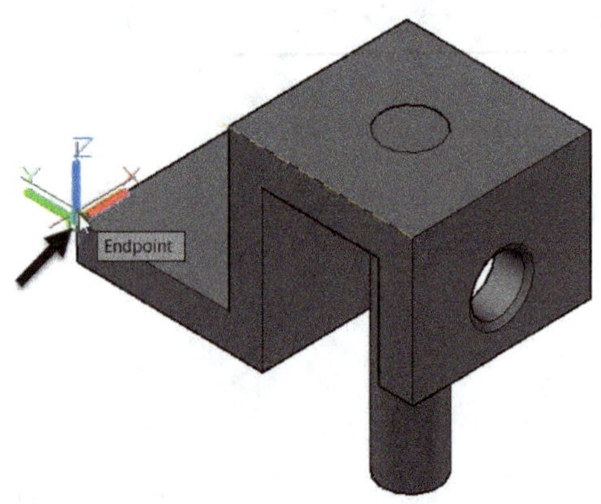

28. Move the pointer backward and select the corner point, as shown.

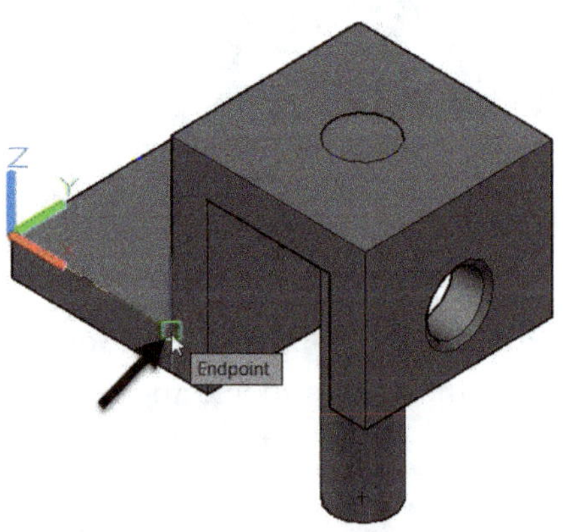

29. Move the pointer toward the right and select the midpoint of the edge, as shown.

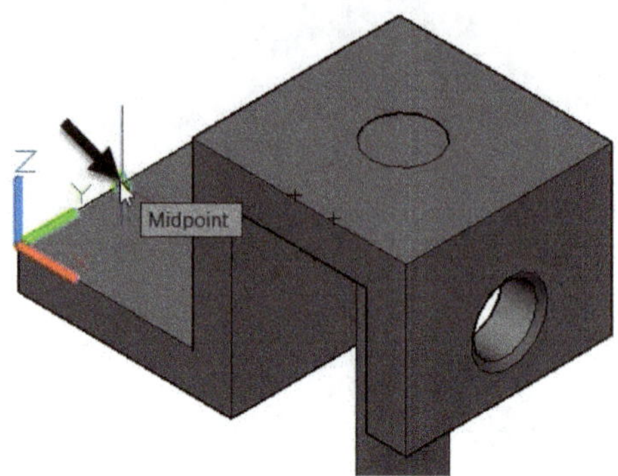

30. On the ribbon, click **Home** tab > **Modeling** panel > **Primitives** drop-down > **Cylinder**.

31. Type 30, 15 in the command line and press ENTER. The centerpoint of the cylinder is defined.

32. Type 5 in the command line and press ENTER to specify the radius of the cylinder.

33. Move the pointer downward and click to create the cylinder.

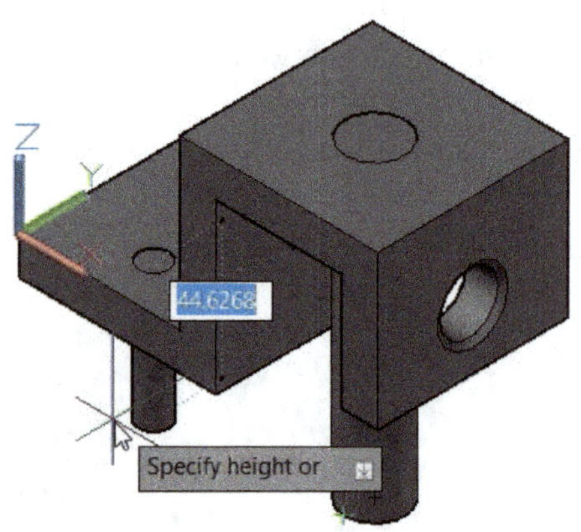

34. On the **Home** tab of the ribbon, expand the **Modify** panel and click the **Mirror** icon.

35. Select the newly created cylinder and press ENTER.

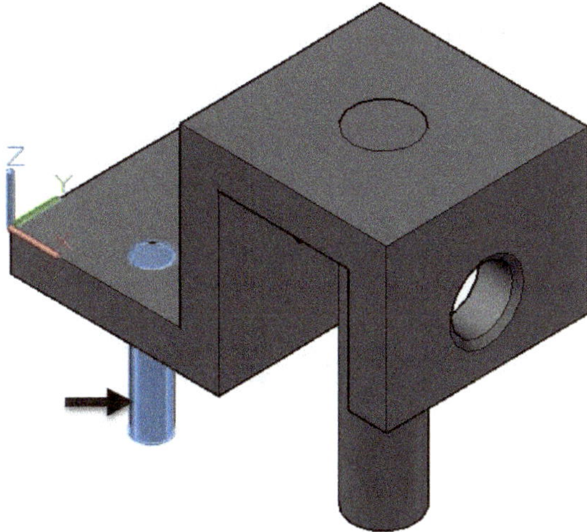

36. Select the midpoint of the horizontal edge of the top face, as shown.

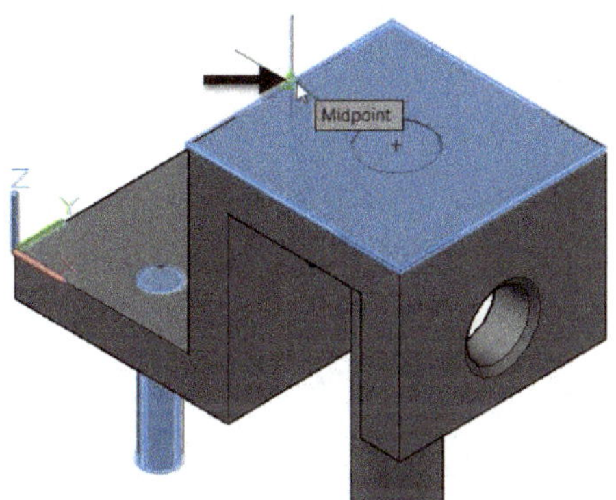

37. Move the pointer backward and select the midpoint of the horizontal edge.

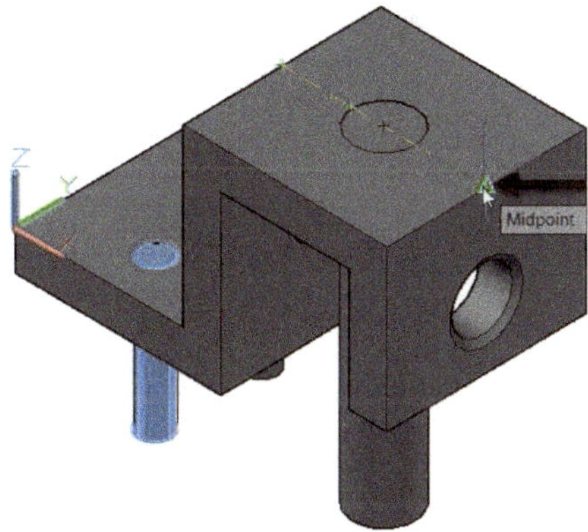

38. Select **No** to keep the source object.

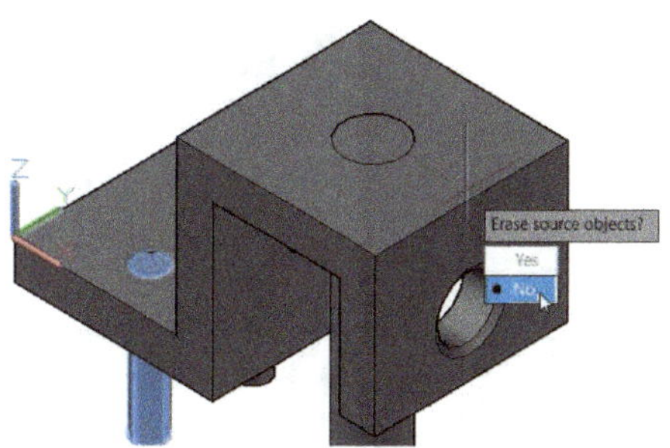

39. Click the front left corner of the ViewCube to change the orientation.

40. On the ribbon, click **Home** tab > **Solid Editing** panel > **Solid, Subtract** .
41. Select the main body and press ENTER.

42. Select the three cylinders and press ENTER. The cylinders are removed from the main body.

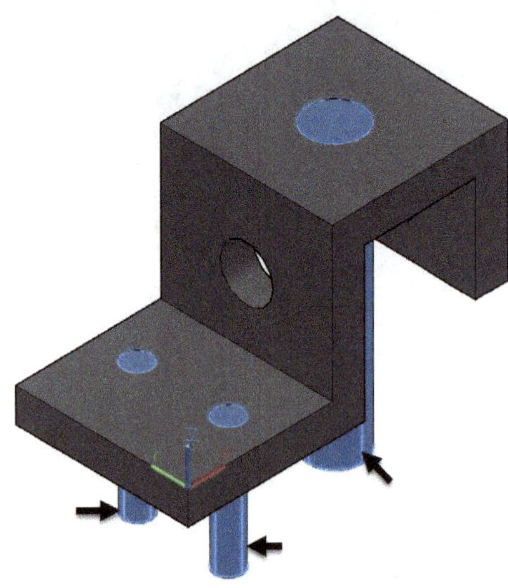

Creating Chamfers and Fillets

1. On the ribbon, click **Solid** tab > **Solid Editing** panel > **Fillet Edge** drop-down > **Chamfer Edge** .

2. Click on the vertical edge of the model, as shown.

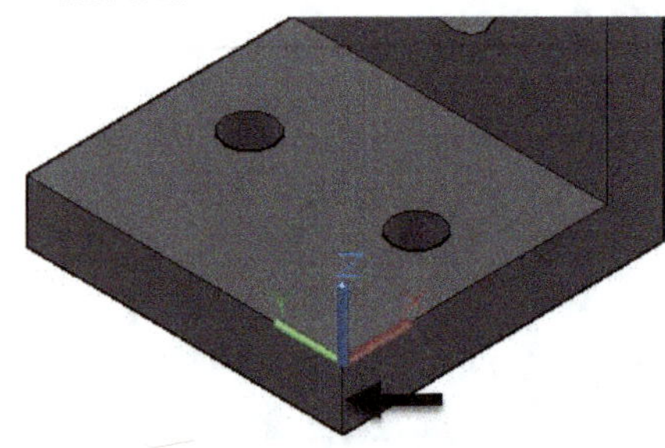

3. Select the **Distance** option from the command line.
4. Type **10** in the command line and press ENTER. Distance 1 is defined.
5. Type **20** in the command line and press ENTER. Distance 2 is defined.
6. Press ENTER twice to create the chamfer.

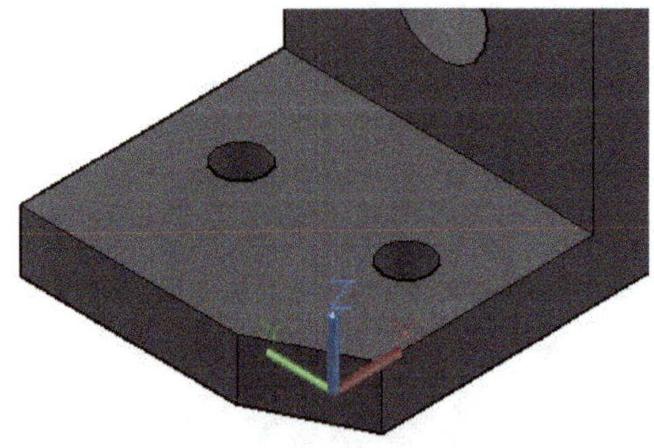

7. On the ribbon, click **Solid** tab > **Solid Editing** panel > **Fillet Edge** drop-down > **Chamfer Edge** .

8. Select the left vertical edge of the model, as shown.

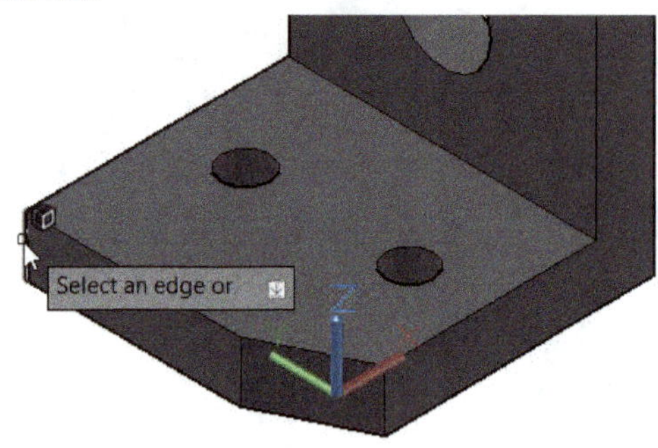

9. Select the **Distance** option from the command line.
10. Type **20** in the command line and press ENTER. Distance 1 is defined.
11. Type **10** in the command line and press ENTER. Distance 2 is defined.
12. Press ENTER twice to create a chamfer.

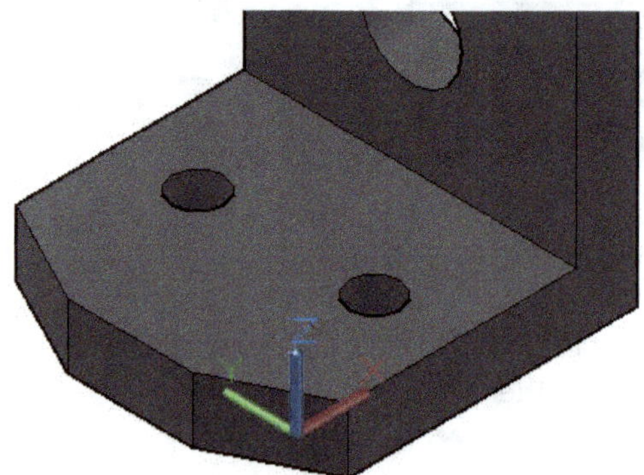

13. On the ribbon, click **Solid** tab > **Solid Editing** panel > **Fillet Edge**.

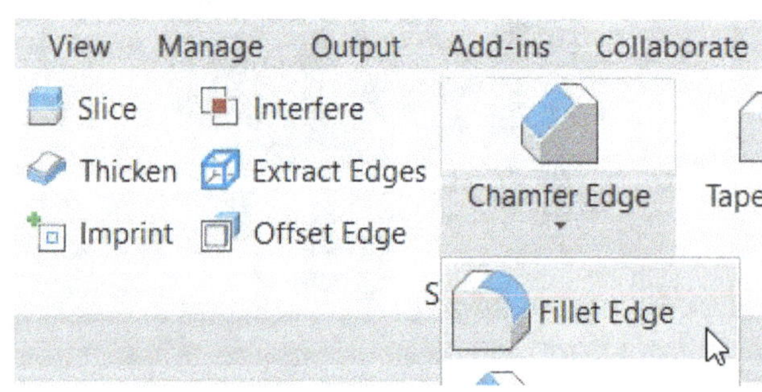

14. Click on the horizontal edge of the geometry, as shown.

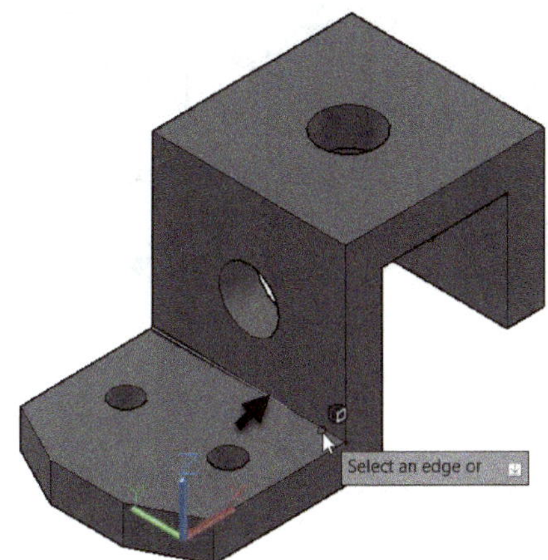

15. Click the bottom front corner of the ViewCube; the view orientation is changed.

16. Select the inner horizontal edge of the model, as shown.

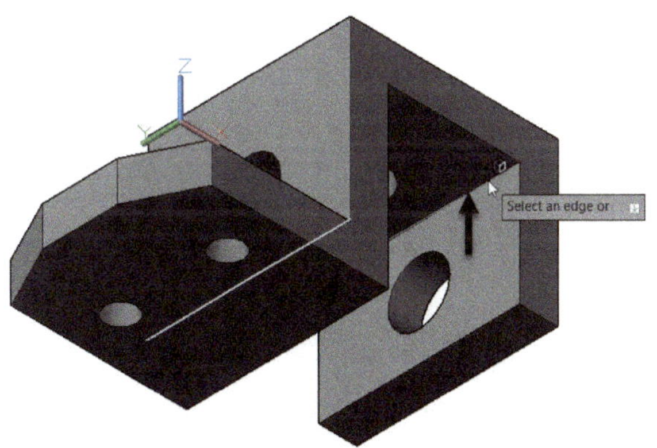

17. Select the bottom-back corner of the ViewCube. The orientation of the model is changed.

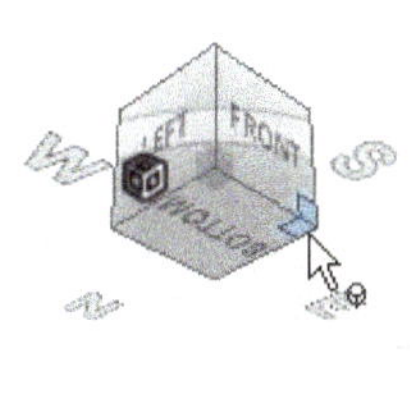

18. Select the visible inner horizontal edge.

19. Select the **Radius** option from the command line.
20. Type 8 and press ENTER thrice.
21. Change the view orientation to SW Isometric.

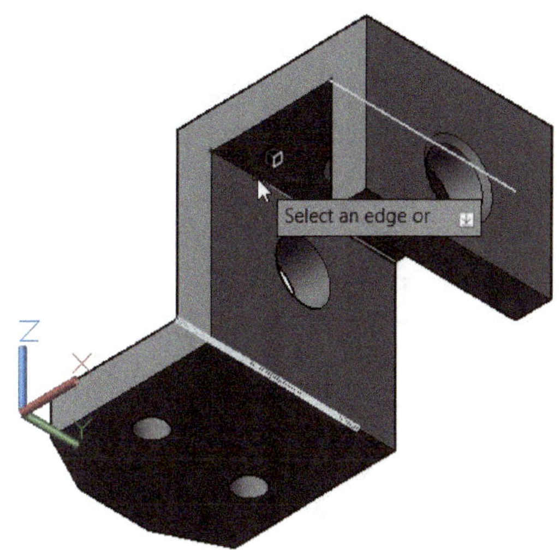

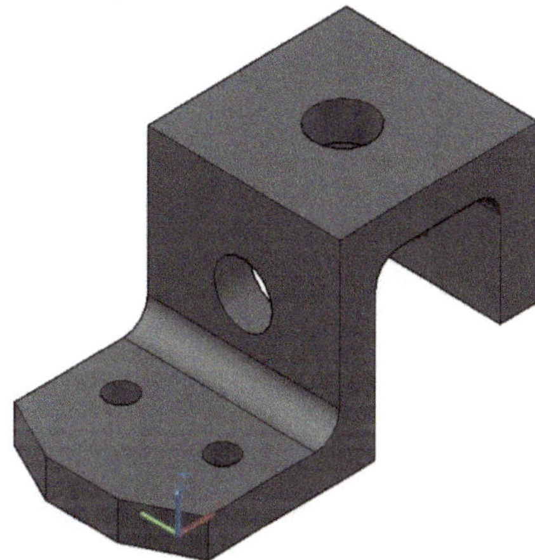

22. On the ribbon, click **Solid** tab > **Solid Editing** panel > **Fillet Edge**.
23. Select the horizontal edges of the model, as shown.

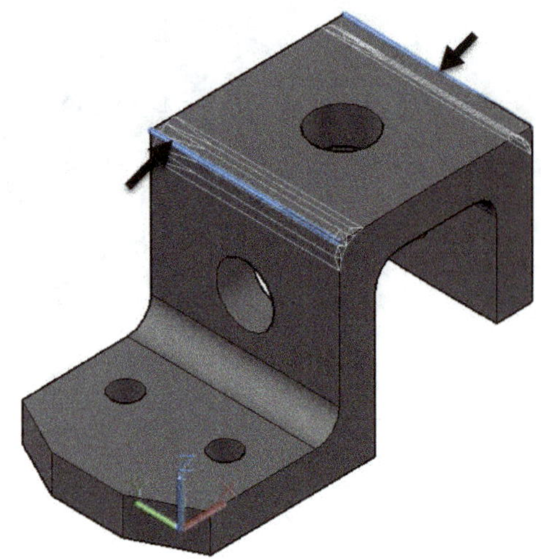

24. Click on the bottom right corner of the ViewCube.

25. Select the bottom horizontal edge of the model.

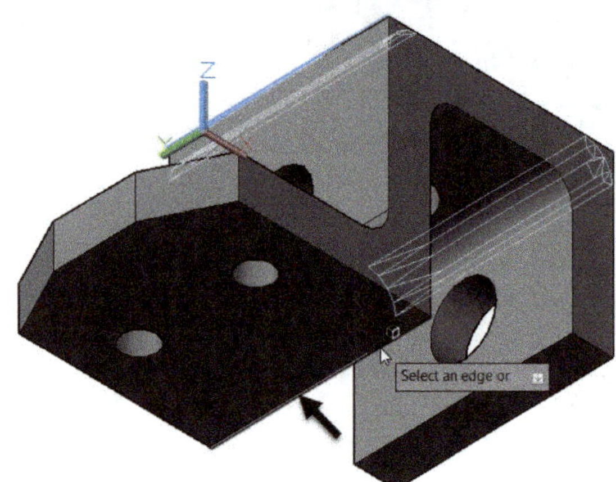

26. Select the **Radius** option from the command line.
27. Type 20 and press ENTER thrice.
28. Change the view orientation to SE Isometric.

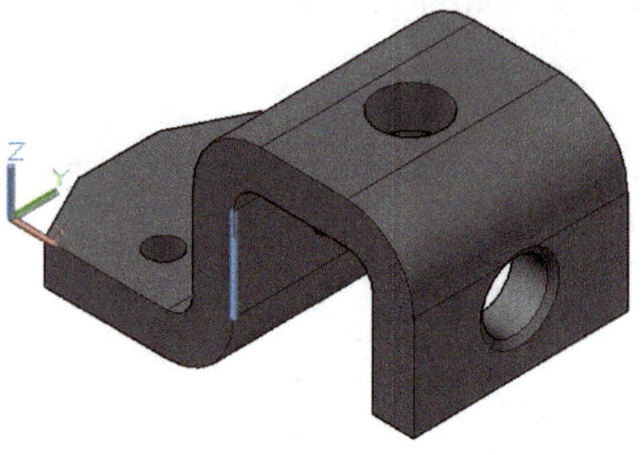

29. Click the **Orbit** tool on the Navigation Bar located at the right of the graphics window.

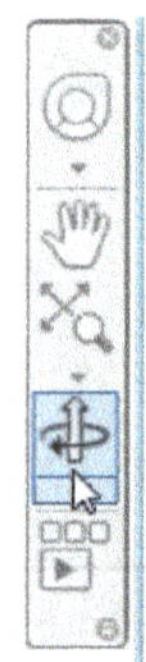

30. Press and hold the left mouse button and drag the pointer upward; the bottom portion is displayed.

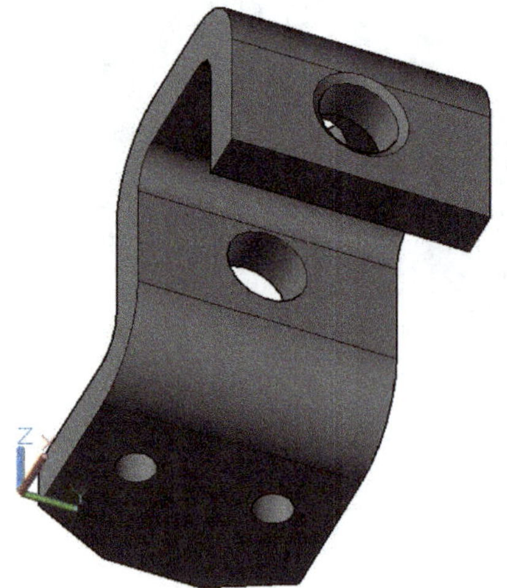

31. Right-click and select **Exit** from the shortcut menu.
32. On the ribbon, click **Solid** tab > **Solid Editing** panel > **Fillet Edge** drop-down > **Chamfer Edge** .

33. Click on the horizontal edges of the model, as shown.

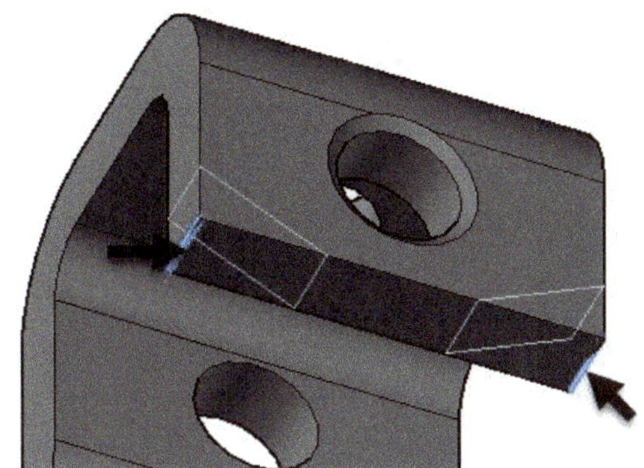

34. Select the **Distance** option from the command line.
35. Type 10 and press ENTER to specify the Distance 1.
36. Press ENTER to specify the Distance 2.
37. Press ENTER twice to create the chamfers.
38. Change the view orientation to SE Isometric.

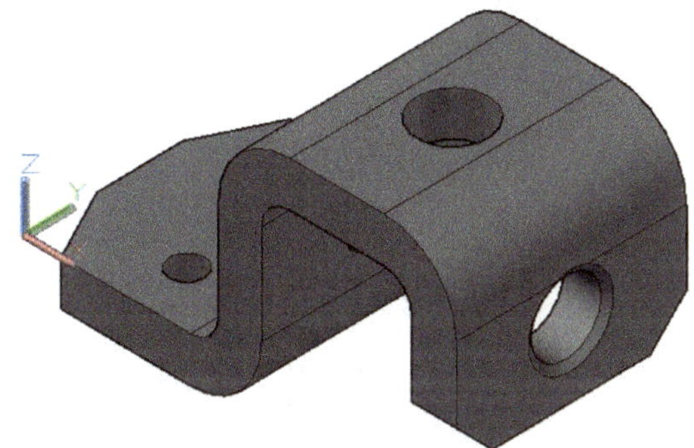

39. Click **Application Menu > Save**.
40. Browse to a location on your computer.
41. Type **Ch3_tutorial1** in the **File name** box.
42. Click the **Save** button.
43. Click **Application Menu > Close > Current Drawing**.

Exercises

Exercise 1 (Millimetres)

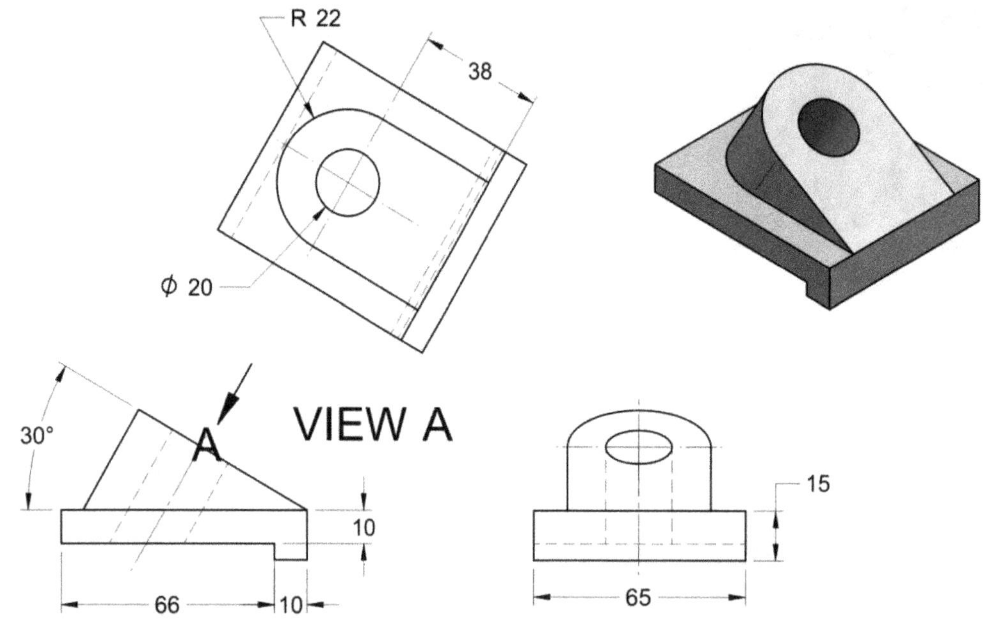

Exercise 2 (Inches)

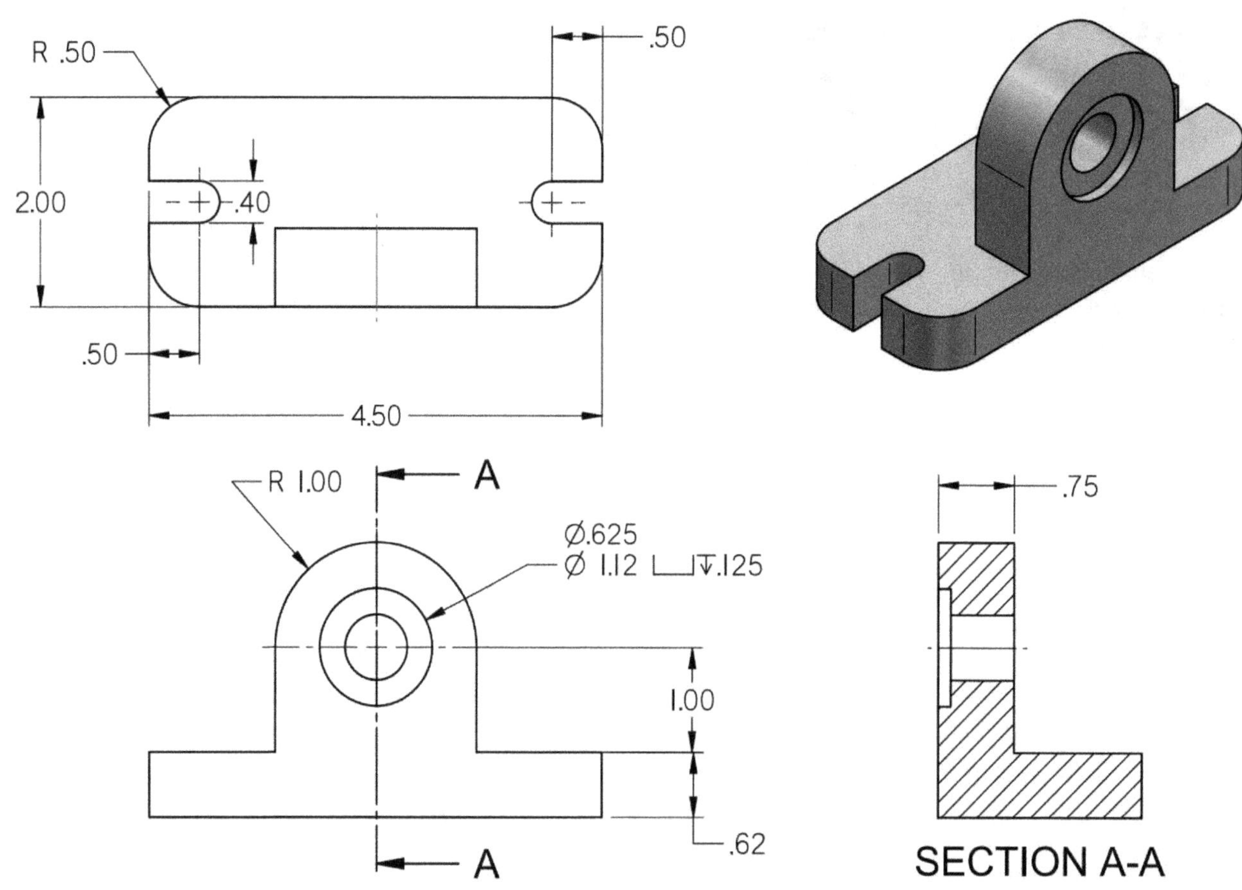

Exercise 3

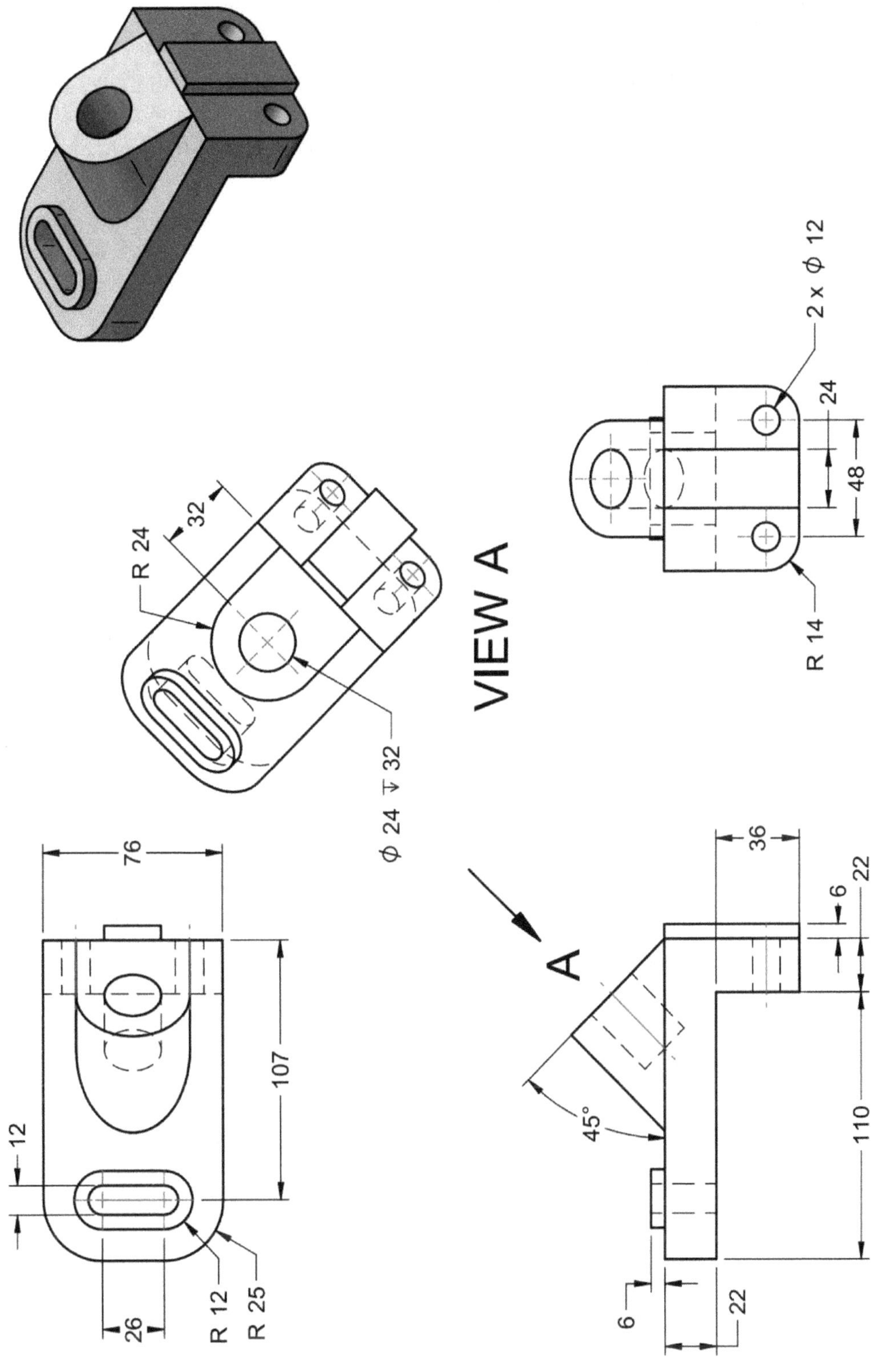

2 x ⌀ 12
24
48
R 14
VIEW A
R 24
32
⌀ 24 ⍌ 32
A
36
6
22
45°
110
6
22
76
107
12
26
R 12
R 25

Chapter 4: Arrayed Geometry

When designing a part geometry, there are often elements of symmetry in each part, or there are at least a few features repeated multiple times. In these situations, AutoCAD offers you some commands that save you time. For example, you can use mirror features to design symmetric parts, which makes designing the part quicker. This is because you only have to design a portion of the part and use the mirror feature to create the remaining geometry.

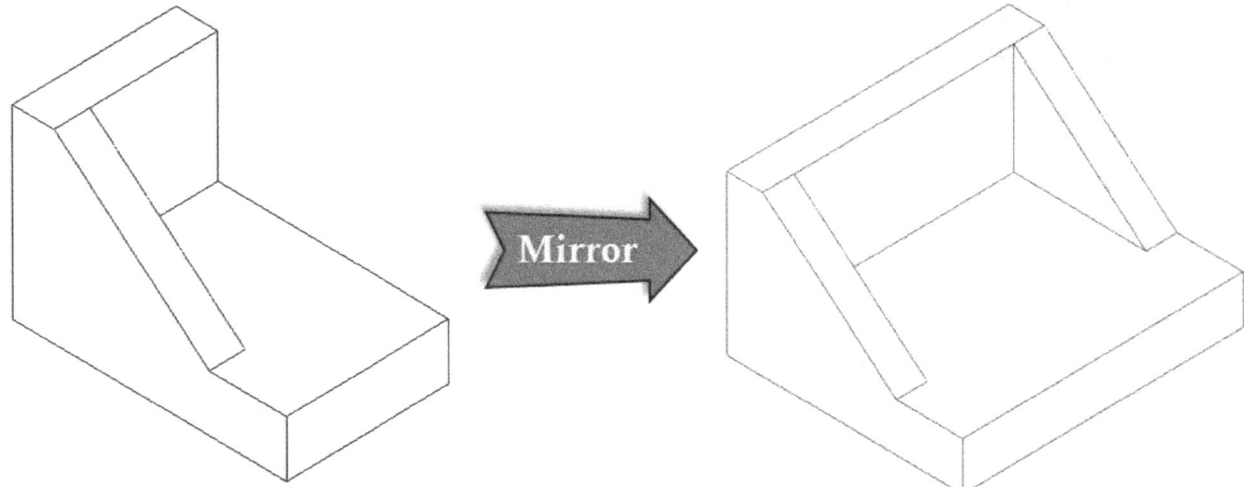

Also, there are some array commands to replicate a feature throughout the part quickly. They save you time from creating additional features individually and help you modify the design easily. If the design changes, you only need to change the first feature, and the rest of the array features will update automatically. In this chapter, you will learn to create the mirrored and array geometries using the commands available in AutoCAD.

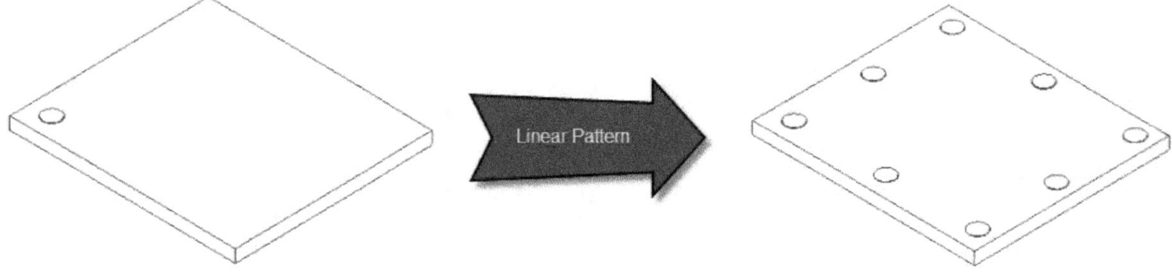

The topics covered in this chapter are:

- *Mirror features*
- *Rectangular Arrays*
- *Polar arrays*
- *Path Arrays*

Mirror

If you are designing a symmetric part, you can save time by using the **Mirror** command. Using this command, you can replicate the individual objects of the entire body or the entire solid body. On the ribbon, click **Home >**

Modify > Mirror . Next, select the object to be mirrored and press ENTER. Now, you need to specify the mirror line in the 3D space. You can specify the mirror line by selecting two points from the graphics window. You can use various snap options to specify the endpoints of the mirror line. For example, turn ON the **OrthoMode** icon on the Status bar. Next, press and hold the SHIFT key and right-click. Next, select the **Mid Between 2 Points** option from the shortcut menu. Select the two points, as shown. The midpoint between the two selected points is selected. Move the pointer in the forward or backward direction and click to specify the mirror line. Next, select **No** from the command line to keep the original object.

3D Mirror

The **3D Mirror** command allows you to mirror an object about the XY, YZ, or ZX planes. In addition, it provides you with many options to specify the mirror plane in the graphics window. On the ribbon, click **Home > Modify > 3D Mirror**. Next, select the object to be mirrored and press ENTER. Next, select the YZ option from the command line. Select a point from the graphics window to specify the location of the YZ plane. Next, select the No option from the command line; the selected object will be mirrored about the YZ plane.

Activate the **3D Mirror** command and select the objects to be mirrored, and then press ENTER. Select the **ZX** plane from the command line and specify the location of the ZX plane, as shown. Next, select the No option from the command line.

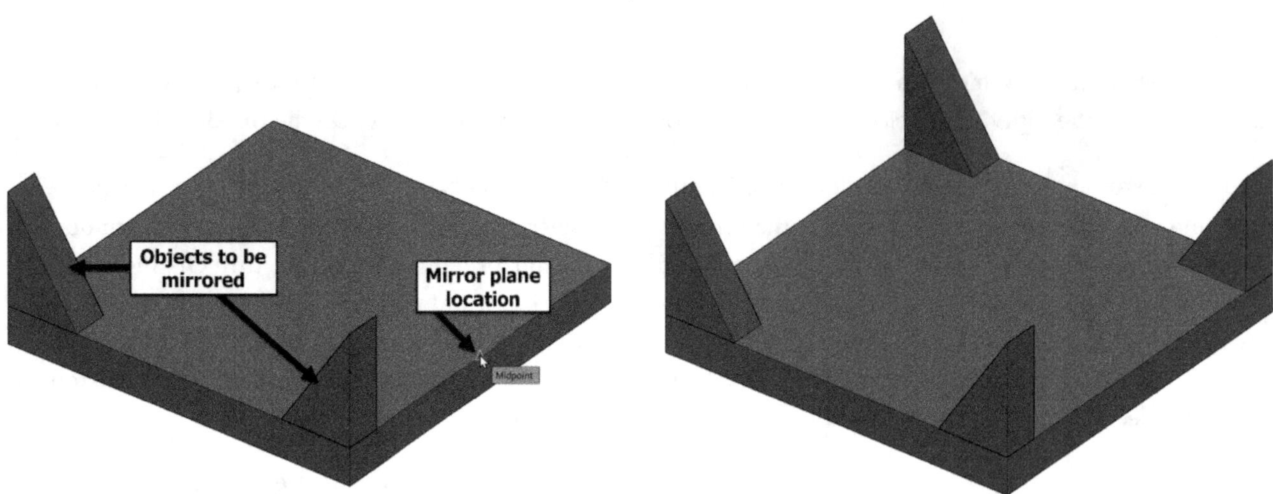

Likewise, mirror the entire solid about the XY plane using the **XY** option.

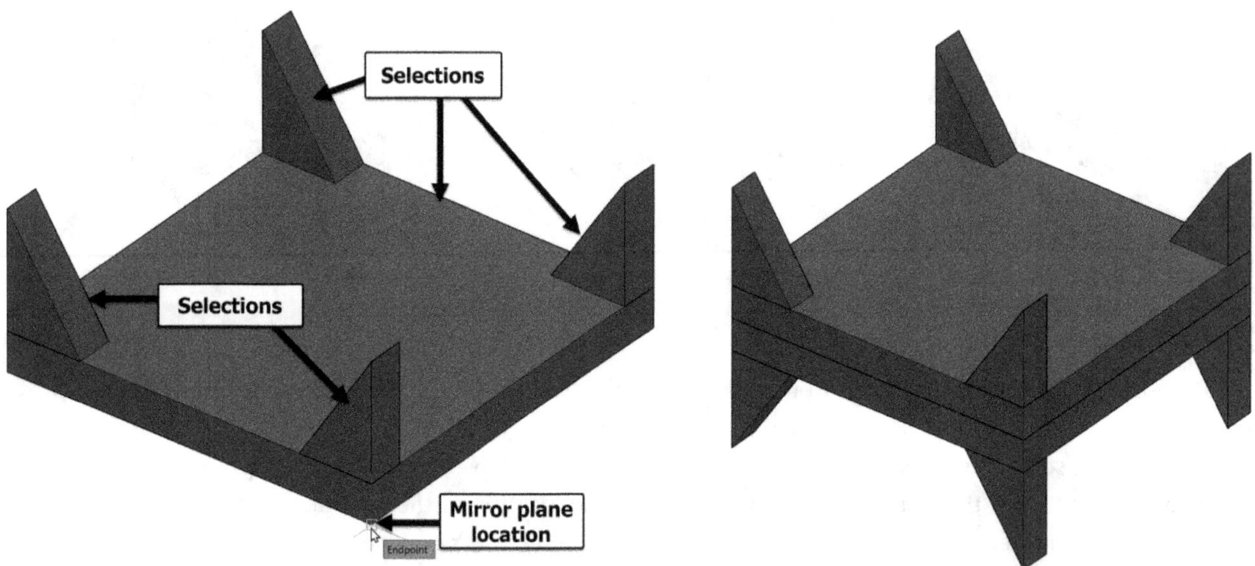

Activate the **3D Mirror** command and select the objects to be mirrored, and then press ENTER. Select the **3Point** plane from the command line and select three points from the graphics window, as shown. An imaginary plane is created passing through the three points. Next, select the **No** option from the command line.

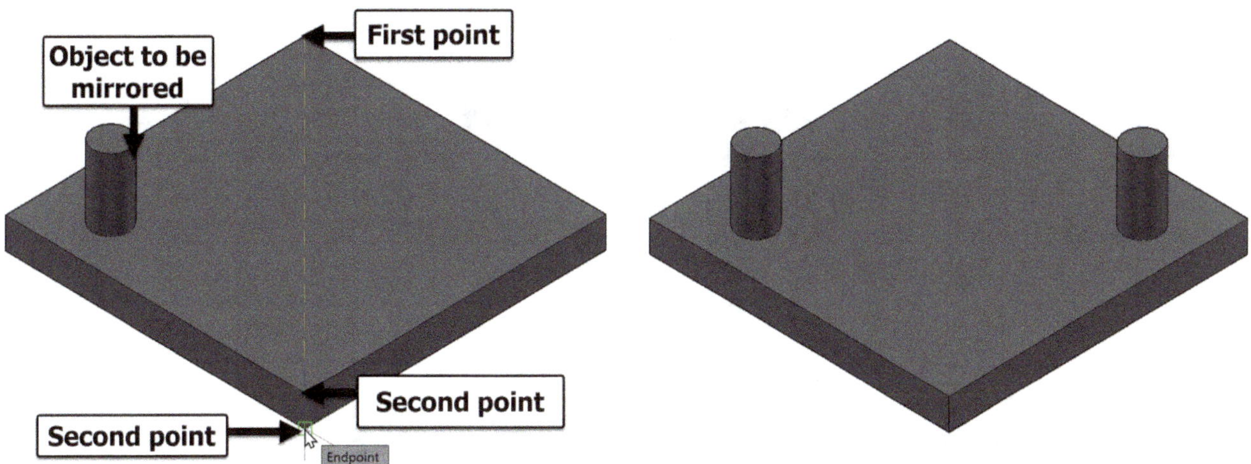

Activate the **3D Mirror** command, select the objects to be mirrored, and then press ENTER. Select the **Zaxis** plane from the command line and select two points from the graphics window, as shown. The Z axis of the imaginary plane is created between the two selected points. Also, the imaginary plane is created perpendicular to the Z axis on the start point of the Z axis. Next, select the **No** option from the command line.

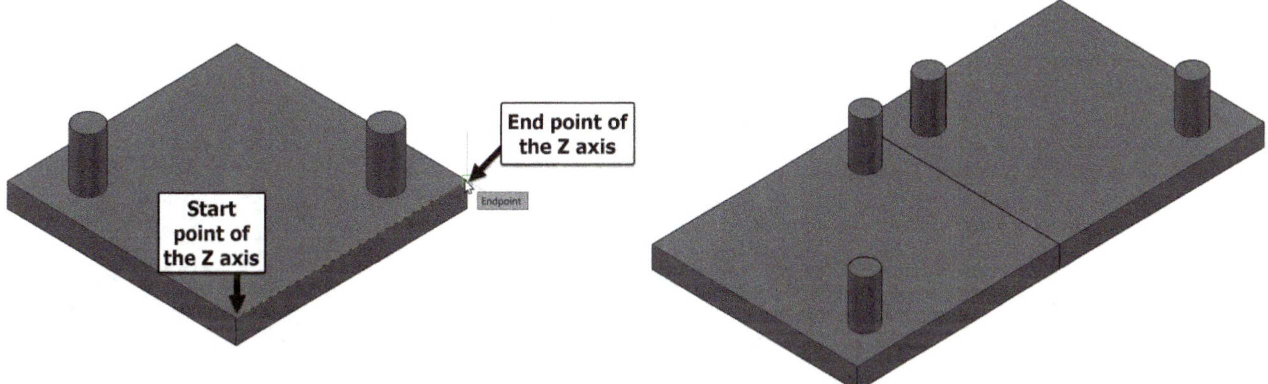

Use the **View** option to mirror the selected objected about the current view of the model. For example, select the Right face of the ViewCube to change the view orientation to right. Next, activate the 3D Mirror command, select the objects to be mirrored, and then press ENTER. Next, select the View option from the command line; the right plane will be used as the mirror plane. Next, select a point from the graphics window to specify the location of the right plane. Select the **No** option from the command line.

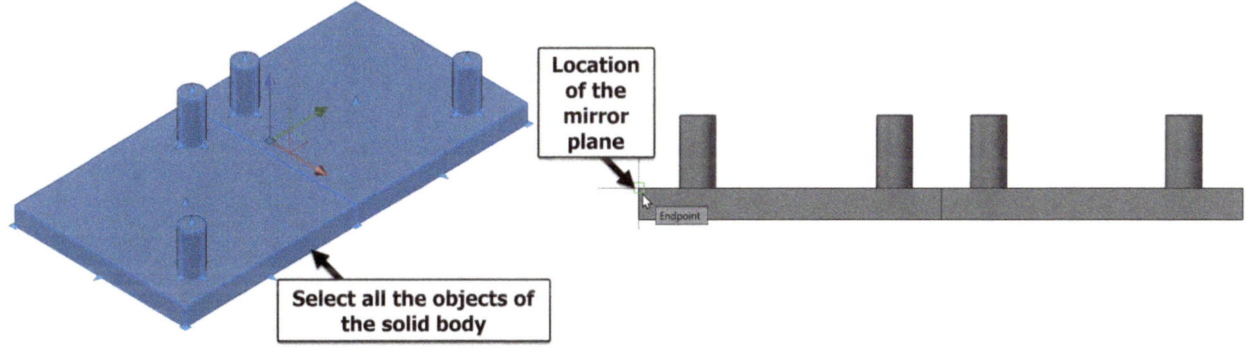

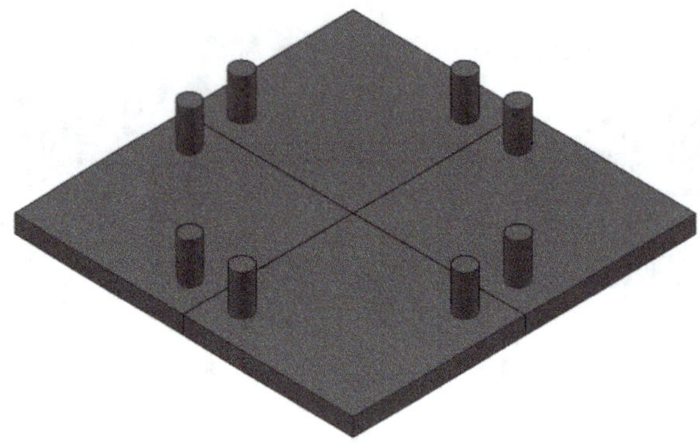

Create Arrays

AutoCAD allows you to replicate a feature using the array commands (**Rectangular Array**, **Polar Array**, and **Path Array**). The following sections explain the different array that can be created using these array commands.

Rectangular Array

To create a rectangular array, you must first activate the **Rectangular Array** command (On the ribbon, click **Home > Modify > Array** drop-down > **Rectangular Array**). Next, select the object to array from the model geometry, and then press ENTER. You will notice that a array preview appears on the model.

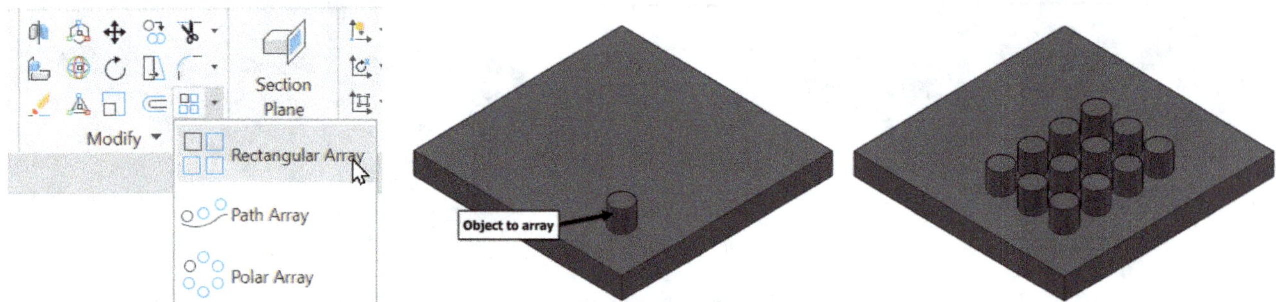

Type-in values in the **Between** and **Columns** boxes available in the **Columns** panel. The Between value specifies the distance between the instances along the column. The Column value specifies the number of instances along the column. You can also type-in a value in the Total box to specify the total distance along the column of the rectangular array. Notice that the **Between** value is calculated automatically as you enter a value in the **Total** box. You can type-in a negative value in the Between or Total boxes, if you want to reverse the array direction. Likewise, set the parameters (**Between** and **Rows**) of the array in **Rows** panel.

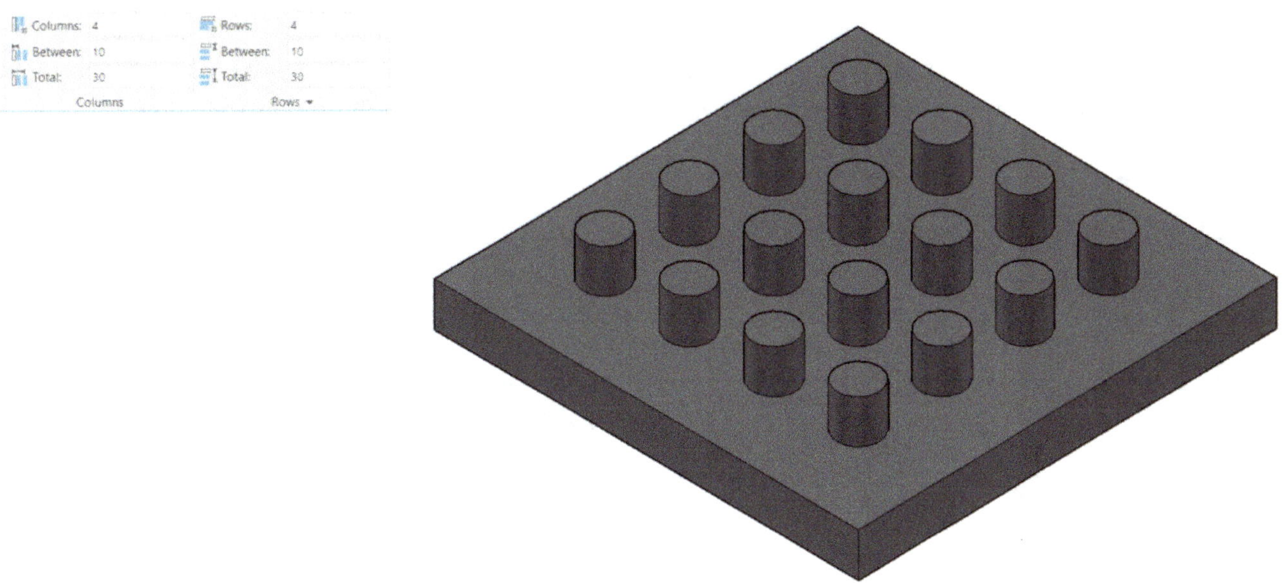

You can also add levels to the pattern along the Z-axis by entering values in the **Levels** panel. Enter a value more than one in the **Level Count** box to add levels to the rectangular pattern. Next, specify the **Between** or **Total** values.

Toggle the **Associative** button on the **Properties** panel if you want create a rectangular pattern that can be edited afterwards. Next, click the **Close Array** button to complete the rectangular array.

Polar Array

The polar array is used to array the selected objects circularly. Activate the **Polar array** command (click **Home**

Modify > Array drop-down > **Polar Array**  on the ribbon) and select the object to array, and then press ENTER. Next, specify the centerpoint of the polar array by selecting a point from the graphics window.

On the **Array Creation** contextual tab of the ribbon, on the **Items** panel, type-in values in the **Items** and **Fill** boxes. The Items value that you specify will be fitted in the **Fill** angle value.

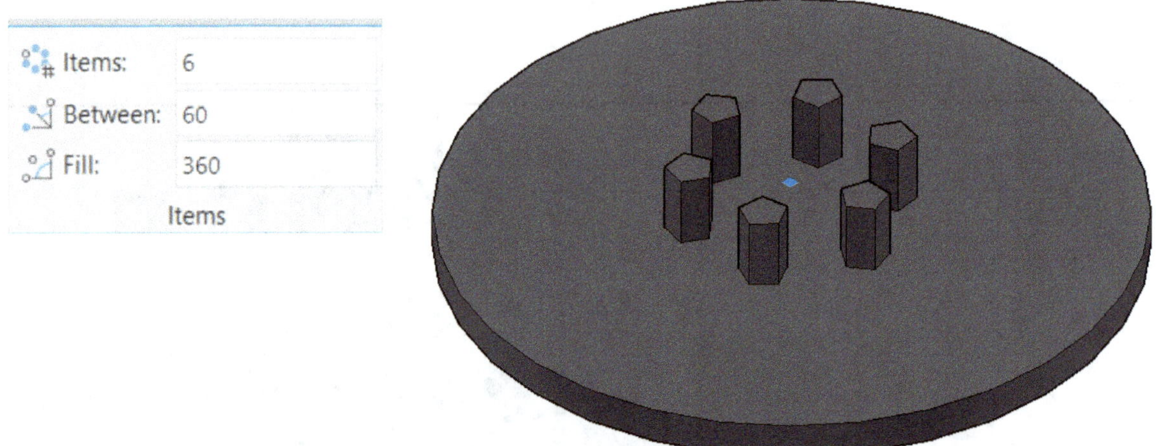

Type in a value in the **Between** box to specify the angle between the instances of the polar array.

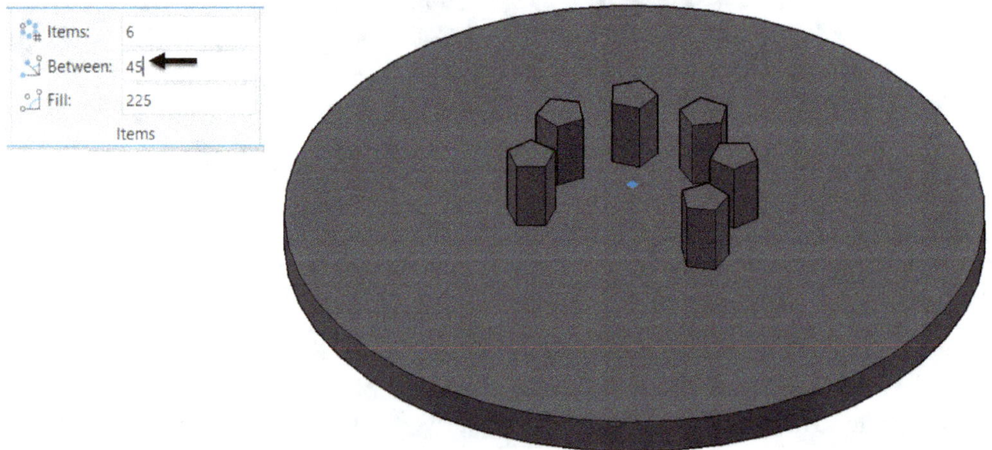

On the **Properties** panel, toggle the **Direction** button to reverse the direction of the array.

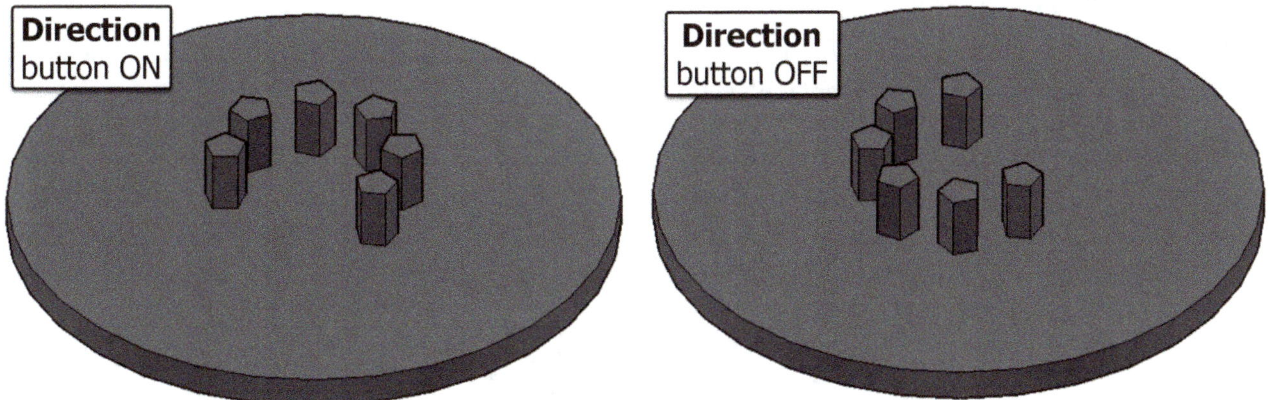

On the **Properties** panel, turn OFF the **Rotate Items** button to array the object with the original orientation. Turn ON the **Rotate Items** button to change the orientation of the instances, as they are arrayed in the circular fashion.

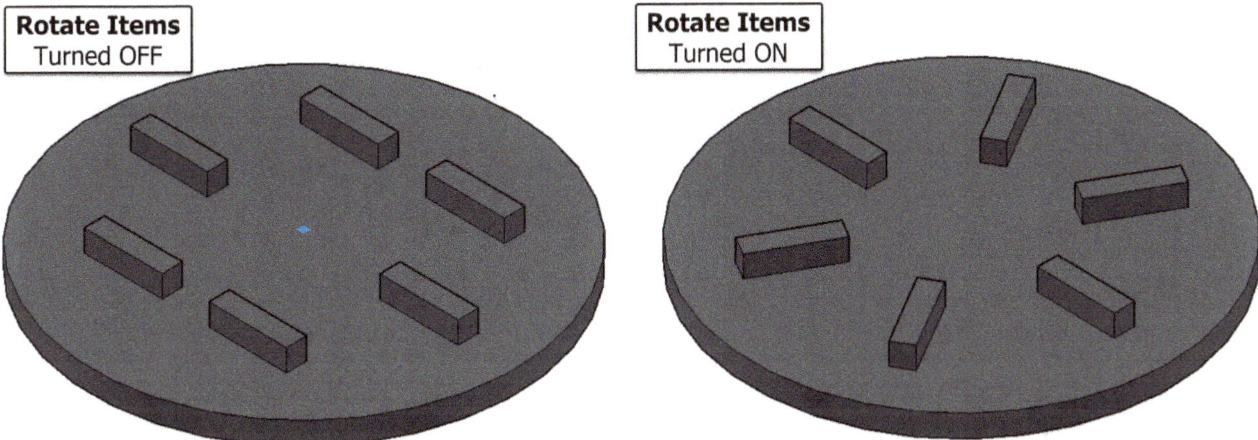

Adding Rows to the array

The **Polar array** command has options to radiate the polar array. On the **Array Creation** contextual tab, type-in values in the **Rows** and **Between** boxes. The **Rows** and **Between** values specify the number of rows and distance between them, respectively.

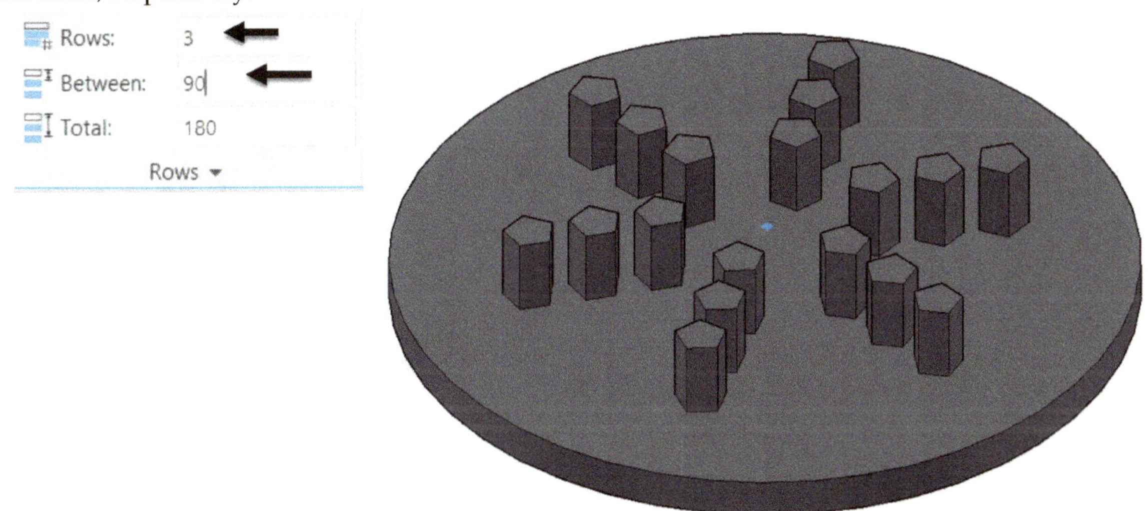

Incremental Elevation

The **Incremental Elevation** option allows you to specify the incremental elevation to the rows. Expand the Rows panel and type-in a value in the **Incremental Elevation** box.

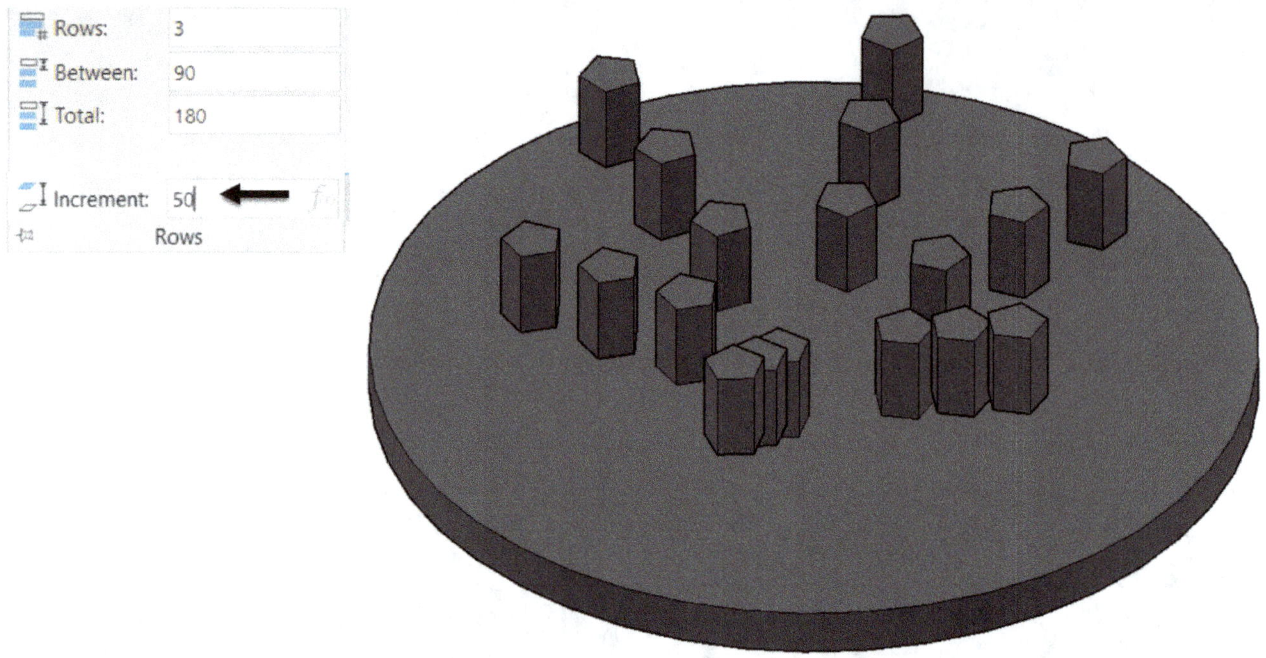

Path Array

You can create an array along a selected curve or edge using the **Path Array** command. Activate the **Path Array** command (click **Home > Modify > Array** drop-down > **Path Array**) and select the object to be arrayed, and then press ENTER. Next, select a 2D or 3D curve from the graphics window. On the **Properties** panel, select **Measure** option. Next, type-in a value in the **Between** box on the **Items** panel; the items are automatically adjusted on the selected path using the value entered in the **Between** box.

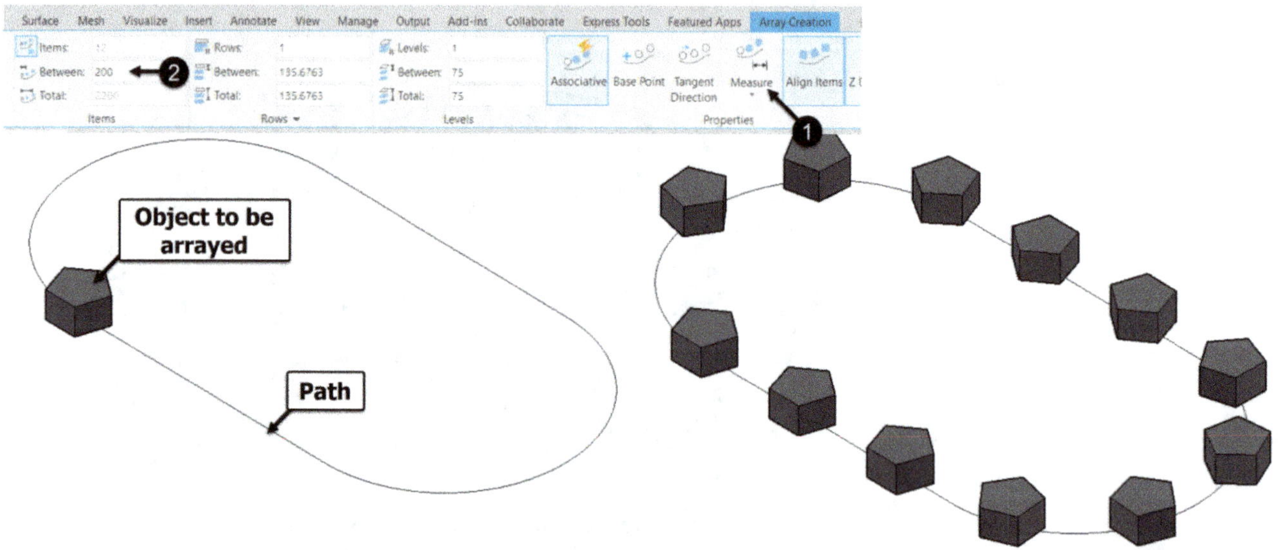

On the **Properties** panel, select **Measure** drop-down > **Divide**. Next, type-in a value in the **Items** box on the **Items** panel; the number of items specified will be divided equally along the selected path.

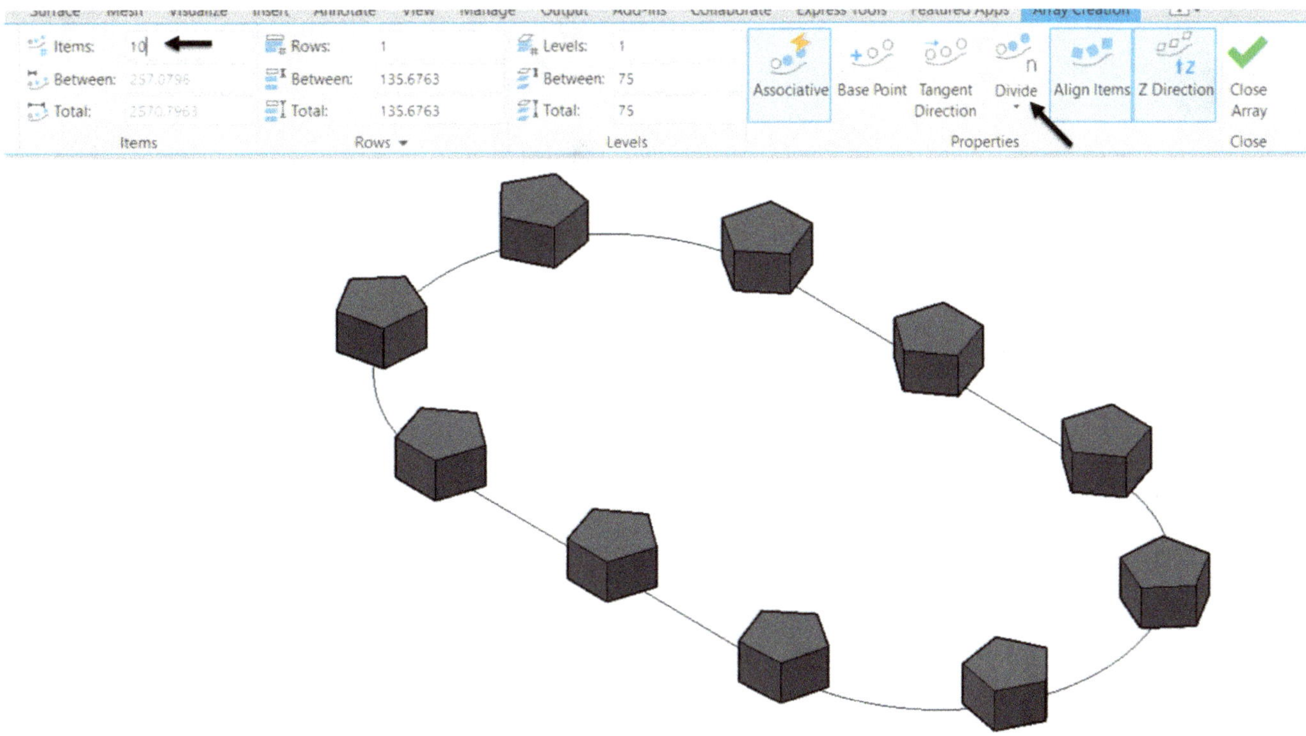

Turn OFF the **Align Items** button on the **Properties** panel to keep the orientation of the instances same as the base object. Turn ON the **Align Items** button to orient the instances tangent to the path.

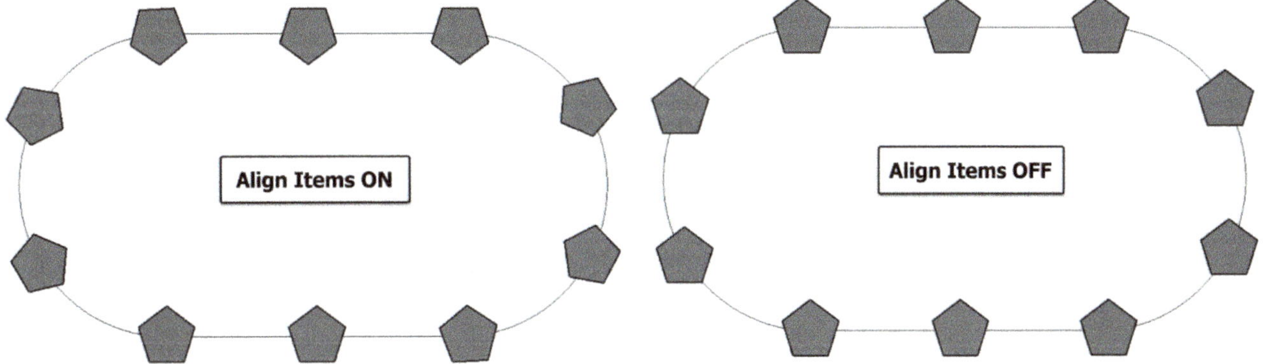

Use the **Tangent Direction** button if you want orient the object along a tangent vector. Click this button and specify the start point of the tangent vector. Next, move the pointer in the required direction and click to specify the end point of the tangent vector.

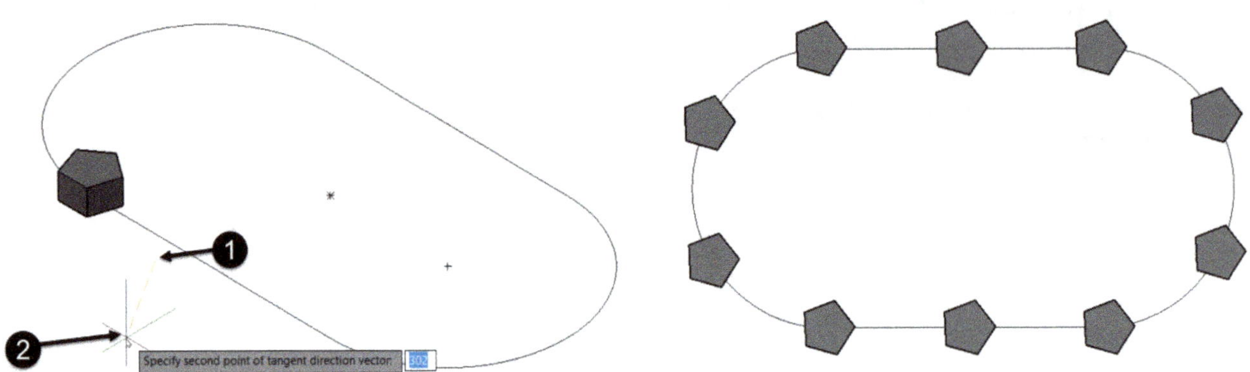

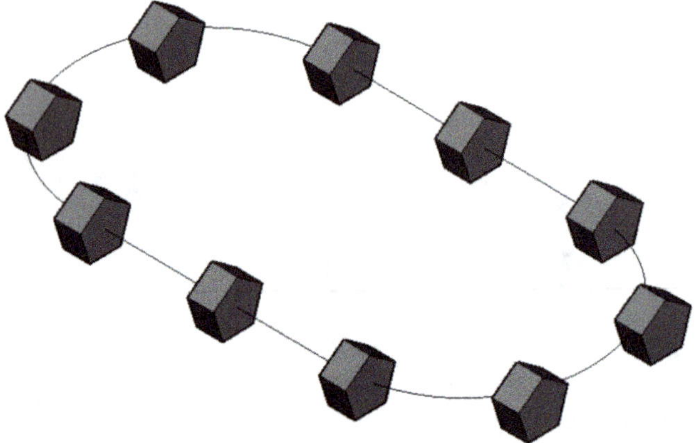

You can also select the **Normal** option from the command line if you want to orient the model normal to the selected path.

Tutorial 1 (Millimeters)

In this example, you create the part shown next.

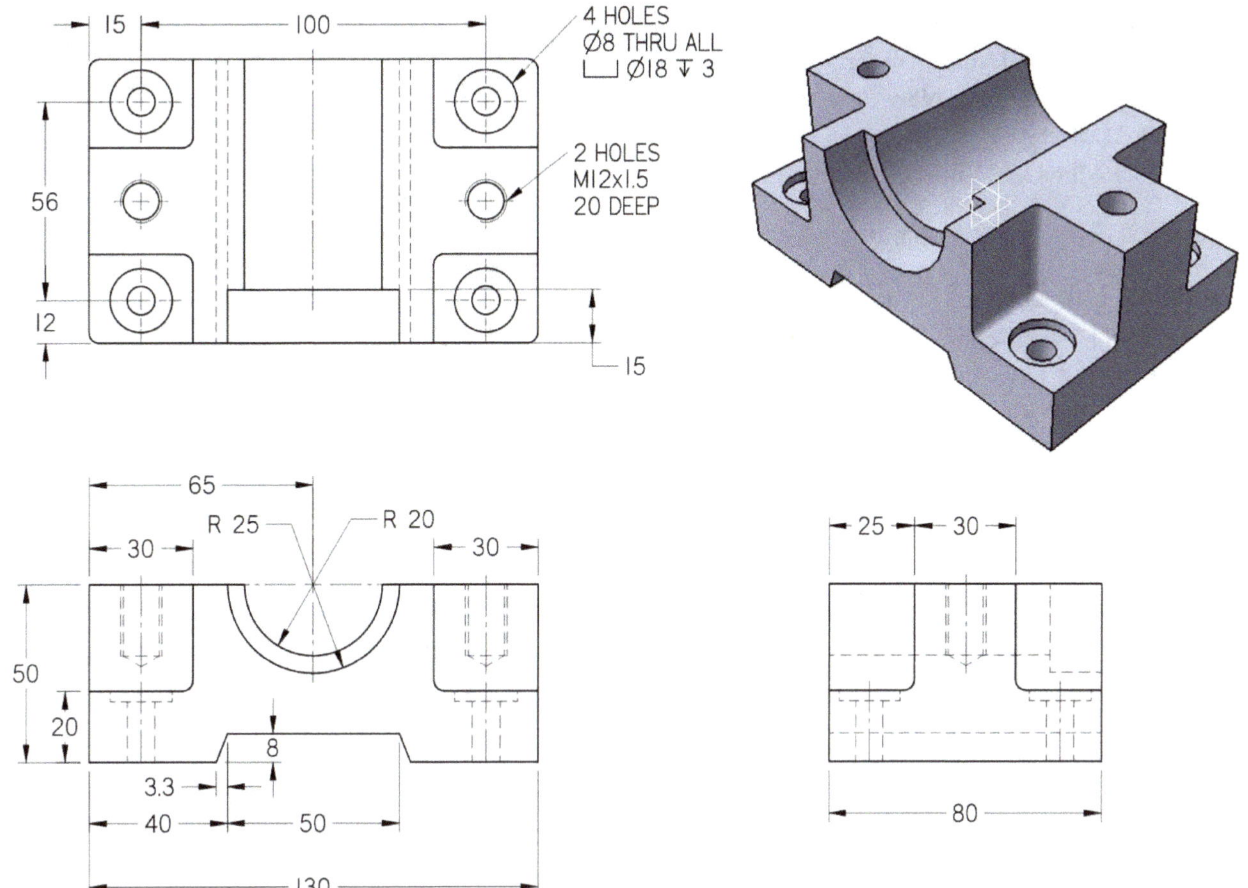
15
100
4 HOLES
Ø8 THRU ALL
Ø18 ▼ 3
2 HOLES
M12x1.5
20 DEEP
56
12
15
65
R 25
R 20
30
30
50
20
8
3.3
40
50
130
25
30
80

Creating a New File

1. Click the **AutoCAD 2025** icon on your desktop.
2. On the **Start** page, click **New** drop-down > **acadiso3D.dwt**.
3. Deactivate the **GRIDMODE** icon on the status bar.

Creating the Box

1. On the ribbon, click **Home** tab > **Modeling** panel > **Primitive** drop-down > **Box**.
2. Type 0,0 in the command line and press ENTER. The first corner of the box is defined.
3. Make sure that the Dynamic Input icon is active on the status bar.
4. Type 130 in the length box and press the TAB key.
5. Type 80 and press ENTER.

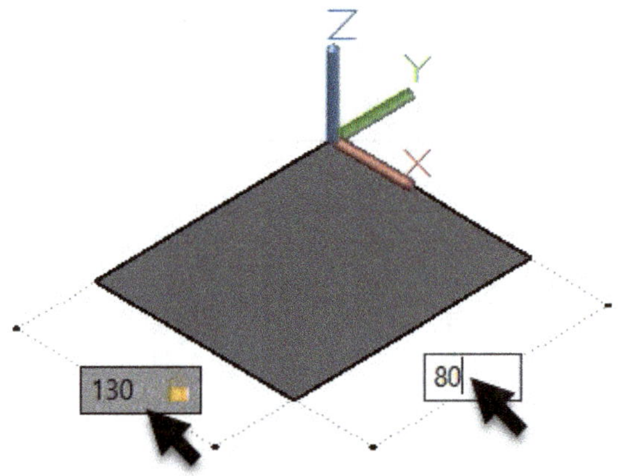

6. Move the pointer upward.
7. Type 50 and press ENTER to create the box.

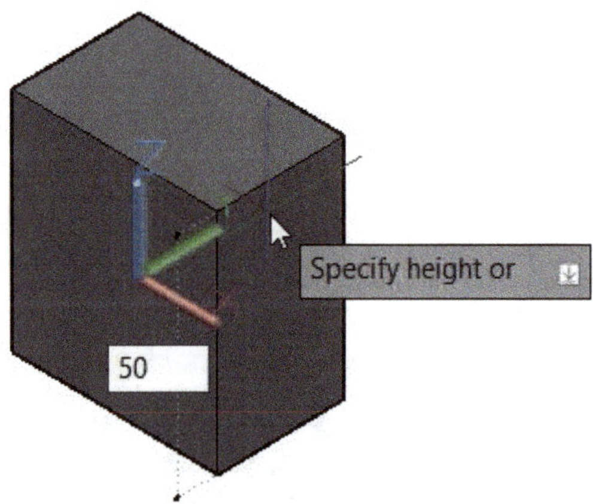

8. Deactivate the **Dynamic Input** icon on the Status bar.

9. Activate the **Orthomode** icon on the Status bar.
10. On the ribbon, click **Home** tab > **Modeling** panel > **Primitive** drop-down > **Box**.
11. Select the top left corner of the box, as shown.

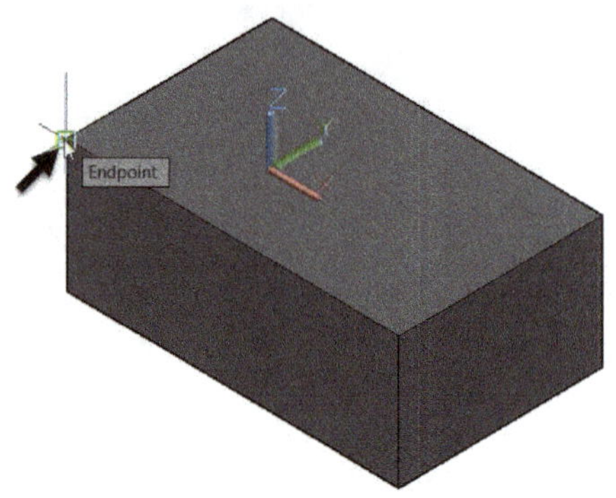

12. Select the **Length** option from the command line.
13. Type 30 and press ENTER.
14. Type -25 and press ENTER to define the width.
15. Type -30 and press ENTER to define the height.

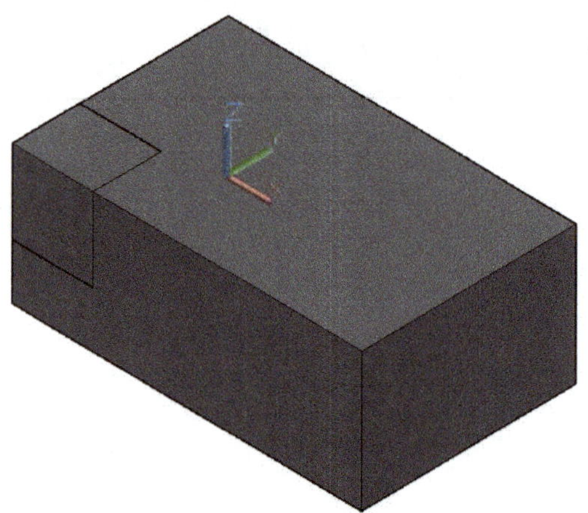

16. Change the **Visual Style** to **Shades of Gray**.

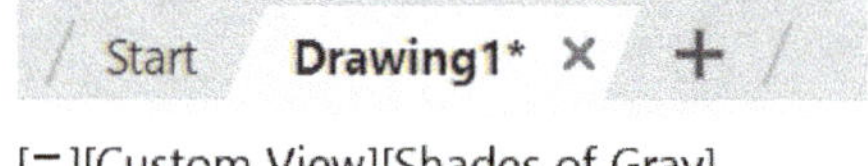

17. Place the pointer on any one of the edges of the small box.
18. Click when the small box is highlighted.

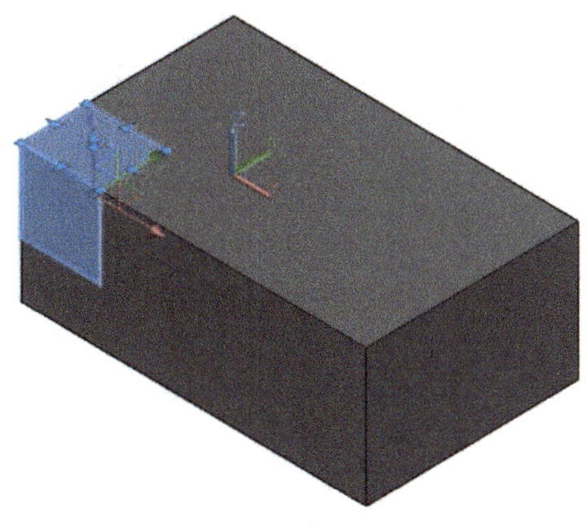

19. On the ribbon, **Home** tab > **Modify** panel > **Array** drop-down > **Rectangular Array**.

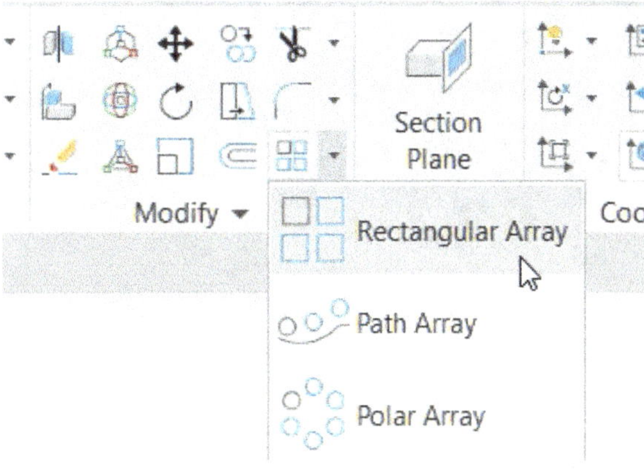

20. On the **Array Creation** tab, type **2** in the **Columns** and **Rows** boxes, respectively.
21. Type **100** in the **Between** box available on the **Columns** panel.

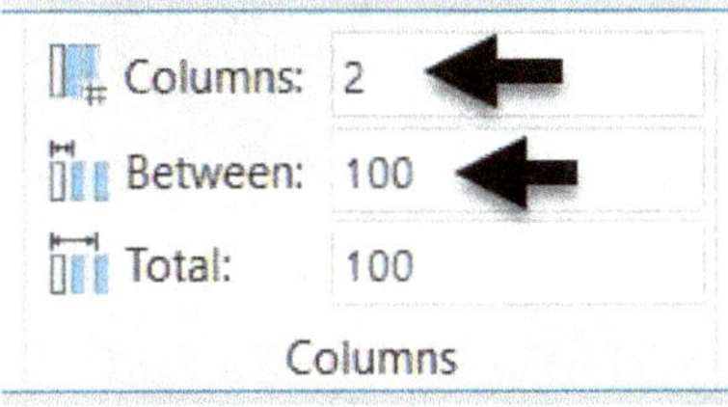

22. Type **55** in the **Total** box available on the **Rows** panel.

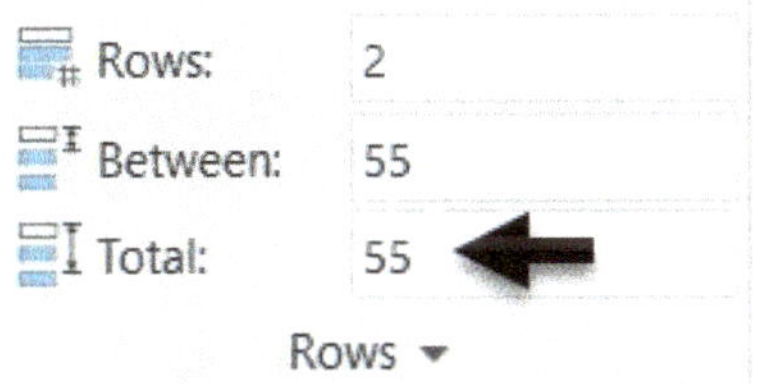

23. Deactivate the **Associative** icon on the ribbon.
24. Click the **Close Array** button on the ribbon.

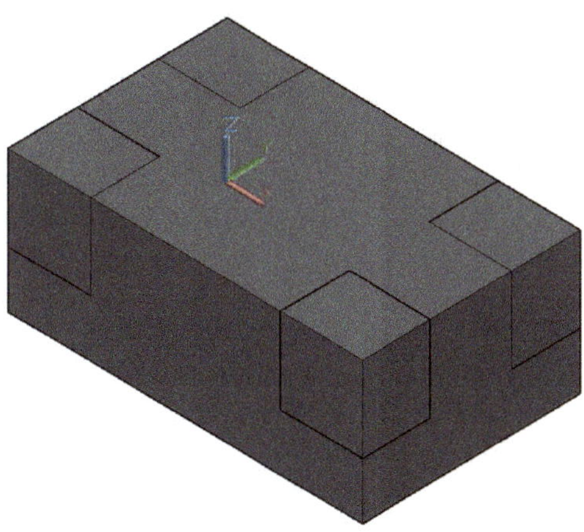

25. On the ribbon, click **Home** tab > **View** panel > **Visual Style** drop-down > **2D Wireframe**.

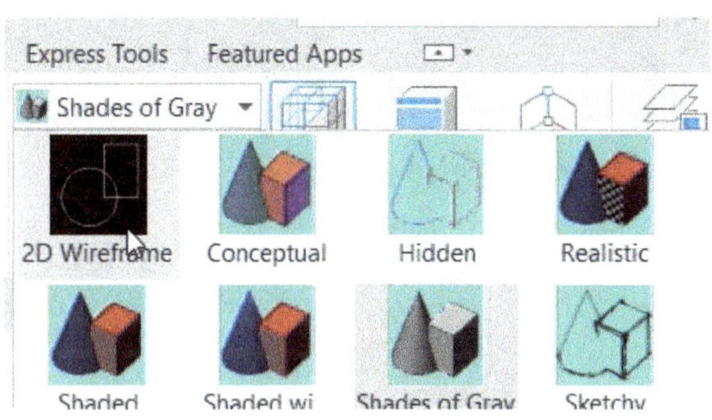

26. On the ribbon, click **Home** tab > **Solid Editing** panel > **Solid, Subtract**.
27. Click on the edge of the large box; the large box is selected.
28. Press ENTER.

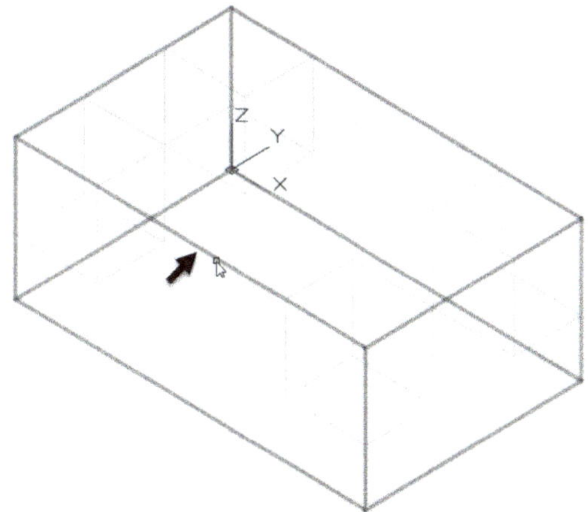

29. Click on the edge of any one of the small boxes.

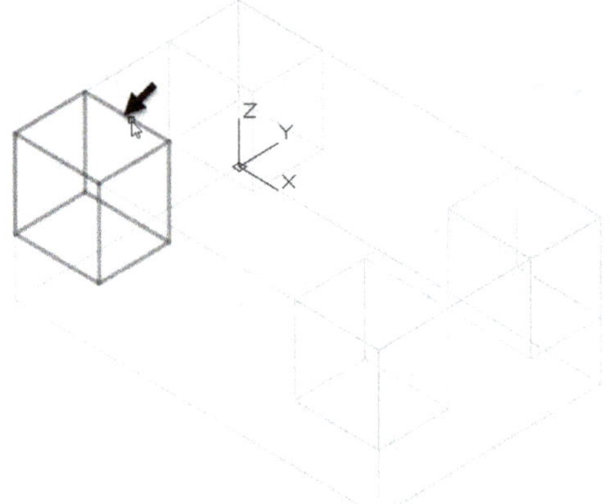

30. Likewise, select the remaining boxes and press ENTER.

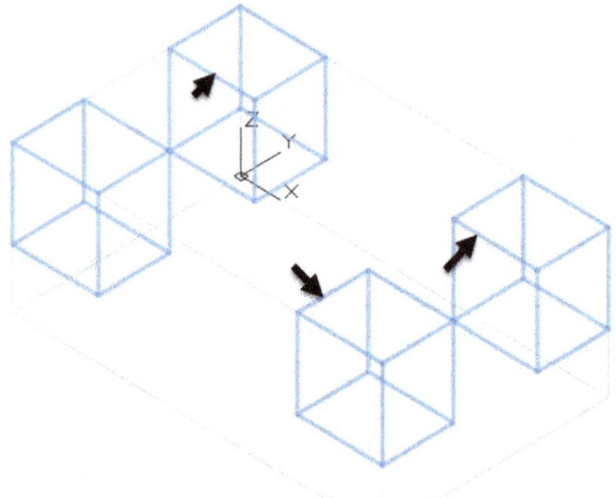

31. In the In-canvas controls, change the **Visual Style** to **Shades of Gray**.

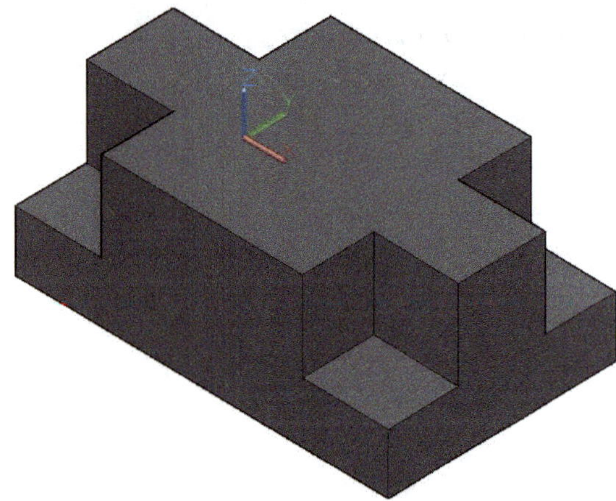

Creating the Hole features

1. On the ribbon, click **Home** tab > **Coordinates** panel > **UCS**.

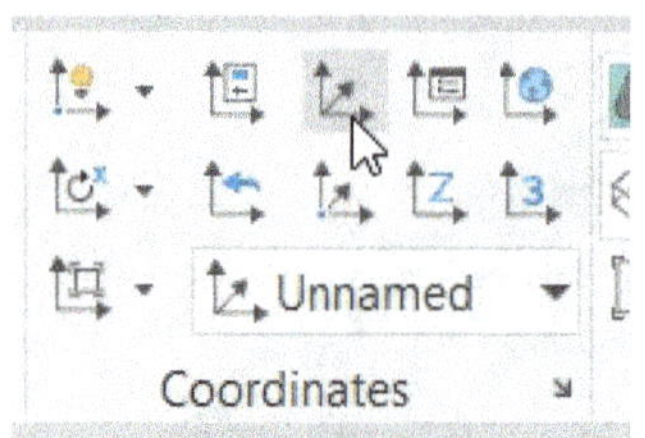

2. Select the lower-left corner of the subtraction to define the origin of the UCS.

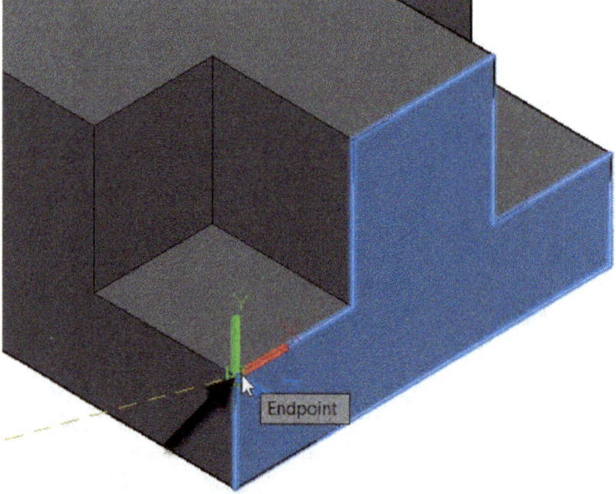

3. Move the pointer toward the right and select the corner point, as shown. The X-axis of the UCS is defined.

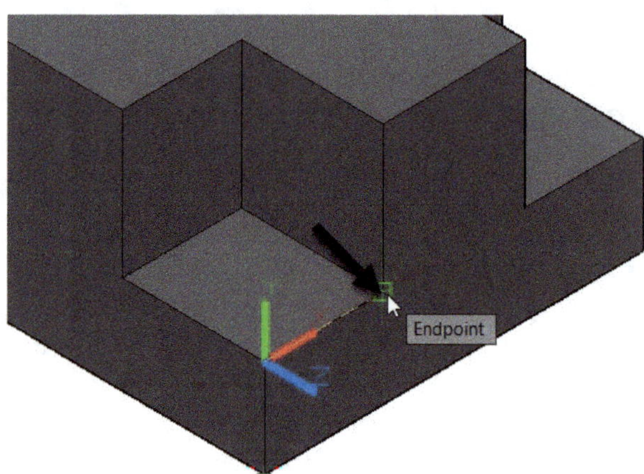

4. Move the pointer in the forward direction and click to define the Y-axis.

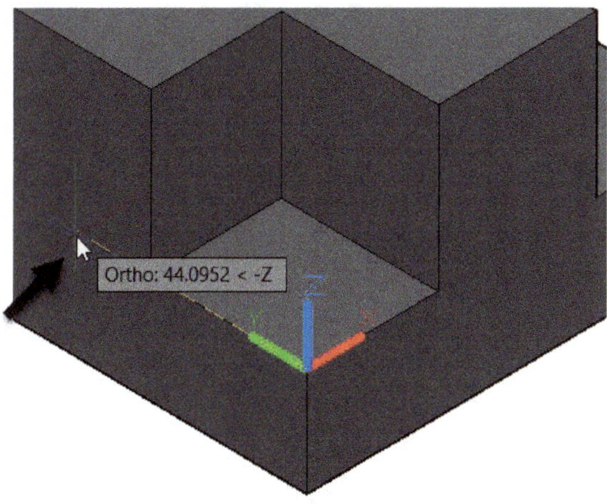

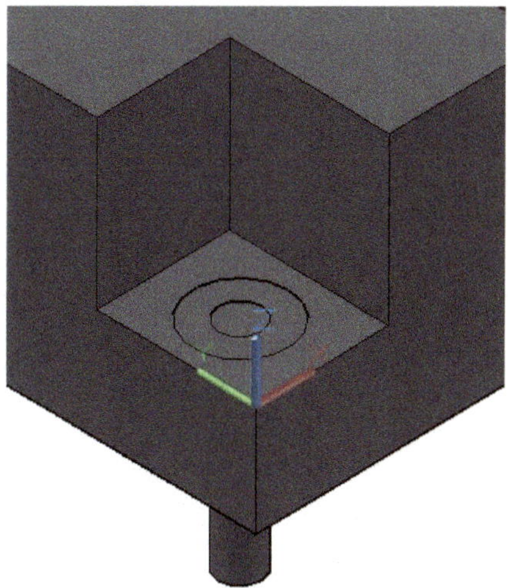

5. On the ribbon, click **Home** tab > **Modeling** panel > **Primitives** drop-down > **Cylinder**.
6. Type 12, 15 in the command line and press ENTER. The centerpoint of the cylinder is defined.
7. Type 4 in the command line and press ENTER.
8. Move the pointer downward and click to create the cylinder.

13. Set the **Visual Style** to **2D Wireframe**.

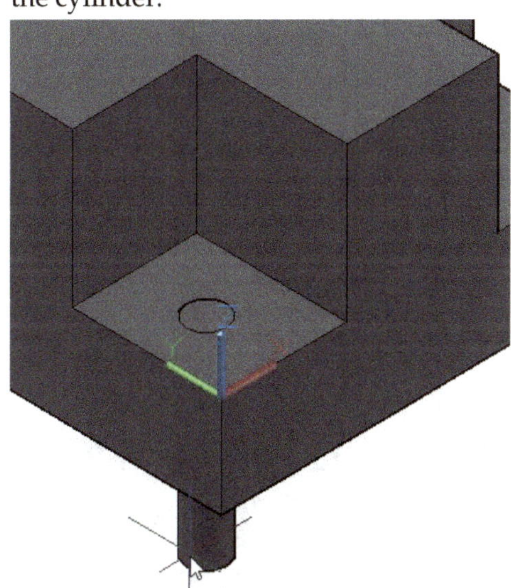

14. Select the two cylinders, as shown.

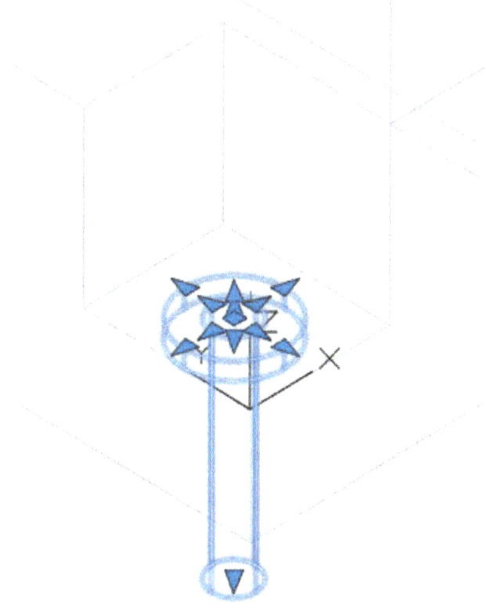

9. On the ribbon, click **Home** tab > **Modeling** panel > **Primitives** drop-down > **Cylinder**.
10. Type 12, 15 in the command line and press ENTER.
11. Type 9 in the command line and press ENTER.
12. Type -3 and press ENTER.

15. On the ribbon, **Home** tab > **Modify** panel > **Array** drop-down > **Rectangular Array**.
16. On the **Array Creation** tab, type **2** in the **Columns** and **Rows** boxes, respectively.
17. Type **56** in the **Between** box available on the **Columns** panel.

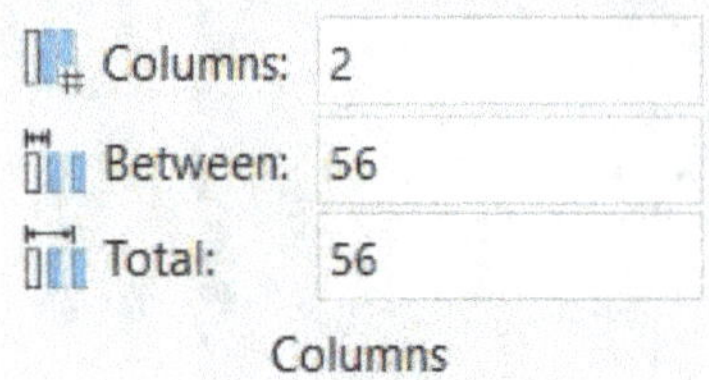

18. Type **100** in the **Between** box available on the **Rows** panel.

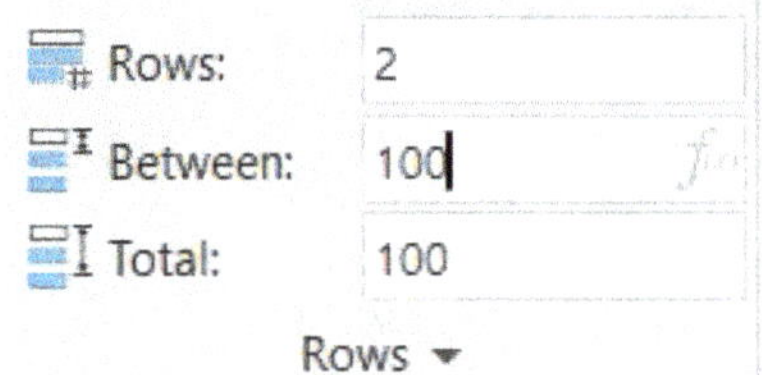

19. Deactivate the **Associative** icon on the ribbon.
20. Click the **Close Array** icon on the ribbon.

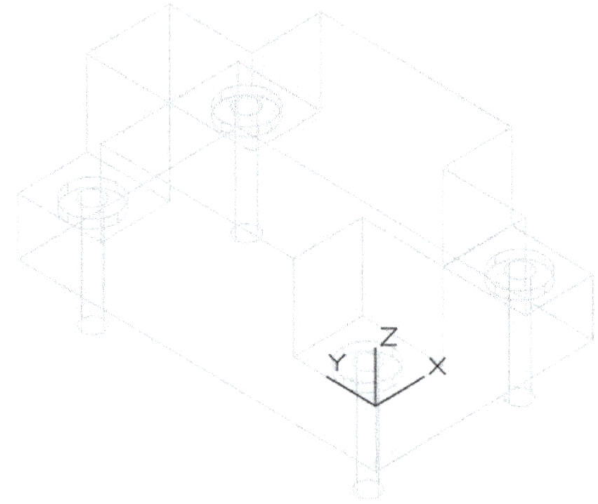

21. On the ribbon, click **Home** tab > **Solid Editing** panel > **Solid, Subtract**.
22. Click on the edge of the main body; the main body is selected.
23. Press ENTER.

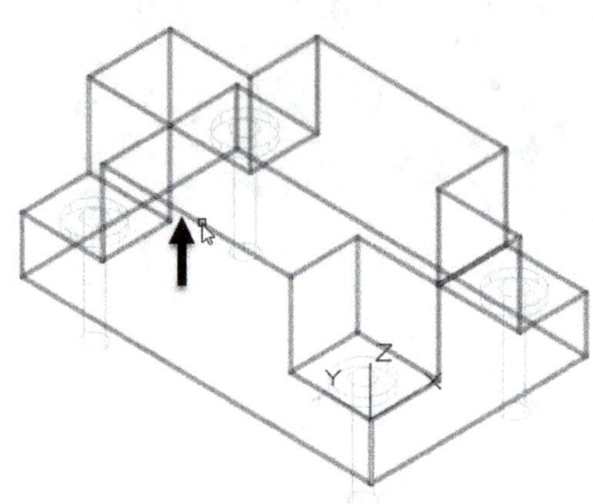

24. Select all the cylinders and press ENTER.

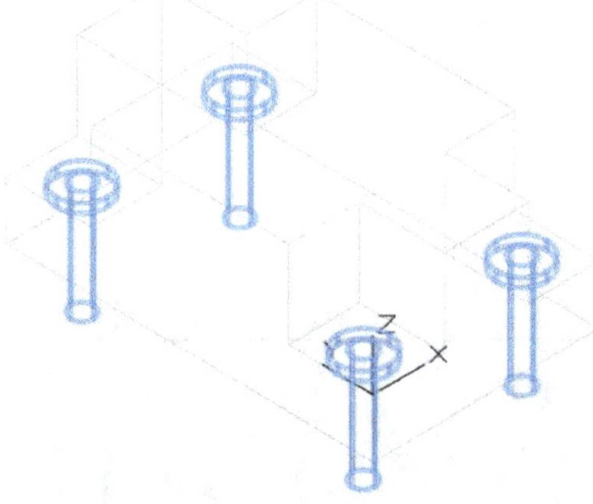

25. Change the **Visual Style** to **Shades of Gray**.

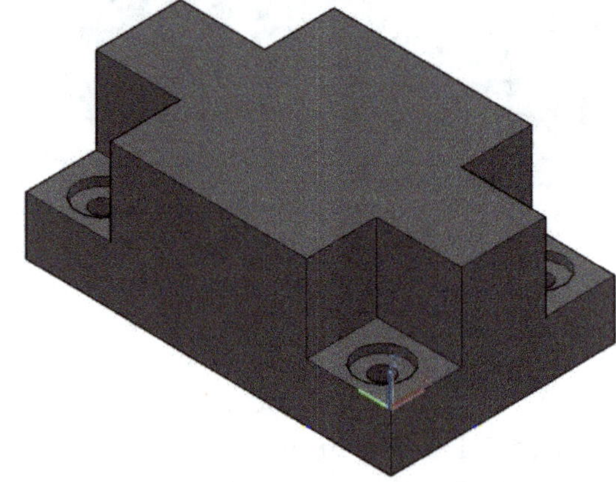

26. On the ribbon, click **Home** tab > **Coordinates** panel > **UCS**.

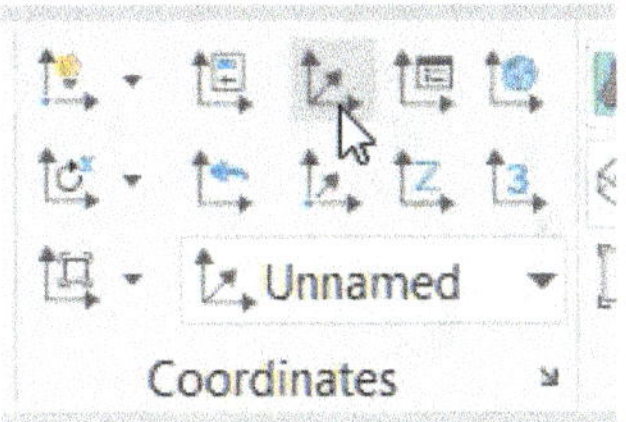

27. Select the corner point, as shown.

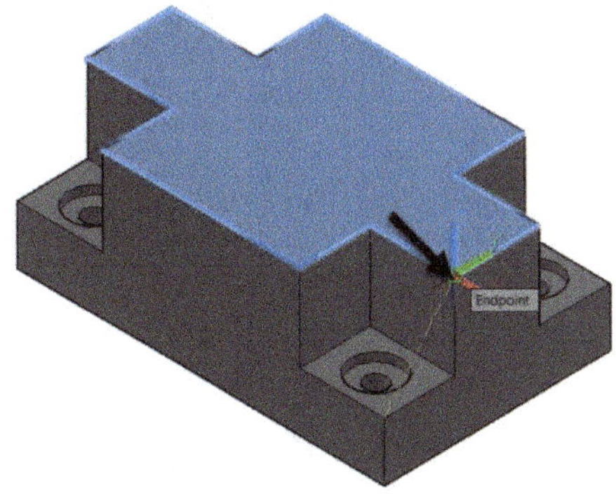

28. Move the pointer toward the right and click. The X-axis of the UCS is defined.

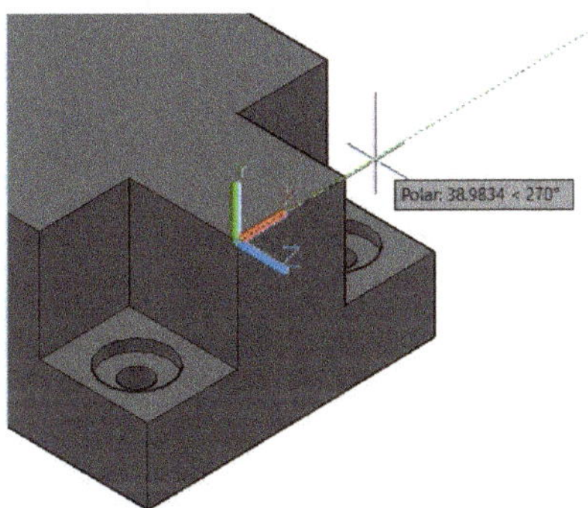

29. Move the pointer in the forward direction and click to define the Y-axis.

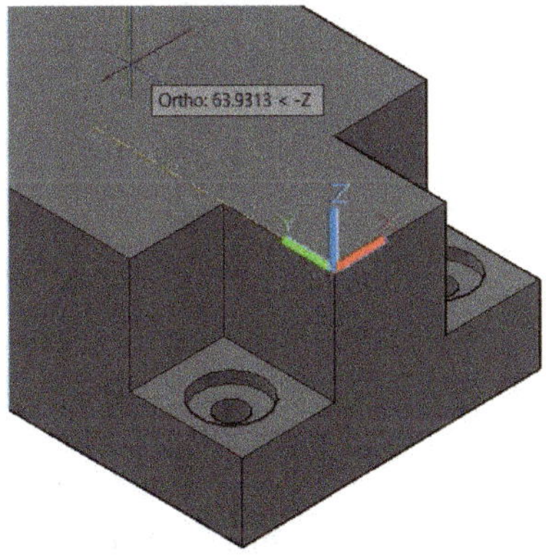

30. On the ribbon, click **Home** tab > **Modeling** panel > **Primitives** drop-down > **Cylinder**.

31. Type 15, 15 in the command line and press ENTER.

32. Type 6 in the command line and press ENTER.

33. Type -20 and press ENTER.

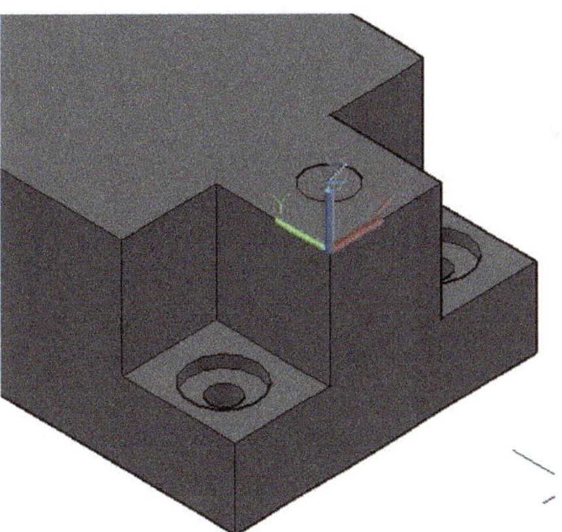

34. On the Status bar, click the down-arrow next to the **Object Snap** icon and select the **Midpoint** option.

35. Set the **Visual Style** to **2D Wireframe**.

36. Select the cylinder, as shown.

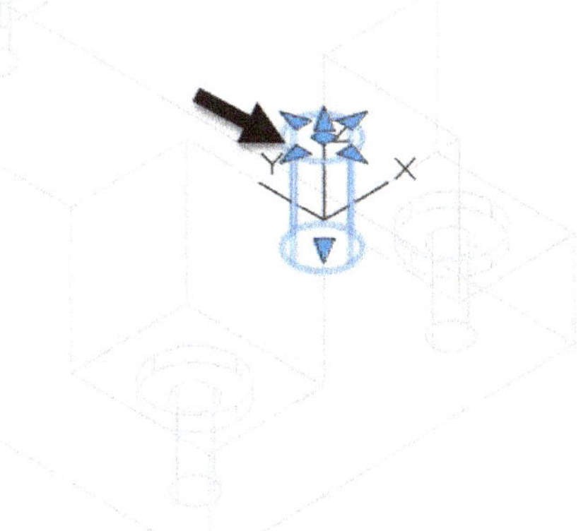

37. On the **Home** tab of the ribbon, expand the **Modify** panel and click the **Mirror** icon.

38. Select the midpoint of the front edge, as shown.

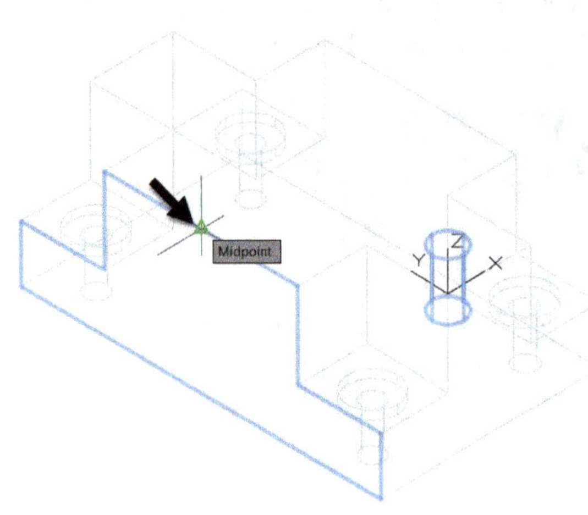

42. Select the corner point of the model, as shown.

39. Move the pointer downward and select the midpoint of the bottom edge.

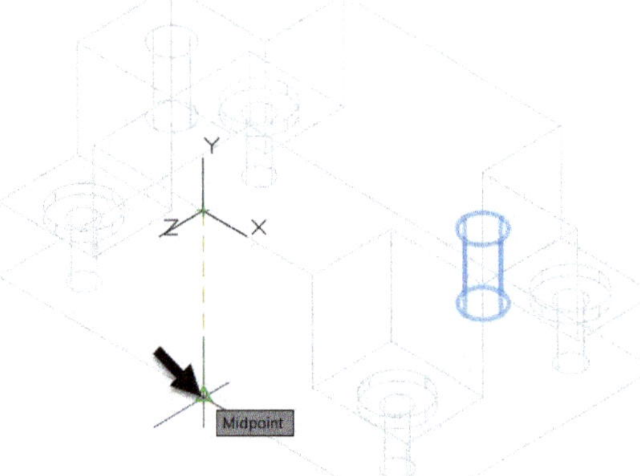

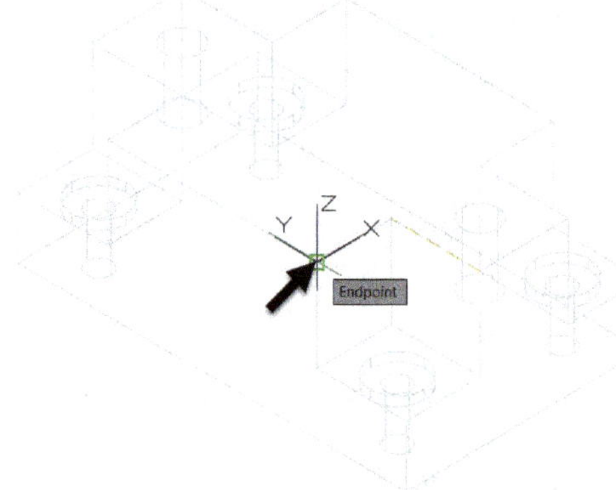

43. Move the pointer toward the right and select the corner point, as shown. The Z-axis of the UCS is defined.

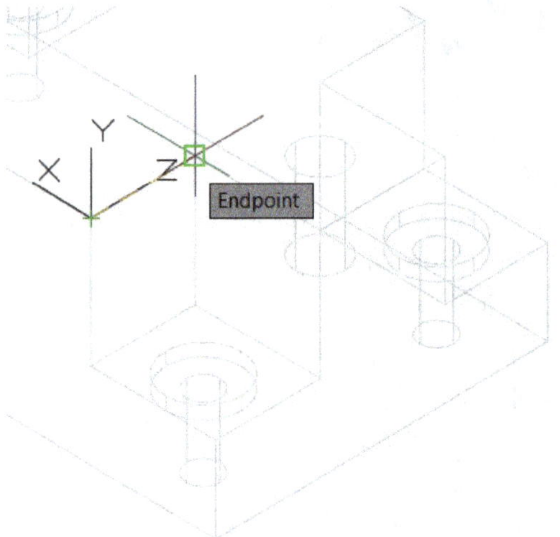

40. Select the **No** option from the command line.

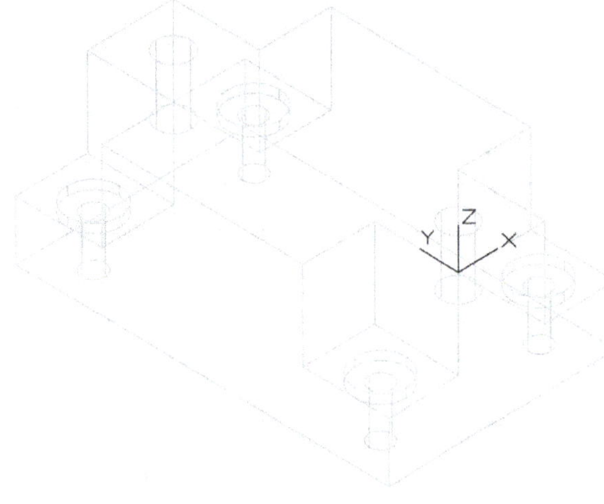

44. On the ribbon, click **Home** tab > **Modeling** panel > **Primitives** drop-down > **Cylinder**.
45. Select the midpoint of the front edge, as shown.

41. On the **Home** tab of the ribbon, click **Coordinates > Z-Axis Vector**.

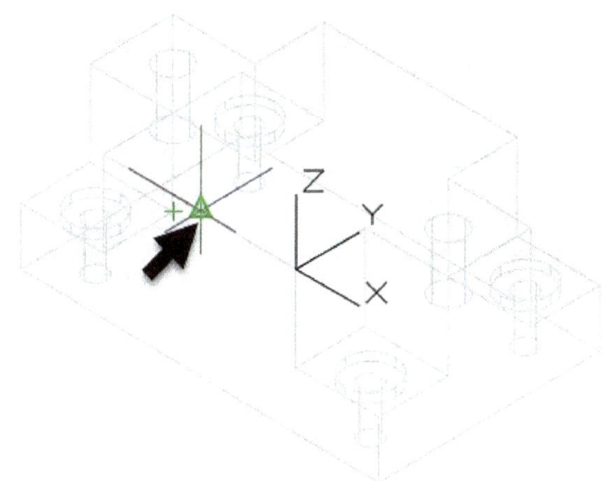

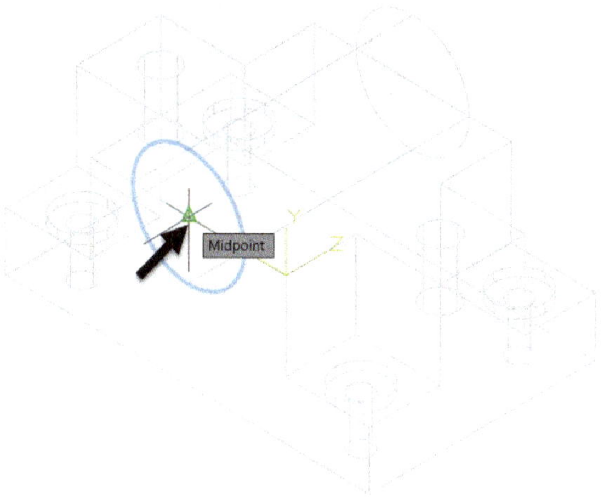

46. Type 20 in the command line and press ENTER.
47. Move the pointer toward the right and select the midpoint of the back edge, as shown.

51. Type 25 in the command line and press ENTER.
52. Move the pointer toward the right.
53. Type 15 and press ENTER.

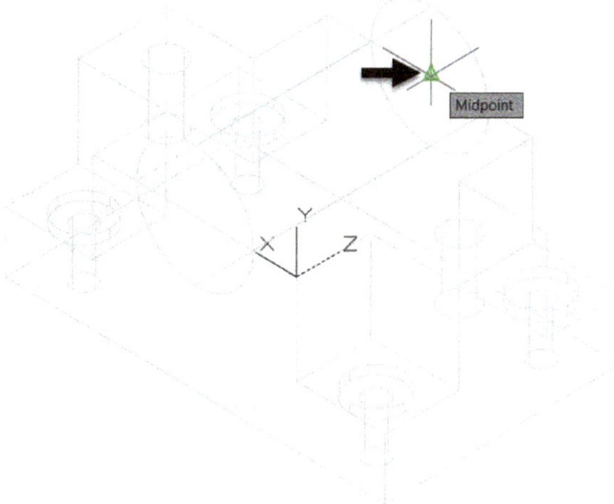

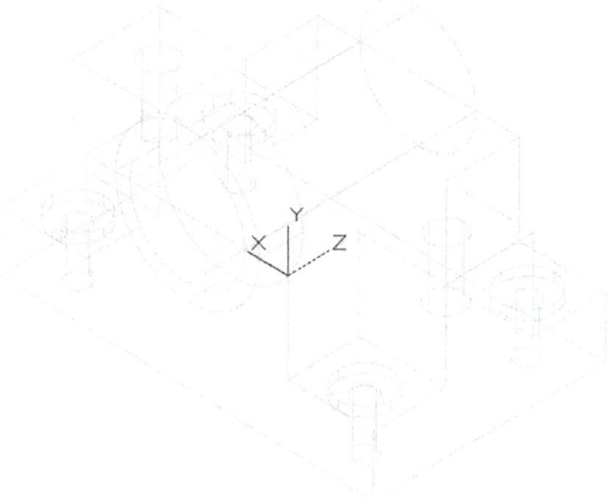

48. Deactivate the **Dynamic UCS** icon on the status bar.
49. On the ribbon, click **Home** tab > **Modeling** panel > **Primitives** drop-down > **Cylinder**.
50. Select the midpoint of the front edge, as shown.

54. On the ribbon, click **Home** tab > **Solid Editing** panel > **Solid, Subtract**.
55. Click on the edge of the main body; the main body is selected.
56. Press ENTER.

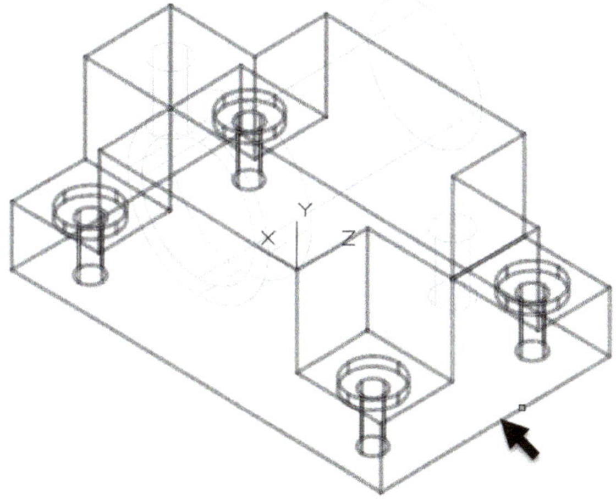

57. Select all the cylinders and press ENTER.

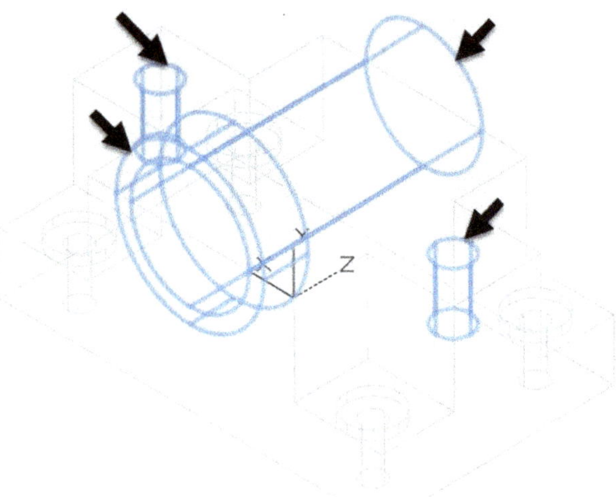

58. Set the **Visual Style** to **Shades of Gray**.

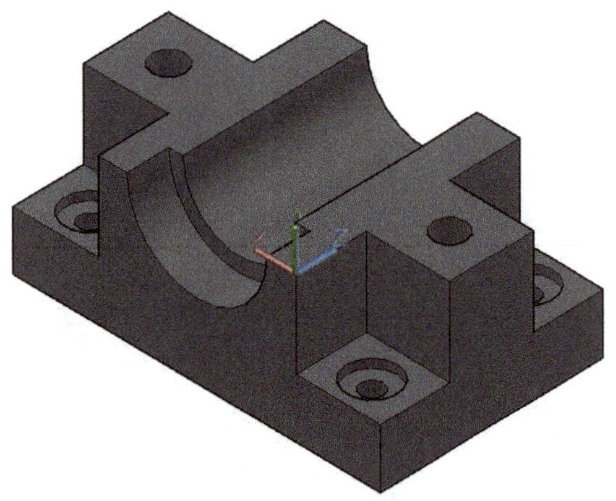

Creating the Presspull feature

1. On the ribbon, click **Home** tab > **Coordinates** panel > **UCS**.

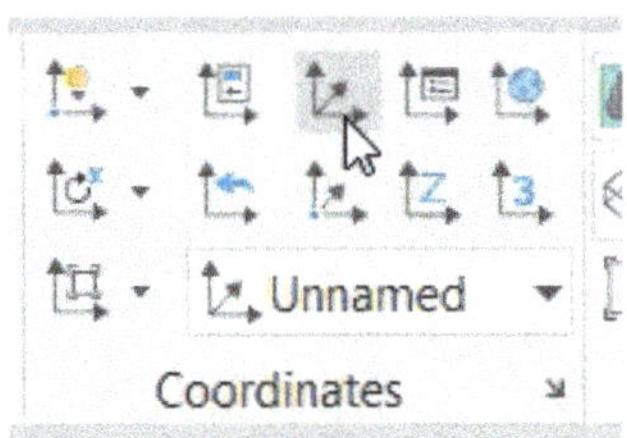

2. Select the lower-left corner of the model to define the origin of the UCS.

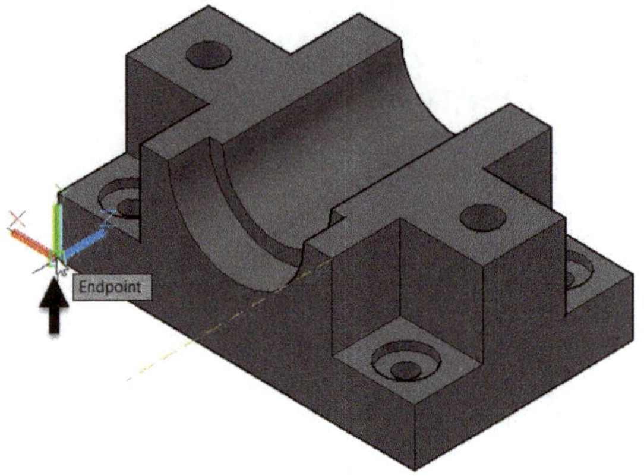

3. Move the pointer backward and select the lower right corner of the model.

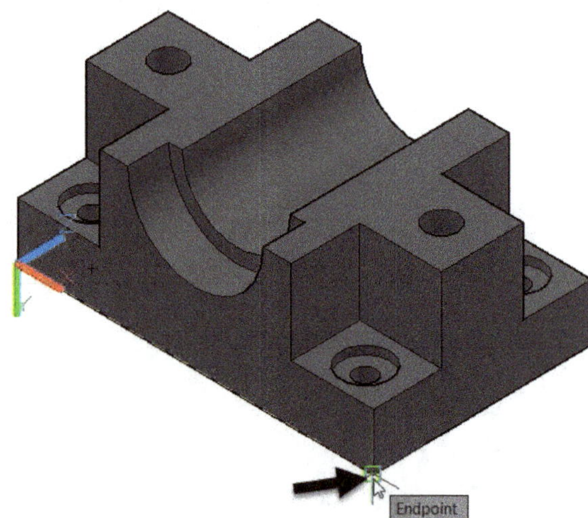

4. Move the pointer upwards and select the corner point, as shown.

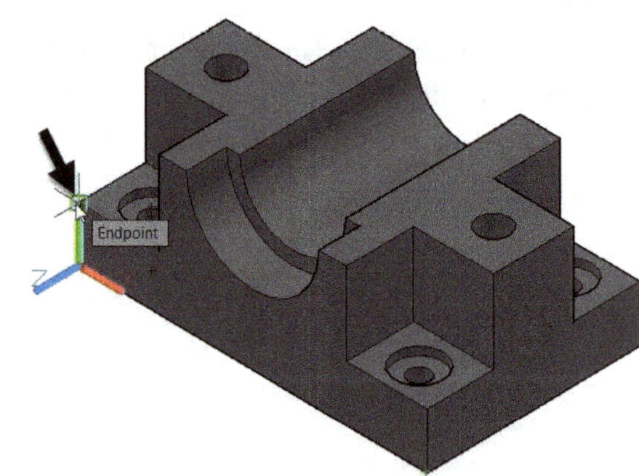

5. On the ribbon, click **Home** tab > **Draw** panel > **Polyline**.

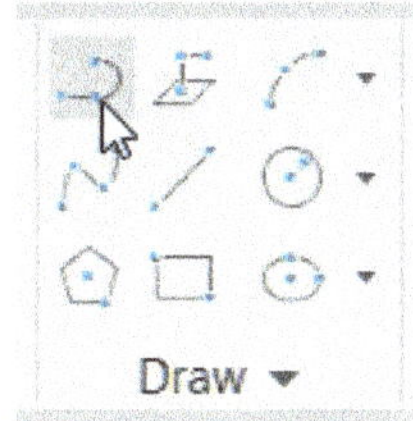

6. Type **36.7, 0** in the command line, and press ENTER.
7. Type **40,8** in the command line and press ENTER.
8. Type **90,8** in the command line and press ENTER.
9. Type **93.3,0** in the command line and press ENTER.
10. Select the **Close** option from the command line.

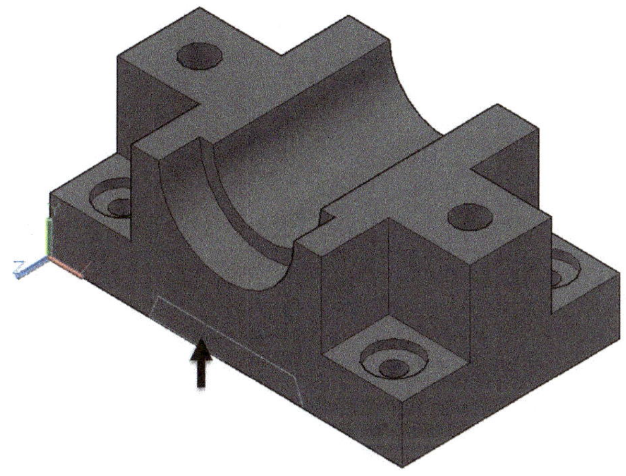

11. On the ribbon, click **Home** tab > **Modeling** panel > **Presspull**.
12. Click in the region bounded by the closed polyline.

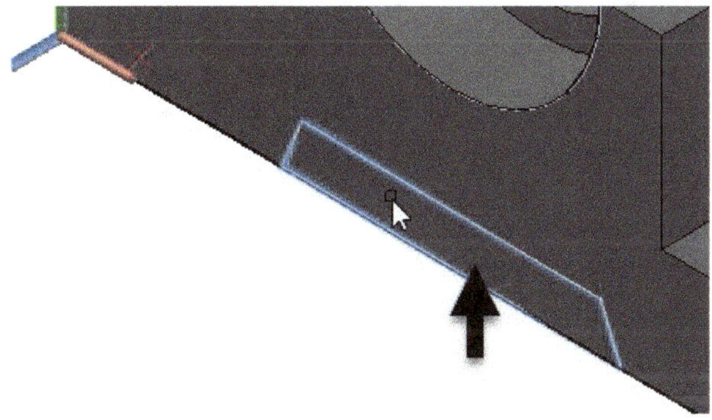

13. Type -80 and press ENTER.

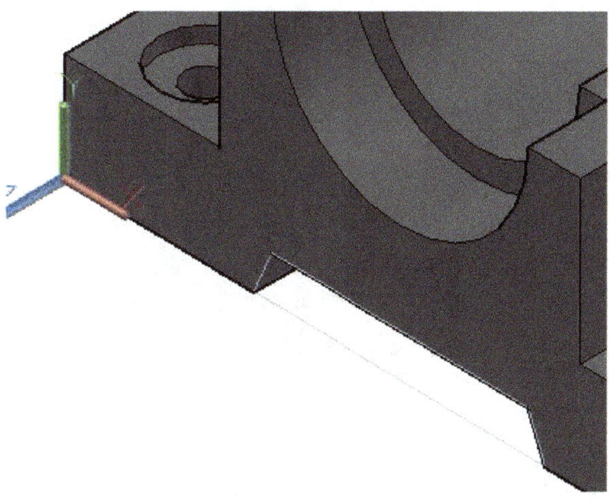

14. Press ESC.
15. Set the **Visual Style** to **2D Wireframe**.
16. On the ribbon, click **Solid** tab > **Solid Editing** panel > **Fillet Edge**.

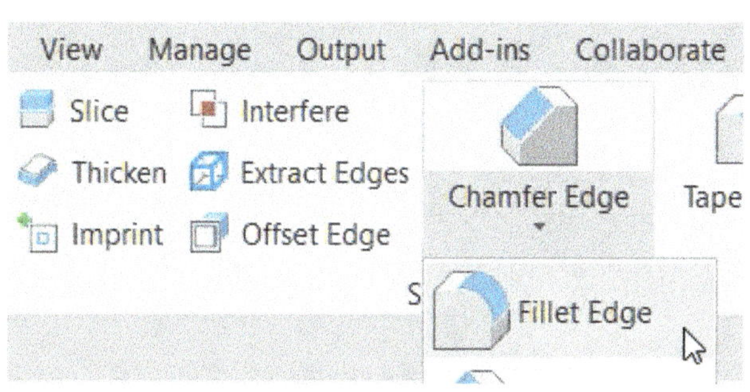

17. Select the inner edges of the subtractions, as shown.

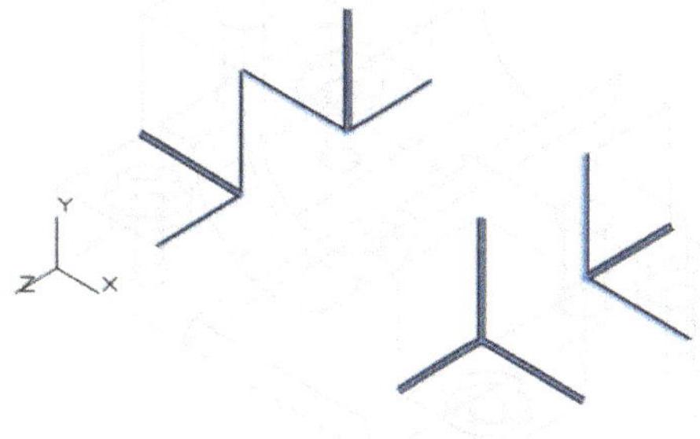

18. Press ENTER.
19. Select the **Radius** option from the command line.
20. Type **2** in the command line and press ENTER.
21. Press ENTER twice to create the fillets.
22. Set the **Visual Style** to **Shades of Gray**.

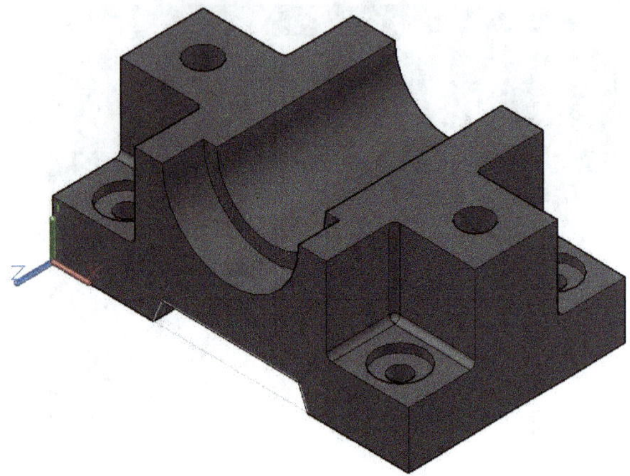

23. Click the **Save** icon on the Quick Access Toolbar.
24. Type **Ch4_tutorial1** in the **File Name** box.
25. Click the **Save** button.
26. Click **Application Menu > Close > Current Drawing**.

Tutorial 2 (Millimetres)

In this example, you create the part shown next.

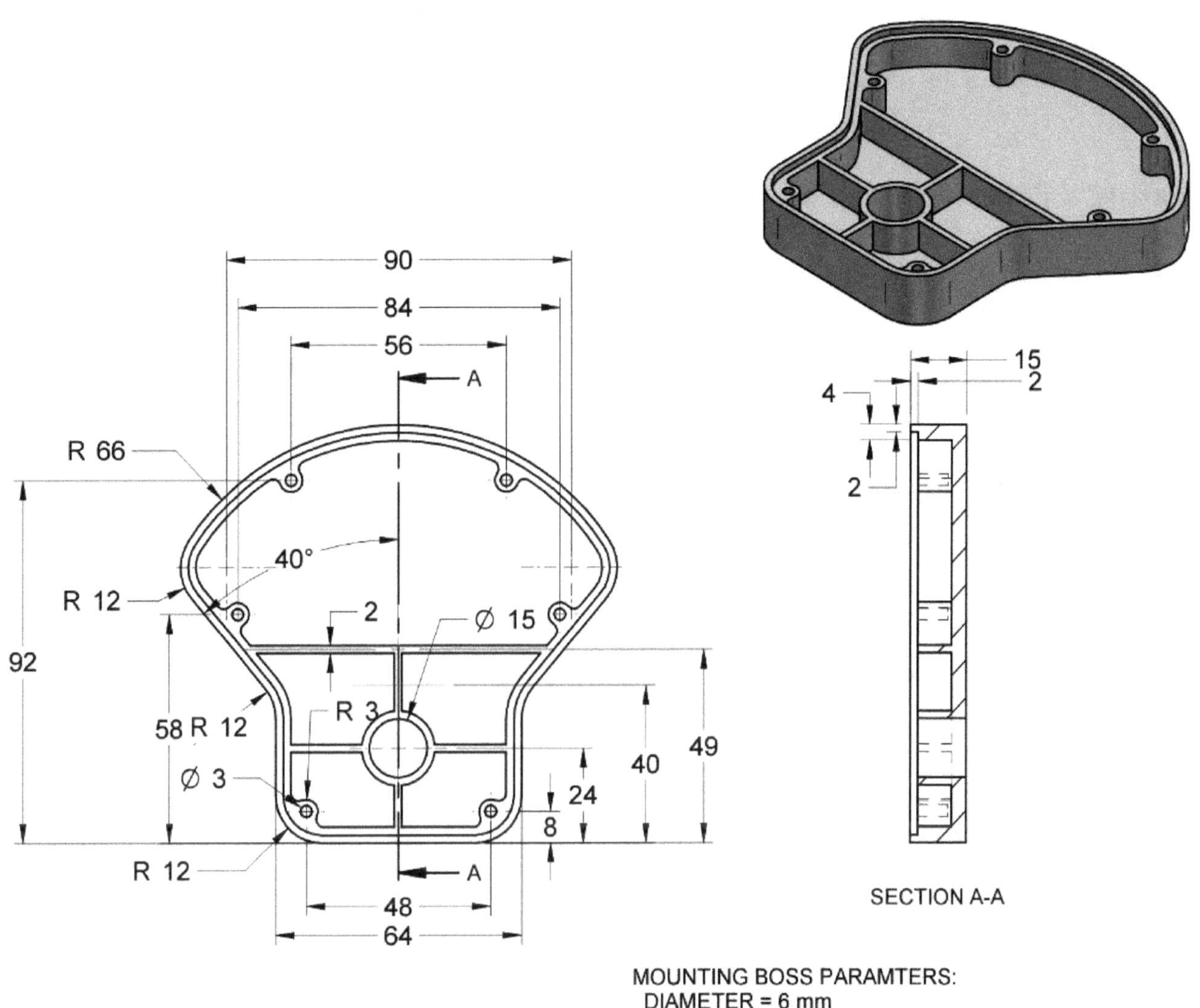

Creating a New File

1. Click the **New** icon on the Quick Access Toolbar.
2. Select the **acadiso3D** template from the **Select template** dialog.
3. Click the **Open** button.
4. Deactivate the **GRIDMODE** icon on the status bar.

Creating a Parametric Sketch

1. On the ribbon, click **Visualize** tab > **Named Views** panel > **Restore View** drop-down > **Top**.

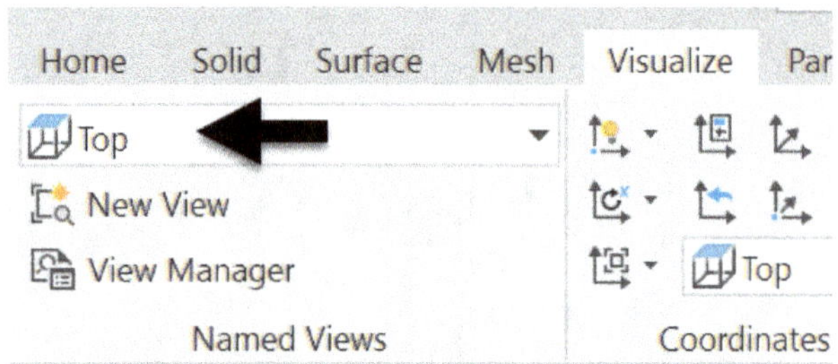

2. Click the **Customization** button on the bottom right corner of the window.

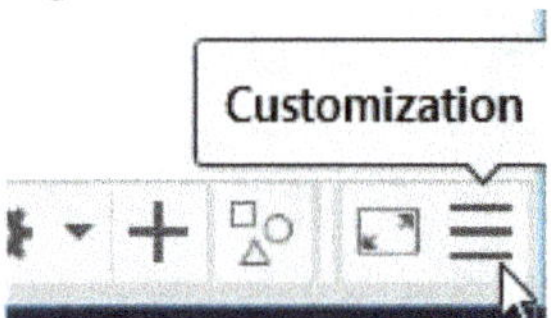

3. Select the **Infer Constraints** option.

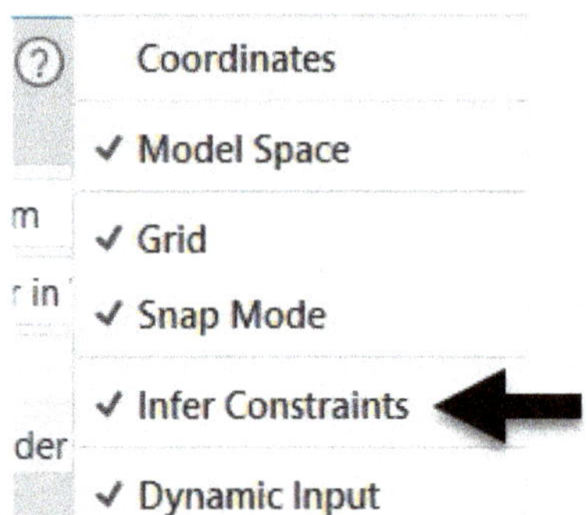

4. Click the **Infer Constraints** icon on the status bar.

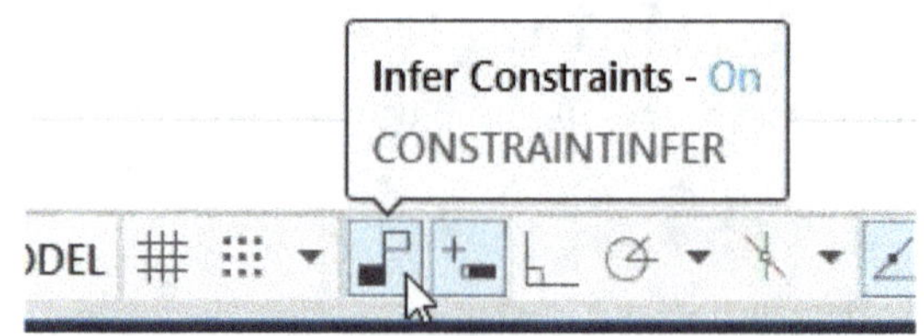

5. On the ribbon, click **Home** tab > **Draw** panel > **Line**.
6. Click in the graphics window to specify the start point of the line.
7. Activate the **Orthomode** icon on the status bar.
8. Move the pointer toward the right.
9. Type 64 and press ENTER.
10. Move the pointer upward.
11. Type 40 and press ENTER.
12. Deactivate the **Orthomode** icon on the status bar.
13. Move the diagonally toward the right and click.

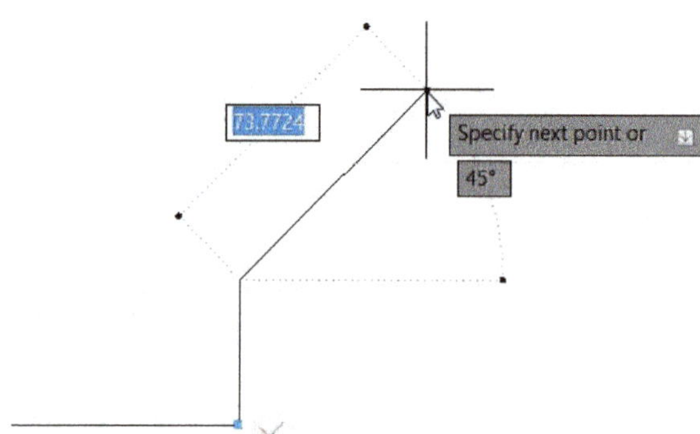

Notice that the infer constraints are created between the endpoints of the lines.

14. On the **Home** tab of the ribbon, expand the **Modify** panel and click the **Mirror** icon.
15. Select the vertical and inclined lines.
16. Press ENTER.
17. Select the midpoint of the horizontal line.
18. Activate the **Orthomode** icon on the status bar.
19. Move the pointer upward and click to specify the mirror line.

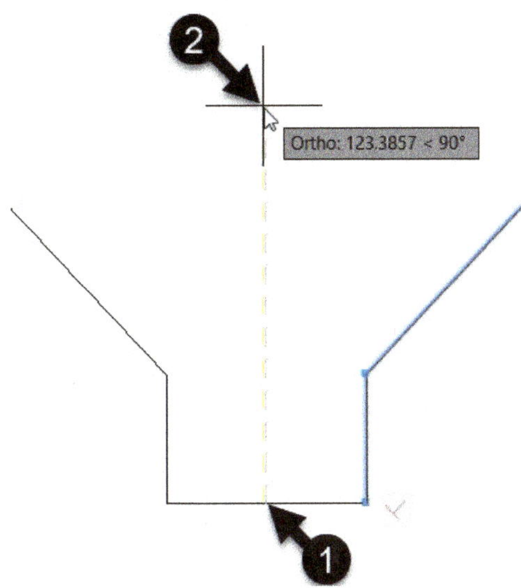

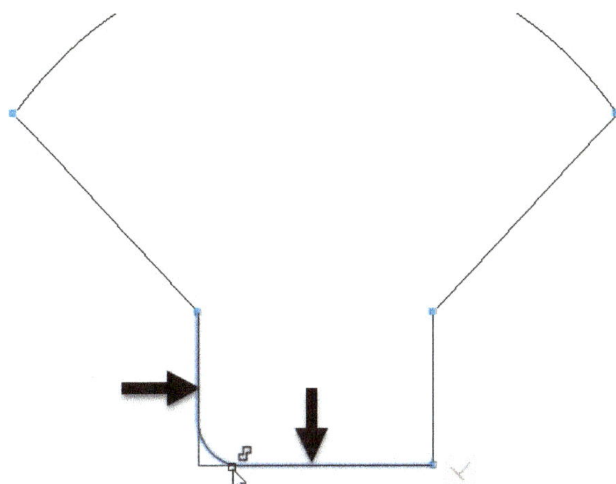

20. Select the **No** option from the command line.
21. Deactivate the **Orthomode** icon on the status bar.
22. On the ribbon, click **Home** tab > **Draw** panel > **Arc** drop-down > **3 Point**.
23. Select the endpoint of the left inclined line, as shown.
24. Move the pointer diagonally toward the right.
25. Click to specify the second point.
26. Select the endpoint of the right inclined line.

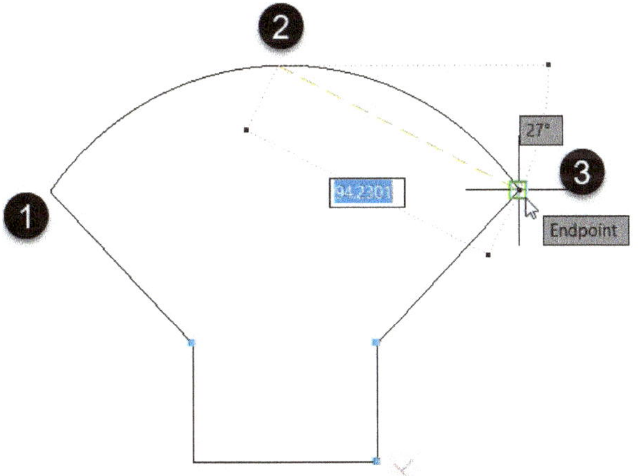

27. On the ribbon, click **Home** tab > **Modify** panel > **Fillet** drop-down > **Fillet**.
28. Select the **Radius** option from the command line.
29. Type 12 in the command line and press ENTER.
30. Select the left vertical line and the horizontal line.

31. Press ENTER to activate the **Fillet** command.
32. Select the right vertical line and the horizontal line.
33. Press ENTER to activate the **Fillet** command.
34. Select the left vertical and left inclined lines.
35. Press ENTER to activate the **Fillet** command.
36. Select the right vertical and right inclined lines.
37. Press ENTER to activate the **Fillet** command.
38. Select the left inclined line and the arc.
39. Press ENTER to activate the **Fillet** command.
40. Select the right inclined line and the arc.

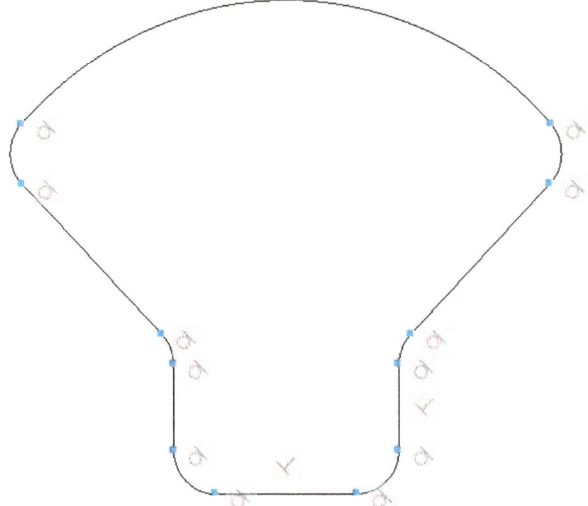

41. On the ribbon, click **Parametric** tab > **Geometric** panel > **Equal**.

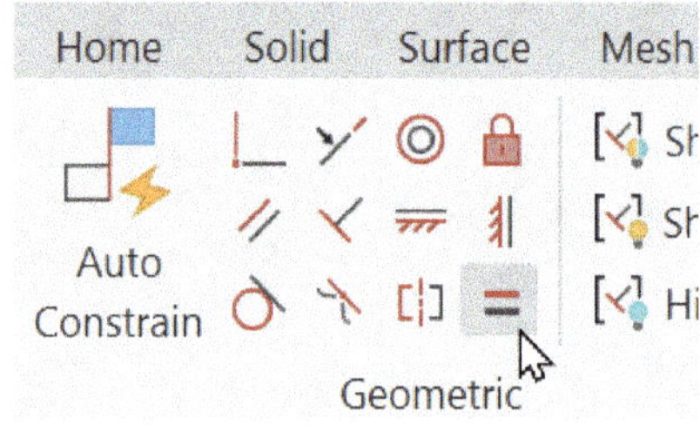

42. Select the two vertical lines.

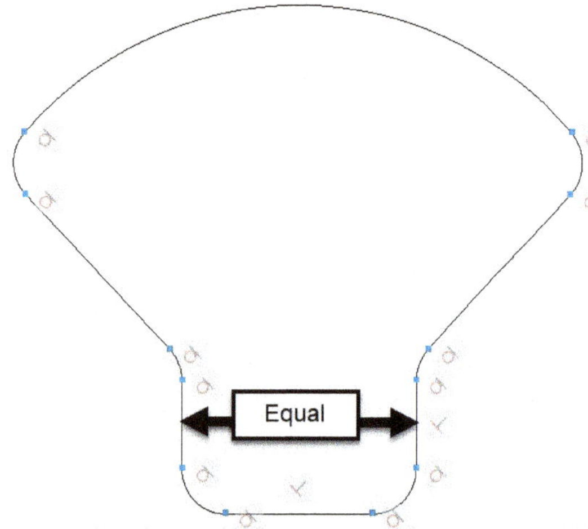

43. Press ENTER to activate the **Equal** command.
44. Select the two inclined lines to make them equal in length.

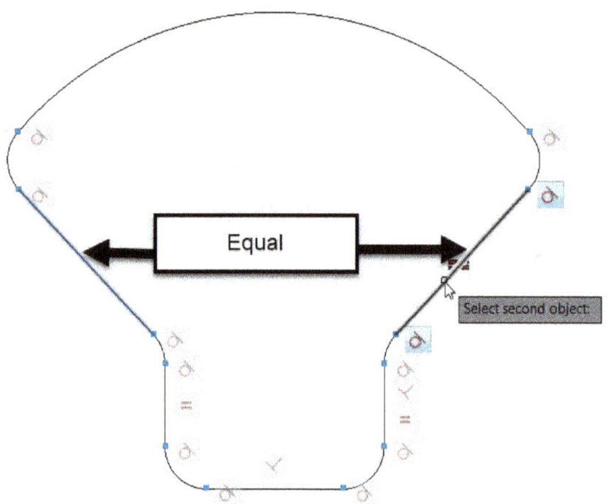

45. Press ENTER to activate the **Equal** command.
46. Select the **Multiple** option from the command line.
47. Select all the fillets and press ENTER.

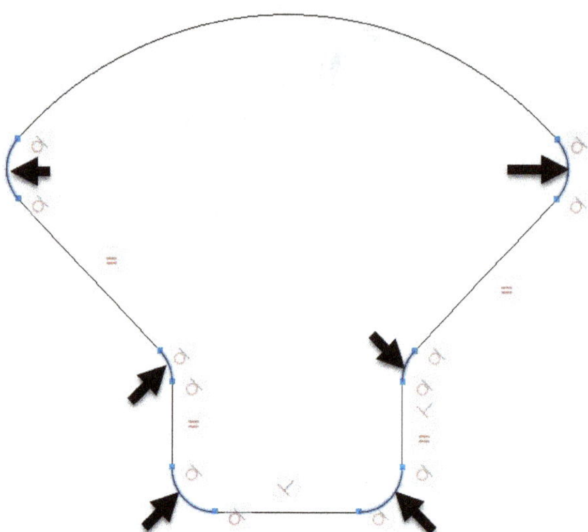

48. On the ribbon, click **Parametric** tab > **Geometric** panel > **Vertical**.

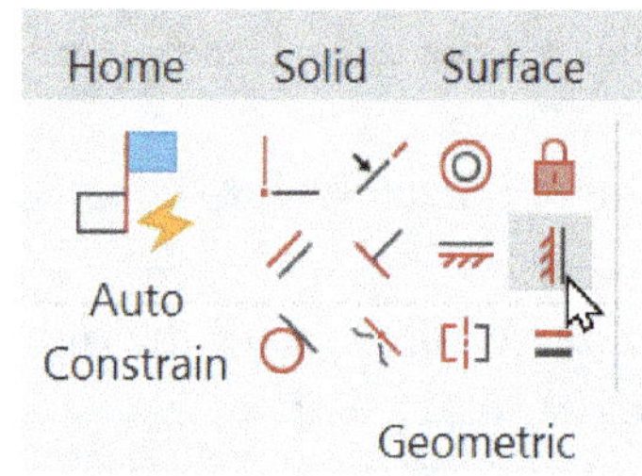

49. Select the left vertical line.

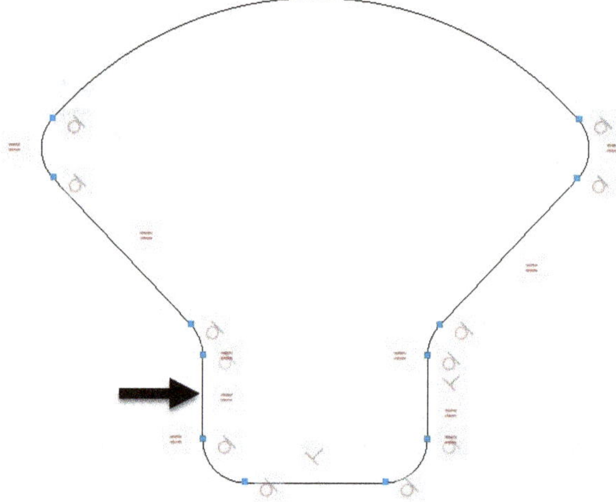

50. On the ribbon, click **Parametric** tab > **Geometric** panel > **Horizontal** .
51. Select the horizontal line.

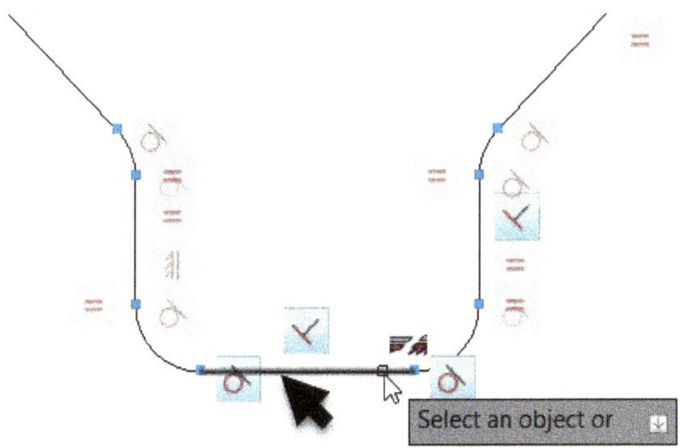

52. On the ribbon, click **Parametric** tab >
    Dimensional panel > **Linear**.

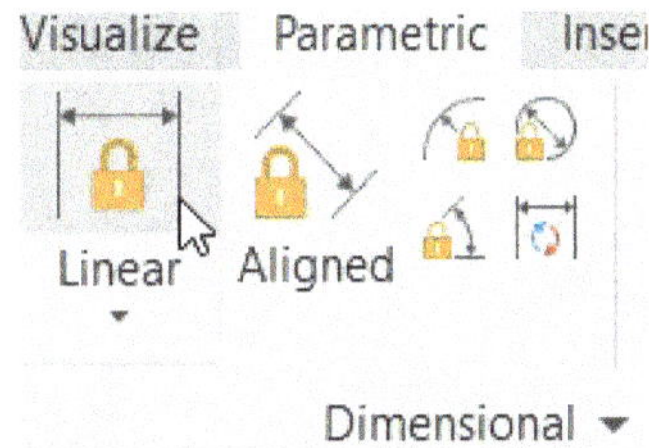

53. Select the lower endpoints of the two vertical
    lines.
54. Move the pointer downward and click.

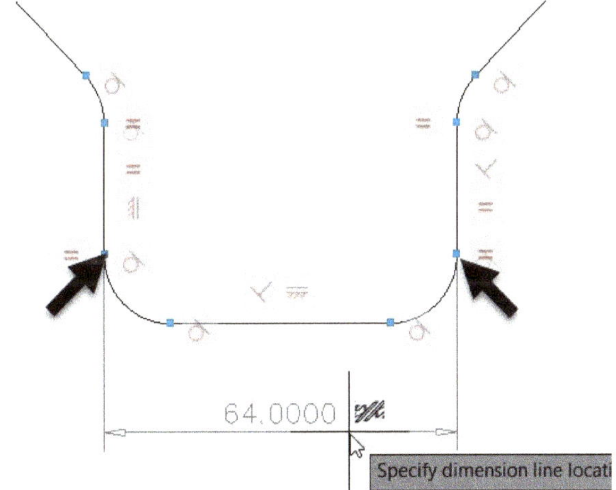

55. Type 64 and press ENTER.
56. On the ribbon, click **Parametric** tab >
    Dimensional panel > **Linear** drop-down >
    Horizontal.

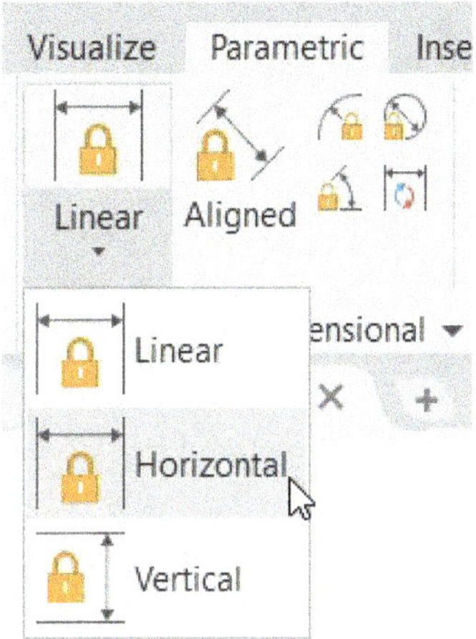

57. Press and hold the Shift key and right-click.
58. Select **Center** from the **Object Snaps** menu.
59. Click on the left fillet, as shown. The center point
    of the fillet is selected.

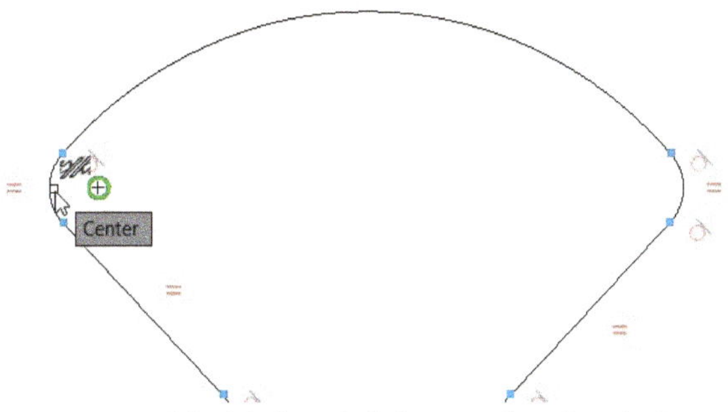

60. Press and hold the Shift key and right-click.
61. Select **Center** from the **Object Snaps** menu.
62. Click on the right fillet, as shown. The center
    point of the fillet is selected.

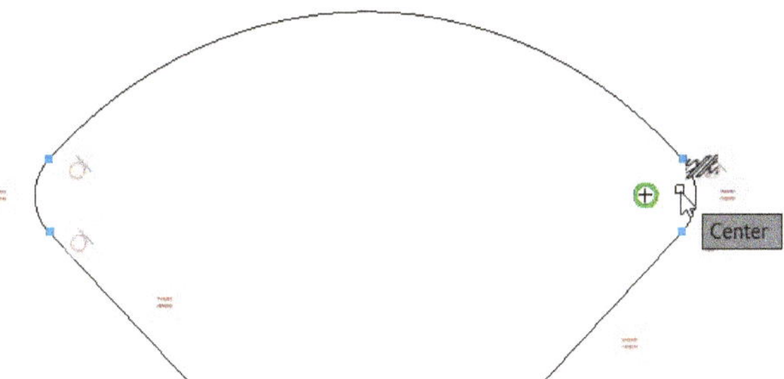

63. Move the pointer upward and click to create the
    horizontal constraint.
64. Click in the graphics window.
65. On the ribbon, click **Parametric** tab >
    Dimensional panel > **Angular**.

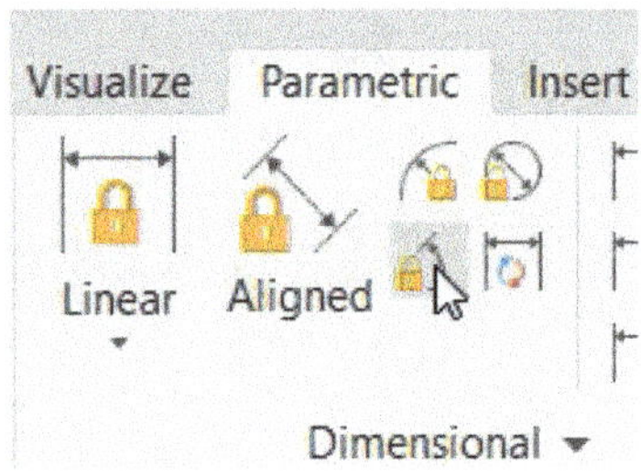

66. Select the left vertical and inclined lines, as shown.
67. Move the pointer toward the left and click.
68. Type 40 and press ENTER.

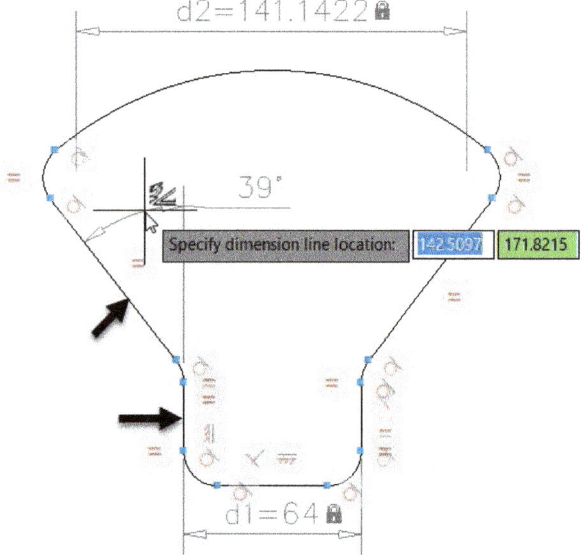

69. On the ribbon, click **Home** tab > **Draw** panel > **Line**.
70. Activate the **Orthomode** icon on the status bar.
71. Select the midpoint of the horizontal line, as shown.
72. Move the pointer vertically upward and click.

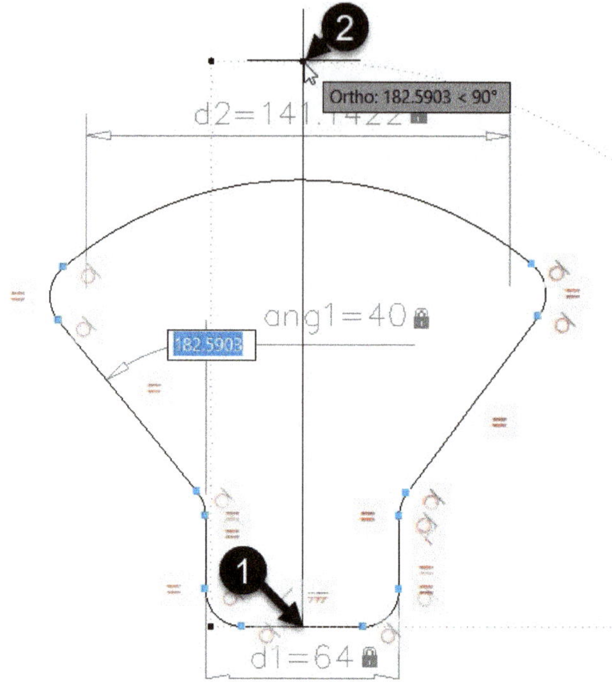

73. On the ribbon, click **Parametric** tab > **Geometric** panel > **Symmetric**.
74. Select the left inclined line to define the first object.
75. Select the right inclined line to define the second object.
76. Select the vertical line to define the symmetry line.

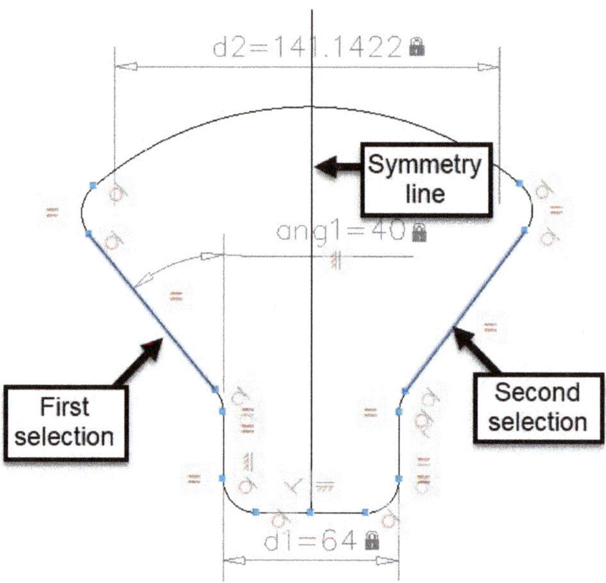

77. On the ribbon, click **Parametric** tab > **Dimensional** panel > **Radius**.

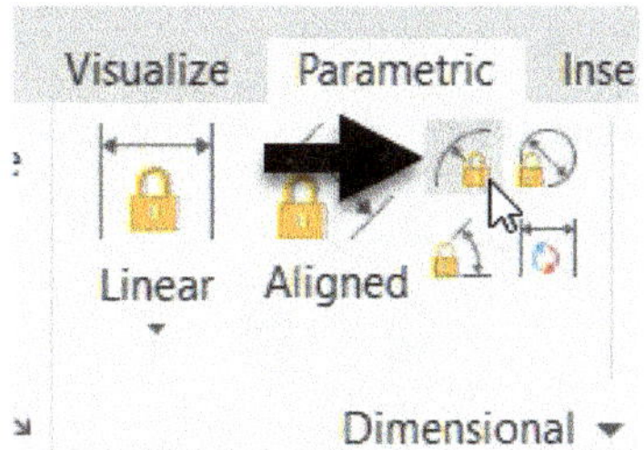

78. Select the large arc.
79. Move the pointer and click.
80. Click in the graphics window

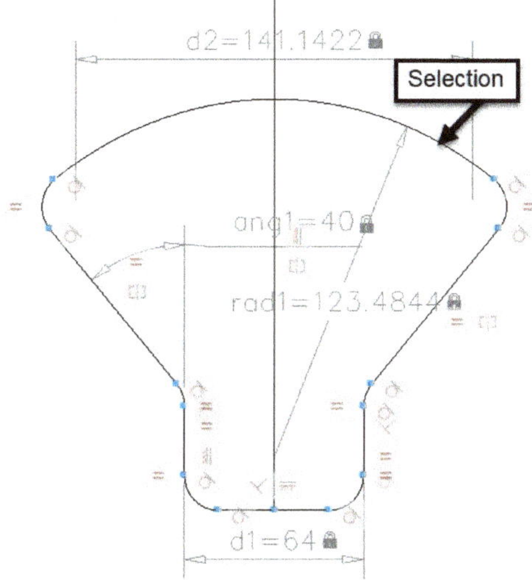

81. On the ribbon, click **Parametric** tab >
    Dimensional panel > **Linear** drop-down >
    Vertical.

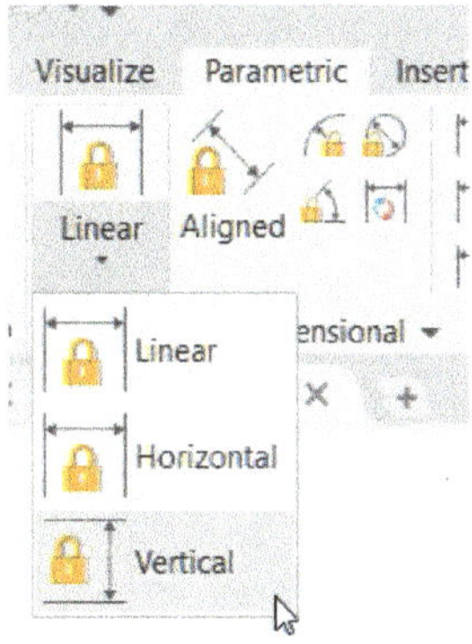

82. Press and hold the Shift key and right-click.
83. Select **Center** from the **Object Snaps** menu.
84. Click on the large arc, as shown. The center
    point of the arc is selected.

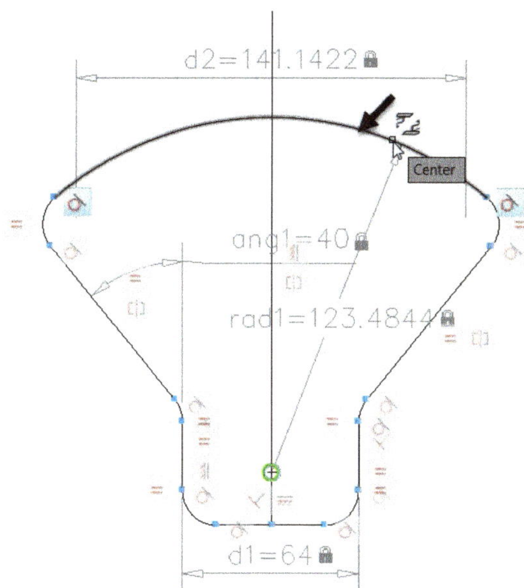

85. Select the right point of the horizontal line, as
    shown.

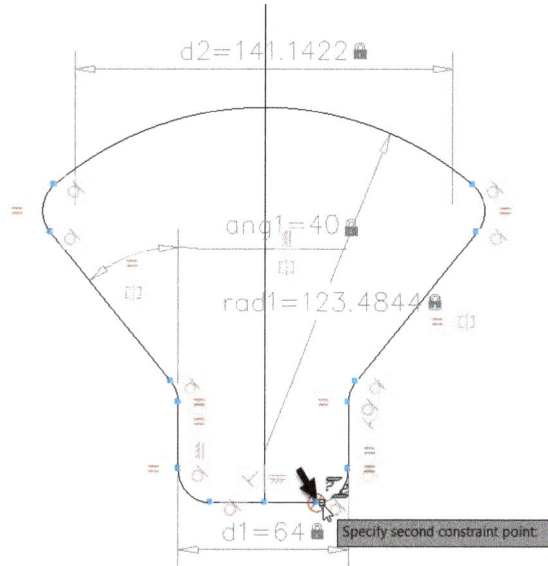

86. Move the pointer toward the right and click.
87. Type 40 and press ENTER.

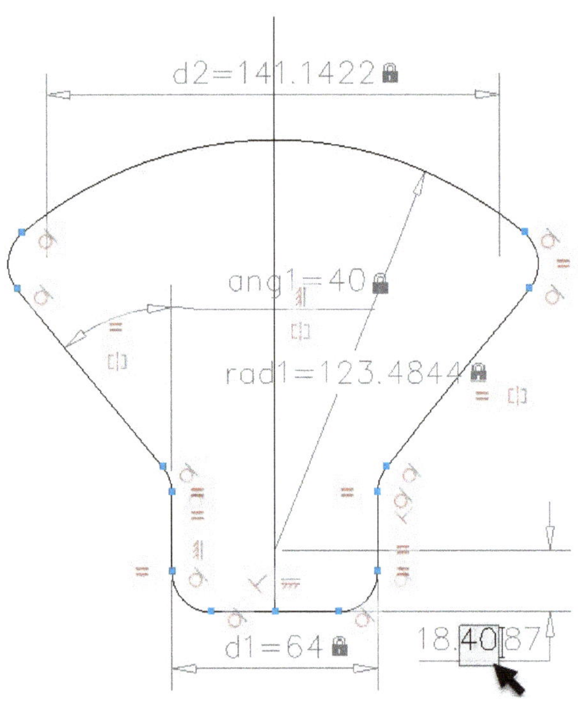

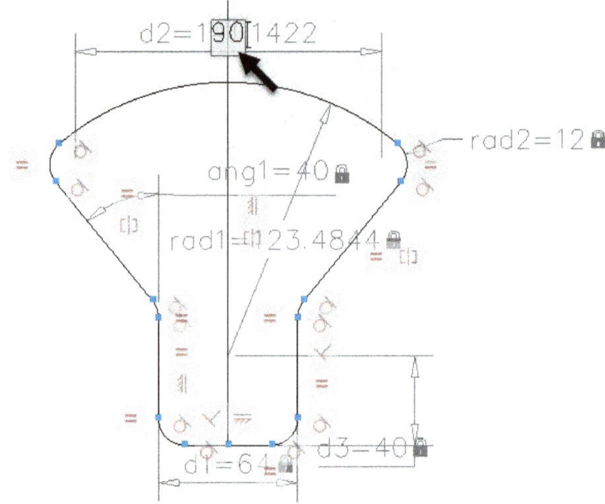

88. On the ribbon, click **Parametric** tab > **Dimensional** panel > **Radius**.
89. Select any one of the fillets.
90. Place the dimensional constraint.
91. Type **12** and press ENTER.

94. Select the radius constraint, as shown.
95. Type 66 and press ENTER.

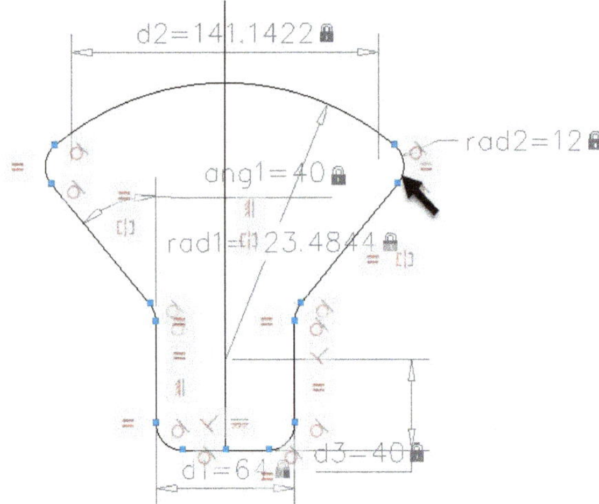

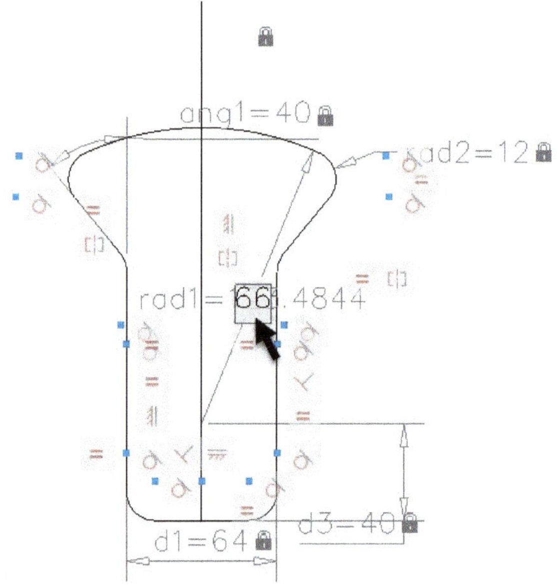

92. Double-click on the horizontal constraint, as shown.
93. Type 90 and press ENTER.

Extruding the Sketch

1. On the **Home** tab of the ribbon, expand the **Draw** panel and click the **Region**.

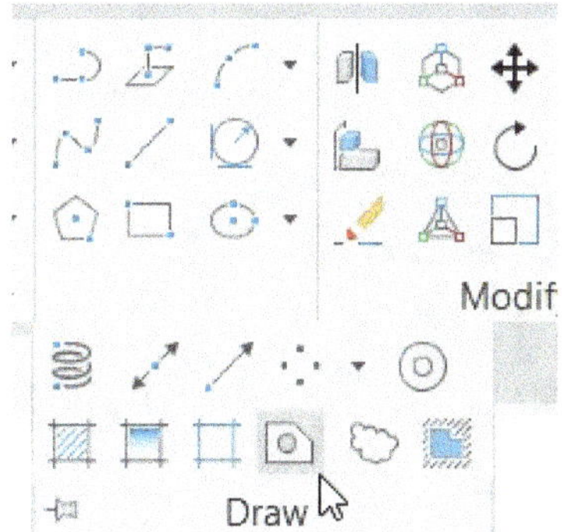

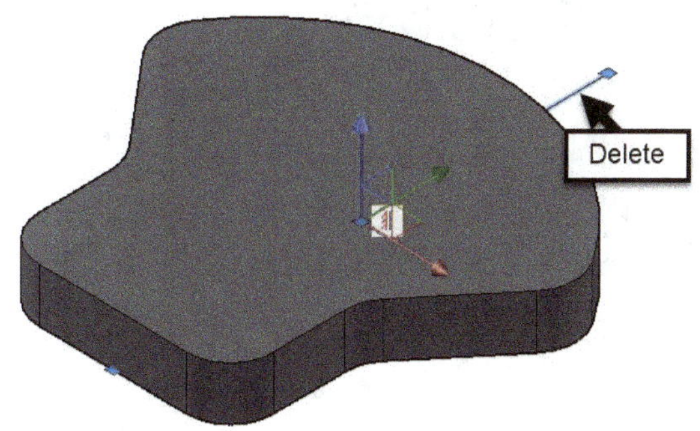

2. Create a selection window from left to right across all the elements of the sketch.

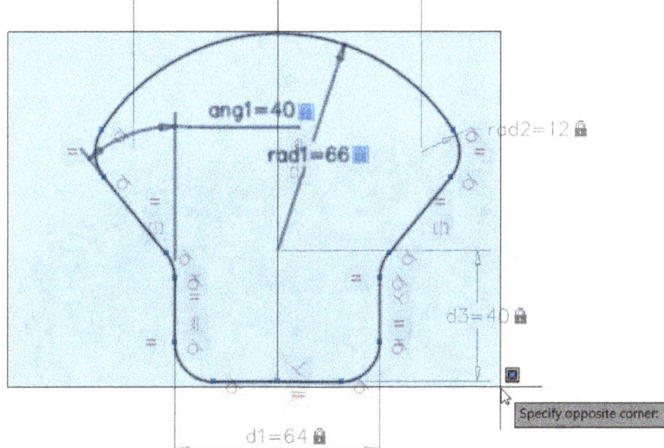

3. Press ENTER to convert the closed sketch into a region.

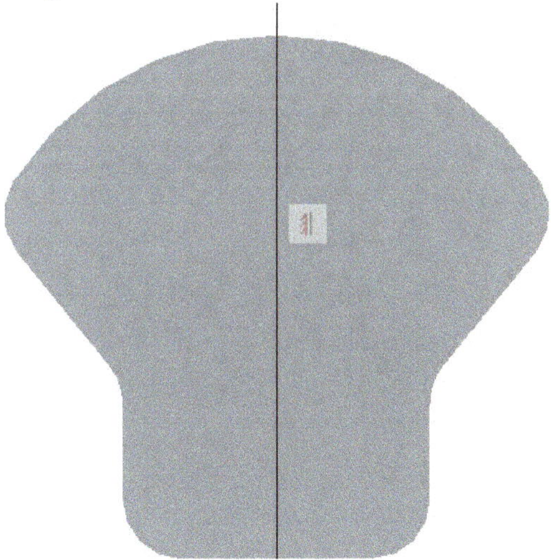

4. Change the view orientation to SE Isometric.
5. On the ribbon, click **Home** tab > **Modeling** panel > **Solids** drop-down > **Extrude**.
6. Select the region and press ENTER.
7. Move the pointer upward.
8. Type 14 and press ENTER.

9. Select the vertical line and press DELETE.

10. On the ribbon, click the **Solid** tab > **Solid Editing** panel > **Offset Edge**.

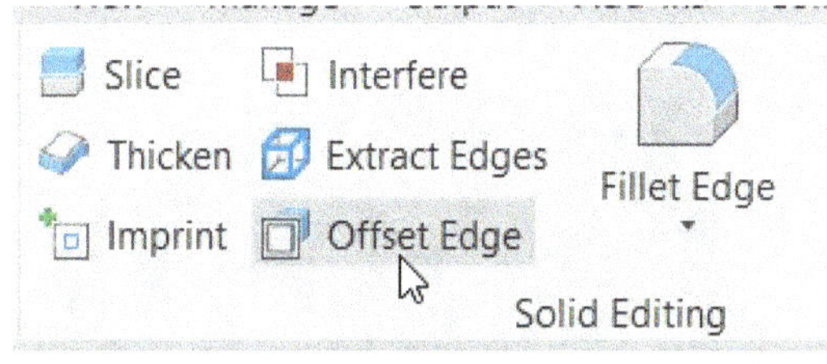

11. Click on the top face of the solid body.
12. Select the **Distance** option from the command line.
13. Type **2** in the command line and press ENTER.
14. Click inside the solid body to specify the direction of the offset edge.

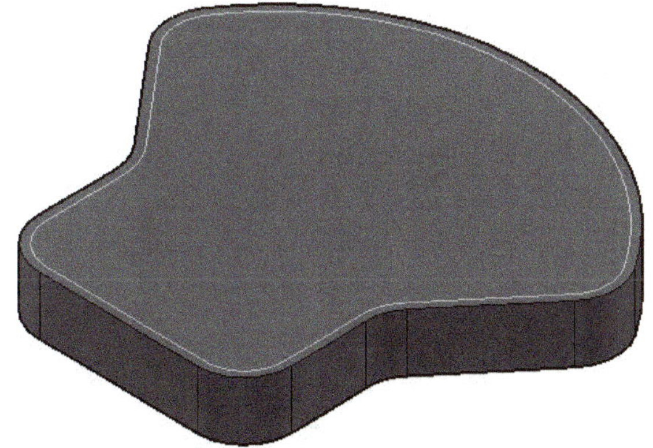

15. On the ribbon, click the **Solid** tab > **Solid Editing** panel > **Shell**.
16. Select the solid body.
17. Click on the top face of the body.
18. Press ENTER.
19. Type **4** in the command line and press ENTER.

20. Press ENTER twice to exit the command.

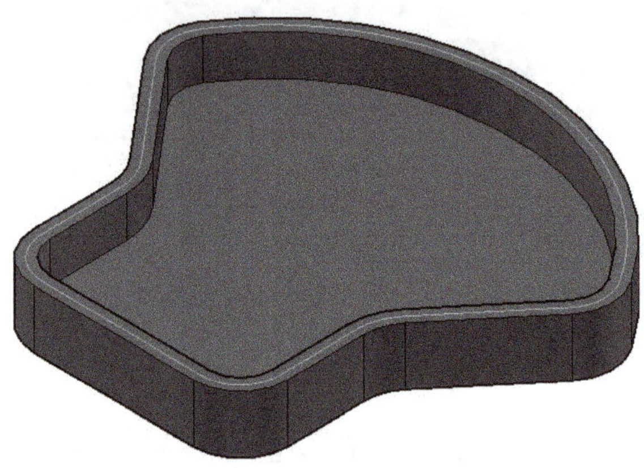

Adding a Lip to the model

1. Select the offset edge.

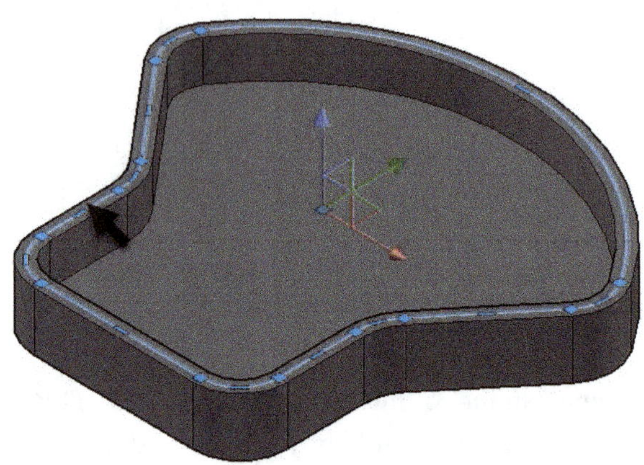

2. On the ribbon, click **Home** tab > **Modeling** panel > **Solids** drop-down > **Extrude**.
3. Move the pointer downward.
4. Type 2 and press ENTER.

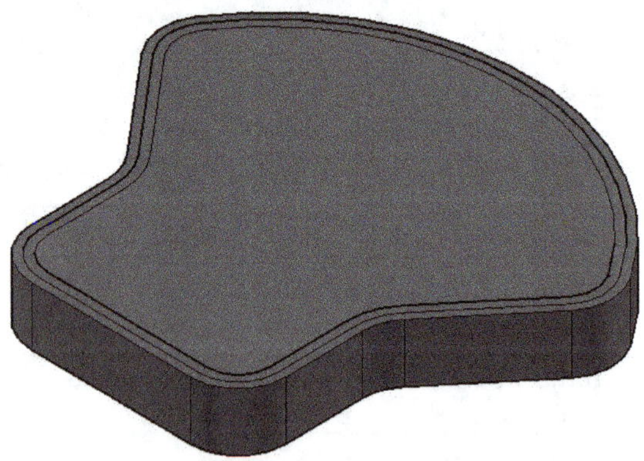

5. On the ribbon, click the **Home** tab > **Modeling** panel > **Solid Editing** drop-down > **Solid, Subtract**.
6. Click on the side face of the model.

7. Press ENTER.
8. Click on the top face of the extruded body.

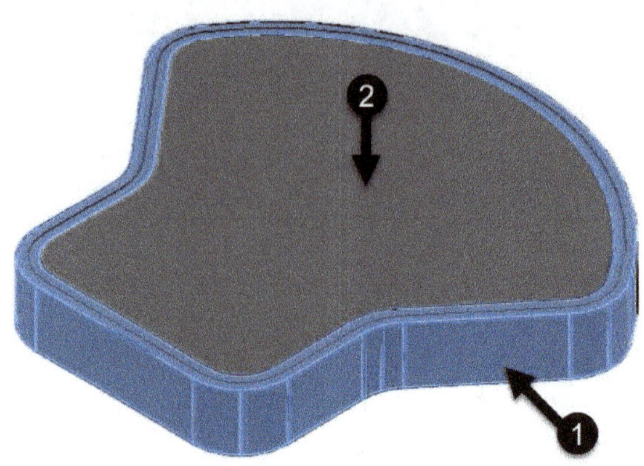

9. Press ENTER.

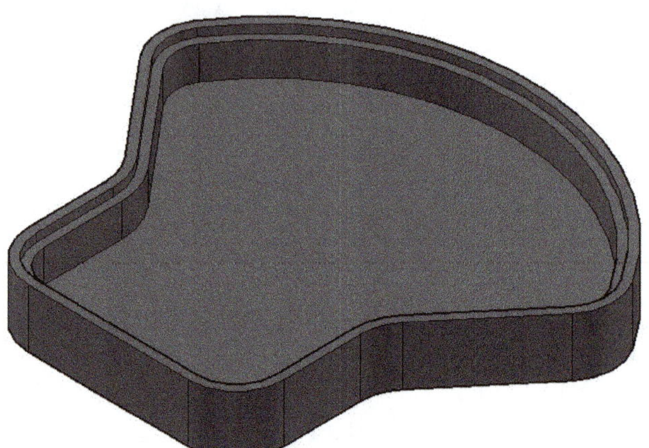

Creating Bosses

1. On the ribbon, click **Home** tab > **Coordinates** panel > **Origin**.

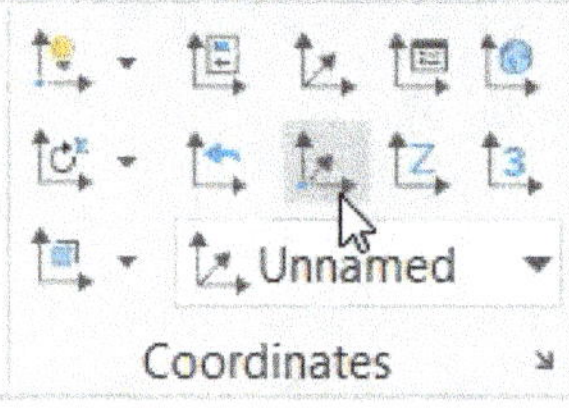

2. Select the midpoint of the horizontal edge, as shown.

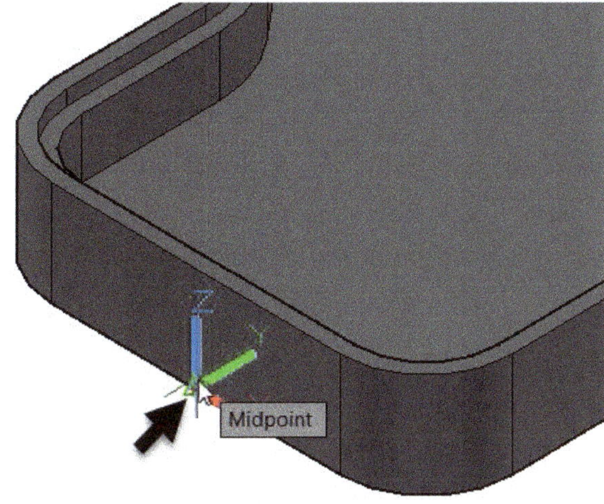

10. Click the Top face of the ViewCube.

11. On the ribbon, click **Home** tab > **Draw** panel > **Circle** drop-down > **Circle, Radius**.

12. Create two circles, as shown.

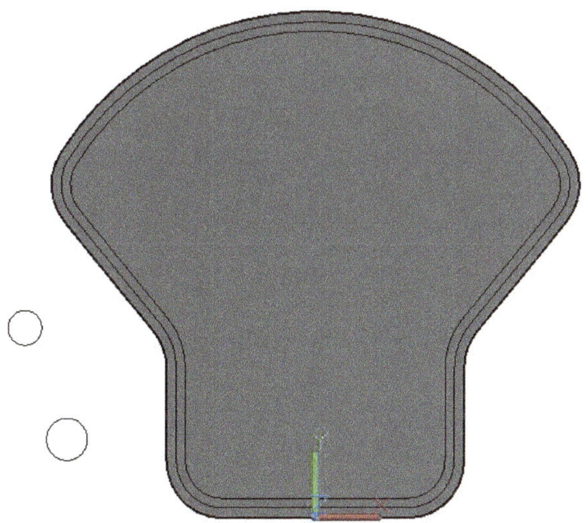

13. On the ribbon, click **Parametric** tab > **Geometric** panel > **Concentric** .

14. Select the two circles to make them concentric.

15. On the ribbon, click **Parametric** tab > **Dimensional** panel > **Diameter**.

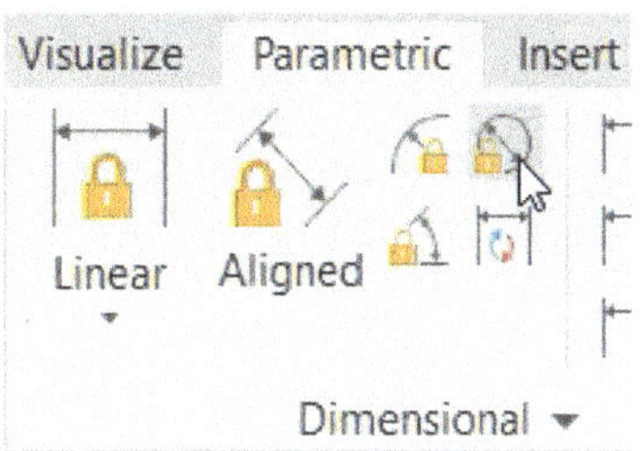

16. Select any one of the circles.

17. Position the dimensional constraint.

18. Type 6 and press ENTER.

19. On the ribbon, click **Parametric** tab > **Dimensional** panel > **Diameter**.

20. Select the other circle.

21. Position the dimensional constraint.

22. Type 3 and press ENTER.

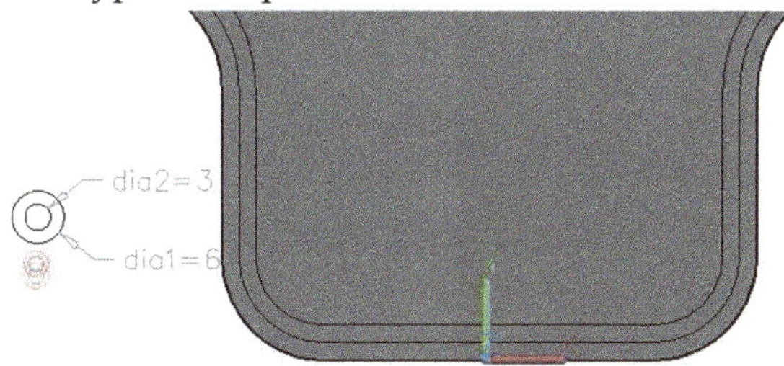

23. Change the **Visual Style** to **2D Wireframe**.

24. On the ribbon, click **Home** tab > **Draw** panel > **Line**.

25. Create a vertical line passing through the origin.

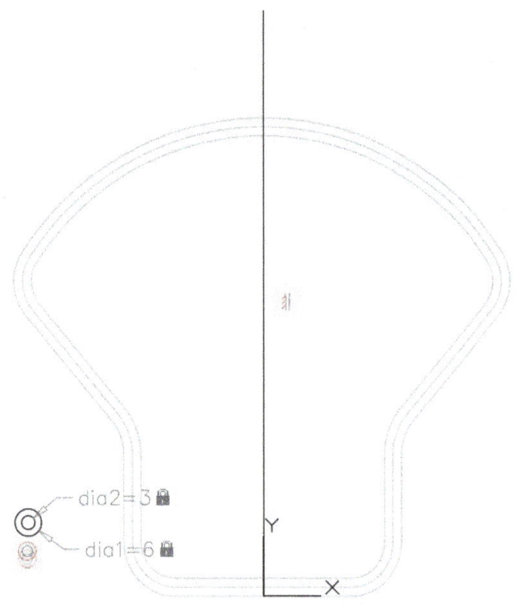

26. On the ribbon, click **Parametric** tab > **Geometric** panel > **Fix** 🔒.
27. Select the lower endpoint of the newly created vertical line.
28. On the ribbon, click **Parametric** tab > **Dimensional** panel > **Linear**.
29. Select the centerpoint of the circle.
30. Select the lower endpoint of the vertical line.
31. Move the pointer downward and click.

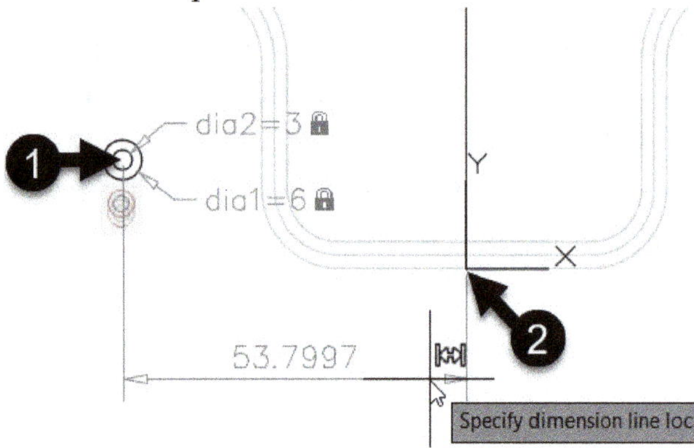

32. Type 24 and press ENTER.

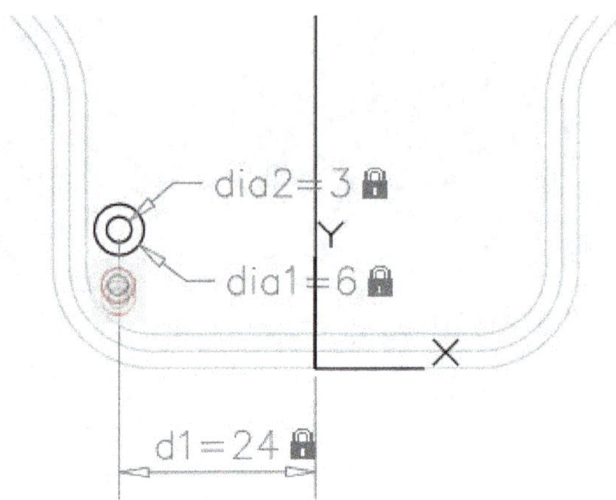

33. On the ribbon, click **Parametric** tab > **Dimensional** panel > **Linear**.
34. Select the lower endpoint of the vertical line.
35. Select the centerpoint of the circle.
36. Move the pointer toward the left and click.

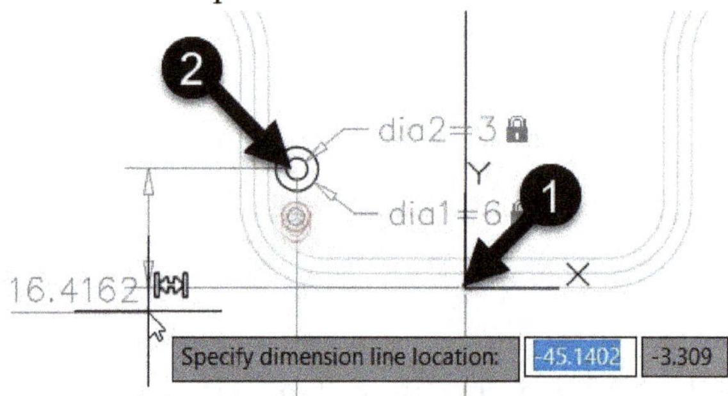

37. Type 8 and press ENTER.

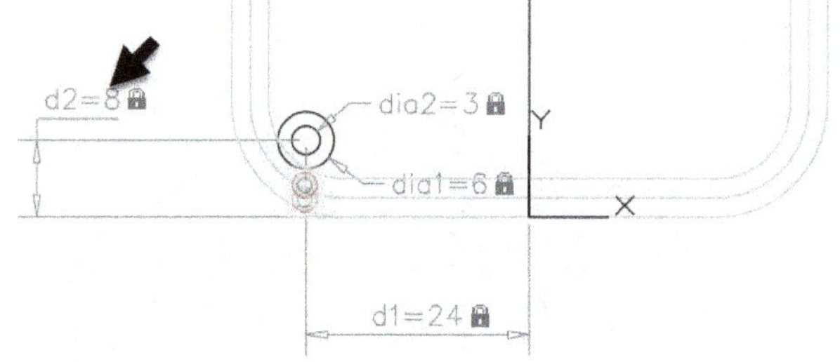

38. On the ribbon, click **Home** tab > **Modify** panel > **Copy**.
39. Select the two circles and press ENTER.
40. Click at an arbitrary point to specify the base point.
41. Move the pointer upward and click.
42. Again, move the pointer upward and click.

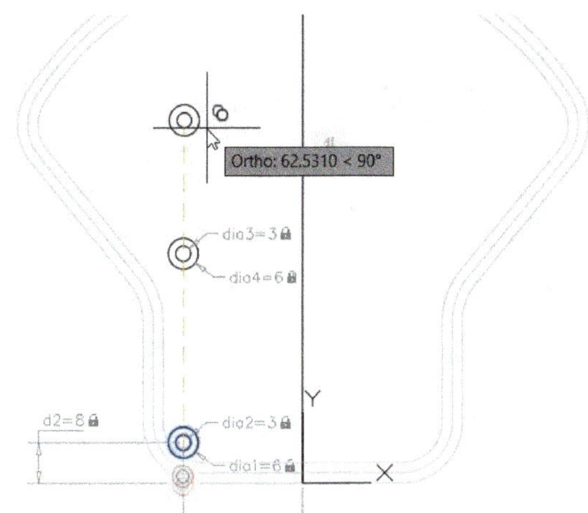

43. Press ESC.
44. Create the Linear dimensional constraints, as shown.

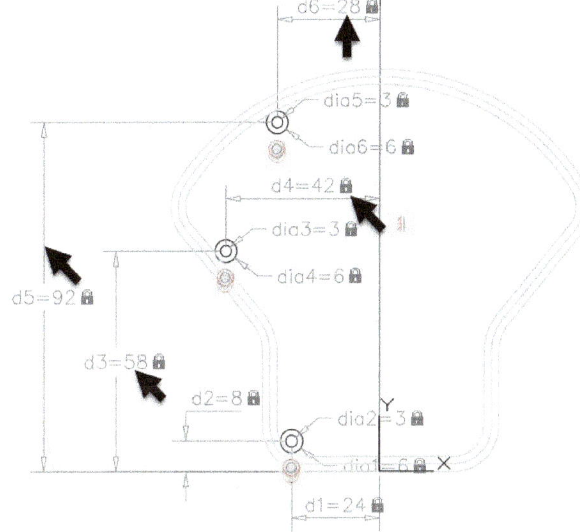

45. On the ribbon, click the **Home** tab > **Modeling** panel > **Extrude**.
46. Select all the large circles and press ENTER.

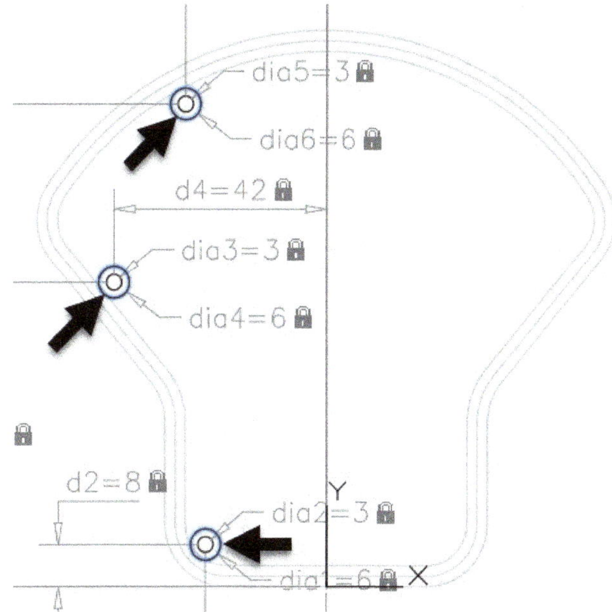

47. Type 12 and press ENTER.
48. On the ribbon, click the **Home** tab > **Modeling** panel > **Extrude**.
49. Select all the small circles and press ENTER.
50. Type 20 and press ENTER.
51. Change the view orientation to SE Isometric.
52. Change the **Visual Style** to **Shades of Gray**.

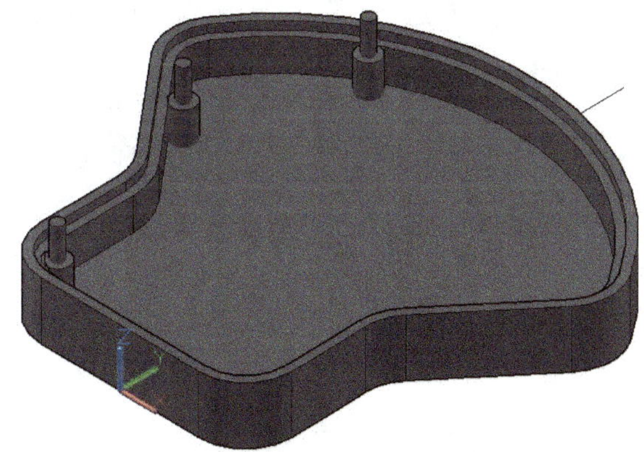

53. Select all the cylinders from the graphics window.
54. On the ribbon, click **Home** tab > **Modify** panel > **3D Mirror**.

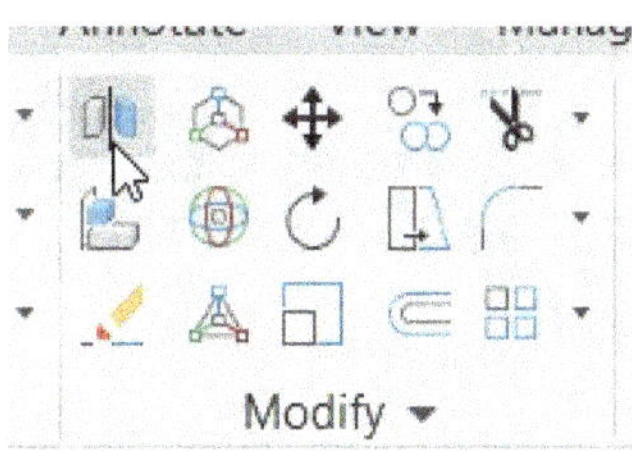

55. Select the **YZ** option from the command line.
56. Select the origin of the UCS to define the location of the mirror plane.
57. Select the **No** option.

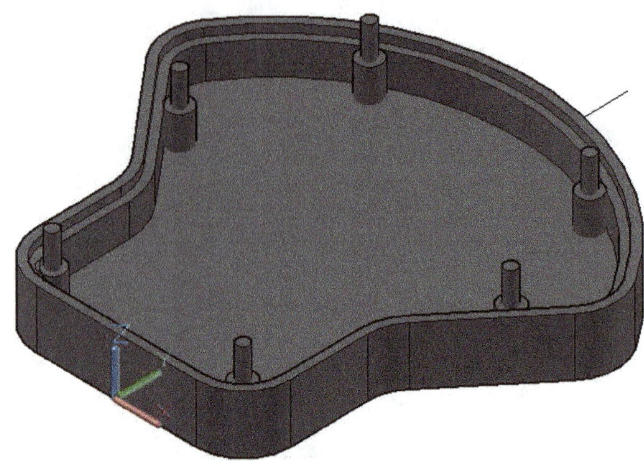

58. On the ribbon, click **Home** tab > **Solid Editing** panel > **Solid, Subtract**.
59. Select the short cylinders and press ENTER.

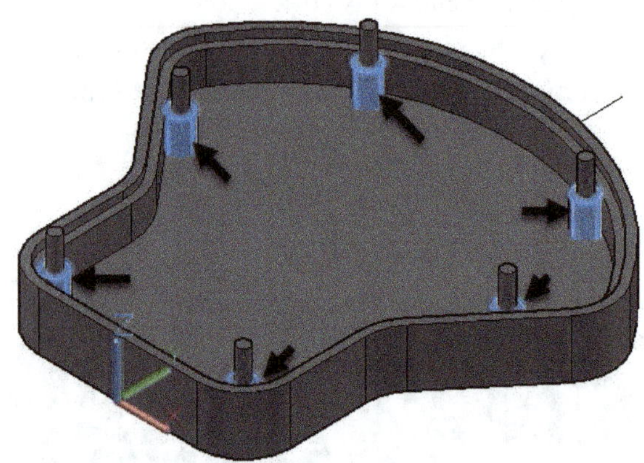

60. Select the tall cylinders and press ENTER.

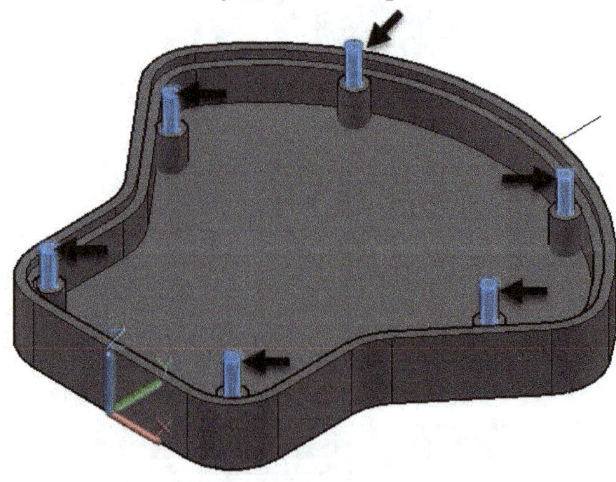

61. Select the vertical line and press DELETE.

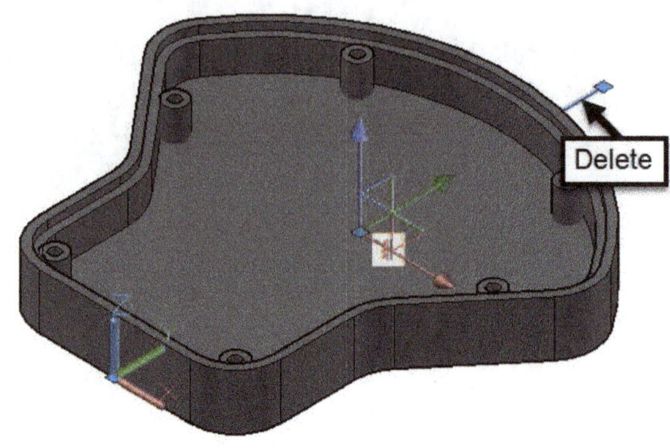

62. On the ribbon, click **Solid** tab > **Boolean** panel > **Union**.
63. Create a selection window across the entire solid body.
64. Press ENTER to combine the bosses and main body.

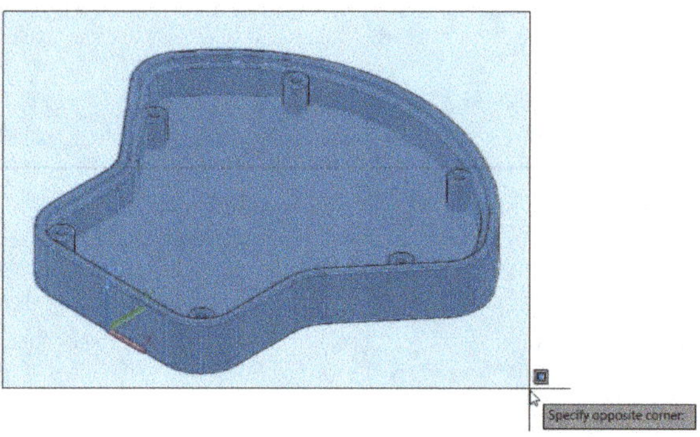

65. Change the **Visual Style** to **2D Wireframe**.
66. On the ribbon, click **Solid** tab > **Solid Editing** panel > **Fillet Edge**.
67. Select the edges between the bosses and the main body.

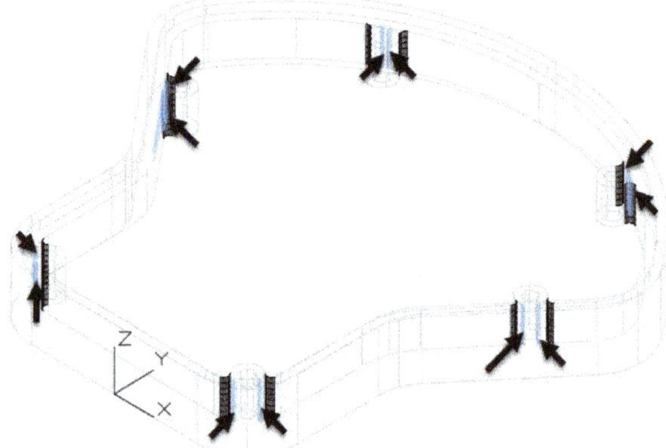

68. Select the **Radius** option from the command line.

69. Type **2** and press ENTER.
70. Press ENTER twice to fillet the edges.

Creating the Rib feature

1. On the ribbon, click **Home** tab > **Coordinates** panel > **Origin**.

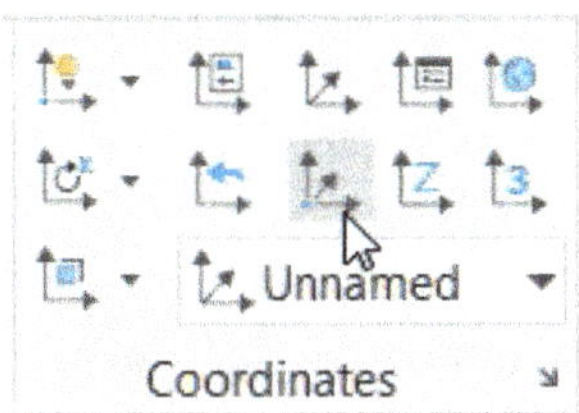

2. Select the midpoint of the inner horizontal edge, as shown.

3. Click the Top face of the ViewCube.
4. On the ribbon, click **Home** tab > **Draw** panel > **Line**.
5. Select the origin point of the UCS.
6. Move the pointer upward.
7. Type 45 and press ENTER.

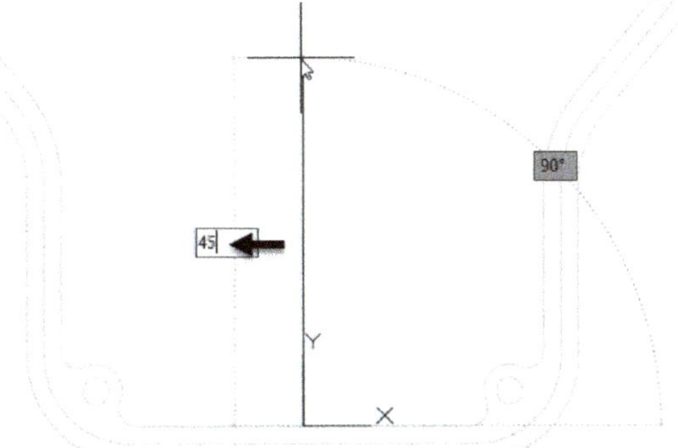

8. Move the pointer toward the right and click outside the model.

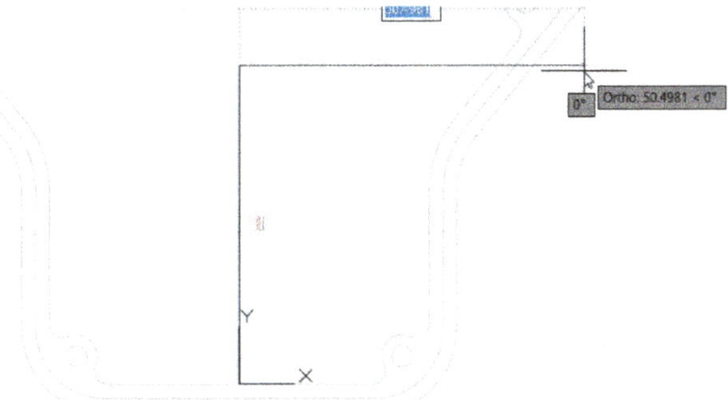

9. Press ESC.
10. On the ribbon, click **Home** tab > **Draw** panel > **Line**.
11. Select the endpoint of the vertical line.
12. Move the pointer toward the left and click outside the model.

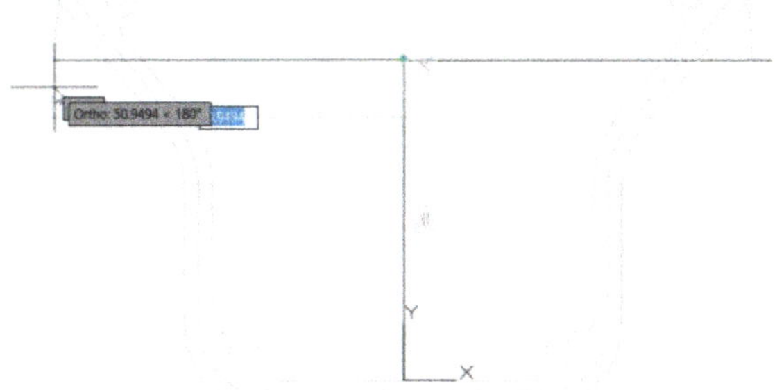

13. On the ribbon, click **Home** tab > **Selection** panel > **Filter** drop-down > **Edge**.

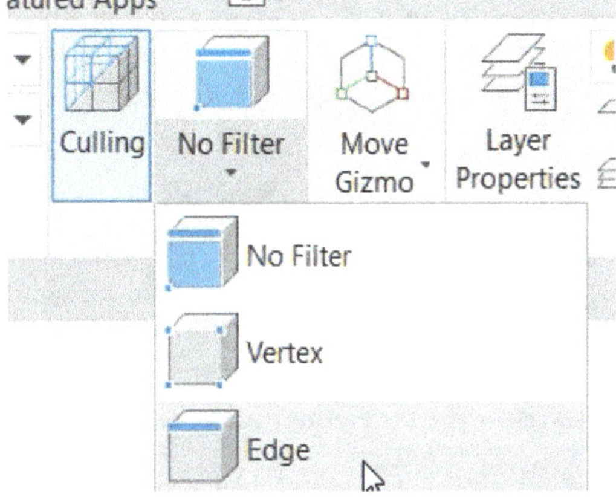

14. On the ribbon, click **Home** tab > **Solid Editing** panel > **Edge** drop-down > **Extract Edges**.

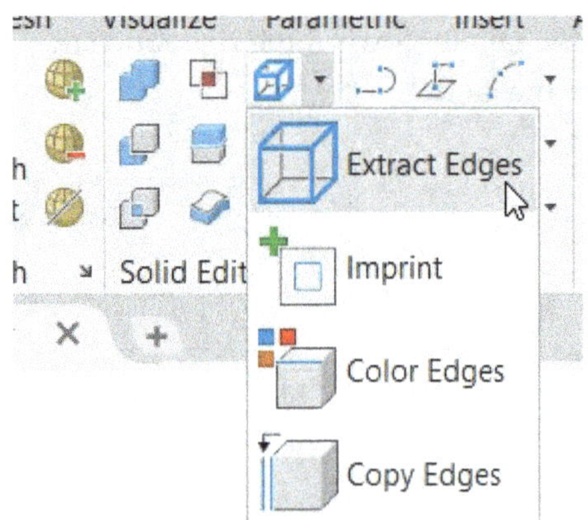

15. Select the edges of the model, as shown.

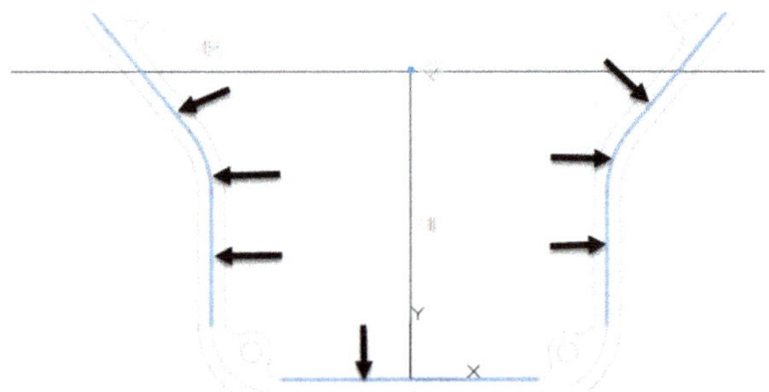

16. Press ENTER.
17. On the ribbon, click the **Home** tab > **Modify** panel > **Offset**.
18. Type 25 and press ENTER.
19. Select the horizontal line, as shown.
20. Move the pointer downward and click.

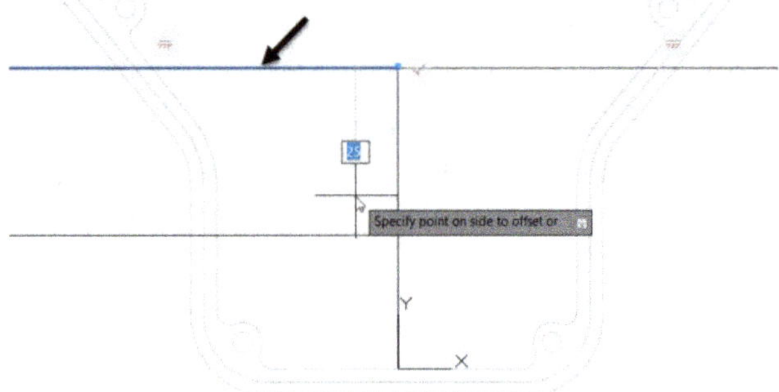

21. Likewise, offset the other horizontal line, as shown.

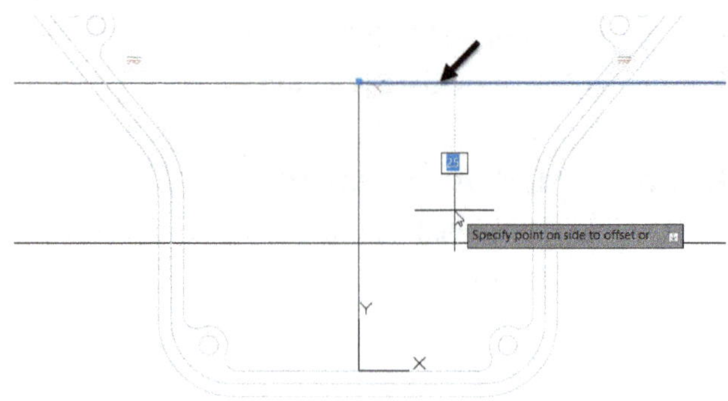

22. On the ribbon, click **Home** tab > **Draw** panel > **Circle** drop-down > **Circle, Diameter**.
23. Select the intersection point between the vertical and horizontal lines.
24. Type 17 and press ENTER.

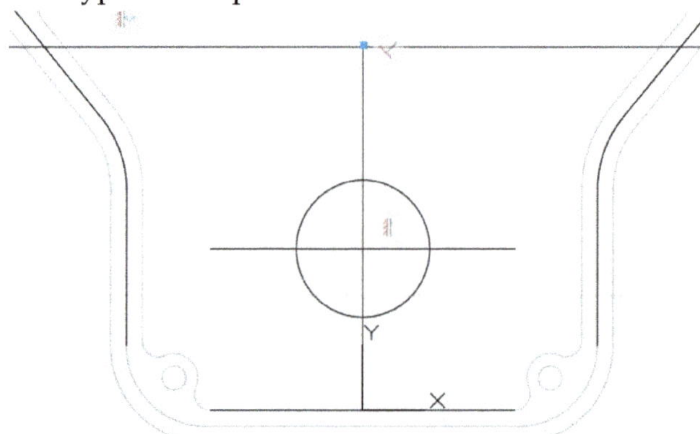

25. On the ribbon, click **Home** tab > **Modify** panel > **Trim/Extend** drop-down > **Trim**.
26. Select the portions of the horizontal line extending outside the model.
27. Select the lines inside the circle.

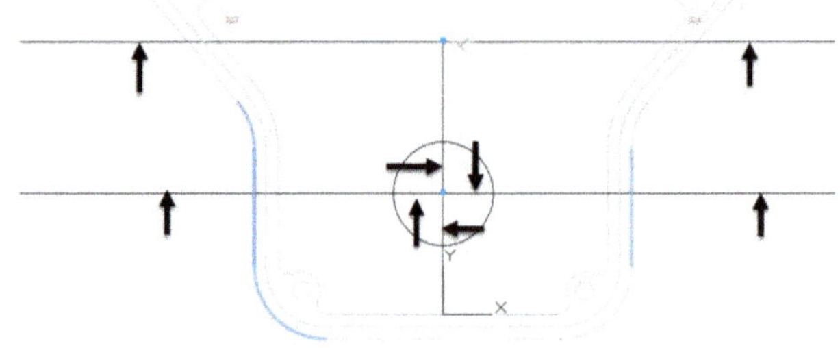

28. Press ESC.

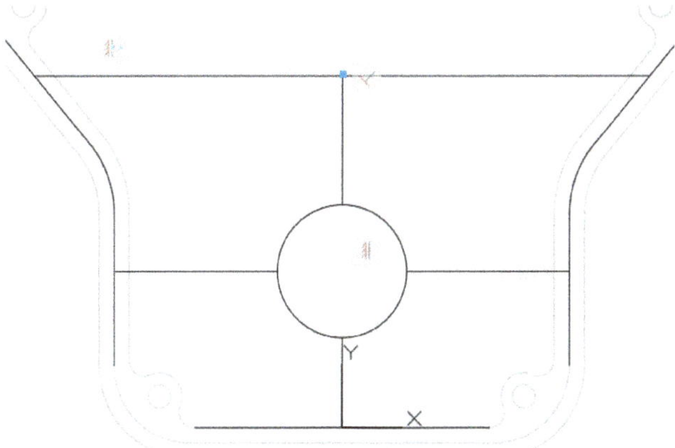

29. On the ribbon, click the **Home** tab > **Modeling** panel > **Polysolid** .
30. Select the **Height** option from the command line.
31. Type 8 and press ENTER.
32. Select the **Width** option from the command line.
33. Type 2 and press ENTER.
34. Select the **Justify** option from the command line.
35. Select the **Center** option from the command line.
36. Select the **Object** option from the command line.
37. Select the horizontal line, as shown.

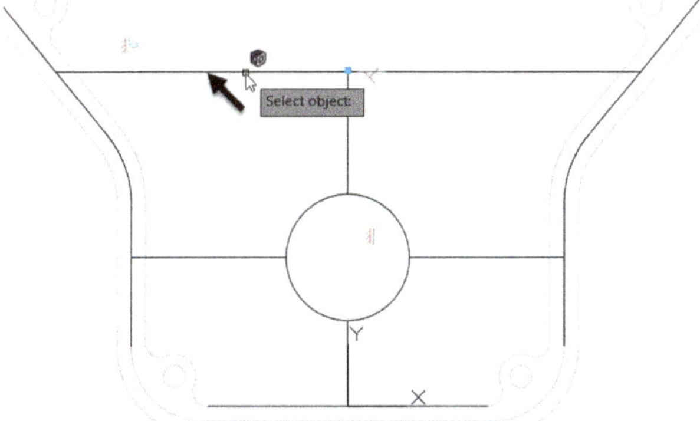

38. Press ENTER and select the **Object** option.
39. Select the next horizontal line, as shown.

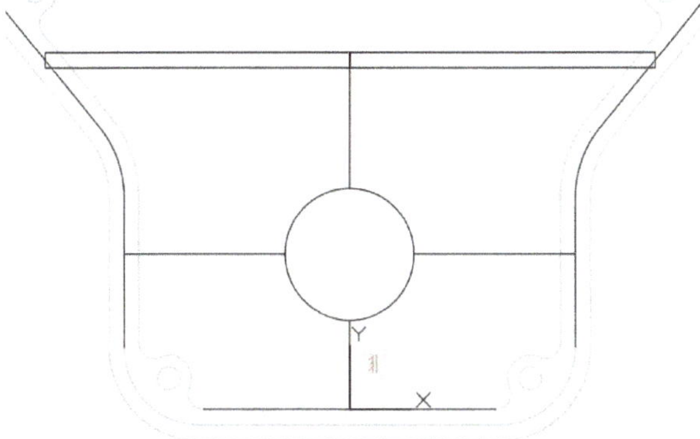

40. Likewise, use the **Polysolid** command and select the remaining lines and circle.

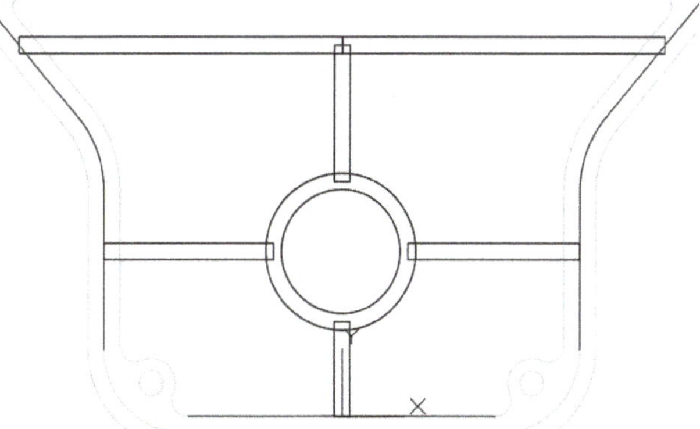

41. Change the view orientation to **SE Isometric**.
42. Change the **Visual Style** to **Shades of Gray**.

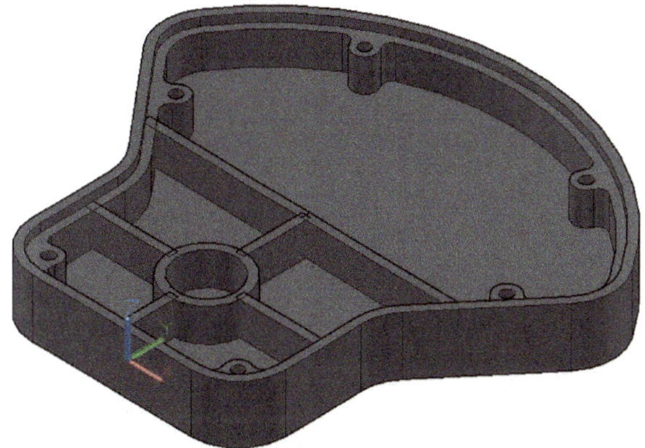

43. On the ribbon, click **Home** tab > **Solid Editing** panel > **Solid, Union**.
44. Create a selection window across all the objects of the model and press ENTER.

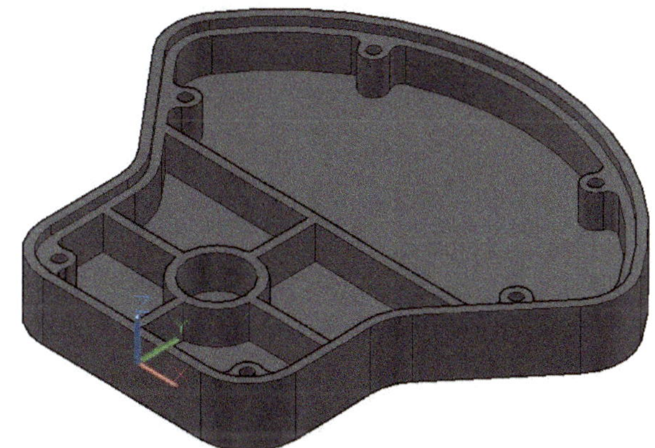

45. Save and close the file.

Tutorial 3 (Inches)

In this example, you create the part shown next.

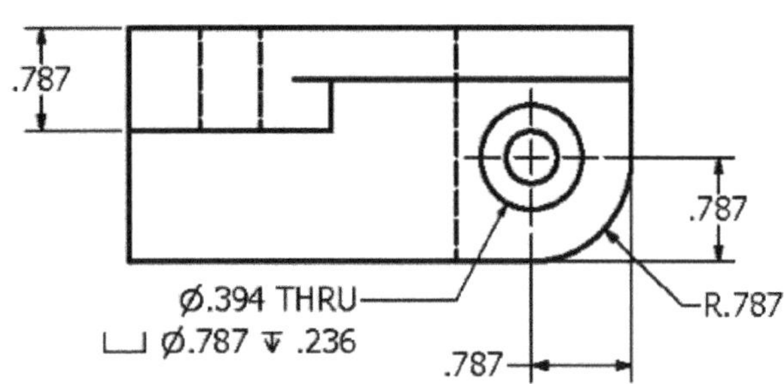

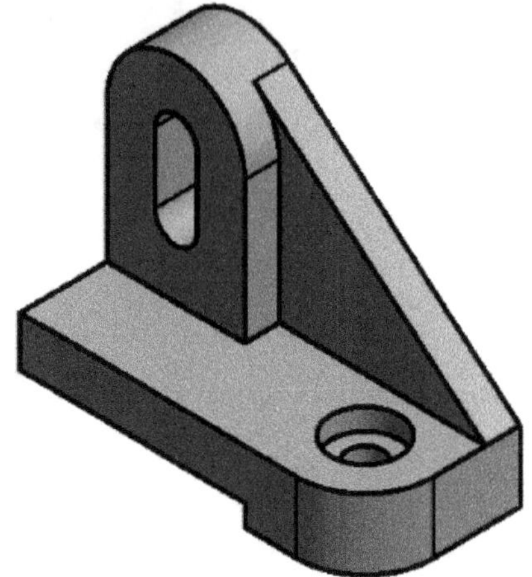

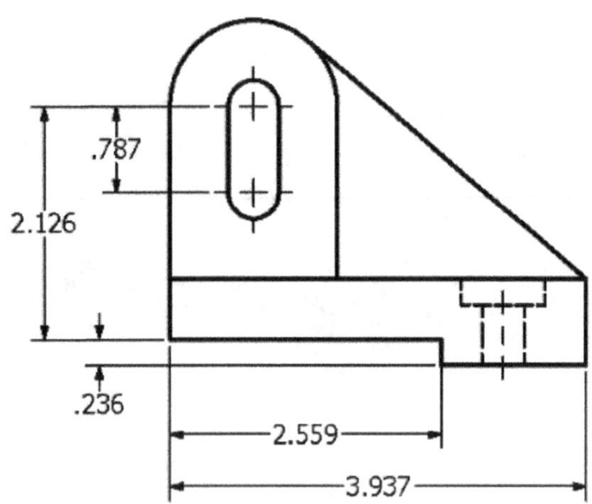

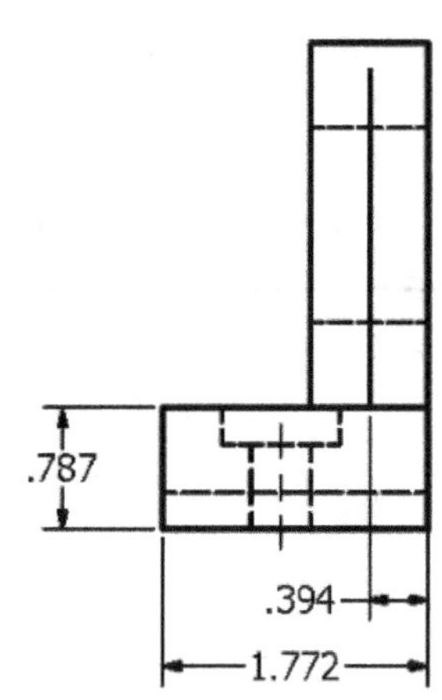

Creating a New File

1. Click the **AutoCAD 2025** icon on your desktop.
2. On the **Start** page, click **New** drop-down > **acad3D.dwt**.
3. On the status bar, click **Workspace Switching** drop-down > **3D Modeling**.
4. Deactivate the **GRIDMODE** icon on the status bar.

Creating Extruded Bodies

1. On the ribbon, click **Home > Draw > Rectangle**.

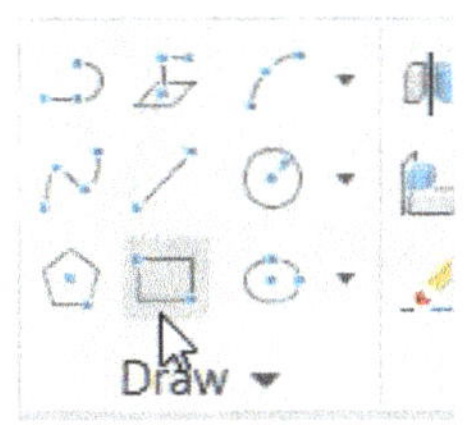

2. Type 0,0 in the command line and press ENTER. The first corner of the rectangle is defined.
3. Select **Dimensions** from the command line.
4. Type **3.937** in the command line and press ENTER. The length of the rectangle is defined.
5. Type **1.772** in the command line and press ENTER. The width of the rectangle is defined.
6. Move the pointer toward the left and click to create the rectangle.
7. On the ribbon, click **Home > Modeling > Extrude**.
8. Select the rectangle and press ENTER.
9. Move the pointer upward.
10. Type **0.787**, and press ENTER.

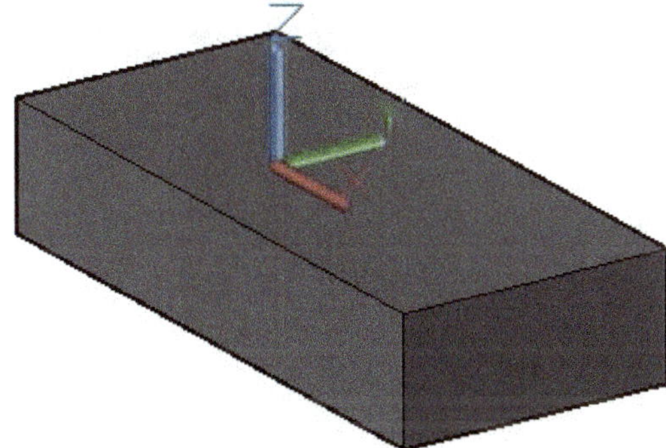

11. On the ribbon, click **Home > Coordinates > Z-Axis Vector**.

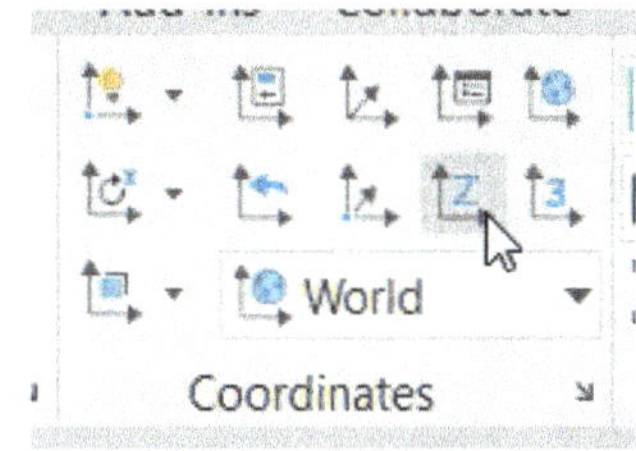

12. Select the back left corner of the extrusion.
13. Select the front left corner of the extrusion.

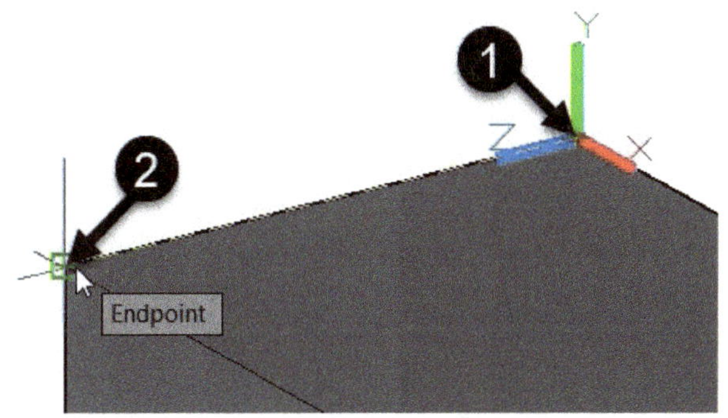

14. On the ribbon, click **Home > Modeling > Primitives** drop-down > **Box**.
15. Type 0,0 and press ENTER.
16. Move the pointer toward the right.
17. Type 1.574 and press the TAB key.
18. Type 1.575, and press ENTER.

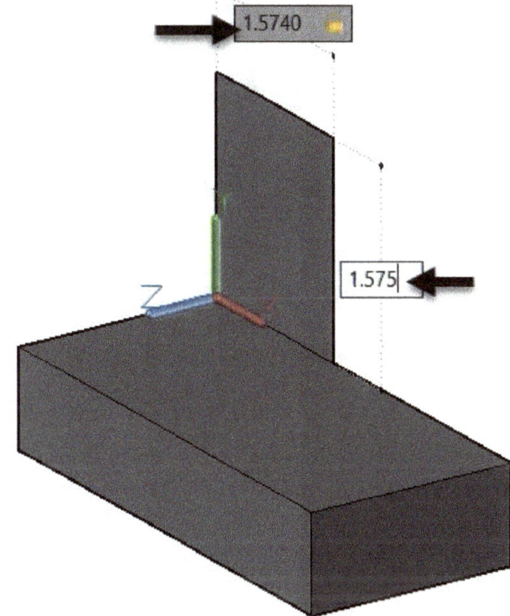

19. Move the pointer toward left.
20. Type .787 and press ENTER.

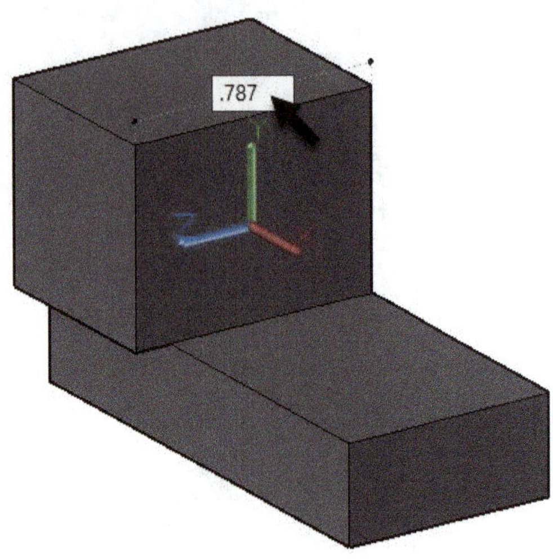

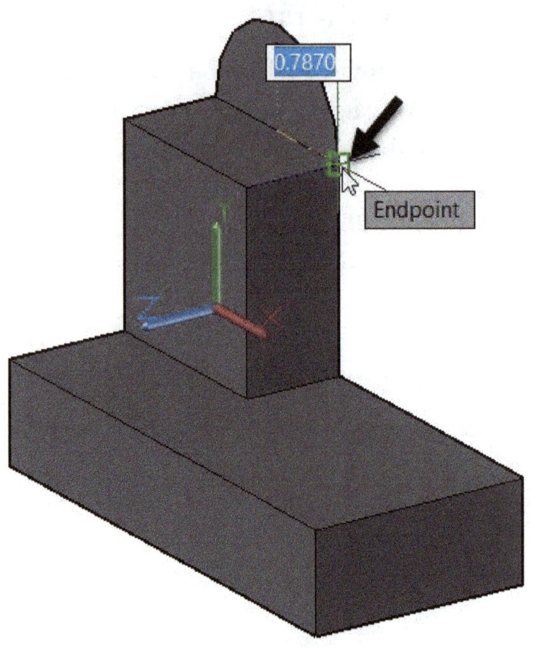

21. On the ribbon, click **Home > Modeling > Primitives** drop-down > **Cylinder**.
22. Select the midpoint of the horizontal back edge, as shown.

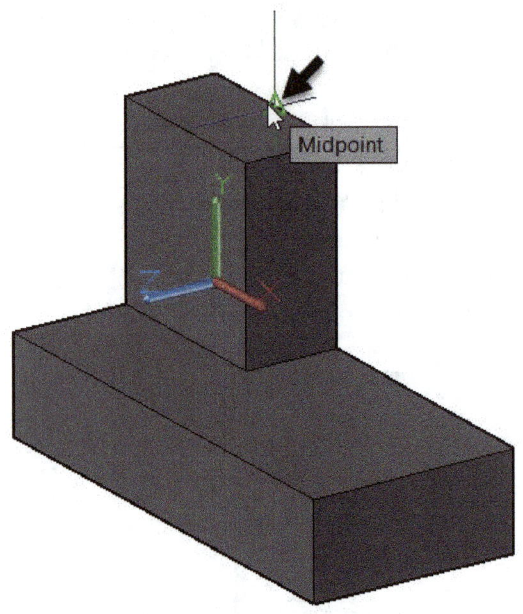

25. Move the pointer toward the left and select the corner point on the front face of the box.

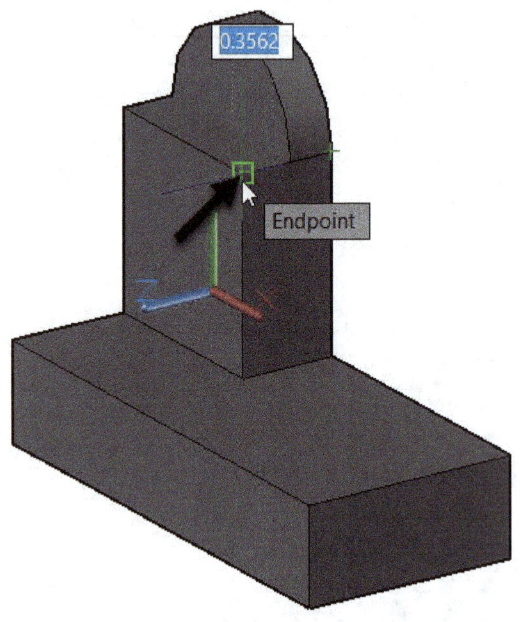

23. Move the pointer outward.
24. Select the corner point of the box, as shown.

26. On the ribbon, click **Home > Solid Editing > Solid, Union**.
27. Select all the objects of the model and press ENTER.

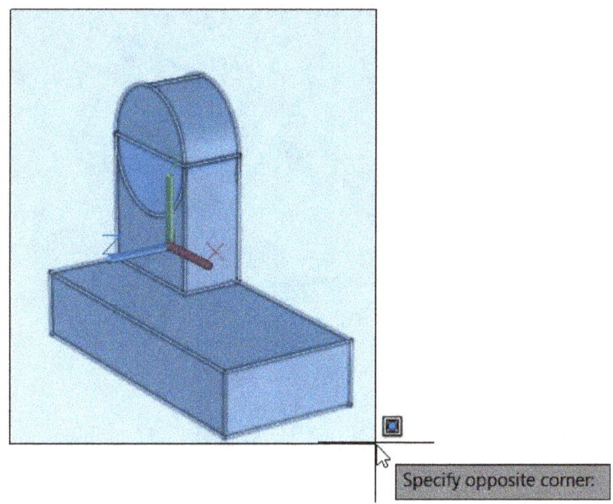

Creating the Rib feature

1. Change the **Visual Style** to **2D Wireframe**.
2. On the ribbon, click **Home** tab > **Selection** panel > **Filter** drop-down > **Edge**.

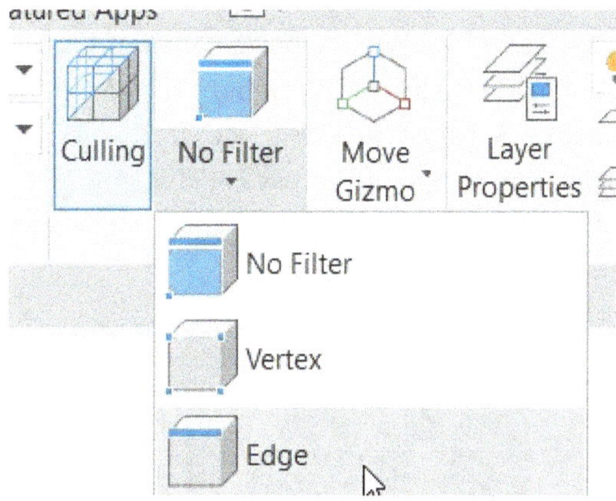

3. On the ribbon, click **Home** tab > **Solid Editing** panel > **Edge** drop-down > **Extract Edges**.

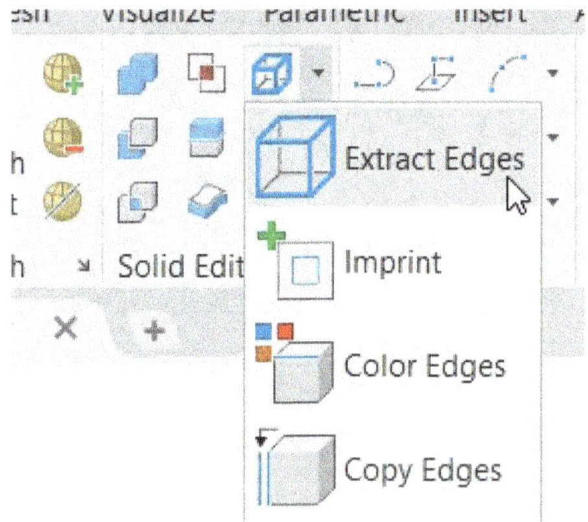

4. Select the edges of the model, as shown.

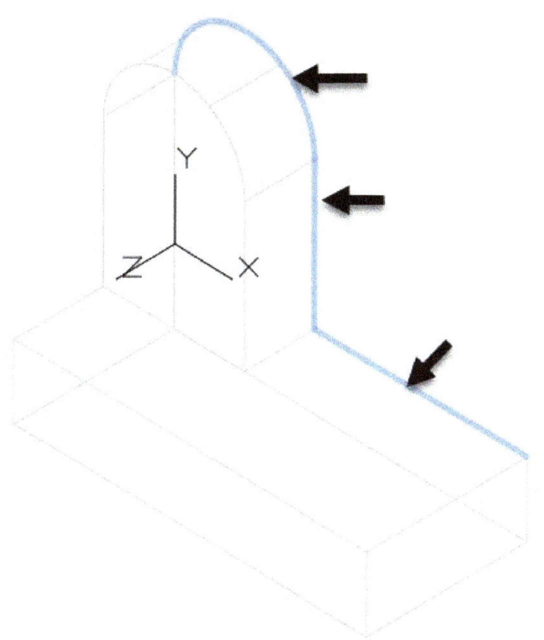

5. Press ENTER.
6. On the ribbon, click **Home** tab > **Draw** panel > **Line**.
7. Select the corner point of the model, as shown.
8. Place the pointer on the extracted arc.
9. Click when the Tangent snap appears.

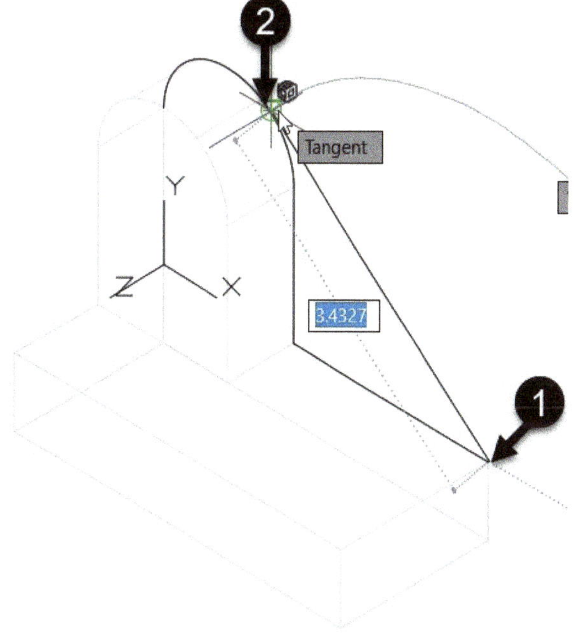

10. Press ESC.
11. On the ribbon, click **Home** tab > **Modify** panel > **Trim/Extend** drop-down > **Trim**.

12. Select the unwanted portion of the arc, as shown.

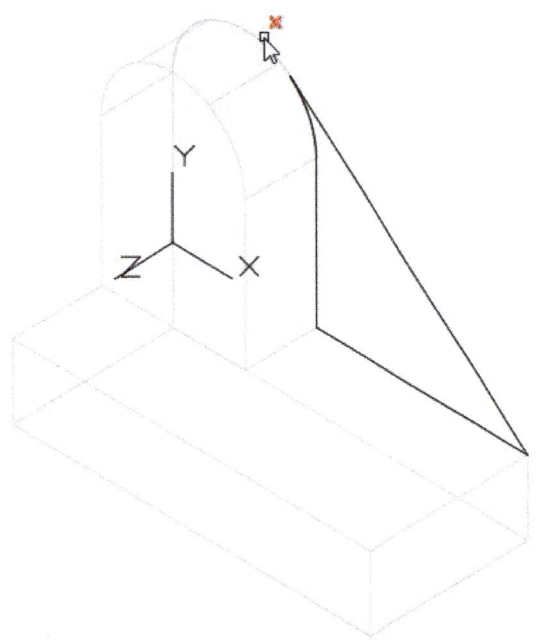

13. On the **Home** tab of the ribbon, expand the **Draw** panel and click the **Region** icon.

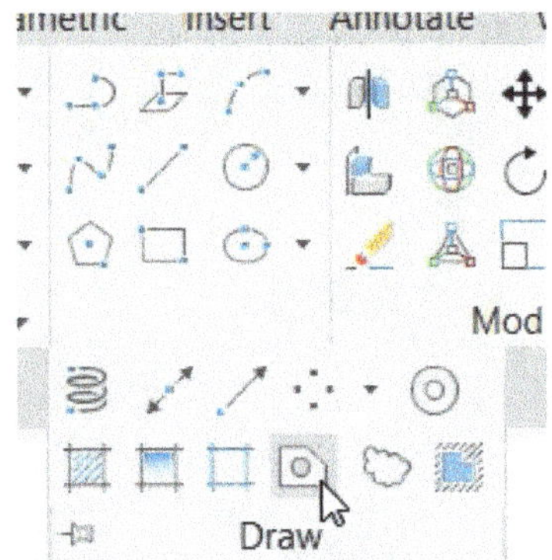

14. Select the extracted edges and the line, as shown.

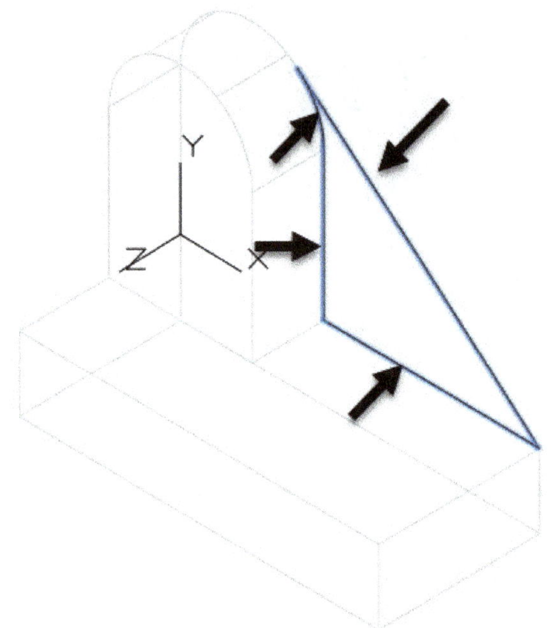

15. Press ENTER.
16. Change the **Visual Style** to **Shades of Gray**.
17. On the **Home** tab of the ribbon, click Modeling panel > **Solids** drop-down > **Extrude**.
18. Select the region and press ENTER.
19. Move the pointer toward left.
20. Type .394 and press ENTER.

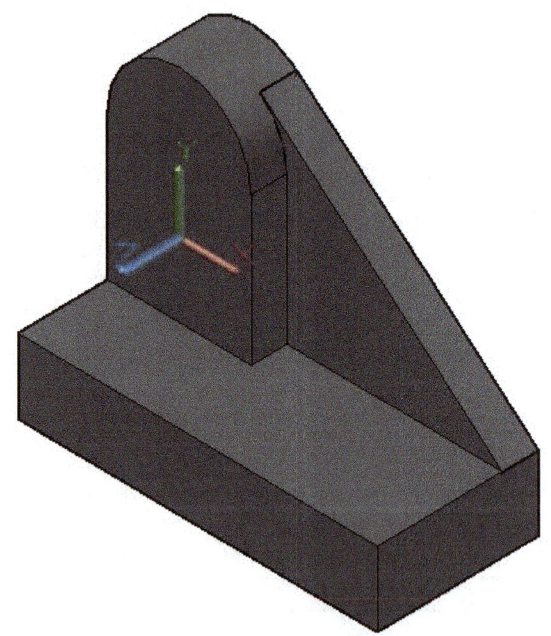

Creating the Slot

1. On the **Home** tab of the ribbon, click

Coordinates > Z-Axis Vector.

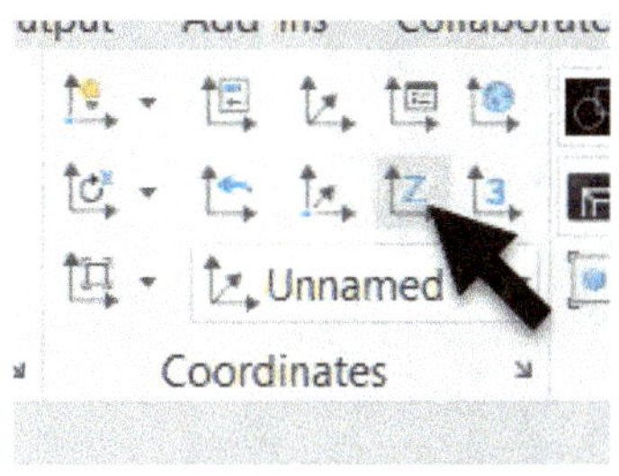

2. Select the corner point of the model, as shown.
3. Move the pointer toward the left and select the corner point, as shown. The Z-axis of the UCS is defined.

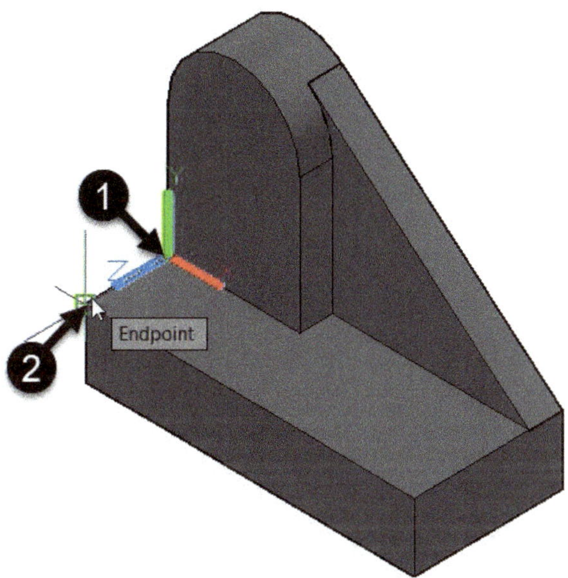

4. On the ribbon, click **Home** tab > **Modeling** panel > **Primitives** drop-down > **Cylinder**.
5. Select the centerpoint of the curved edge, as shown. The centerpoint of the cylinder is defined.

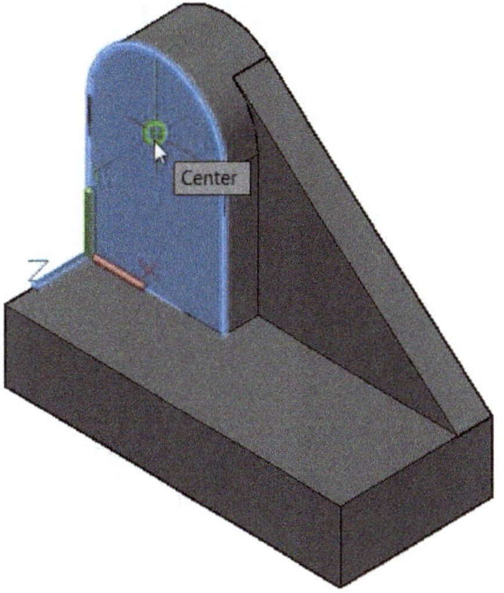

6. Type **.237** in the command line and press ENTER. The radius of the cylinder is defined.
7. Move the pointer toward the right and click outside the model.

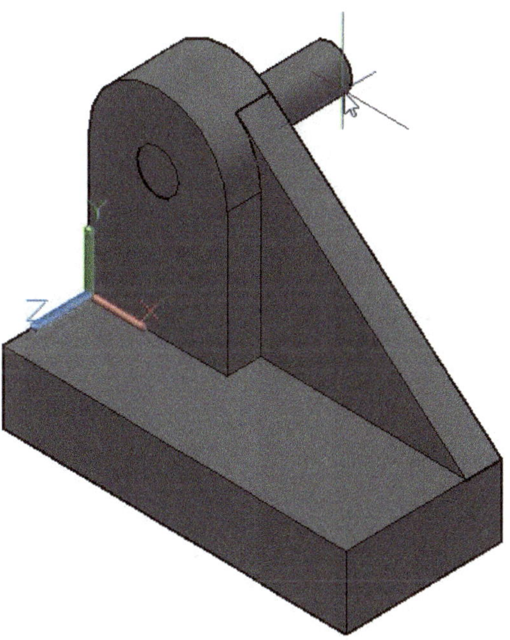

8. Select the newly created cylinder.
9. On the ribbon, click **Home** tab > **Modify** panel > **Copy**.
10. Select the center point of the cylinder to define the base point.
11. Activate the **Orthomode** icon on the Status bar.
12. Move the pointer downward.

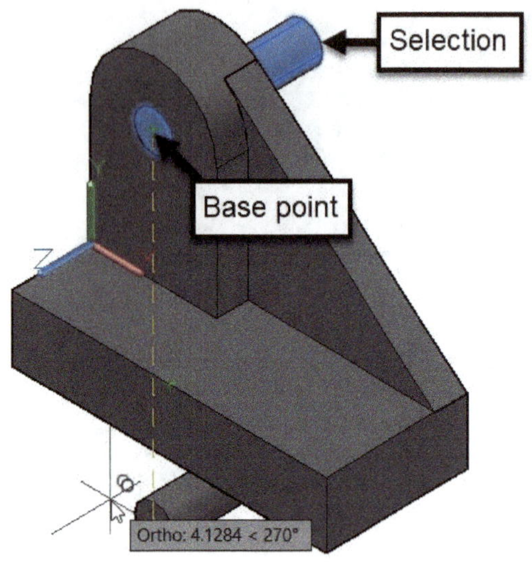

13. Type .787 and press ENTER.

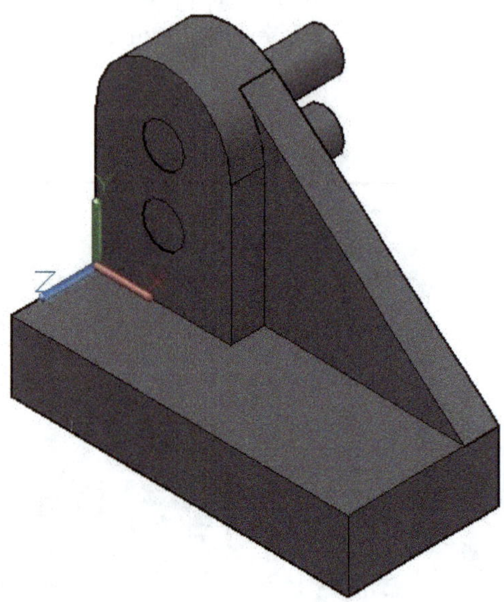

14. On the ribbon, click **Home** tab > **Modeling** panel > **Primitives** drop-down > **Box**.
15. On the status bar, click **Object Snap** drop-down > **Quadrant**.
16. Select the left quadrant point of the first cylinder.
17. Move the pointer downward.
18. Select the right quadrant point of the second cylinder.

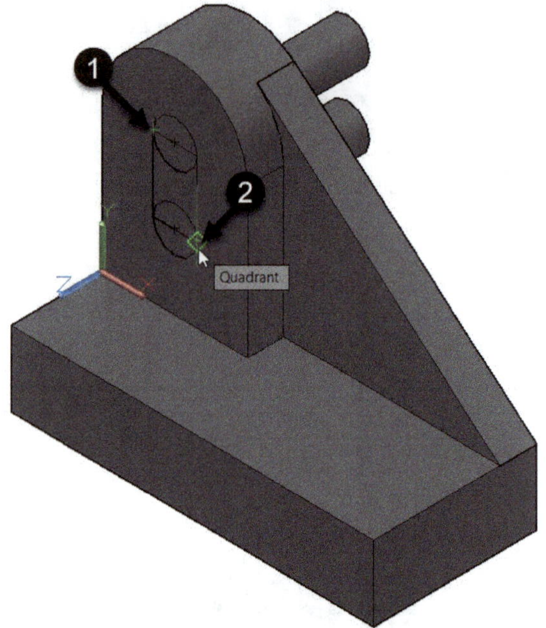

19. Move the pointer toward the right and click outside the model.

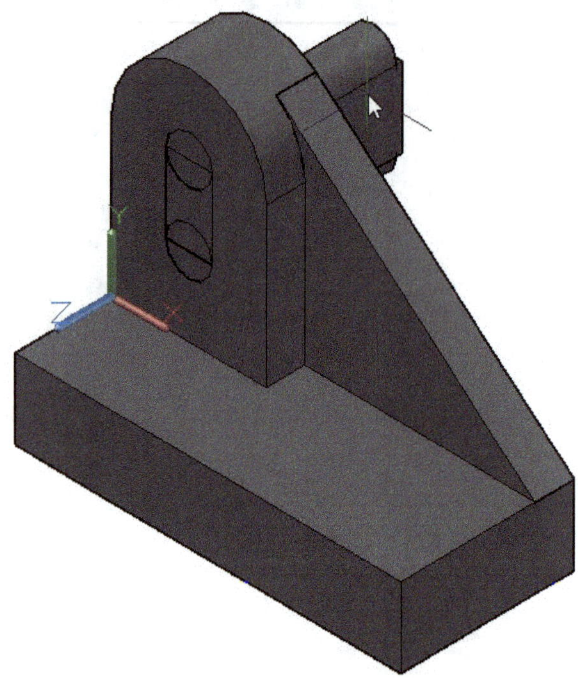

20. On the ribbon, click **Home** tab > **Solid Editing** panel > **Solid, Subtract**.
21. Select the main body and press ENTER.

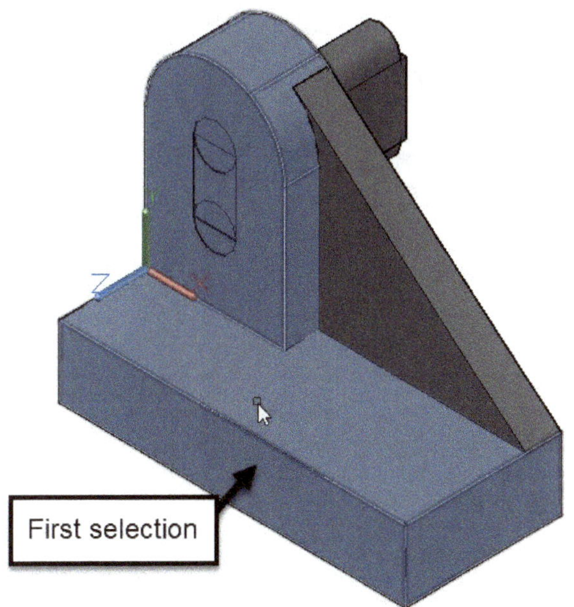

22. Select the two cylinders and the box.

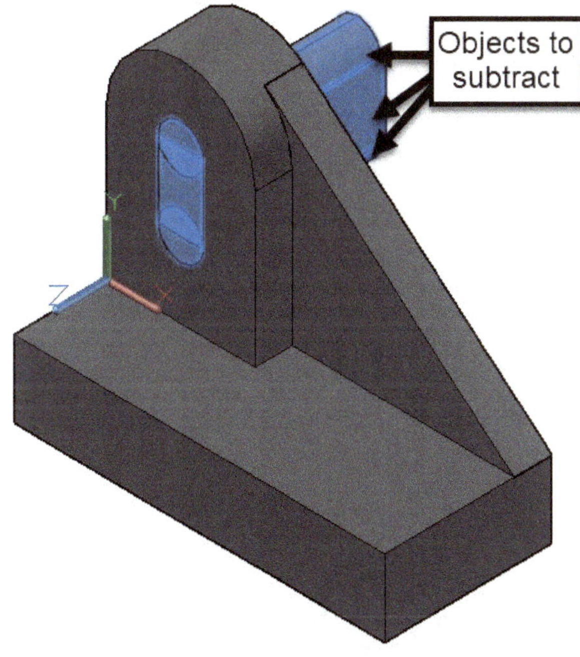

23. Press ENTER to subtract the cylinders and box from the main body.

24. On the ribbon, click **Solid** tab > **Solid Editing** panel > **Fillet Edge** drop-down > **Fillet Edge**.

25. Select the right vertical edge of the model, as shown.

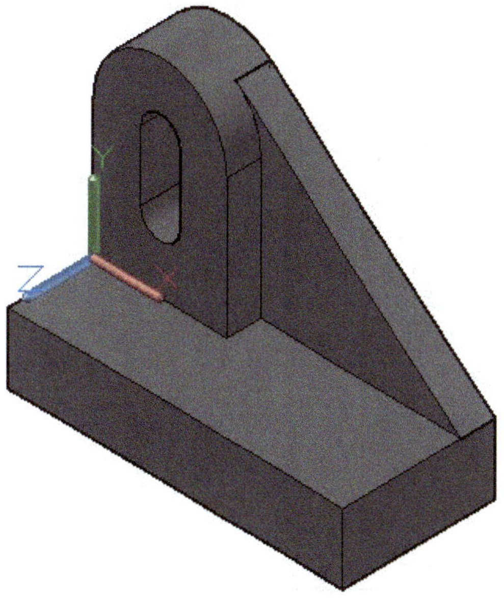

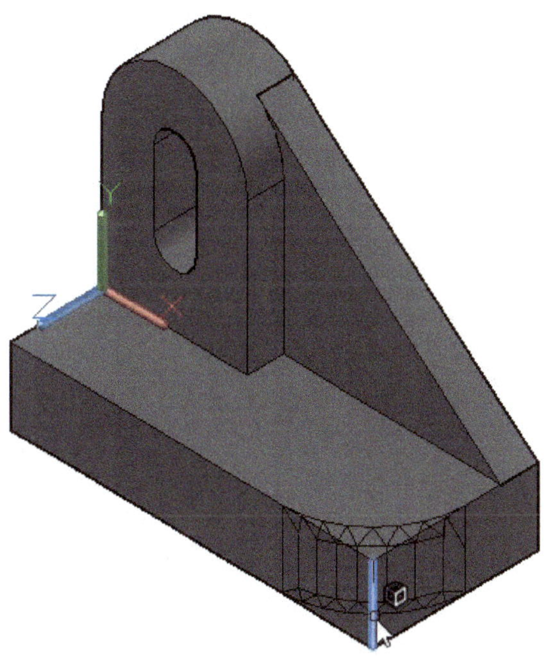

26. Select the **Radius** option from the command line.

27. Type .787 and press ENTER.

28. Press ENTER twice to create the fillet.

29. On the ribbon, click **Home** tab > **Coordinates** panel > **Z-Axis Vector**.

30. Select the centerpoint of the fillet to define the origin of the UCS.

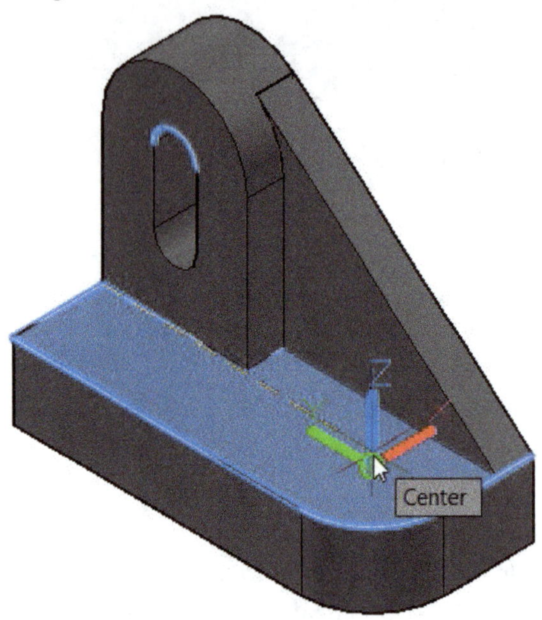

31. Move the pointer vertically downward and click.

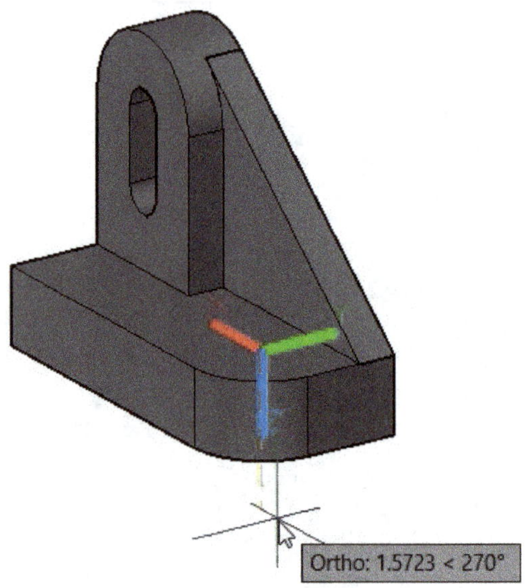

32. On the ribbon, click **Home** tab > **Modeling** panel > **Primitives** drop-down > **Cylinder**.
33. Type 0,0 and press ENTER.
34. Type .3935 and press ENTER.
35. Type 0.236, and press ENTER.

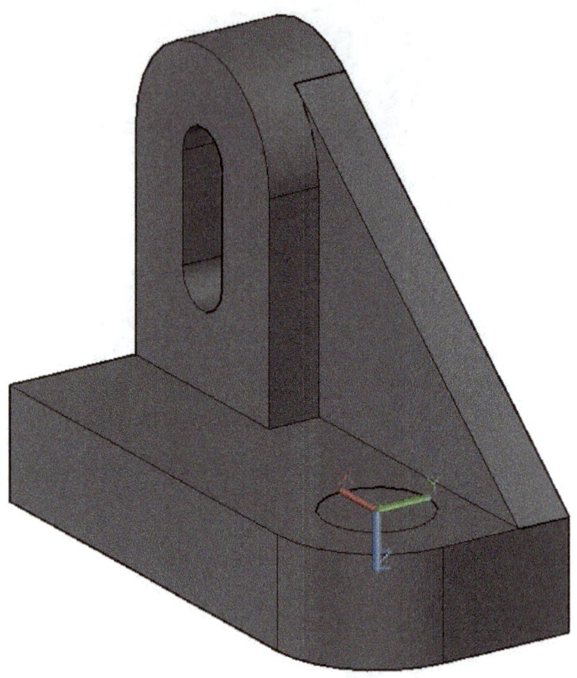

36. On the ribbon, click **Home** tab > **Modeling** panel > **Primitives** drop-down > **Cylinder**.
37. Type 0,0 and press ENTER.
38. Type .197 and press ENTER.
39. Move the pointer downward and click outside the model.

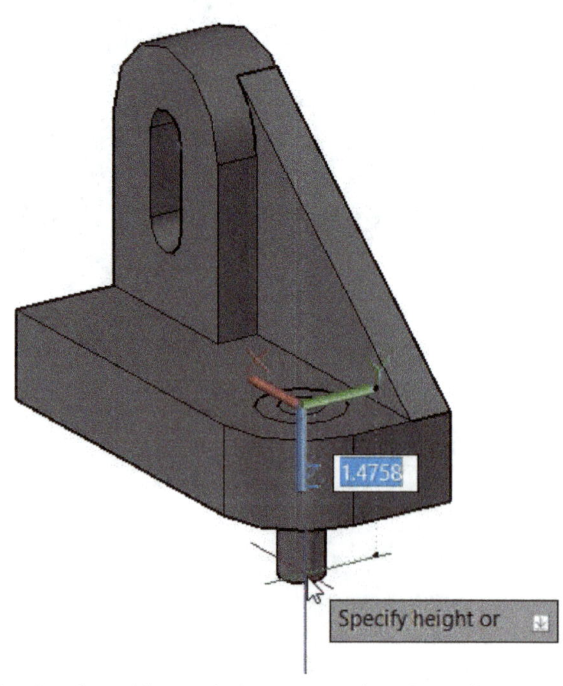

40. On the ribbon, click **Home** tab > **Coordinates** panel > **UCS, World**.

41. Deactivate the **Dynamic Input** icon on the status bar.
42. On the ribbon, click **Home** tab > **Modeling** panel > **Primitives** drop-down > **Box**.
43. Select the lower-left corner of the model.

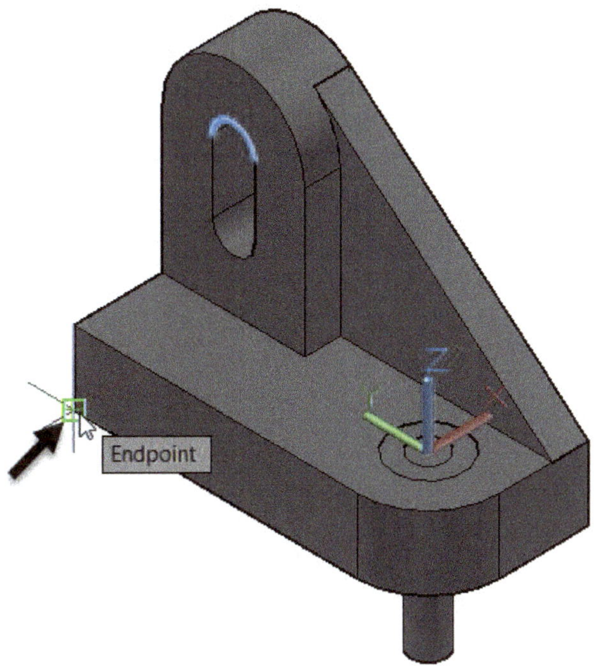

44. Select the **Length** option from the command line.
45. Type 2.559, and press ENTER.
46. Move the pointer toward the right and click outside the model.

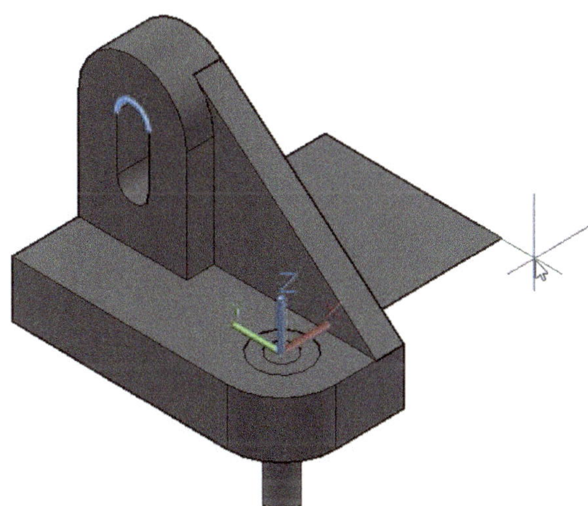

47. Type 0.236 and press ENTER to specify the height of the box.

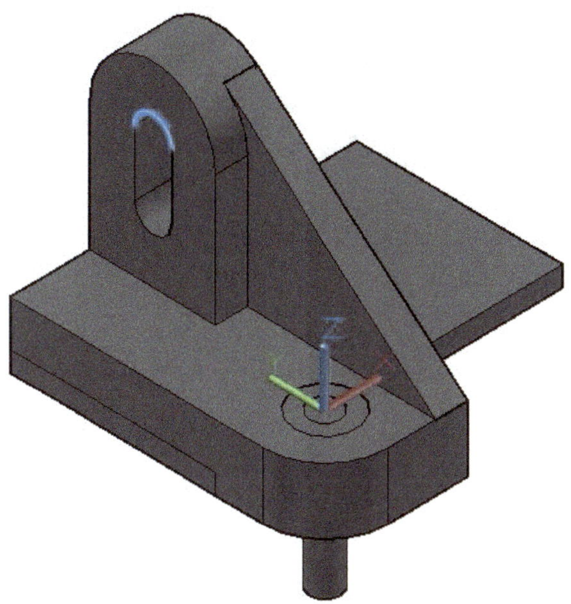

48. On the ribbon, click **Home** tab > **Solid Editing** panel > **Solid, Subtract**.
49. Select the main body and press ENTER.

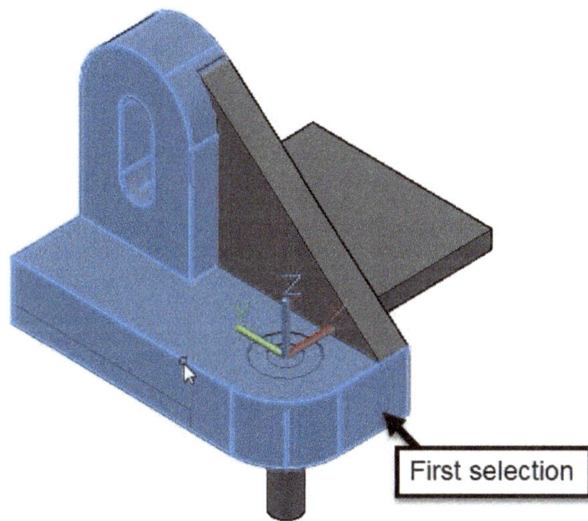

50. Select the two cylinders and the box.

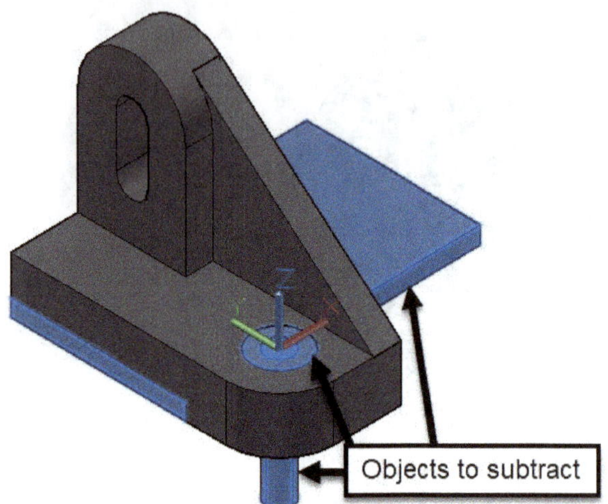

51. Press ENTER to subtract the objects from the main body.

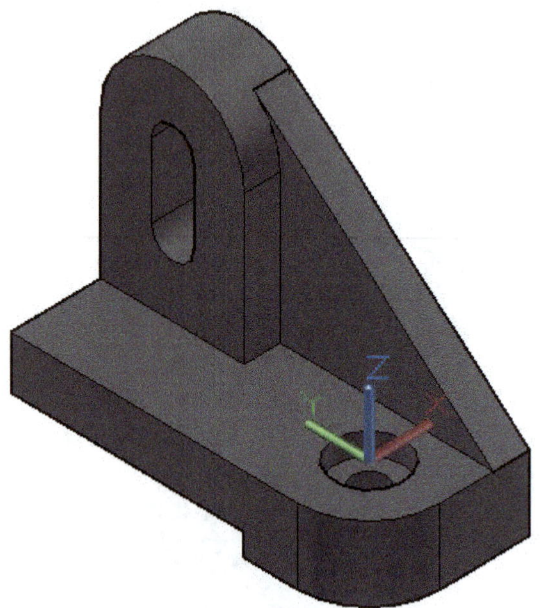

52. Save and close the file.

Exercises

Exercise 1

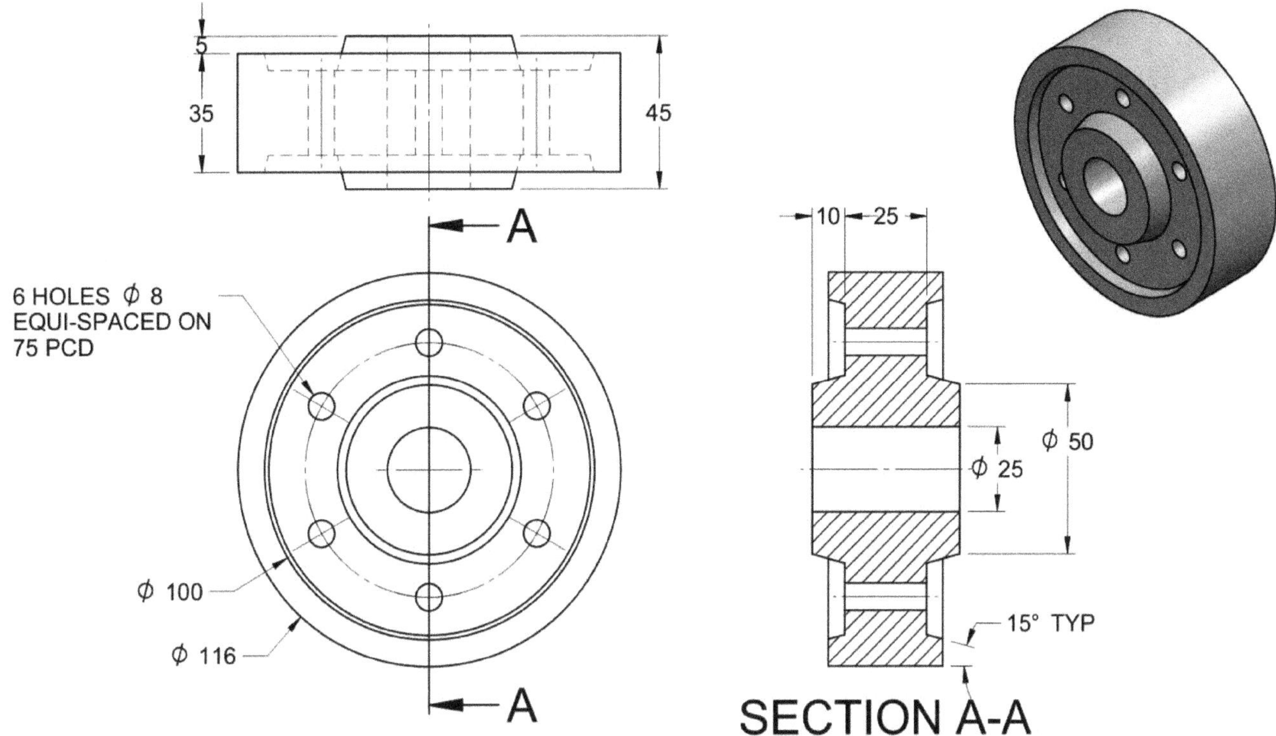

Exercise 2 (Inches)

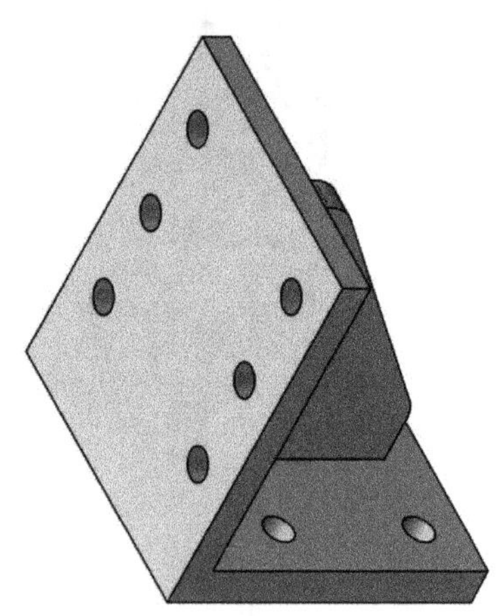

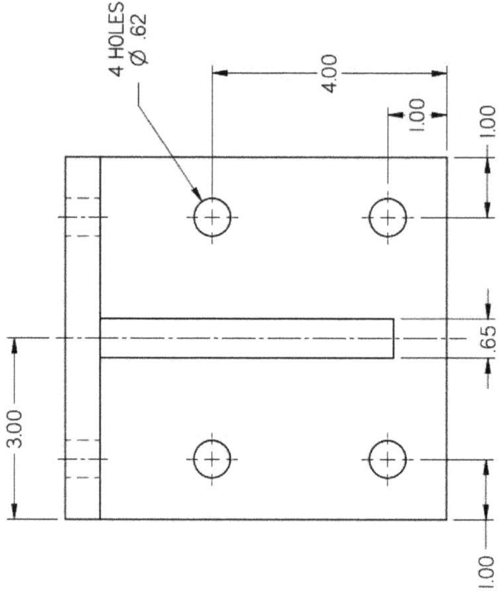

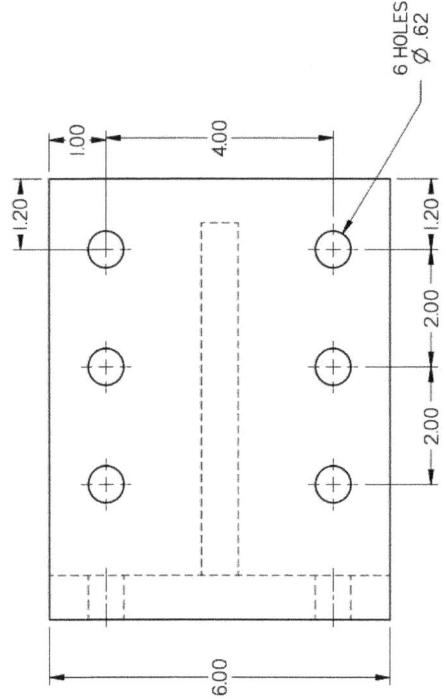

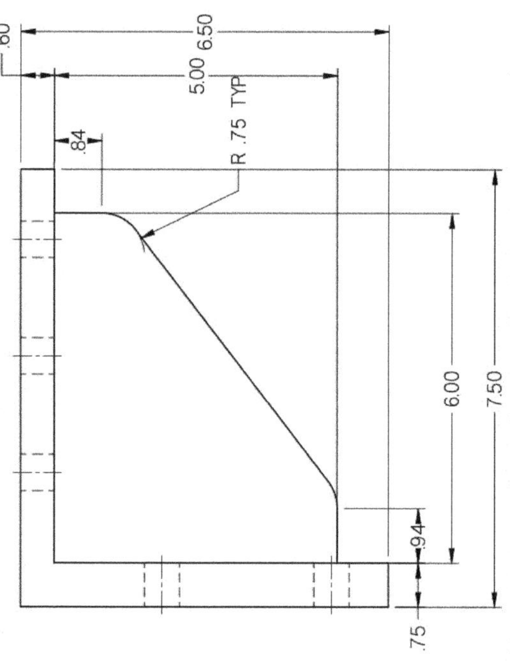

Chapter 5: Sweep Features

The Sweep Feature

The **Sweep** command is one of the basic commands available in AutoCAD that allow you to generate solid geometry. It can be used to create simple geometry as well as complex shapes. A sweep is composed of two items: a cross-section and a path. The cross-section controls the shape of the sweep while the path controls its direction. For example, take a look at the angled sweep feature shown in the figure. This is created using a simple sweep with the ellipse as the profile and an angled line as the path.

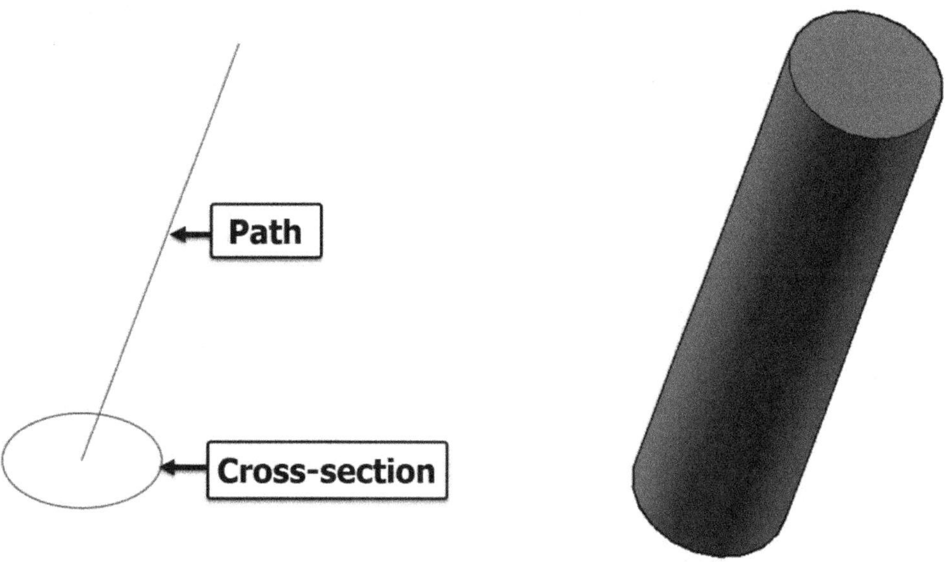

By making the path a bit more complicated, you can see that a sweep allows you to create shapes you would not be able to create using commands such as Extrude or Revolve.

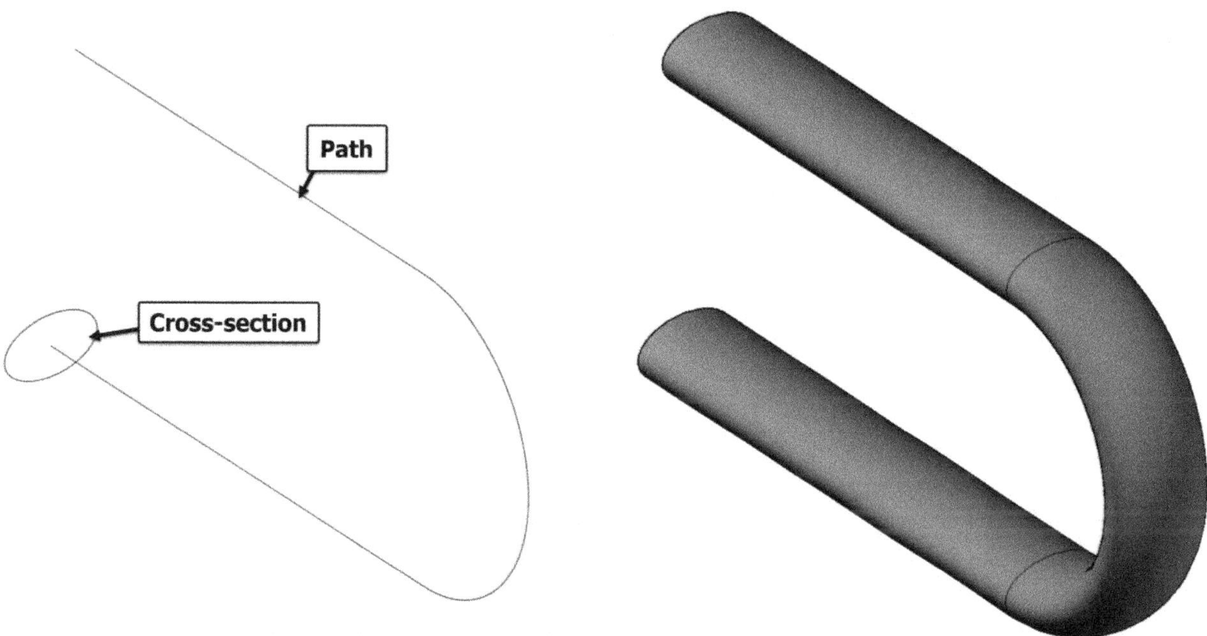

The topics covered in this chapter are:

- *Path sweeps*
- *Scaling and twisting the profile along the path*

Creating a Swept Solid

A swept solid requires two elements: a cross-section and path. The cross-section defines the shape of the sweep along the path. A path is used to control the direction of the profile. A path can be a 2D or 3D curve. To create a sweep, you must first create a path and a cross-section. Create a path by drawing a 2D or 3D curve. It can be an open or closed object. However, if you have created a path curve using more than one element, then you need to join the all the elements such that the path is single element. To do this, expand the Modify panel on the Home tab of the ribbon and click the **Join** tool. Next, select all the elements of the path and press ENTER.

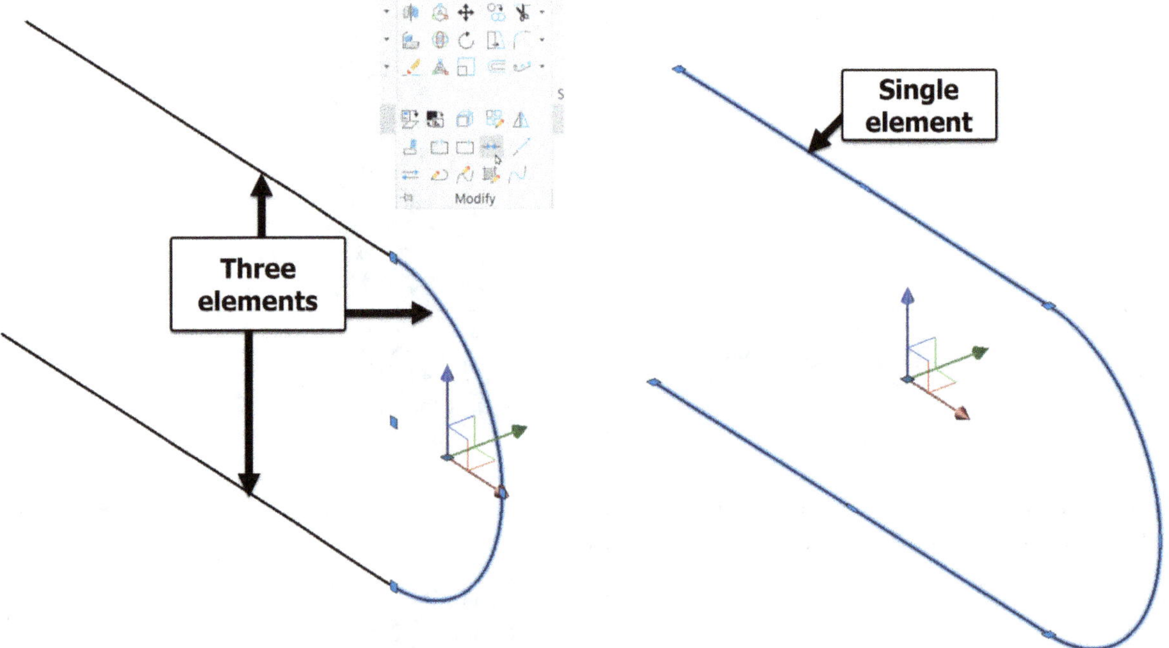

Next, click **Home > Coordinates** panel **> Z-Axis Vector** on the ribbon. Next, select the endpoint of the path, move the pointer along the direction of the path and click; a new UCS is created with its XY plane normal to the path. Next, activate a drawing command and create a closed cross-section.

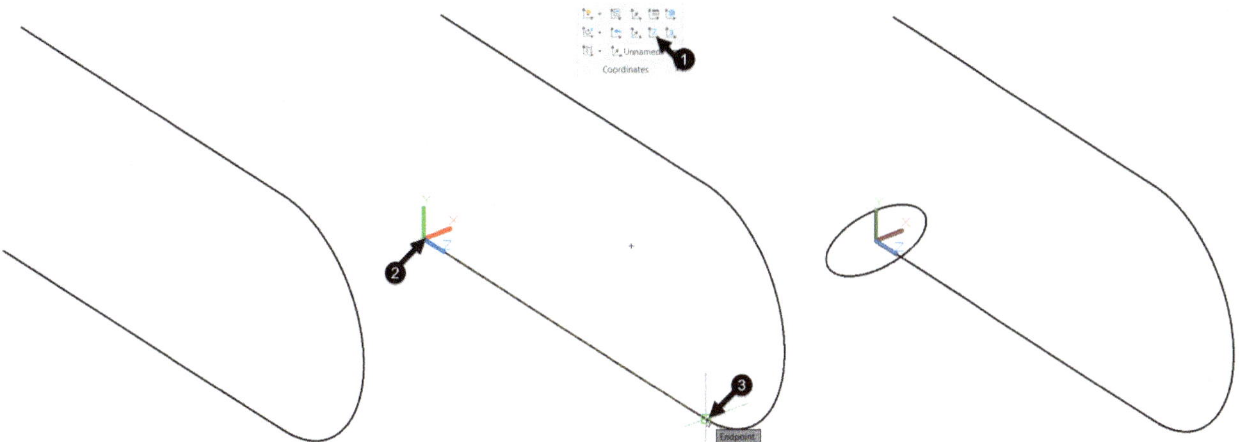

Click **Home > Modeling panel > Sweep** on the ribbon and then select the cross-section from the graphics window. Press ENTER and select the path.

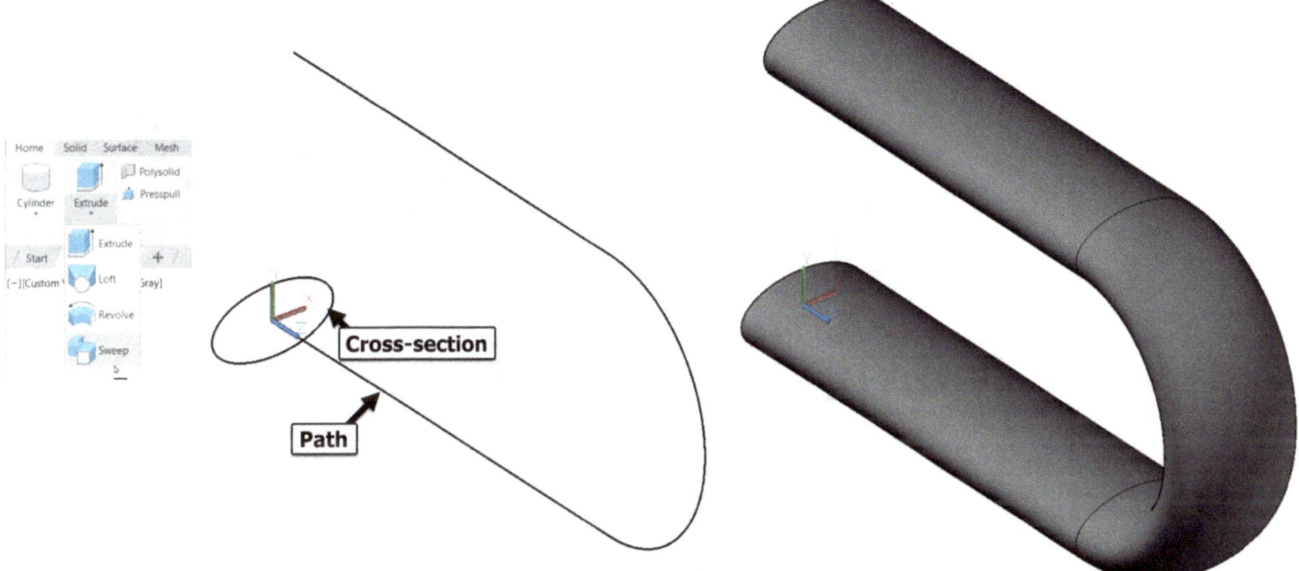

A profile must be created as a sketch. However, a path can be a 2D or 3D curve. The following illustrations show various types of paths and resultant sweep features.

2D Curve

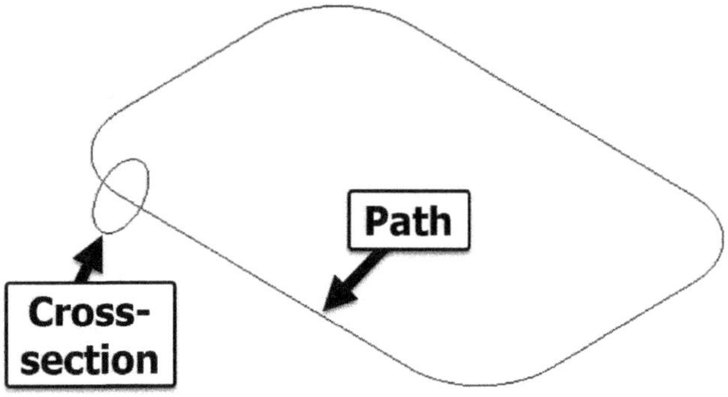

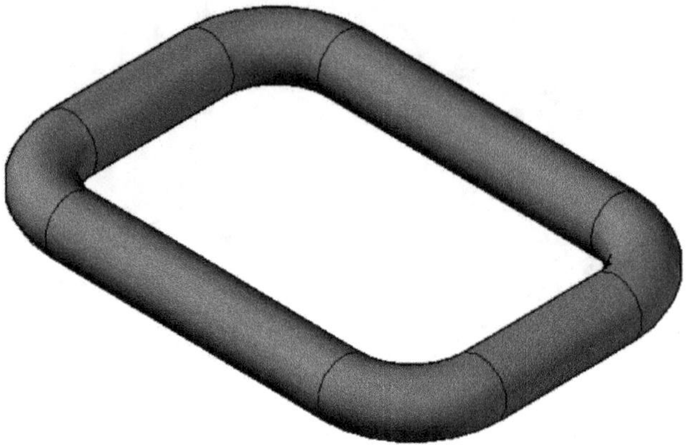

3D Curve

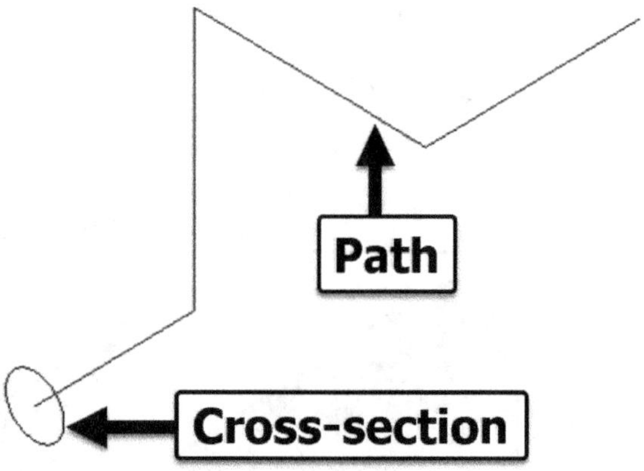

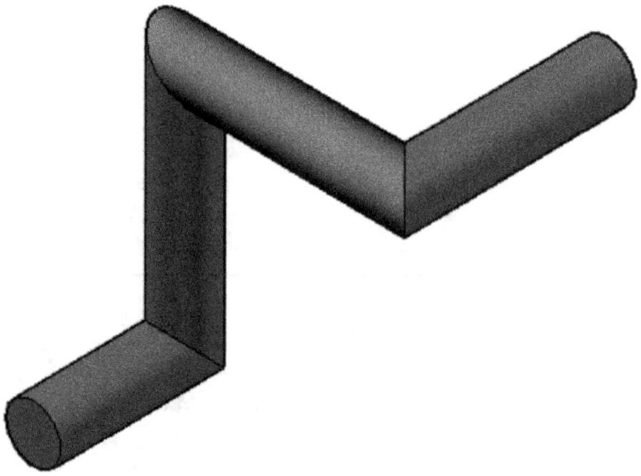

Alignment

The **Alignment** option allows you to create a swept solid even when the cross section and the path are created on a same plane. For example, create a path and the cross-section on the same plane, as shown. Activate the **Sweep** command and select the cross-section and press ENTER. Next, select the **Alignment** option from the command line and select the **Yes** option. Select the path from the graphics window; the cross-section will be swept along the selected path in the direction perpendicular to the path.

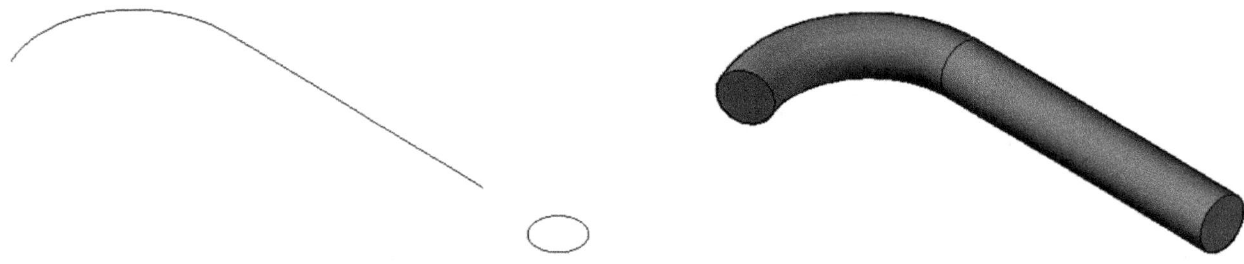

Twist

AutoCAD allows you to twist the profile along the path. Select the profile and press ENTER. Next, select the **Twist** option from the command line. Type-in the twist angle and press ENTER. Next, select the path along the profile will be swept. The profile is twisted by the specified twist angle. The following figure shows a swept solid twisted at three different angles.

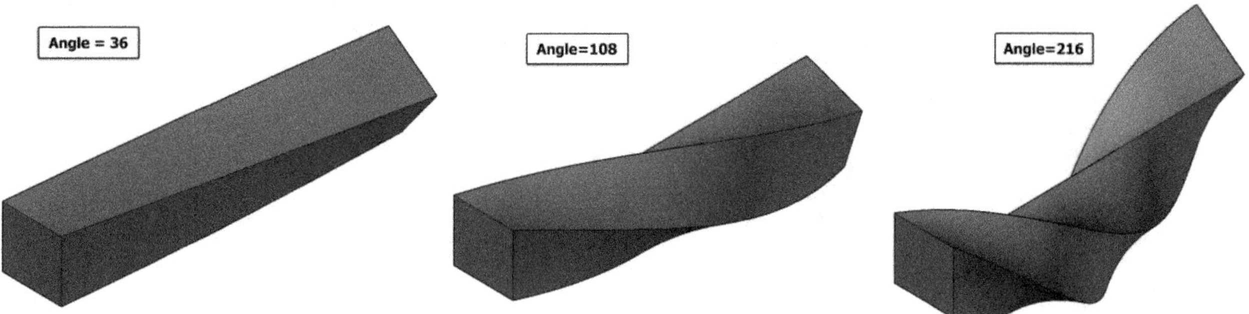

Scale

AutoCAD allows you to taper the sweep along the path. Select the profile and press ENTER. Next, select the Scale option from the command line and type-in the scale value. For example, you type 0.5 the profile will be scaled to half of its size. Next, press ENTER and select the path from the graphics window.

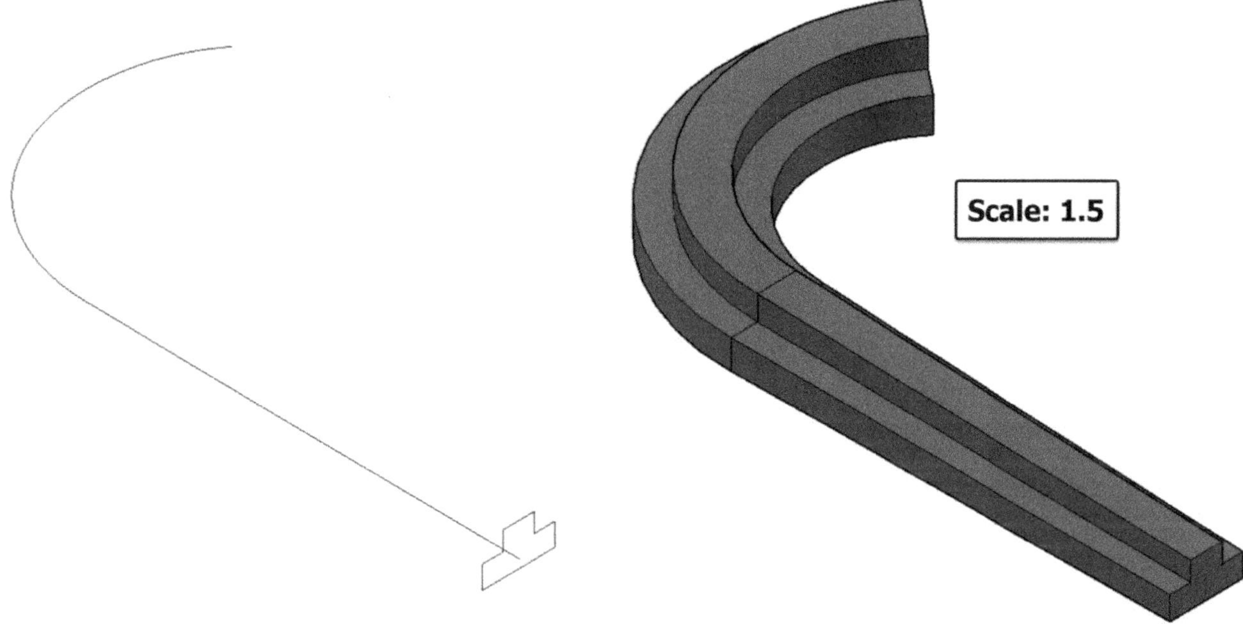

Tutorial 1

In this example, you create the part shown below.

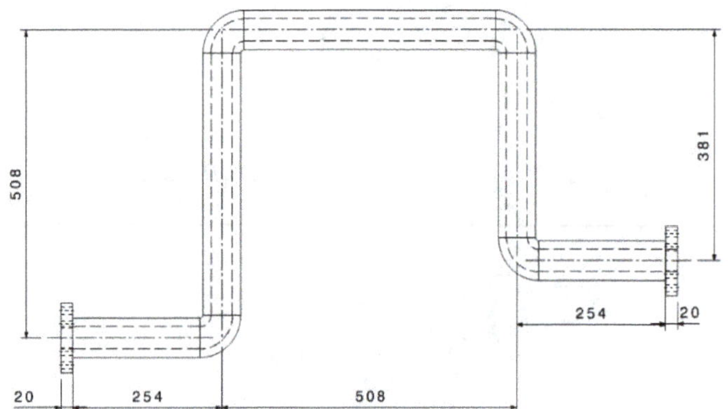

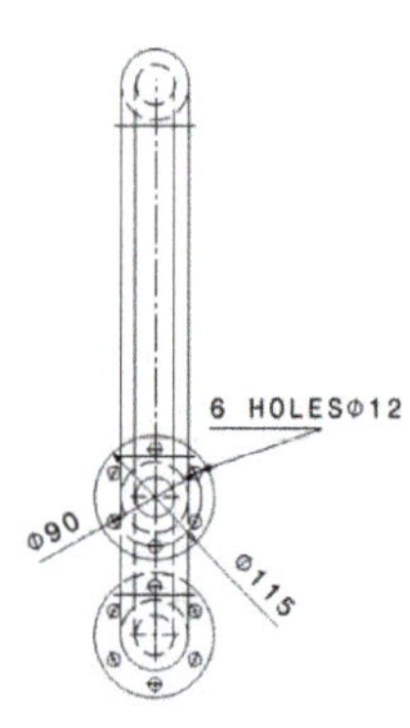

PIPE I.D. 51

PIPE O.D. 65

Creating a New File

1. Click the **AutoCAD 2025** icon on your desktop.
2. On the **Start** page, click **New** drop-down > **acadiso3D.dwt**.
3. Deactivate the **GRIDMODE** icon on the status bar.

Creating the Swept Solid

1. On the ribbon, click **Home** tab > **View** panel > **Restore View** drop-down > **Front**.

2. On the ribbon, click **Home** tab > **Draw** panel > **Polyline**.
3. Type 0,0 in the command line and press ENTER. The first point of the polyline is defined.
4. Make sure that the **Dynamic Input** and **Orthomode** icons are active on the status bar.
5. Move the pointer toward the right.
6. Type 254, and press ENTER.
7. Move the pointer upward.
8. Type 508, and press ENTER.
9. Move the pointer toward the right.
10. Type 508, and press ENTER.
11. Move the pointer downward.
12. Type 381, and press ENTER.
13. Move the pointer toward the right.
14. Type 254, and press ENTER.
15. Press ESC.

16. On the ribbon, click **Home** tab > **Modify** panel > **Fillet** drop-down > **Fillet**.

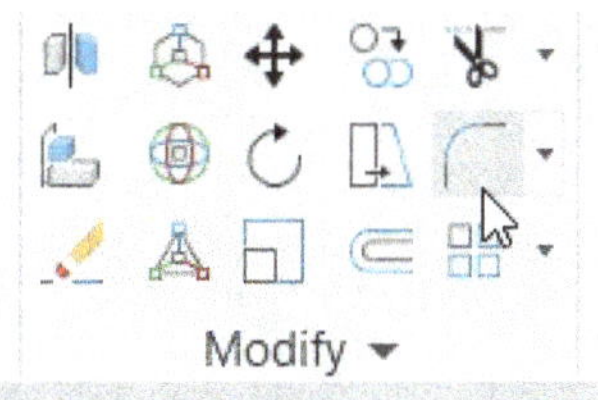

17. Select the **Radius** option from the command line.
18. Type **38** in the command line and press ENTER.
19. Select Vertical and horizontal lines meeting at the corner, as shown.

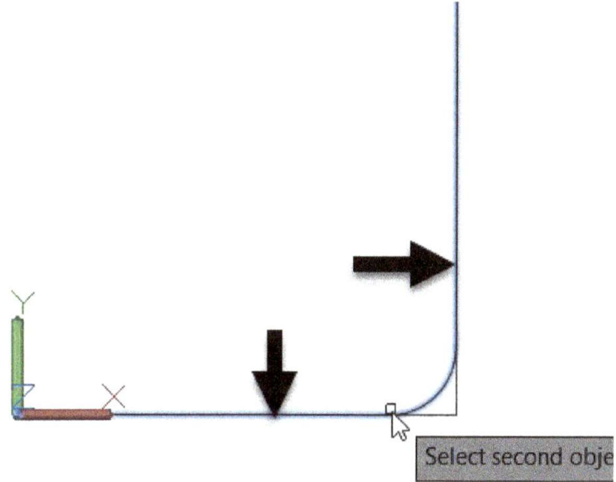

20. Press ENTER to activate the **Fillet** command.
21. Select the vertical and horizontal lines meeting at the corner, as shown.

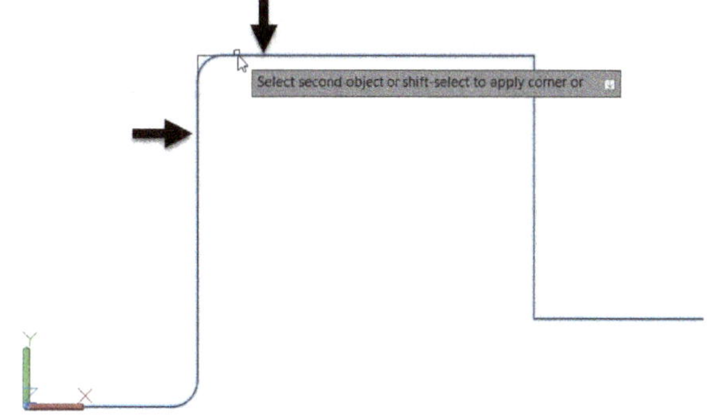

22. Likewise, create fillets at the corners, as shown.

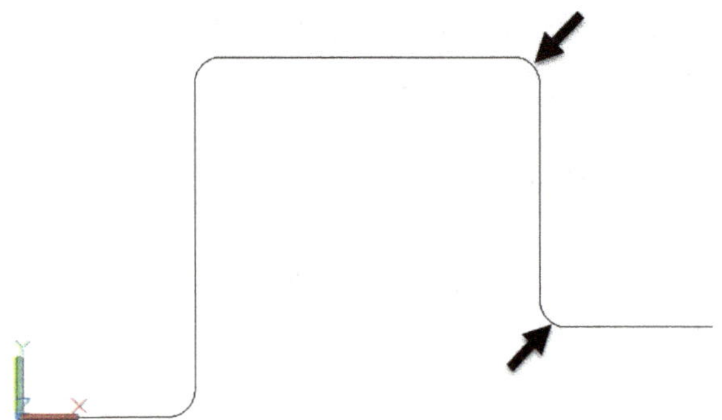

23. Change the view orientation to SE Isometric.
24. On the ribbon, click **Home** tab > **Coordinates** panel > **Z-Axis Vector**.

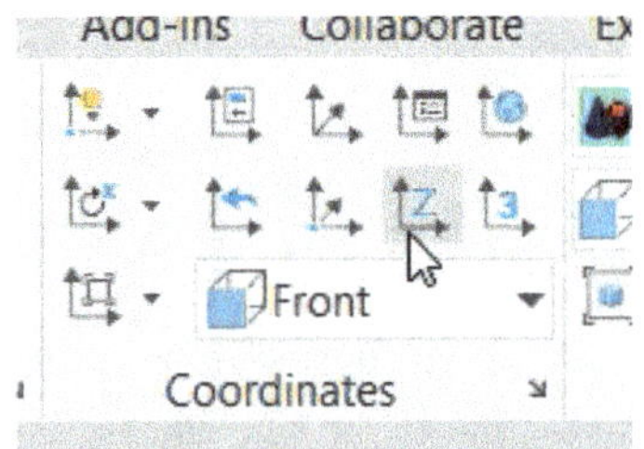

25. Select the endpoint of the polyline.

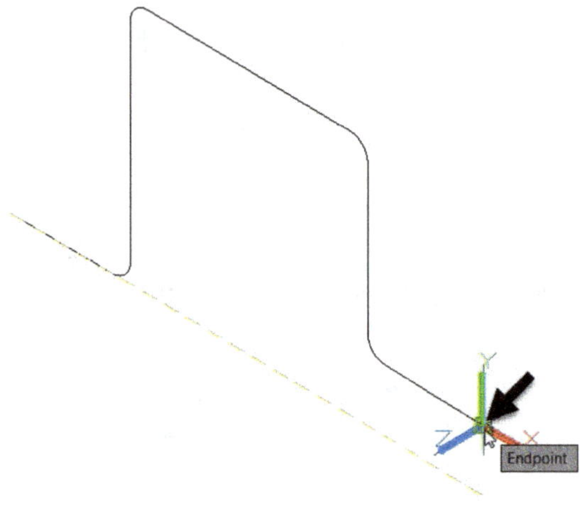

26. Move the pointer along the horizontal line and select its endpoint, as shown.

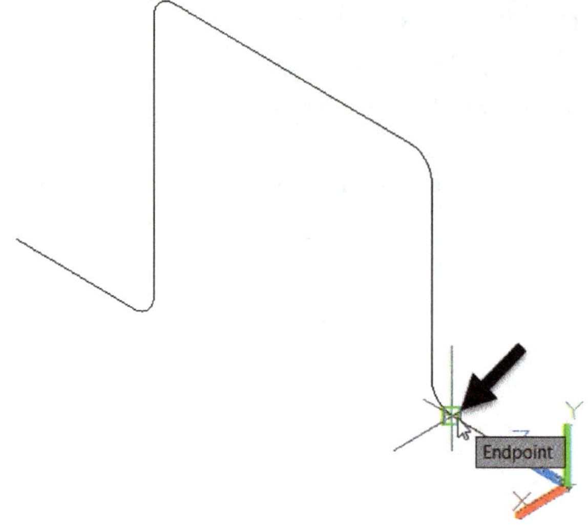

27. On the ribbon, click **Home** tab > **Draw** panel > **Circle** drop-down > **Circle, Diameter**.

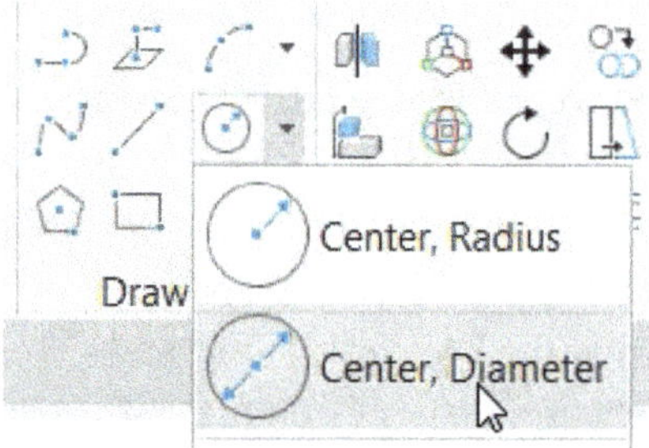

28. Type 0,0 and press ENTER.
29. Type 65 and press ENTER.

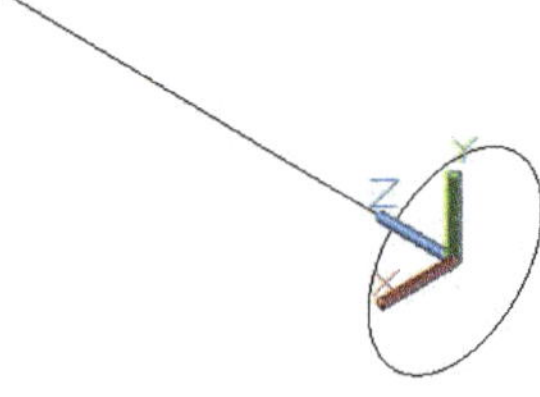

30. On the ribbon, click the **Home** tab > **Modeling** panel > **Solids** drop-down > **Sweep** .
31. Select the circle and press ENTER to define the object to sweep.
32. Select the polyline to define the path.

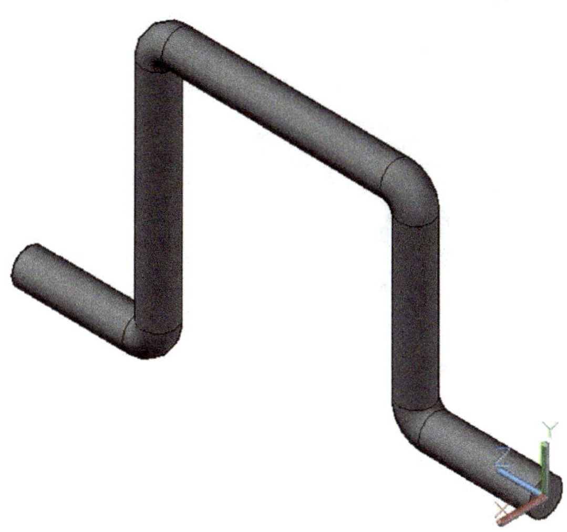

Shelling the Solid

1. On the ribbon, click **Solids** tab > **Solid Editing** panel > **Shell**.

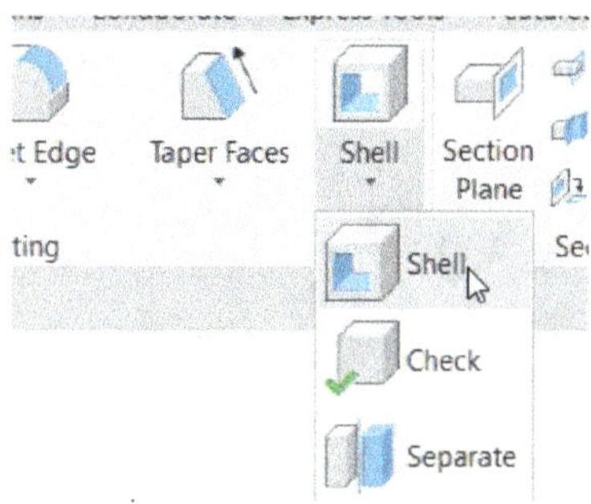

2. Click on the swept solid.
3. Click on the front end of the swept solid.

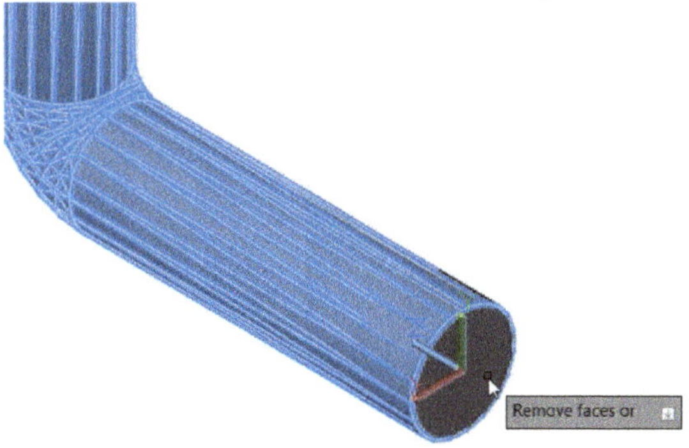

4. On the Navigation Bar, click the **Orbit** icon.
5. Press and hold the left mouse button and drag the pointer toward the right.
6. Scroll the mouse wheel backward.
7. Right-click and select Exit.

8. Click on the back end face of the swept solid.

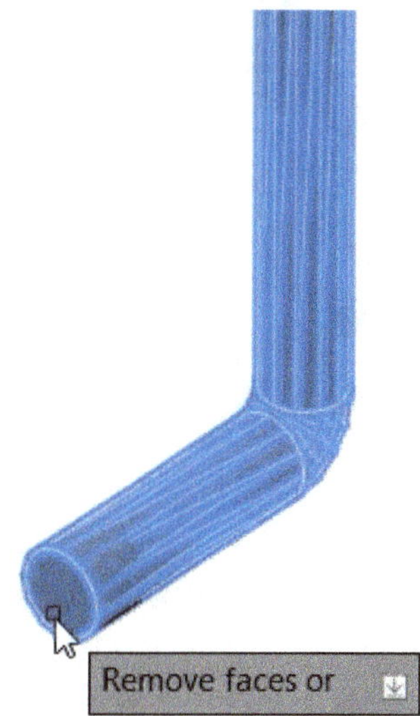

9. Press ENTER to accept the selection.
10. Type 7 in the command line and press ENTER. The shell thickness is defined.
11. Select **eXit** from the command line.
12. Select **eXit** from the command line.
13. Change the view orientation to SE Isometric.

Adding the Flange

1. On the ribbon, click **Home** tab > **Draw** panel > **Circle** drop-down > **Circle, Diameter**.

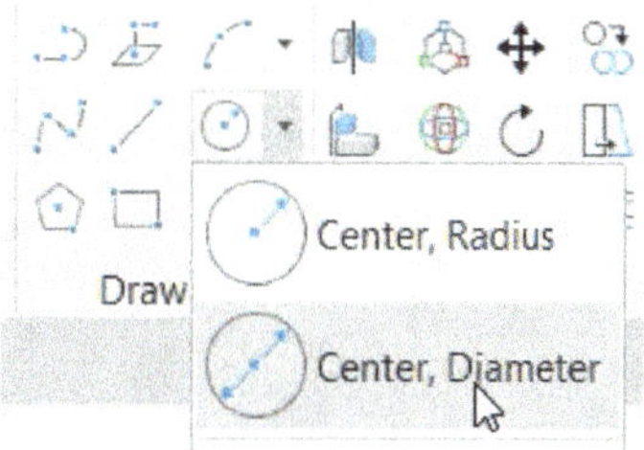

2. Type 0,0 and press ENTER.
3. Type 115, and press ENTER.

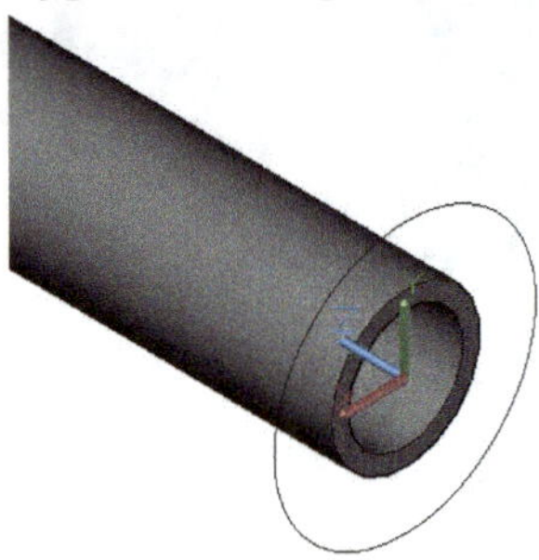

4. Activate the **Dynamic Input** icon on the status bar.
5. On the ribbon, click **Home** tab > **Modeling** panel > **Presspull**.
6. Click on the end face of the swept solid.

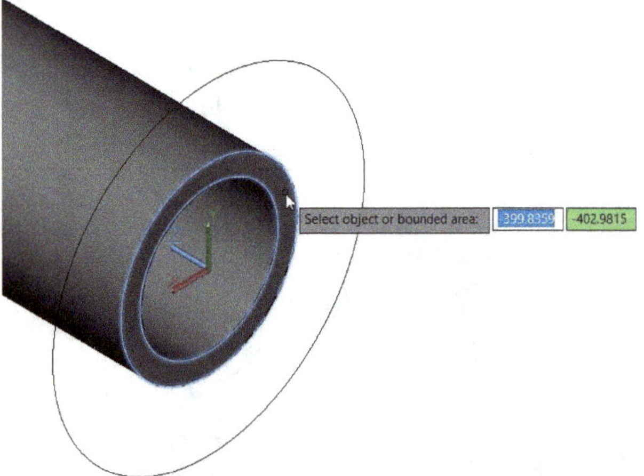

7. Move the pointer toward the right.
8. Type 20 and press ENTER.

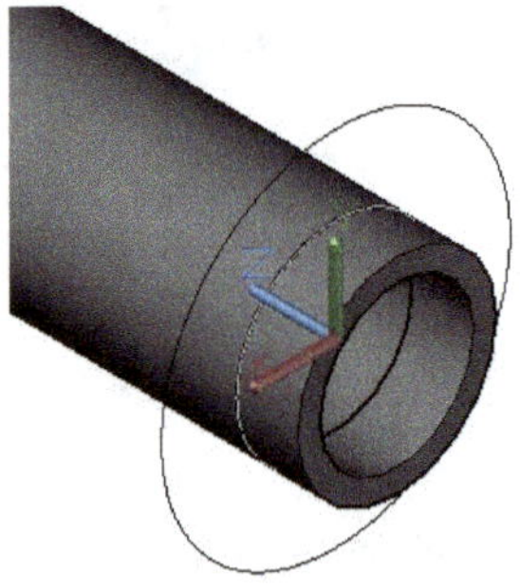

9. Click inside the circle and move pointer toward the right.
10. Type 20 and press ENTER.

Creating the Polar array

1. On the ribbon, click **Home** tab > **Modeling** panel > **Primitives** drop-down > **Cylinder**.
2. Type 0, 45 in the command line and press ENTER. The centerpoint of the cylinder is defined.
3. Type 6 in the command line and press ENTER.
4. Move the pointer toward the right.
5. Type 20 and press ENTER to create the cylinder.

6. Set the **Visual Style** to **2D Wireframe**.
7. Select the small cylinder, as shown.

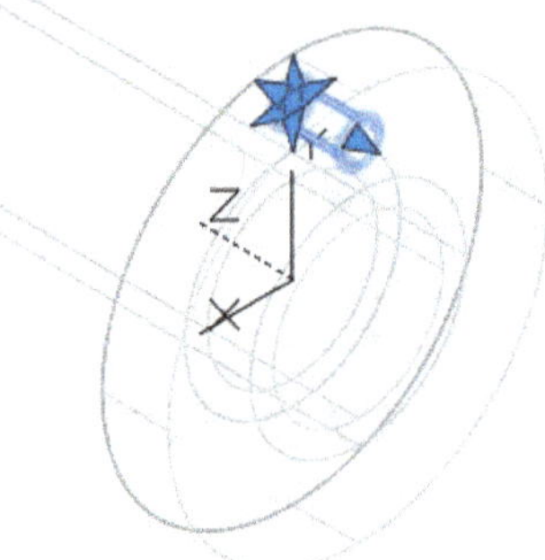

8. On the ribbon, **Home** tab > **Modify** panel > **Array** drop-down > **Polar Array**.

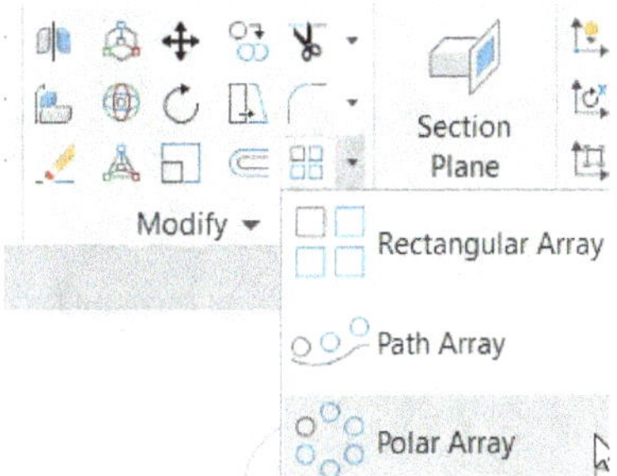

9. Select the centerpoint of the press pulled solid; the centerpoint of the polar array is defined.

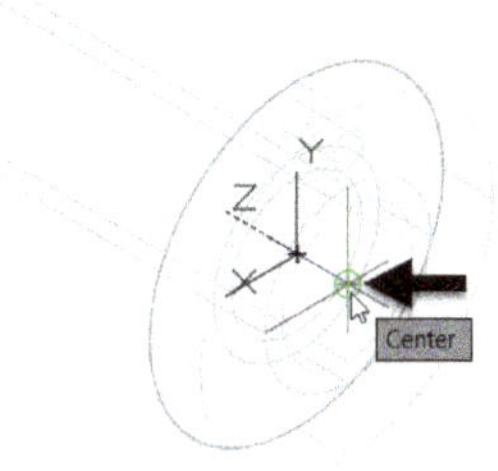

10. On the **Array Creation** tab, type **6** and **360** in the **Items** and **Fill** boxes, respectively.

11. Deactivate the **Associative** icon on the ribbon.
12. Click the **Close Array** icon on the ribbon.

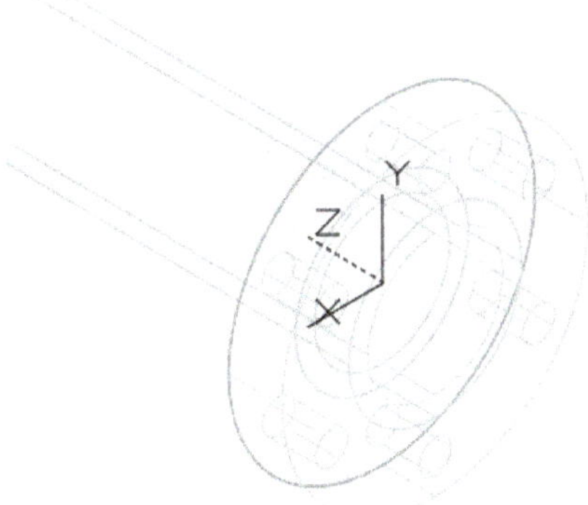

13. On the ribbon, click **Home** tab > **Solid Editing** panel > **Solid, Subtract**.
14. Click on the edge of the press pulled solid; the press pulled solid is selected.
15. Press ENTER.

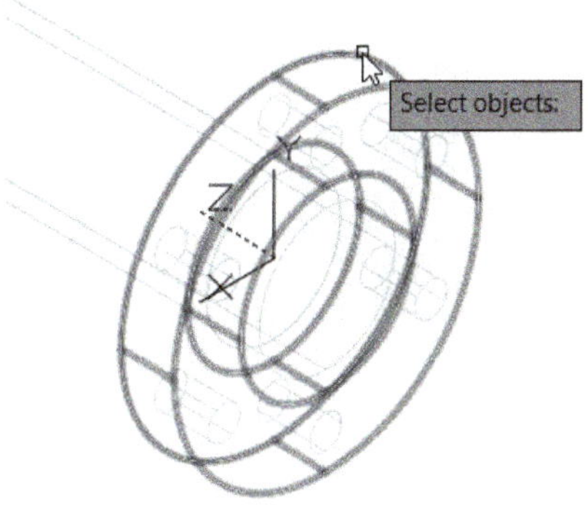

16. Select all the cylinders of the polar array and press ENTER.

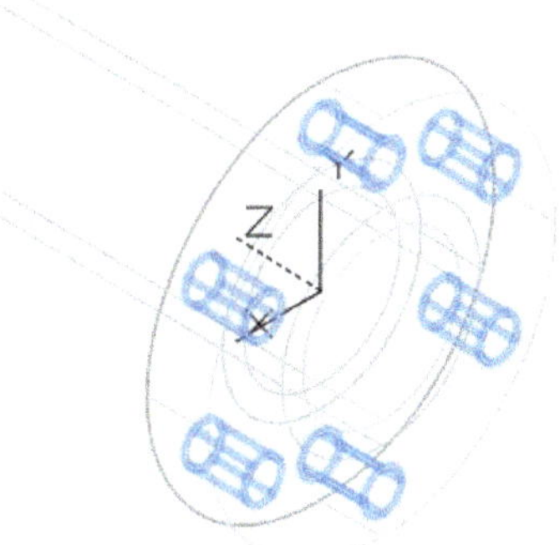

17. Change the **Visual Style** to **Shades of Gray**.

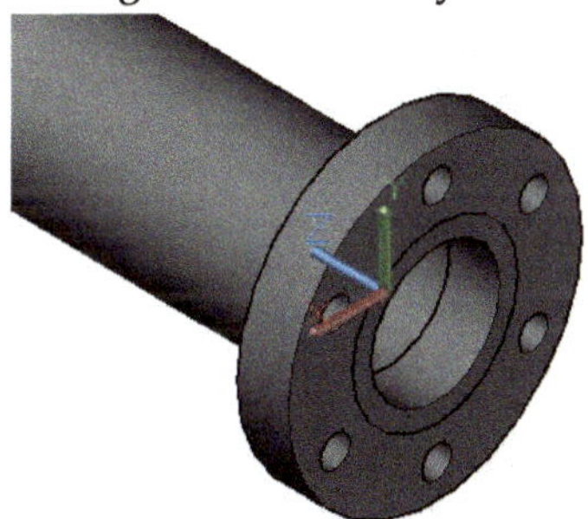

18. Select the two press pulled solids, as shown.

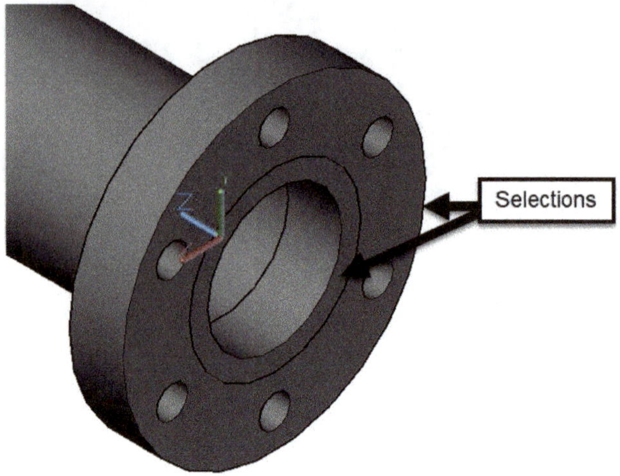

19. On the ribbon, **Home** tab > **Modify** panel > **Copy**.

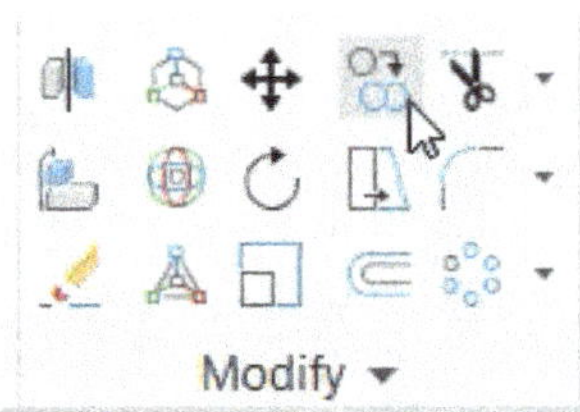

20. Select the centerpoint of the press pulled solid to define the base point.

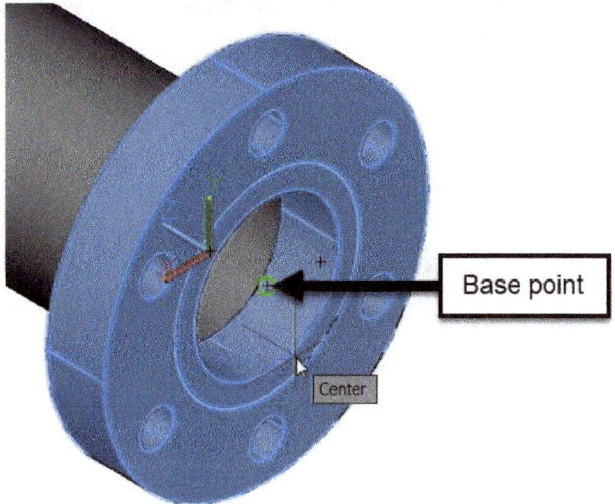

21. Move the pointer in the forward direction.
22. Select the centerpoint of the circular edge on the backside, as shown.

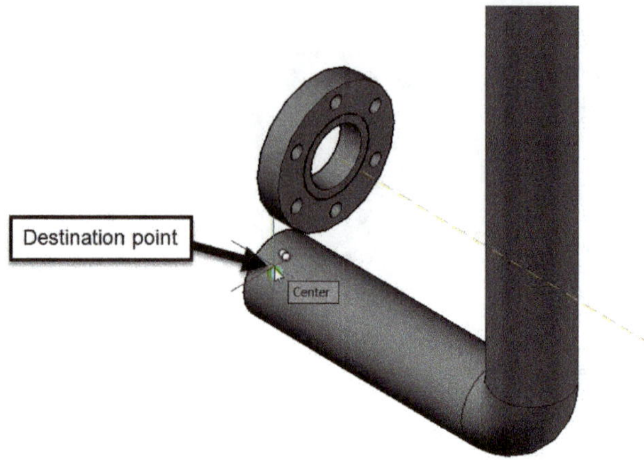

23. Press ESC.
24. On the ribbon, click **Home** tab > **Solid Editing** panel > **Solid, Union**.

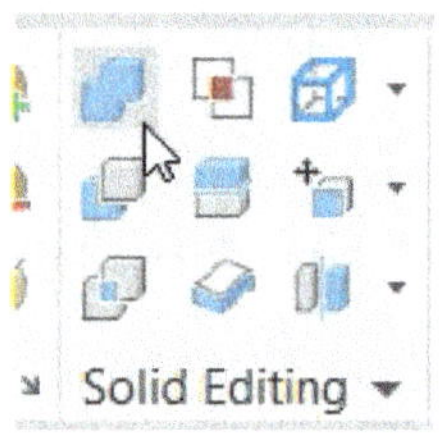

25. Create a selection window across the entire model.

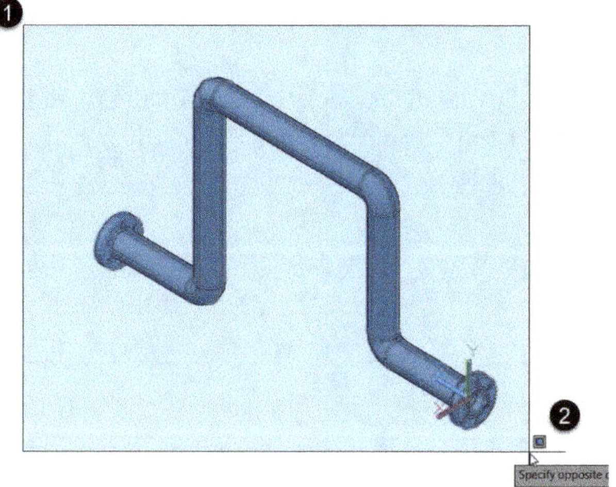

26. Press ENTER. All the solids are combined into a single solid.
27. Click the **Save** icon on the Quick Access Toolbar.
28. Type **Ch5_tutorial1** in the **File Name** box.
29. Click the **Save** button.
30. Click **Application Menu > Close > Current Drawing**.

Tutorial 2

In this example, you create the assembly shown below.

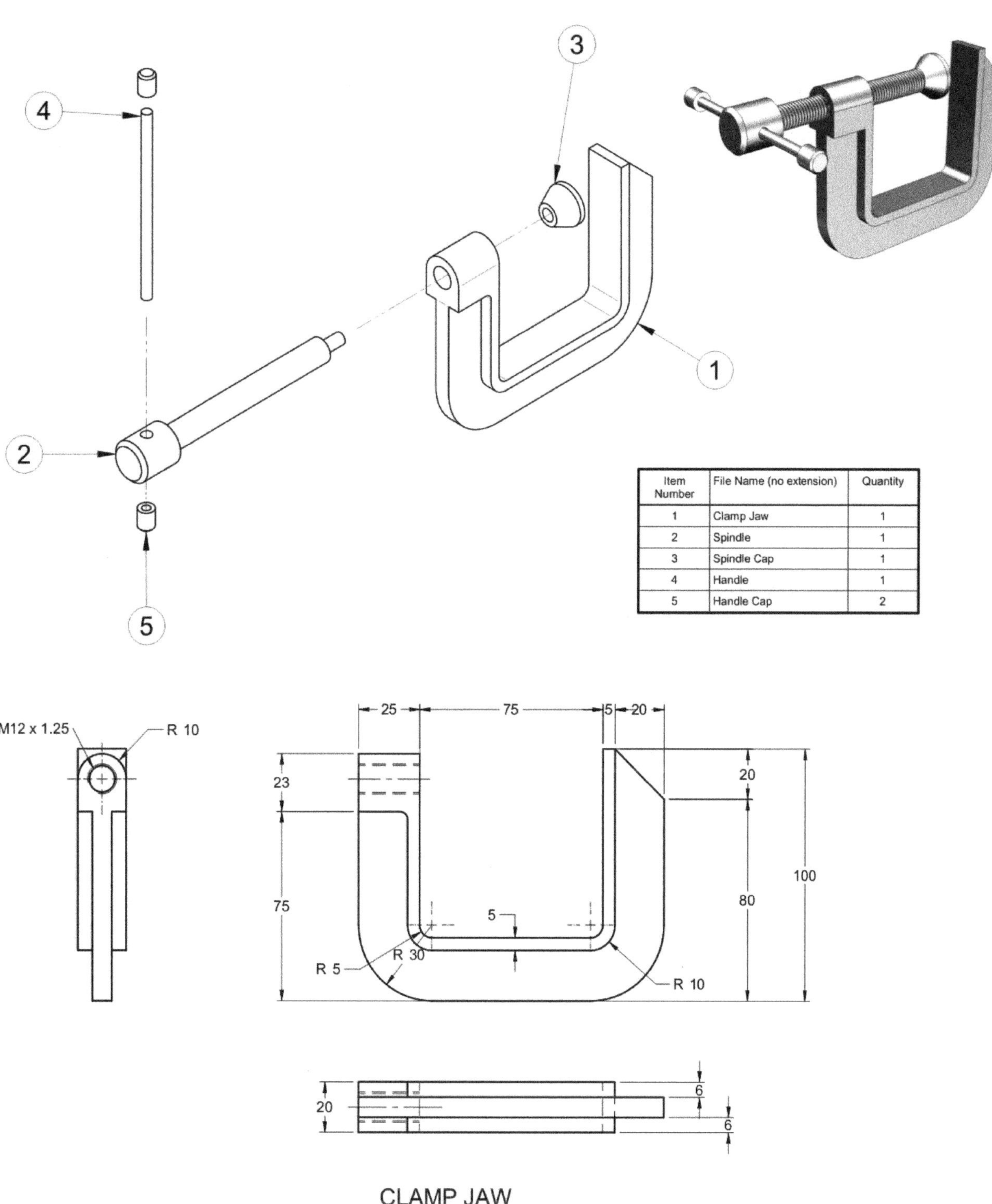

Item Number	File Name (no extension)	Quantity
1	Clamp Jaw	1
2	Spindle	1
3	Spindle Cap	1
4	Handle	1
5	Handle Cap	2

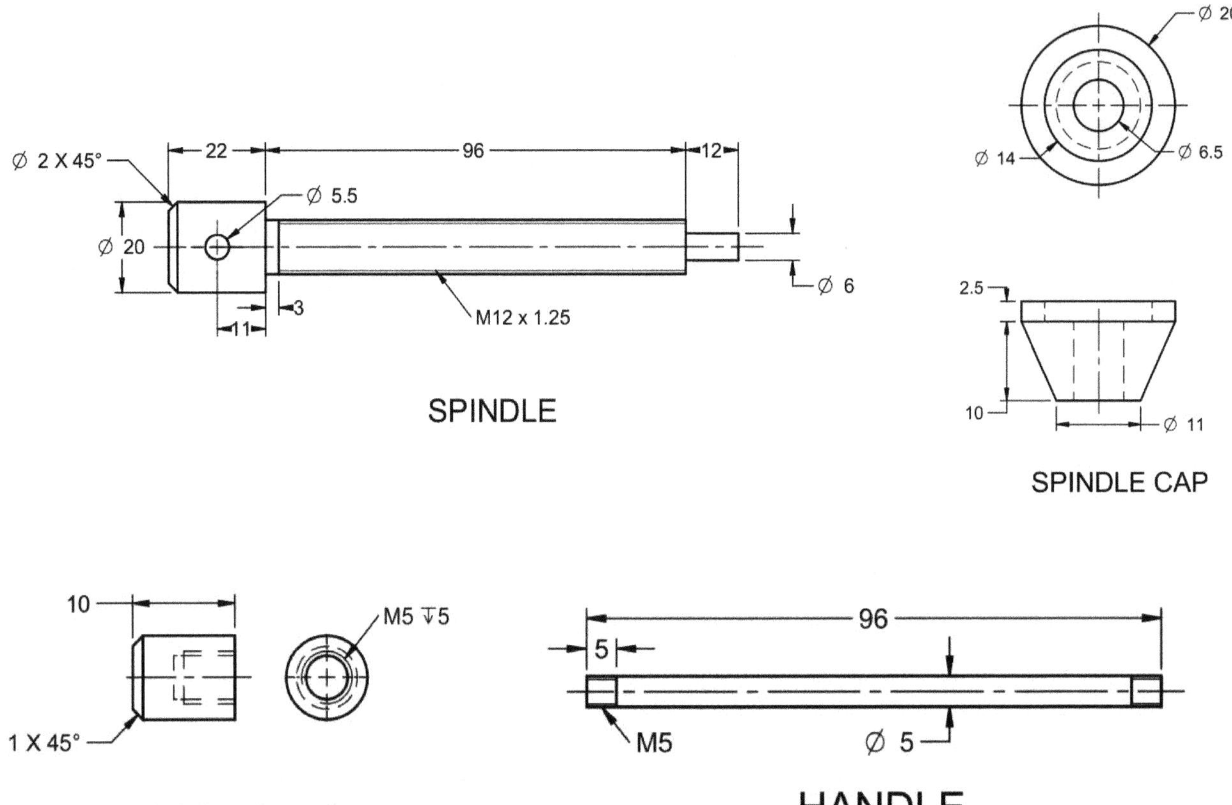

Ø 2 X 45°
22
96
12
Ø 5.5
Ø 20
Ø 6
11
3
M12 x 1.25
SPINDLE
Ø 20
Ø 14
Ø 6.5
2.5
10
Ø 11
SPINDLE CAP
10
M5 ↧5
1 X 45°
HANDLE CAP
96
5
M5
Ø 5
HANDLE

Creating a New File

1. Click the **New** icon on the Quick Access Toolbar.
2. Select the **acadiso3D** template from the **Select template** dialog.
3. Click the **Open** button.
4. Deactivate the **GRIDMODE** icon on the status bar.

Creating the Clamp Jaw

1. On the **Home** tab of the ribbon, click **Coordinates > Z-Axis Vector**.

2. Press ENTER to specify 0,0,0 as the origin of the UCS, as shown.
3. Activate the Orthomode icon on the status bar.
4. Move the pointer toward the left and click. The Z-axis of the UCS is defined.

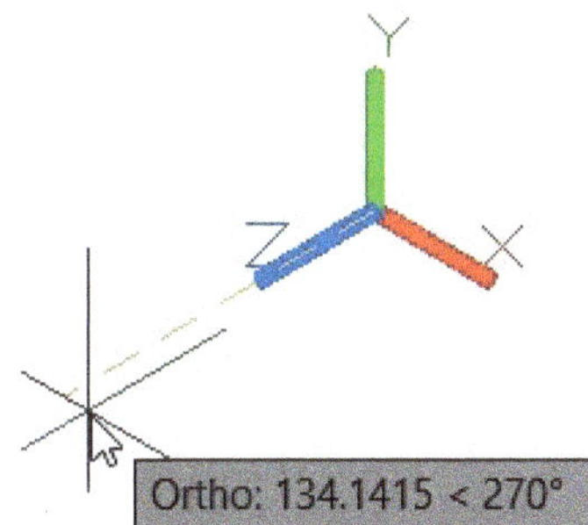

5. On the ribbon, click **Home** tab > **Modeling** panel > **Primitives** drop-down > **Cylinder**.
6. Type 0,88 and press ENTER to define the centerpoint if the cylinder.
7. Type 10 and press ENTER to define the radius of the cylinder.
8. Type -25 and press ENTER.

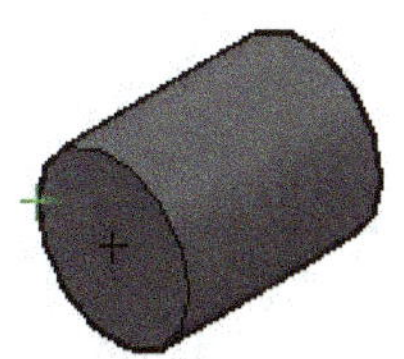

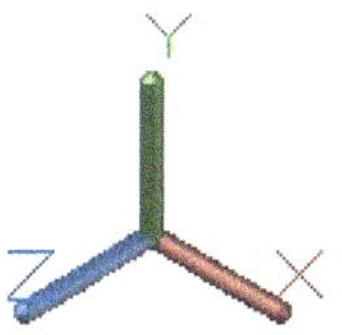

9. On the ribbon, click **Home** tab > **Modeling** panel > **Primitives** drop-down > **Box**.
10. Select the left quadrant point of the cylinder, as shown.

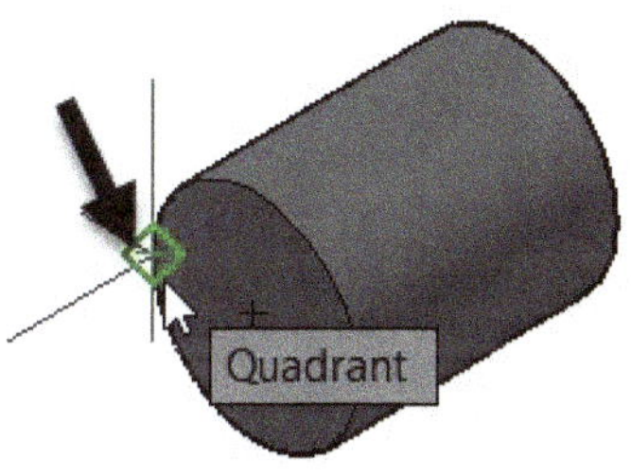

11. Select the **Length** option from the command line.
12. Move the pointer toward the right and select the right quadrant point.

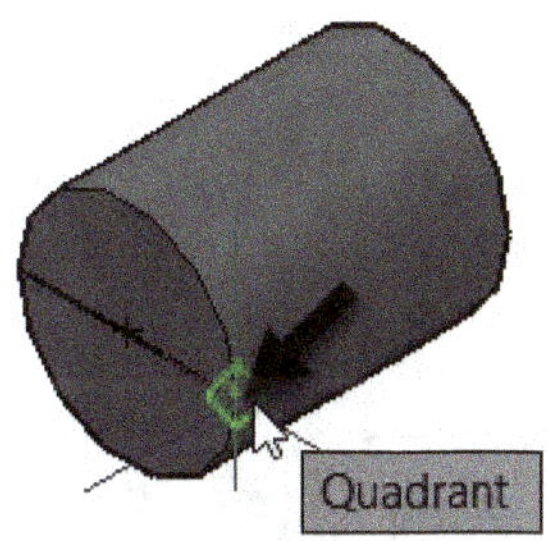

13. Move the pointer downward.
14. Type 13 and press ENTER
15. Move the pointer toward the right and select the quadrant point on the back face of the cylinder.

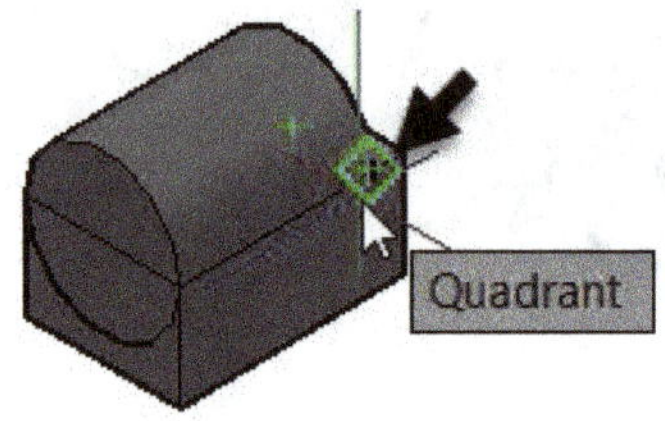

16. On the ribbon, click **Home** tab > **Solid Editing** panel > **Solid, Union**.

17. Select the cylinder and box, and then press ENTER.

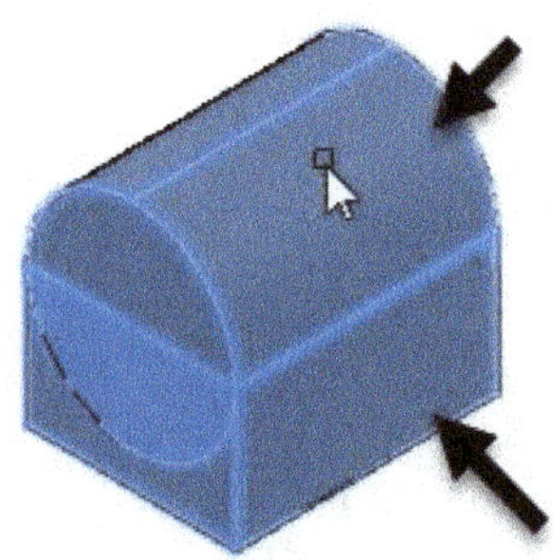

Creating the Swept Solid

1. On the **Home** tab of the ribbon, click **Coordinates > Z-Axis Vector**.

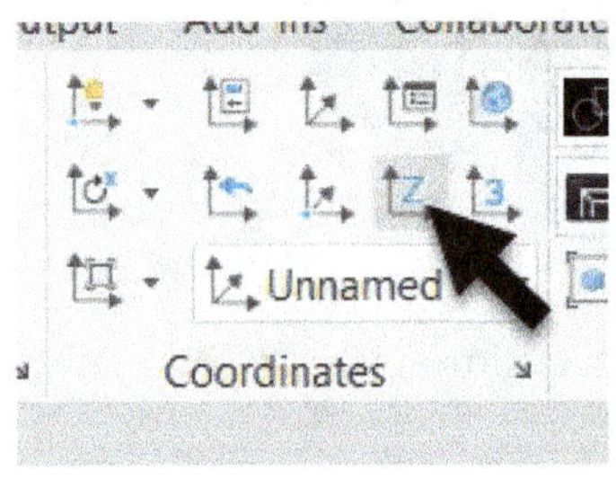

2. Orbit the model and select the midpoint of the bottom-front edge.

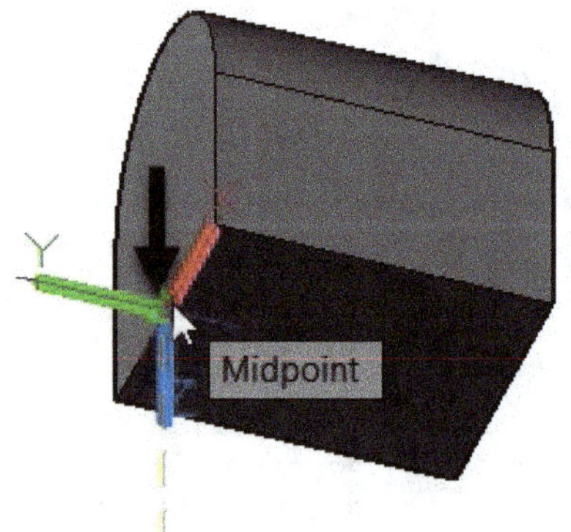

3. Move the pointer downward and click to specify the Z-axis.

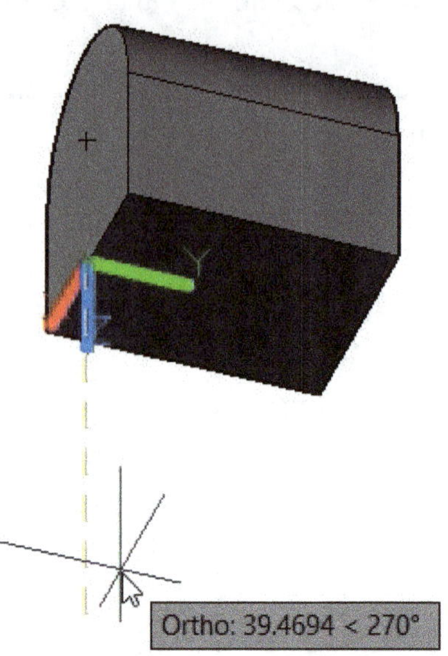

4. Change the **Visual Style** to **2D Wireframe**.

5. On the ribbon, click **Home** tab > **Selection** panel > **Filter** drop-down > **Edge**.

6. On the ribbon, click **Home** tab > **Solid Editing** panel > **Edge** drop-down > **Extract Edges**.

7. Select the edges of the bottom face of the model, as shown.

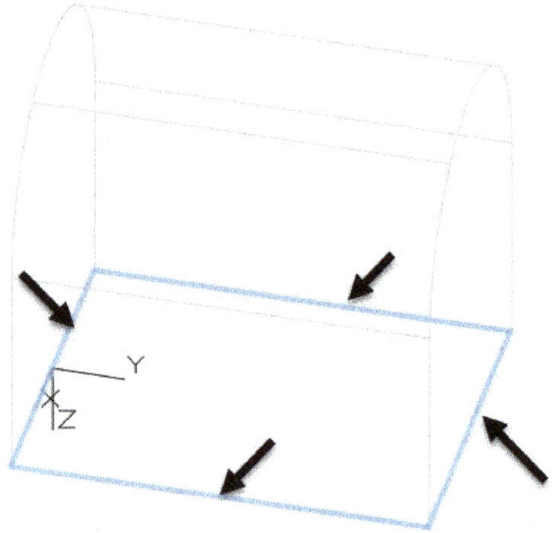

8. Press ENTER.

9. On the ribbon, click **Home** tab > **Selection** panel > **Filter** drop-down > **No Filter**.

10. On the ribbon, click the **Home** tab > **Modify** panel > **Offset**.

11. Type 5 in the command line and press ENTER. The offset distance is defined.

12. Select the extracted edge, as shown.

13. Move the pointer inside the model and click.

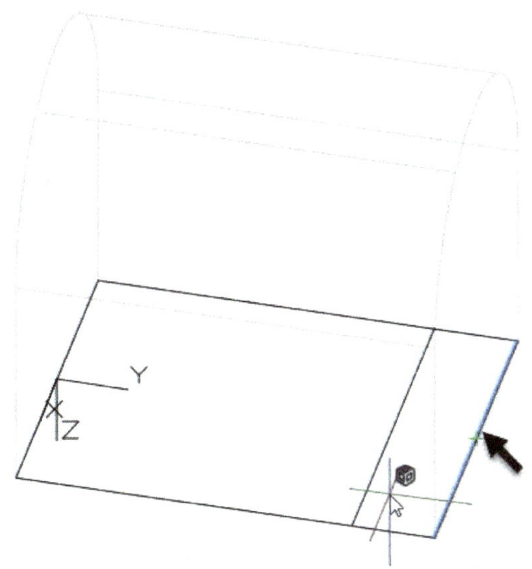

14. Press ENTER twice.
15. Type 6 and press ENTER.
16. Select the extracted edge, as shown.

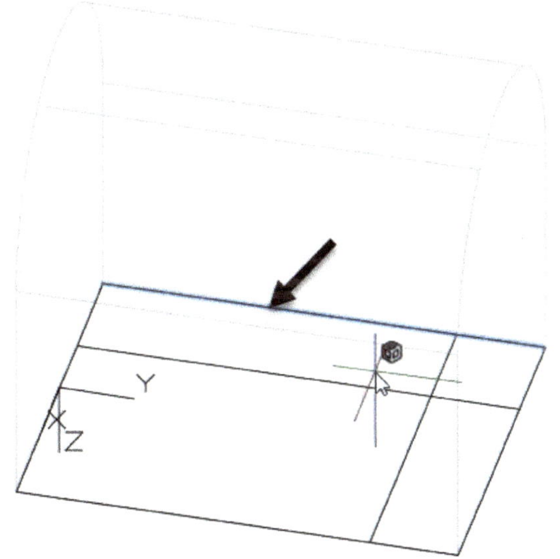

17. Move the pointer inside the model and click.
18. Select the extracted edge, as shown.
19. Move the pointer inside the model and click.

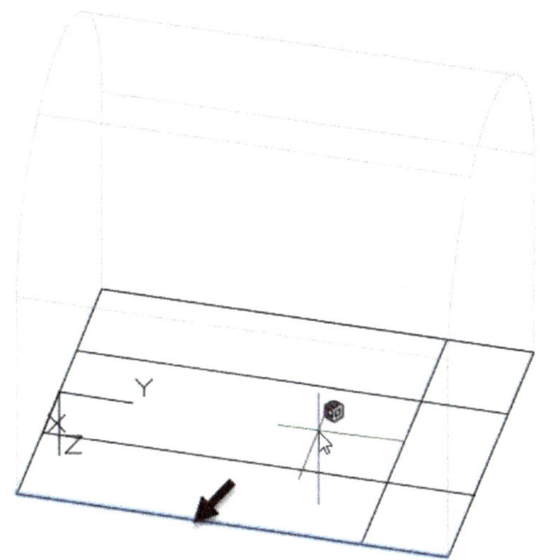

20. On the ribbon, click **Home** tab > **Modify** panel > **Trim/Extend** drop-down > **Trim**.
21. Select the portions of the horizontal line extending outside the model.

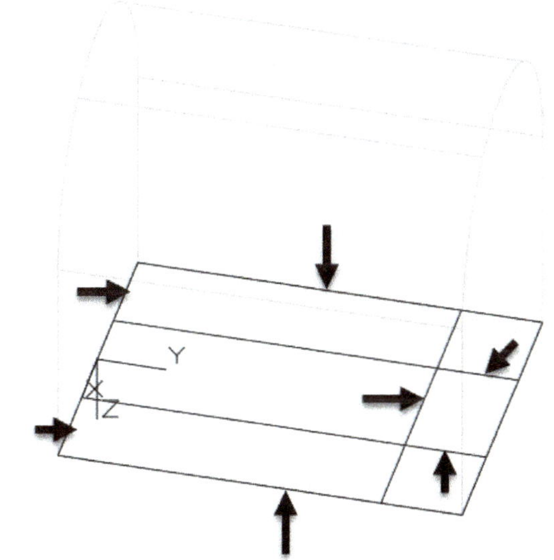

22. Press ESC.

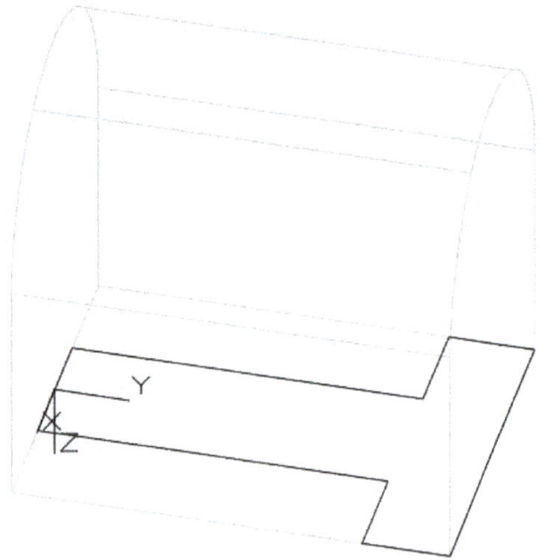

23. On the **Home** tab of the ribbon, click
    Coordinates > Z-Axis Vector.

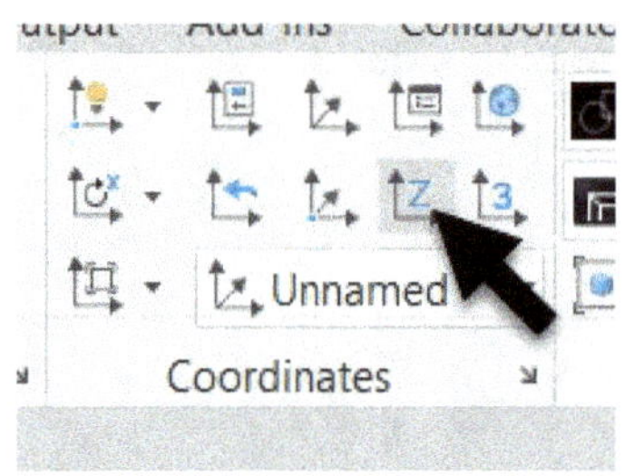

24. Orbit the model and select the midpoint of the
    bottom back edge.

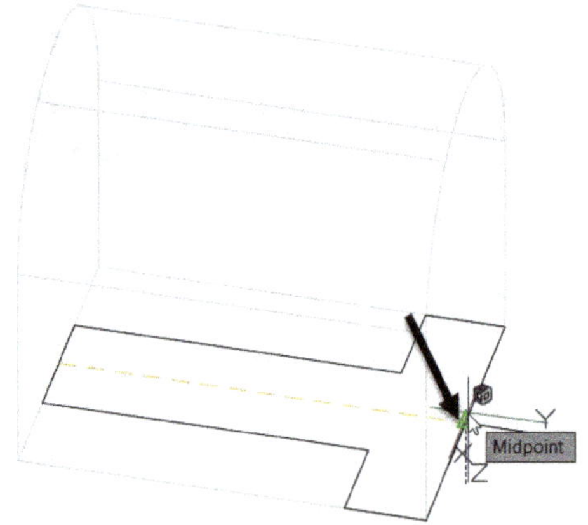

25. Select the corner point of the model, as shown.

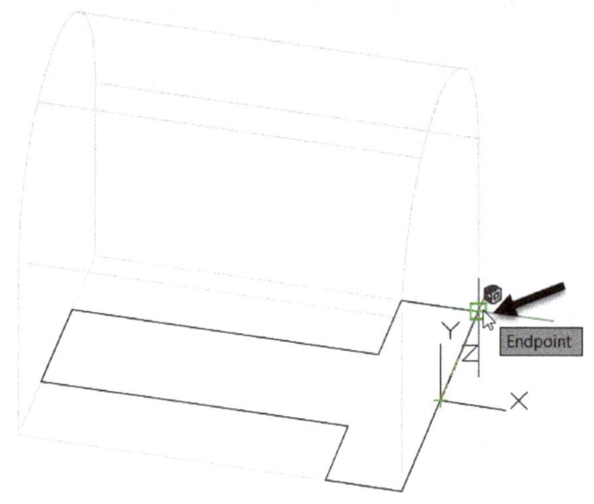

26. Change the View orientation to SE Isometric.
27. On the ribbon, click **Home** tab > **Draw** panel >
    Polyline.
28. Type 0,0 in the command line and press ENTER.
29. Turn ON the Dynamic Input and
    ORTHOMODE icons on the status bar.
30. Move the pointer downward.
31. Type 50 and press ENTER.

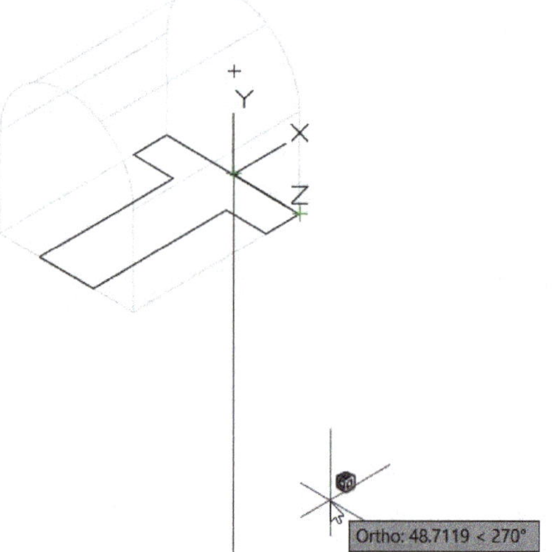

32. Move the pointer toward the right.

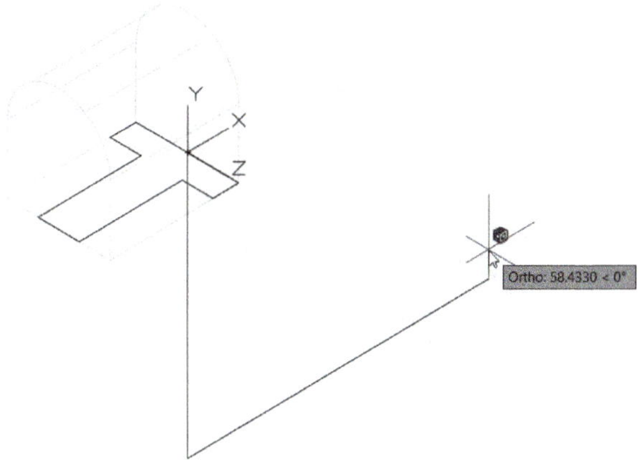

33. Type 75 and press ENTER.
34. Move the pointer upward.

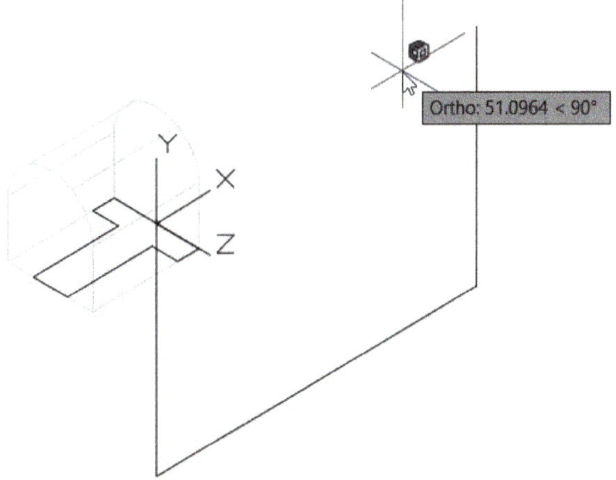

35. Type 75 and press ENTER.
36. Press ESC.
37. On the ribbon, click **Home** tab > **Modify** panel > **Fillet** drop-down > **Fillet**.

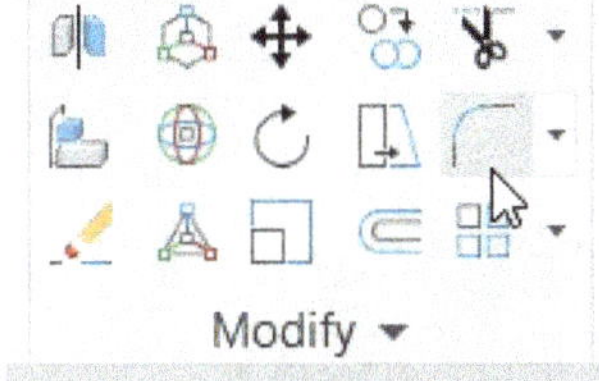

38. Select the **Radius** option from the command line.
39. Type **5** in the command line and press ENTER.
40. Select Vertical and horizontal lines meeting at the corner, as shown.

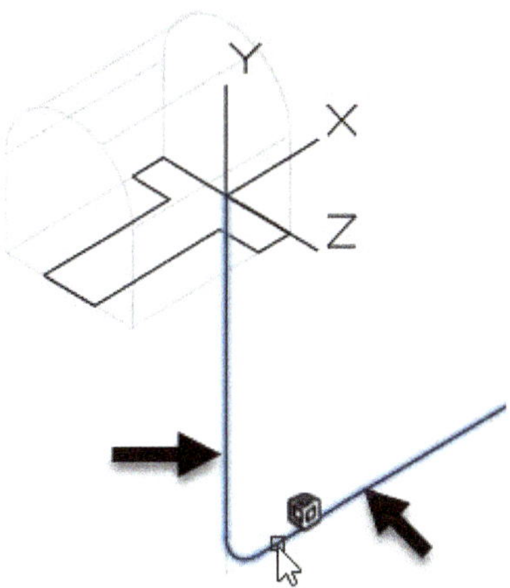

41. Press ENTER to activate the Fillet command.
42. Select Vertical and horizontal lines meeting at the corner, as shown.

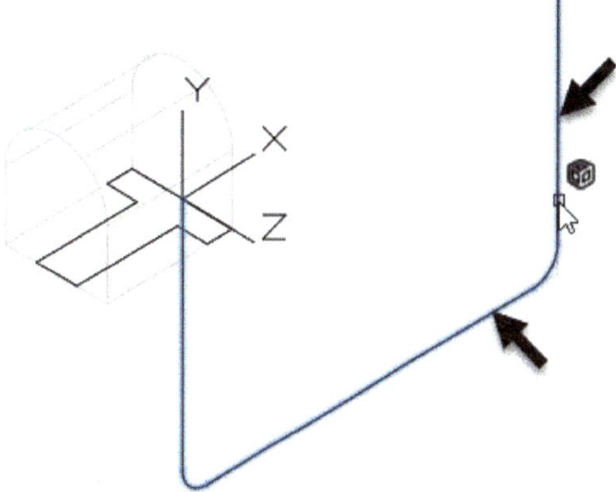

43. On the **Home** tab of the ribbon, expand the **Draw** panel and click the **Region** icon.
44. Select all the entities, as shown.

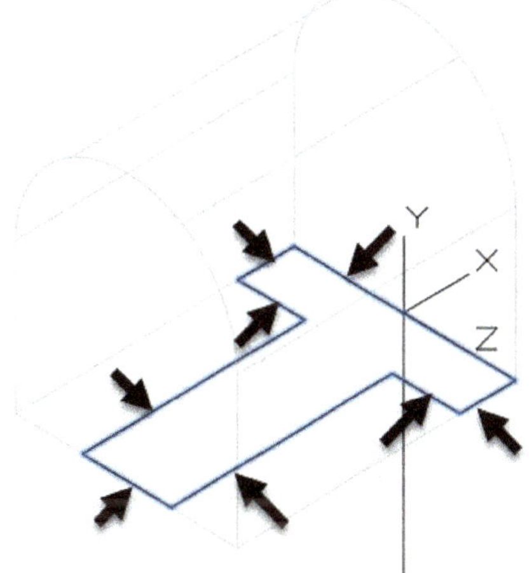

45. Press ENTER to convert all the 2D elements into a region.

46. On the ribbon, click the **Home** tab > **Modeling** panel > **Solids** drop-down > **Sweep**.
47. Select the region and press ENTER to define the object to sweep.

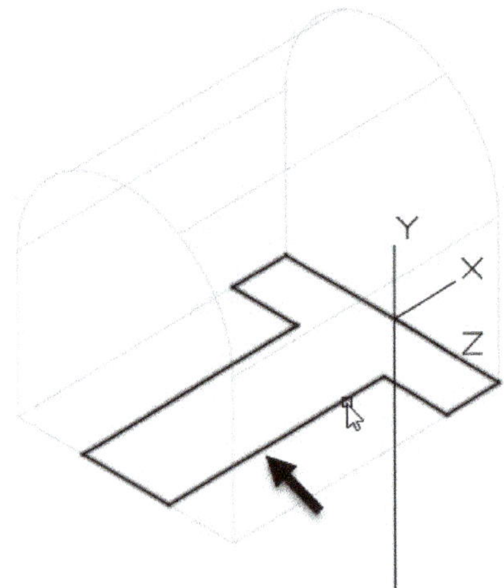

48. Select the polyline and press ENTER to define the path.

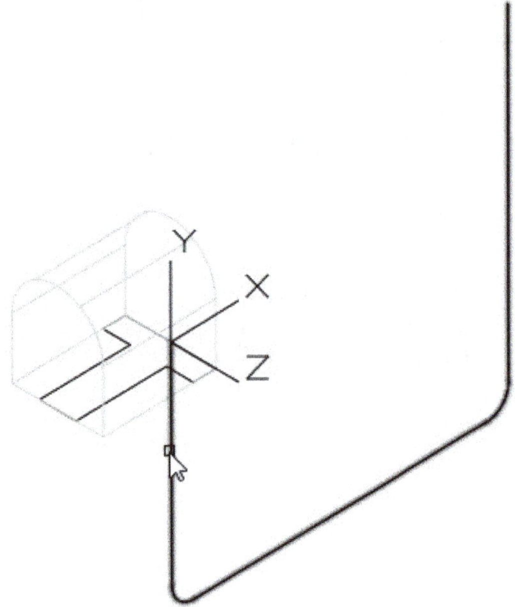

Creating the Hole

1. Change the **Visual Style** to **Shades of gray**.
2. On the ribbon, click **Home** tab > **Coordinates** panel > **Z-Axis Vector**.
3. Select the centerpoint of the circular edge, as shown.

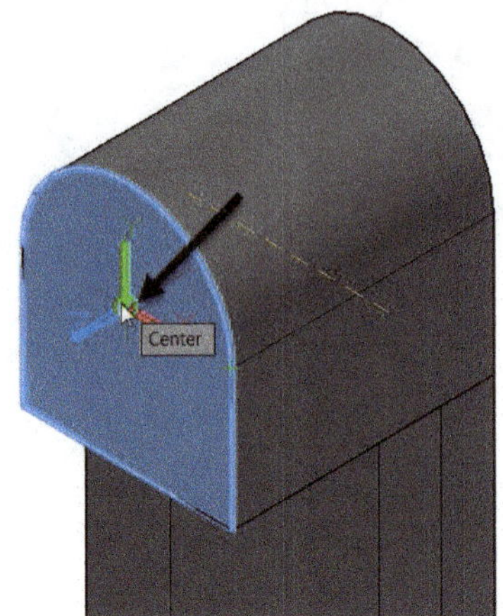

4. Move the pointer toward the left and click to define the Z-axis.

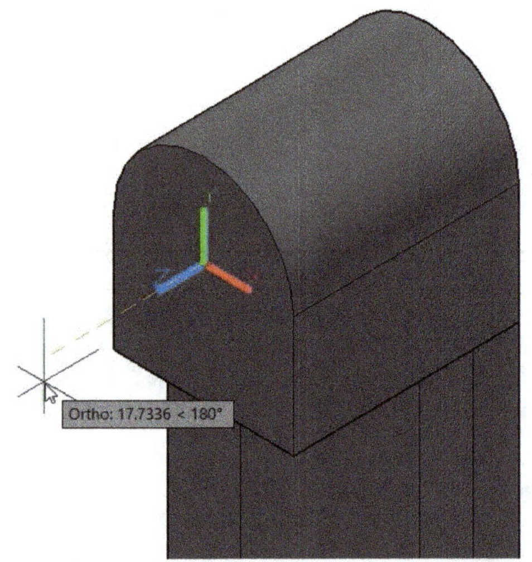

5. On the ribbon, click **Home** tab > **Modeling** panel > **Primitives** drop-down > **Cylinder**.
6. Select the centerpoint of the circular edge, as shown.

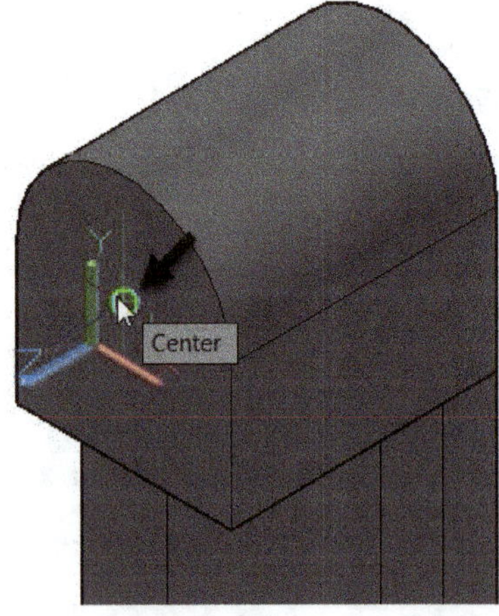

7. Type 6 and press ENTER to define the radius of the cylinder.
8. Move the pointer toward the right and click.

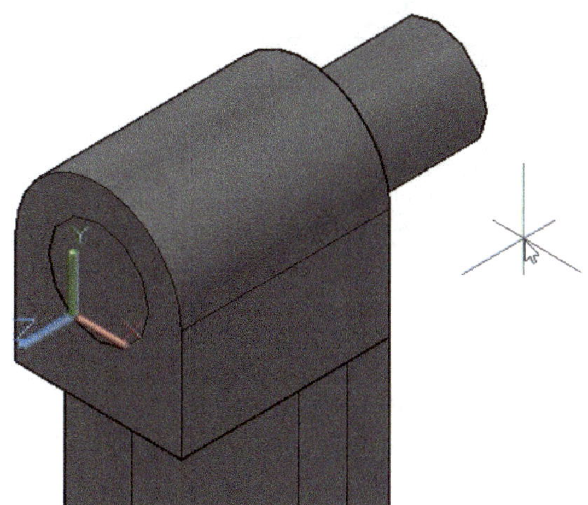

9. On the ribbon, click **Home** tab > **Solid Editing** panel > **Solid, Subtract**.
10. Select the body, as shown.

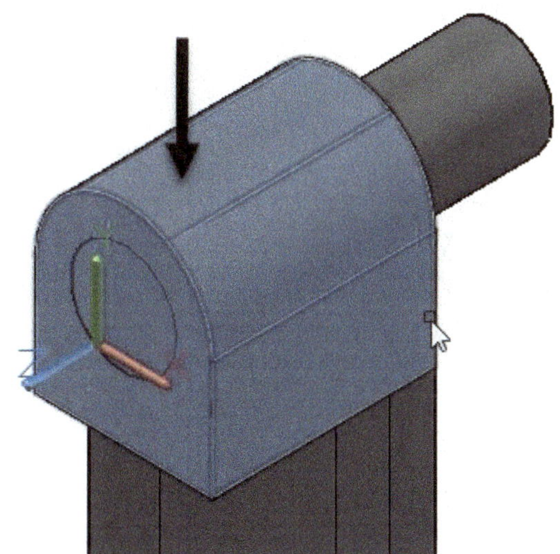

11. Press ENTER.
12. Select the cylinder and press ENTER.

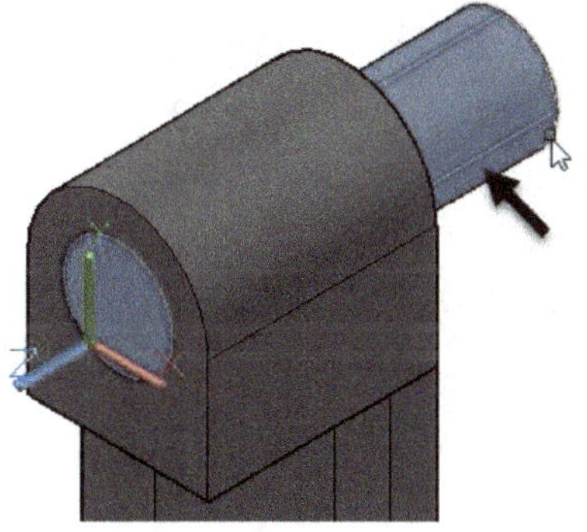

Creating the Chamfers and Fillets

1. On the ribbon, click the **Solid** tab > **Solid Editing** panel > **Fillet Edge** drop-down > **Chamfer Edge**.
2. Select the horizontal edge, as shown.

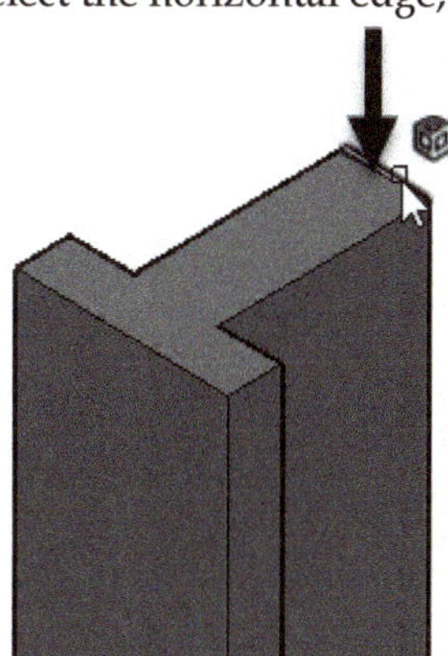

3. Select the **Distance** option from the command line.
4. Type **20** in the command line and press ENTER. Distance 1 is defined.
5. Type **20** in the command line and press ENTER. Distance 2 is defined.
6. Press ENTER twice to create the chamfer.

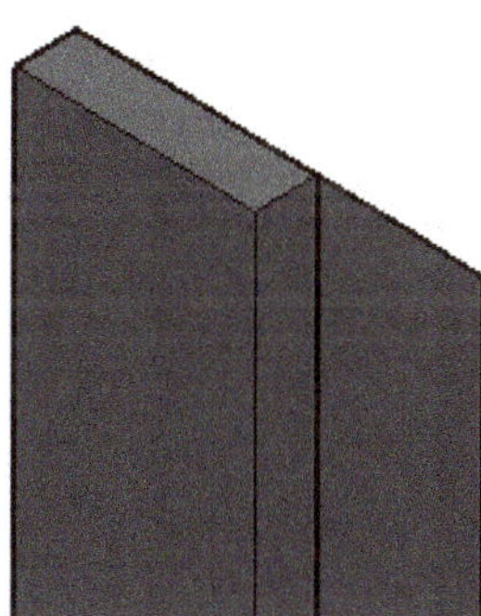

7. On the ribbon, click **Home** tab > **Solid Editing** panel > **Solid, Union**.
8. Select all the bodies and press ENTER.
9. On the ribbon, click **Solid** tab > **Solid Editing** panel > **Fillet Edge**.
10. Click the bottom front corner of the ViewCube; the view orientation is changed.

11. Select the inner horizontal edge of the model, as shown.

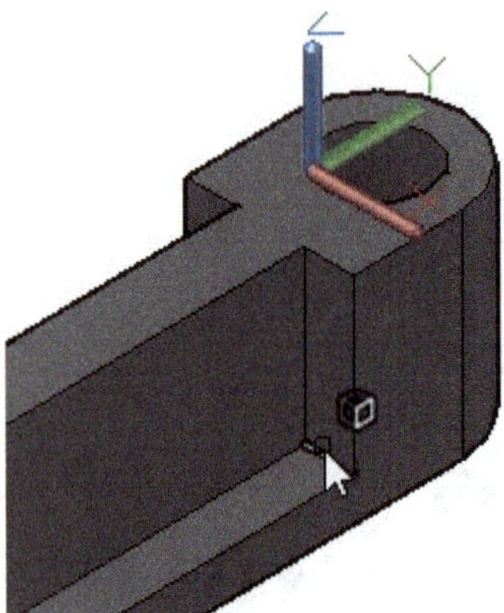

12. Select the top-left corner of the ViewCube. The orientation of the model is changed.

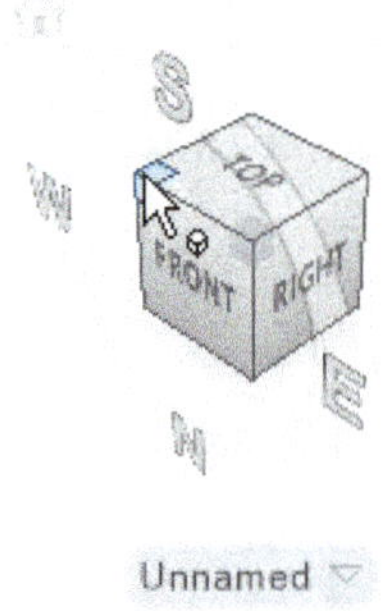

13. Select the visible inner horizontal edge.

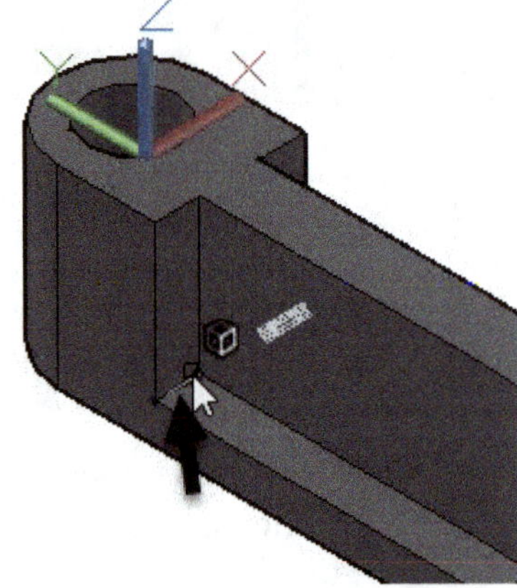

14. Select the **Radius** option from the command line.
15. Type 2 and press ENTER thrice.

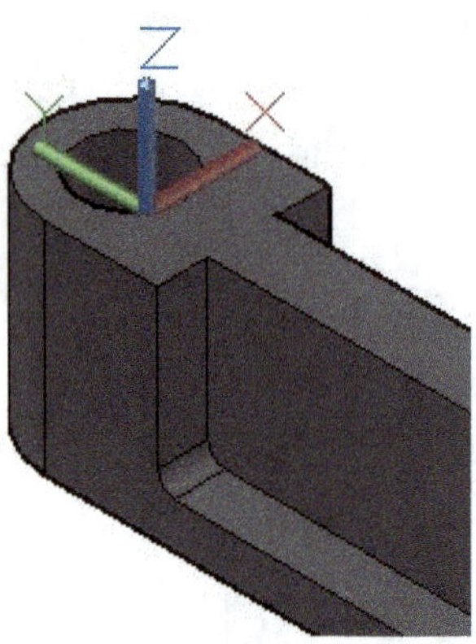

16. Change the View orientation to SE Isometric.

Creating the Spindle

1. On the ribbon, click **Home** tab > **Modeling** panel > **Primitives** drop-down > **Cylinder**.
2. Select the centerpoint of the circular edge, as shown.

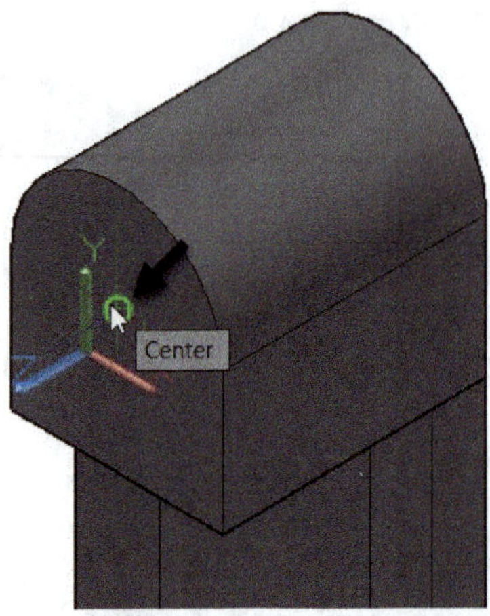

3. Type 6 and press ENTER to define the radius of the cylinder.
4. Type -96 and press ENTER.

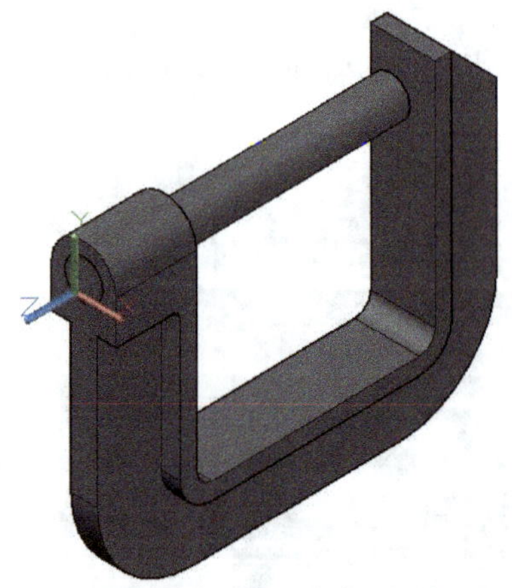

5. Select the newly created cylinder.
6. Select the Y-axis of the move gizmo.

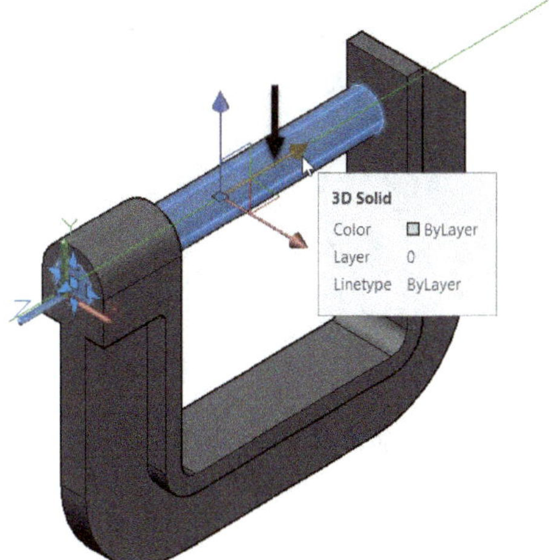

7. Move along the selected axis toward left.

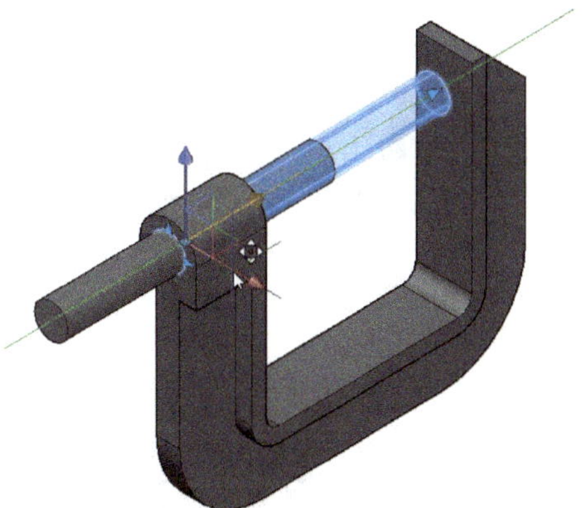

8. Type 16 and press ENTER.
9. On the ribbon, click **Home** tab > **Modeling** panel > **Primitives** drop-down > **Cylinder**.
10. Select the centerpoint of the front face of the cylinder.

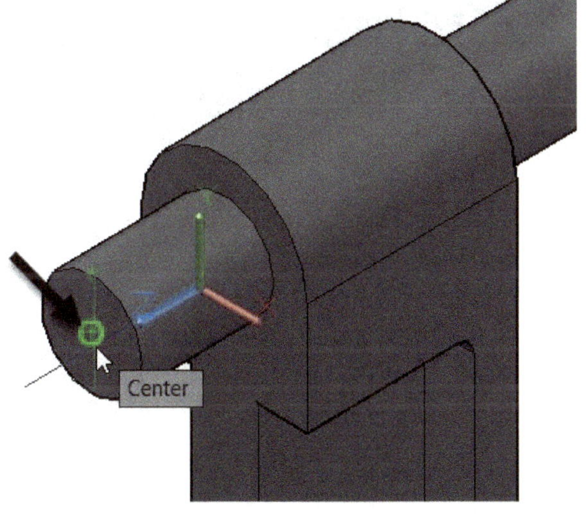

11. Type 10 and press ENTER to define the radius of the cylinder.
12. Type 22 and press ENTER to define the height of the cylinder.

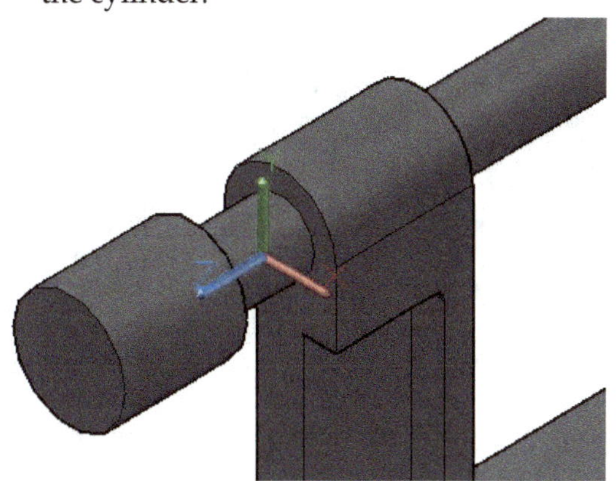

13. Change the View orientation to **NW Isometric**.

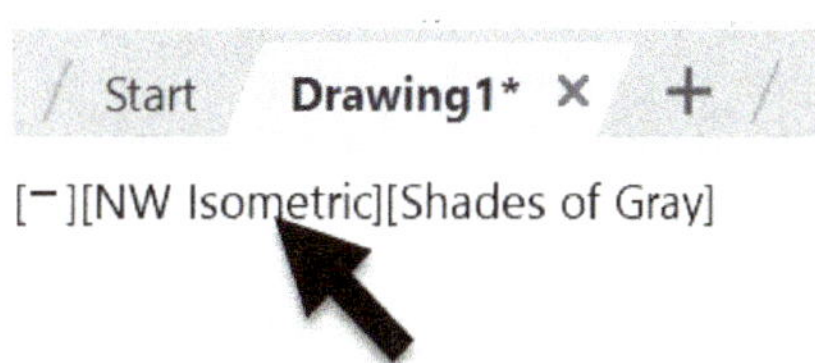

14. On the ribbon, click **Home** tab > **Modeling** panel > **Primitives** drop-down > **Cylinder**.
15. Select the centerpoint of the end face of the cylinder.

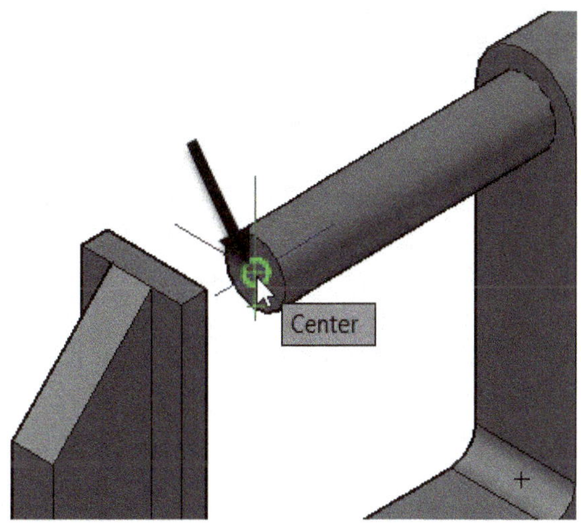

16. Type 3 and press ENTER to define the radius of the cylinder.
17. Type -12 and press ENTER to define the height of the cylinder.

18. Change the View orientation to **SE Isometric**.
19. On the ribbon, click the **Solid** tab > **Solid Editing** panel > **Fillet Edge** drop-down > **Chamfer Edge**.
20. Select the circular edge of the cylinder.

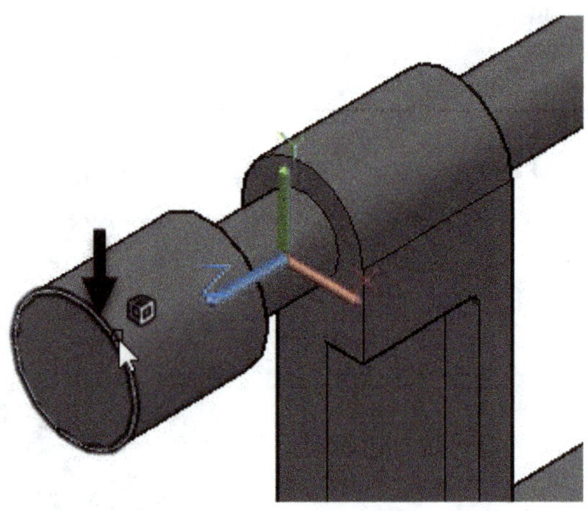

21. Select the **Distance** option from the command line.
22. Type **2** in the command line and press ENTER. Distance 1 is defined.
23. Type **2** in the command line and press ENTER. Distance 2 is defined.
24. Press ENTER twice to create the chamfer.

25. On the **Home** tab of the ribbon, click **Coordinates > Z-Axis Vector**.

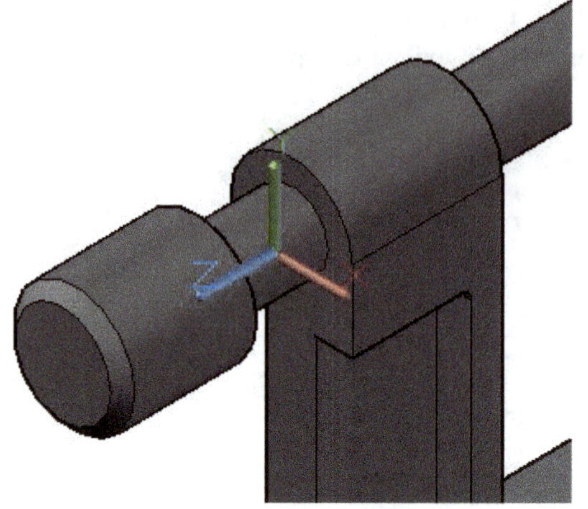

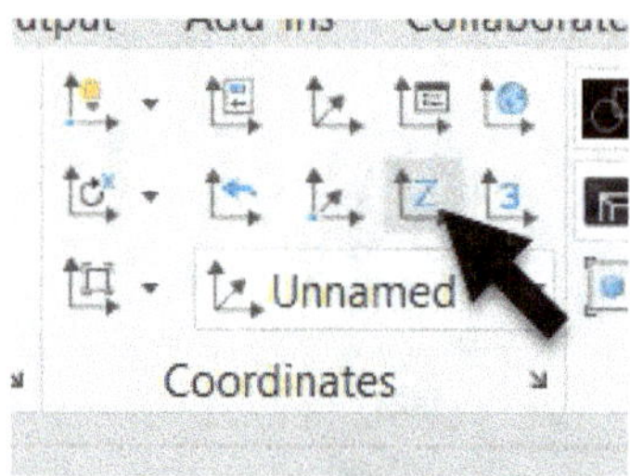

26. Select the quadrant point of the circular edge, as shown.

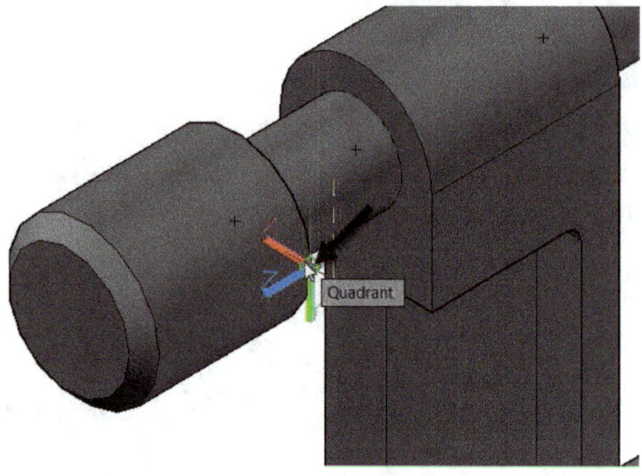

27. Move the pointer backward and click. The Z-axis of the UCS is defined.

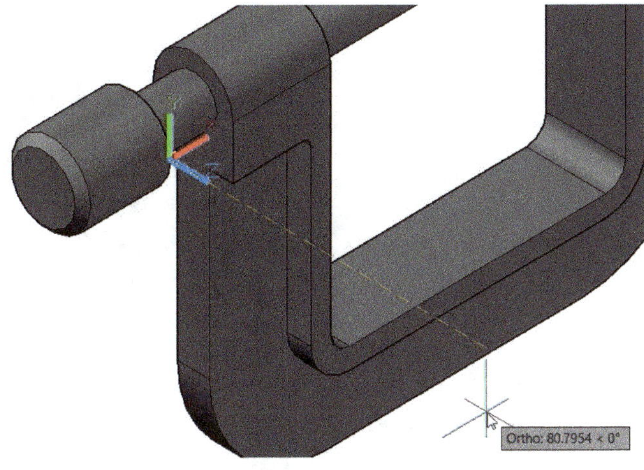

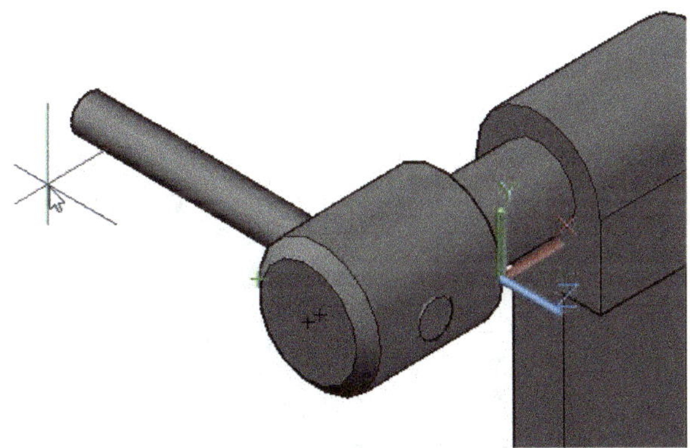

28. On the ribbon, click **Home** tab > **Modeling** panel > **Primitives** drop-down > **Cylinder**.
29. Type -11,0 and press ENTER to define the centerpoint of the cylinder.
30. Select the **Diameter** option from the command line.
31. Type 5.5 in the command line and press ENTER.
32. Move the pointer toward the left and click outside the model.

33. On the ribbon, click **Home** tab > **Solid Editing** panel > **Solid, Subtract**.
34. Select the large cylinder and press ENTER.
35. Select the small cylinder and press ENTER.

36. On the ribbon, click **Home** tab > **Solid Editing** panel > **Solid, Union**.
37. Select the three cylinders and press ENTER.

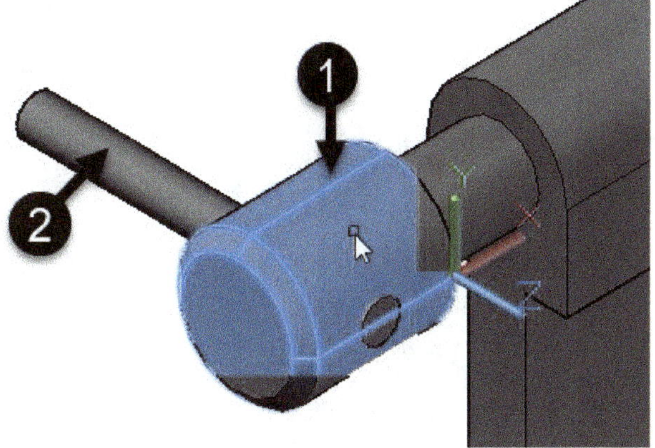

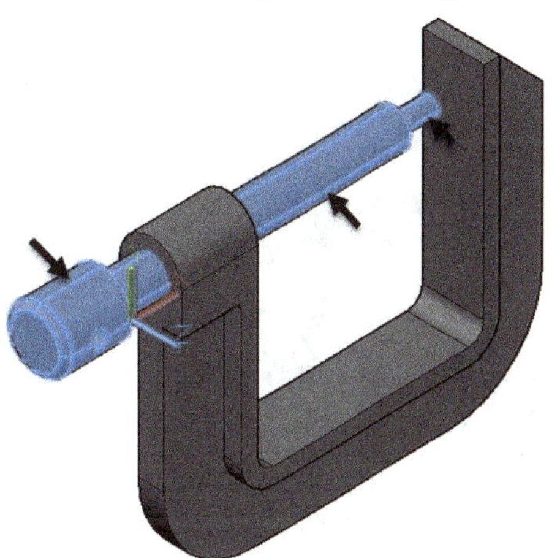

Creating the Spindle Cap

1. Change the View orientation to NW Isometric.
2. On the **Home** tab of the ribbon, click **Coordinates > Z-Axis Vector**.

3. Select the center point of the circular edge, as shown.

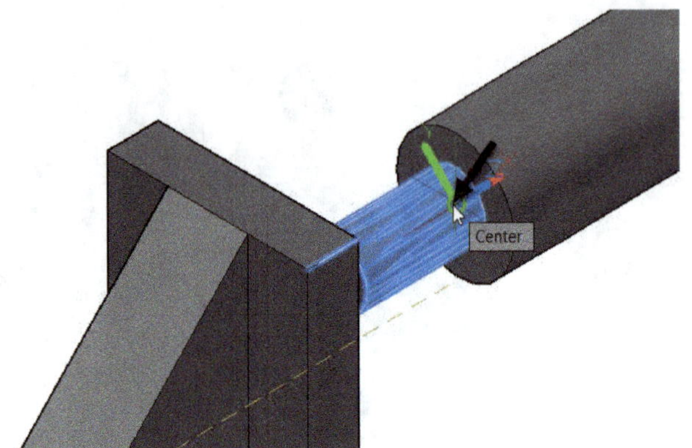

4. Move the pointer toward the left and click. The Z-axis of the UCS is defined.

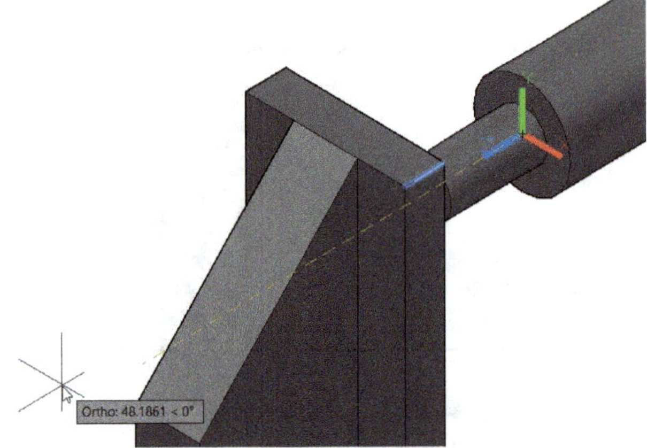

5. On the ribbon, click **Home** tab > **Modeling** panel > **Primitives** drop-down > **Cylinder**.
6. Select the centerpoint of the circular edge, as shown.

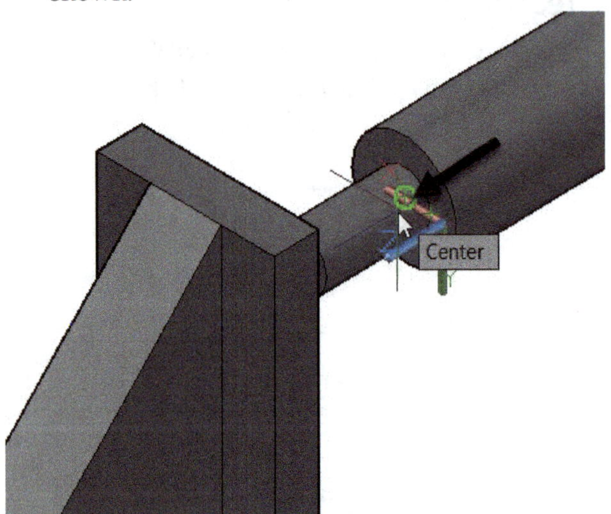

7. Select the **Diameter** option from the command line.
8. Type 11 and press ENTER to define the radius of the cylinder.

9. Type 10 and press ENTER.

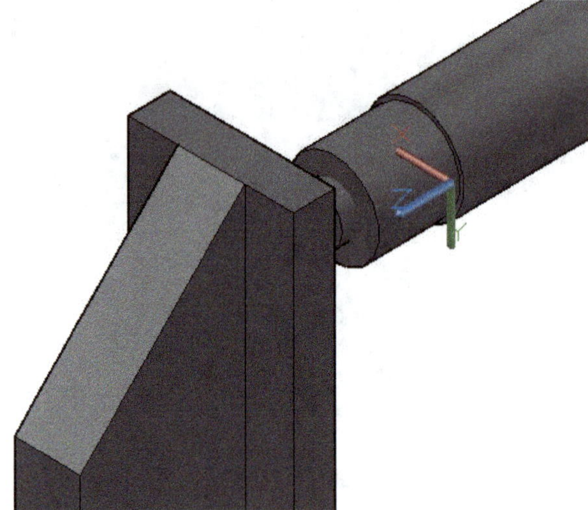

10. On the **Solid** tab of the ribbon, click **Solid Editing** panel > **Taper Faces**.

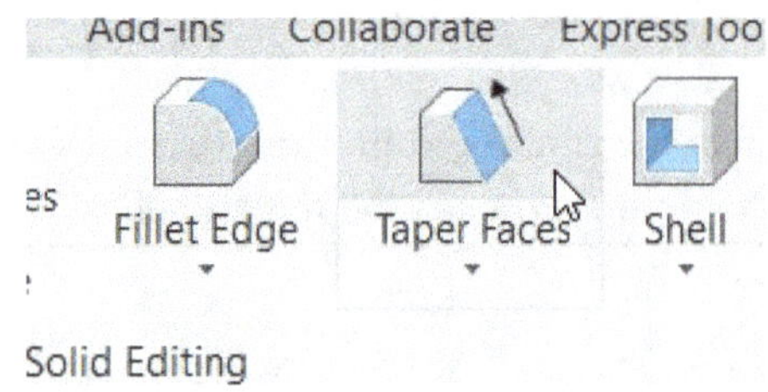

11. Select the cylindrical face, as shown.

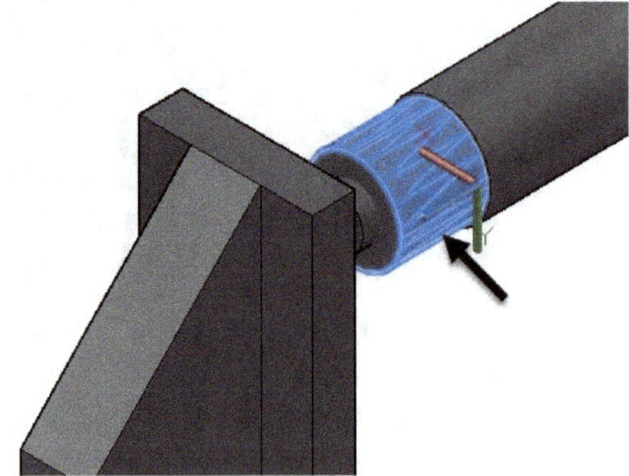

12. Press ENTER.
13. Select the centerpoint of the circular edge, as shown.

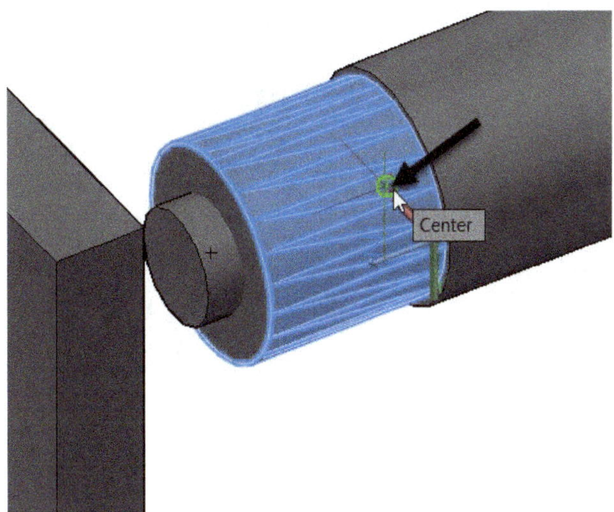

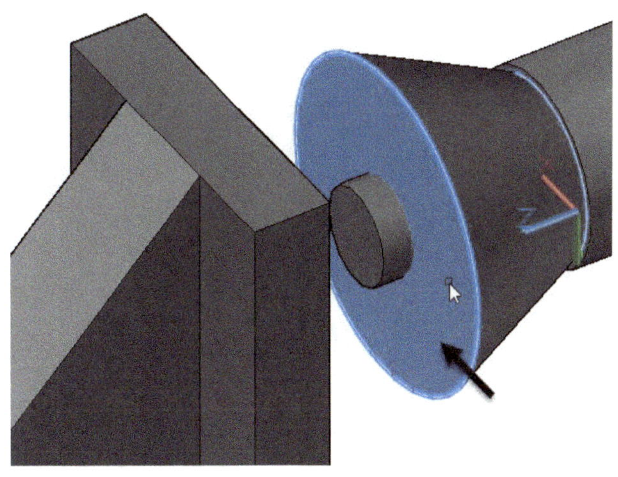

14. Move the pointer in the Z direction of the UCS, and then click to specify the axis.

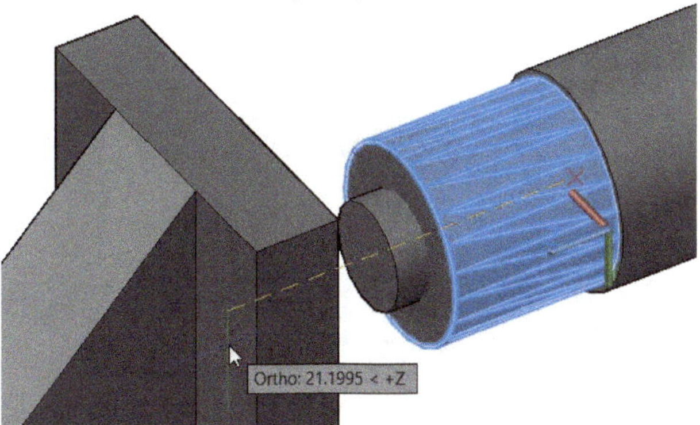

15. Type -24.228 and press ENTER to specify the taper angle.

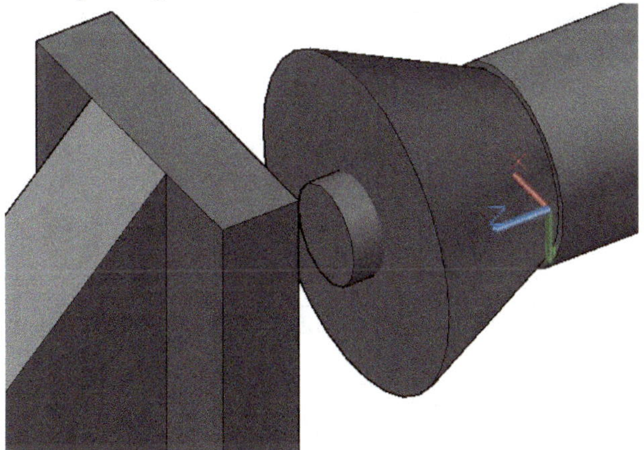

16. Select the **Extrude** option from the command line.
17. Select the end face of the spindle cap.

18. Press ENTER
19. Type 2.5 and press ENTER.
20. Press ENTER.

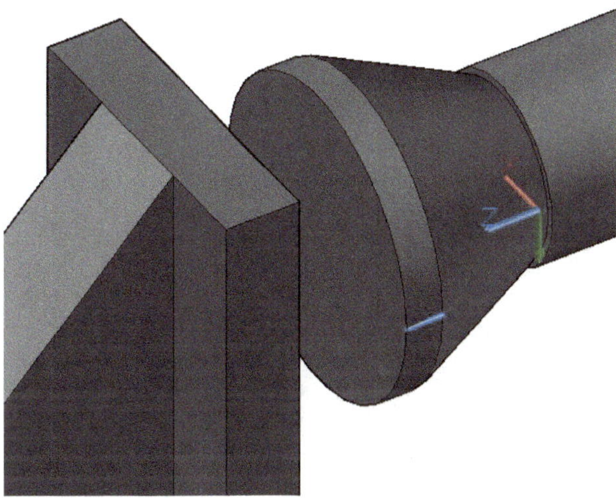

21. Press ESC.
22. Deactivate the **Dynamic Input** icon on the status bar.
23. On the ribbon, click **Home** tab > **Modeling** panel > **Primitives** drop-down > **Cylinder**.
24. Select the centerpoint of the circular edge, as shown.

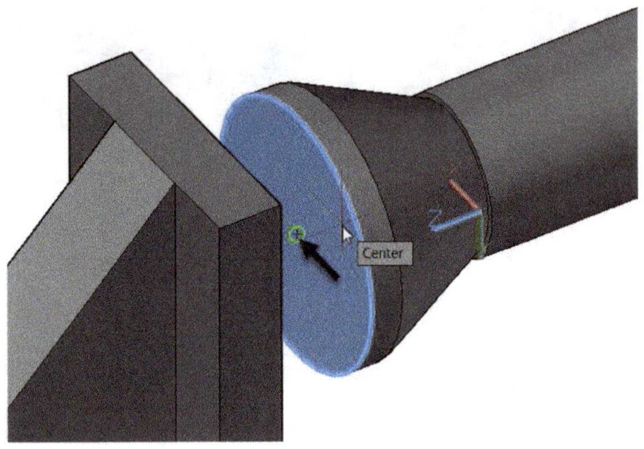

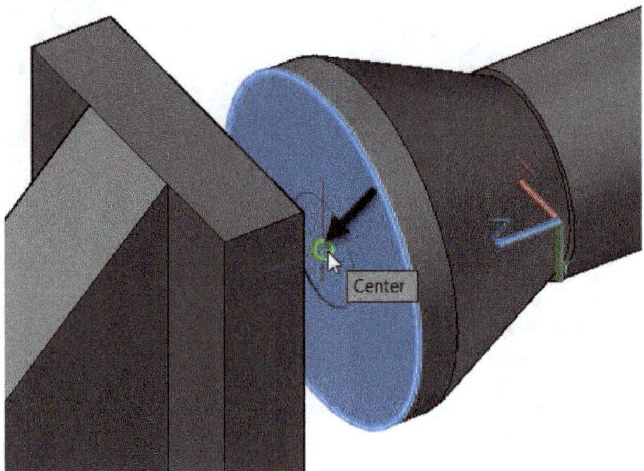

25. Select the **Diameter** option from the command line.
26. Type 6.5 in the command line and press ENTER.
27. Type -12.5 in the command line and press ENTER.

30. Type 7 in the command line and press ENTER.
31. Type -2.5 in the command line and press ENTER.

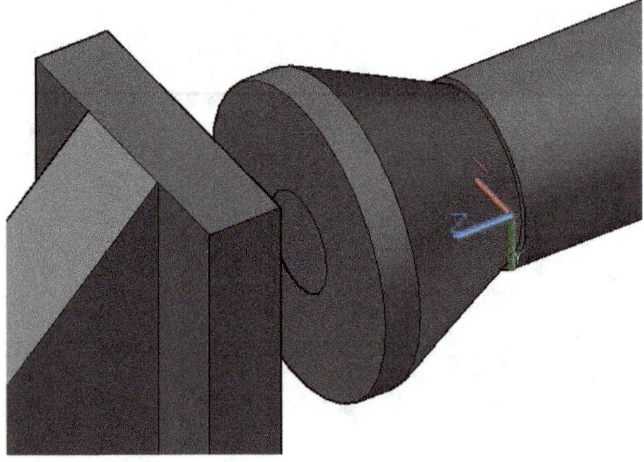

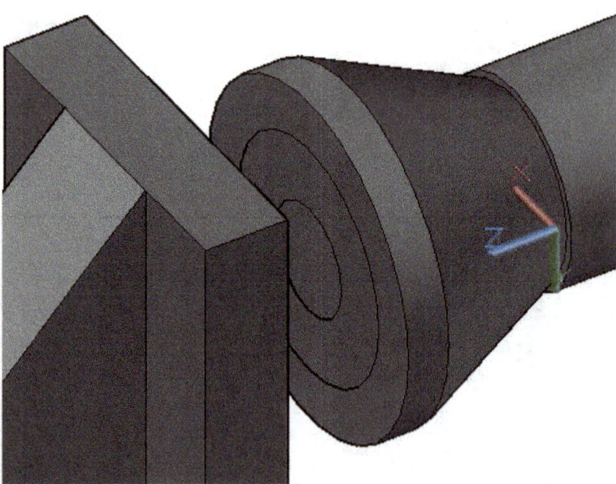

28. On the ribbon, click **Home** tab > **Modeling** panel > **Primitives** drop-down > **Cylinder**.
29. Select the centerpoint of the circular edge, as shown.

32. On the ribbon, click **Home** tab > **Solid Editing** panel > **Solid, Subtract**.
33. Select the tapered cylinder and press ENTER.

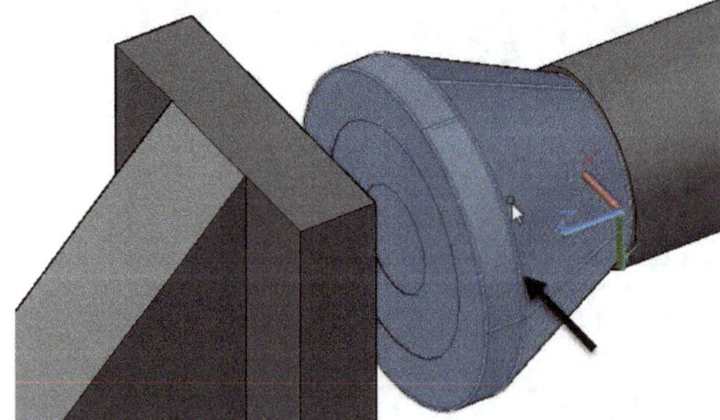

34. Select the two cylinders inside the tapered cylinder, as shown.

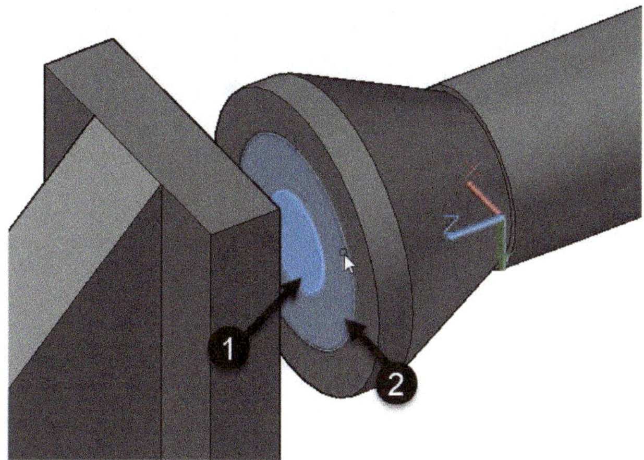

35. Press ENTER.

Creating the Handle

1. Change the View orientation to **SE Isometric**.
2. On the ribbon, click **Home** tab > **Coordinates** panel > **UCS, Previous**. The UCS is moved to its previous location.

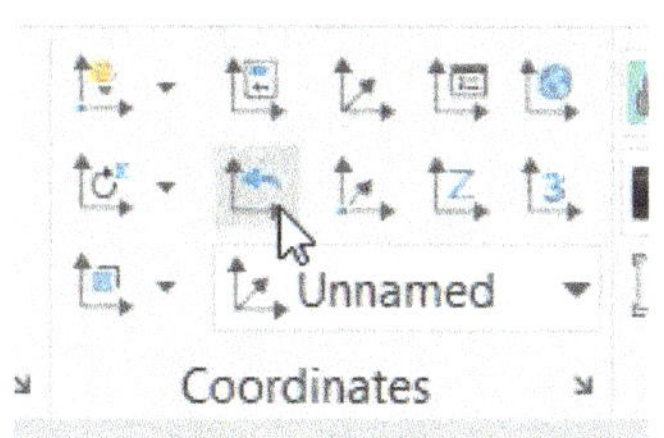

3. On the ribbon, click **Home** tab > **Modeling** panel > **Primitives** drop-down > **Cylinder**.
4. Type -11,0 and press ENTER to define the centerpoint of the cylinder.
5. Select the **Diameter** option from the command line.

6. Type 5 in the command line and press ENTER.
7. Type 96 and press ENTER.

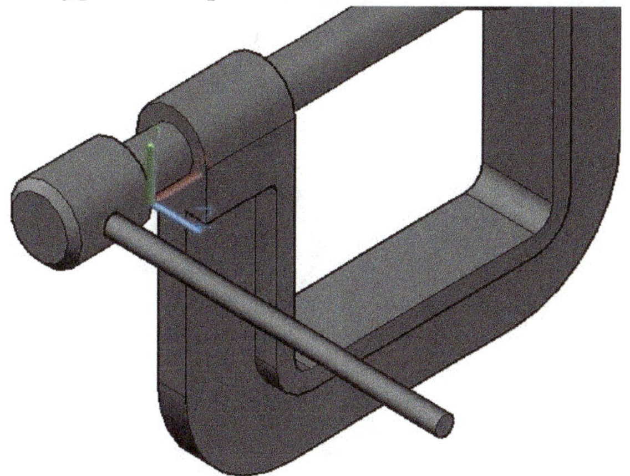

8. Select the newly created cylinder.
9. Click on the X-axis of the move gizmo and move toward left.

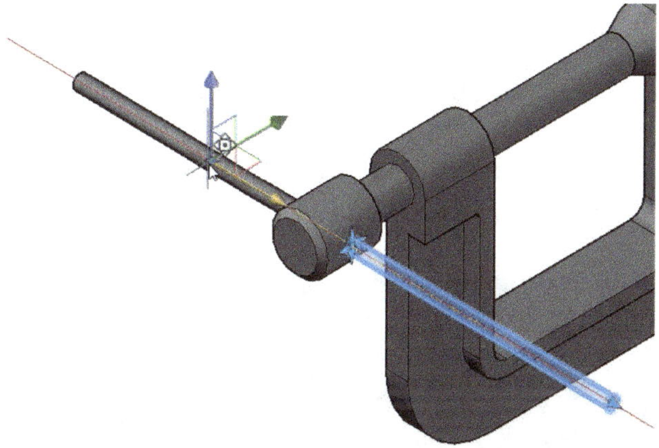

10. Type 58 and press ENTER.

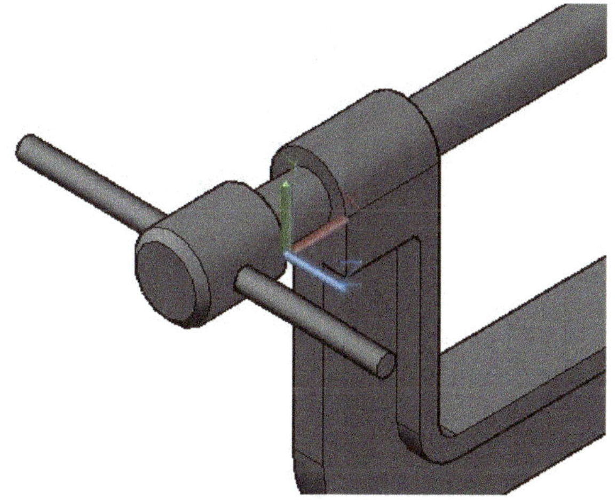

Creating the Handle Cap

1. On the ribbon, click **Home** tab > **Modeling** panel > **Primitives** drop-down > **Cylinder**.
2. Select the centerpoint of the circular edge, as shown.

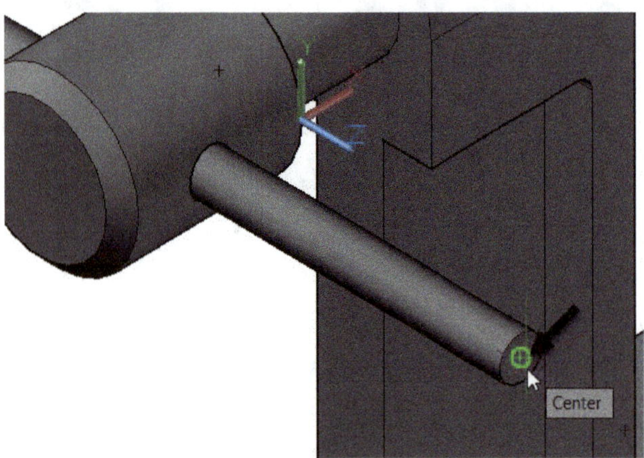

3. Select the **Diameter** option from the command line.
4. Type 8 in the command line and press ENTER.
5. Type 10 and press ENTER.

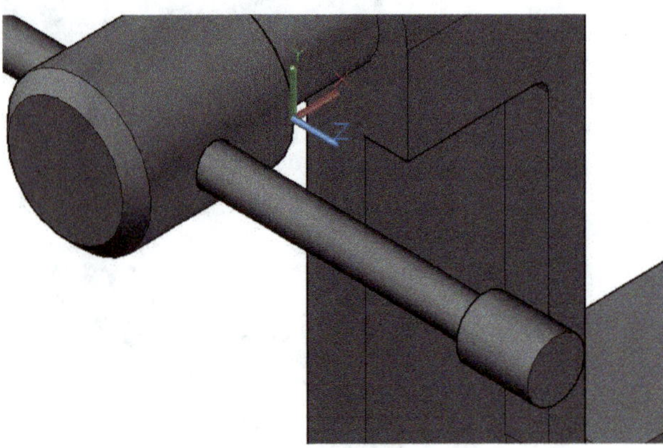

6. On the ribbon, click **Home** tab > **Modeling** panel > **Primitives** drop-down > **Cylinder**.
7. Select the centerpoint of the circular edge, as shown.

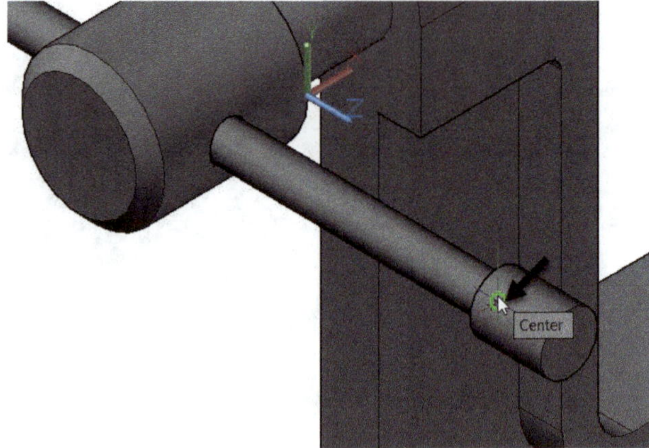

8. Select the **Diameter** option from the command line.
9. Type 5 in the command line and press ENTER.
10. Type 5 and press ENTER.
11. Change the **Visual Style** to **2D Wireframe**.
12. On the ribbon, click **Home** tab > **Solid Editing** panel > **Solid, Subtract**.
13. Select the large cylinder, as shown.

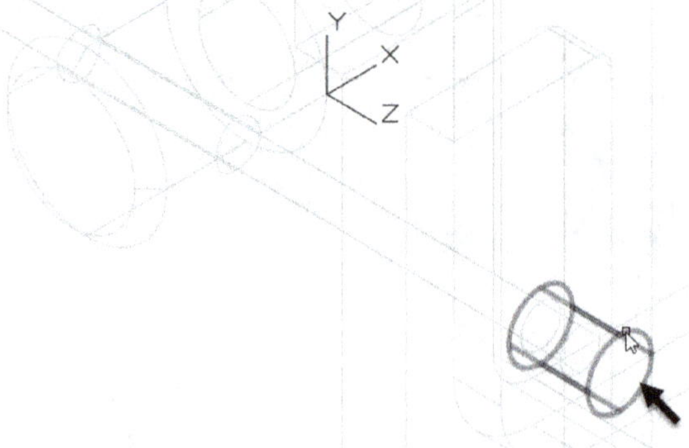

14. Press ENTER.
15. Select the small cylinder, as shown.

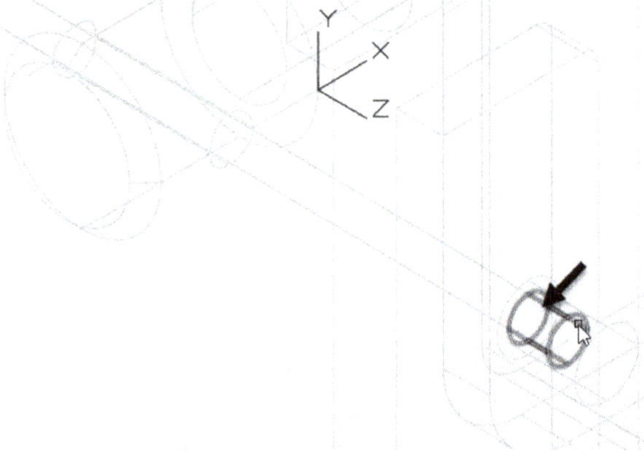

16. Press ENTER.
17. Change the **Visual Style** to **Shades of Gray**.
18. Select the handle cap.
19. Click on the X-axis of the Move gizmo.

20. Move along the selected axis toward left.
21. Type 5 and press ENTER.

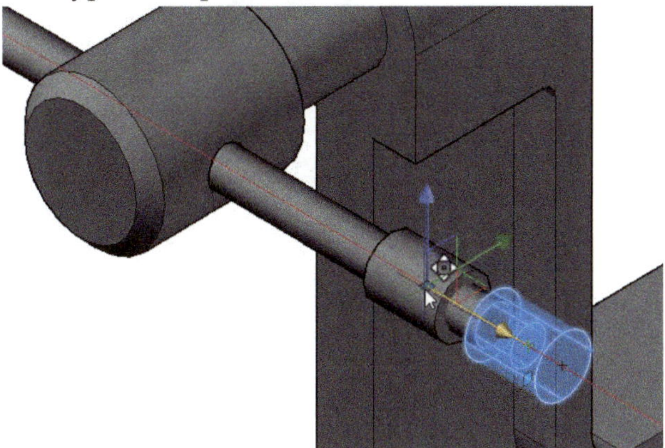

22. On the ribbon, click the **Solid** tab > **Solid Editing** panel > **Fillet Edge** drop-down > **Chamfer Edge**.
23. Select the circular edge of the cylinder.

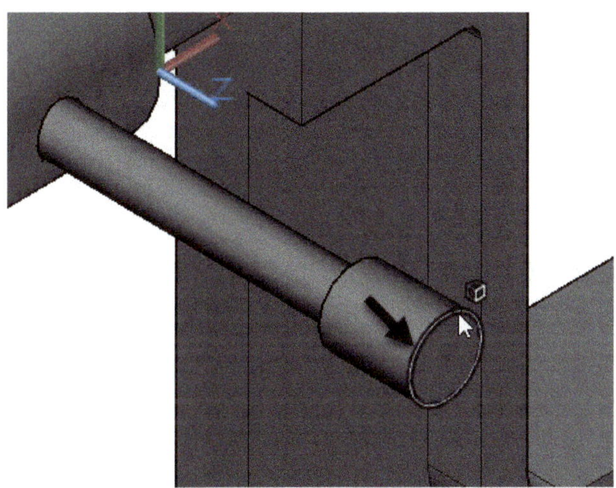

24. Select the **Distance** option from the command line.
25. Type **1** in the command line and press ENTER. Distance 1 is defined.
26. Type **1** in the command line and press ENTER. Distance 2 is defined.
27. Press ENTER twice to create the chamfer.

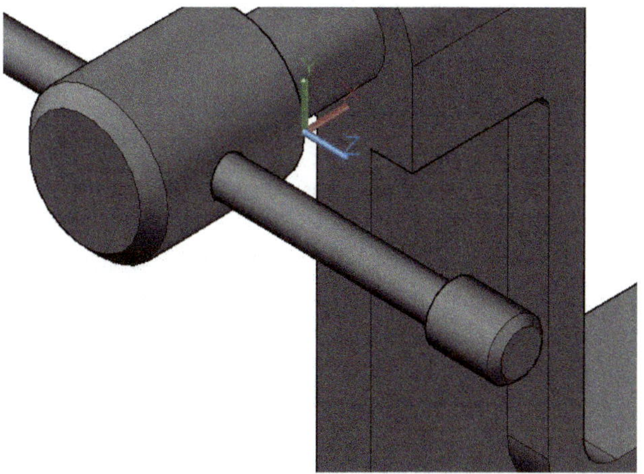

28. On the ribbon, click **Home** tab > **Coordinates** panel > **UCS, World**.

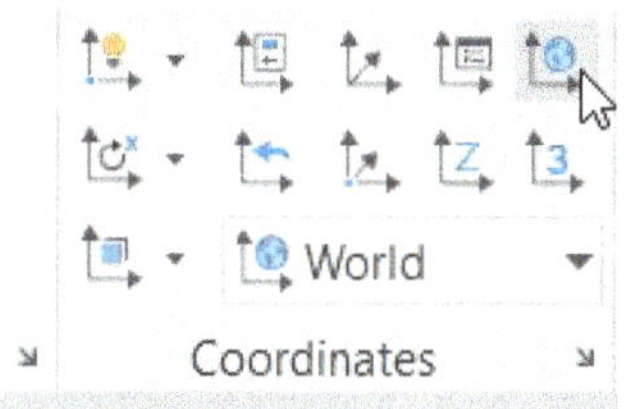

29. Select the handle cap.

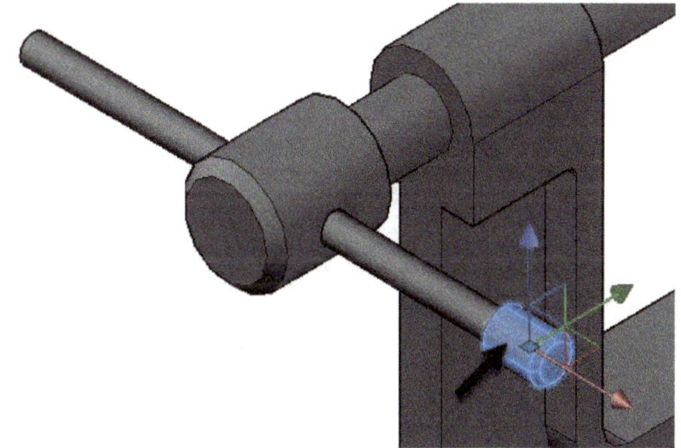

30. On the ribbon, click **Home** tab > **Modify** panel > **3D Mirror**.

31. Select the **YZ** option from the command line.
     The orientation of the mirror plane is defined
32. Press ENTER to define 0,0,0 as the location of
     the mirror plane.
33. Select **No** from the command line to keep the
     original object.

34. Save and close the drawing file.

Exercises

Exercise1

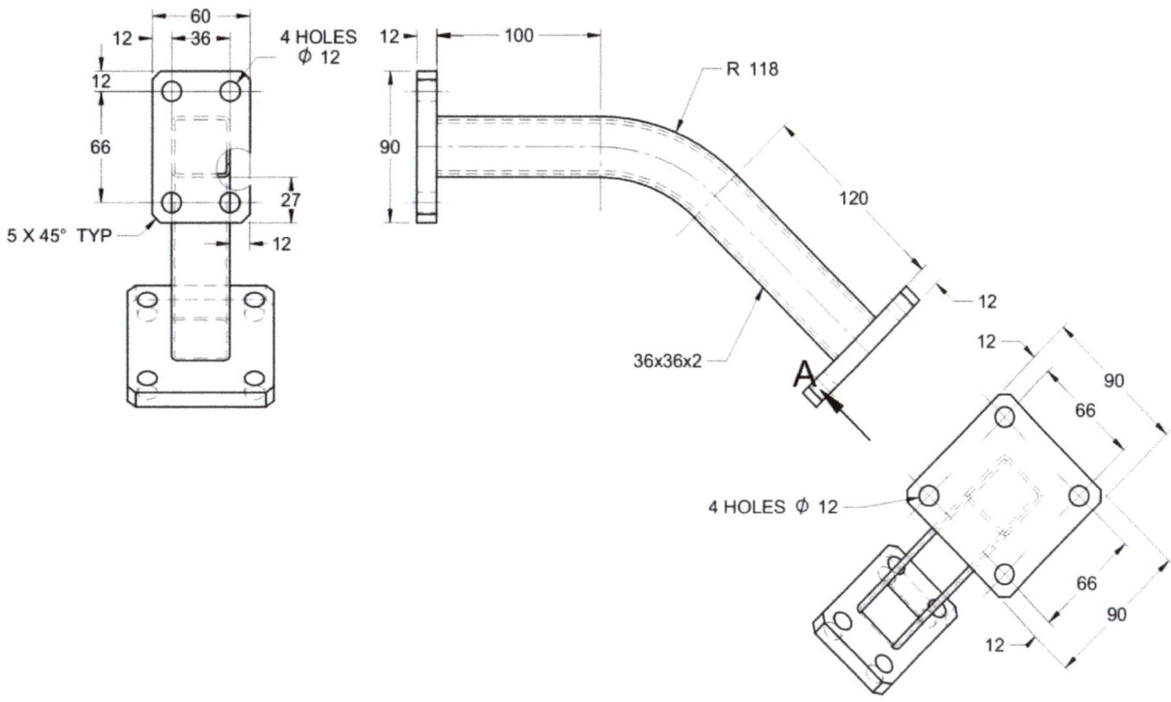

Exercise 2

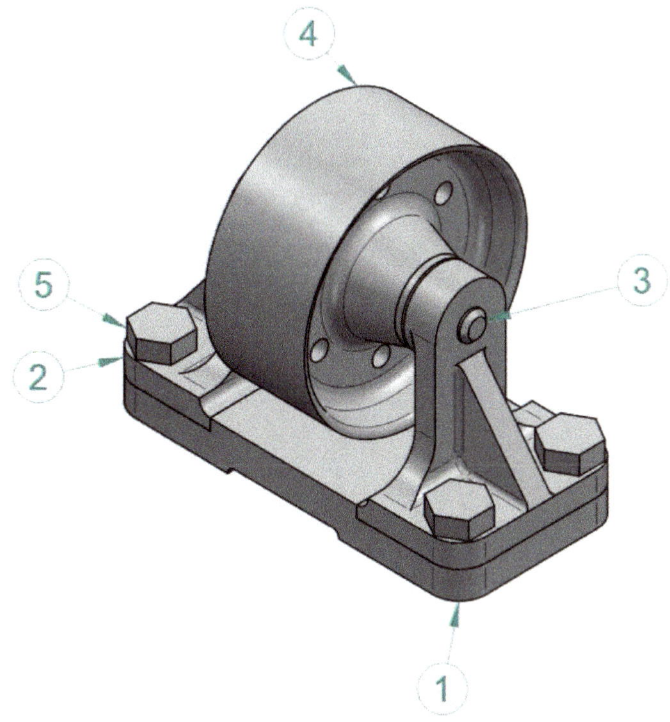

Item Number	File Name (no extension)	Quantity
1	Base	1
2	Bracket	2
3	Spindle	1
4	Roller-Bush assembly	1
5	Bolt	4

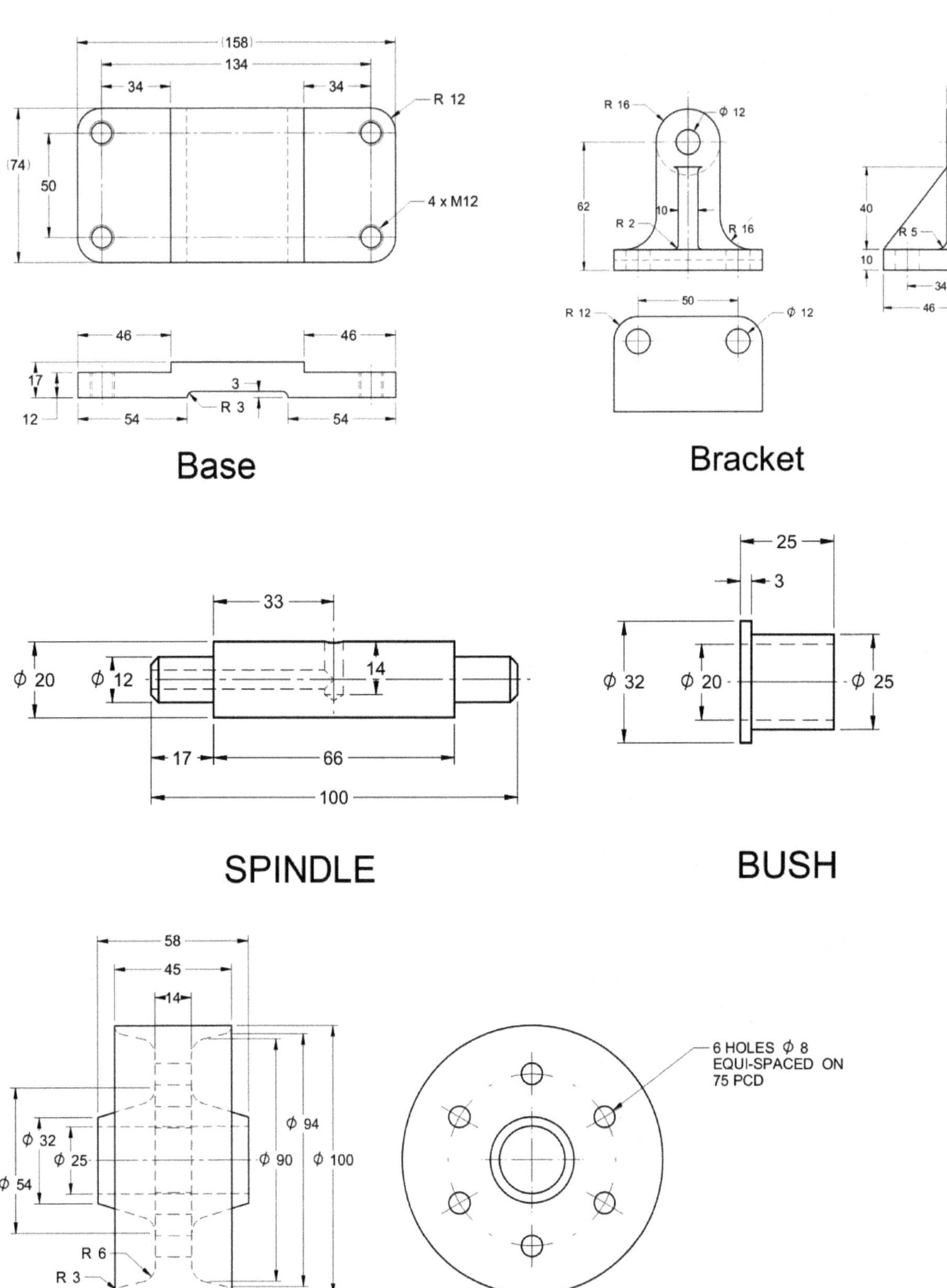

(158)
134
34
34
R 12
(74)
50
4 x M12
46
46
17
3
R 3
12
54
54
Base
R 16
Φ 12
14
62
10
R 2
R 16
40
R 5
5
10
R 5
5
R 12
50
Φ 12
34
46
Bracket
33
14
Φ 20
Φ 12
17
66
100
SPINDLE
25
3
Φ 32
Φ 20
Φ 25
BUSH
58
45
14
Φ 94
Φ 32
Φ 25
Φ 90
Φ 100
Φ 54
R 6
R 3
6 HOLES Φ 8
EQUI-SPACED ON
75 PCD
Roller

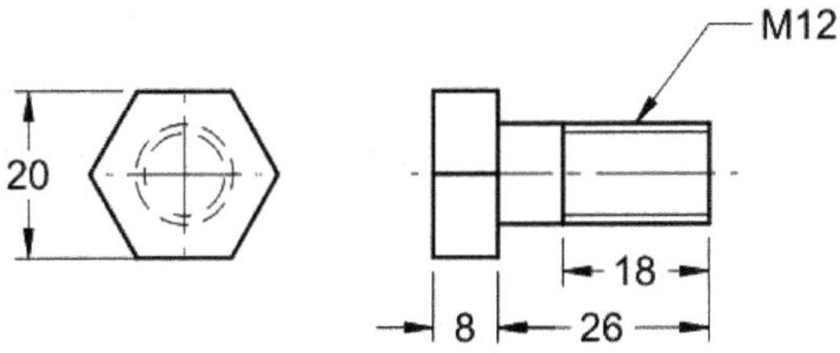

Bolt

Chapter 6: Loft Features

The **Loft** command is one of the advanced commands available in AutoCAD that allows you to create simple and complex shapes. A basic loft is created by defining two profiles and joining them together. For example, if you create a loft feature between a circle and a square, you can quickly change the solid's cross-sectional shape. This ability is what separates the loft feature from the sweep feature.

The topics covered in this chapter are:

- *Basic Lofts*
- *Loft profiles*
- *Profile geometry*
- *Surface Controls*
- *Guides*
- *Path*

Loft

This command creates a loft feature between different profiles. To create a loft, first, create two or more profiles on different planes. The planes can be parallel or perpendicular to each other. Click **Home > Modeling > Solids** drop-down > **Loft** on the ribbon. Next, select two or more cross-sections from the graphics window. Press ENTER twice to create a lofted solid.

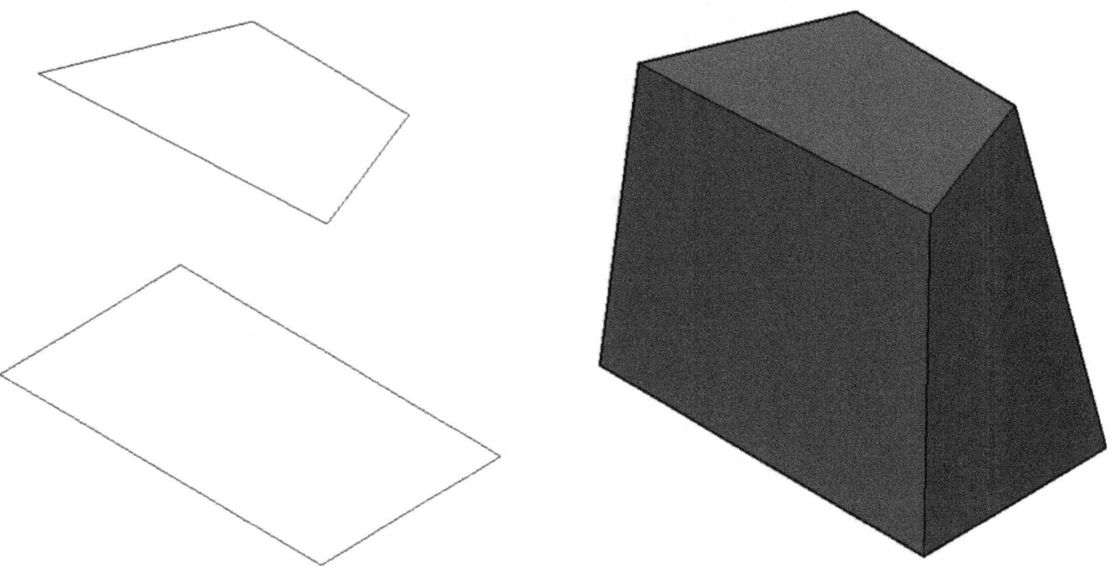

Loft Profiles

In addition to 2D sketches, you can also define loft profiles by using different element types. For instance, you can use existing model faces, surfaces, curves, and points. The only restriction is that the points can be used at the beginning or end of a loft.

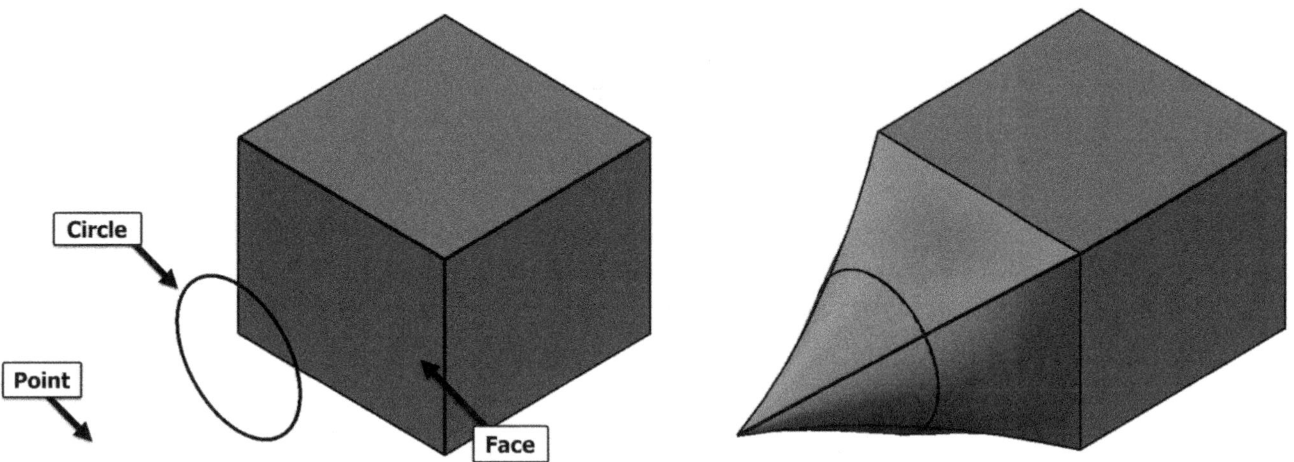

Profile Geometry

Profiles used for creating lofts should have a matching number of segments. For example, a four-sided profile will loft nicely to another four-sided profile despite the differences in the individual segments' shape. The **Loft** command generates smooth faces to join them.

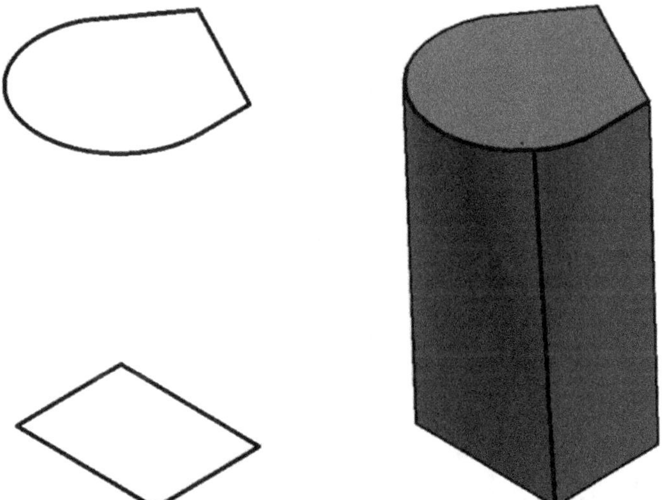

In addition to that, a five-sided profile will loft nicely to a two-sided profile.

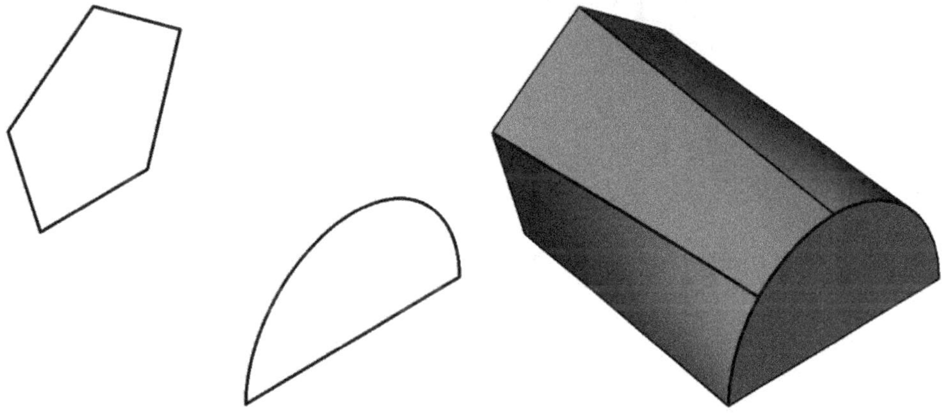

Surface Control

The shape of a loft is controlled by the profile sketches and the plane location. However, the options on the **Loft Settings** dialog can control the side faces' behavior. If you would like to change the side faces' appearance, you can specify the settings at the beginning of the loft, or at the end of the lofts, or both.

Select the cross-sections from the graphics window and press ENTER. Next, select the **Settings** option from the command line; the **Loft Settings** dialog appears. In this dialog, select the **Smooth Fit** option; it creates a smooth connection between the cross-sections. If you select the **Ruled** option, the lofted solid or surface has sharp edges.

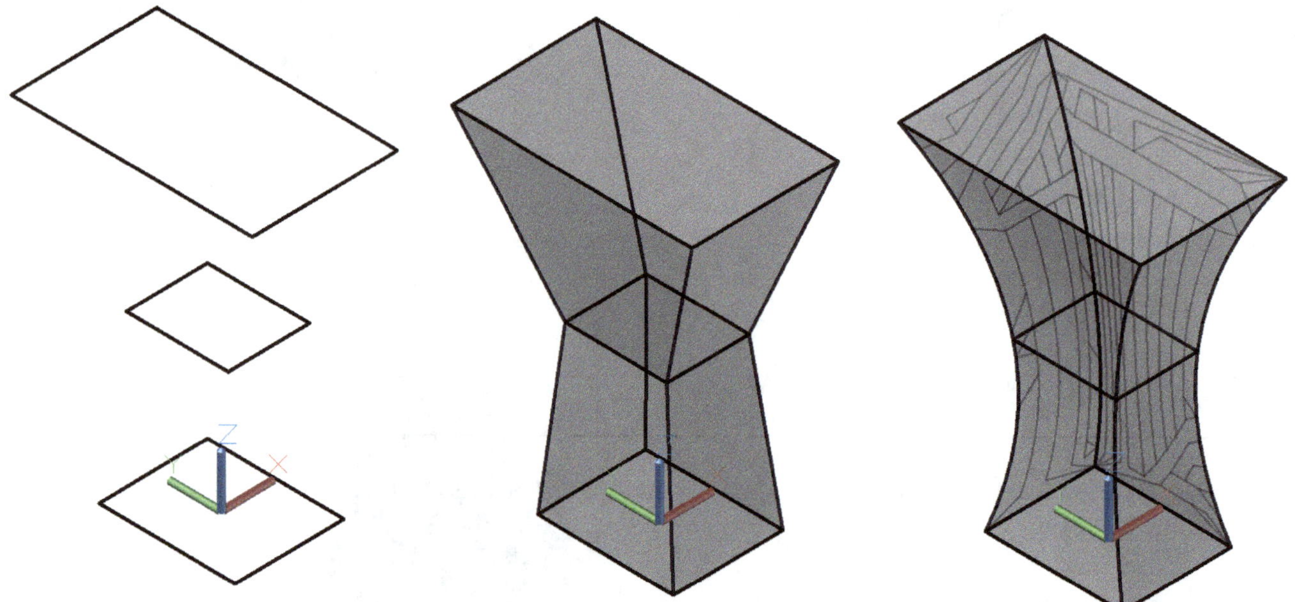

The **Normal to** option creates a solid or surface normal to the cross-section. You can select the loft solid or surface to be normal to **All cross sections**, or **Start Cross Section** or **End Cross Section** or **Start and End Cross Sections**.

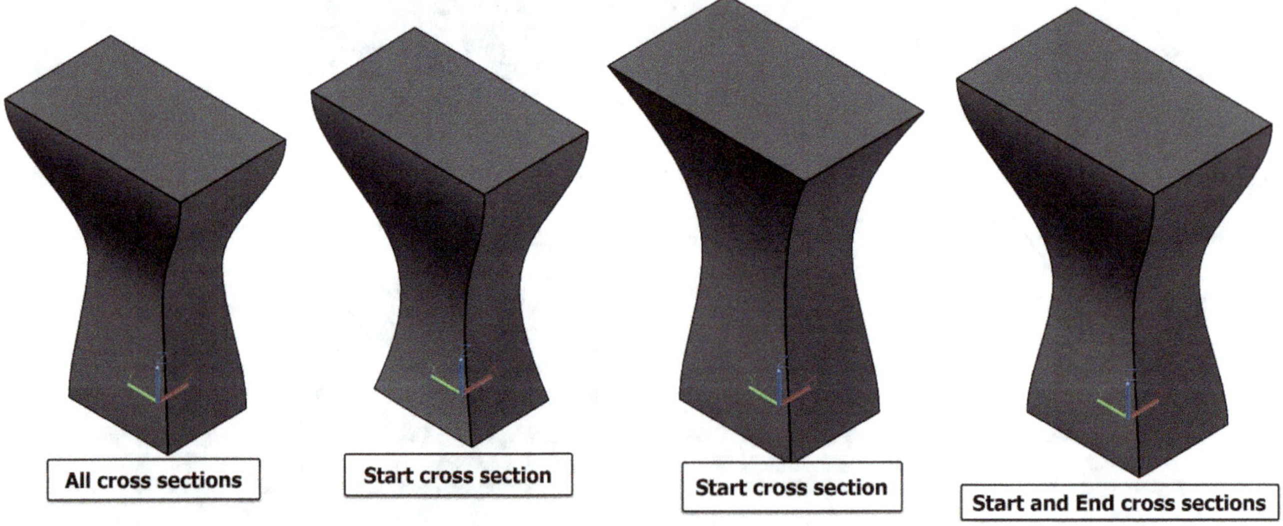

The **Draft angles** option defines the draft angle and magnitude at start and end cross-sections. The draft angle is the beginning direction of the loft surface. If you set the draft angle to 90 degrees, the loft surface starts vertically from the cross-section, and the 0-draft angle starts loft surface horizontally. The Magnitude is the relative distance up to which the loft surface will follow the draft angle before it bends.

The **Close surface or solid** option connects the start and end section of the lofted object.

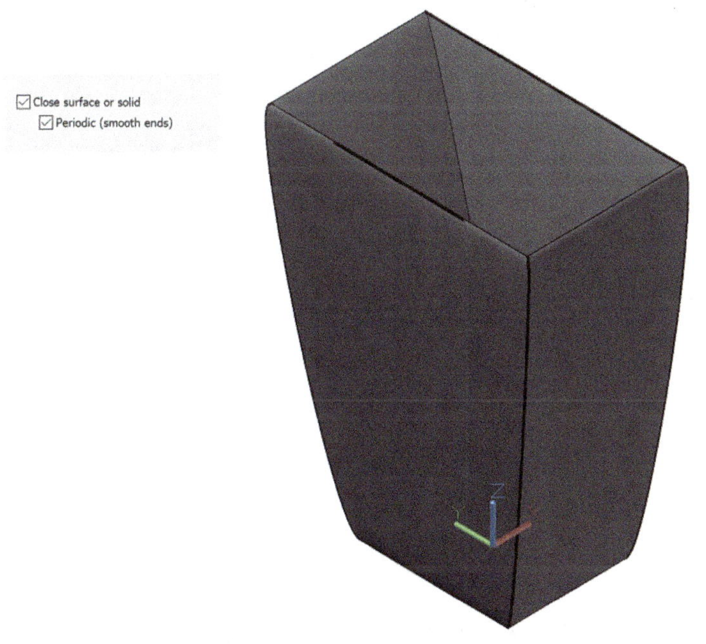

Guide

Similar to the **Surface Control** options, guides allow you to control a loft's behavior between profiles. You can create curves by using 2D or 3D sketches. For example, create two cross-sections, as shown. Next, click Home > Modify > 3D Move on the ribbon, and then select the outer ellipse.

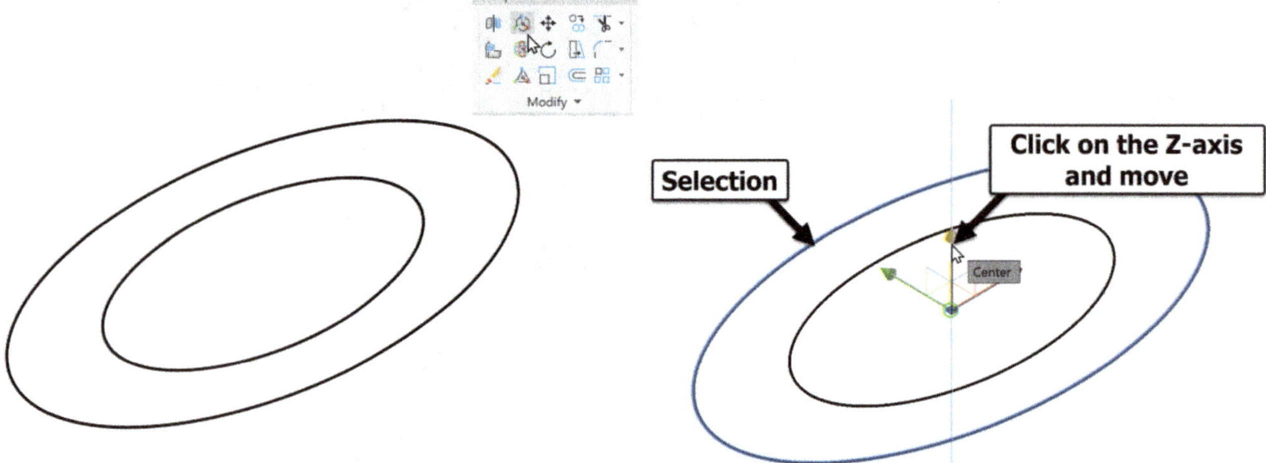

Click on the Z -axis of the Move gizmo, move the pointer upward up to the required distance, and then click.

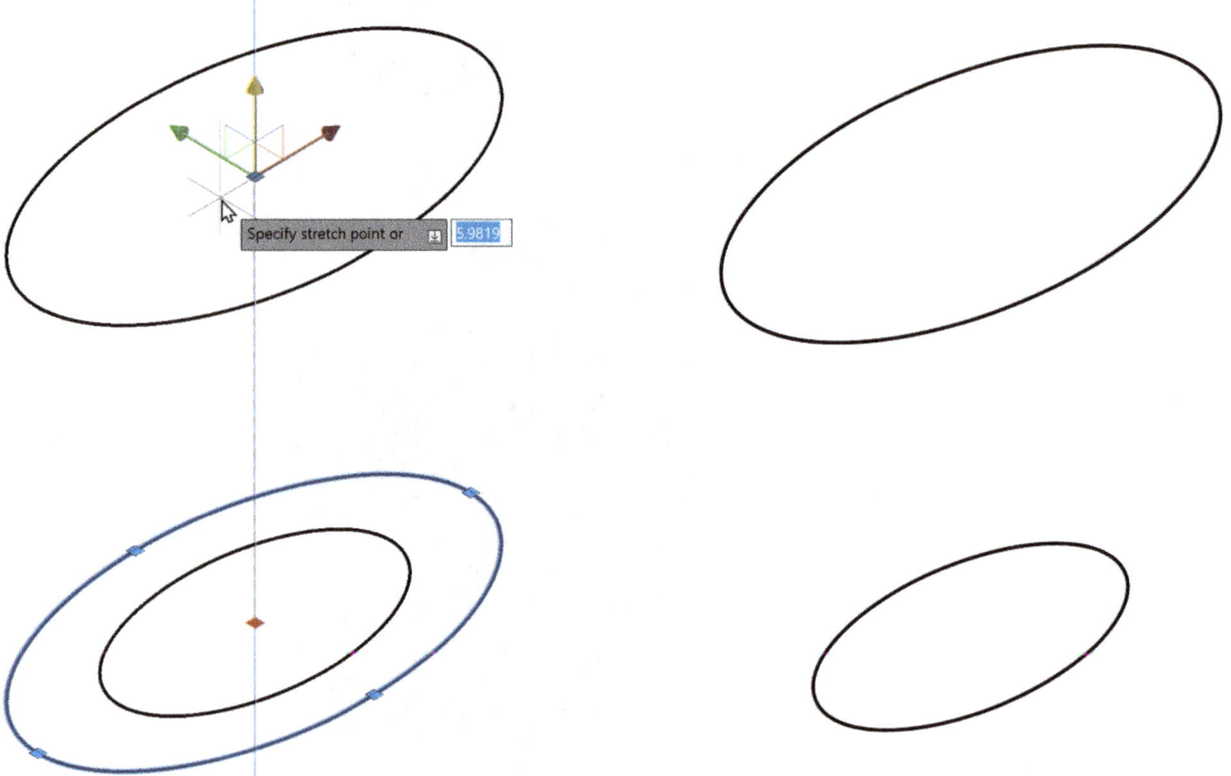

Next, you need to create a UCS on the quadrant point of the ellipse. To do this, click **Home > Coordinates > Z-Axis Vector**. Select the quadrant point of the small ellipse to define the origin point of the UCS. Make sure that the **Ortho Mode** icon is turned ON on the status bar. Move the pointer toward the back of the model and click. Next, click **Home > Draw > Spline** and select the origin point of the UCS. Next, specify the two more points of the spline, as shown. Press ENTER to create the spline. Likewise, create another spline, as shown.

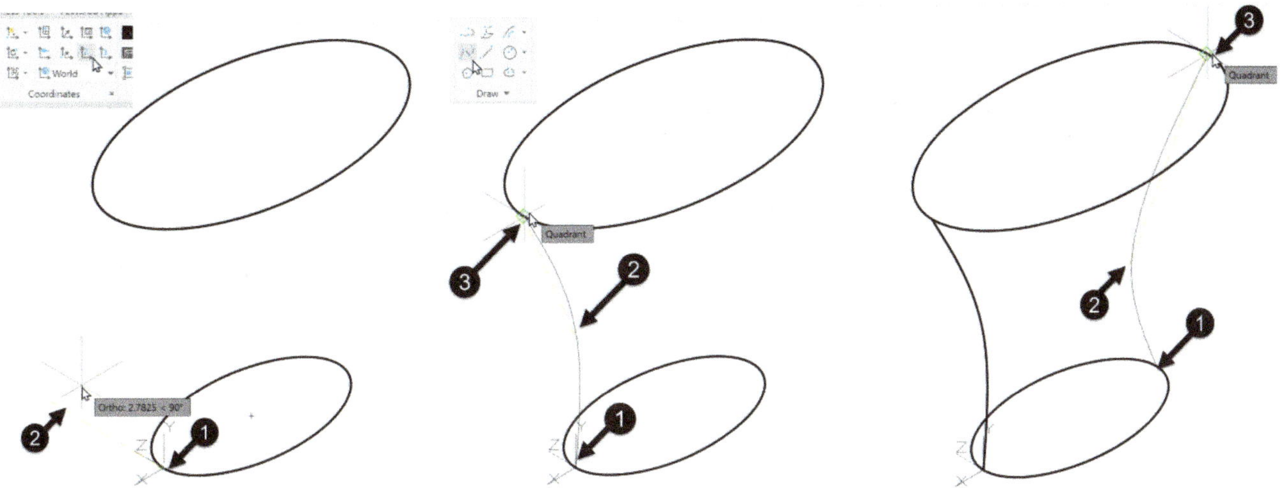

Now, activate the **Loft** command and select the cross-section. Press and select the **Guides** option from the command line. Next, select the guide curves; you will see the preview updates.

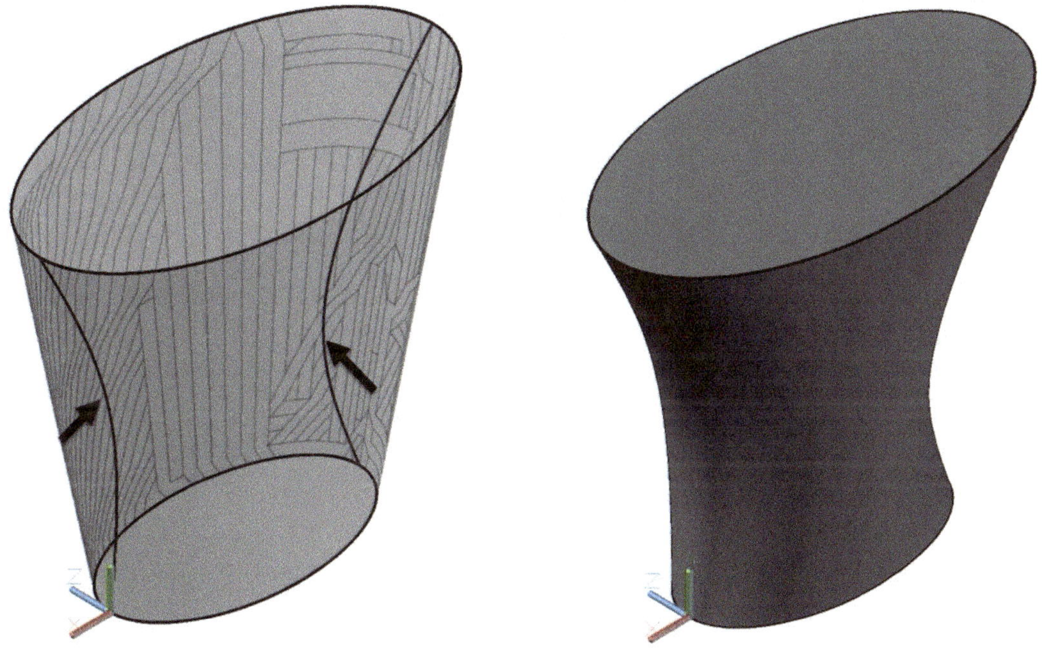

Path

The **Path** option helps you create a loft feature with the help of path passing through the selected profiles. First, create a path, as shown. Next, activate the **Loft** command and select the profiles. Next, press ENTER and select the Path option from the command line. Select the path to create a loft feature passing through it.

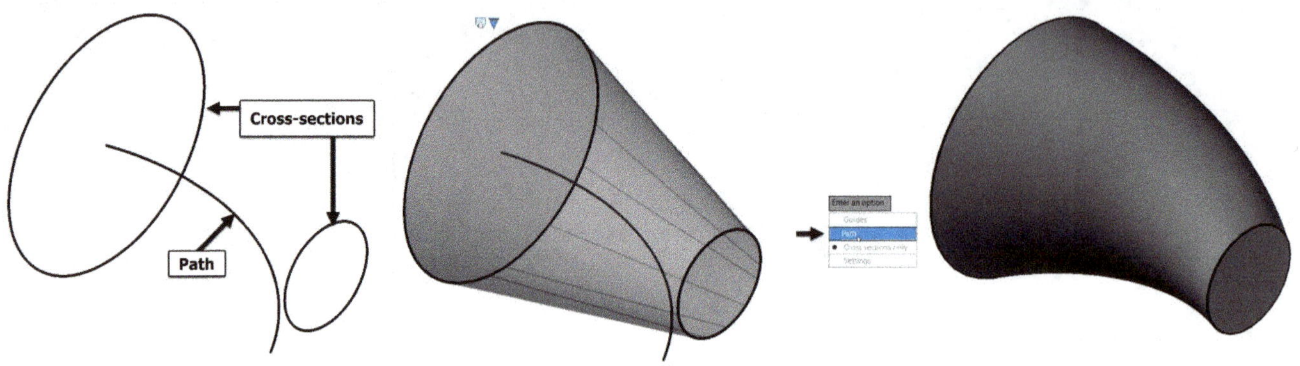

Tutorial 1

In this example, you create the part shown below.

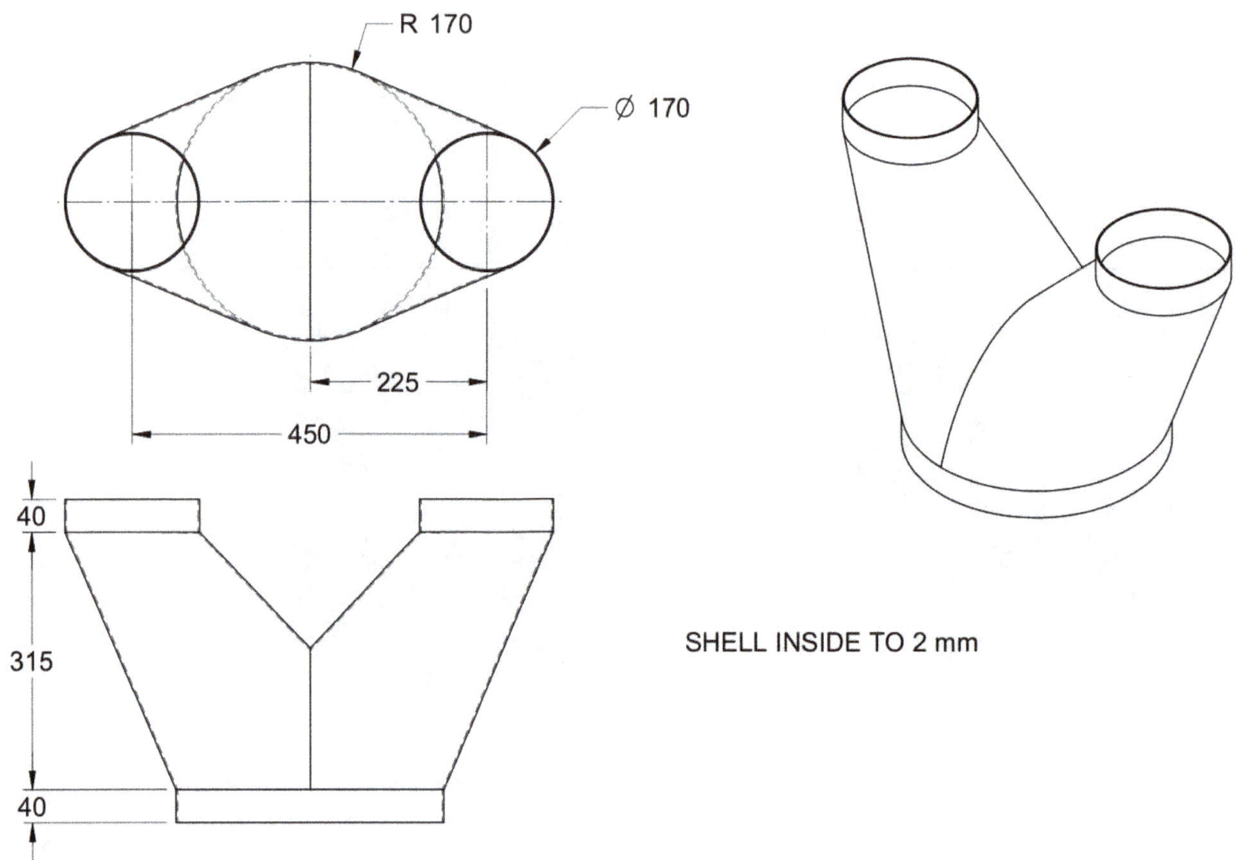

Creating a New File

1. Click the **New** icon on the Quick Access Toolbar.
2. Select the **acadiso3D** template from the **Select template** dialog.
3. Click the **Open** button.
4. Deactivate the **GRIDMODE** icon on the status bar.

Creating a Loft Feature

1. On the ribbon, click **Home** tab > **Modeling** panel > **Primitives** drop-down > **Cylinder**.
2. Type 0, 0 in the command line and press ENTER. The centerpoint of the cylinder is defined.
3. Type 170 in the command line and press ENTER.
4. Move the pointer upward.
5. Type 40 and press ENTER to create the cylinder.

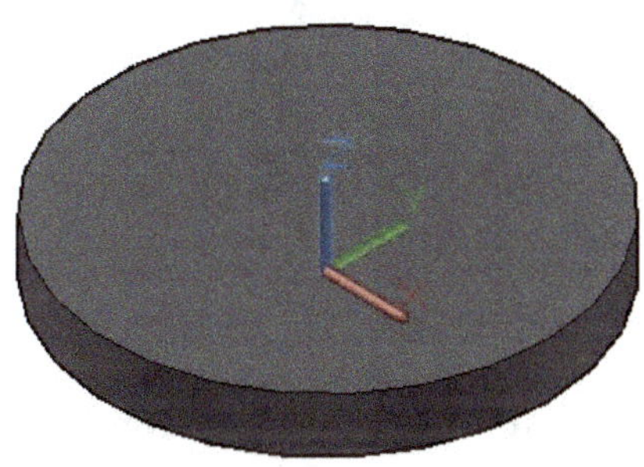

6. On the ribbon, click **Home** tab > **Coordinates** panel > **Origin**.
7. Type 0,0,315 in the command line and press ENTER. The UCS is moved up to 315 distance in the Z-direction.

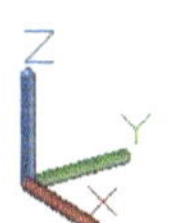

8. On the ribbon, click **Home** tab > **Draw** panel > **Circles** drop-down > **Circle, Diameter**.
9. Type 225,0 in the command line and press ENTER.
10. Type 170 in the command line and press ENTER. The diameter of the circle is specified.

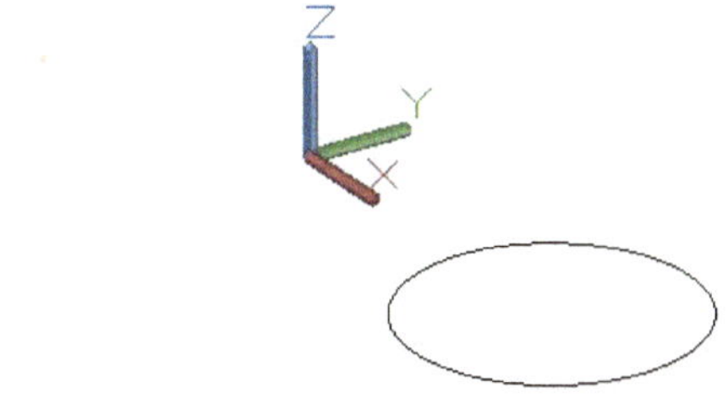

11. On the ribbon, click **Home** tab > **Coordinates** panel > **View** drop-down > **Face**.

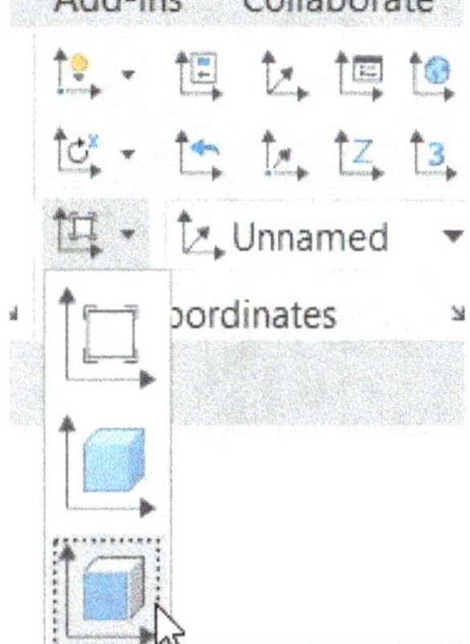

12. Click on the top face of the cylinder.

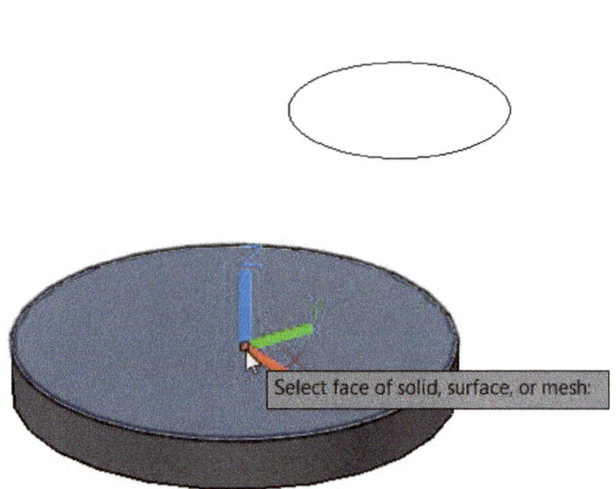

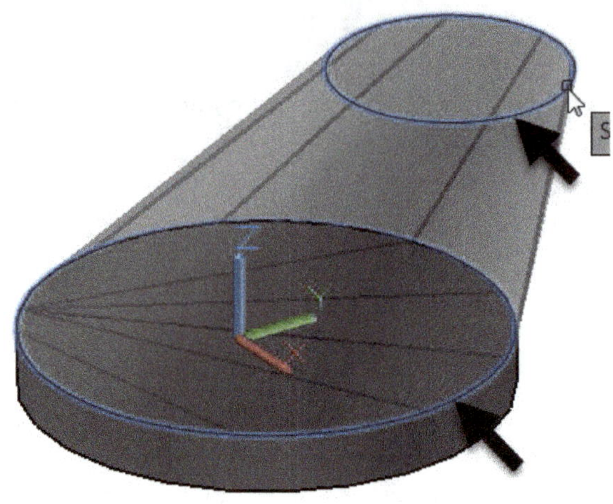

13. Press ENTER to accept the selection. The UCS is placed on the selected face.
14. On the ribbon, click **Home** tab > **Draw** panel > **Circles** drop-down > **Circle, Diameter**.
15. Place the pointe on the circular edge of the cylinder; the center point of the cylinder is highlighted.
16. Select the center point of the cylinder.

20. Press ENTER twice to create the *Loft* feature.

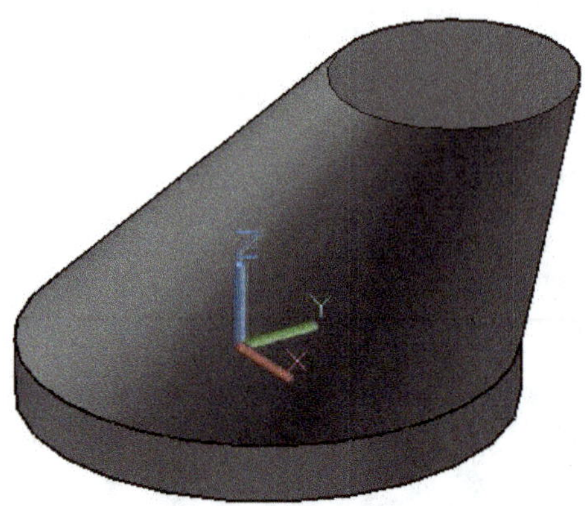

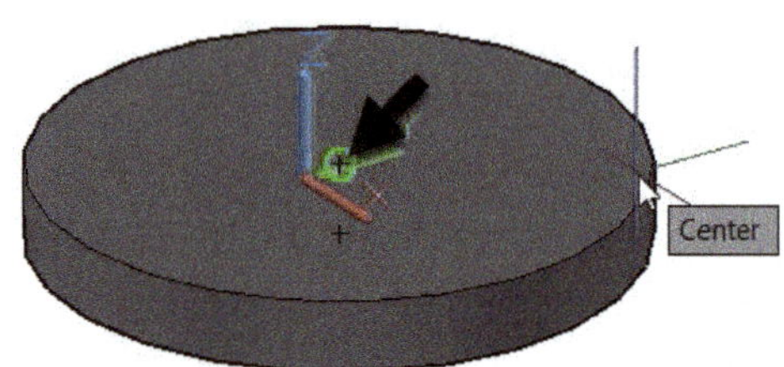

17. Type 340 in the command line and press ENTER.
18. On the ribbon, click the **Home** tab > **Modeling** panel > **Solids** drop-down > **Loft**.
19. Select the two circles.

Extruding a Planar Face of the Model

1. On the ribbon, click the **Home** tab > **Solid Editing** panel > **Edit Faces** drop-down > **Extrude Faces**.

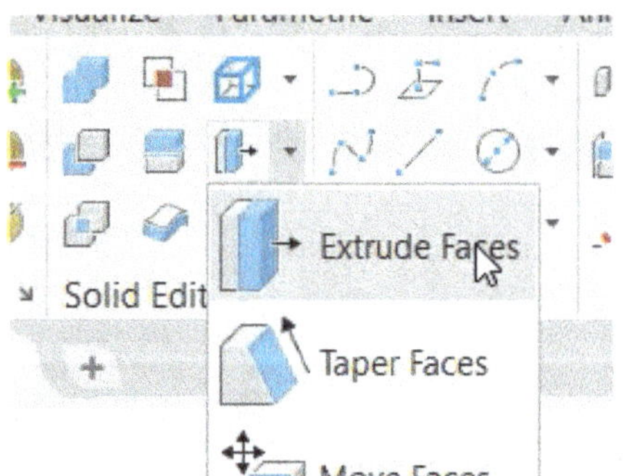

2. Click on the top face of the *Loft* solid.

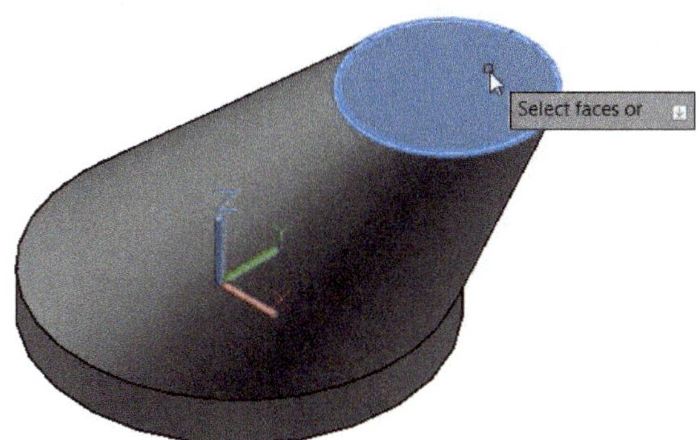

3. Press ENTER to accept the selection.
4. Type 40 and press ENTER to specify the extrusion height.
5. Press ENTER to accept 0 as the taper angle.
6. Press ENTER twice to extrude the face.

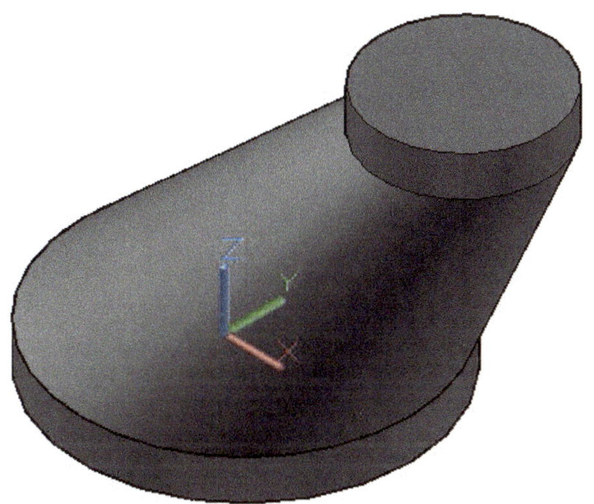

Mirroring the Loft solid.

1. On the status bar, click the down arrow next to the **Object Snap** icon, and then select the **Quadrant** option.

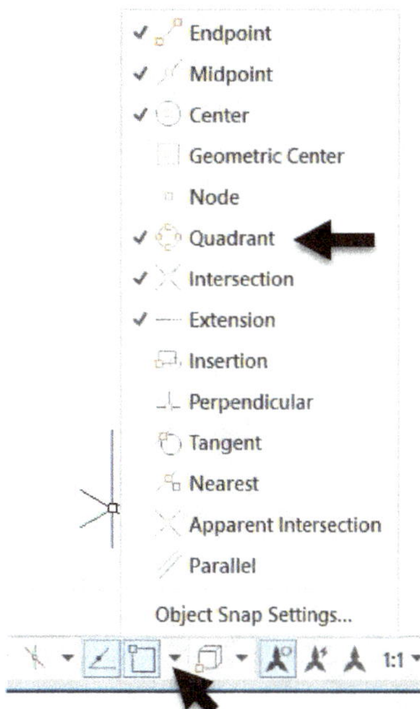

2. Select the loft solid.

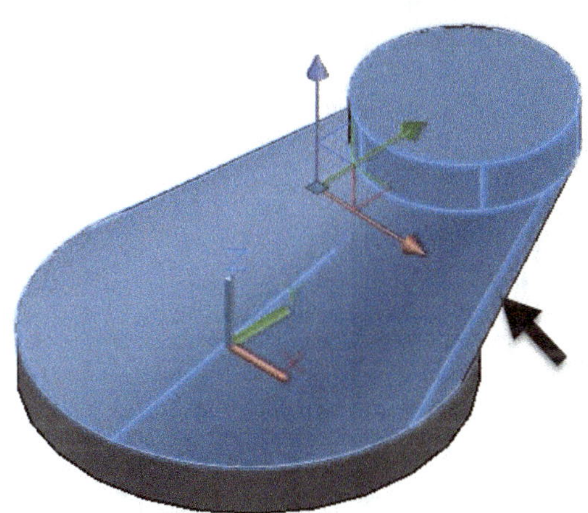

3. On the ribbon, click **Home** tab > **Modify** panel > **3D Mirror**.

4. Select the **YZ** option from the command line. The orientation of the mirror plane is defined

5. Select the quadrant point of the circular edge, as shown. The location of the mirror plane is defined.

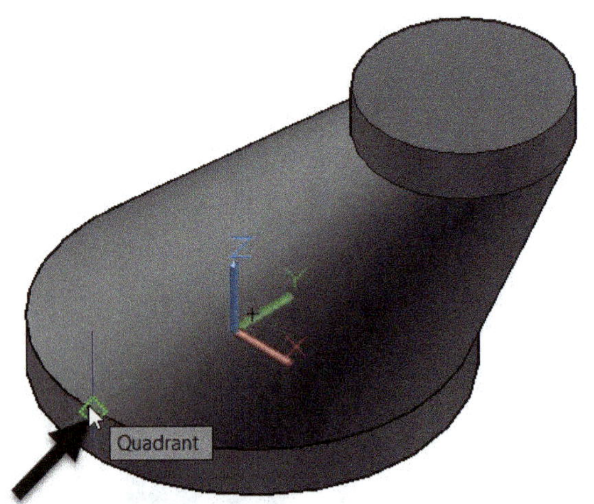

6. Select **No** from the command line to keep the original object.

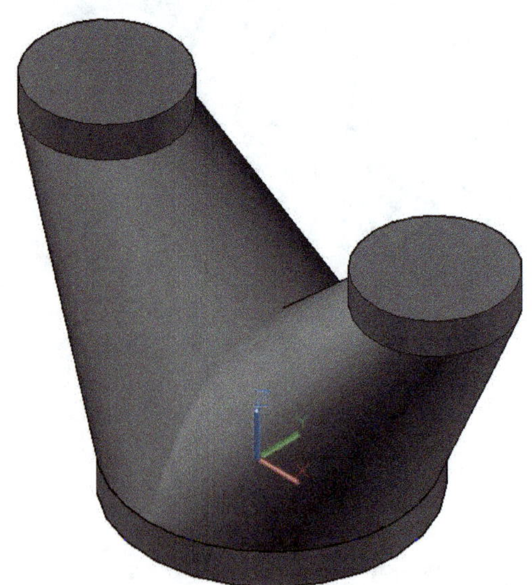

7. On the ribbon, click **Home** tab > **Solid Editing** panel > **Solid, Union**.

8. Create a selection window across all the elements of the model.

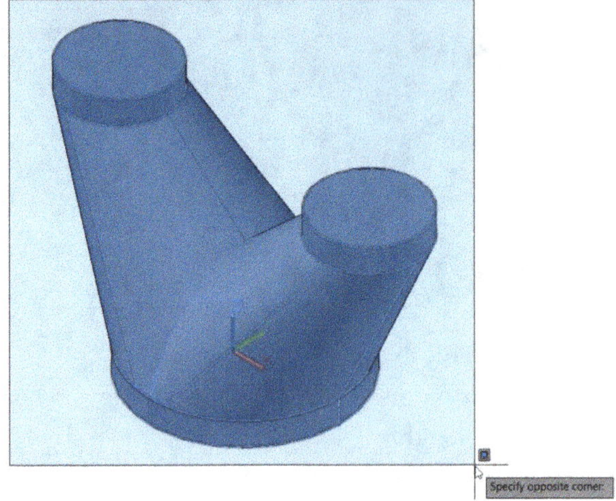

9. Press ENTER to combine all the objects.

Shelling the Model geometry

1. On the ribbon, click **Solids** tab > **Solid Editing** panel > **Shell**.

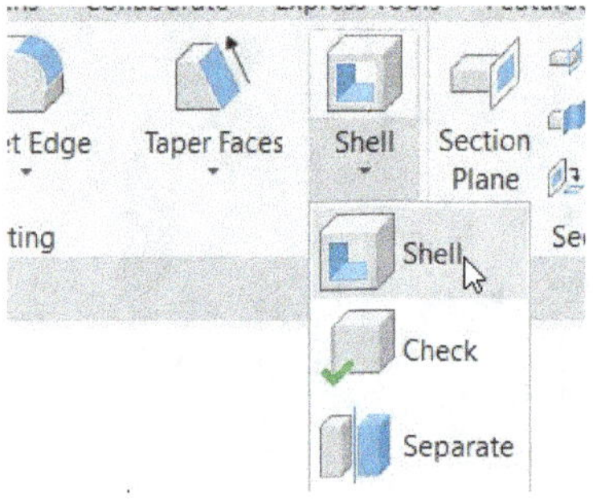

2. Click on the model.
3. Click on the top faces of the model.

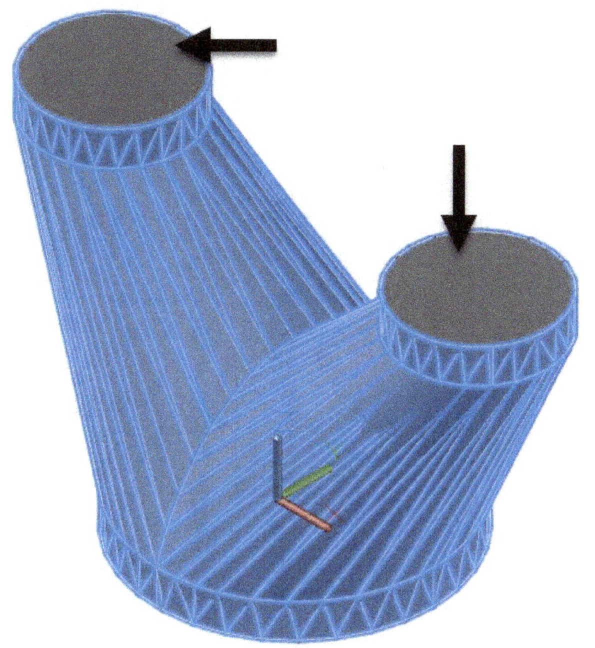

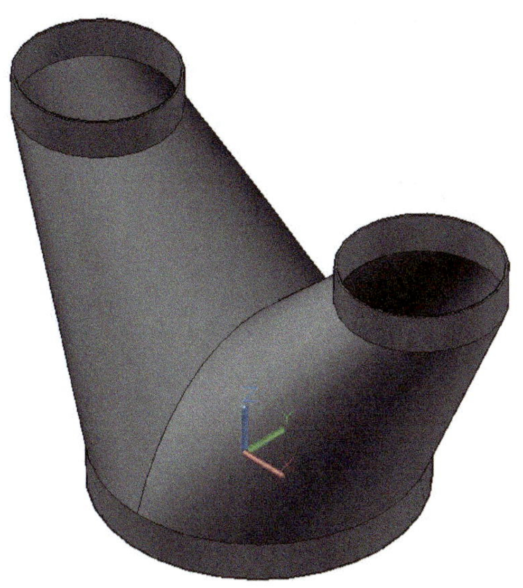

4. On the Navigation Bar, click the **Orbit** icon.
5. Press and hold the left mouse button and drag the pointer upward.
6. Right-click and select Exit.
7. Click on the bottom face of the model.

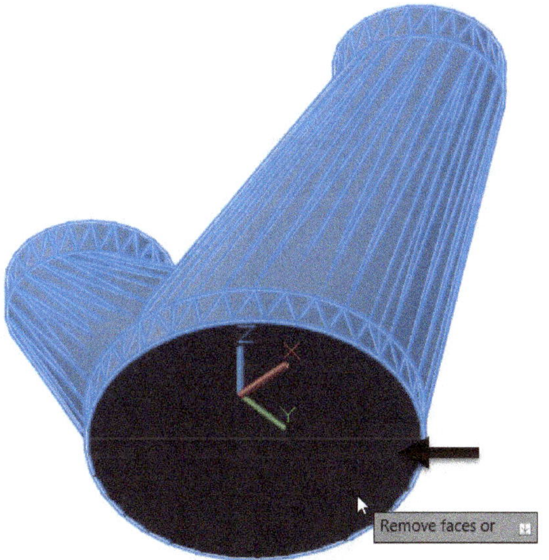

13. Click the **Save** icon on the Quick Access Toolbar.
14. Type **Ch6_tutorial1** in the **File Name** box.
15. Click the **Save** button.
16. Click **Application Menu > Close > Current Drawing**.

8. Press ENTER to accept the selection.
9. Type 2 in the command line and press ENTER. The shell thickness is defined.
10. Select **eXit** from the command line.
11. Select **eXit** from the command line.
12. Change the view orientation to SE Isometric.

Tutorial 2 (Inches)

In this example, you will create the part shown below.

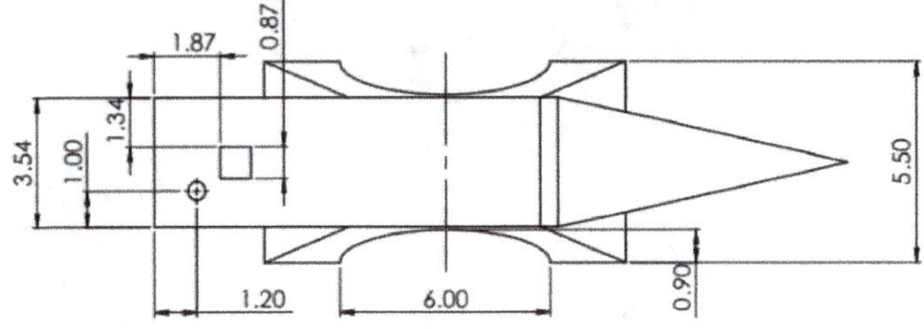

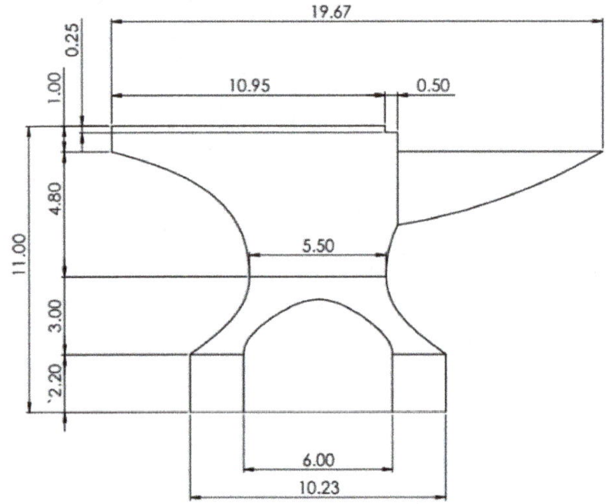

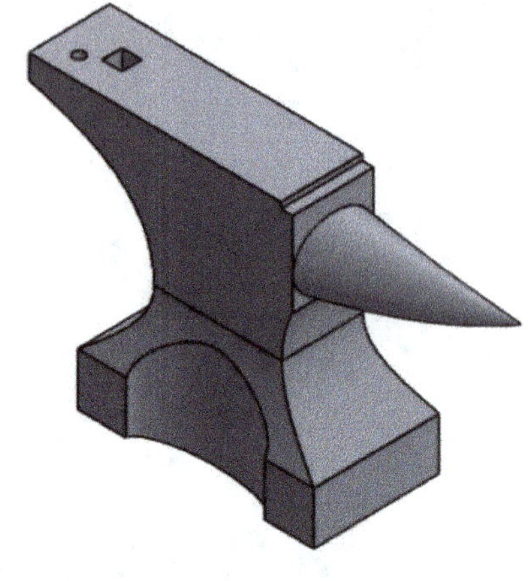

1. Start **Autodesk AutoCAD 2025**.
2. On the **Application Menu**, click the **New** icon; the **Select Template** dialog appears.

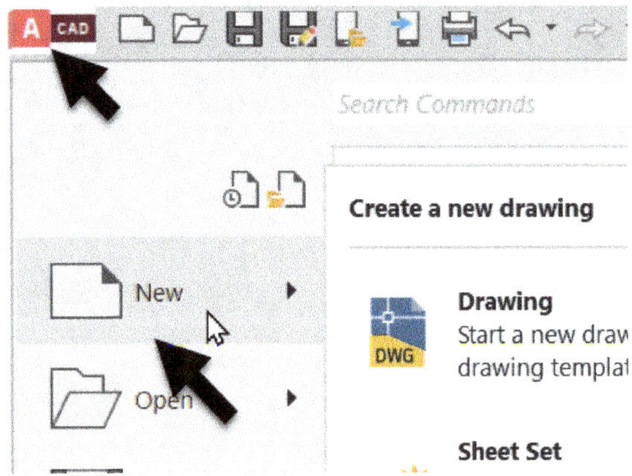

3. On this dialog, click **acad3D**, and then click the **Open** button.
4. Deactivate the **GRIDMODE** icon on the status bar.

5. On the ribbon, click **Home** tab > **Modeling** panel > **Primitive** drop-down > **Box**.
6. Type 0,0 in the command line and press ENTER. The first corner of the box is defined.
7. Type 10.23, 5.5 in the command line, and press ENTER. The second corner of the box is defined.
8. Type 2.2 in the command line and press ENTER. The height of the box is specified.
9. Click the **Zoom Extents** icon on the Navigation Bar to fit the box into the graphics window.

Create the Lofted solid

1. Change the **Visual Style** to **2D Wireframe**.
2. On the ribbon, click **Home** tab > **Selection** panel > **Filter** drop-down > **Edge**.

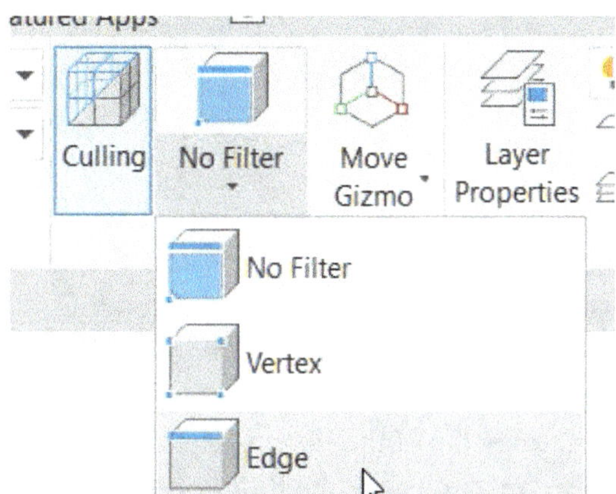

3. On the ribbon, click **Home** tab > **Solid Editing** panel > **Edge** drop-down > **Extract Edges**.

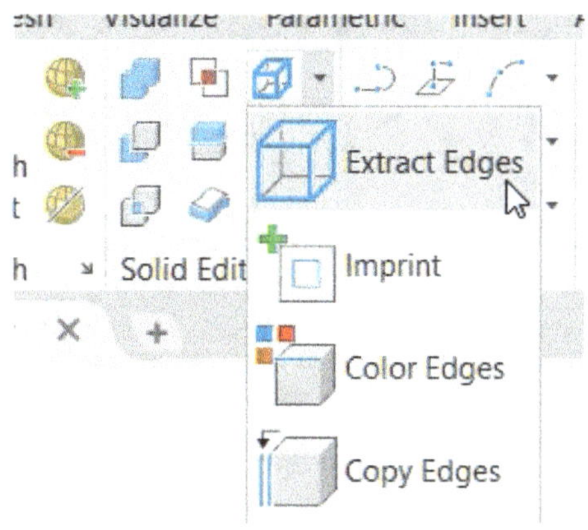

4. Select the edges of the model, as shown.

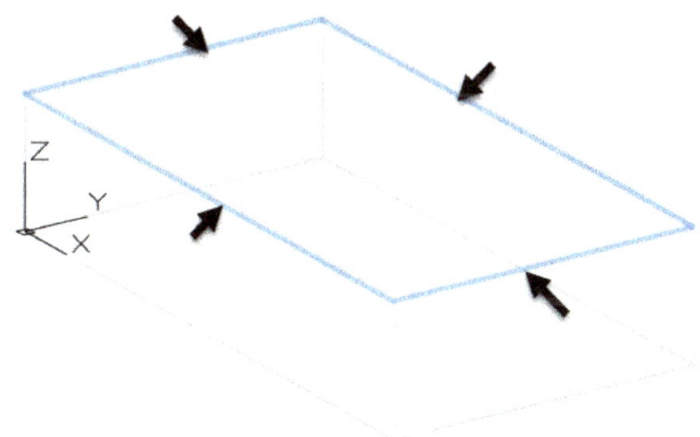

5. Press ENTER.
6. On the ribbon, click the **Home** tab > **Modify** panel > **Offset**.

7. Type 2.365, and press ENTER.
8. Select the extracted left edge.
9. Move the pointer toward the right and click.

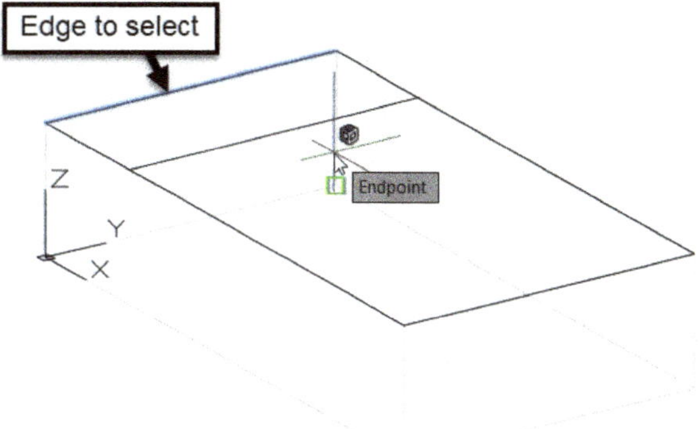

10. Select the extracted right edge.
11. Move the pointer toward the left and click.

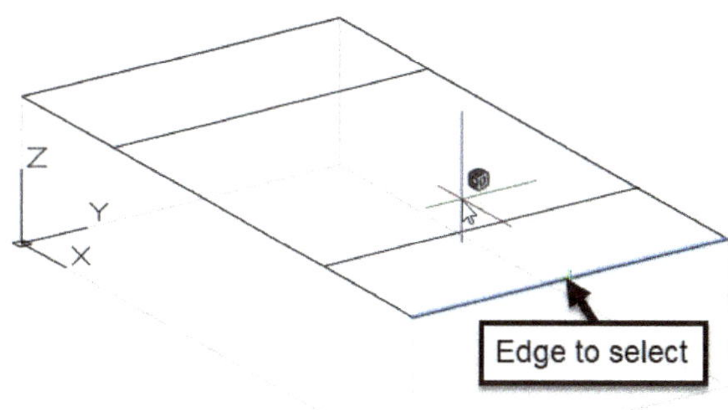

12. Press ENTER twice.
13. Type 0.98 and press ENTER.
14. Select the front edge.
15. Move the pointer backward and click.

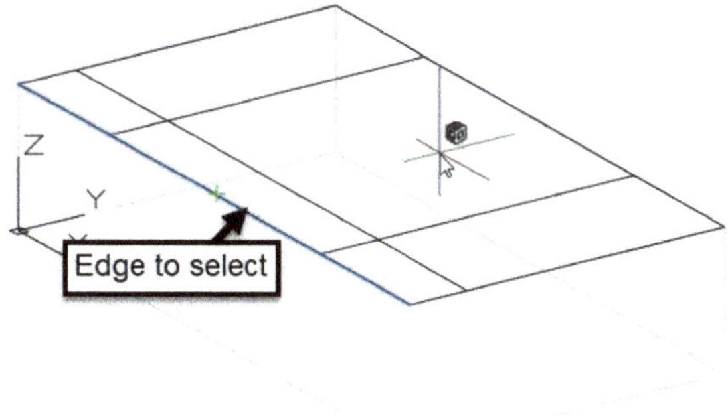

16. Select the back edge.
17. Move the pointer forward and click.

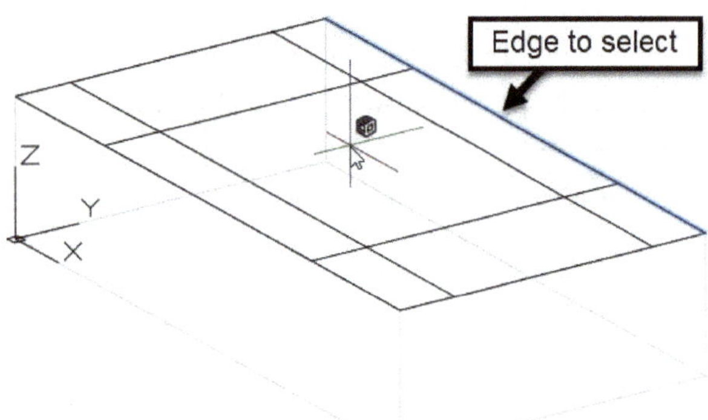

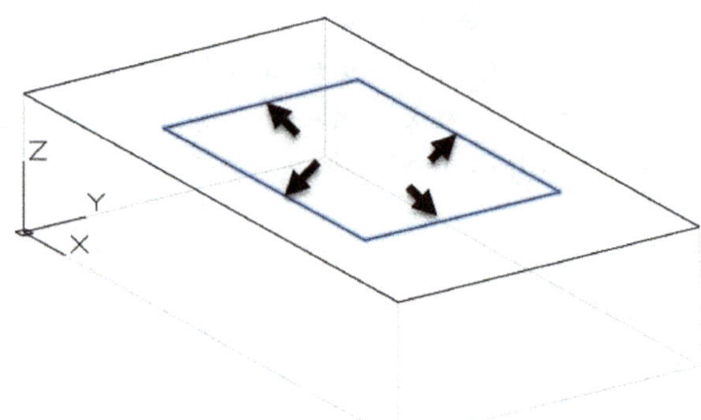

18. On the ribbon, click **Home** tab > **Modify** panel > **Trim/Extend** drop-down > **Trim**.
19. Select the portions of the offset lines, as shown.

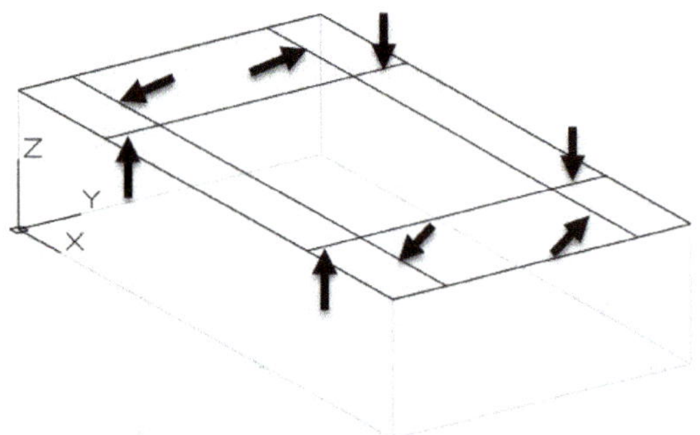

20. On the **Home** tab of the ribbon, expand the **Modify** panel and click the **Edit Polyline** icon.

21. Select the **Multiple** option from the command line.
22. Select the trimmed lines, as shown.

23. Press ENTER.
24. Select the **Yes** option from the command line.
25. Select the **Join** option from the command line.
26. Press ENTER.
27. On the **Home** tab of the ribbon, expand the **Modify** panel and click the **Edit Polyline** icon.
28. Select the **Multiple** option from the command line.
29. Select the extracted lines, as shown.

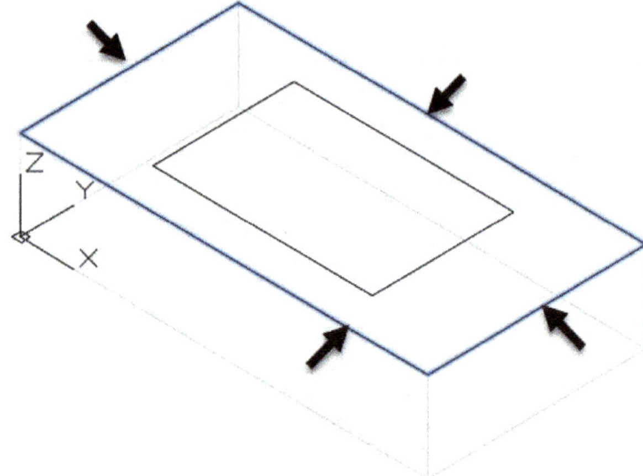

30. Press ENTER.
31. Select the **Yes** option from the command line.
32. Select the **Join** option from the command line.
33. Press ENTER.
34. Press ESC.
35. On the ribbon, click **Home** tab > **Selection** panel > **Filter** drop-down > **No Filter**.
36. On the ribbon, click **Home** tab > **Modify** panel > **3D Move**.
37. Select the newly created region and press ENTER.

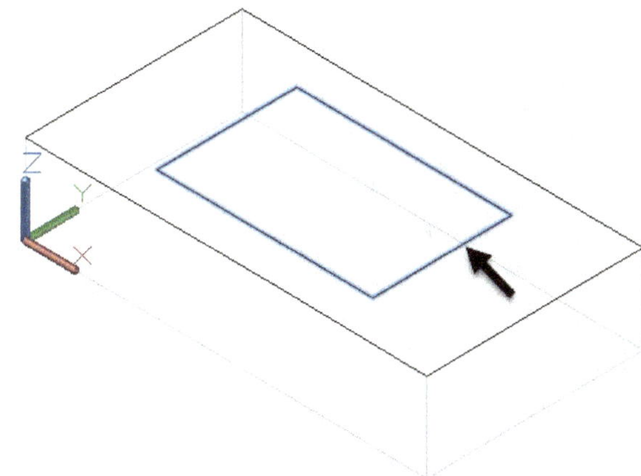

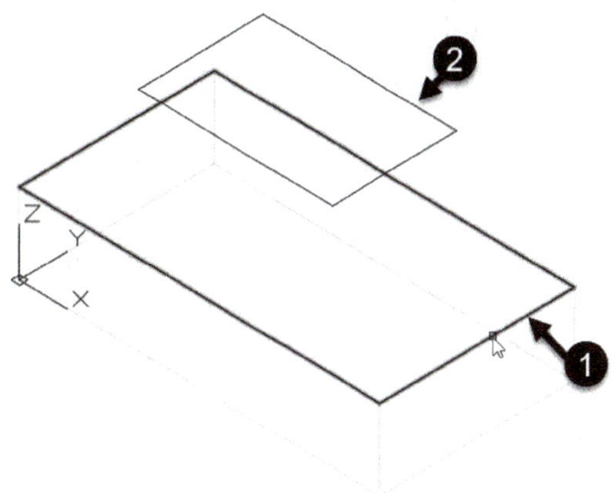

38. Select the Z-axis of the move gizmo.

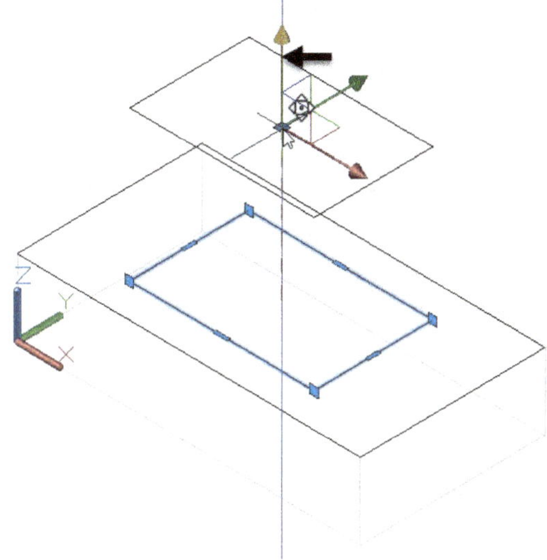

39. Move upward.
40. Type 3 and press ENTER.
41. On the ribbon, click the **Home** tab > **Modeling** panel > **Solids** drop-down > **Loft**.
42. Select the large rectangle.
43. Select the small rectangle and press ENTER.

44. Select the **Settings** option from the command line.
45. On the **Loft Settings** dialog, select the **Draft angles** option.
46. Type **90** in the **Start angle** and **End angle** boxes.
47. Type **0.1** in the **Start magnitude** box.
48. Click **OK**.

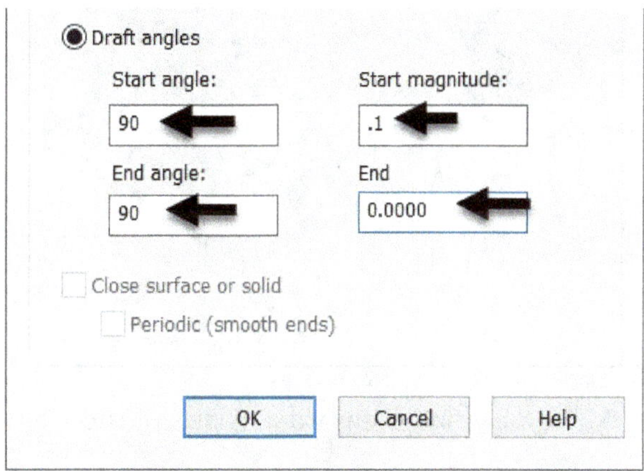

49. Change the **Visual Style** to **Shades of Gray**.

50. On the ribbon, click **Home** tab > **Solid Editing** panel > **Solid, Union**.
51. Create a selection window across all the elements of the model.
52. Press ENTER to combine all the objects.
53. Activate the **Orthomode** icon on the status bar.
54. On the ribbon, click **Home** tab > **Modeling** panel > **Primitives** drop-down > **Cylinder**.
55. Select the **Elliptical** option from the command line.
56. Select the **Center** option from the command line.
57. Select the midpoint of the front horizontal edge, as shown.

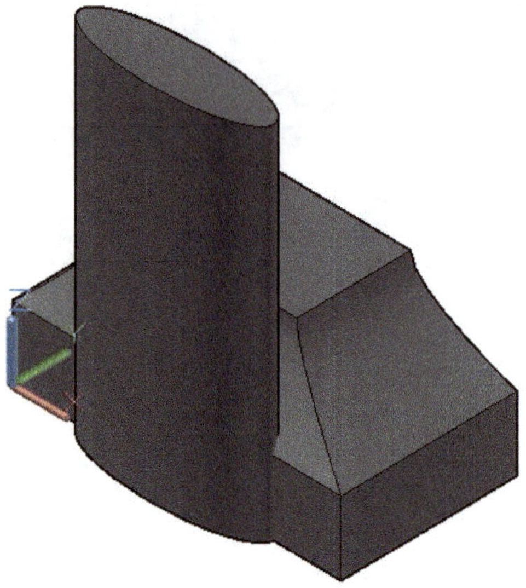
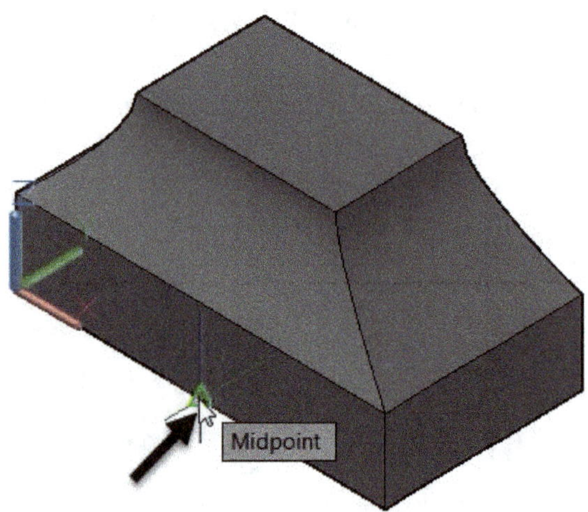

58. Type .9 and press ENTER.
59. Type 3 and press ENTER.
60. Move the pointer **upward** and click outside the model.

61. Select the elliptical cylinder.
62. On the ribbon, click **Home** tab > **Modify** panel > **3D Mirror**.
63. Select the **ZX** option from the command line. The orientation of the mirror plane is defined
64. Select the midpoint of the bottom-right edge, as shown. The location of the mirror plane is defined.

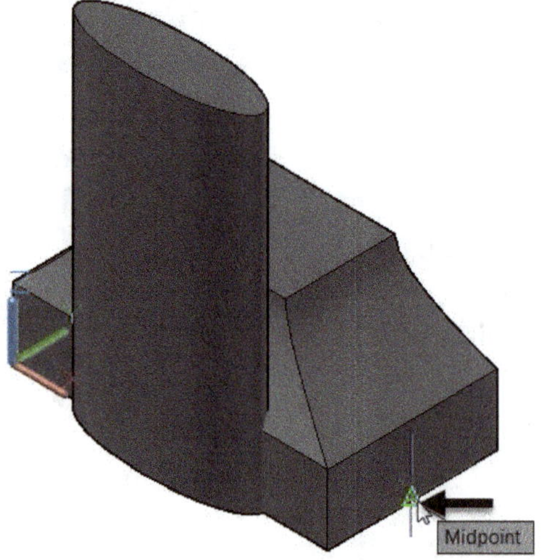

65. Select the **No** option from the command line.

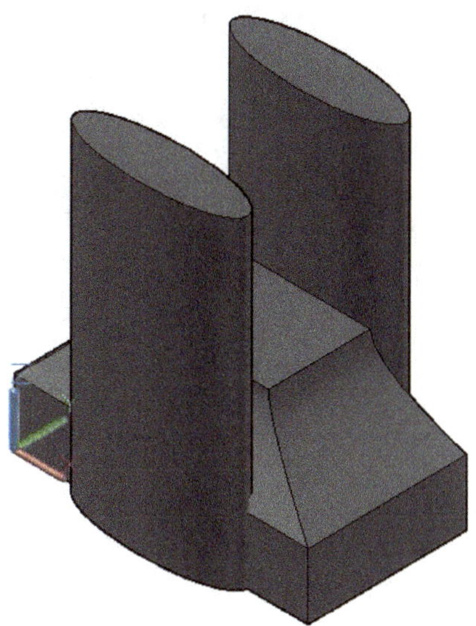

66. On the ribbon, click the **Home** tab > **Modeling** panel > **Solid Editing** drop-down > **Solid, Subtract**.
67. Click on the main body
68. Press ENTER.
69. Select the two elliptical cylinders.
70. Press ENTER.

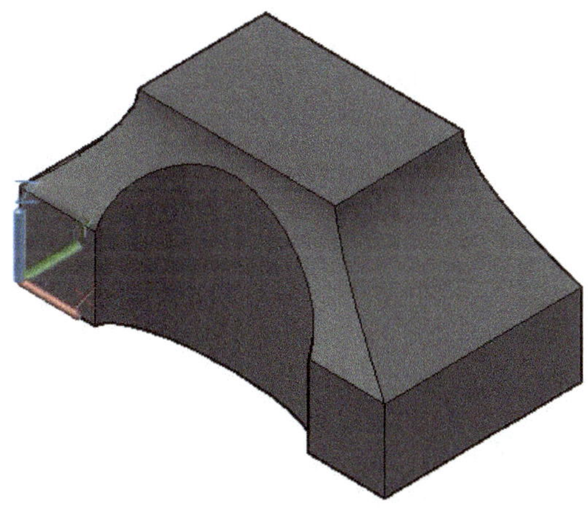

71. Change the **Visual Style** to **2D Wireframe**.
72. On the ribbon, click **Home** tab > **Selection** panel > **Filter** drop-down > **Edge**.
73. On the ribbon, click **Home** tab > **Solid Editing** panel > **Edge** drop-down > **Extract Edges**.
74. Select the edges of the model, as shown.

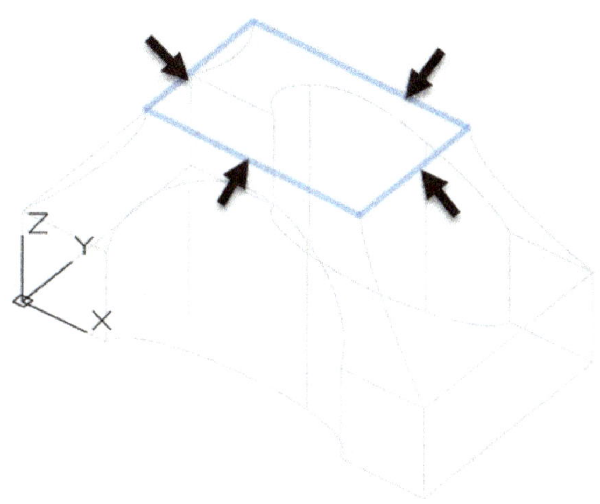

75. Press ENTER.
76. On the ribbon, click the **Home** tab > **Modify** panel > **Offset**.
77. Type 5.475, and press ENTER.
78. Select the extracted left edge.
79. Move the pointer toward the left and click.

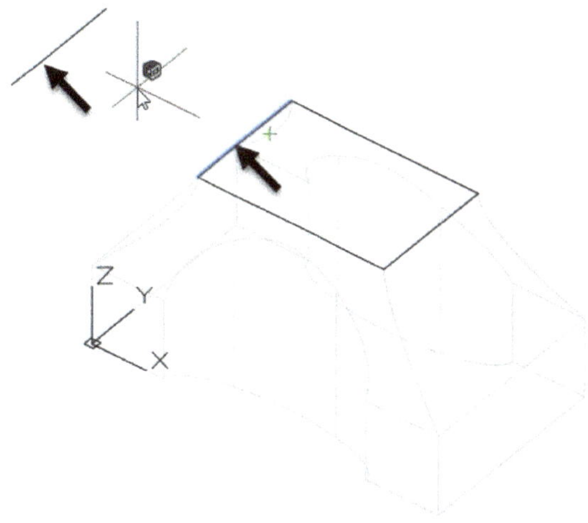

80. Select the extracted right edge.
81. Move the pointer toward the right and click.

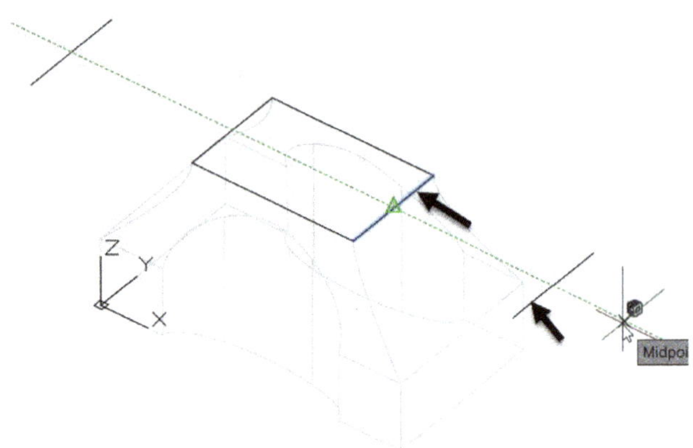

82. Press ESC.
83. Type L in the command line and press ENTER.
84. Select the front endpoints of the two offset lines.

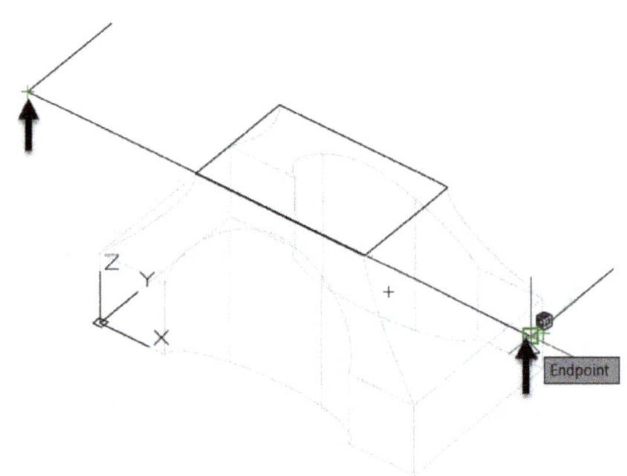

85. Press ENTER twice.
86. Select the back endpoints of the two offset lines.

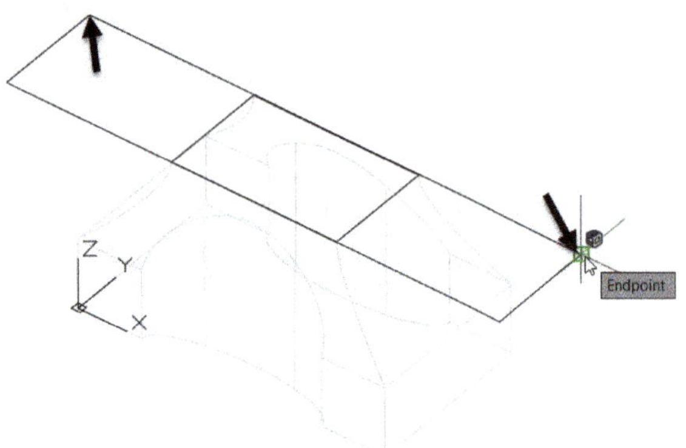

87. Press ESC.
88. On the **Home** tab of the ribbon, expand the **Modify** panel and click the **Edit Polyline** icon.
89. Select the **Multiple** option from the command line.

90. Select the offset and newly created lines, as shown.

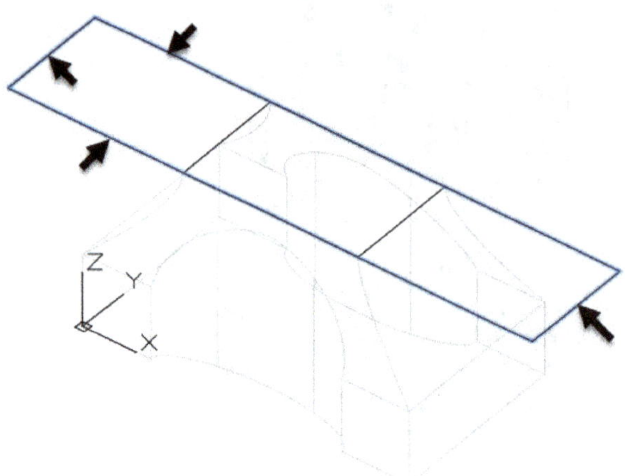

91. Press ENTER.
92. Select the **Yes** option from the command line.
93. Select the **Join** option from the command line.
94. Press ENTER.
95. Press ESC.
96. On the ribbon, click **Home** tab > **Modify** panel > **3D Move**.
97. Select the newly created polyline and press ENTER.
98. Select the Z-axis of the move gizmo.

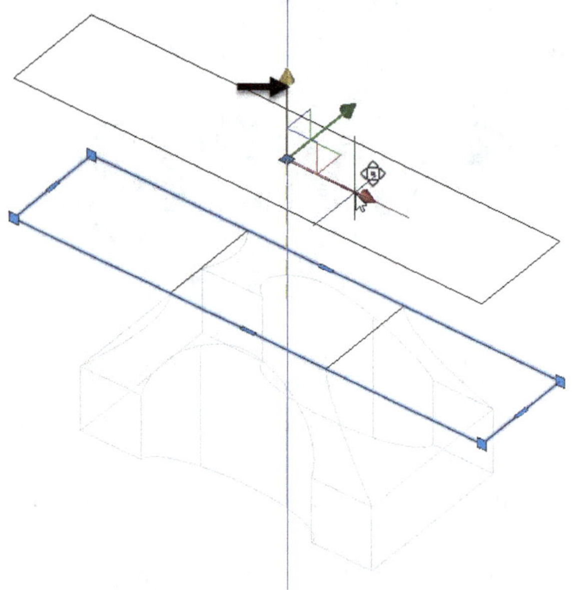

99. Move upward.
100. Type 4.8 and press ENTER.

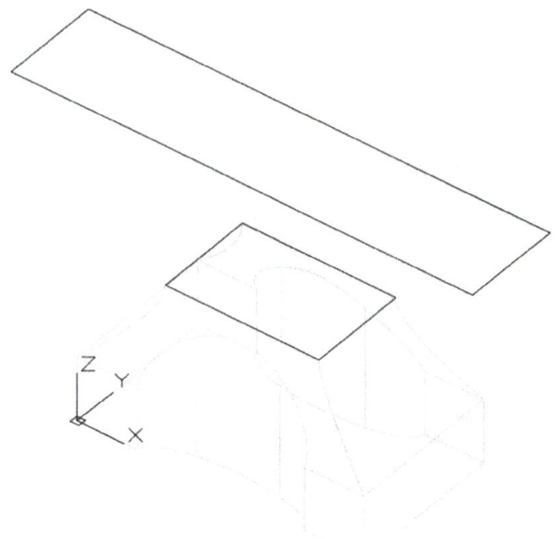

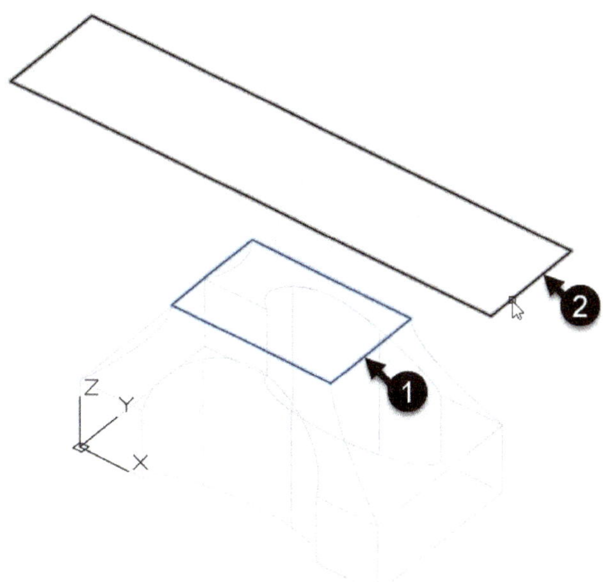

101. On the **Home** tab of the ribbon, expand the **Modify** panel and click the **Edit Polyline** icon.
102. Select the **Multiple** option from the command line.
103. Select the extracted lines, as shown.

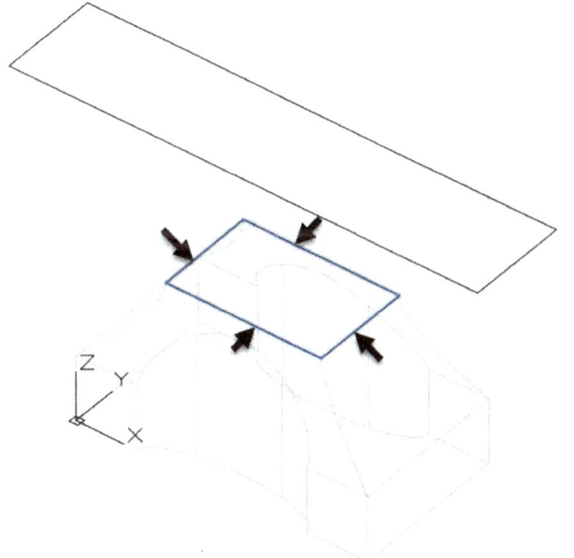

104. Press ENTER.
105. Select the **Yes** option from the command line.
106. Select the **Join** option from the command line.
107. Press ENTER.
108. On the ribbon, click the **Home** tab > **Modeling** panel > **Solids** drop-down > **Loft**.
109. Select the small rectangle.
110. Select the large rectangle and press ENTER.

111. Select the **Settings** option from the command line.
112. On the **Loft Settings** dialog, select the **Normal to** option.
113. Select the **Start cross section** option from the drop-down.
114. Click **OK**.
115. Change the **Visual Style** to **Shades of Gray**.

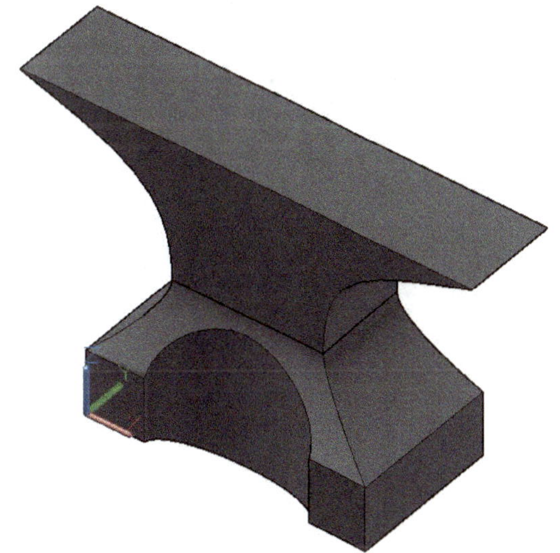

116. On the ribbon, click **Home > Modeling > Primitives** drop-down > **Box**.
117. Select the corner point of the loft solid, as shown.

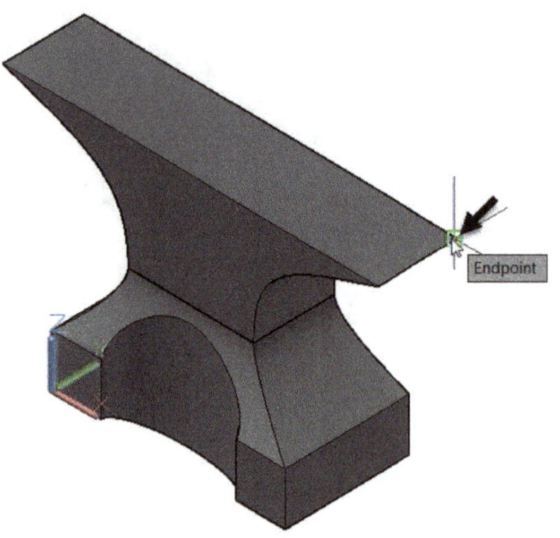

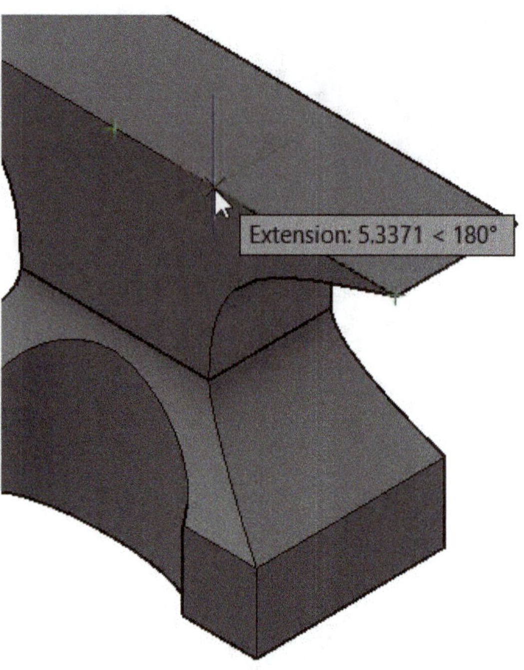

118. Select the **Length** option from the command line.
119. Select the other corner point of the loft solid, as shown; the length of the box is defined.

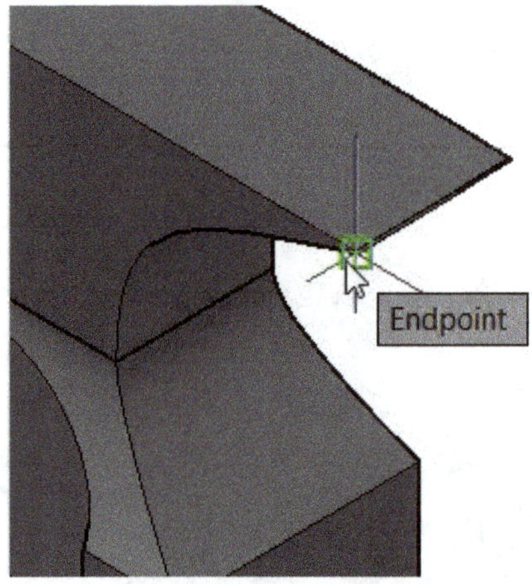

121. Move the pointer downward and select the lower corner point of the loft, as shown.

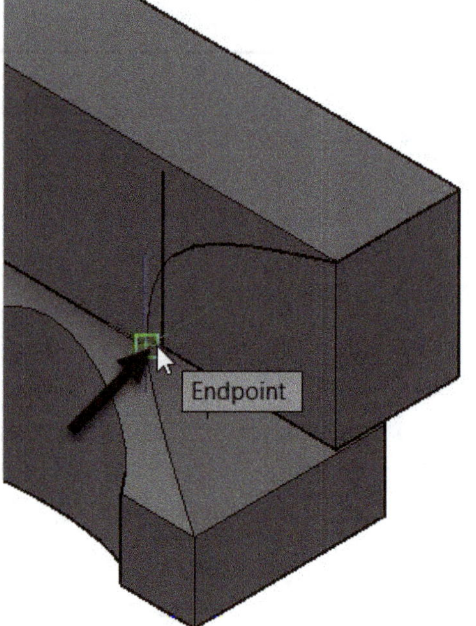

120. Move the pointer toward left and type 5.

122. On the ribbon, click **Home** tab > **Solid Editing** panel > **Solid, Subtract**.
123. Select the lofted solid and press ENTER.
124. Select the box and press ENTER.

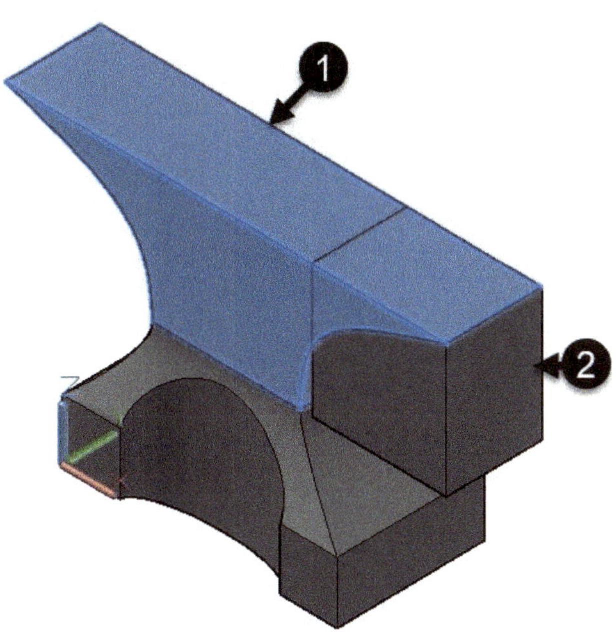

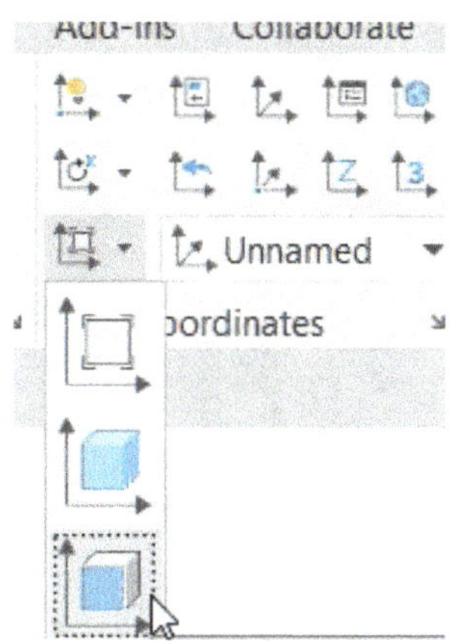

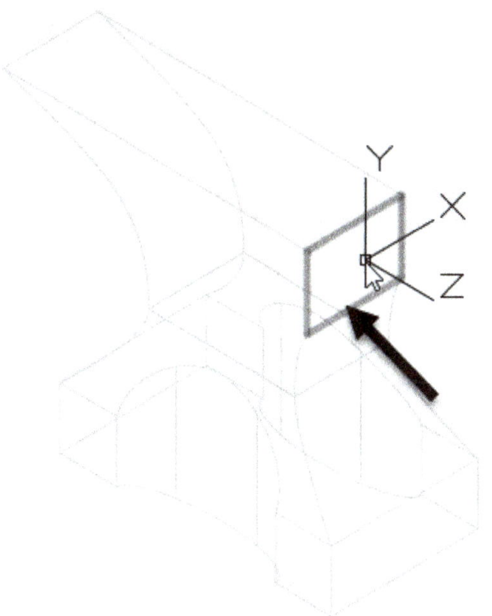

Creating a Loft with Guide Curves

1. Change the **Visual Style** to **2D Wireframe**.
2. On the ribbon, click **Home** tab > **Coordinates** panel > **View** drop-down > **Face**.

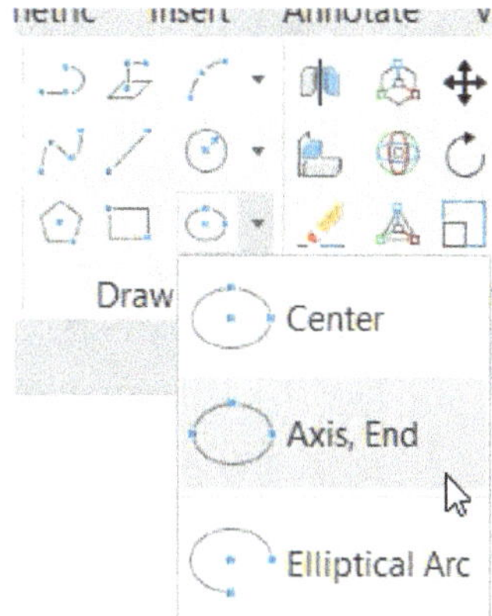

3. Click on the right-side face of the model.

4. Press ENTER to accept the selection. The UCS is placed on the selected face.
5. On the **Home** tab of the ribbon, click **Draw > Ellipse** drop-down > **Axis, End**.

6. Select the midpoint of the left vertical edge, as shown.

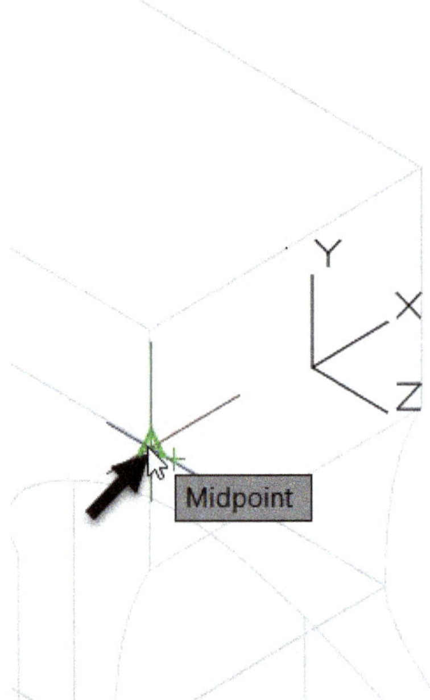

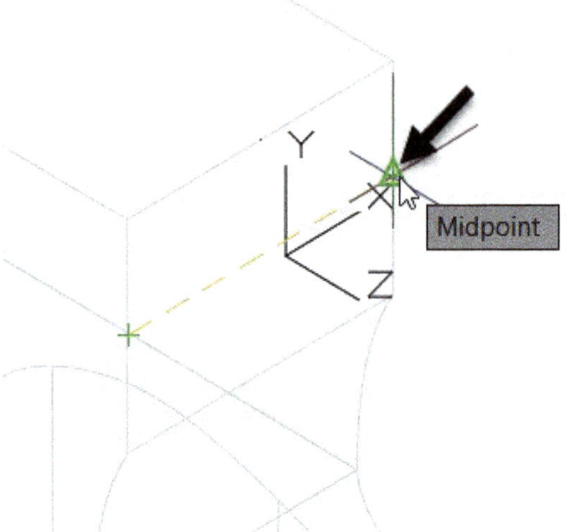

7. Select the midpoint of the right vertical edge, as shown.

8. Select the midpoint of the lower horizontal edge, as shown.

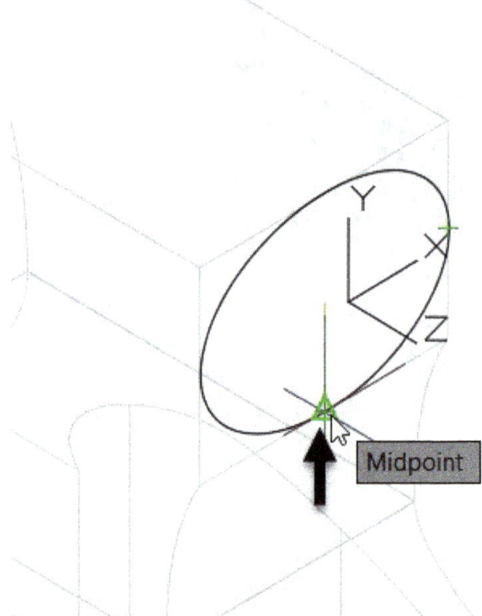

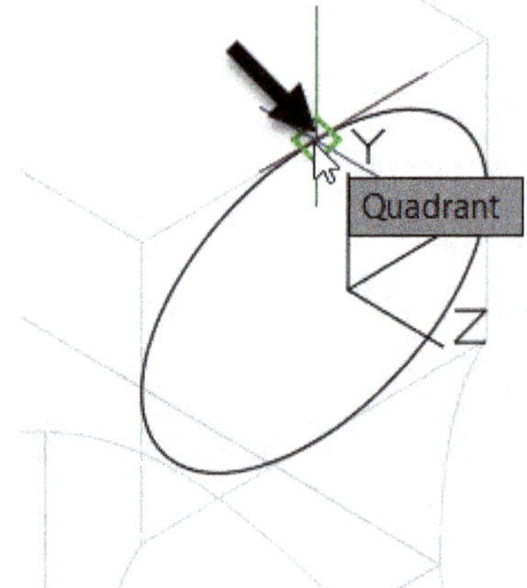

9. On the **Home** tab of the ribbon, click **Modeling > Primitives** drop-down > **Sphere** .

10. Select the **2P** option from the command line.

11. Select the top quadrant point of the ellipse.

12. Move the pointer vertically downward.

13. Type 0.5 and press ENTER.

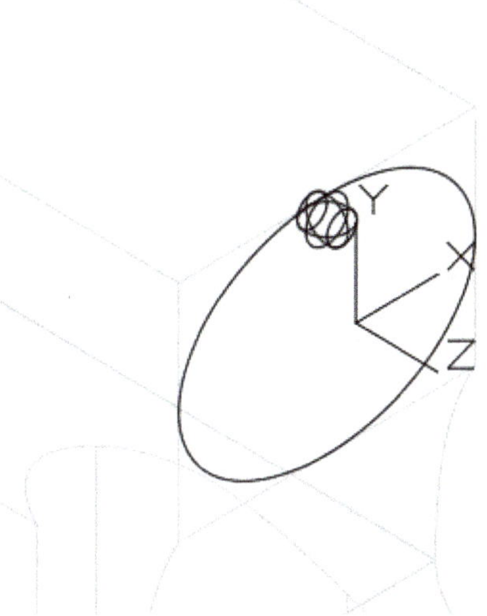

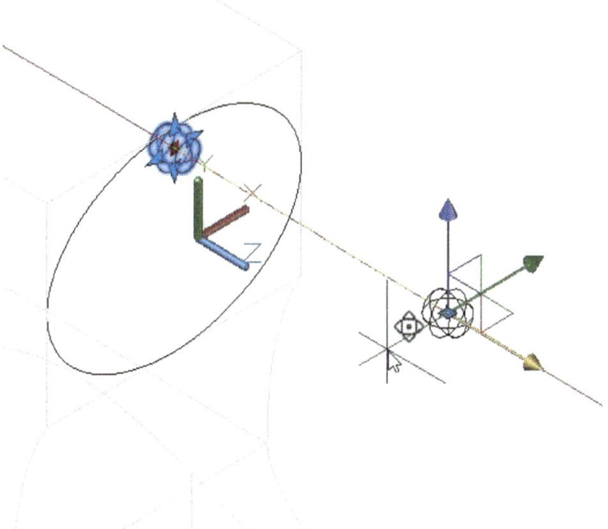

14. On the ribbon, click **Home** tab > **Modify** panel > **3D Move**.
15. Select the newly created sphere and press ENTER.
16. Click on the X-axis (Red arrow) of the move gizmo.

18. Type 7.72 and press ENTER.

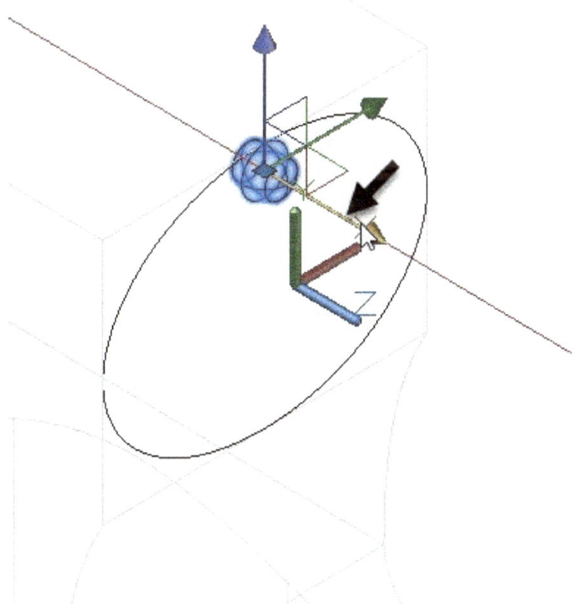

19. On the **Home** tab of the ribbon, click **Draw > Circle** drop-down > **Circle, Diameter**.
20. Select the centerpoint of the sphere.

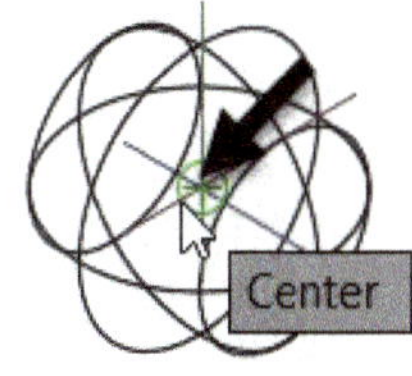

21. Move the pointer outward.

17. Move along the selected axis.

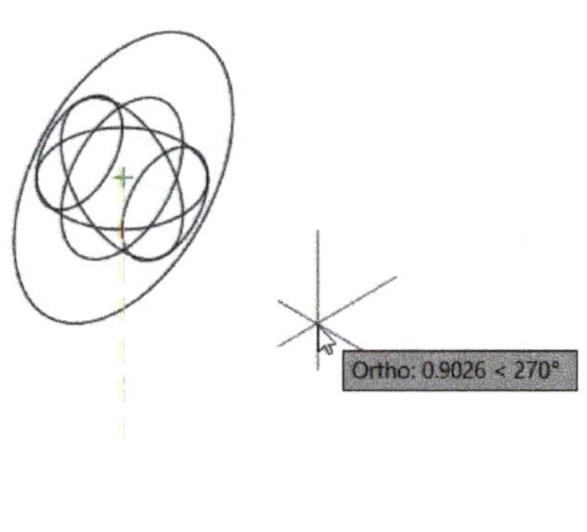

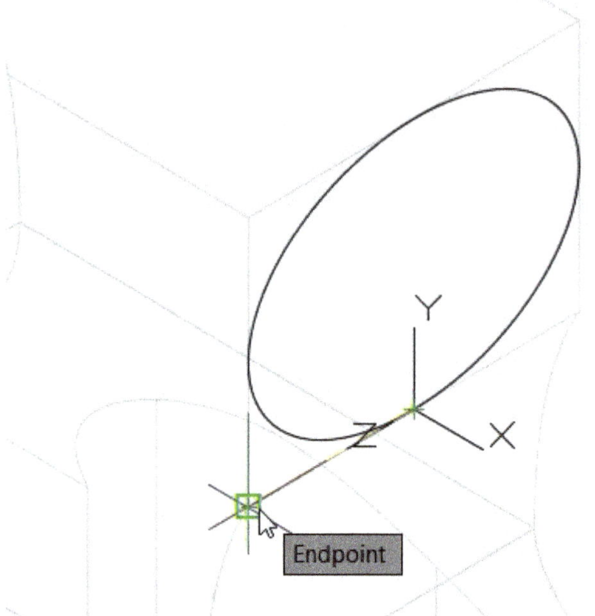

ircle: .5

22. Type .5 and press ENTER.
23. On the **Home** tab of the ribbon, click **Coordinates > Z-Axis Vector**.
24. Select the midpoint of the lower horizontal edge, as shown.

26. On the **Home** tab of the ribbon, click **Draw** panel > **Polyline**.
27. Select the origin point of the UCS.

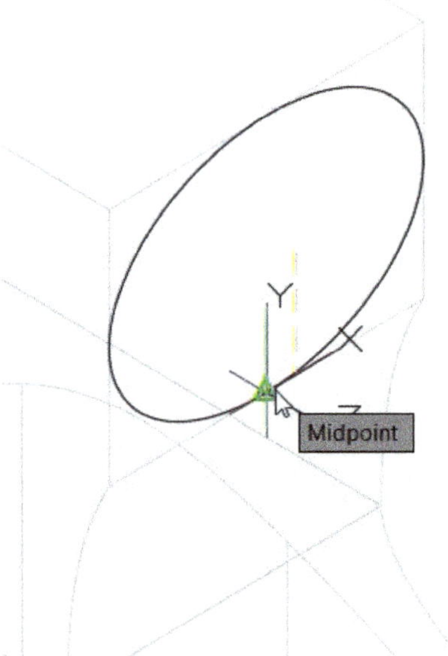

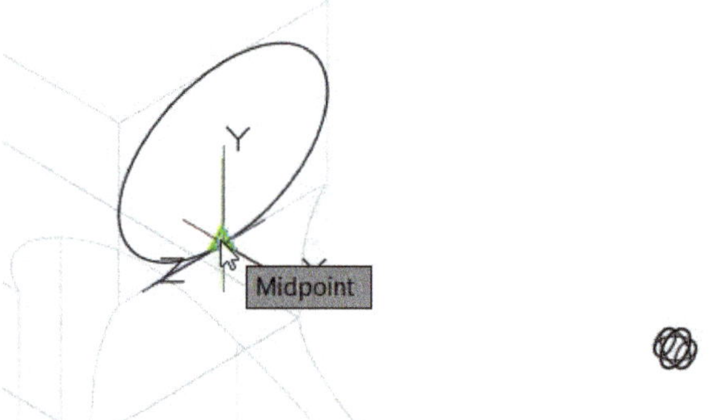

28. Move the pointer backward.

25. Move the pointer toward the left and select the corner point, as shown.

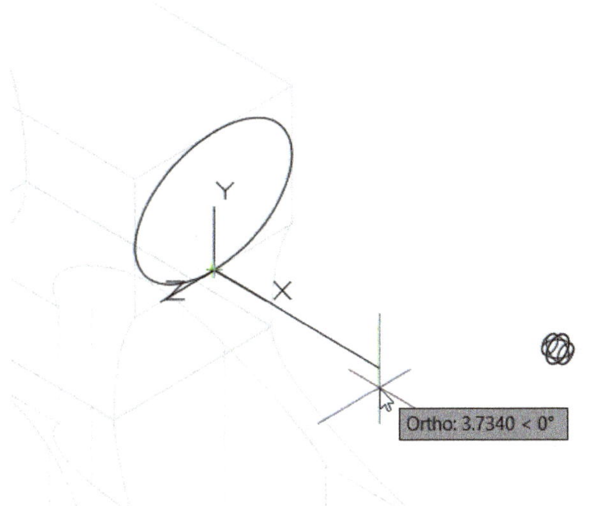

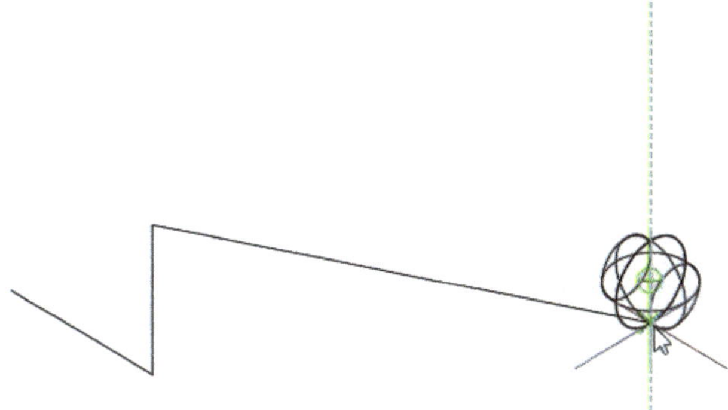

36. Press ESC.
37. On the **Home** tab of the ribbon, click **Draw** panel
    > Spline

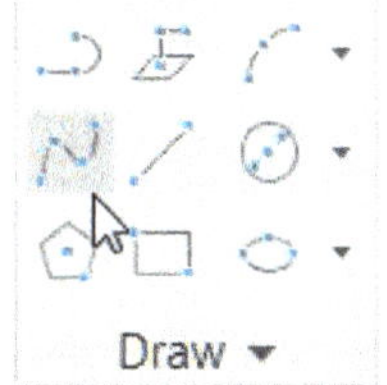

29. Type 4.11 and press ENTER.
30. Move the pointer upward.

38. Select the **Method** option from the command
    line.
39. Select the **Fit** option from the command line.
40. Select the points of the polyline, as shown.

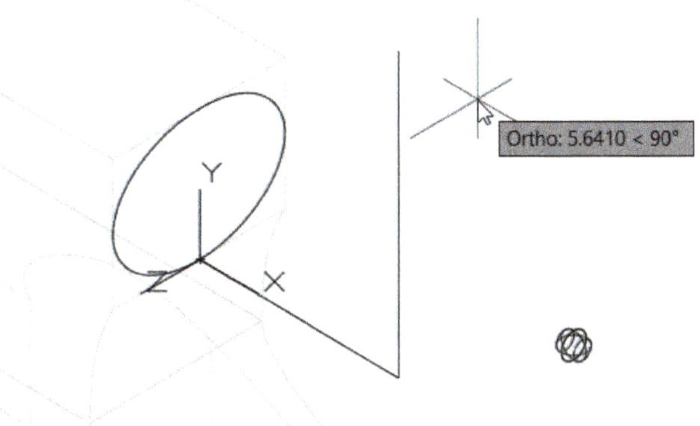

31. Type 0.9 and press ENTER.
32. Deactivate the Orthomode icon on the status
    bar.
33. Place the pointer on the centerpoint of the
    sphere.
34. Move the pointer downward; the trace line
    appears.
35. Select the intersection point between the trace
    line and circle, as shown.

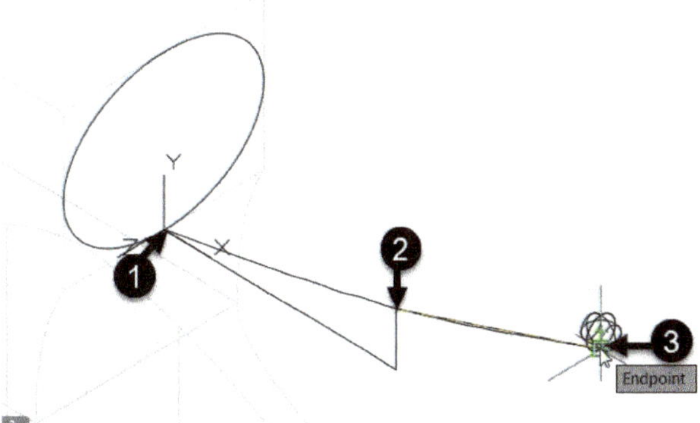

41. Right-click and select Enter.
42. Select the polyline and press DELETE.

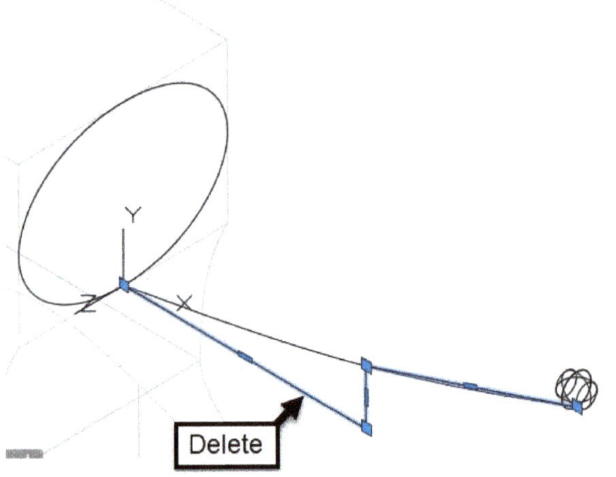

43. On the **Home** tab of the ribbon, click **Draw** panel > **Line**.
44. Select the top quadrant point of the ellipse.
45. Place the pointer on the centerpoint of the sphere.
46. Move the pointer upward.
47. Select the intersection point between the trace line and the circle.

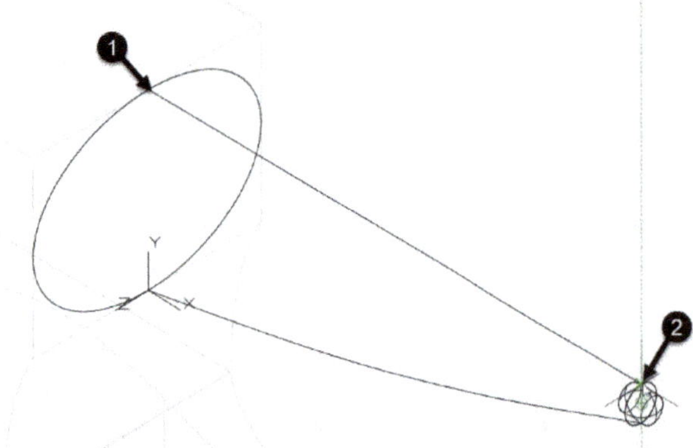

48. Press ESC.
49. On the **Home** tab of the ribbon, click **Modeling** > **Solids** drop-down > **Loft**.
50. Select the ellipse and circle. Next, press ENTER.

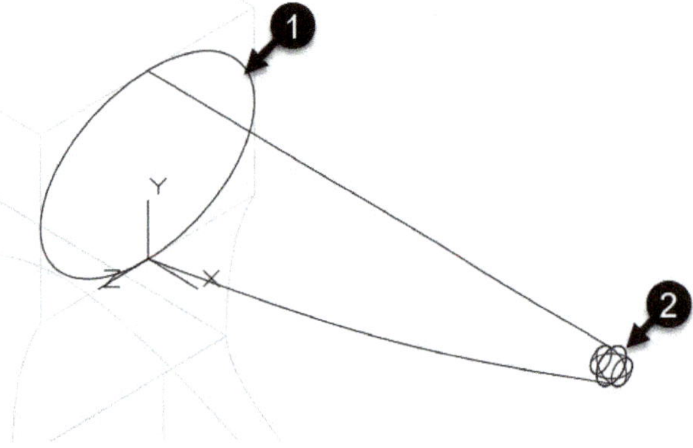

51. Select the **Guides** option.
52. Select the spline and line. Next, press ENTER.

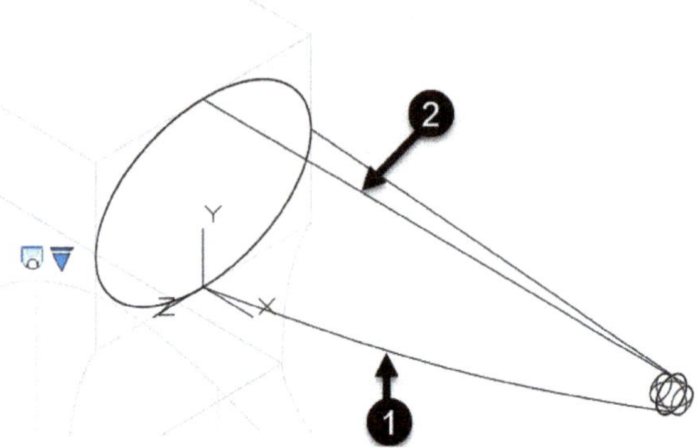

53. Change the **Visual Style** to **Shades of Gray**.

Extruding the Face

1. On the **Home** tab of the ribbon, click **Solid Editing > Face Editing** drop-down > **Extrude Faces**.

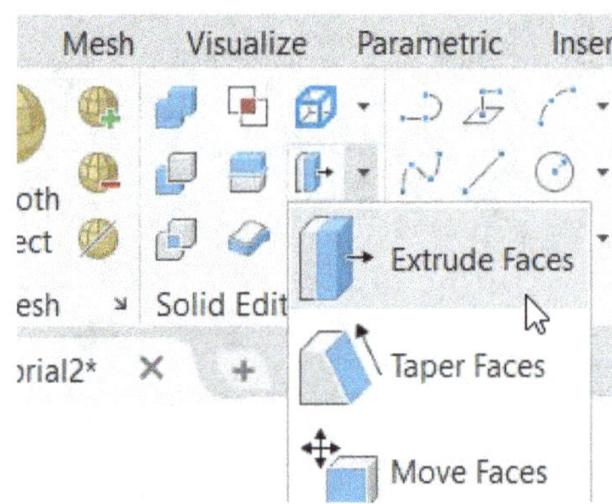

2. Click on the top face of the model.
3. Press ENTER.

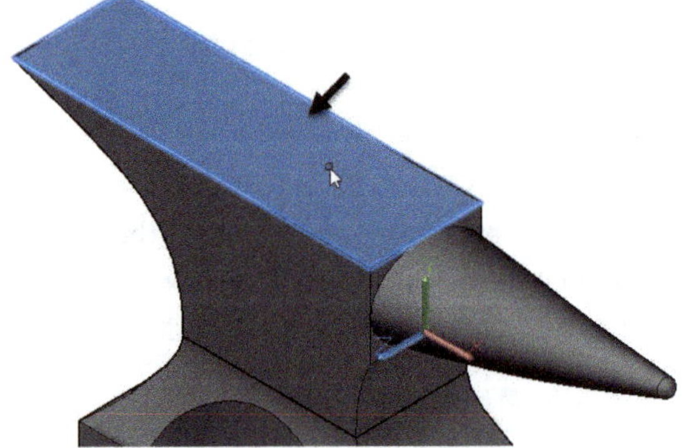

4. Type 1 and press ENTER to define the height of the extrusion.
5. Press ENTER to define 0 as the taper angle.

6. Press ESC.

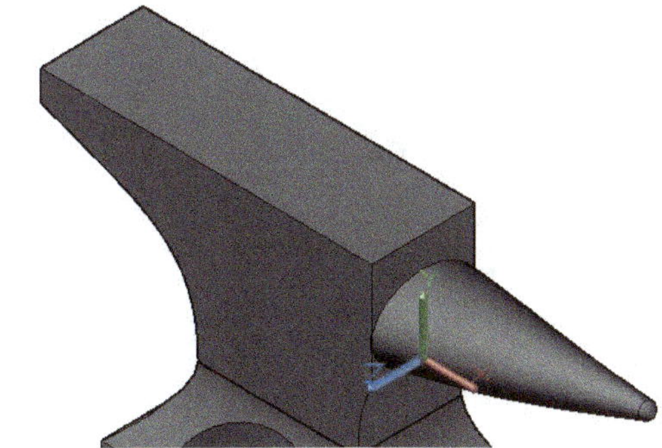

Creating the Extruded Cuts

1. On the **Home** tab of the ribbon, click **Draw** panel
    > **Rectangle**.
2. Select the corner point of the model, as shown.

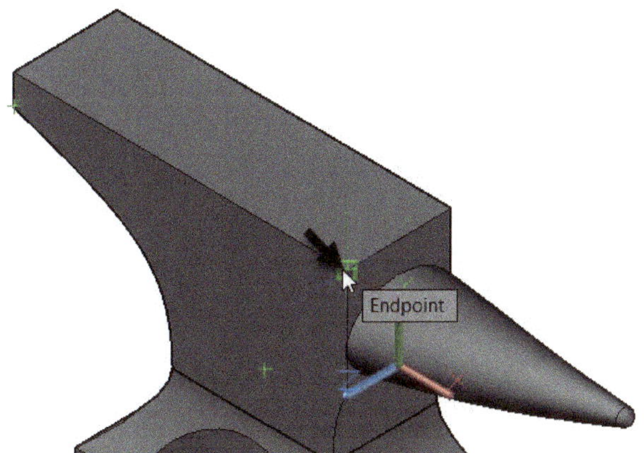

3. Select the **Dimensions** option from the
    command line.
4. Type 0.5 and press ENTER.
5. Type 0.25 and press ENTER.
6. Move the pointer toward left and downward,
    and then click.

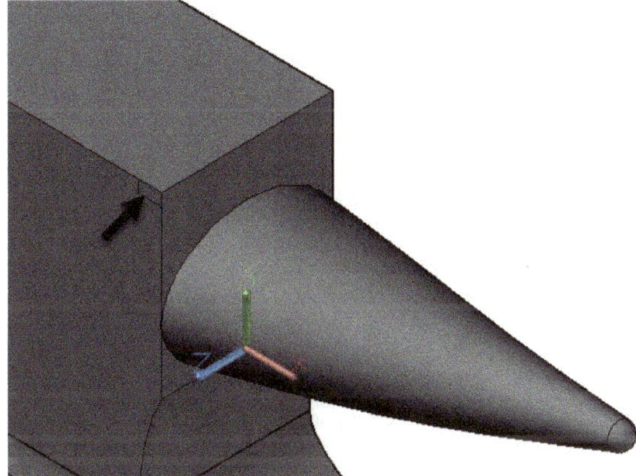

7. On the **Home** tab of the ribbon, click **Modeling**
    > **Solid** drop-down > **Extrude**.

8. Click in the region enclosed by the rectangle.

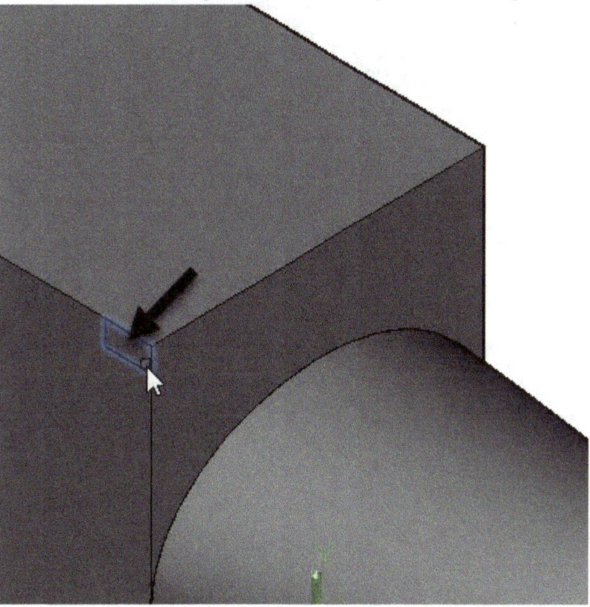

9. Move the pointer toward the right and click
    outside the model.

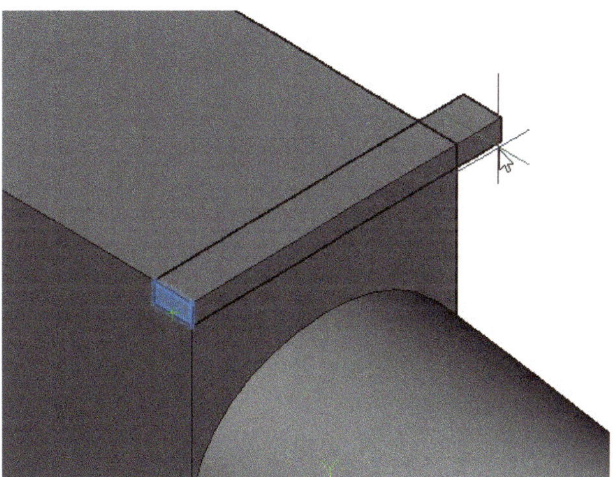

10. On the ribbon, click the **Home** tab > **Modeling**
    panel > **Solid Editing** drop-down > **Solid,
    Subtract**.
11. Click on the loft body.
12. Press ENTER.
13. Select the extrusion.
14. Press ENTER.

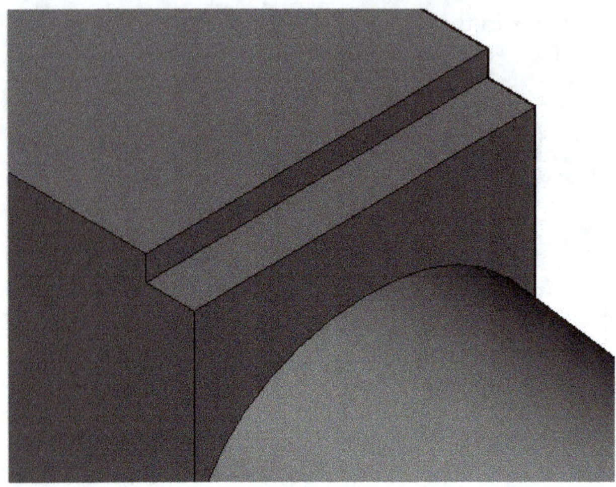

15. On the ribbon, click **Home** tab > **Coordinates** panel > **View** drop-down > **Face**.

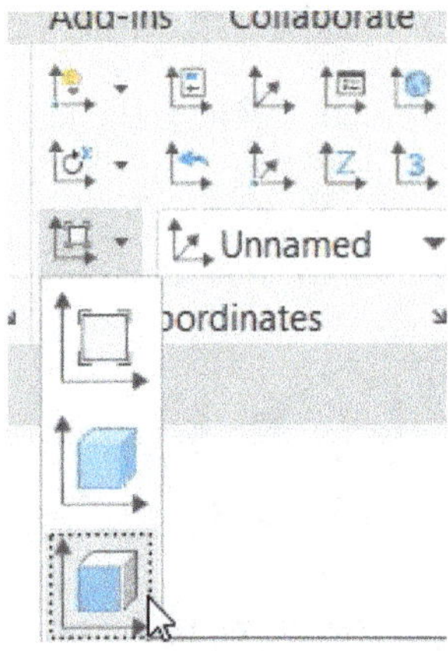

16. Click on the top face of the model.

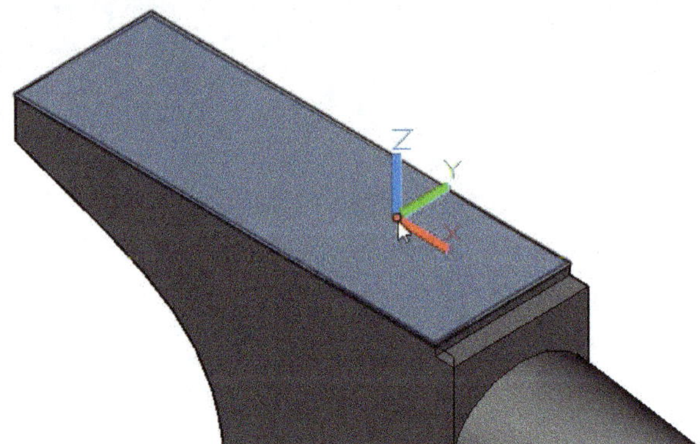

17. Press ENTER to accept the selection. The UCS is placed on the selected face.
18. Activate the Orthomode icon on the status bar.
19. On the ribbon, click **Home > Modeling > Primitives** drop-down > **Box**.

20. Select the corner point of the extrusion, as shown.

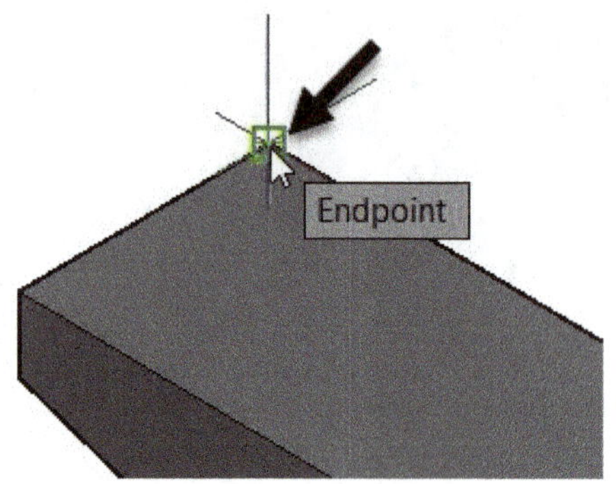

21. Select the **Length** option from the command line.
22. Type **.87**, and press ENTER.
23. Type **.87**, and press ENTER.
24. Move the pointer downward and click outside the model.

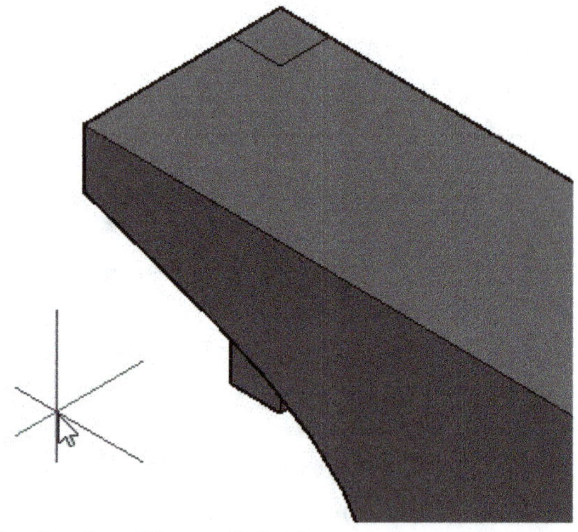

25. On the ribbon, click **Home** tab > **Modeling** panel > **Primitives** drop-down > **Cylinder**.
26. Select the corner point of the model, as shown.

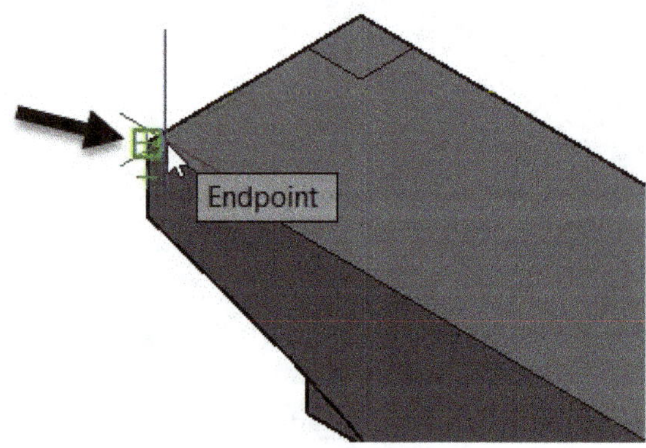

27. Type .25, and press ENTER.

28. Move the pointer downward and click outside the model.

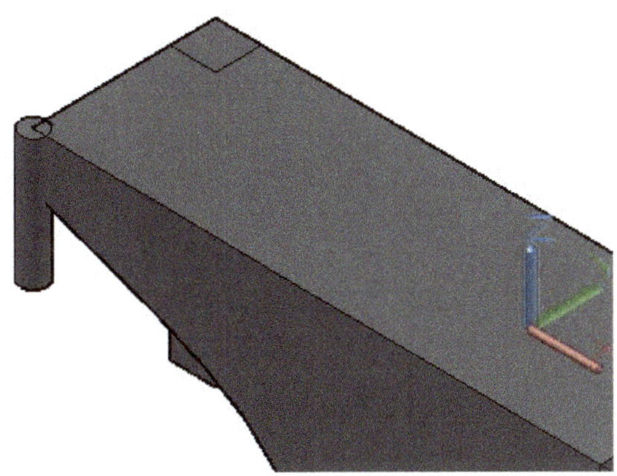

29. Select the cylinder.
30. Click on the X-axis of the move gizmo.
31. Move the pointer along the selected axis.

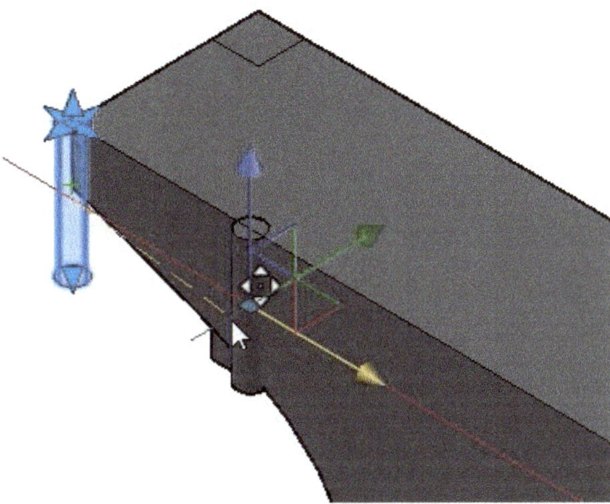

32. Type 1.2 and press ENTER.
33. Click on the Y-axis of the move gizmo.
34. Move the pointer along the selected axis.

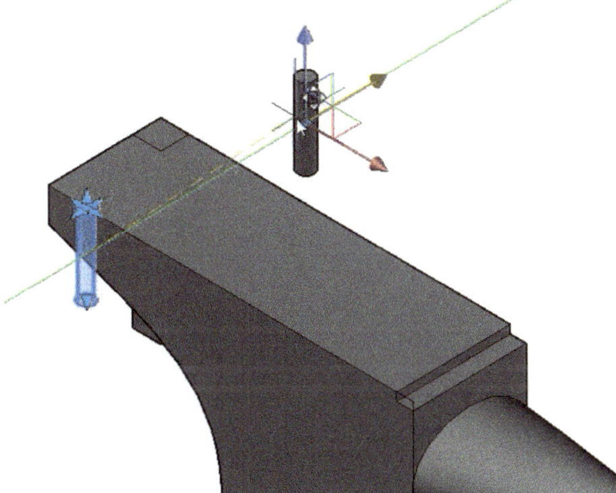

35. Type 1 and press ENTER.
36. Press ESC.
37. Select the box.
38. Click on the X-axis of the move gizmo.
39. Move the pointer along the selected axis.

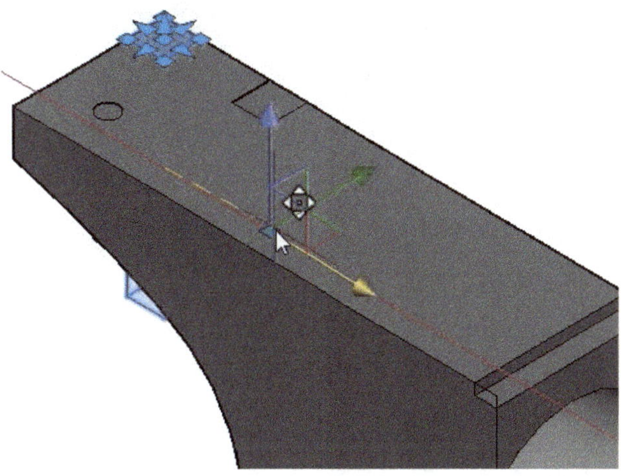

40. Type 1.87 and press ENTER.
41. Click on the Y-axis of the move gizmo.
42. Move the pointer toward left along the selected axis.

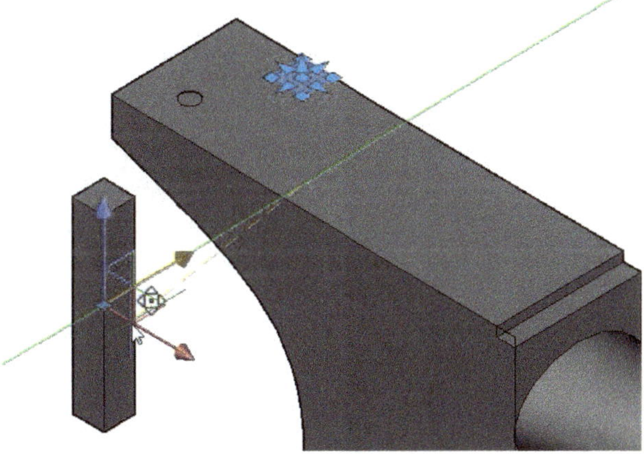

43. Type 1.34 and press ENTER.
44. Press ESC.
45. On the ribbon, click the **Home** tab > **Modeling** panel > **Solid Editing** drop-down > **Solid, Subtract**.
46. Click on the loft body.

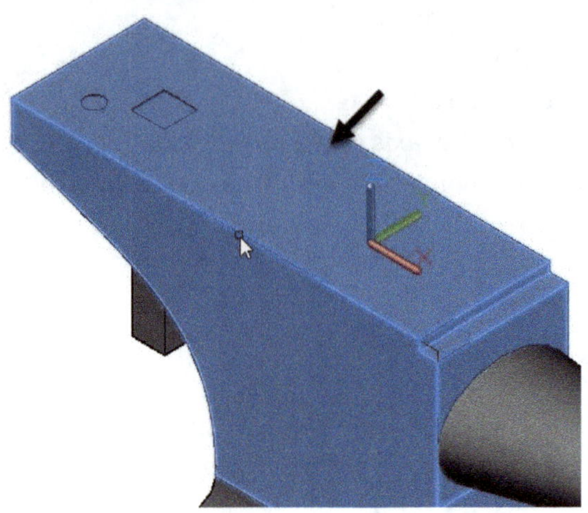

47. Press ENTER.
48. Select the cylinder and box.
49. Press ENTER.

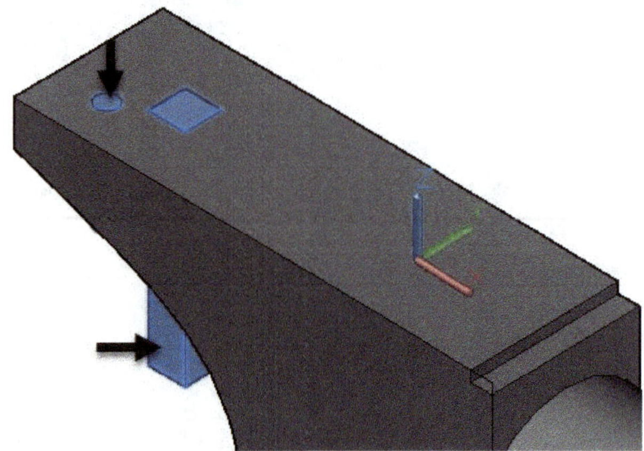

50. On the ribbon, click the **Home** tab > **Modeling** panel > **Solid Editing** drop-down > **Solid, Union**.
51. Create a selection window across all the objects.
52. Press ENTER.
53. Save and close the file.

Exercises

Exercise 1

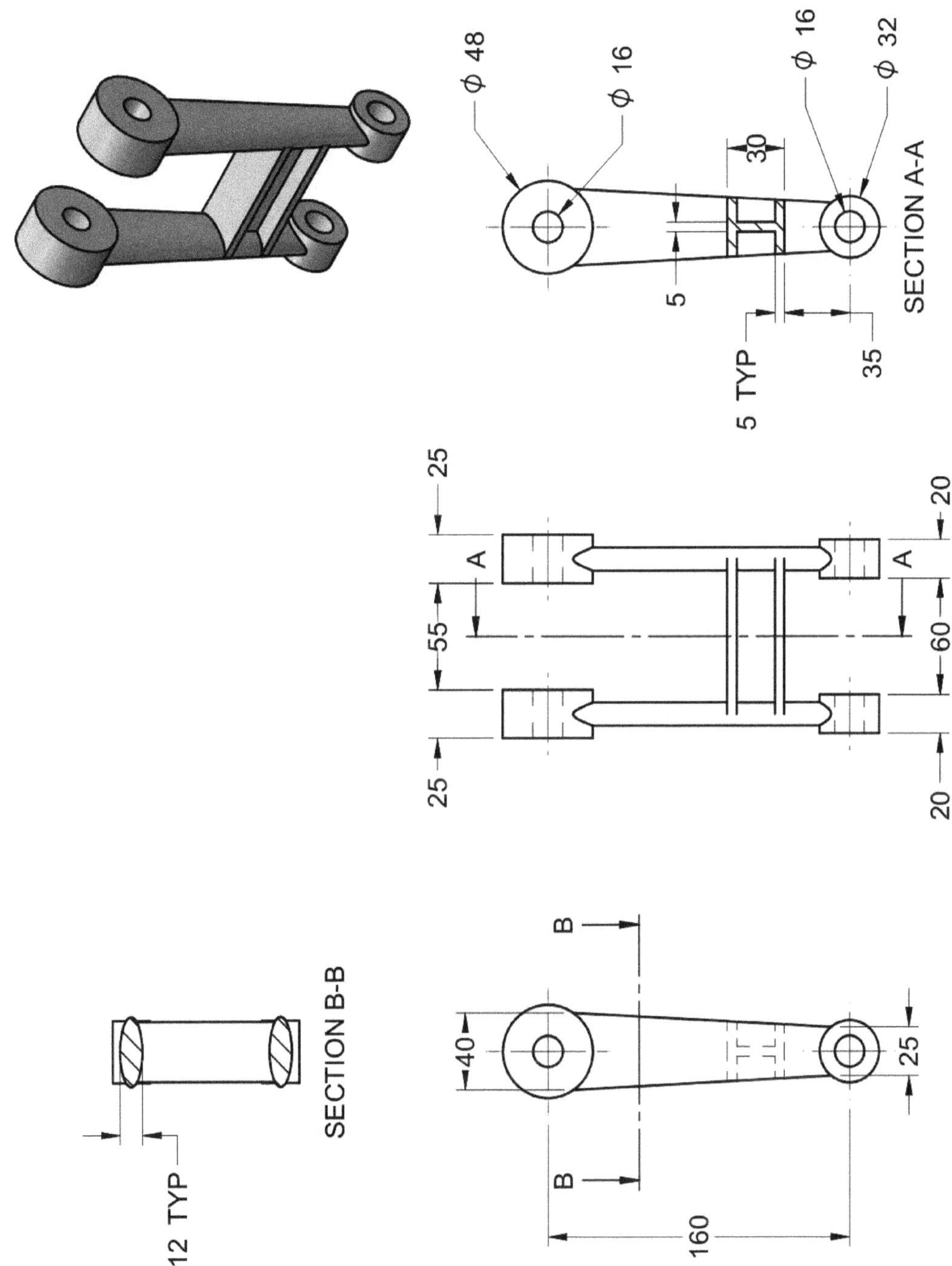

Chapter 7: Modifying Parts

In the design process, it is not required to achieve the final model in the first attempt. There is always a need to modify the existing parts to get the desired part geometry. In this chapter, you will learn various commands and techniques to make changes to a part.

The topics covered in this chapter are:

- *Offset Faces*
- *Move faces*
- *Rotate faces*
- *Extrude faces*
- *Delete faces*

The SOLIDEDIT command

AutoCAD provides you with a special tool called **SOLIDEDIT** to modify faces and planes of part geometry. You can perform various operations using this tool: **Offset**, **Translate**, **Rotate**, **Extrude,** and **Delete** faces.

Offset Faces

The **Offset Faces** option moves the selected face in the direction perpendicular to it. To offset a face, select the **Offset** option from the **Solid Editing** drop-down available on the **Solid Editing** panel of the **Home** tab of the ribbon. Next, click on the face to offset, and press ENTER. Type in a value in the command line and press ENTER. You can offset the face in the opposite direction by entering a negative offset distance value in the command line. Press ESC.

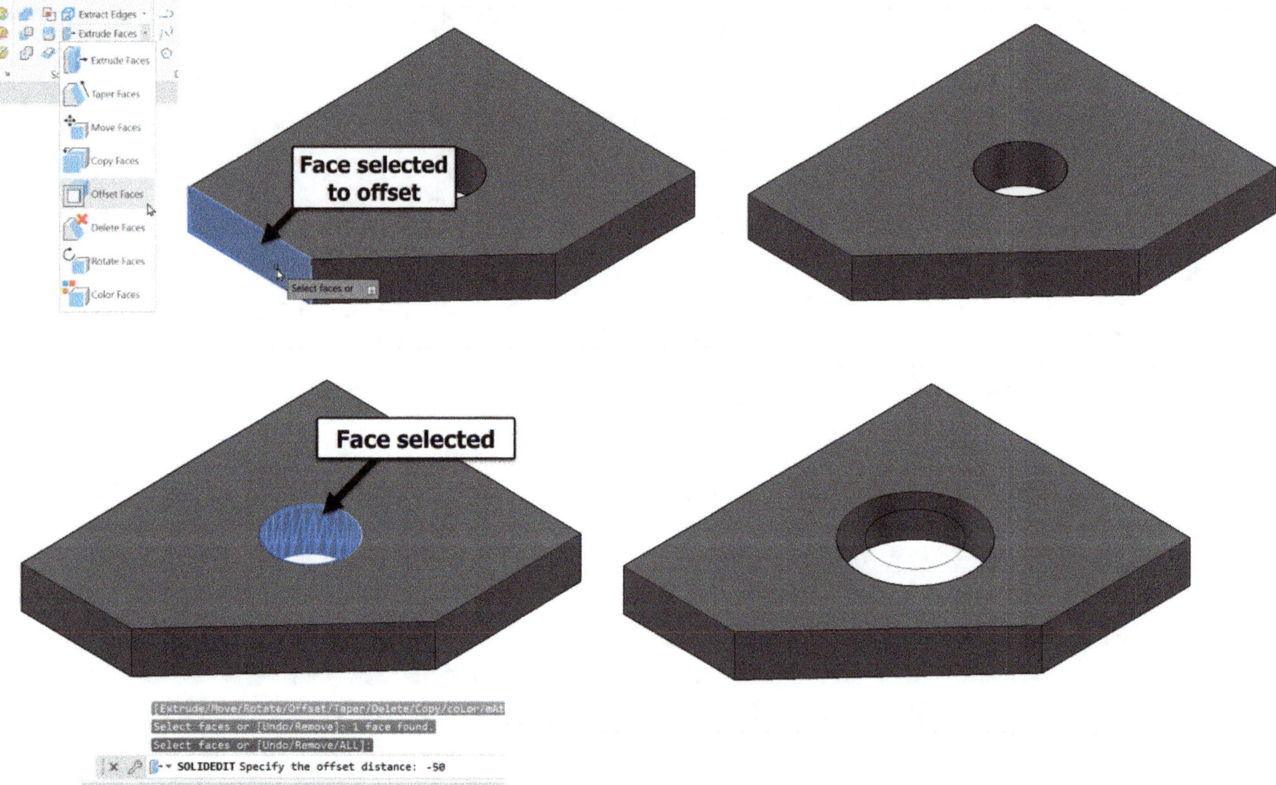

Move Faces

The **Move Faces** option allows you to move the selected face(s) along the perpendicular direction. To move faces, select the **Move Faces** option from the **Solid Editing** drop-down on the **Solid Editing** panel. Next, click on the face to move, and then press ENTER. Specify the base point by selecting a vertex from the 3D model. Next, move the pointer and click to specify the destination point (or) type-in the displacement value and press ENTER.

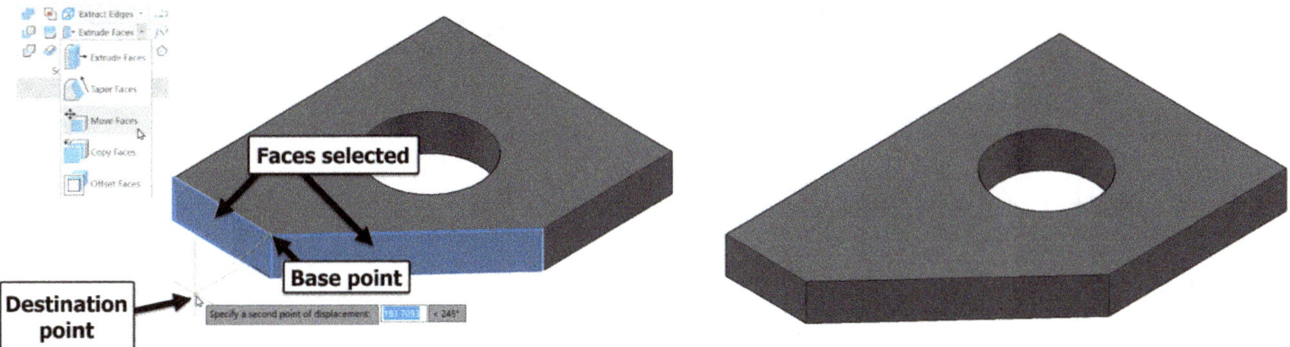

Rotate faces

The **Rotate Faces** option helps you to rotate the selected faces about an axis. On the ribbon, click **Home** tab > **Solid Editing** panel > **Solid Editing** drop-down > **Rotate Faces**. Select the face to rotate and press ENTER. Next, you need to define the axis of rotation by specifying the start and end points. Specify the start and endpoints of the axis, as shown. Next, type-in the rotation angle and press ENTER.

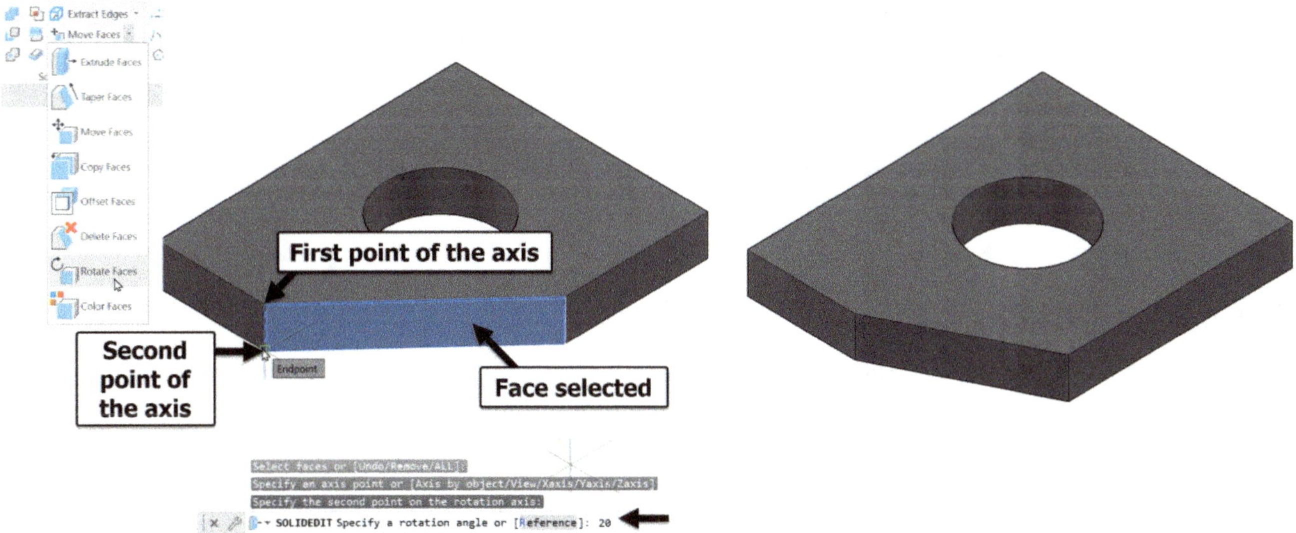

Extrude Face

Use the **Extrude Face** command (on the ribbon, click **Home** > **Solid Editing** panel > **Solid Editing** drop-down > **Extrude Face**), if you want to pull the selected face and add new faces to the model. Activate the Extrude Face command select the face to be extruded. Next, press ENTER and type-in the extrusion height in the command line. Next, you need to specify the taper angle of the extrusion. You can press ENTER to specify the taper angle as zero.

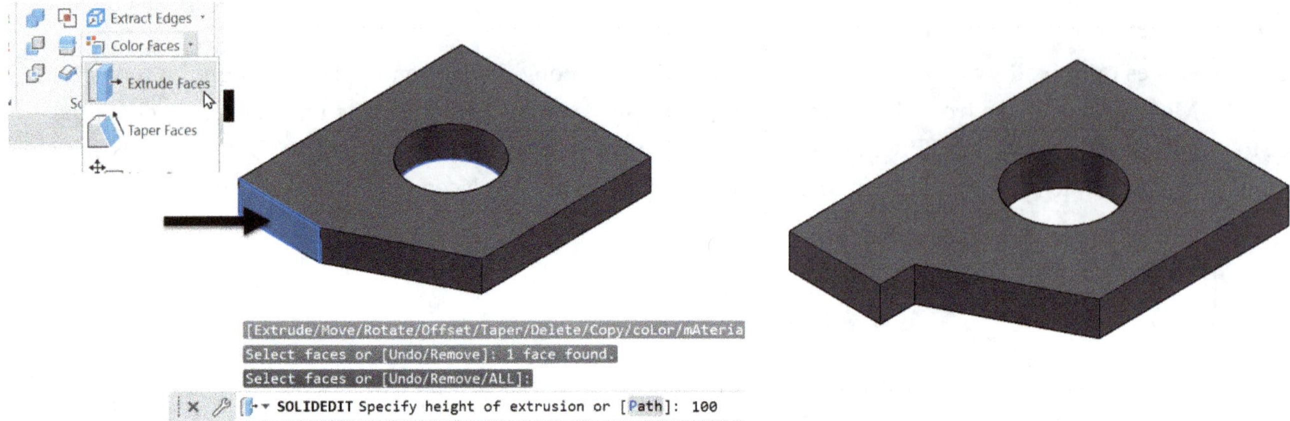

The new faces will be added perpendicular to the extruded face.

Delete Face

This option deletes the selected set of faces and adjusts the side faces. On the ribbon, click **Home > Solid Editing** panel > **Solid Editing** drop-down > **Delete Faces**. Next, select the faces to delete.

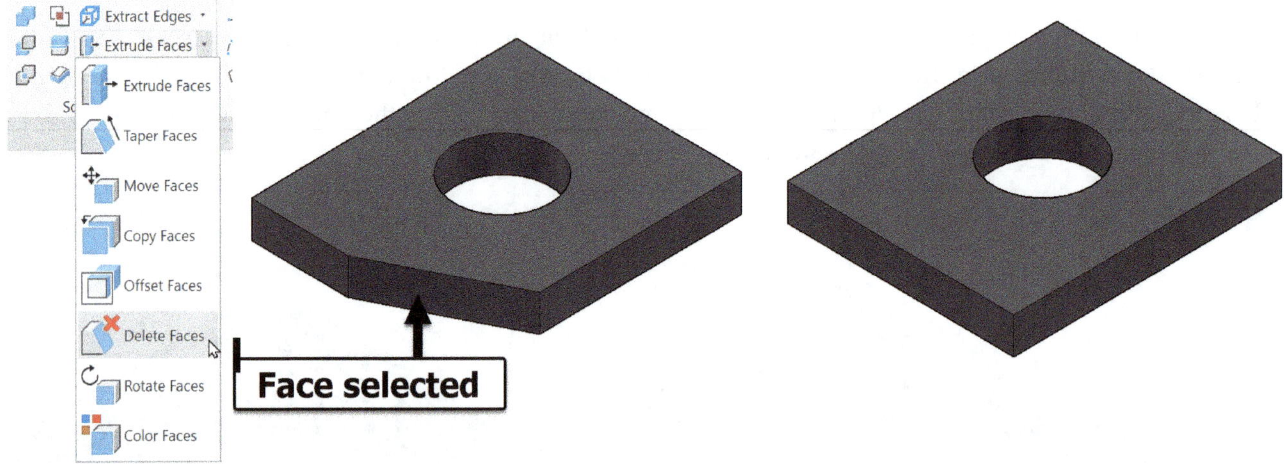

Tutorial 1 (Millimetres)

In this example, you create the part shown below and then modify it using the editing tools.

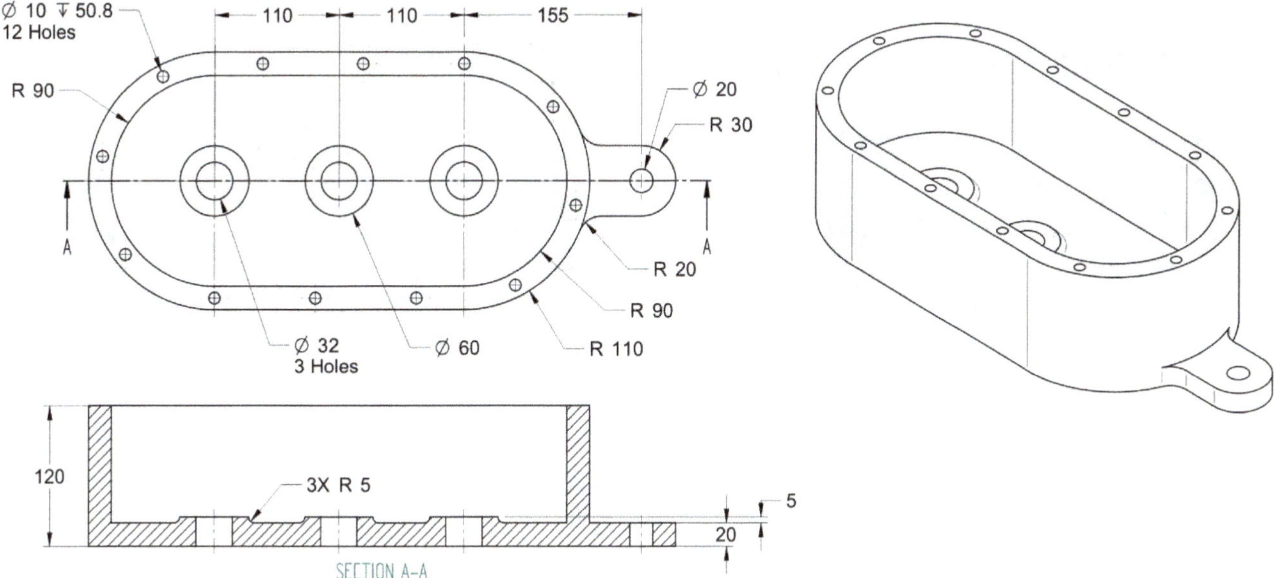

Creating a New File

1. Click the **New** icon on the Quick Access Toolbar.
2. Select the **acadiso3D** template from the **Select template** dialog.
3. Click the **Open** button.
4. Deactivate the **GRIDMODE** icon on the status bar.

Creating the Base

1. Activate the **Orthomode** icon on the status bar.
2. On the ribbon, click **Home** tab > **Modeling** panel > **Primitives** drop-down > **Box**.
3. Type 0,0 and press ENTER to specify the first corner of the box.
4. Select the **Length** option from the command line.
5. Type 220, and press ENTER.
6. Type 220, and press ENTER.
7. Type 120, and press ENTER.
8. On the ribbon, click **Home** tab > **Modeling** panel > **Primitives** drop-down > **Cylinder**.
9. Select the midpoint of the top-left edge, as shown.

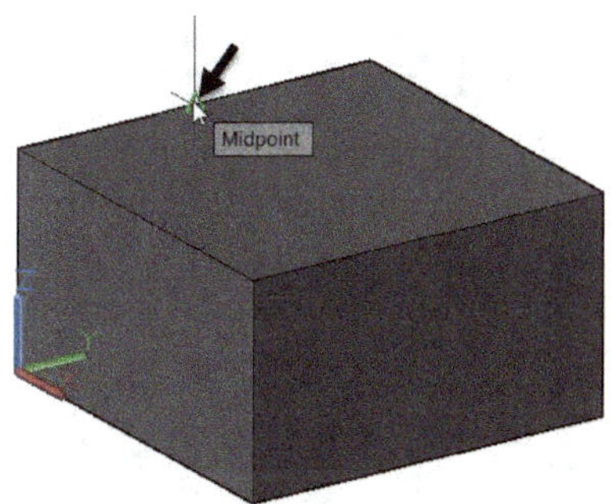

10. Select the top-left corner of the box.

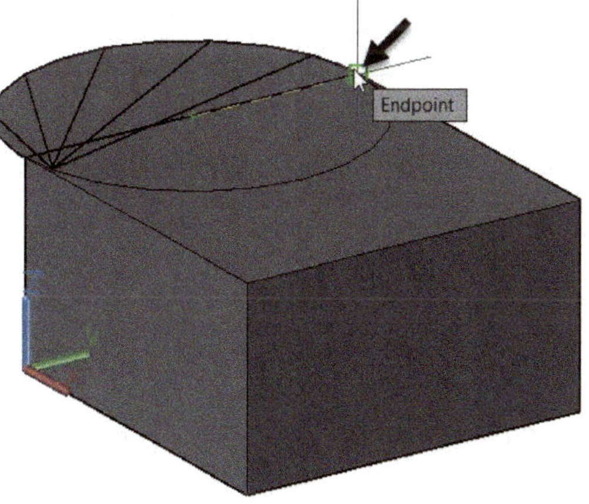

11. Move the pointer downward and select the bottom corner of the box.

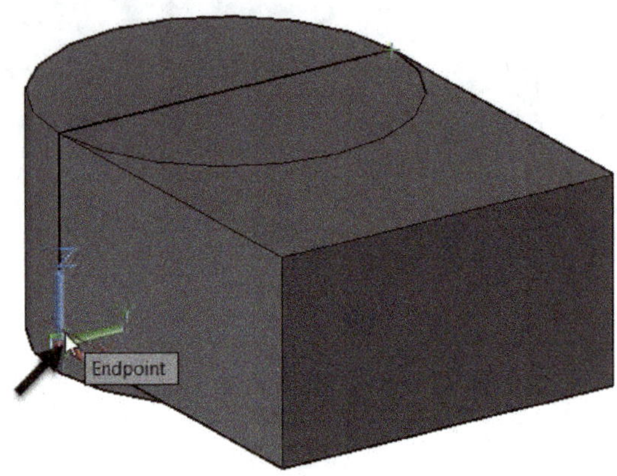

12. Likewise, create another cylinder on the right side of the box.

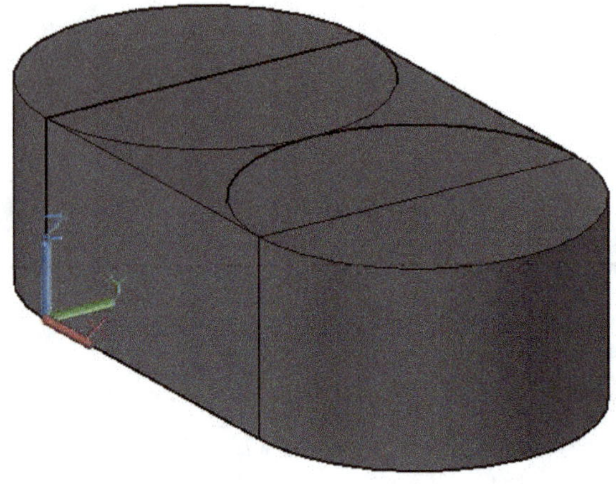

13. On the ribbon, click **Home** tab > **Solid Editing** panel > **Solid, Union**.
14. Create a selection window across all the elements of the model.
15. Press ENTER to combine all the objects.
16. On the ribbon, click the **Solid** tab > **Solid Editing** panel > **Shell**.
17. Select the solid body.
18. Click on the top face of the body.
19. Press ENTER.
20. Type **20** in the command line and press ENTER.

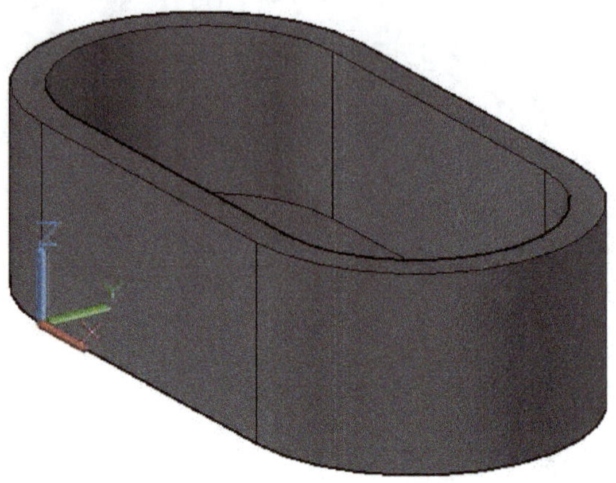

Adding Features and Holes

1. On the ribbon, click **Home** tab > **Modeling** panel > **Primitives** drop-down > **Cylinder**.
2. Select the midpoint of the curved bottom edge, as shown.

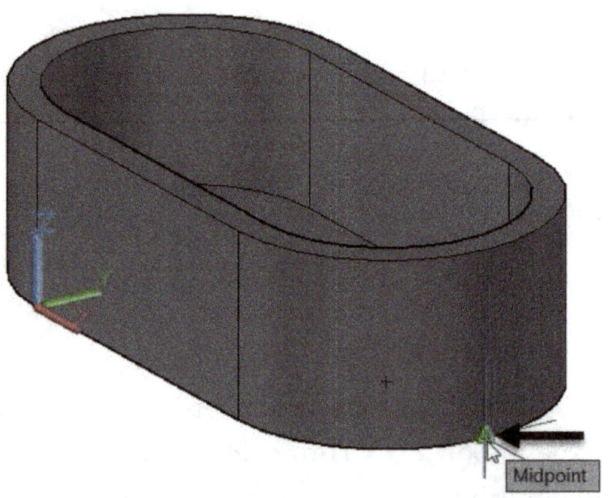

3. Type 30 and press ENTER to specify the radius.
4. Type 20 and press ENTER to specify the height.

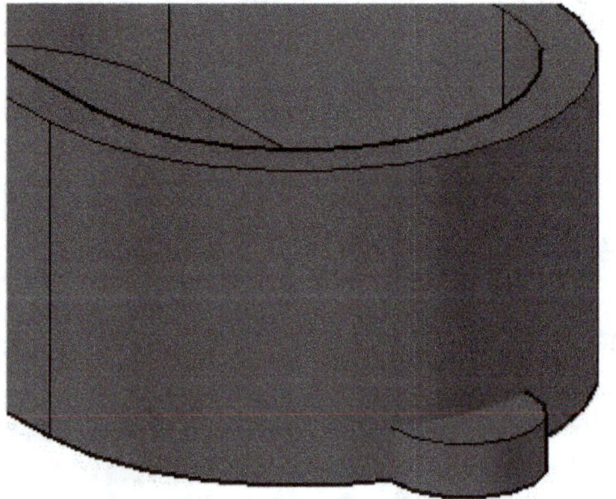

5. Select the newly created cylinder.
6. Select the X-axis of the move gizmo.

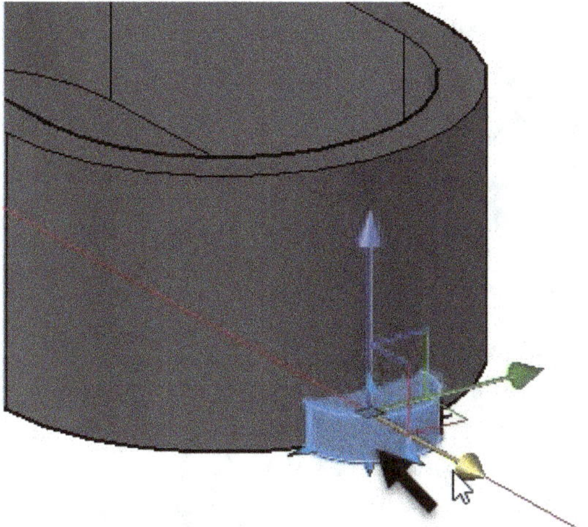

7. Move along the selected axis.

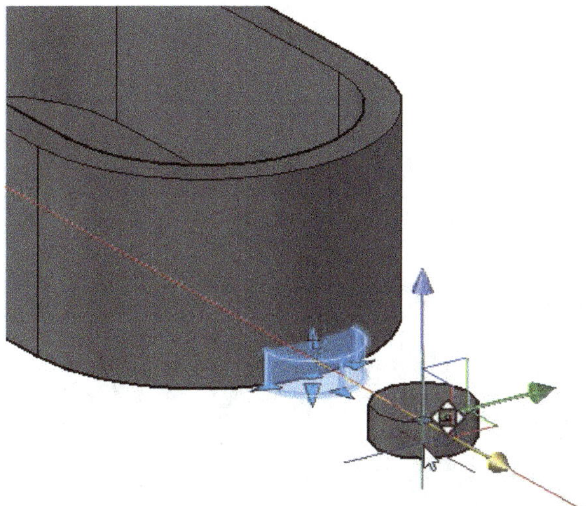

8. Type 45 and press ENTER.

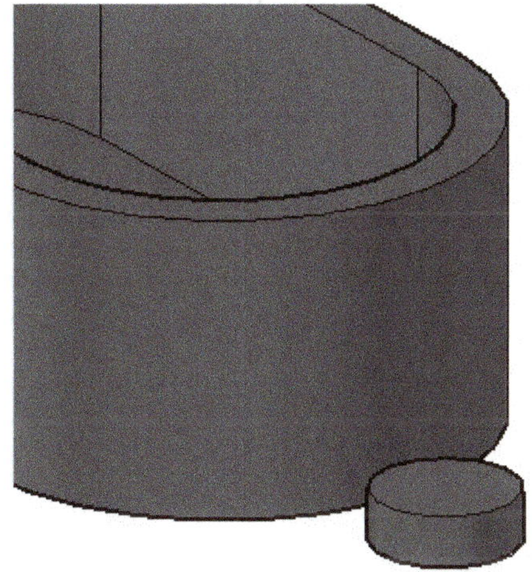

9. On the ribbon, click **Home** tab > **Modeling** panel > **Primitives** drop-down > **Box**.

10. Select the quadrant point of the lower circular edge of the cylinder.

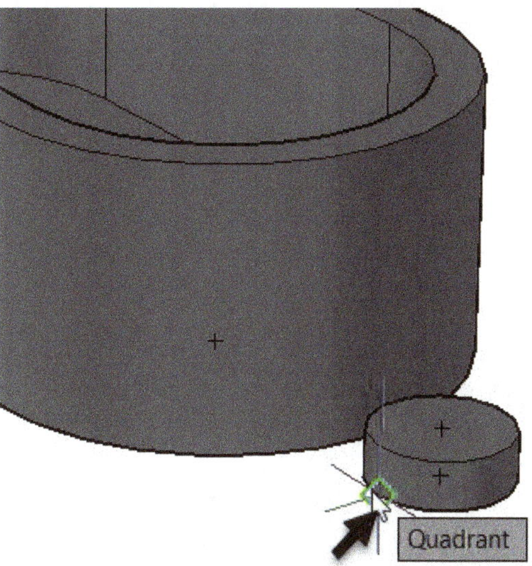

11. Select the **Length** option from the command line.
12. Type -60 and press ENTER.
13. Type -60 and press ENTER.
14. Type 20 and press ENTER.

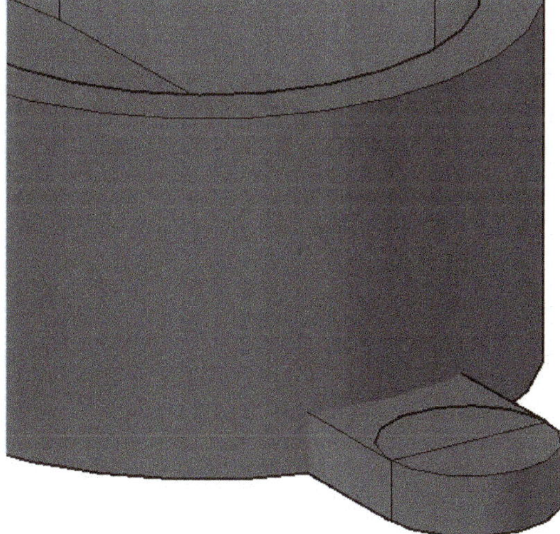

15. On the ribbon, click **Home** tab > **Coordinates** panel > **View** drop-down > **Face**.

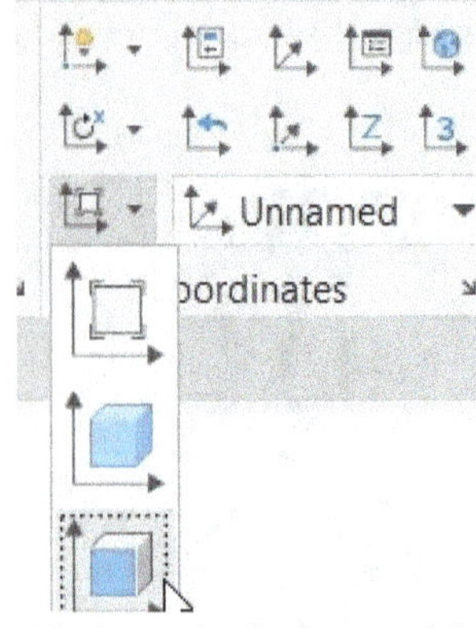

16. Click on the horizontal face of the shell.

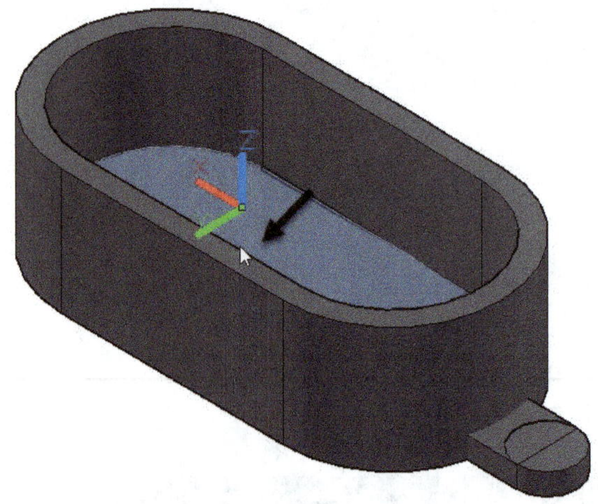

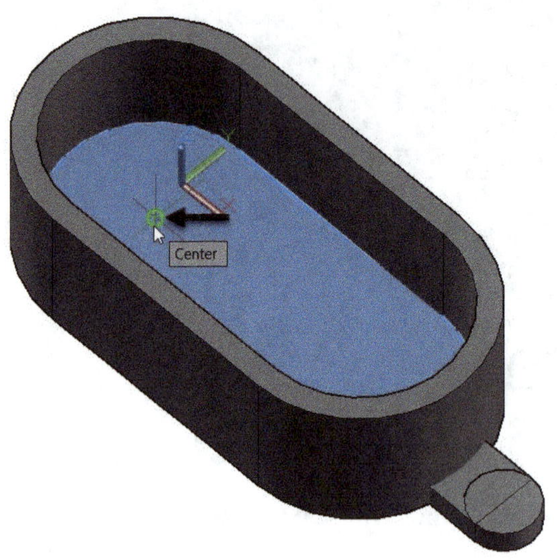

17. Press ENTER to accept the selection. The UCS is placed on the selected face.
18. On the ribbon, click **Home** tab > **Modeling** panel > **Primitives** drop-down > **Cylinder**.
19. Place the pointer on the circular edge on the left side; the centerpoint of the circular edge is displayed.
20. Select the centerpoint of the circular edge.

21. Type 30 and press ENTER.
22. Type 5 and press ENTER.

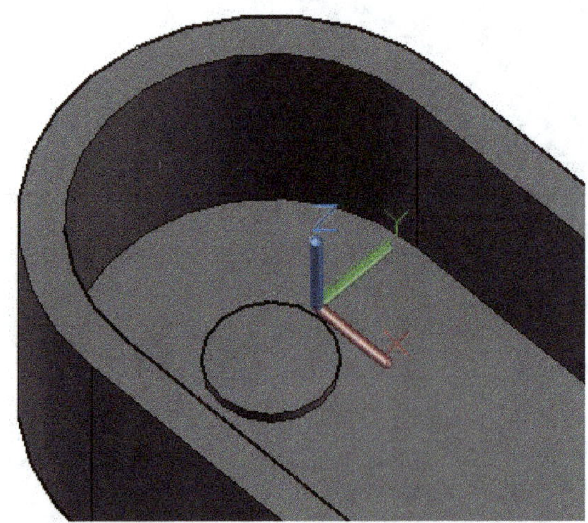

23. Select the newly created cylinder.
24. On the ribbon, click **Home** tab > **Modify** panel > **Array** drop-down > **Rectangular Array**.
25. On the **Array Creation** tab of the ribbon, type **3**, and **1** in the **Columns** and **Rows** boxes, respectively.
26. Type **110** in the **Between** box on the **Columns** panel.
27. Click the **Close Array** icon.

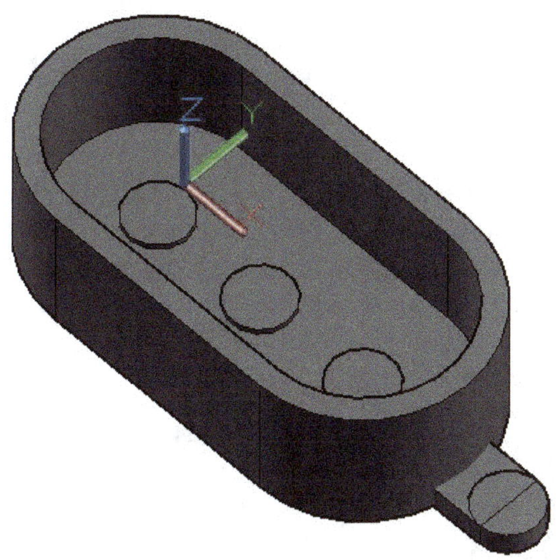

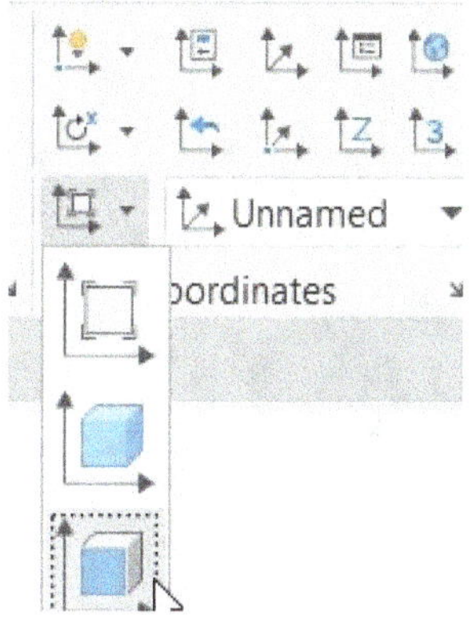

28. On the ribbon, click **Home** tab > **Solid Editing** panel > **Solid, Union**.
29. Create a selection window across all the objects of the model, and press ENTER.

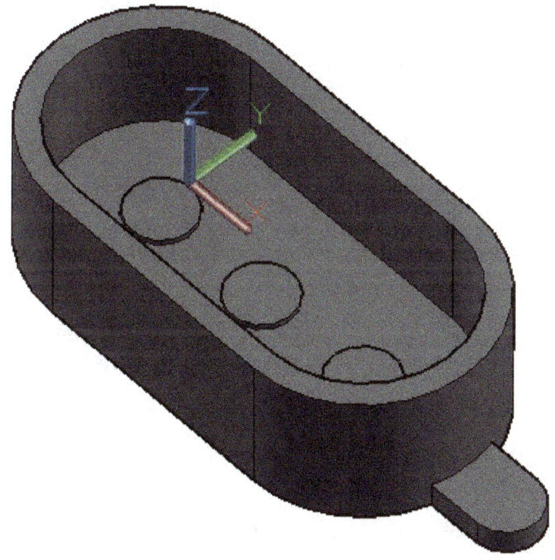

30. On the ribbon, click **Home** tab > **Coordinates** panel > **View** drop-down > **Face**.

31. Click on the top face of the newly created cylinder.

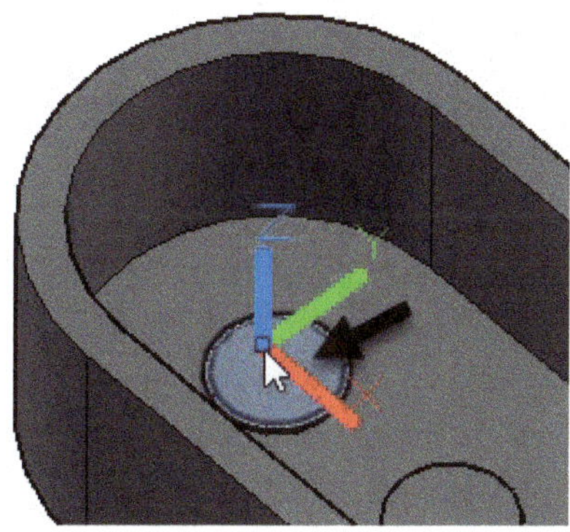

32. Press ENTER to accept the selection. The UCS is placed on the selected face.
33. On the ribbon, click **Home** tab > **Modeling** panel > **Primitives** drop-down > **Cylinder**.
34. Place the pointer on the circular edge of the cylinder; the centerpoint of the circular edge is displayed.
35. Select the centerpoint of the circular edge.

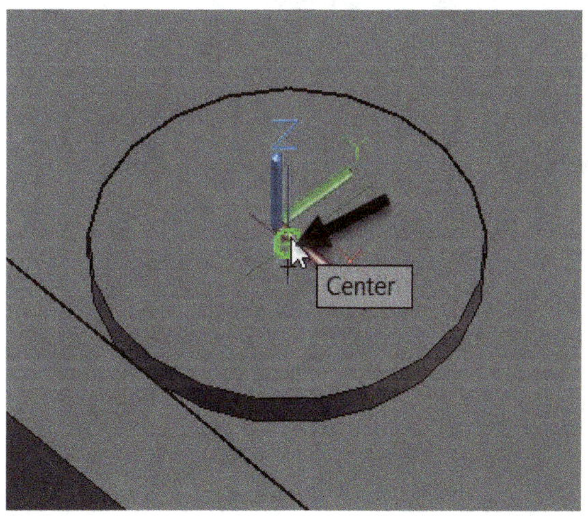

36. Type 16 and press ENTER.
37. Move the pointer downward and click outside the model.

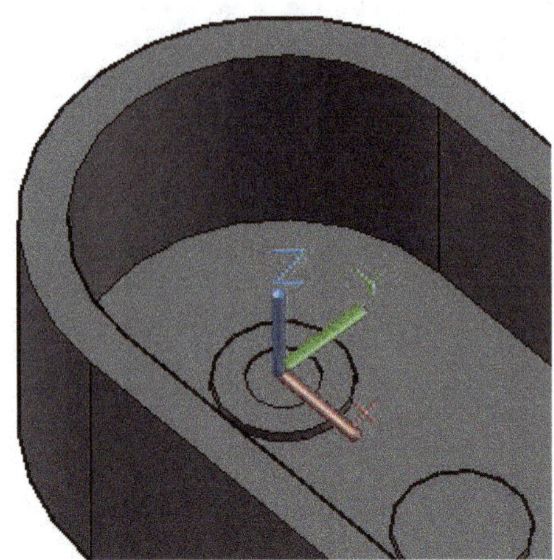

38. Select the newly created cylinder.
39. On the ribbon, click **Home** tab > **Modify** panel > **Array** drop-down > **Rectangular Array**.
40. On the **Array Creation** tab of the ribbon, type **3,** and **1** in the **Columns** and **Rows** boxes, respectively.
41. Type **110** in the **Between** box on the **Columns** panel (enter a negative value if the array is displayed in the reverse direction).
42. Click the **Close Array** icon.

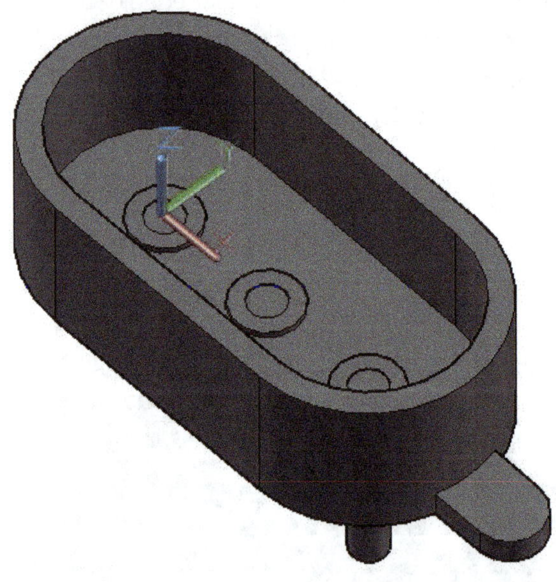

43. On the ribbon, click **Home** tab > **Modeling** panel > **Primitives** drop-down > **Cylinder**.
44. Place the pointer on the circular edge on the right side; the centerpoint of the circular edge is displayed.
45. Select the centerpoint of the circular edge.
46. Type 10 and press ENTER.
47. Move the pointer downward and click outside the model.

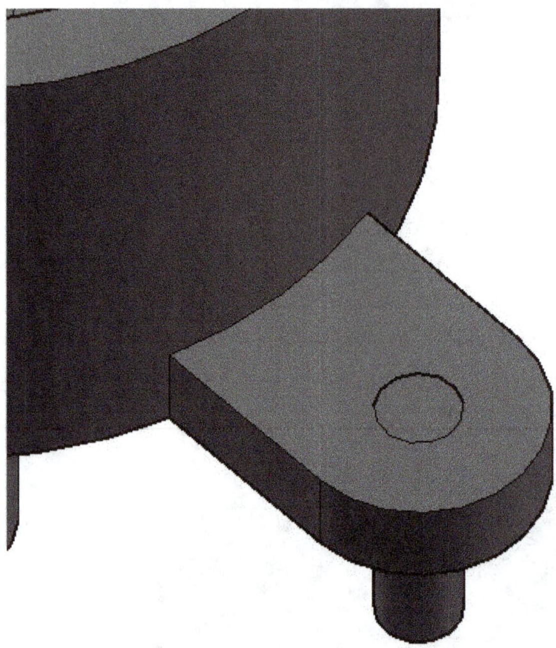

48. On the ribbon, click **Home** tab > **Modeling** panel > **Primitives** drop-down > **Cylinder**.
49. Press and hold the SHIFT key.
50. Right-click and select the **Mid Between 2 Points** option.
51. Select the vertices of the model, as shown.

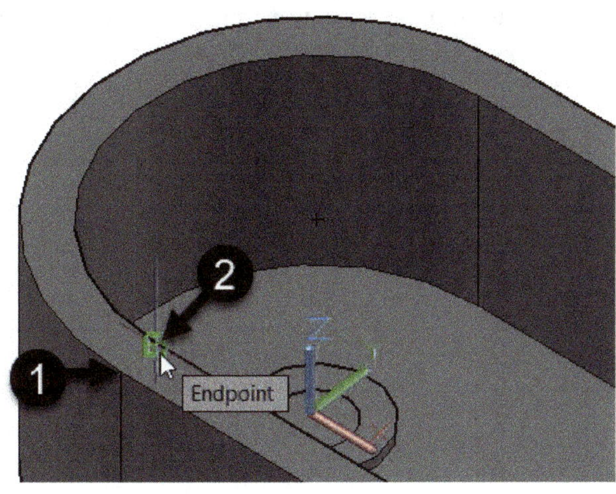

52. Type 5 and press ENTER.
53. Type -50.8 and press ENTER.

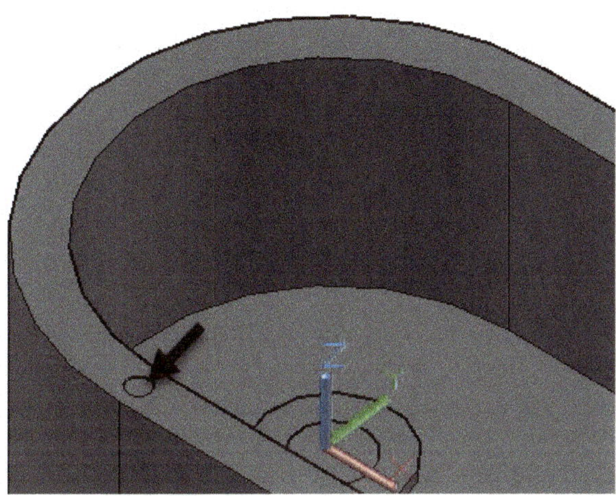

54. Change the **Visual Style** to **2D Wireframe**.
55. On the ribbon, click **Home** tab > **Selection** panel > **Filter** drop-down > **Edge**.

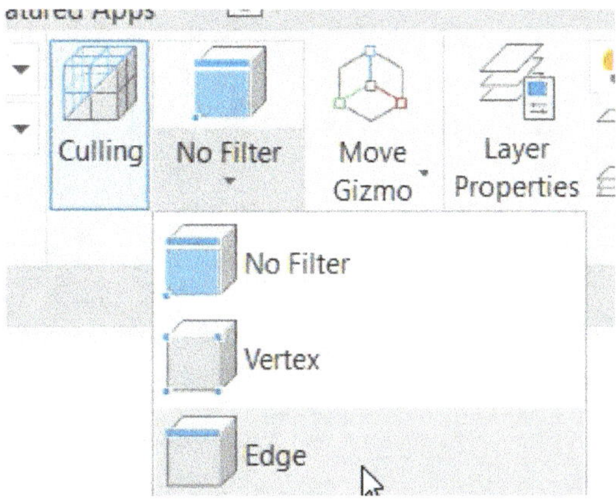

56. On the ribbon, click **Home** tab > **Solid Editing** panel > **Edge** drop-down > **Extract Edges**.

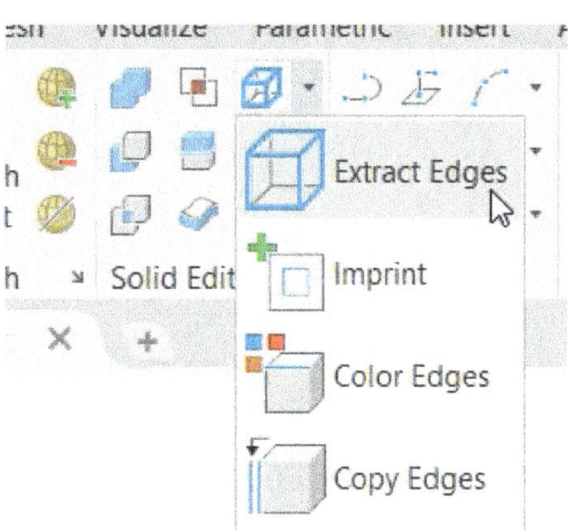

57. Select the edges of the model, as shown.

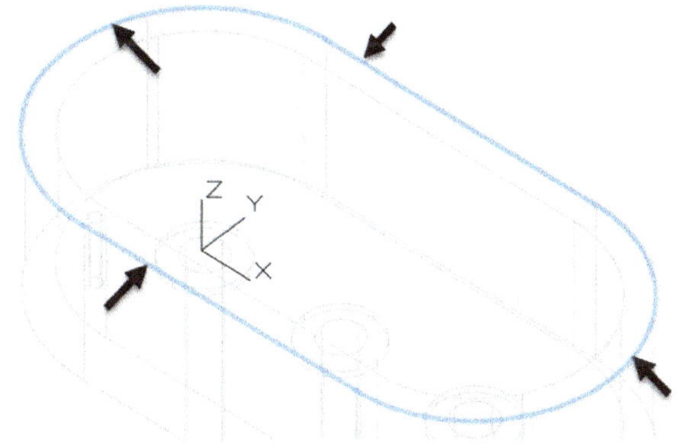

58. Press ENTER.
59. On the ribbon, click the **Home** tab > **Modify** panel > **Offset**.
60. Type 10 and press ENTER.
61. Select the extracted horizontal edge.
62. Move the pointer inside the model and click.
63. Likewise, offset the other edges, as shown.

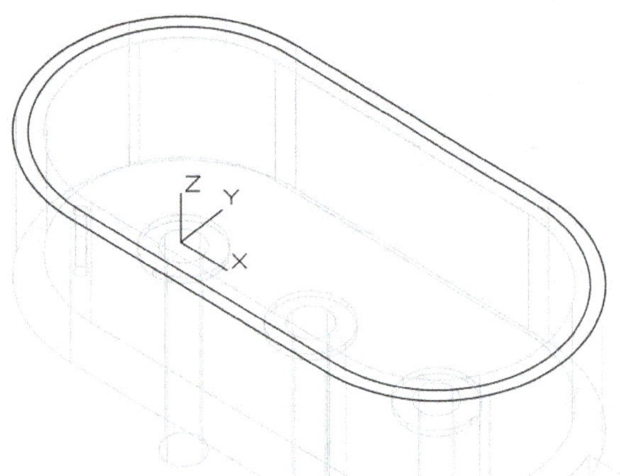

64. On the **Home** tab of the ribbon, expand the **Modify** panel and click the **Edit Polyline** icon.

65. Select the **Multiple** option from the command line.
66. Select all the offset entities and press ENTER.

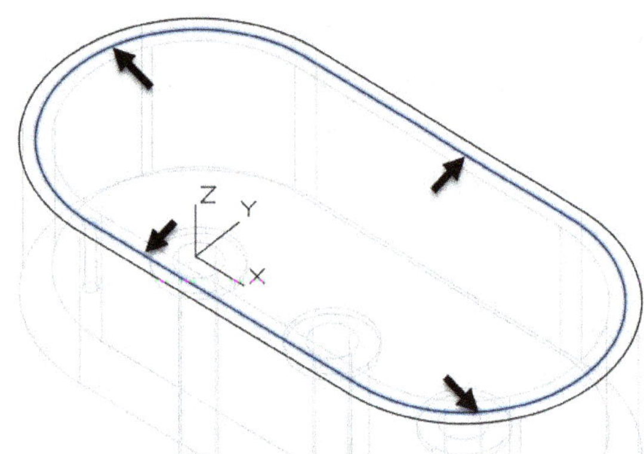

67. Select **Yes** from the command line.
68. Select the **Join** option from the command line.
69. Press ENTER to specify 0 as the fuzz distance.
70. Press ESC.

71. On the ribbon, click **Home** tab > **Selection** panel > **Filter** drop-down > **No Filter**.
72. On the ribbon, click **Home** tab > **Modify** panel > **Array** drop-down > **Path Array**.

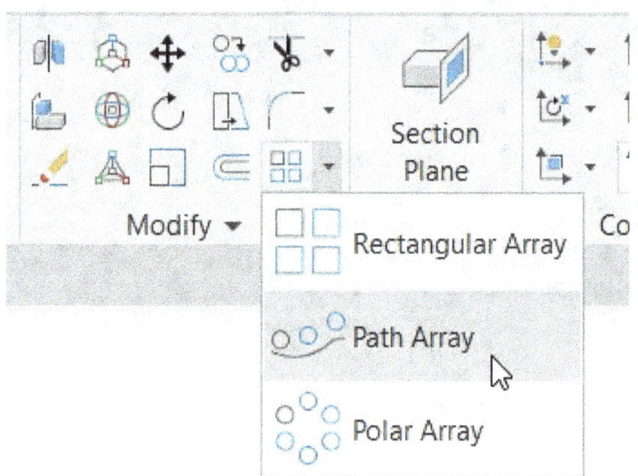

73. Select the cylinder and press ENTER.

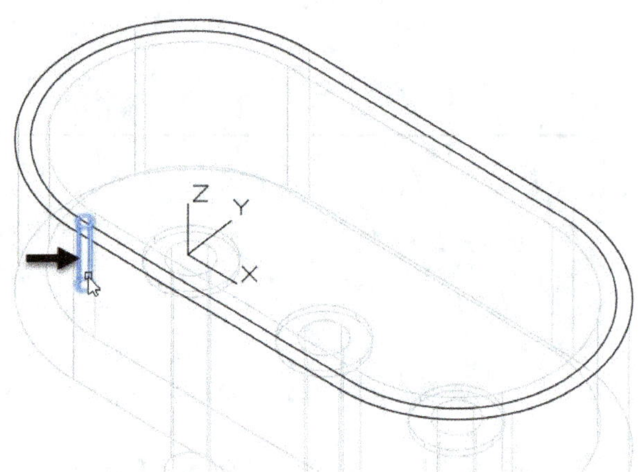

74. Select the polyline created using the **Edit Polyline** command.

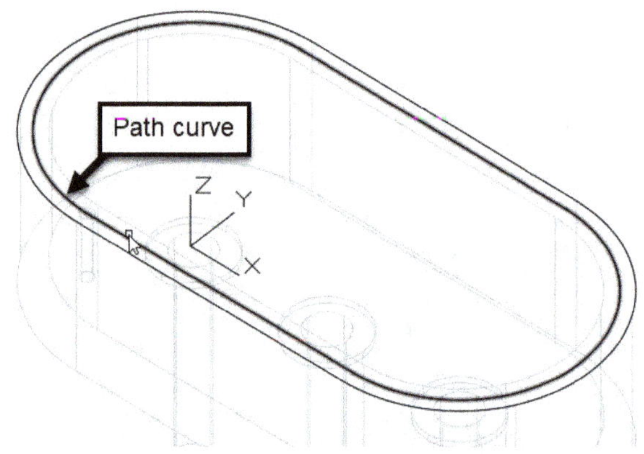

75. Click the **Base Point** icon on the **Properties** panel.

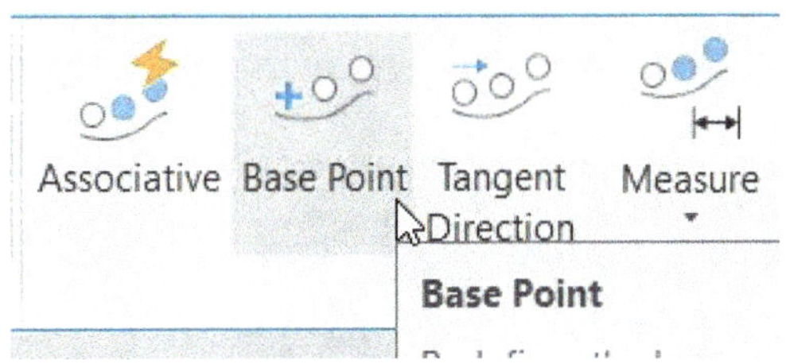

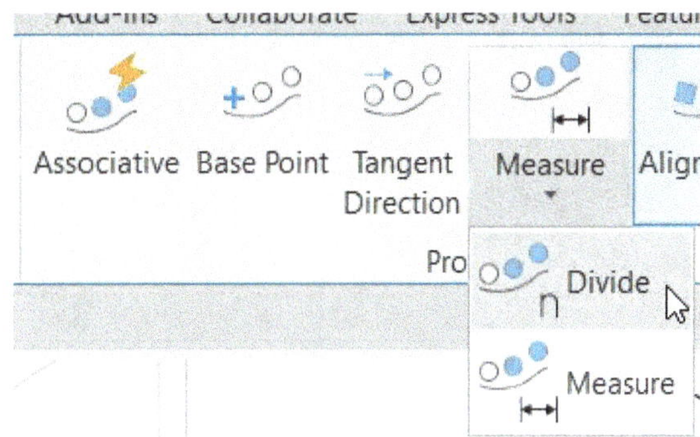

76. Select the centerpoint of the cylinder to be arrayed.

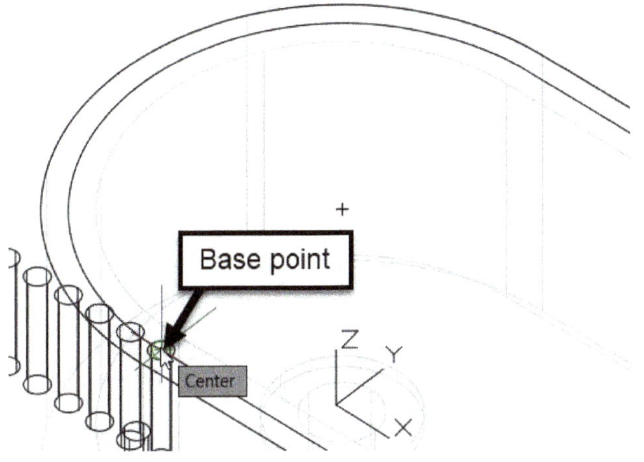

77. Click the **Item Count** icon on the **Items** panel.

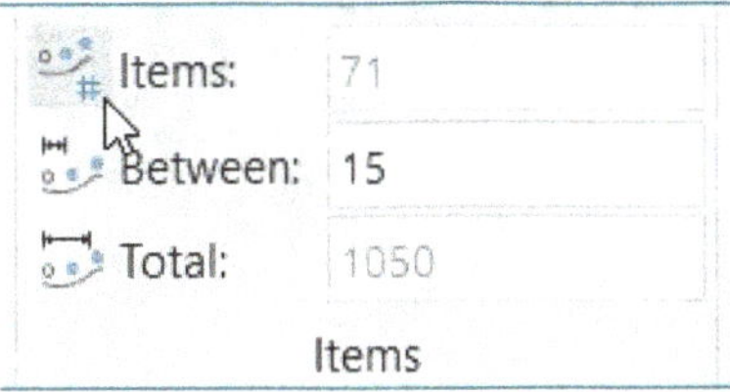

78. Type **12** in the **Items** box on the **Items** panel.

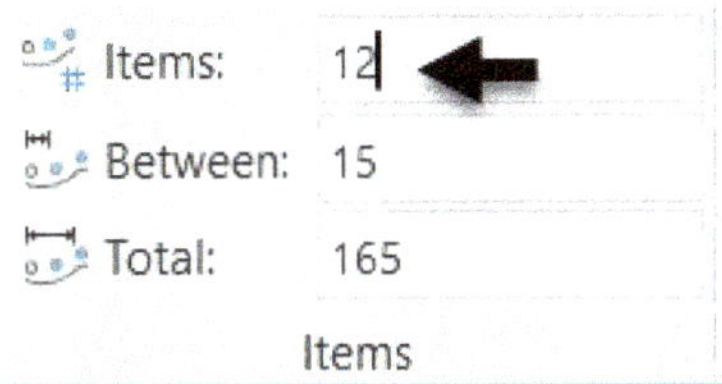

79. Click **Measure Method** drop-down > **Divide** on the **Properties** panel.

80. Click the **Close Array** icon.
81. Select the polyline and the extracted edges.
82. Press DELETE.

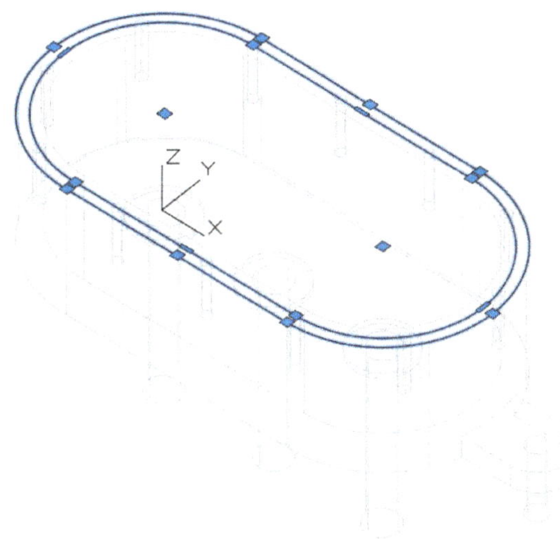

83. On the ribbon, click **Home** tab > **Solid Editing** panel > **Solid, Subtract**.

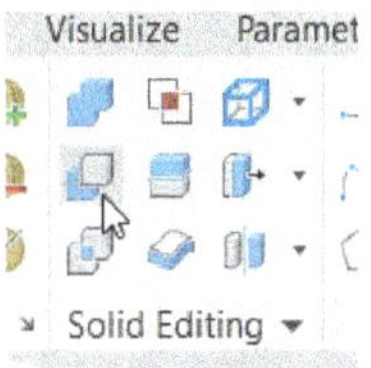

84. Select the main body and press ENTER.

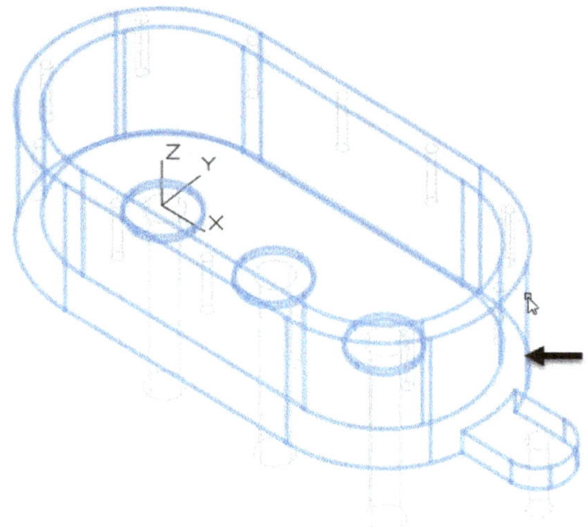

85. Select all the cylinders and press ENTER.

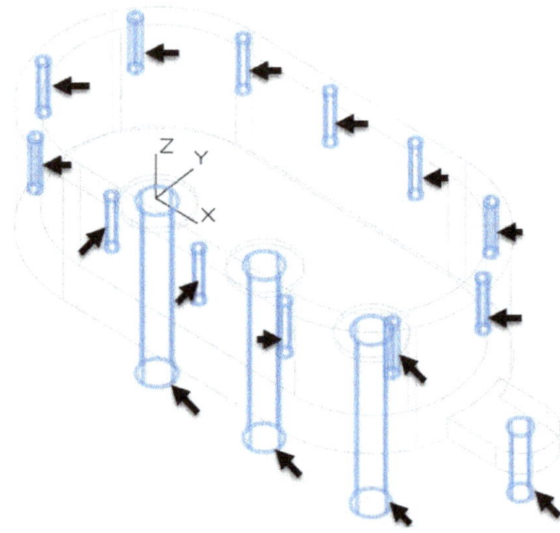

86. Change the **Visual Style** to **Shades of Gray**.

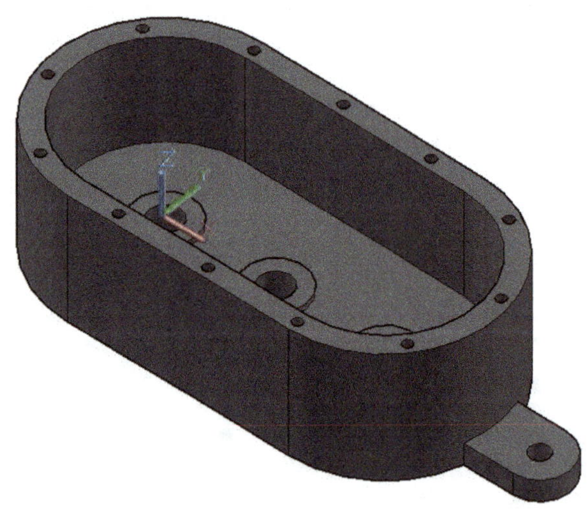

Creating Edge Fillets

1. On the ribbon, click **Solid** tab > **Solid Editing** panel > **Fillet Edge**.
2. Click on the vertical edges of the geometry, as shown.

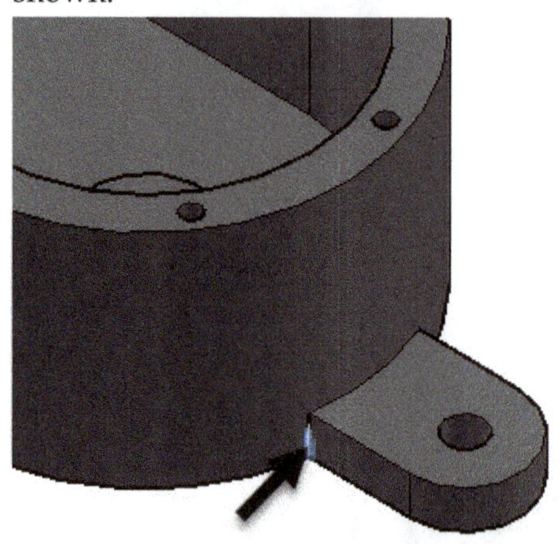

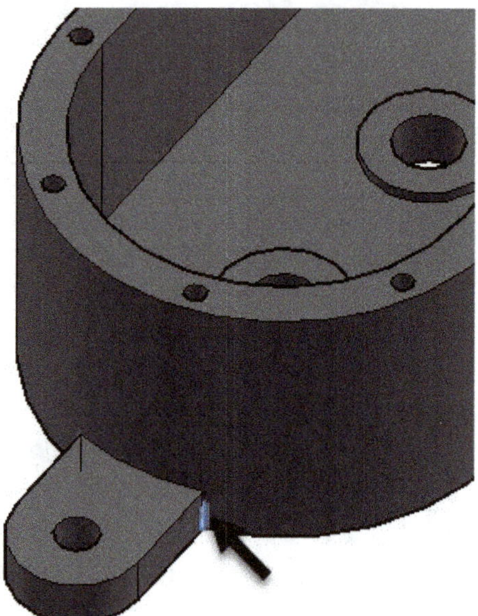

3. Select the **Radius** option from the command line.
4. Type 20 and press ENTER thrice.

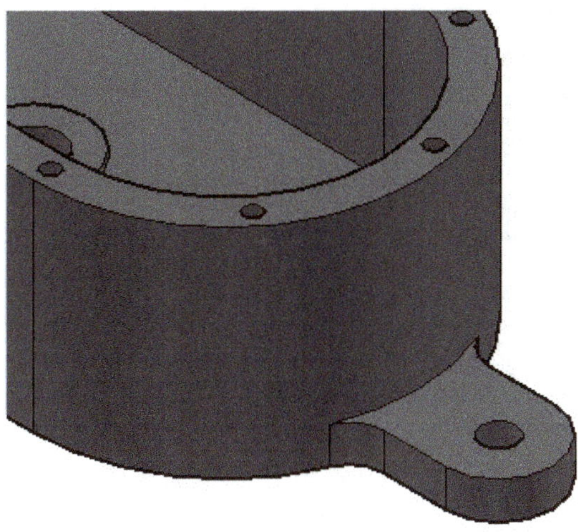

5. On the ribbon, click **Solid** tab > **Solid Editing** panel > **Fillet Edge**.

6. Click on the circular edges of the geometry, as shown.

7. Select the **Radius** option from the command line.

8. Type 5 and press ENTER thrice.

Moving Faces

1. On the ribbon, click the **Home** tab > **Solid Editing** panel > **Solid Editing** drop-down > **Move Faces**.

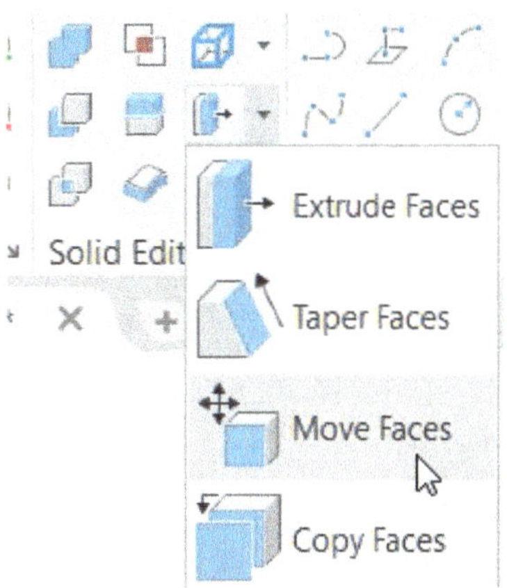

2. Select the cylindrical faces of the model, as shown.

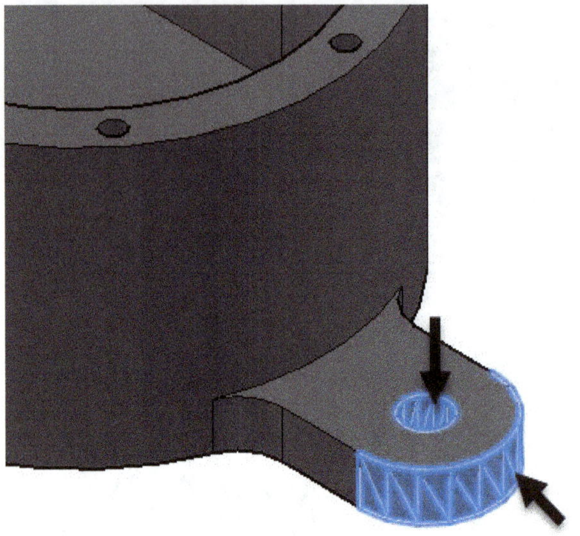

3. Press ENTER.
4. Select the endpoint of the circular edge.

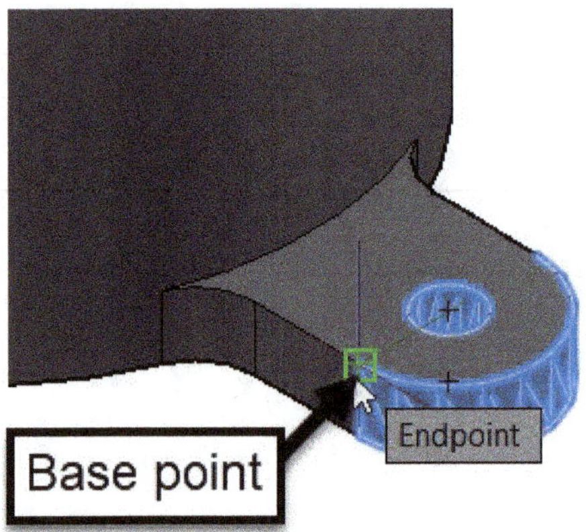

5. Move the pointer backward.

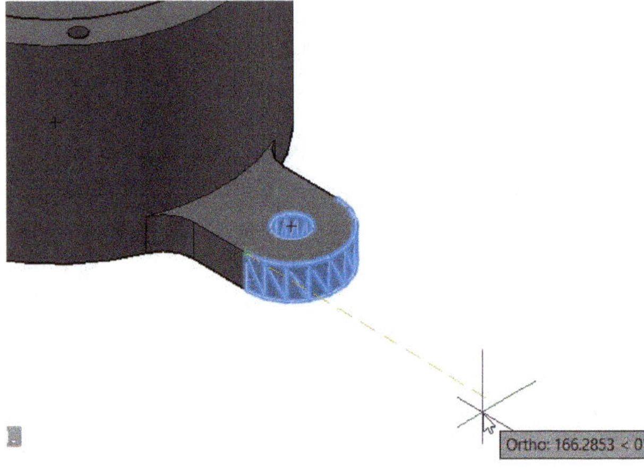

6. Type 20 and press ENTER.

7. Select the **Move** option from the command line.
8. Select the top face of the model.

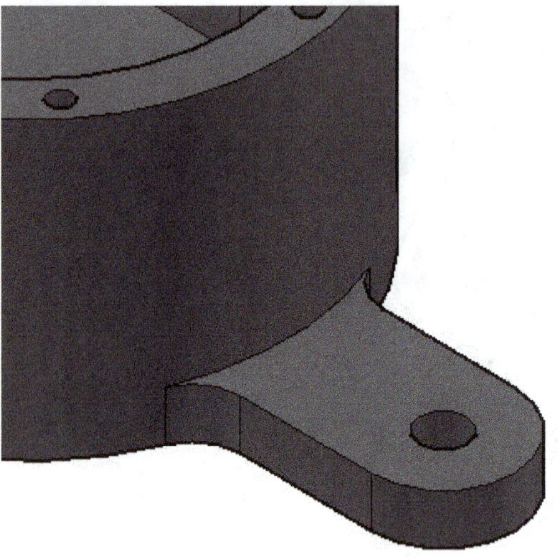

9. Press ENTER.
10. Select the endpoint of the vertical edge, as shown.

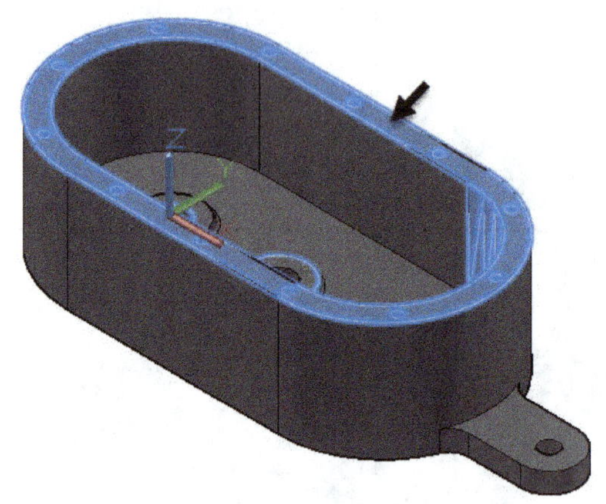

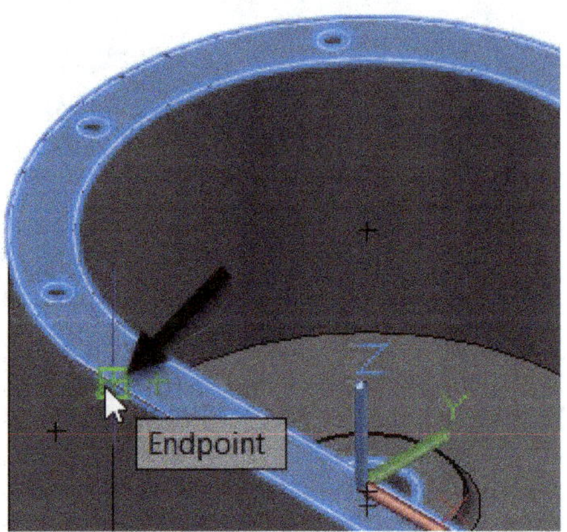

11. Move the pointer downward.

12. Type 40 and press ENTER.

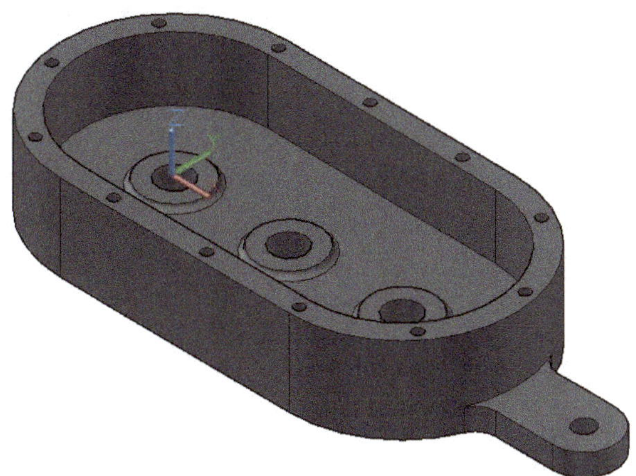

13. Click the **Orbit** tool on the Navigation Bar located at the right of the graphics window.

14. Press and hold the left mouse button and drag the pointer downward; the top portion is displayed.
15. Right-click and select **Exit**.
16. Select the **Move** option from the command line.
17. Select the bottom faces of the holes.
18. Press ENTER.

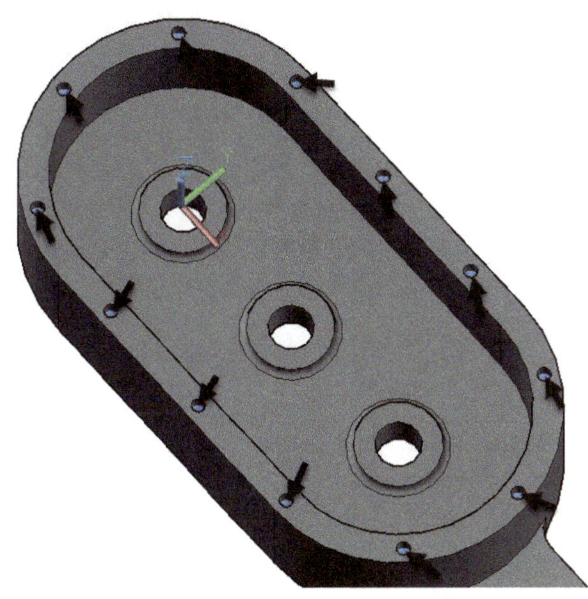

19. Select the endpoint of the vertical edge, as shown.

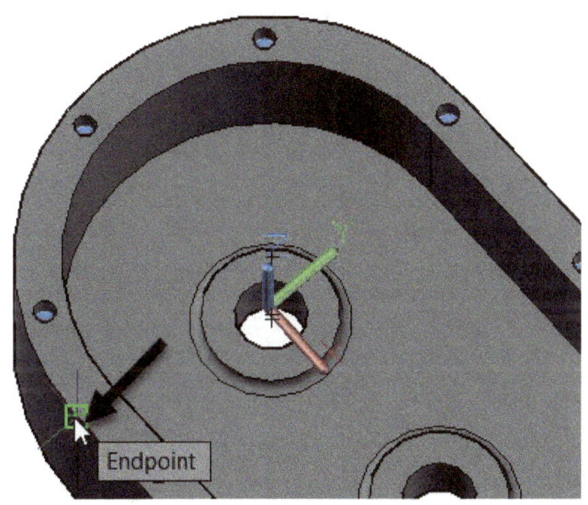

20. Move the pointer downward.
21. Type 40 and press ENTER.
22. Save and close the file.

Exercises

Exercise 1

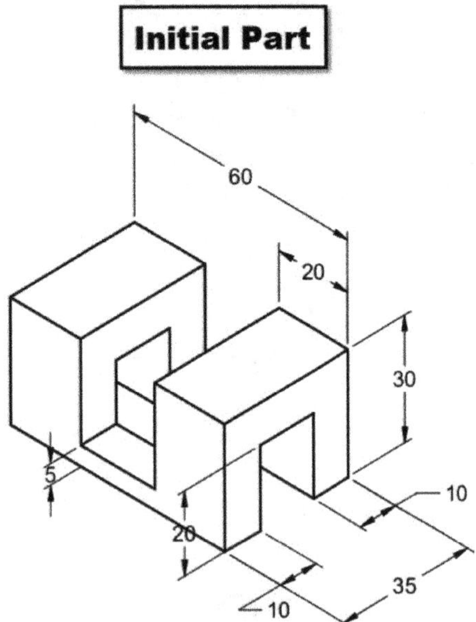

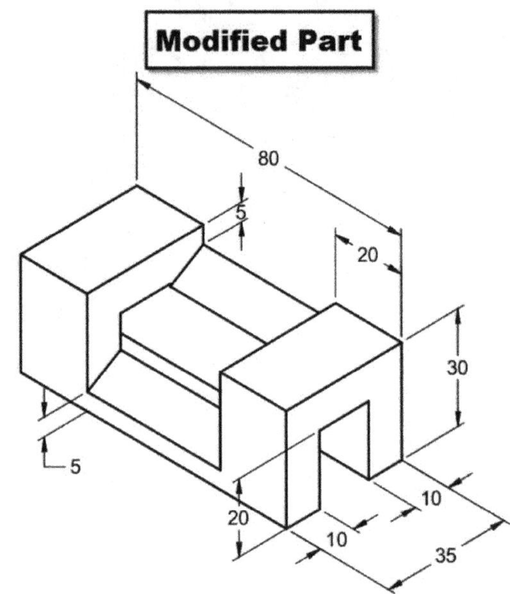

Exercise 2

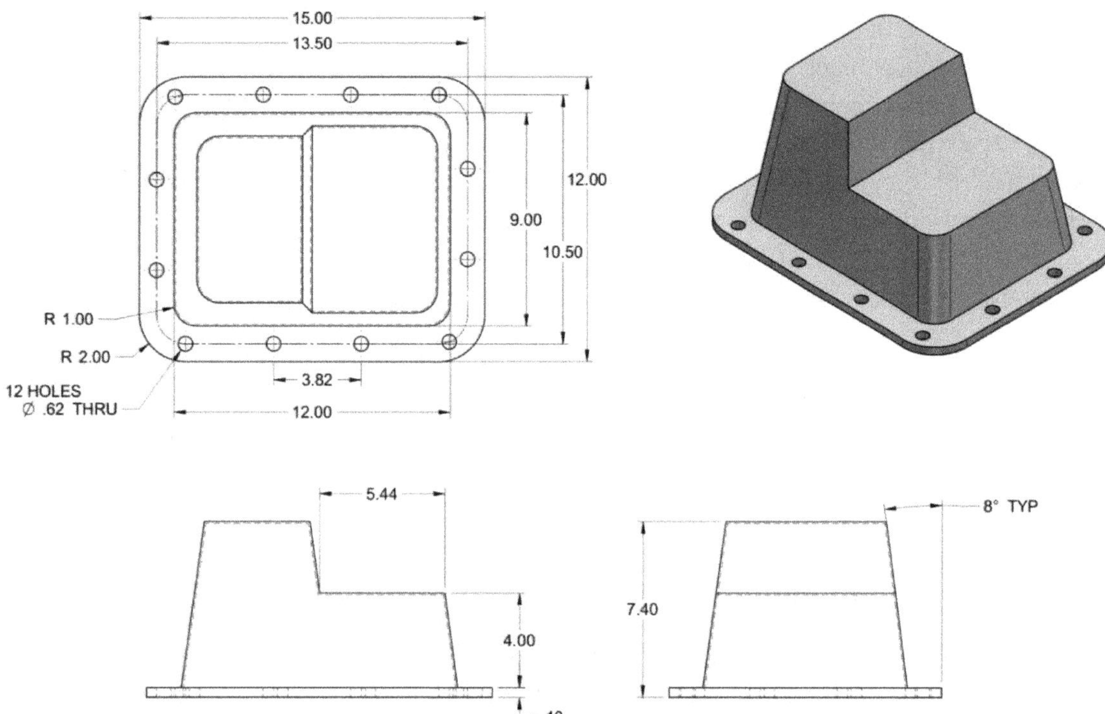

SHEET THICKNESS = 0.079 in

Chapter 8: Drawings

Drawings are used to document your 3D models in the traditional 2D format including dimensions and other instructions useful for the manufacturing purpose. In AutoCAD, you first create 3D models and assemblies, and then use them to generate the drawing. There is a direct association between the 3D model and the drawing. When changes are made to the model, every view in the drawing will be updated. This relationship between 3D model and the drawing makes the drawing process fast and accurate.

The topics covered in this chapter are:

- *Create model views*
- *Projected views*
- *Sections views*
- *Detail views*

Setting the Drafting Standard

Before you start generating the drawing views of the 3D model, you need to specify the drafting standard. It defines the way the views will be generated. To specify the drafting standard, click **Home > View > Drafting Standard (inclined arrow)** on the ribbon; the **Drafting Standard** dialog appears. In the **Drafting Standard** dialog, select the required option from the **Projection type** section.

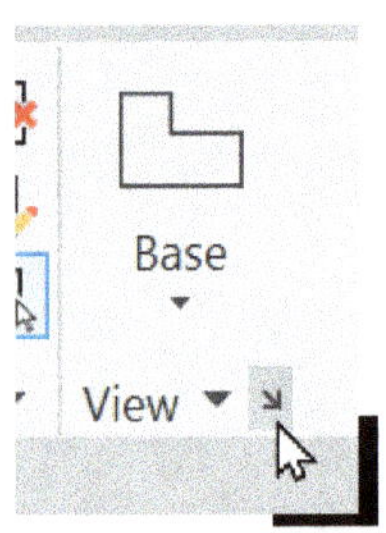

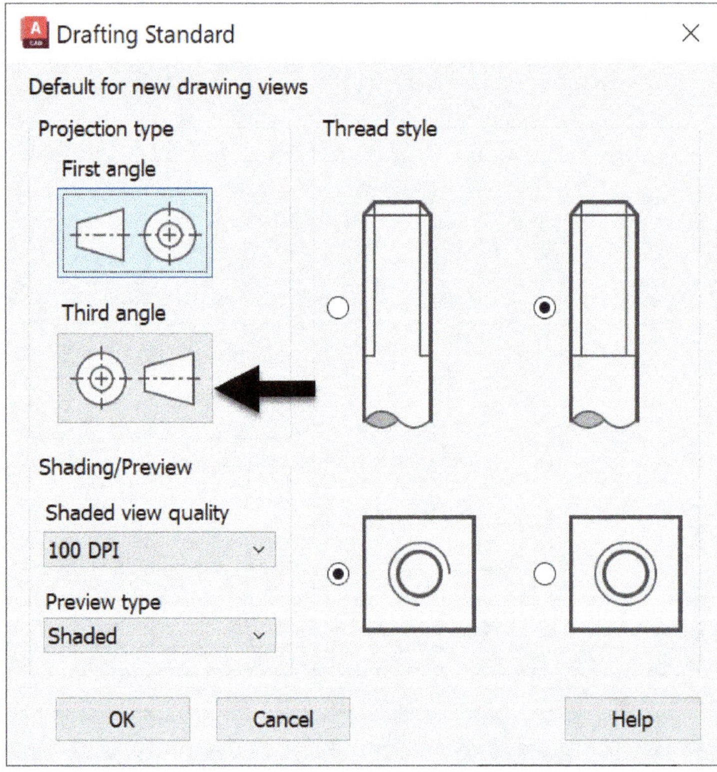

Examine the other options in the dialog, as they are self-explanatory. Click the **OK** button.

Creating a Base View

The base view will be the first view of the drawing. It can be any view (front, top, right, left, bottom, or back view) of the model. But commonly, the front or top views of the model are generated first. To generate the base view of the model, click **Home > View > Base > From Model Space** on the ribbon.

Select the **Entire model** option from the command line; the model in the model space will be selected and the message, "Enter new or existing layout name to make current or [?] <Layout1>:" appears in the command line. Press ENTER to select **Layout 1**; the base view will be attached to the pointer and the message, "Specify location of base view or [Type/sElect/Orientation/Hidden lines/Scale/Visibility] <Type>:" appears in the command line. Also, the **Drawing View Creation** tab appears in the ribbon. Specify the location of the view in the paper space.

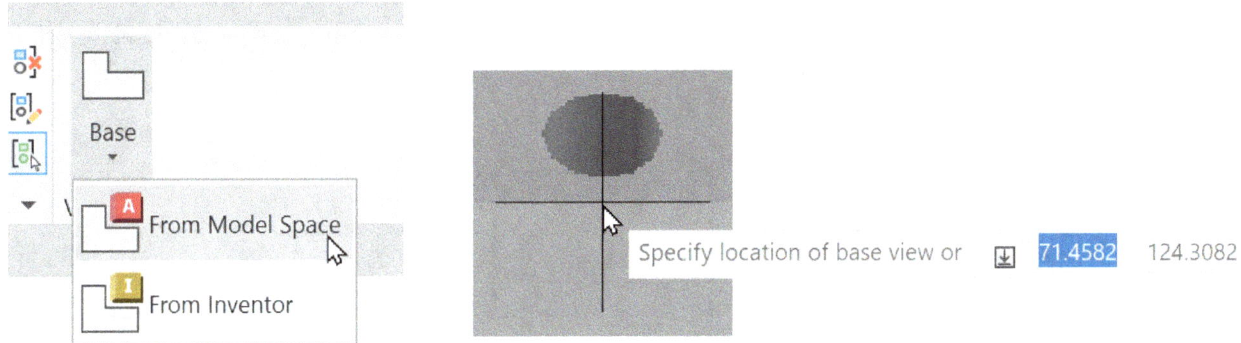

In the **Drawing View Creation** tab, select an option from the **Orientation** panel. Select the **Visible Lines** option from the **Hidden Lines** drop-down.

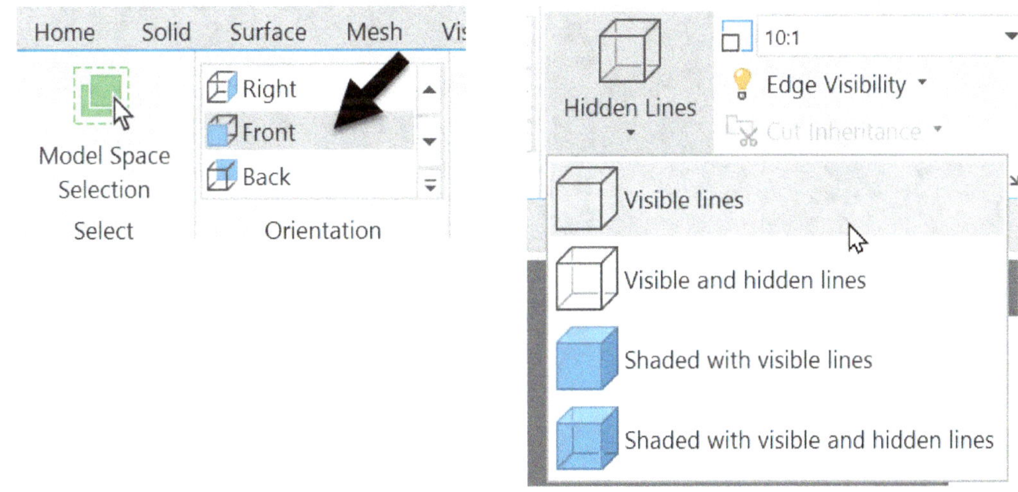

Set the **Scale** value in the **Appearance** panel. Click the **OK** button on the **Create** panel to create the base view; a projected view will be attached to the pointer, and you will be asked to specify its location. You will learn to create projected views in the next section. Press ENTER to exit the command.

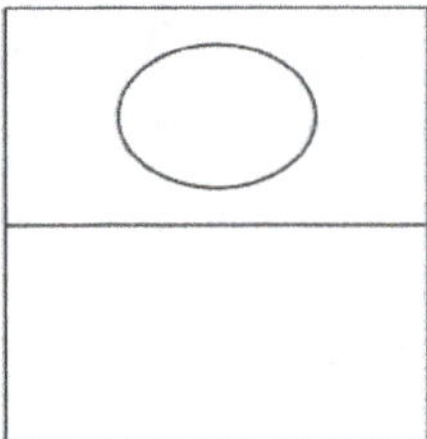

Creating a Projected View

A projected view can be created from an existing view. It can be an orthographic view or isometric view generated by projecting from a base view or any other existing view. To create a projected view, click **Layout > Create View > Projected** on the ribbon, and then select the base view from **Layout 1**; the projected view will be attached to the pointer.

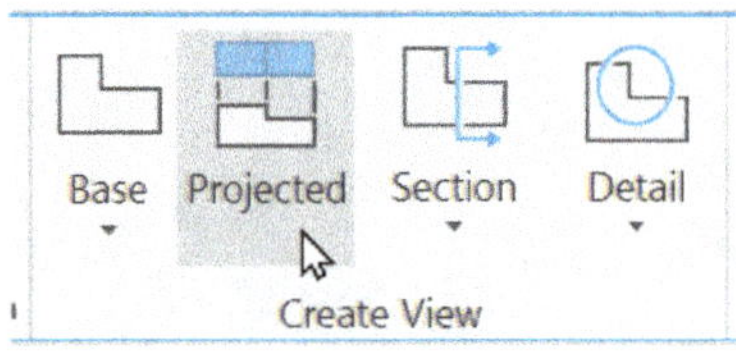

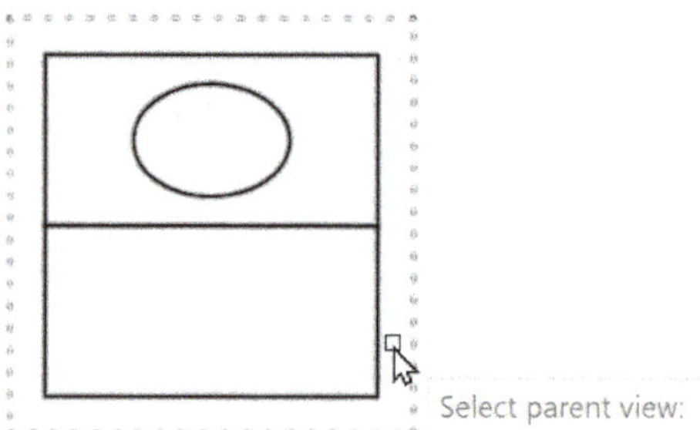

Move the pointer toward right and click to specify the location of the projected view, as shown. Select the **eXit** option from the command line to exit the command.

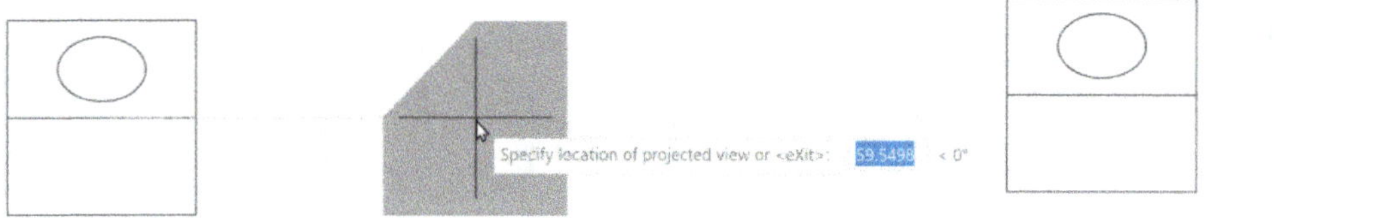

Creating Section Views

One of the common views used in 2D drawings is the section view. Before creating a section view, you need to specify the section view style.

Creating the Section View Style

Section View Style defines the display of the section view and the cutting plane. To create a section view style,

click **Layout > Styles and Standards > Section View Style** on the ribbon; the **Section View Style Manager** dialog appears. Click the **New** button in the **Section View Style Manager** dialog; the **Create New Section View Style** dialog appears. Type **Example** in the **New Style Name** box and click **Continue; the New Section View Style** dialog appears. In this dialog, click the **Cutting Plane** tab and select the **Show cutting plane lines** option.

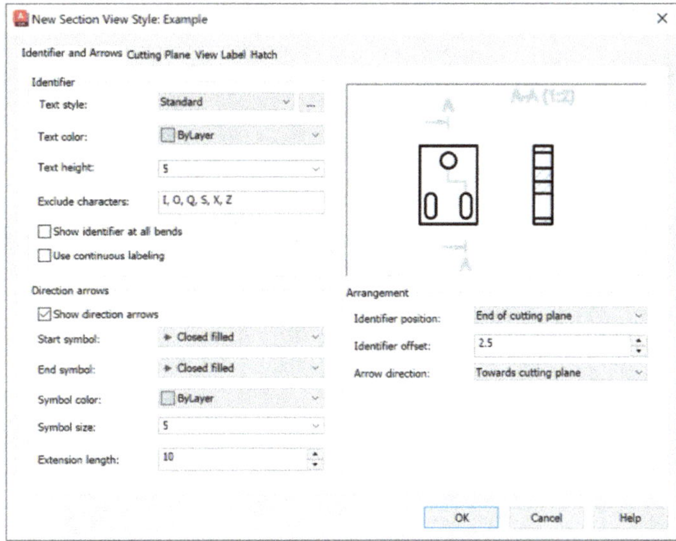

Click the **Hatch** tab and set the **Hatch Scale** to **0.5** and click **OK**. Click the **Set current** button on the **Section View Style Manager** dialog and click **Close**.

Creating a Full Section View

To create a full section view, click **Layout > Create Views > Section > Full** on the ribbon. Next, select the base view from the layout. After selecting the base view, you need to specify the start and endpoints of the cutting plane. Select the start point of the cutting plane, as shown.

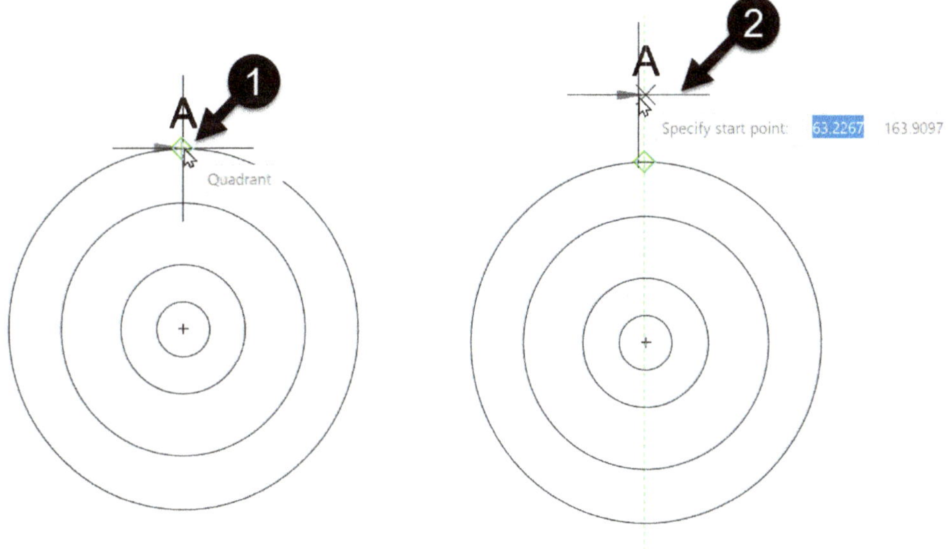

Move the pointer vertically downward and specify the endpoint of the cutting plane. Move the pointer toward the right and click to specify the location of the section view. Select the **eXit** option to create the section view.

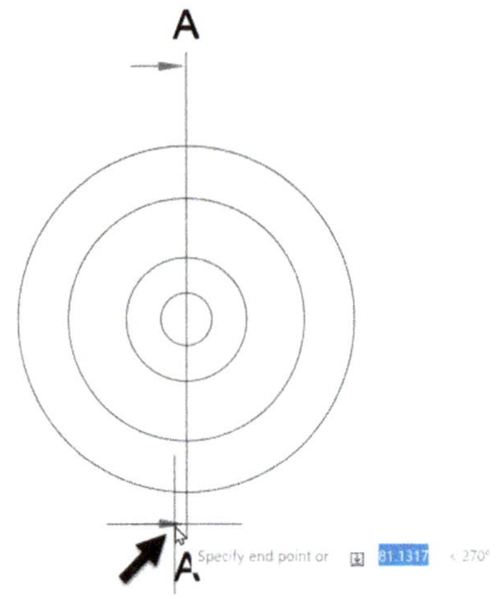

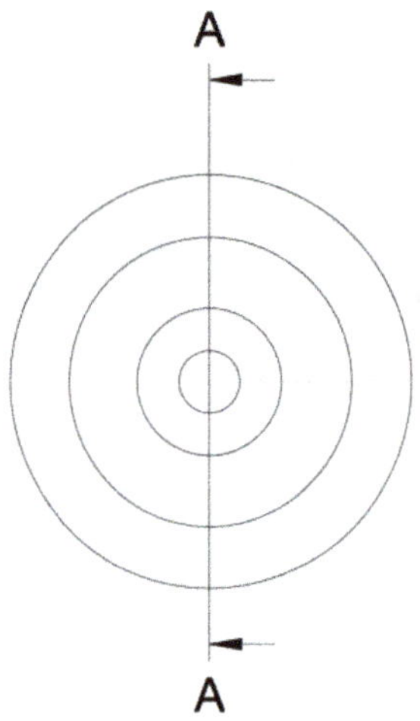

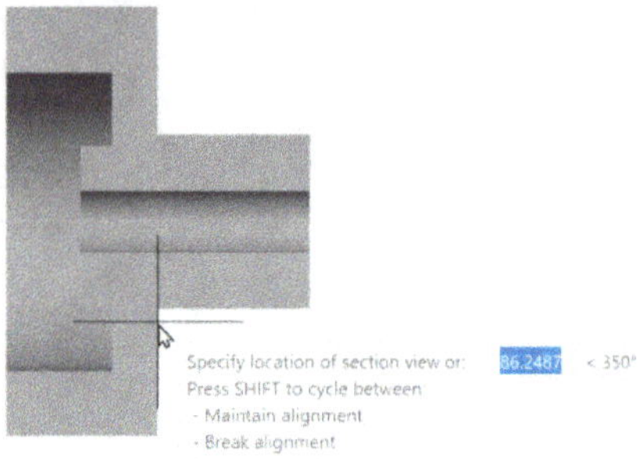

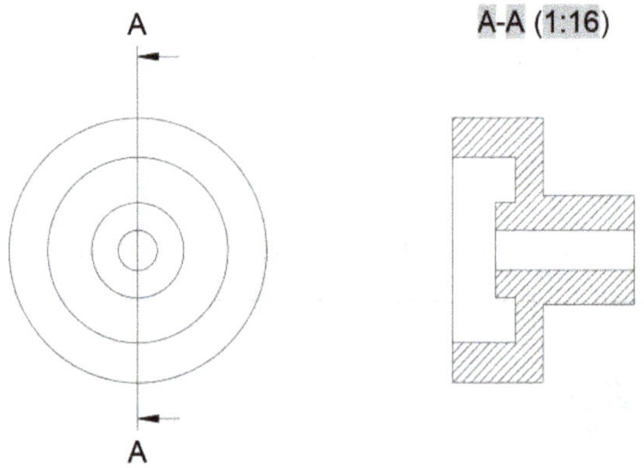

A

A

A

A

A

A

A-A (1:16)

A

A

Creating a Half Section View

To create a half section view, click **Layout > Create Views > Section > Half** on the ribbon. Next, select the base view from the layout. Select the start point of the cutting plane, as shown. Move the pointer and select the next point of the cutting plane. Next, move the pointer in the perpendicular direction to the first line segment of the cutting plane and then click. Move the pointer toward right and click to place the section view. Select the **eXit** option to create the half section view.

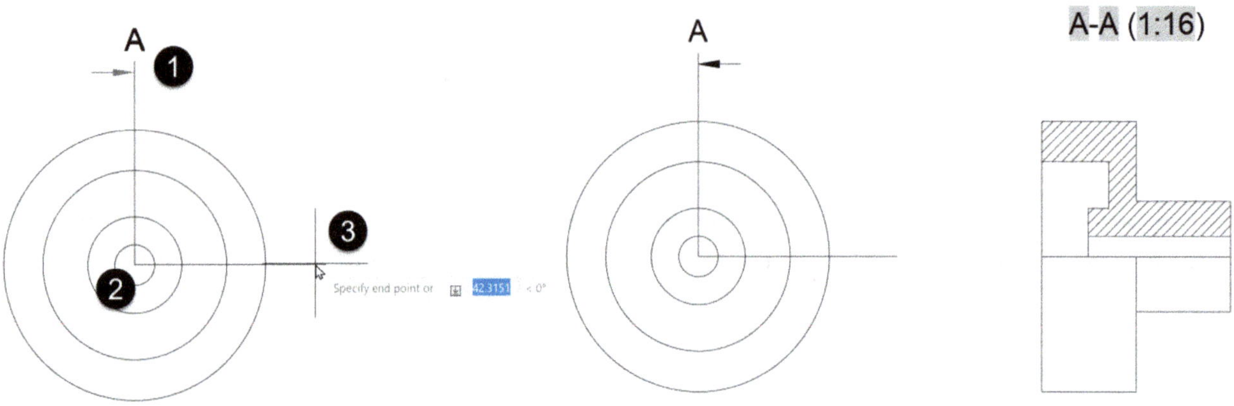

Creating an Aligned Section View

To create an aligned section view, click **Layout > Create Views > Section > Aligned** on the ribbon. Next, select the base view from the layout. Select the start point of the cutting plane, as shown. Move the pointer and select the next point of the cutting plane. Next, move the pointer at angle to the first line segment of the cutting plane click. Select Done from the command line. Move the pointer toward right and click to place the section view. Select the **eXit** option to create the half section view.

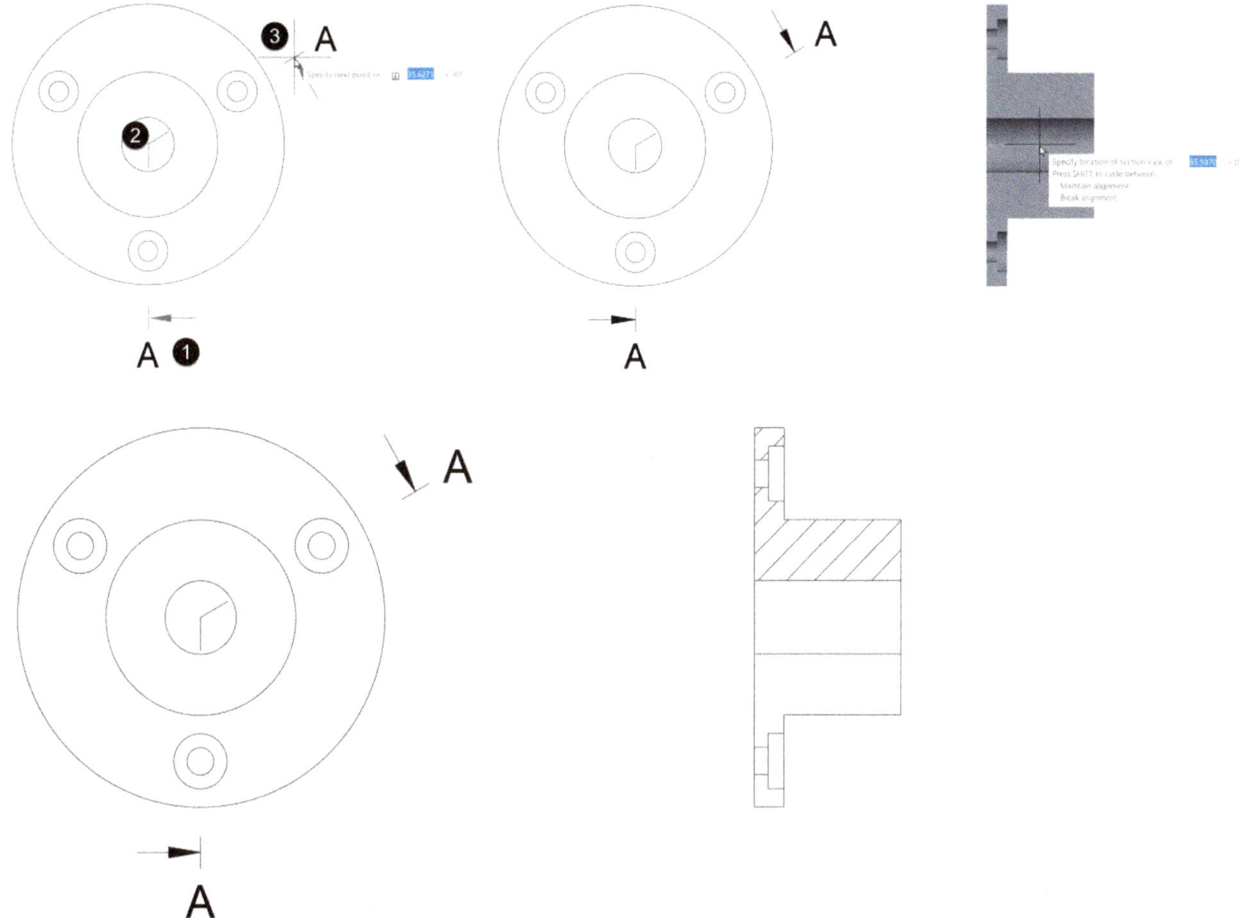

Creating an Offset Section View

The Offset Section View command creates a section view using a cutting plane passing through multiple features of the model. To create an offset section view, click **Layout > Create Views > Section > Offset** on the ribbon and select the base view from the layout. Next, you need to create a multi-segment cutting plane. For example, you need to create a cutting plane passing through the holes, as shown.

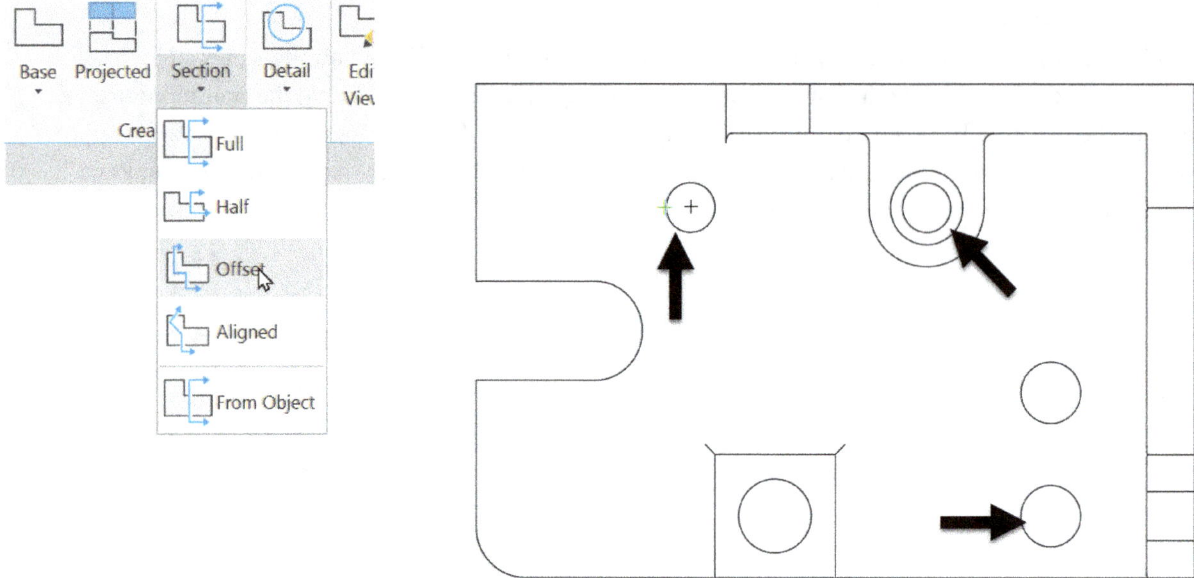

Place the pointer on the left quadrant point of the top-left circle. Next, move the pointer horizontally toward left along the traceline. Click to specify the start point of the cutting plane. Move the pointer horizontally toward right and click at the location, as shown.

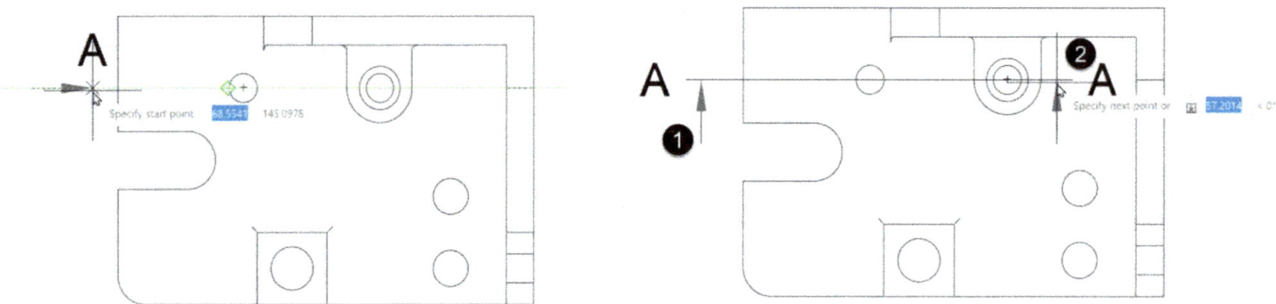

Move the downward and select the center point of the bottom-right circle. Move the pointer toward right and click outside the model, as shown. Select the **Done** option from the command line.

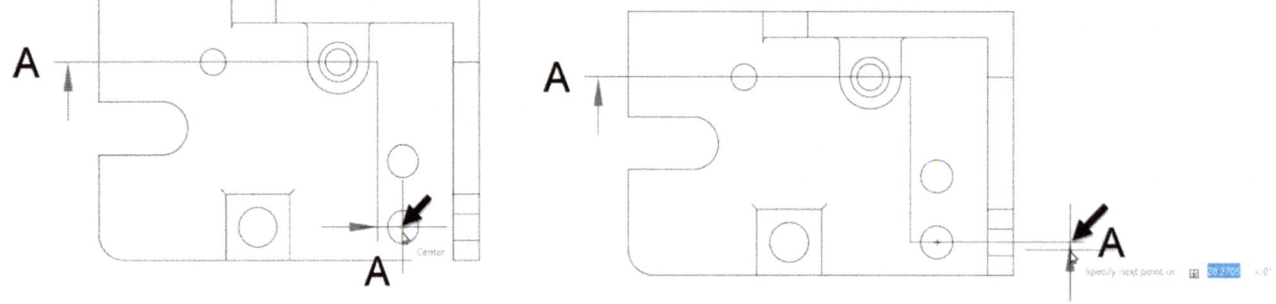

Next, move the pointer downward and click to place the section view. Select **eXit** from the command line.

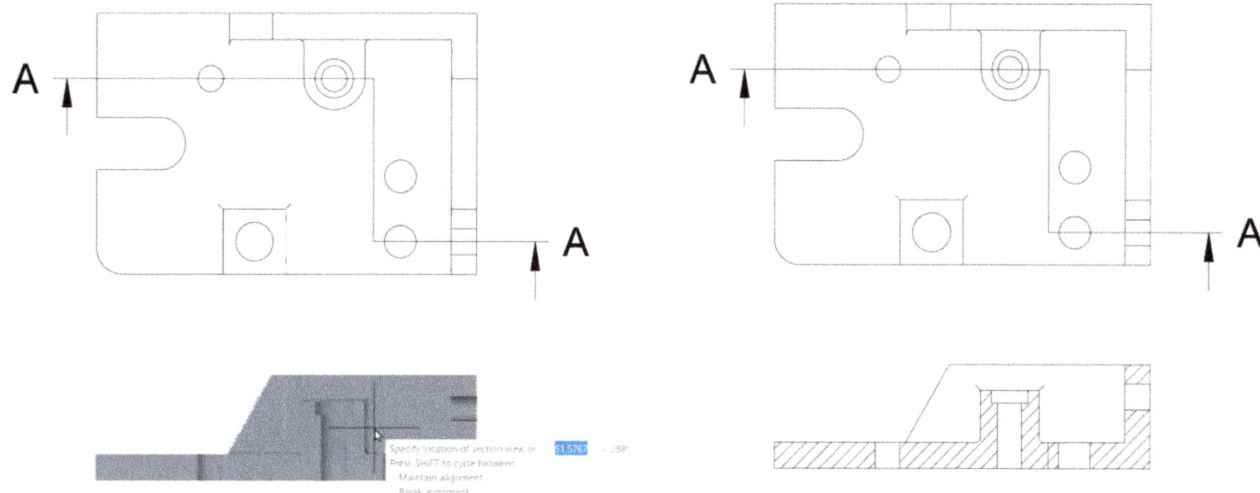

Creating a Detailed View

A detailed view is created to enlarge and view small portions of a drawing. To create a detailed view, click
Layout > Create Views > Detail > Circular on the ribbon. Next, select the base view from the layout; this
automatically activates the circle tool. If you want a rectangular boundary, then click the **Rectangular** icon under
the **Boundary** panel of the **Detail View Creation** ribbon tab. Draw a circle or rectangle to identify the area that
you wish to zoom into. Once the fence shape is drawn, select a value from the **Scale** drop-down available on the
Appearance panel; the scale factor scales the detail view.

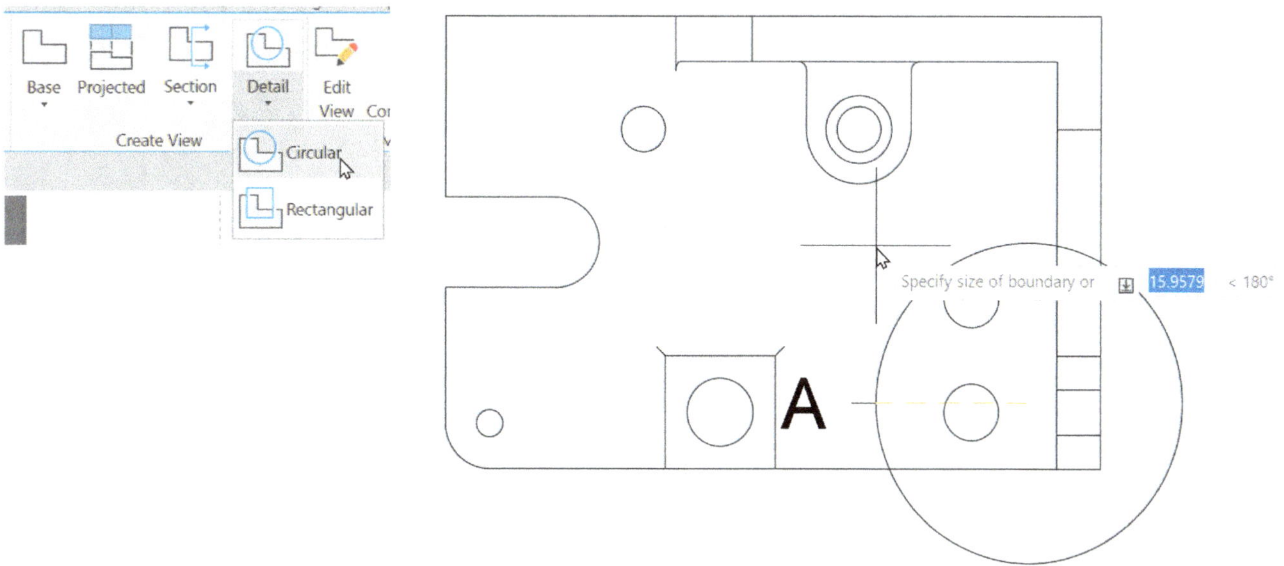

Next, click on any one of the icons available in the **Model Edge** panel. You can select the **Smooth, Smooth with
border, Smooth with connection line,** or **Jagged** icon. The **Smooth** option creates a smooth cut edge. The **Jagged**
option creates a jagged cut edge.

The **Smooth with border** option allows you to display a full detail boundary. You can show a connection line
between the detail view and the base view by clicking the **Smooth with connection line** option. Next, move the

pointer and click to locate the view; the detail view will appear with a label. Select eXit from the command line to create the detail view.

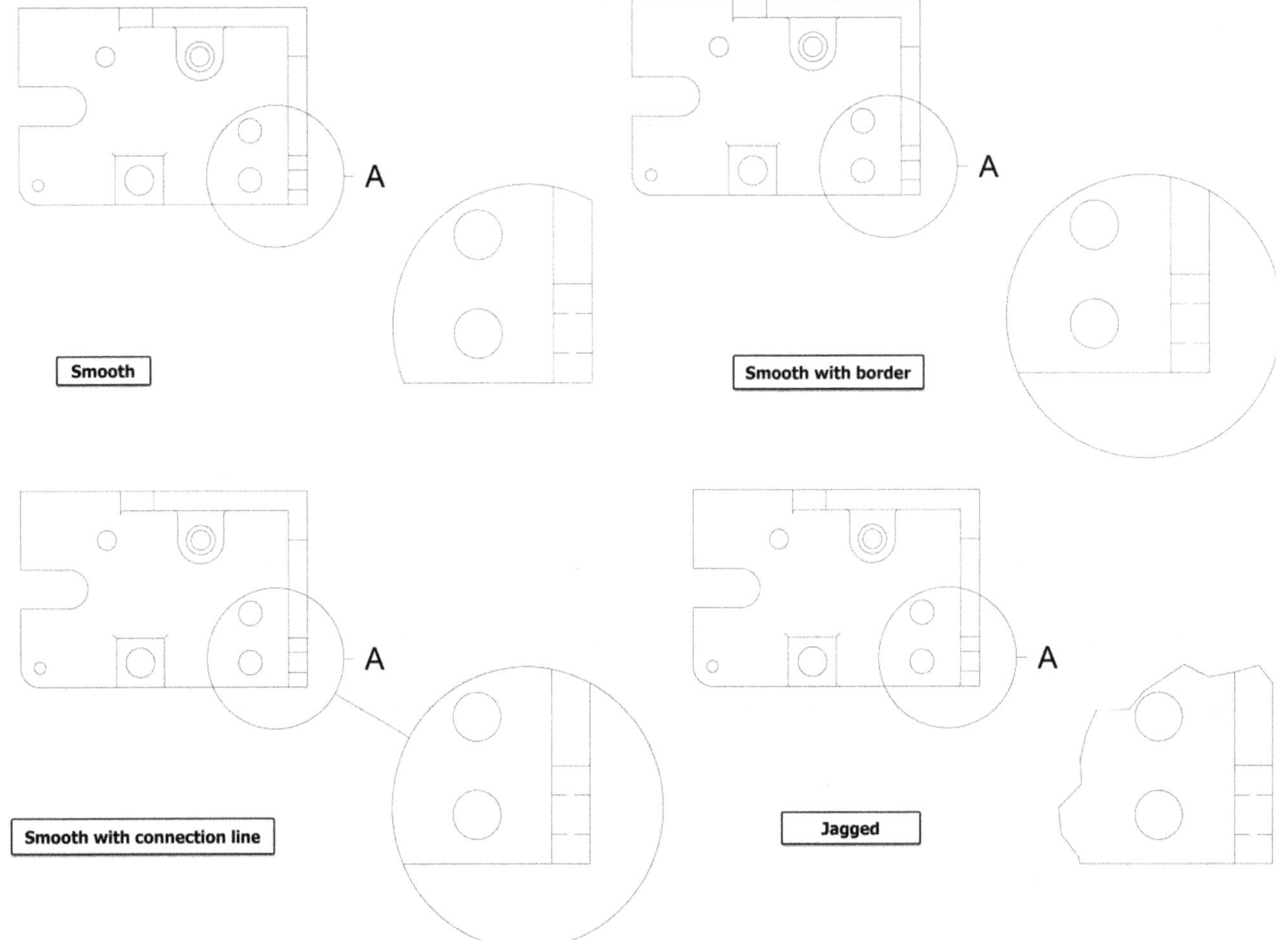

AutoCAD allows you to change the boundary and model edge even after creating the detail view. To do this, click **Layout > Modify View > Edit View** on the ribbon, and then select the detail view; the **Detail View Editor** panel is displayed. Next, select the different options from the **Boundary** and **Model Edge** panel, and then click **OK**.

Tutorial 1

In this example, you create the 2D drawing of the part shown below.

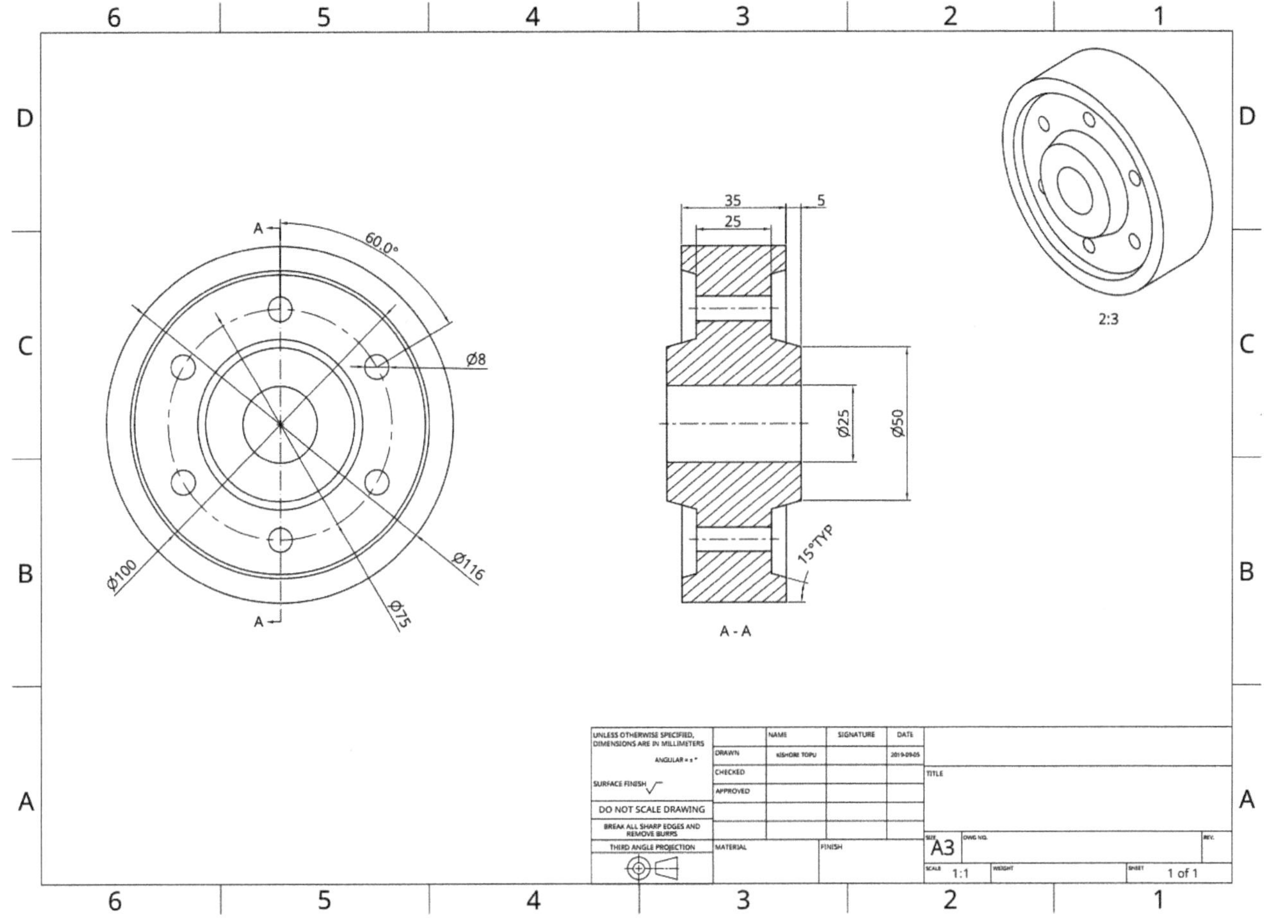

6 5 4 3 2 1
D
A
60.0°
Ø8
Ø100
Ø116
Ø75
A
C
B
35
25
5
Ø25
Ø50
15°TYP
A - A
2:3
UNLESS OTHERWISE SPECIFIED,
DIMENSIONS ARE IN MILLIMETERS
ANGULAR = ± °
SURFACE FINISH
DO NOT SCALE DRAWING
BREAK ALL SHARP EDGES AND
REMOVE BURRS
THIRD ANGLE PROJECTION
NAME
SIGNATURE
DATE
DRAWN
KISHORE TOPU
2019-09-05
CHECKED
APPROVED
MATERIAL
FINISH
TITLE
SIZE
A3
DWG NO.
REV.
SCALE
1:1
WEIGHT
SHEET
1 of 1

Creating the Drawing from a 3D Model

1. Download the **Chapter 10** part file from the companion website. Next, extract the zip file.
2. Open the Ch10_Tutorial1 file.

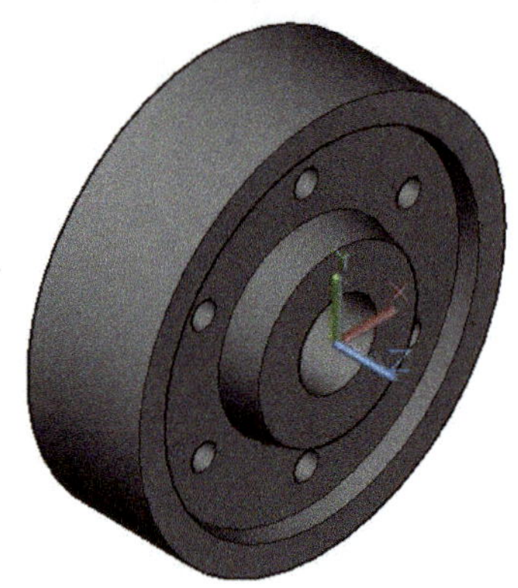

3. Click the right mouse button on the **Layout 1** tab.
4. Select the **Drafting Standard Setup** option.

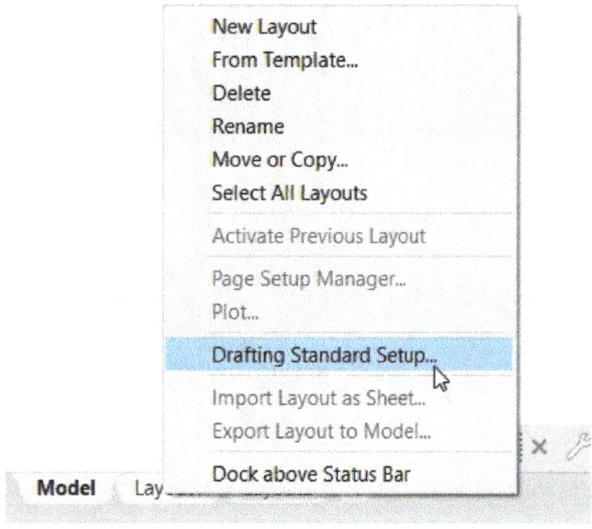

5. On the **Drafting Standard** dialog, select the **Third angle** option from the **Projection type** section.
6. Click **OK**.

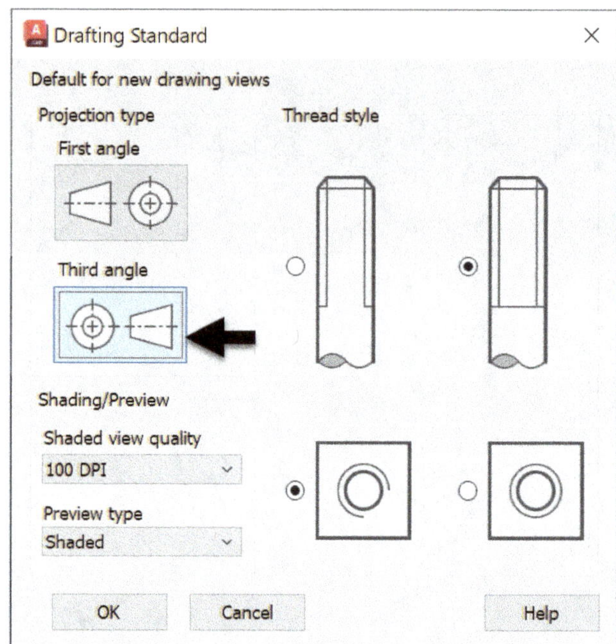

7. Click the **Layout 1** tab, and then select the **Page Setup Manager** option.
8. Select the **Layout 1** and click the **Modify** button.
9. On the **Page Setup** dialog, select **Paper size > ISO A3 (420.00 x 297.00 MM)**.
10. Click **OK**.
11. Close the **Page Setup Manager** dialog.
12. Select the viewport on the layout and press DELETE.

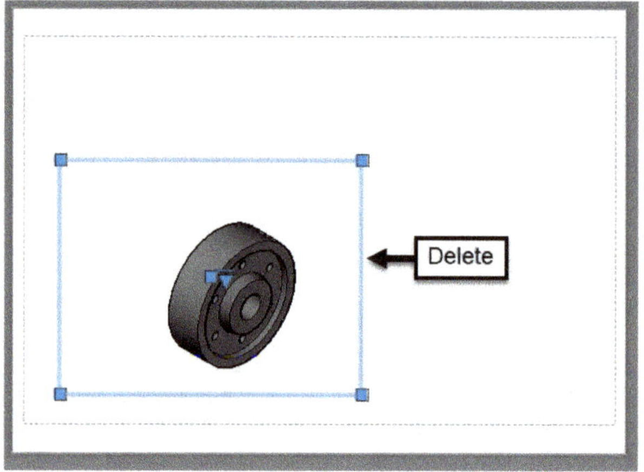

13. Click the **Model** tab.
14. On the ribbon, click **Home** tab > **View** panel > **Base** drop-down > **From Model Space**.

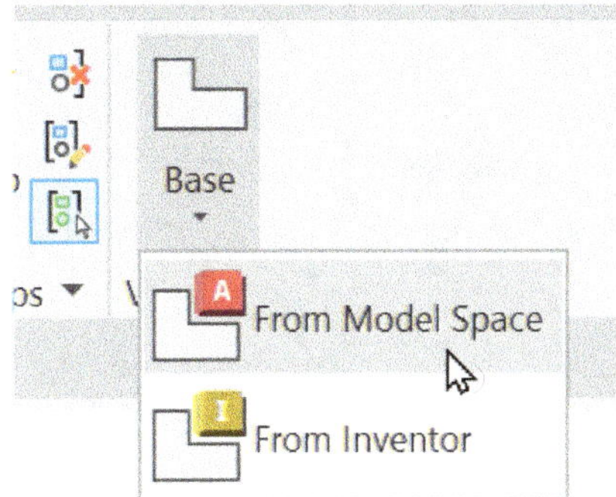

15. Press ENTER to select the entire model.
16. Press ENTER to select **Layout 1** as the current layout.
17. On the **Drawing View Creation** tab of the ribbon, select the **Right** option from the **Orientation** panel.

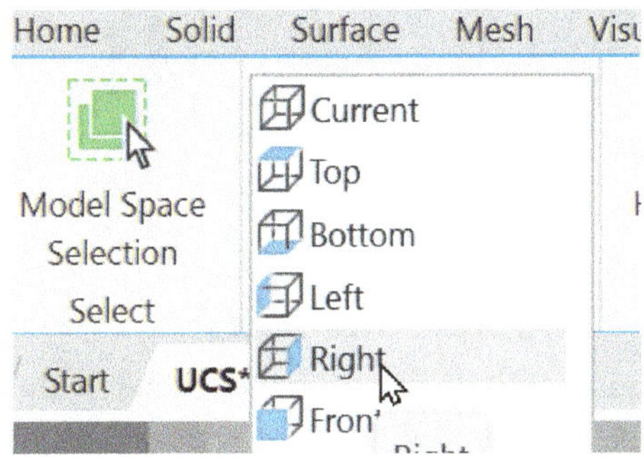

18. On the **Appearance** panel, set the **Scale** to **1:1**.

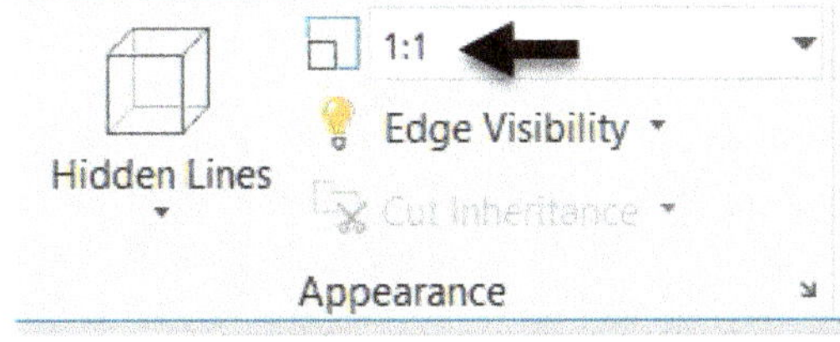

19. Select the **Visible Lines** option from the drop-down available on the **Appearance** panel.

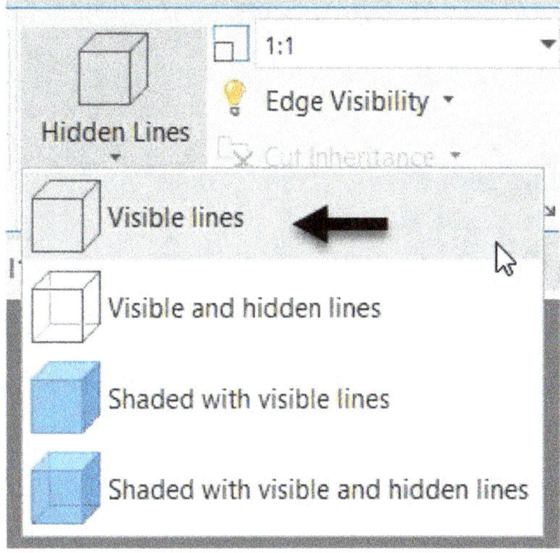

20. Click on the left side of the layout, as shown.

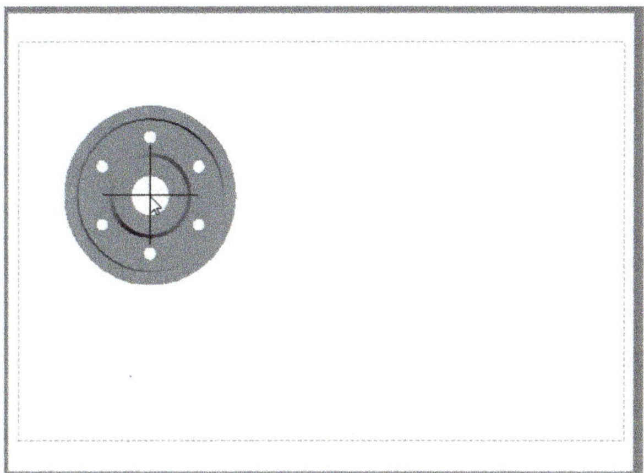

21. Click **OK** on the **Create** panel.

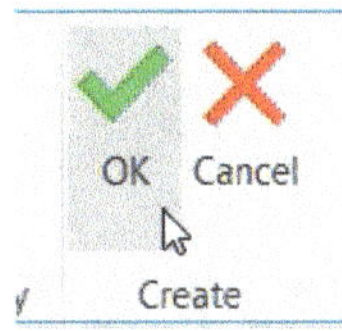

22. Move the pointer toward the top left corner and click to position the Isometric view, as shown.

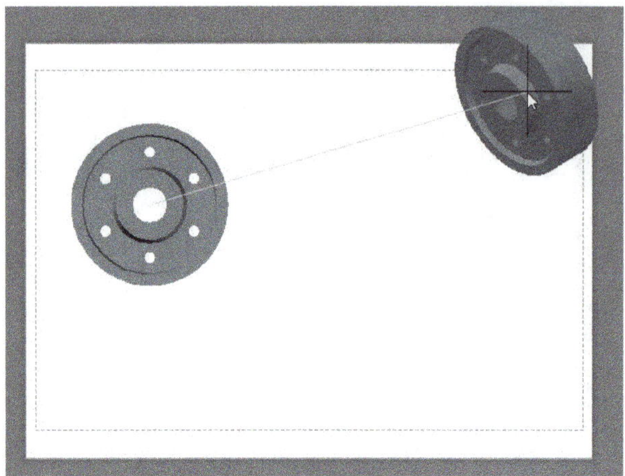

23. Press ENTER.
24. Select the Isometric view.
25. Click on the square grip of the select view.
26. Move the pointer inside the layout boundary and click.

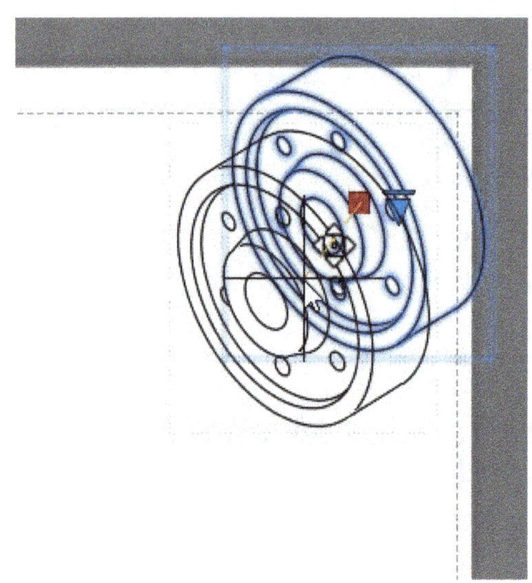

27. Select the isometric view.
28. On the ribbon, click **Edit > Edit View**.

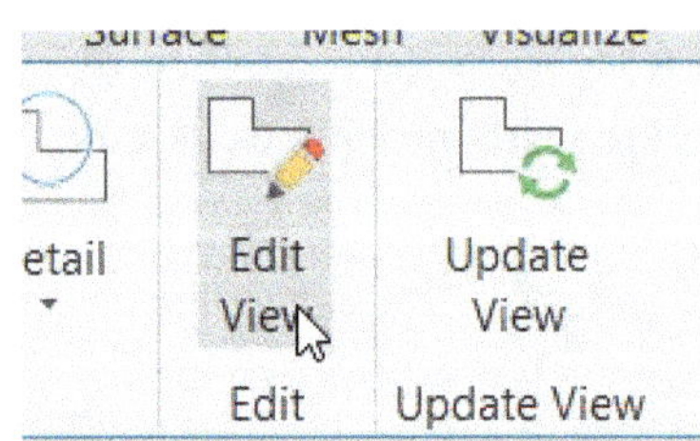

29. Type **2:3** in the **Scale** box on the **Appearance** panel.

30. Click the **OK** button.

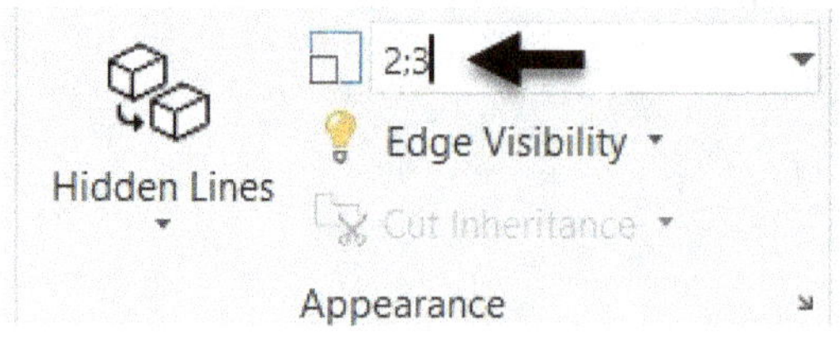

31. Move the Isometric to the top right corner.

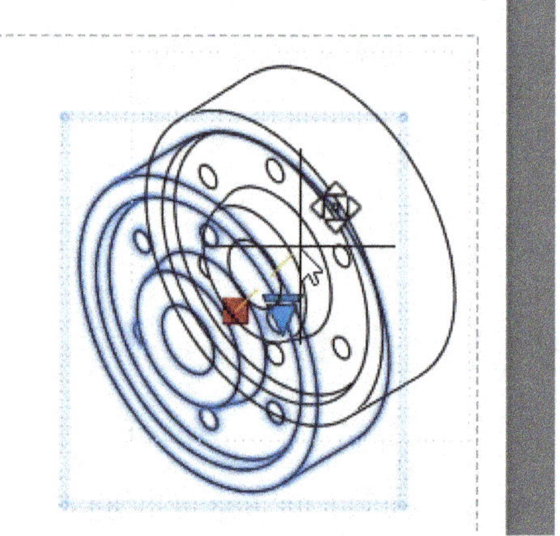

Creating the Section view

1. On the **Layout** tab of the ribbon, click **Create New** panel > **Section View** drop-down > **Full**.

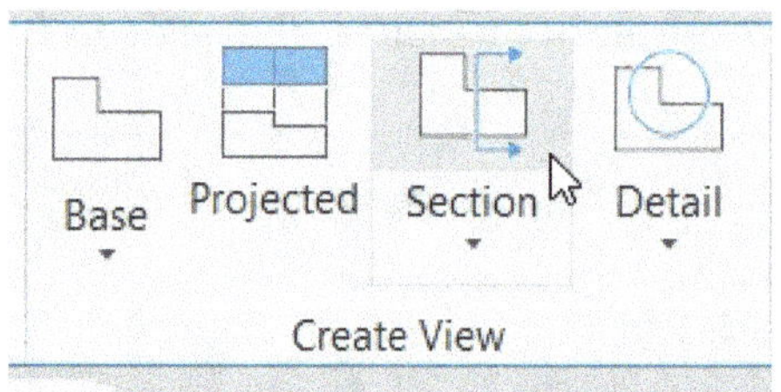

2. Select the Right view.
3. Place the pointer on the centerpoint of the selected view.

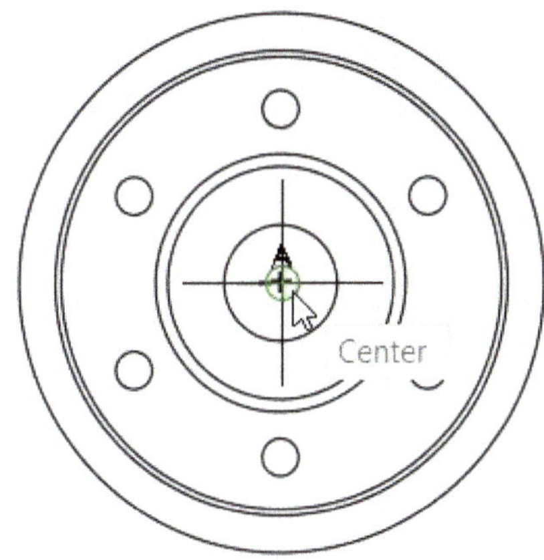

4. Move the pointer vertically upward. A dotted line appears from the center point of the selected view.
5. Click on the dotted line.

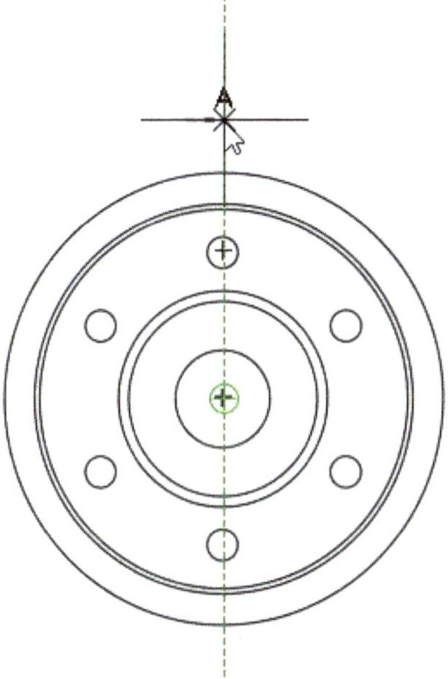

6. Move the pointer vertically downward.
7. Click below the selected view.
8. Press ENTER.

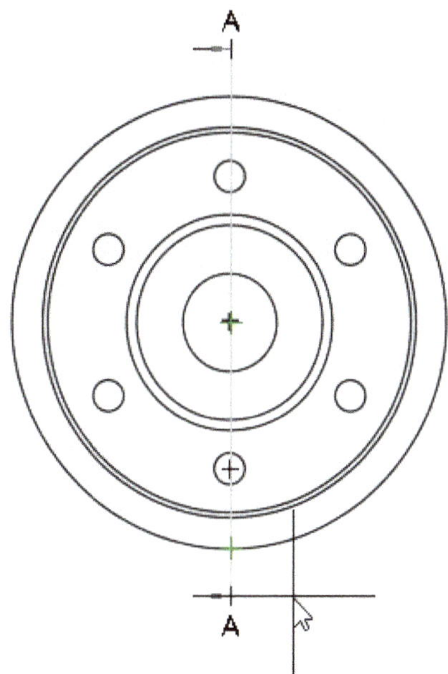

9. Move the pointer toward the right and click.

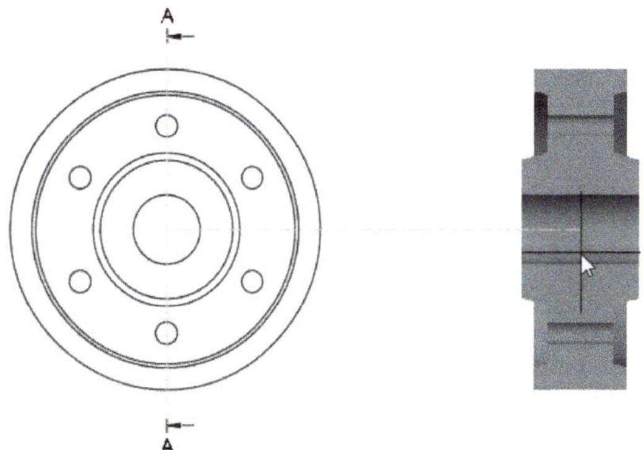

10. Click **OK** on the **Create** panel of the ribbon.

Adding Centerlines and Center Marks

1. On the ribbon, click **Home** tab > **Layers** panel > **Layer Properties**.
2. Click the **New Layer** icon on the Layer Properties Manager.
3. Type **Centerlines** in the **Name** box.
4. Change the layer **Color** to Black.
5. Set the Linetype to **CENTER**.
6. Make the layer current.

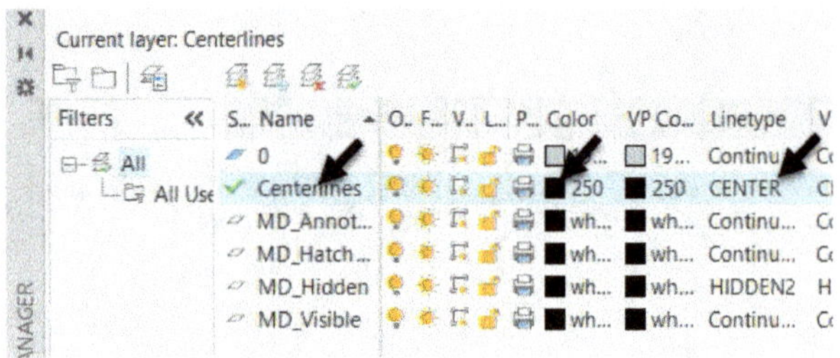

7. Close the Layer Properties Manager.

8. On the ribbon, click **Annotate** tab > **Centerlines** panel > **Centerline**.

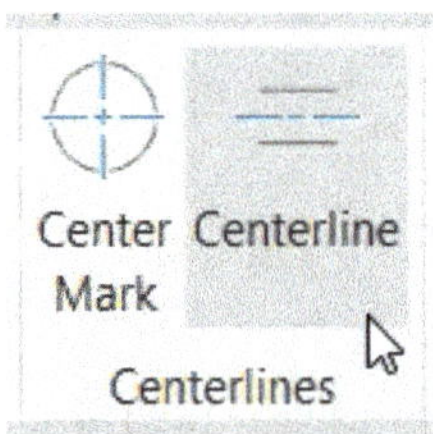

9. Select the horizontal edges of the large hole.

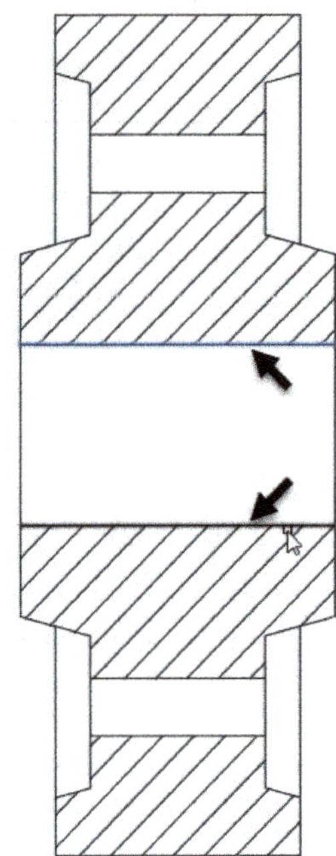

10. Likewise, create centrelines for the small holes.

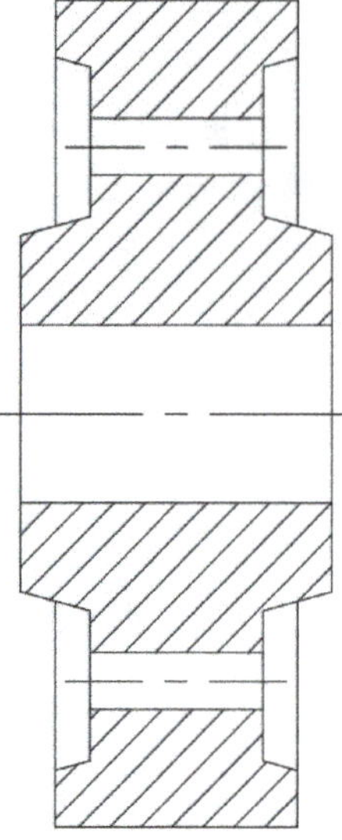

11. On the ribbon, click **Home** tab > **Draw** panel > **Circle** drop-down > **3 Point**.

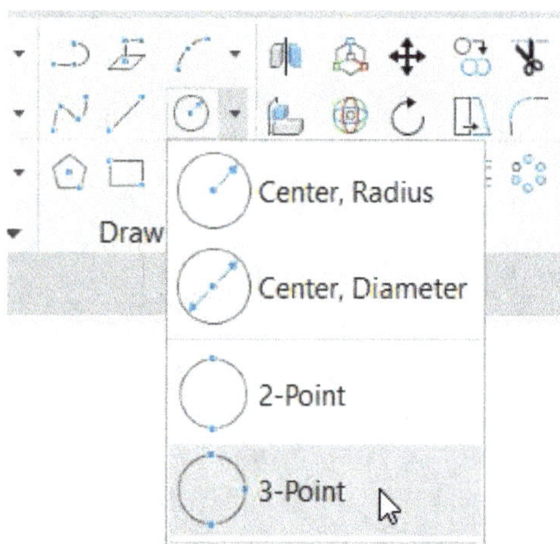

12. Select the centerpoints of the three circles, as shown.

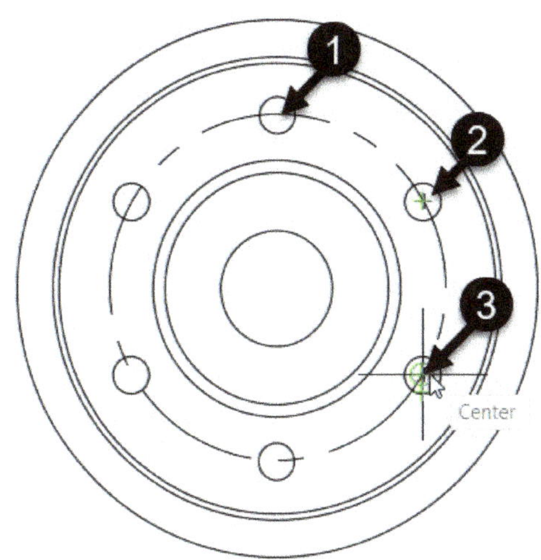

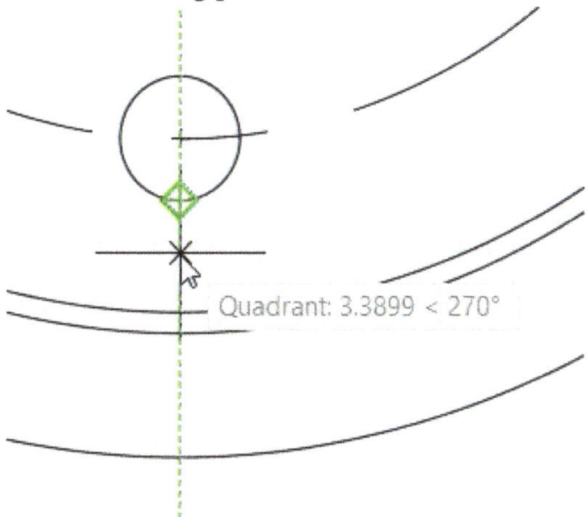

13. On the ribbon, click **Home** tab > **Draw** panel > **Line**.
14. Place the pointer on the lower quadrant point of the lower circle, as shown.
15. Move the pointer downward and click to specify the starting point of the line.
16. Move the pointer vertically upward and click to define the endpoint of the line.

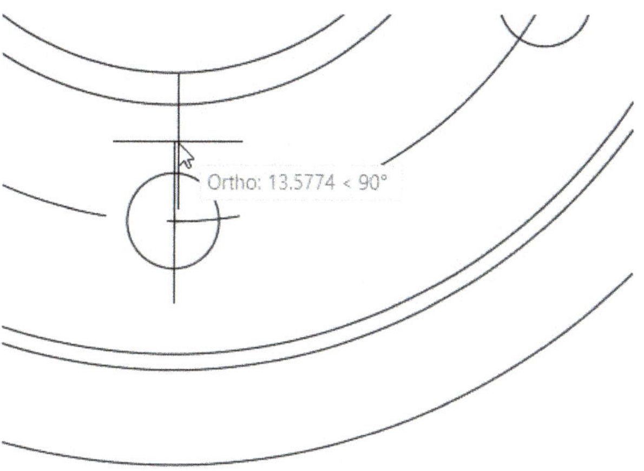

32. Press ESC.
33. On the ribbon, **Home** tab > **Modify** panel > **Array** drop-down > **Polar Array**.

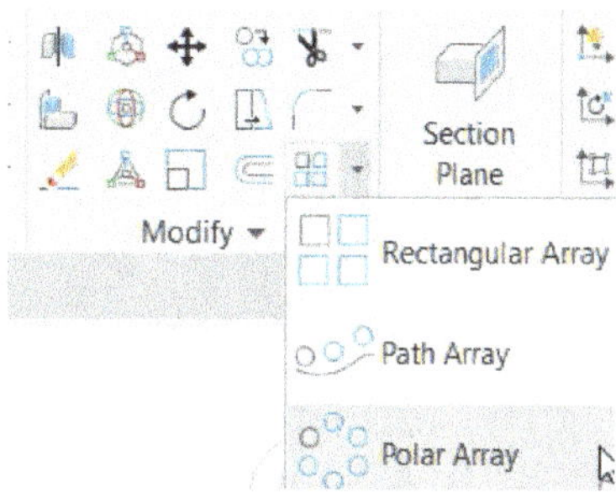

34. Select the newly created line and press ENTER.
35. Select the centerpoint of the center circle; the centerpoint of the polar array is defined.

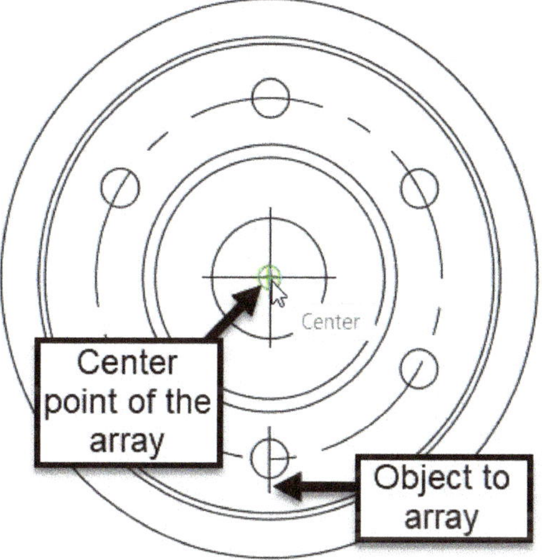

36. On the **Items** panel, type **6**, and **360** in the **Items** and **Fill** boxes, respectively.

37. Make sure that the **Rotate Items** icon is selected on the **Properties** panel.

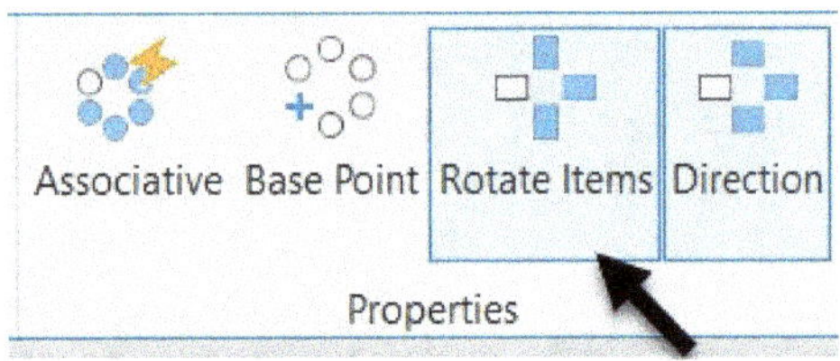

38. Click **Close Array**.

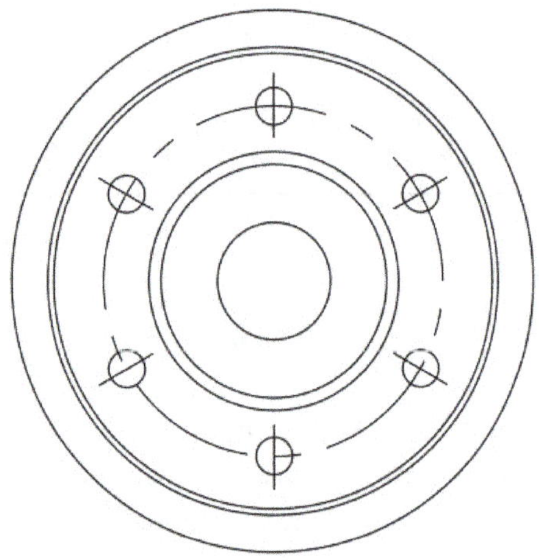

39. On the ribbon, click **Annotate** tab > **Centerlines** panel > **Center Mark**.

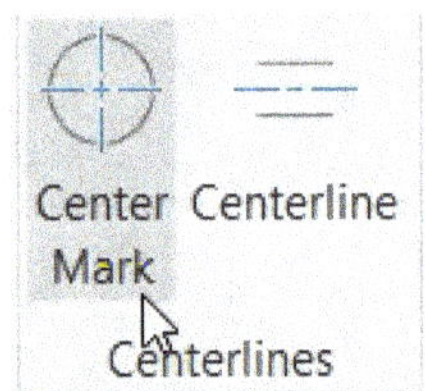

40. Select the center hole.

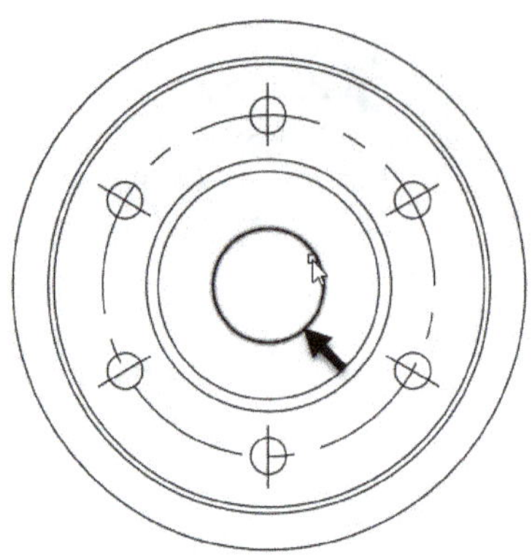

41. Press ENTER.

Adding Dimensions

Now, you add the dimensions to the drawing views.

1. Create the **Dimension** layer and make it as current.

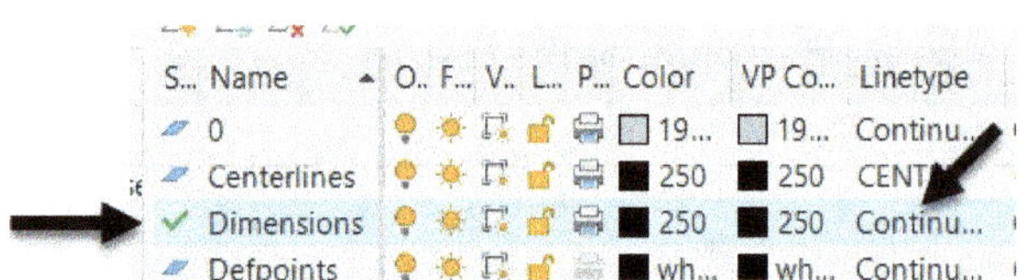

2. Click **Dimension** drop-down > **Linear** on the **Dimension** panel of the **Annotate** ribbon tab.

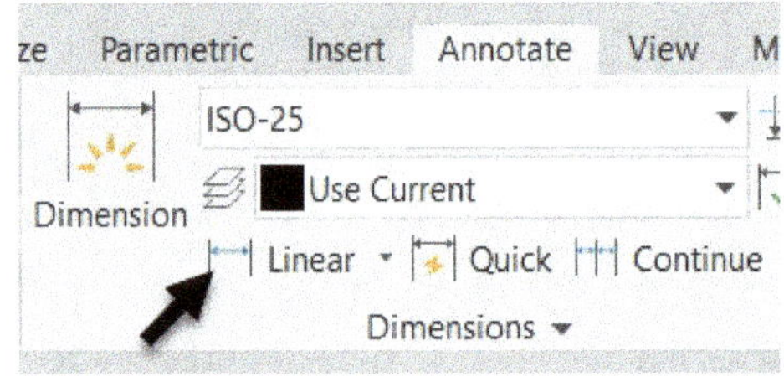

3. Select the two points of the section view, as shown.

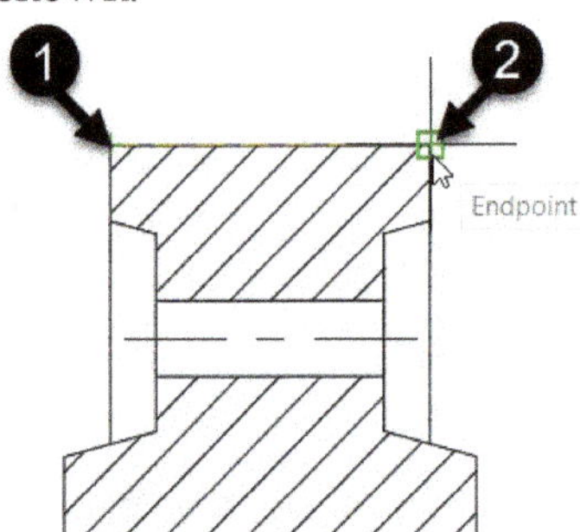

4. Move the pointer upwards and click to add dimension.

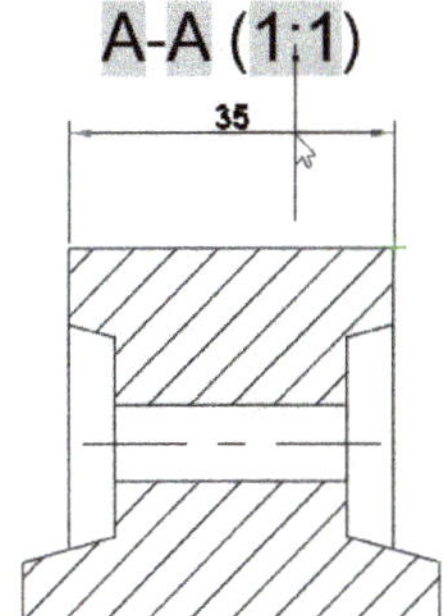

5. Click **Dimensions** panel > **Continuous** on the ribbon.

6. Select the corner point of the line of the section view, as shown.

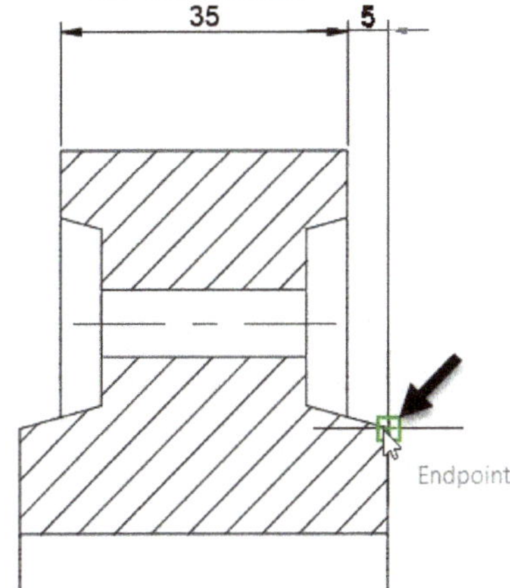

7. Press ESC.

8. Click **Dimensions** panel > **Dimension** on the **Annotate** tab of the ribbon.

9. Select the endpoints of the two parallel edges of the section view, as shown. Next, move the pointer upward and click to position the dimension.

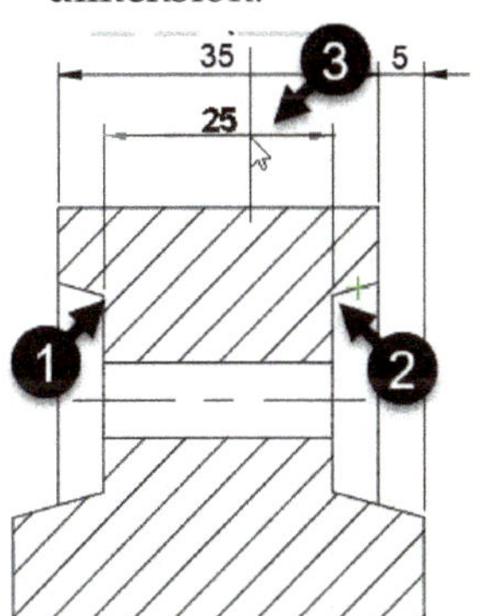

10. Click the **Dimension** icon on the **Dimensions** panel of the **Annotate** ribbon tab.

11. Select the endpoints of the two horizontal edges of the section view, as shown.

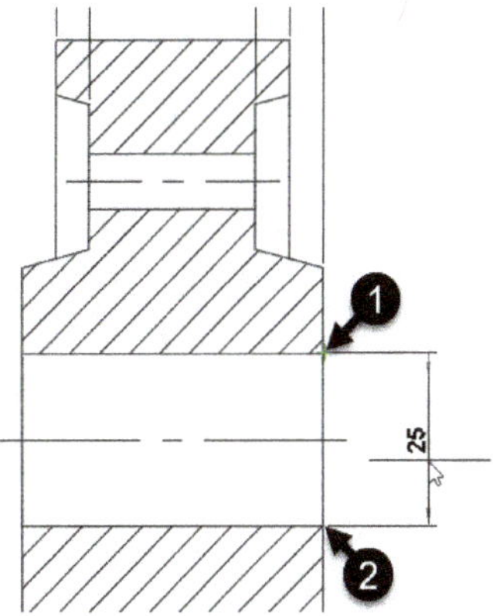

12. Select the **MText** option from the command line.

13. On the **Text Editor** tab of the ribbon, select Insert panel > **Symbol** drop-down > **Diameter**.

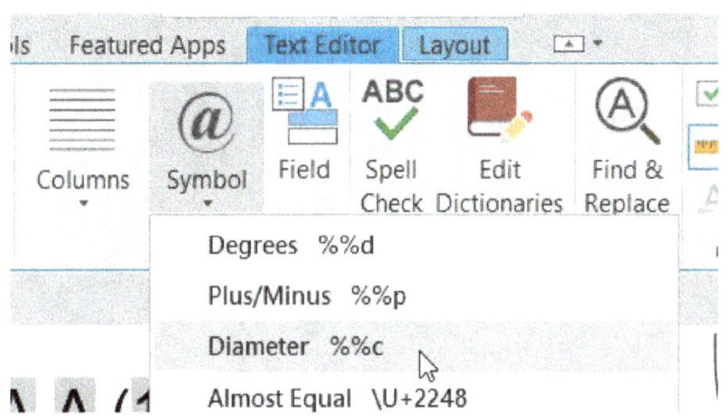

14. Click in the graphics window.

15. Move the pointer toward the right and click to position the dimension.

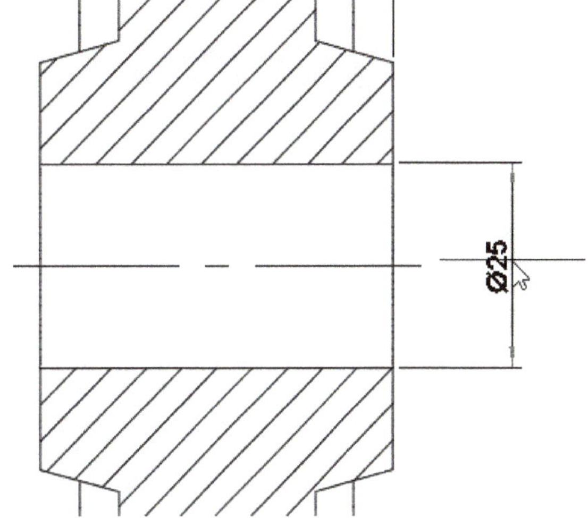

16. Press ESC.

17. Likewise, add another dimension to the section view, as shown.

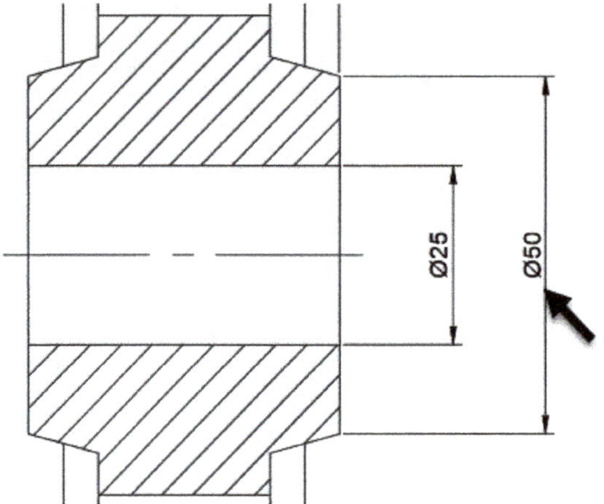

18. Click **Dimensions** panel > **Dimensions** drop-down > **Angular** on the **Annotate** tab of the ribbon.

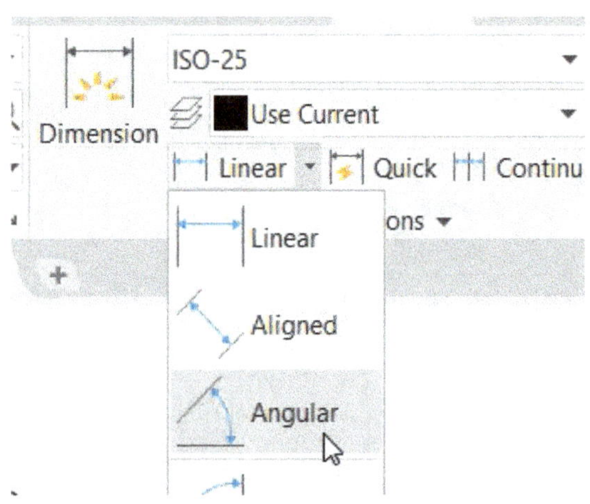

19. Select the two edges of the section view, as shown.

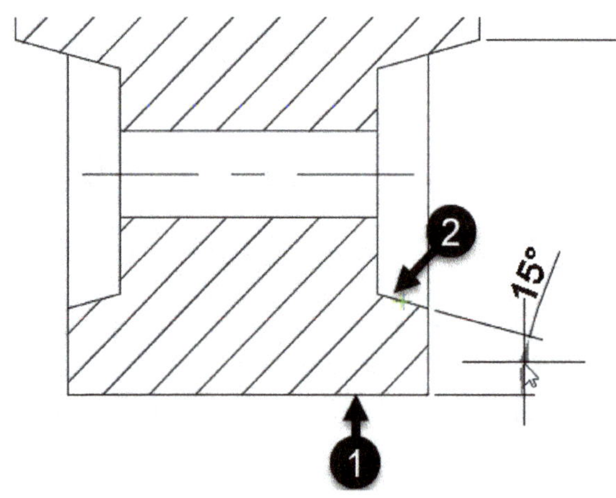

20. Select the **MText** option from the command line.
21. Expand the text editor by dragging the arrow displayed next to it.
22. Click next to the dimension value.
23. Type TYP and click in the graphics window.

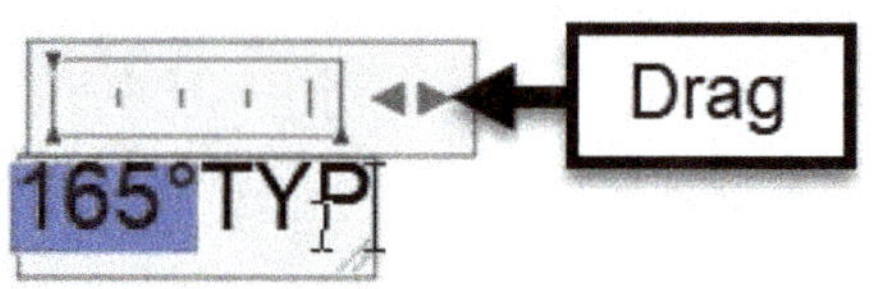

24. Move the pointer toward the right and click to position the angular dimension.

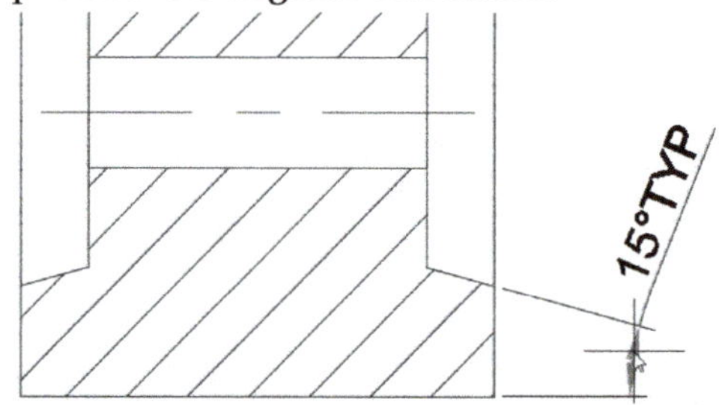

25. Click **Dimension** drop-down > **Diameter** on the **Dimensions** panel of the **Annotate** ribbon tab.

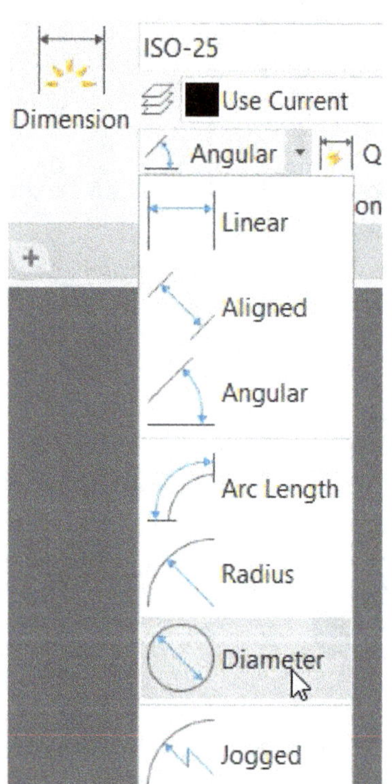

26. Select the outer circular edge, as shown.

27. Move the pointer and click to position the dimension at the location, as shown.

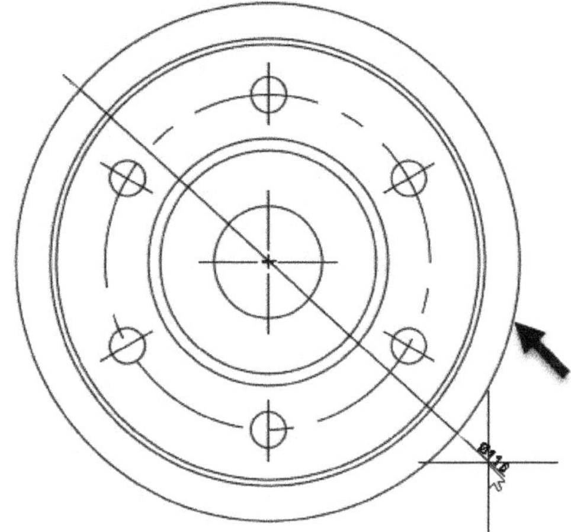

28. Likewise, create other diameter dimensions, as shown.

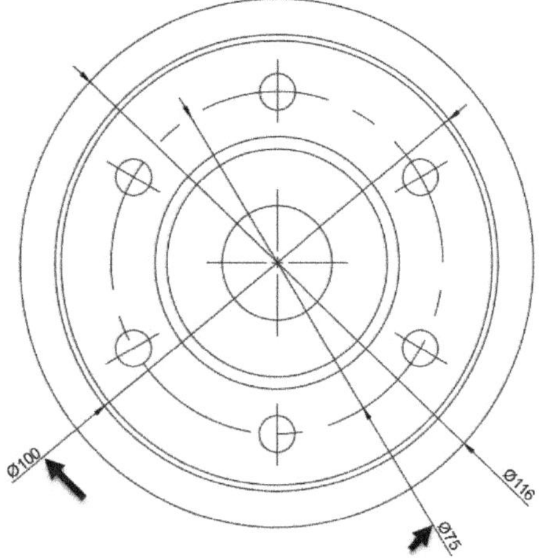

29. Click **Dimension** drop-down > **Diameter** on the **Dimensions** panel of the **Annotate** ribbon tab.

30. Select the small hole on the front view, as shown.

31. Move the pointer diagonally and click to place the diameter dimension.

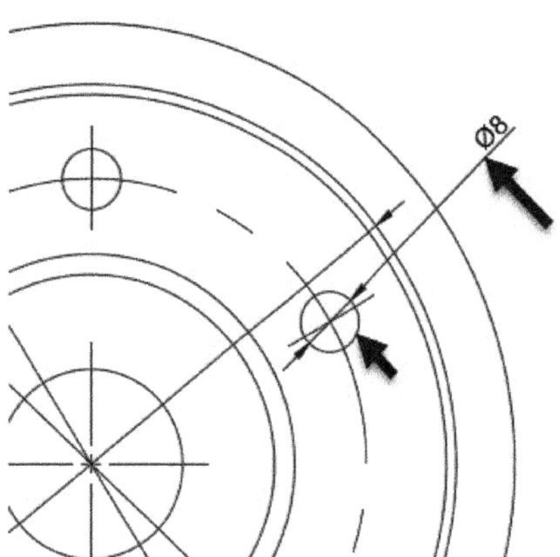

32. Click **Dimensions** panel > **Dimensions** drop-down > **Angular** on the **Annotate** tab of the ribbon.

33. Select the two centerlines of the circles, as shown.

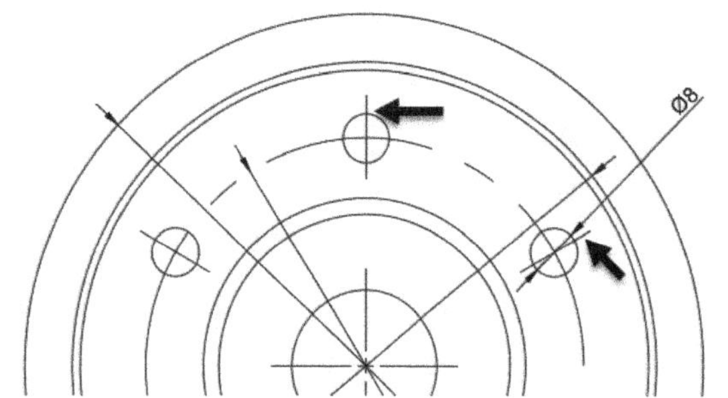

34. Move the pointer outward and click to position the angular dimension.

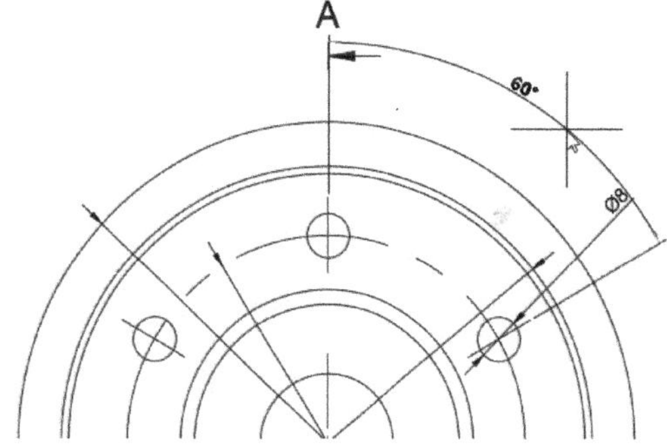

35. Save and close the drawing.

Exercise 2

Create orthographic views and an auxiliary view of the part model shown below. Add dimensions and annotations to the drawing.

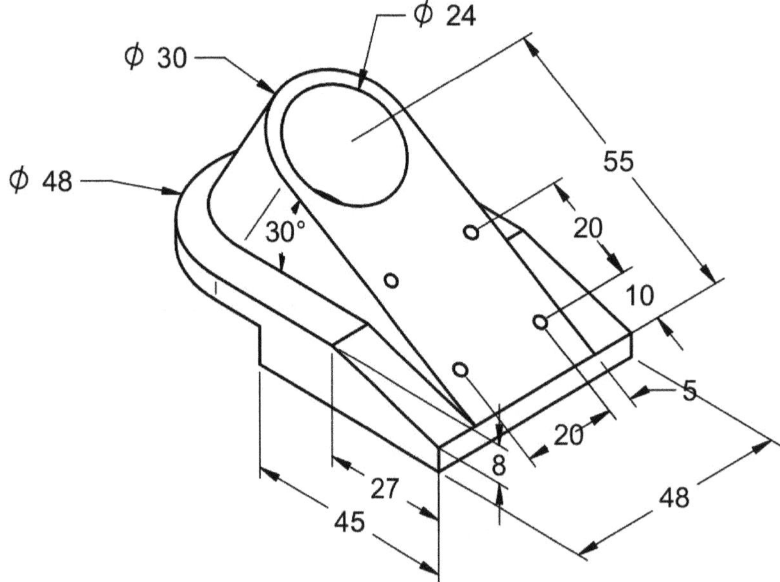

Chapter 9: Surface Design

The topics covered in this chapter are:

- *Extruded Surfaces*
- *Revolved surfaces*
- *Lofted surfaces*
- *Patch surfaces*
- *Swept surfaces*
- *Offset surfaces*
- *Trim Surfaces*
- *Extend Surfaces*

AutoCAD Surfacing commands can be used to create complex geometries that are very difficult to create using standard extruded features and revolve features. Surface modeling can also be used to edit and fix the broken imported parts. In this chapter, you learn the basics of surfacing commands that are mostly used. The surfacing commands are available in the **Surface** tab of the ribbon.

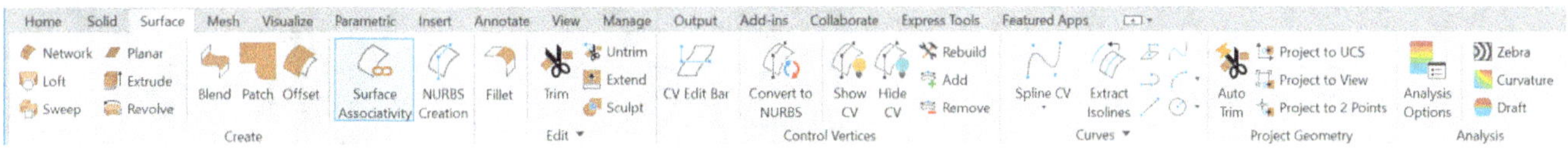

AutoCAD offers a rich set of surface design commands. A surface is an infinitely thin piece of geometry. For example, consider a cube shown in the figure. It has six faces. Each of these faces is a surface, an infinitely thin piece of geometry that acts as a boundary in 3D space. Surfaces can be simple or complex shapes. The advantage of using the surfacing commands is that you can design a model with more flexibility.

Extruded Surface

To create an extruded surface, first, create single or multiple 2D objects using the drawing tools. Next, select click **Surface > Create > Extrude** on the ribbon and select the 2D object(s) from the graphics window. Note that you can select single objects by clicking on them (or) multiple objects by creating selection window. If you want a connected surface, convert all the connected objects into a single object either by using the PLINEEDIT command or REGION command in case of closed profile. Press ENTER to accept the selection. Next, type-in a value in command line and press ENTER to create the extruded surface. You will notice that the extrusion is not capped at the ends.

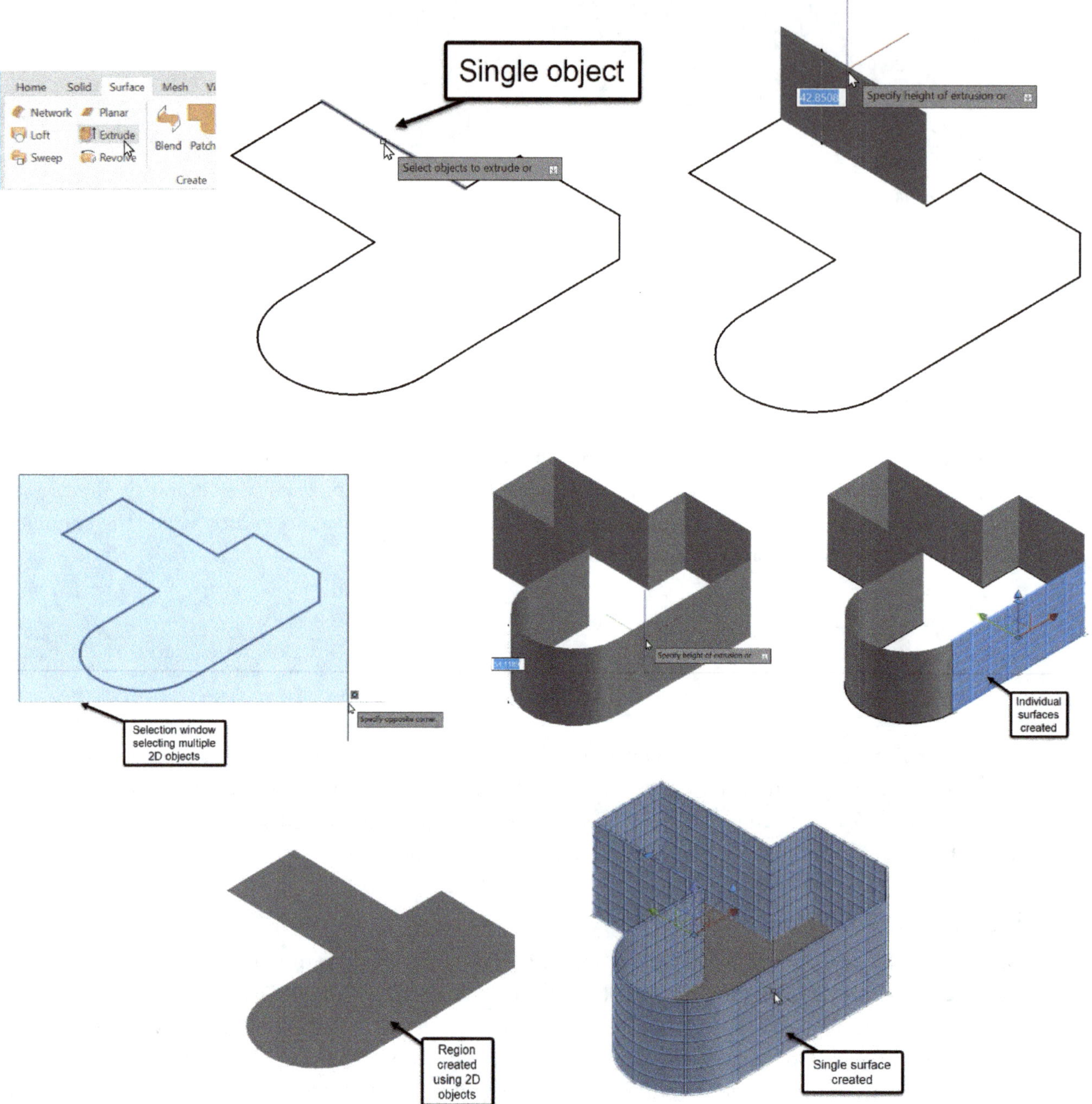

Revolved Surface

To create a revolved surface, first, create an open or closed section and the axis of revolution. Next, click **Surface tab > Create** panel **> Revolve** on the ribbon. Select the revolved profile and press ENTER. Next, select the Object option from the command line and select the revolution axis. Type-in the revolution angle and press ENTER (or) simply press ENTER to create a full 360 degrees revolved solid.

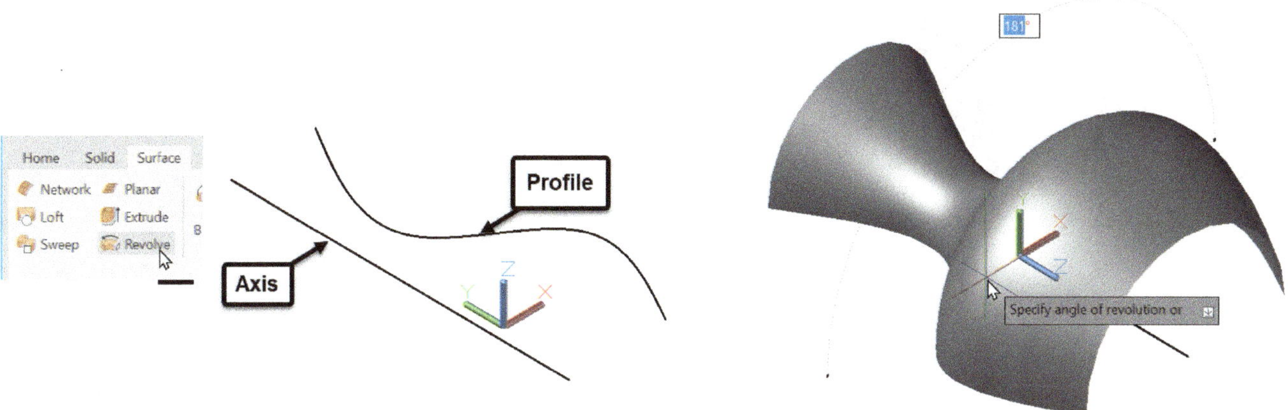

Loft

This command creates a surface body through multiple sections. The shape of the geometry adjusts automatically to pass through the sections. Create atleast two cross-sections using the drawing tools such as circles, rectangles, polylines, or splines. The cross-sections can parallel or perpendicular to each other. Next, click **Surface > Create > Loft** on the ribbon. Next, select two or more cross-sections from the graphics window. Press ENTER twice to create a lofted surface.

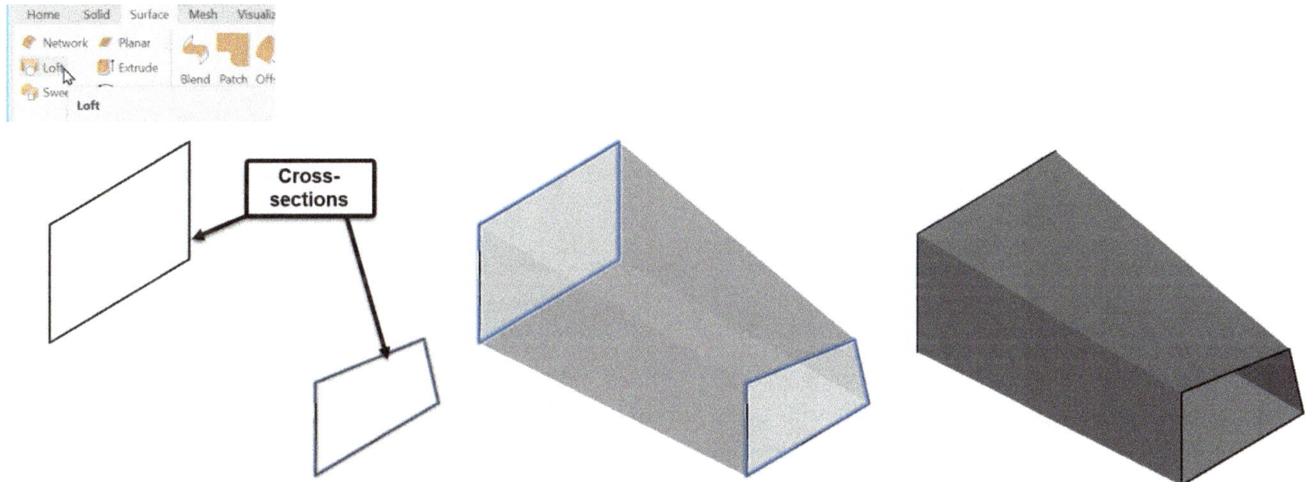

Join multiple Edges

The Join multiple Edges option of the Loft command allows you to create loft surface between the edges of the two or more surfaces. It can be tangent or curvature, continuous in both directions. To create this type of surface, activate the **Loft** command, and then select the **Join multiple edges** option from the command line. Select the edge of the first surface, and then right-click to accept the selection. Select the Join multiple edges option from the command line. Next, select the edge of the second surface, and then right-click. Likewise, use the Join multiple edges option and select the edges of the other surfaces. The preview of the transition surface is displayed.

Press ENTER and notice the grips on the selected edge. Using these edges, you can specify how the loft surface will be connected to the selected edges. These options are already discussed in Chapter 6: Loft Features. After specifying the continuity type, press ENTER to create the lofted surface.

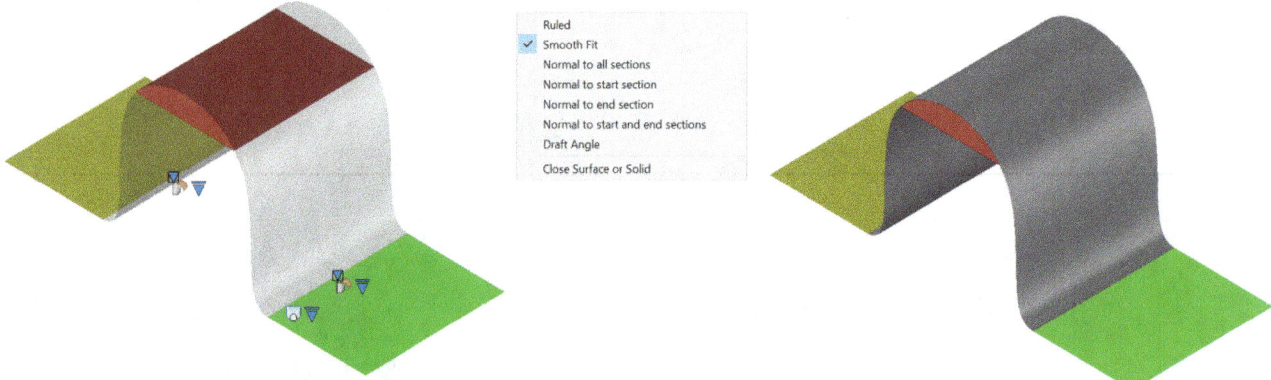

Sweep

This command creates a surface by sweeping a section along a path. First, create a sweep section and a path, and then activate the **Sweep** command (on the ribbon, click **Surface > Create > Sweep**). Select the profile, and then press ENTER. Select the path; the swept surface appears.

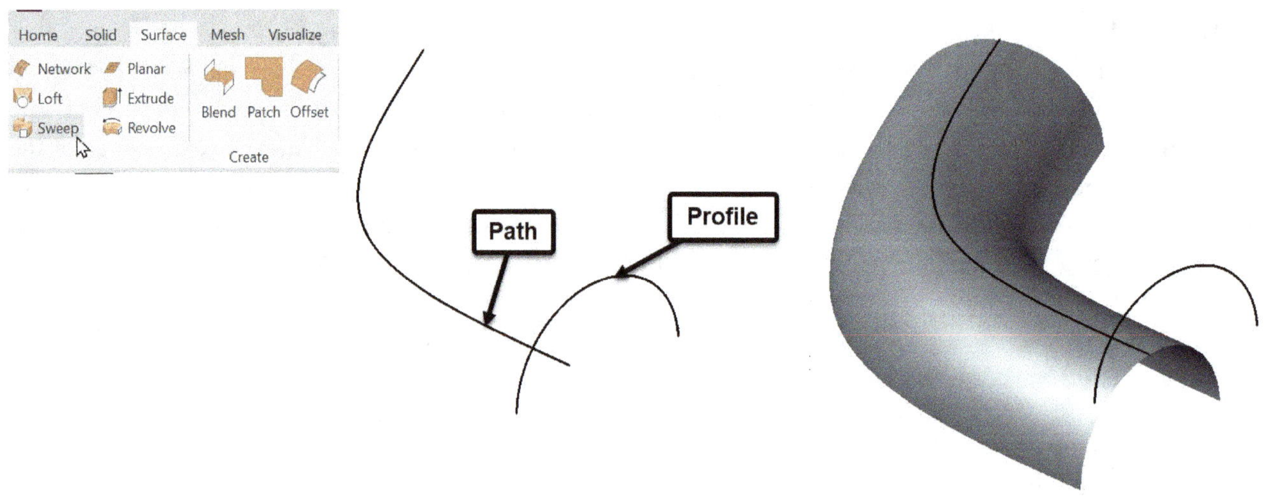

Patch

To create a patch surface, Activate the **Patch** command (on the ribbon, click **Surface > Create > Patch**) and select a closed loop of edges. Next, press ENTER to accept the selection.

Select the **COntinuity** option from the command line. Next, select **G0**, **G1**, or **G2** option from the command line. The **G0** option creates the patch surface by precisely aligning with the boundary curves or surfaces, ensuring a perfect fit. However, there is no smooth connection where the patch surface meets at the boundaries; they join together abruptly, which may create a noticeable edge or corner.

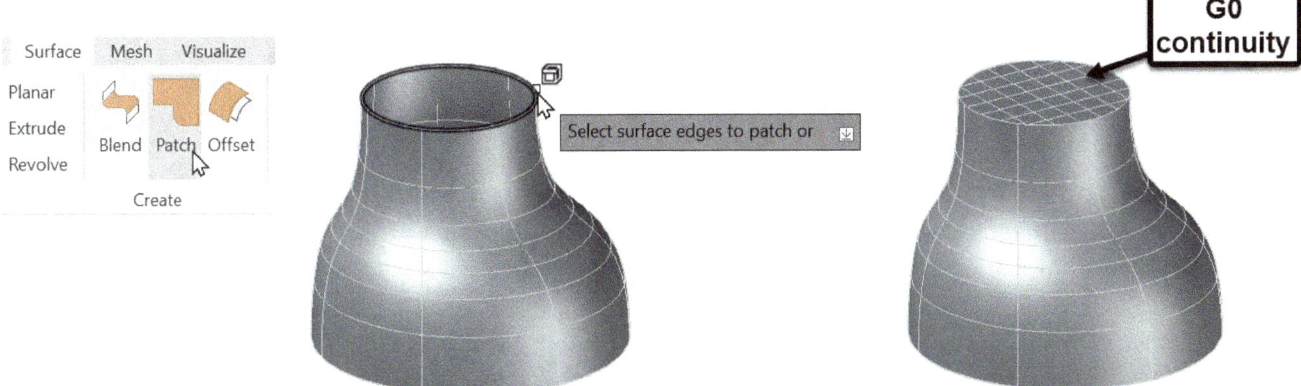

The **G1** option creates a tangential connection between the patch surface and the boundary curves or surfaces, resulting in a smoother transition than **G0**. However, a noticeable change in curvature may still occur. Ideal for situations where a smoother visual transition is desired, but perfect curvature matching is not required.

The **G2** option create a patch surface that aligns with the boundary curves or surfaces, ensuring a match in curvature. This results in the smoothest possible transition, eliminating any visible edges or corners. This is especially useful in applications that require high-quality surface modeling with seamless transitions, like in the design of cars or products. G2 provides the smoothest results but may require more processing power and time.

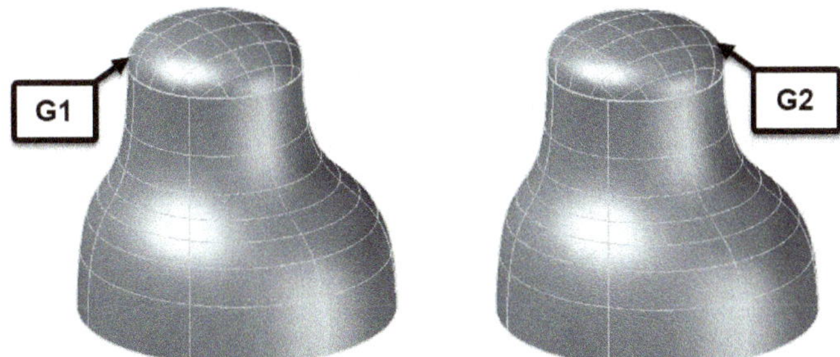

After specifying the continuity option, select the Bulge Magnitude option. This option modifies the surface curvature by specifying the bulge factor. Essentially, it influences how much the surface protrudes out.

Upon selecting this option, you'll be prompted to input a value for the bulge magnitude, which dictates the extent of bulging or curvature: Enter a value to make the surface bulge outwards. Enter 0 to create a flat surface.

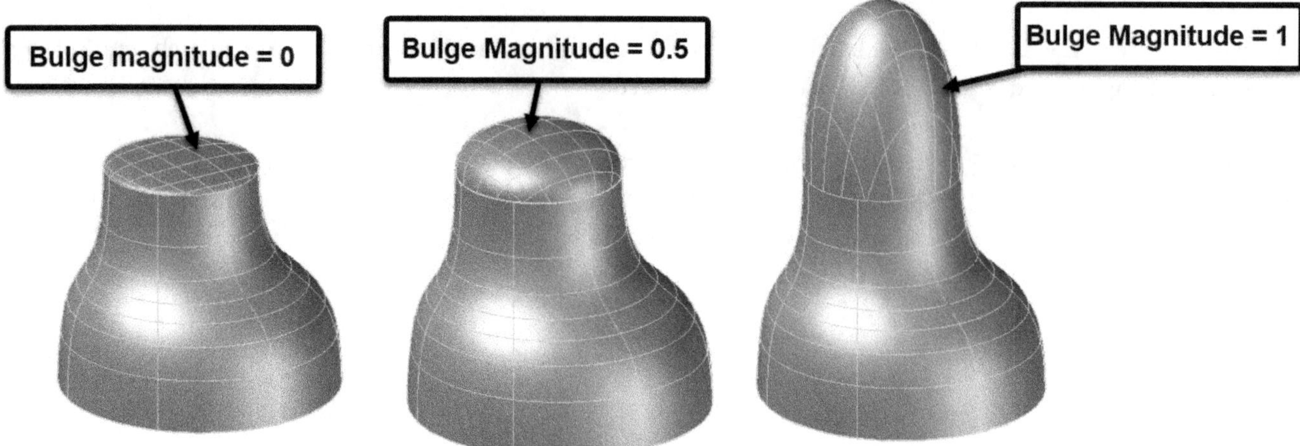

Creating a Patch surface using Guide Curves

The **Guides** feature within the **Patch** command allows you to shape the patch surfaces using additional curves. The patch surface follows the guides, giving you more control over the final 3D surface shape.

To begin, activate the **Patch** command and select the **Curves** option. Next, select the objects that will form the patch boundary. These can be closed polylines, splines, or any other edge set defining the surface perimeter. Once the boundary is selected, press ENTER to accept the selection.

To activate the **Guides** option, type 'G' or 'Guides' and hit Enter. You'll then be prompted to choose the curves to function as guides. These guides will impact the patch's shape.

Select the curves, lines, or splines you wish to use as guides for the patch surface. For multiple guide selection, hold down the Shift key while selecting. After choosing the guides, press Enter. AutoCAD will then generate the patch surface, taking into account both the boundary and the guide curves.

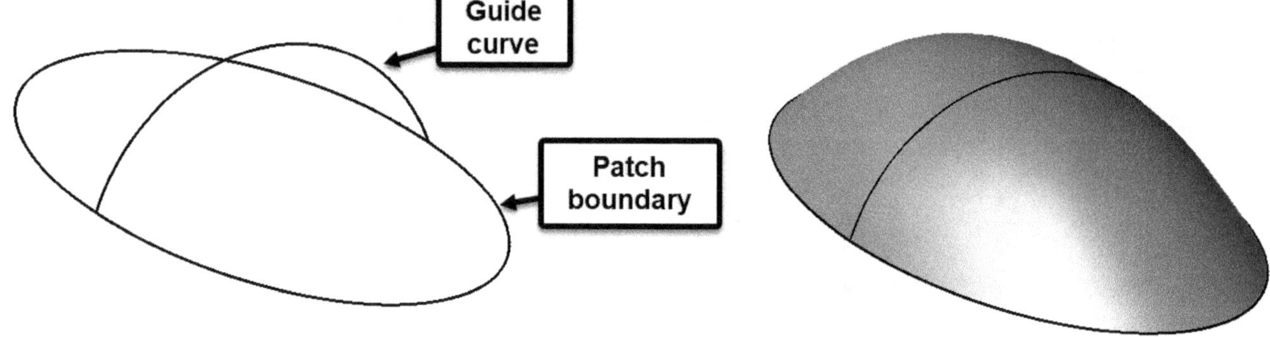

Trim

This command trims a portion of a surface using a trimming tool. The trimming tool can be a surface, plane, or a sketched entity. Activate this command (click **Surface > Edit > Trim** on the ribbon) and select the object to trim. Press ENTER to accept the selection. Select the cutting tool. Next, select the portion of the surface to be removed. Press ENTER to exit the command.

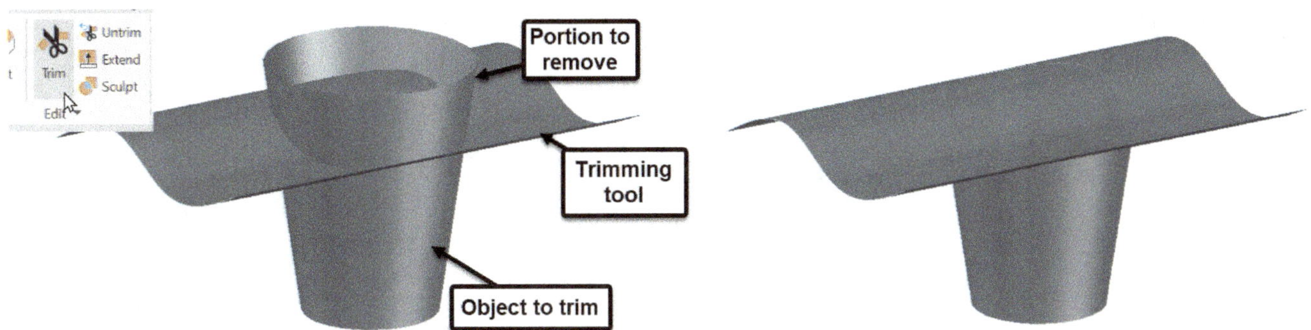

You can also trim a surface using a curve. Activate the **Trim** command and select the curve. You will notice that the trimming boundary is created normal to the surface. Also, the trim boundary is created throughout the model. Click inside the area to trim. Press ENTER to trim the surface.

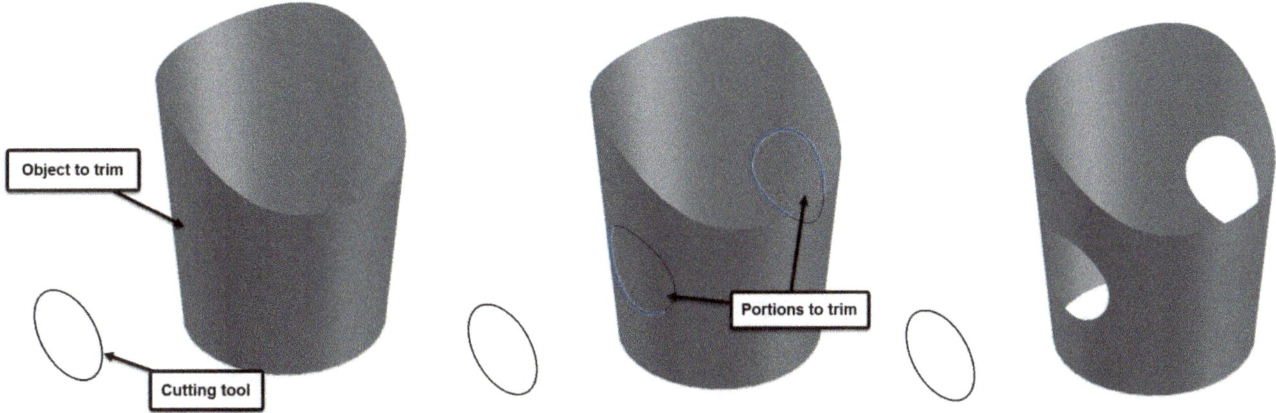

Untrim

You can untrim a trimmed surface using the **Untrim** command. Activate this command (on the ribbon, click **Surface > Edit > Untrim**) and click on the edges of the trimmed portions of the surface. If the surface contains multiple trimmed sections, select the 'SUrface' option from the command line and click on the entire surface.

Offset

To create an offset surface, activate the **Offset** command (click **Surface > Create > Offset** on the ribbon) and select the faces to offset. Press ENTER to accept the selection. Notice the options in the command line. The **Flip Direction** option allows you flip offset direction of the surface. The **Both sides** option allows you to offset on both sides of the original surface. The **Connect** option connects the offset surfaces. After specifying the desired options, type-in the offset value in the command line.

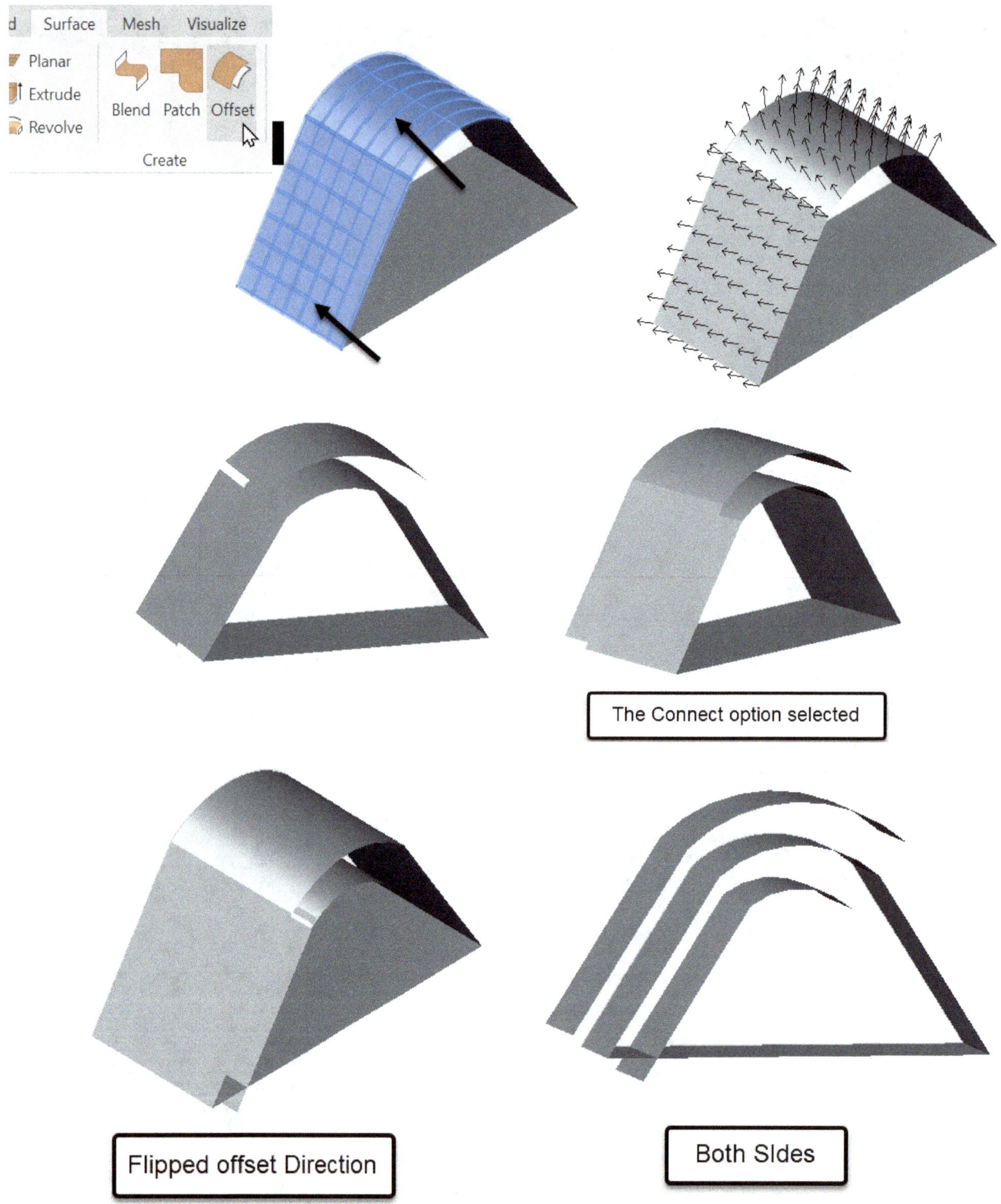

Adding Thickness to the Surface

Creating a solid from a surface can be accomplished by simply thickening a surface. To add thickness to a surface, activate the **Offset** command (on the ribbon, click **Surface > Create > Offset**) and select the surfaces to be thickened. Press ENTER to accept the selection. Next, select the **Solid** option from the command line. Use the Flip Direction option if you want to change the direction of the offset. Enter the offset value in the command line and press ENTER.

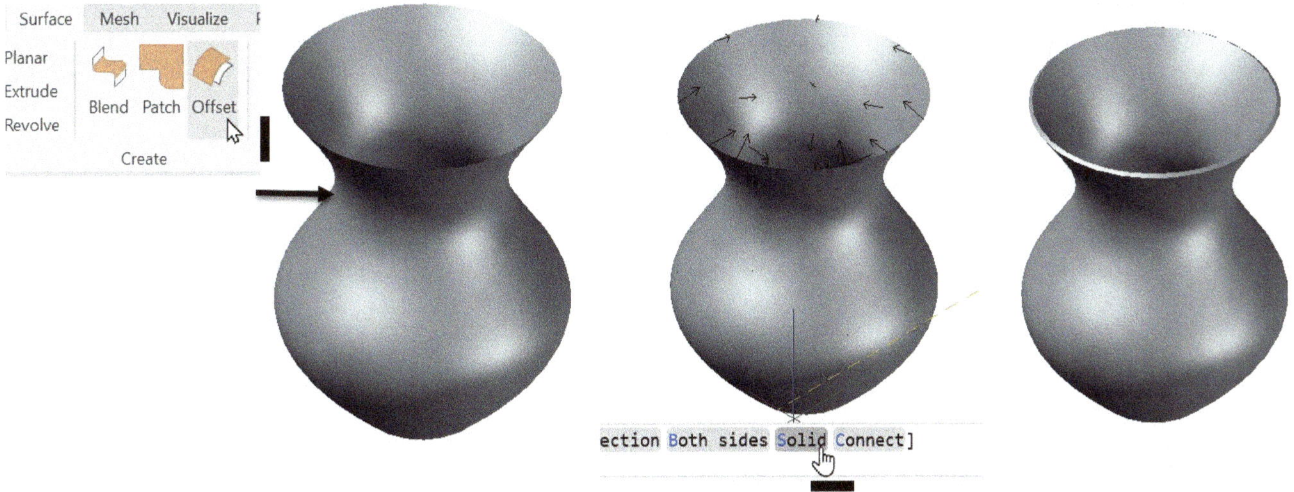

Surface Blend

The **Surface Blend** command is a tool that generates a surface to bridge the gap between two existing surfaces. This bridge can be either tangent or curvature continuous in both directions. To create a blend surface, follow these steps:

- Activate the **Surface Blend** command. You can find this on the ribbon by clicking **Surface > Create > Blend**.
- Select the first edge. If you have multiple connected edges, use the **CHain** option to select them all at once. Press ENTER to confirm your selection.
- Select the edge of the second surface and press ENTER.

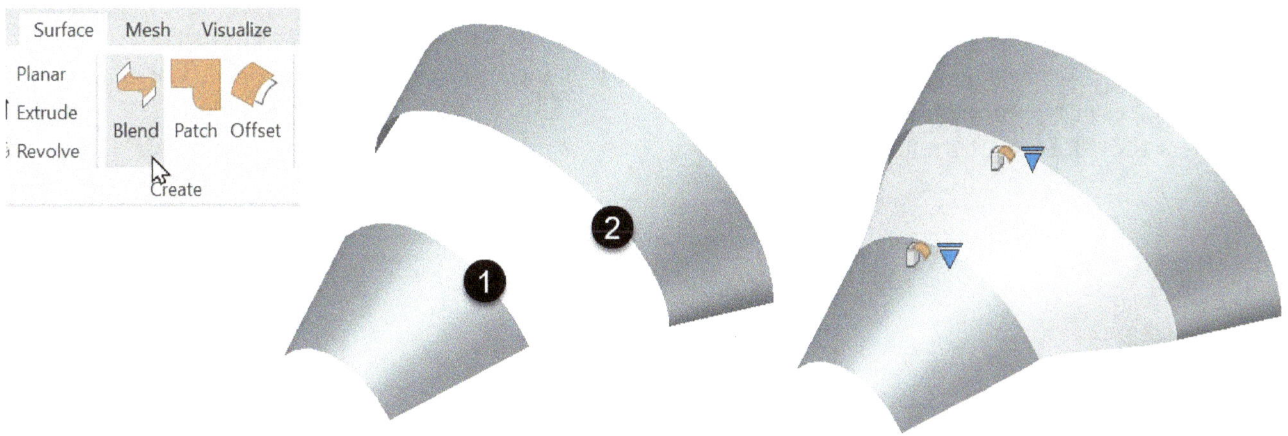

To specify how the boundary surface connects to the selected edges:
- Click the grip displayed on the first edge.
- Choose your continuity type. You can select G1 (Tangent) to maintain tangency between the first edge and the bridge surface. Alternatively, you can select G0 (Position) or G2 (Curvature).
- Repeat these steps for the second edge.

To define the bulge magnitude:
- Select the **Bulge magnitude** option from the command line.
- Enter a value in the command line and press ENTER.

Press ENTER once more to finalize and create the blend surface.

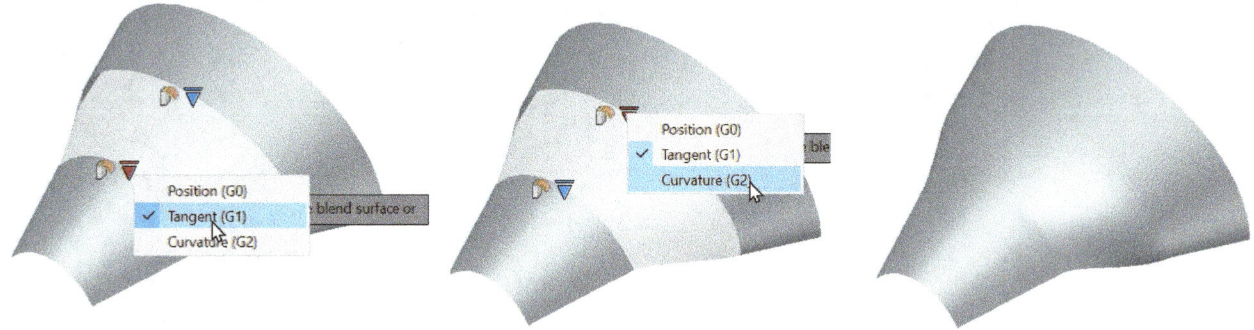

Surface Fillets

Surface Fillets serve multiple purposes. They can bridge gaps between faces, aid in blending intricate surfaces, and be determined by a boundary curve instead of a radius. For instance, you can create a face blend to bridge a gap between two faces.

1. Activate the **Surface Fillets** command. You can find this on the ribbon by clicking **Surface > Edit > Surface Fillets**.
2. Choose the **Radius** option. Enter the radius value and confirm it by selecting two points from the graphics window. A helpful tip: select vertices of the two surfaces to automatically set the minimum distance between them as the fillet radius.
3. Once the fillet radius is set, select the first face surface.
4. Next, select the second surface. If necessary, adjust the fillet radius by dragging the Fillet grip displayed on the fillet. Ensure the radius is equal to or greater than the distance between the two surfaces.
5. Choose the **Trim surface** option to decide whether to trim the surfaces to the fillet edge or not. Select either **Yes** or **No** from the command line.
6. Press ENTER to finalize and create the fillet.

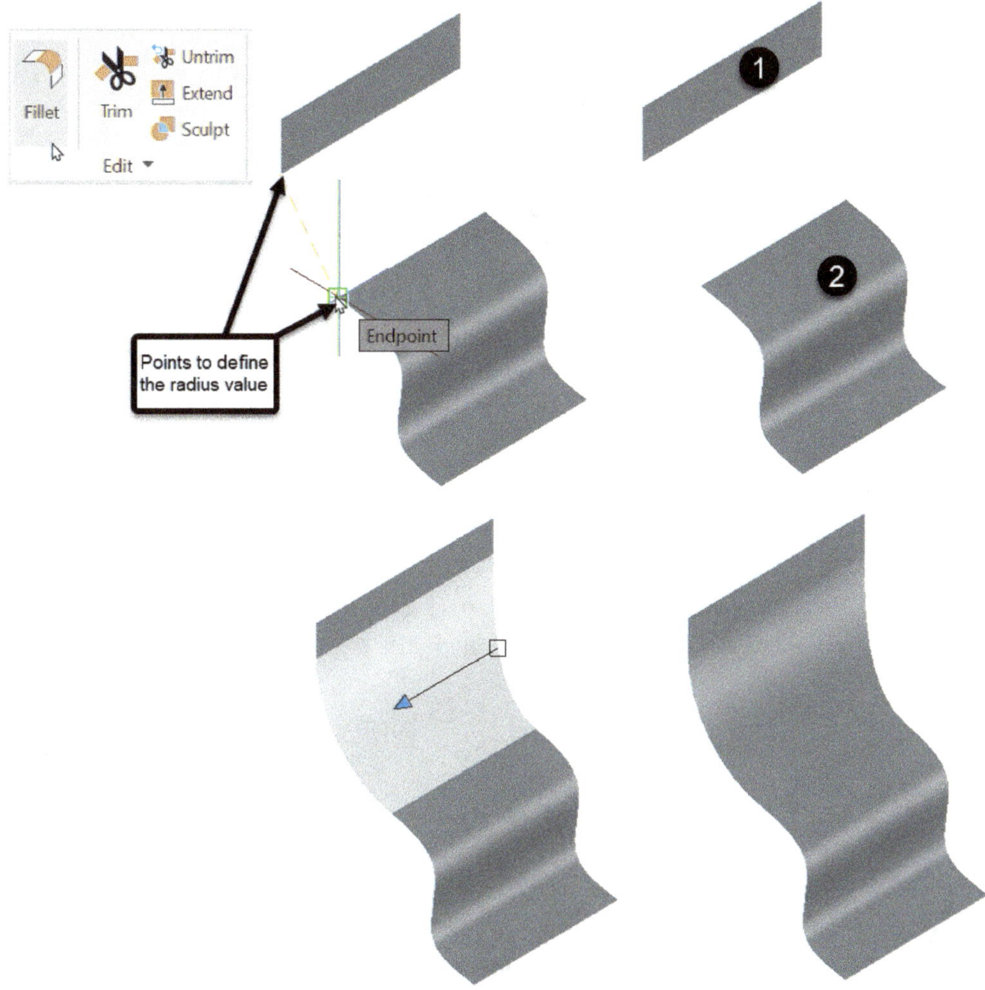

Extend

During the design process, you may sometimes need to extend a surface. You can extend a surface using the **Extend** command. Activate this command (On the ribbon, click **Surface > Edit > Extend**) and select the edge of the surface to be extended. Next, press ENTER to accept the selection. Select the **Modes** option from the command line. Next, select the **Extend** or **Stretch** option from the command line. The **Extend** option lets you make a surface longer along its natural direction. The **Stretch** option lets you move the edges of a surface to a new spot, making the surface bigger.

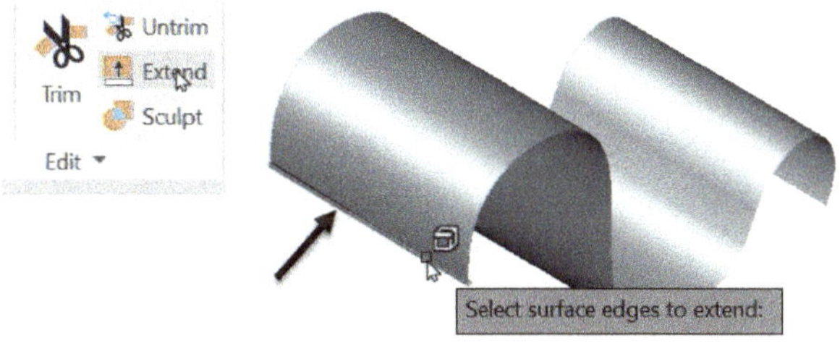

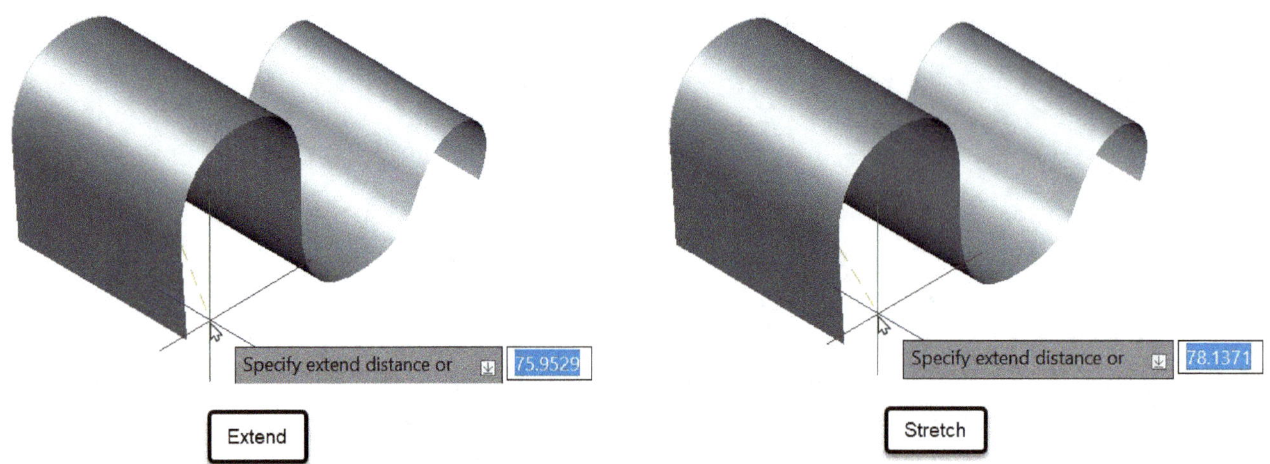

Next, select the **Merge** or **Append** option. The **Merge** option lets you extend a surface and blend the new part smoothly with the old one, keeping it as a single entity.

The **Append** option also extends a surface but creates a separate new part, attaching it to the existing surface without blending. This is useful when you want distinct surface sections or when merging isn't suitable for complex surface modeling.

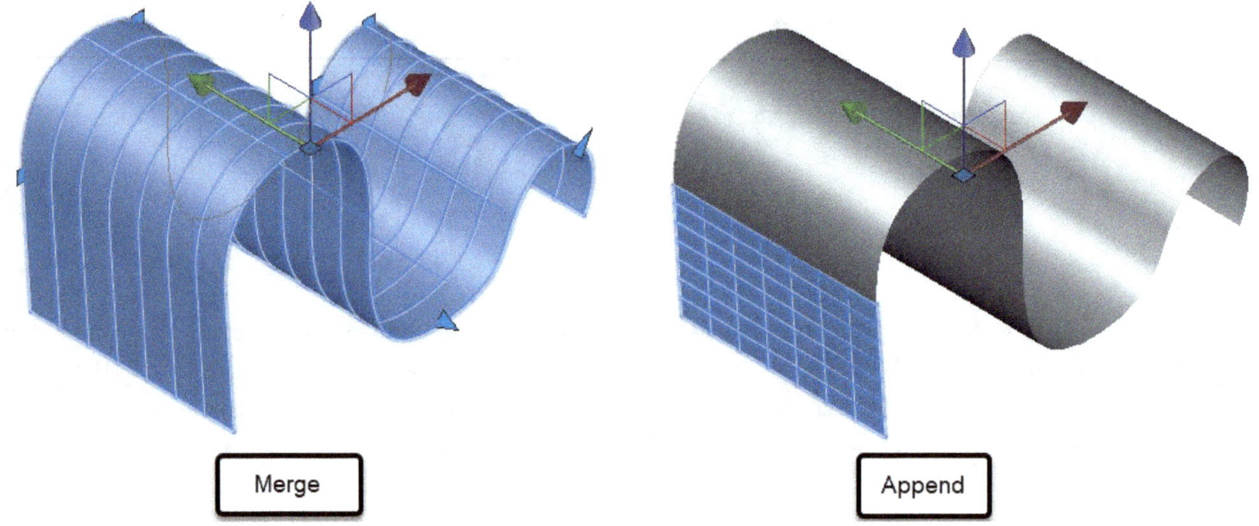

Type-in extend distance value and press ENTER.

Sculpt

The **Sculpt** command is used to trim multiple surfaces at a time and create a closed solid. For example, you can use this option for the following case.

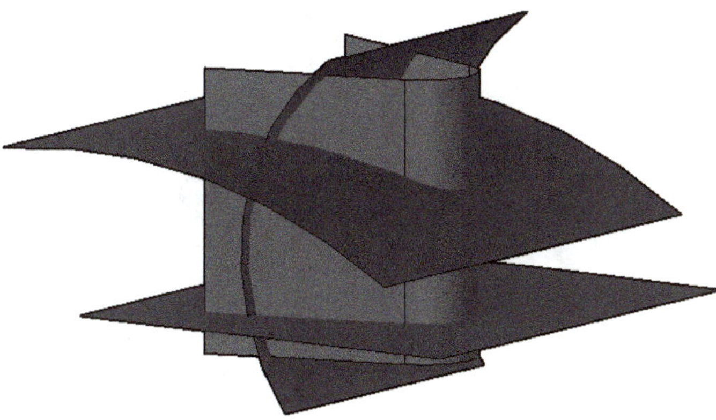

Activate the **Sculpt** command (on the ribbon, click **Surface > Edit > Sculpt**). Select the required surfaces from the model (All surfaces in this case). Press ENTER the surfaces and create a closed solid.

Network

The **Network Surface** command allows you to generate a surface by specifying a network of curves. You this command, you can create intricate three-dimensional models by specifying a grid-like pattern of curves to define the shape of a surface. This results in a smooth, continuous surface that accurately represents the desired design.

- In the top right corner of the graphics window, click **View Controls > Right** from the **In-Canvas Controls**.
- On the ribbon, click **Home > Draw > Spline**.
- Click in the graphics window to define the first point of the spline.
- Move the pointer slightly toward bottom right corner up to a small distance and click to specify the second point.

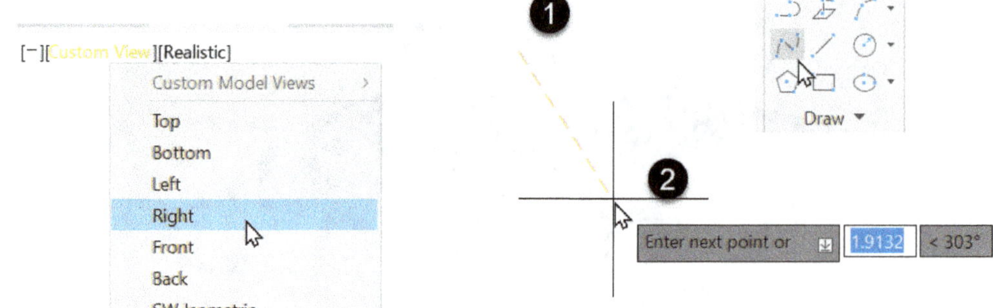

- Move the pointer slightly toward bottom left corner up to a small distance and click to specify the third point.
- Move the pointer downward toward the bottom right corner and click to define the endpoint of the spline.
- Press ENTER to create the spline.

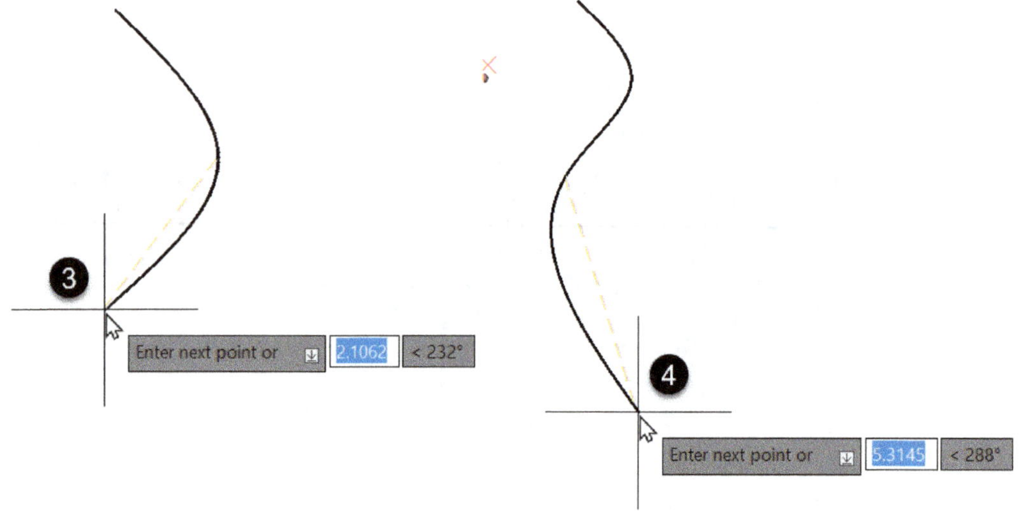

- On the ribbon, click **Home > Modify > Copy** and select the spline, and then press ENTER.
- Select the lower endpoint of the spline to define the base point of the spline.
- Move the pointer toward right up to a small distance and click to create the copy the spline.
- Select the copied spline and click **Home > Modify > 3D Scale** on the ribbon.
- Select the midpoint of the spline to define the base point.
- Move the pointer and type-in 0.8 as the scale factor. Next, press ENTER to scale the copied spline.

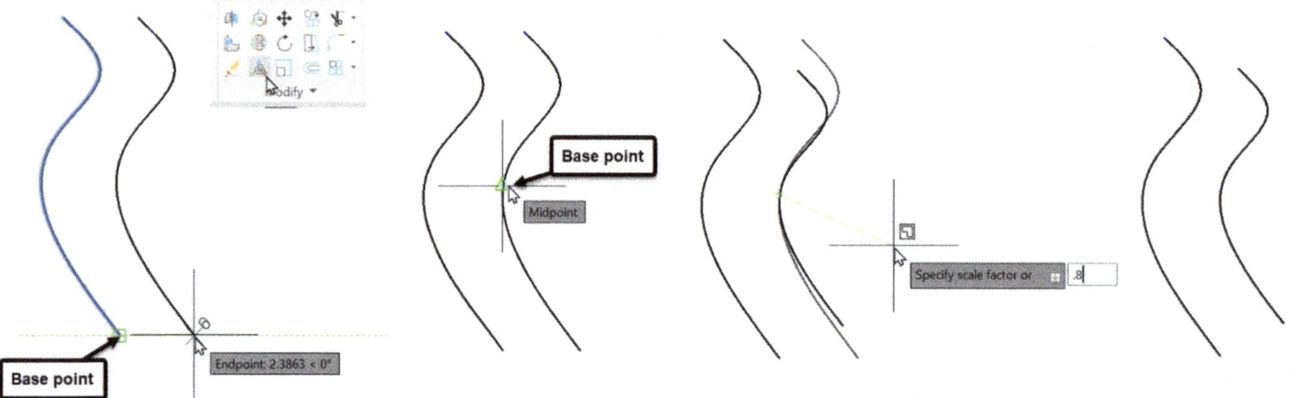

- In the top right corner of the graphics window, click **View Controls > SE Isometric** from the **In-Canvas Controls**.
- Select the copied spline to display 3D Move gizmo on it.
- Click on the X-axis of the 3D Move gizmo and drag the pointer toward right up to a small distance, and then click.

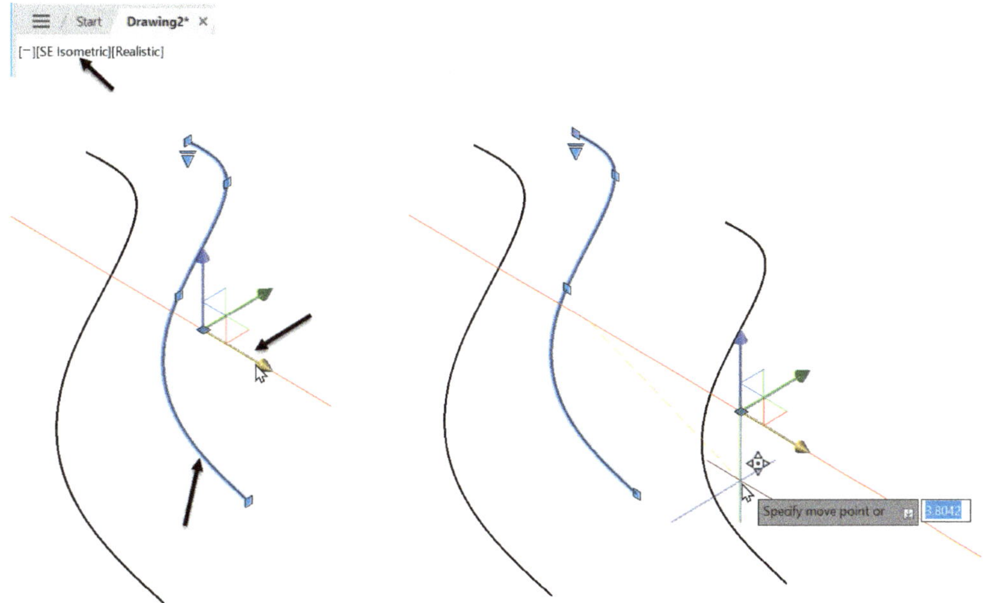

- Select the copied spline and click **Home > Modify > 3D Mirror** on the ribbon.
- Select the **XY** option from the command line.
- Select the lower endpoint of the first spline to define the origin point of the mirror plane.
- Select the **No** from the command line to keep the original object.

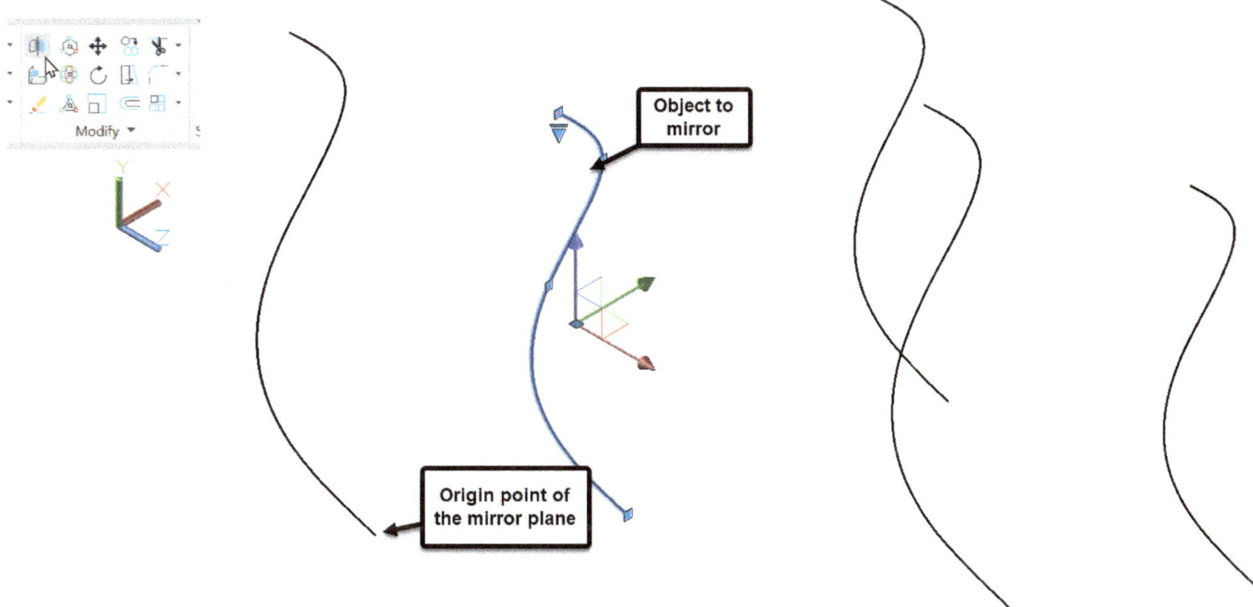

- On the ribbon, click **Home > Draw > Spline**.

- Select the top endpoints of the splines. Next, press ENTER to create a spline connecting all three endpoints.

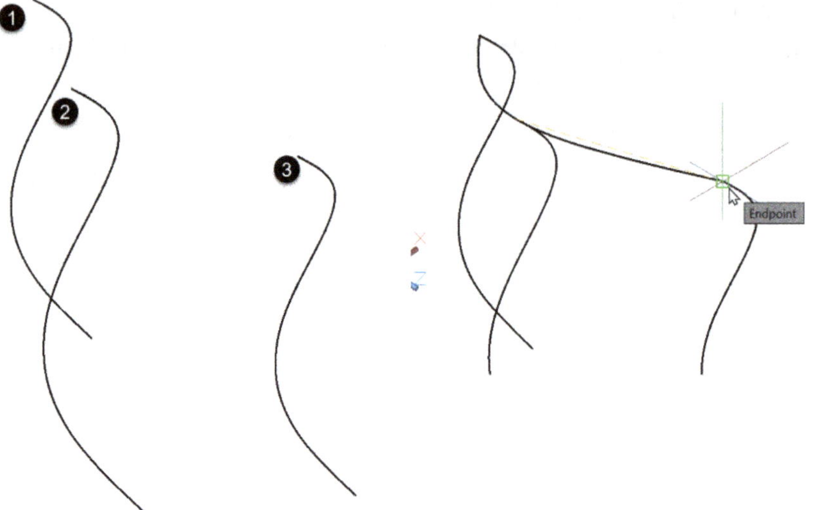

- Select the midpoints of the three splines and press ENTER.
- Select the lower endpoints of the three splines and press ENTER.

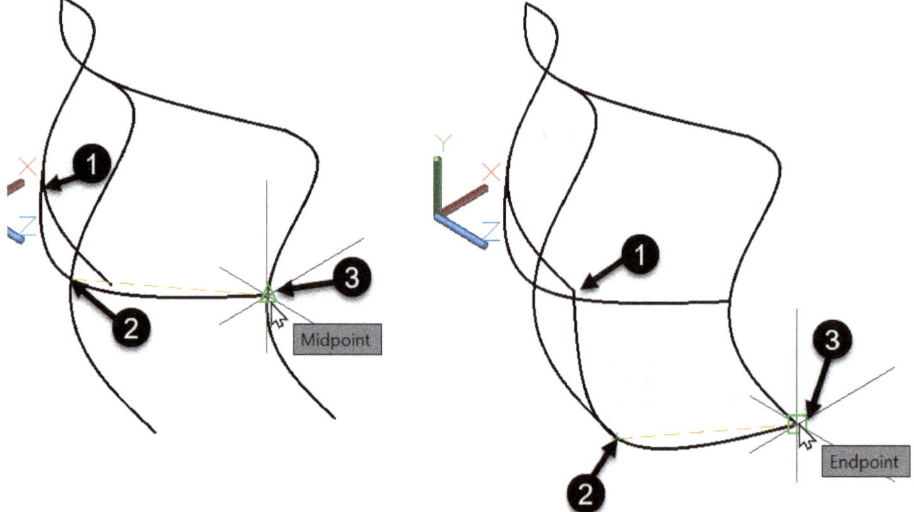

- On the ribbon, click **Surface > Create > Network** and select the splines displayed in the vertical direction. Next, press ENTER.
- Select the splines displayed in the horizontal direction, and then press ENTER.

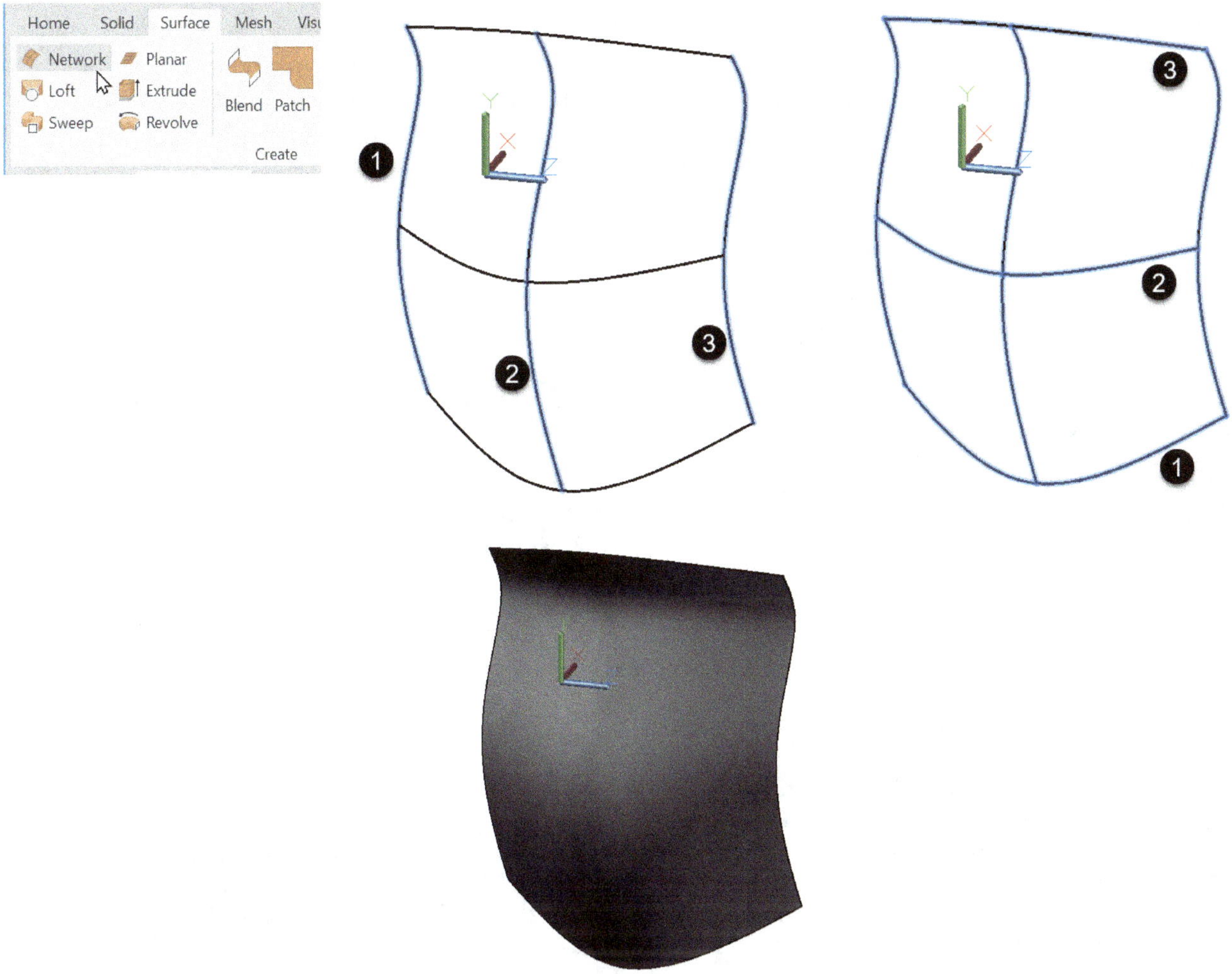

Planar Surface

To create a planar surface, initiate the command by selecting **Surface > Create > Planar Surface** on the ribbon. Then, define the surface by clicking on two diagonal corner points. Alternatively, use the **Object** option to choose 2D objects that form a closed profile, which will generate a planar surface from your selection.

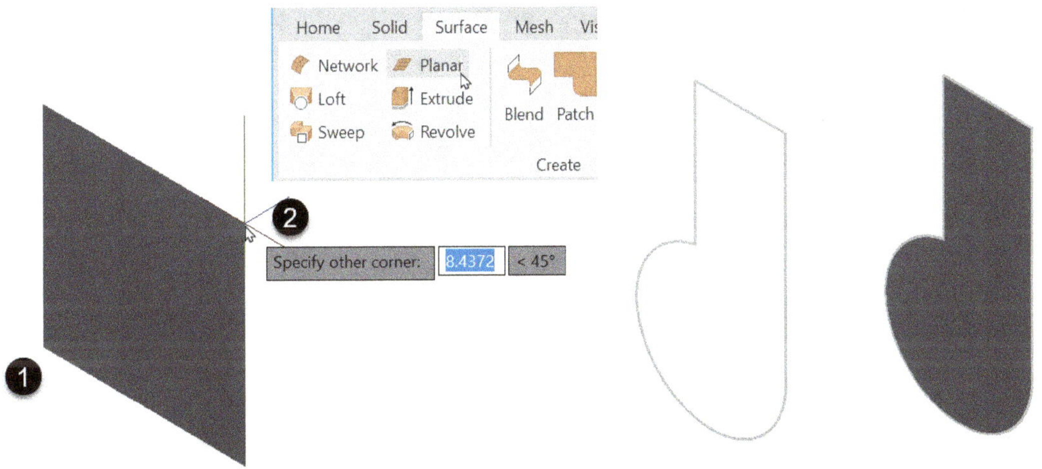

Extract Isolines

This command creates isolines on the selected face. Isolines are curves on a surface that represent constant values of a function, like curvature or elevation. They help you to understand the shape and topography of a surface, aiding in analysis and visualization. Activate this command (on the ribbon, click **Surface** tab > **Curves** group > **Extract Isolines**) and select the surface. Next, move the pointer on the selected surface and click to position the isoline. Select the **Direction** option from the command line to change the direction to perpendicular in which the isolines are created.

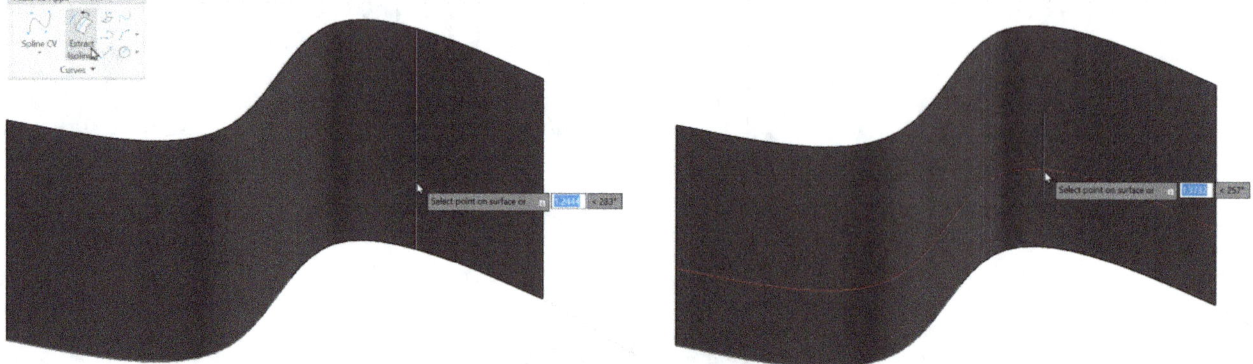

The **Spline points** option creates splines on the surface. Select this option from the command line. Start selecting points on the surface. On the command line, select the **Close** option if you want to close the curve.

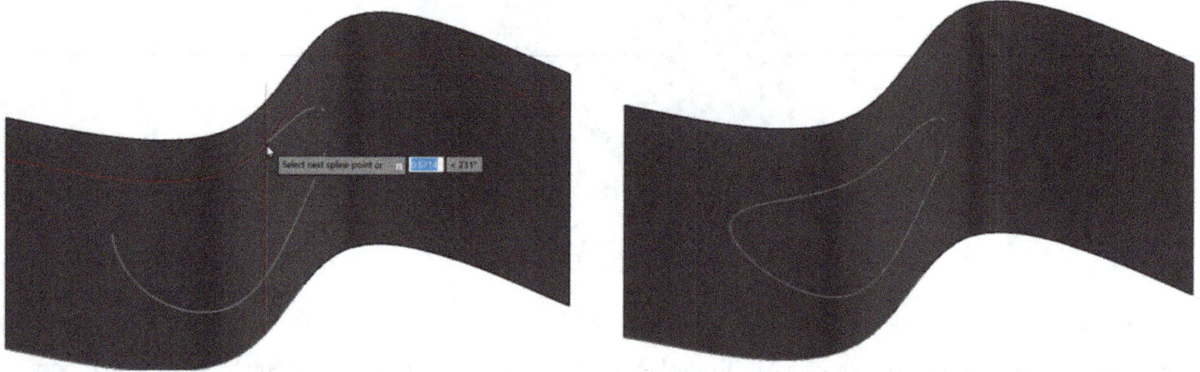

Extract Intersection

The **Extract Intersection** command creates a curve at the intersection of the surface and plane, or two surfaces, or solid and surface, or solid and plane. Activate the **Extract Intersection** command (on the ribbon, click **Surface >**

Edit > Extract Intersection) and select the two intersecting surfaces. Press ENTER and select the Yes option from the command line.

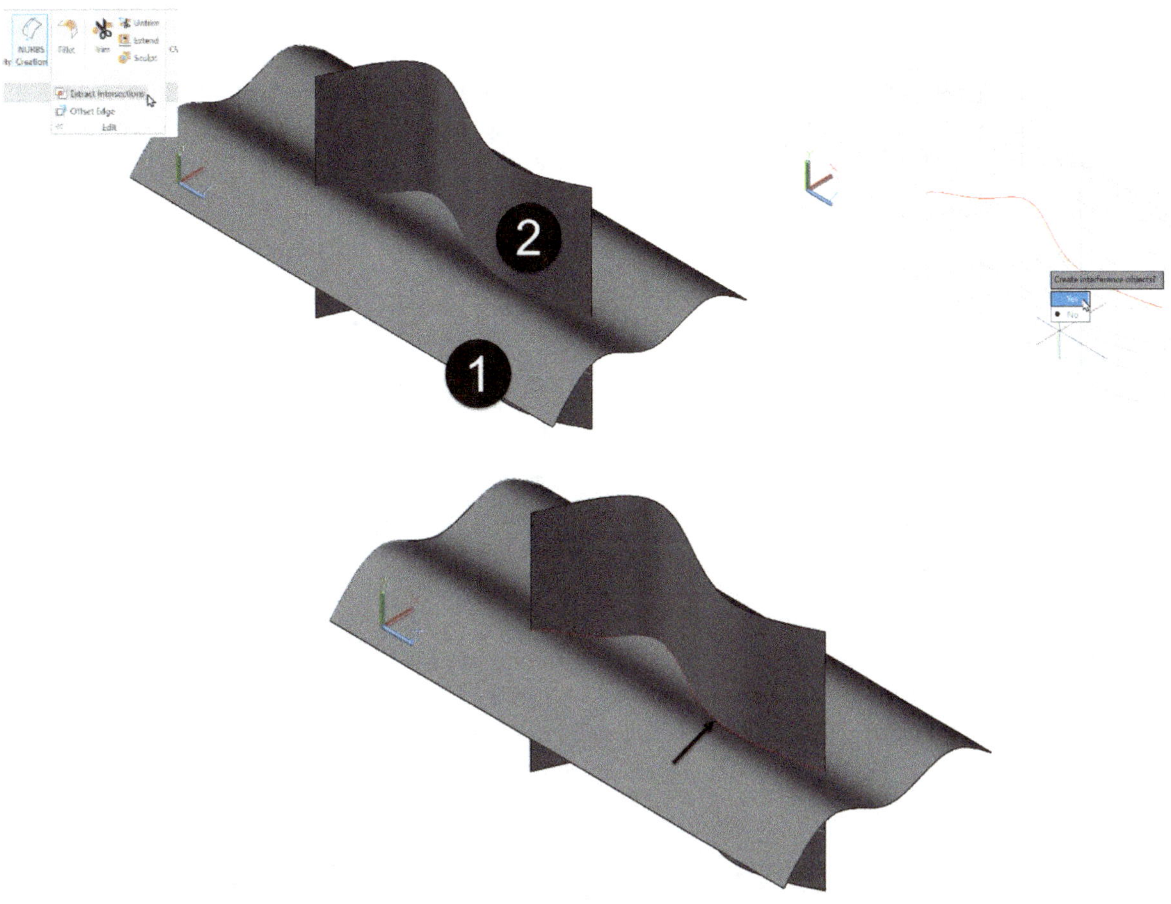

Surface Projection UCS

The **Surface Projection UCS** command takes a 2D curve and maps it onto a surface. The direction in which the 2D curve is projected will be dependent on the current UCS orientation. On the ribbon, click **Surface > Project Geometry > Surface Projection UCS** and select the curve to project. Press and ENTER and select the surface onto which the curve will be mapped.

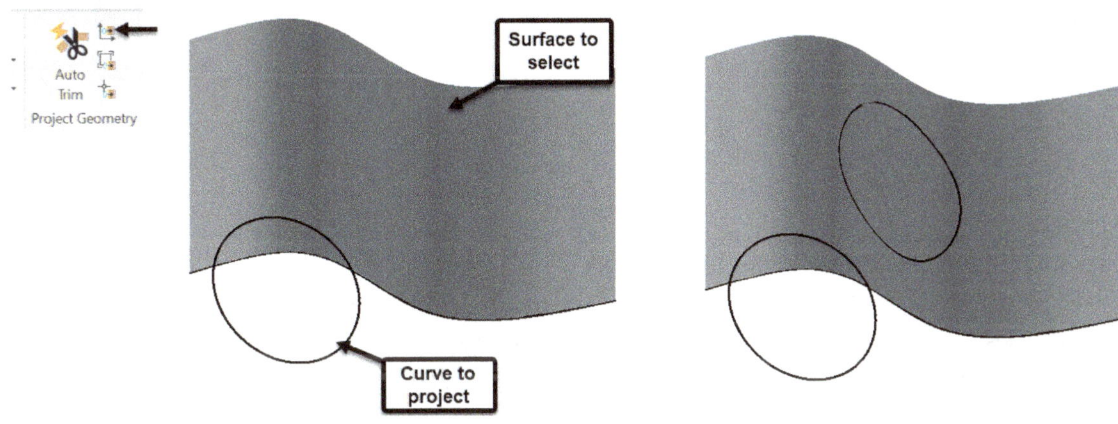

If you want to trim the surface using the projected geometry, automatically, then click the **Auto Trim** icon on the **Projected Geometry** panel of the **Surfaces** ribbon tab.

Surface Projection View

The **Surface Projection View** command projects the selected geometry along the current view direction. Adjust your viewpoint to the angle you wish to project from using the **VIEW** command or the view cube and navigation tools. Activate the **Surface Projection View** command and select the objects to project. Press ENTER and select the surface onto which the curve will be projected.

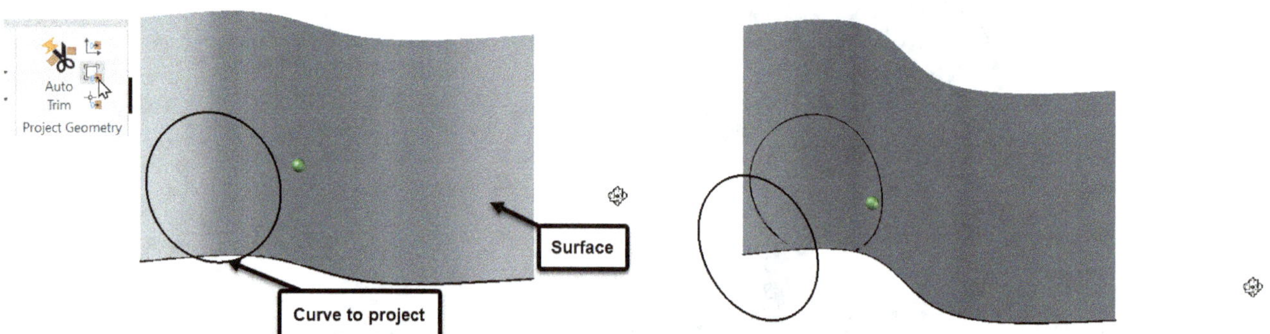

Surface Projection Vector

The **Surface Projection Vector** command projects the selected geometry along a custom direction. You can determine the direction of the projection by specifying two points. On the ribbon, click **Surface > Project Geometry > Surface Projection Vector**. Next, select two points from the graphics window to specify the direction. Select the curve to project and press ENTER. Next, select the surface.

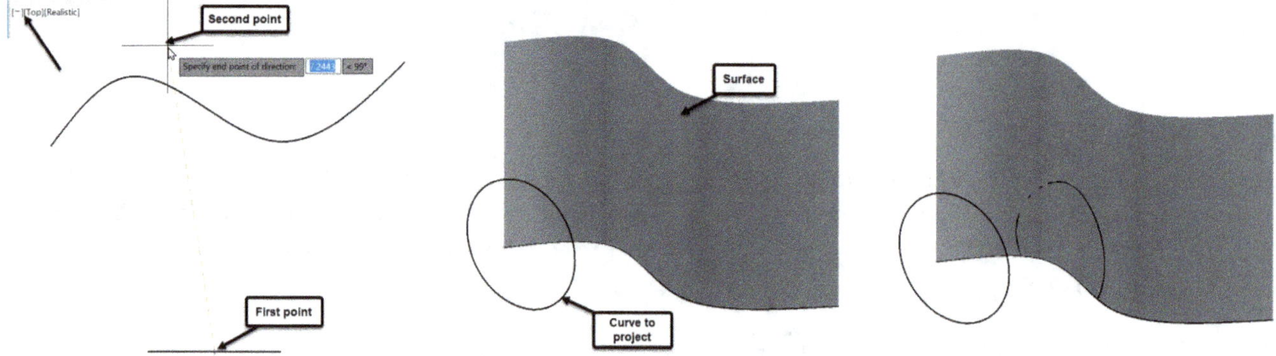

Example 1

In this example, you will create a headphone surface model.

1. Start **AutoCAD 2025**.
2. Click **New drop-down > acadiso3D.dwt** on the **Start** screen.
3. On the ribbon, click **Home > Layers > Layers Properties Manager**.
4. On the Layers Properties Manager, click the **New Layer** icon. Next, type Curves in the Layer name box.
5. Click the **Color** swatch and select the Black color from the **Select Color** dialog. Click **OK**.
6. Likewise, create two more layers Surfaces and Solid.
7. Double-click on the **Curves** layer to activate it. Next, close the Layers Properties Manager.

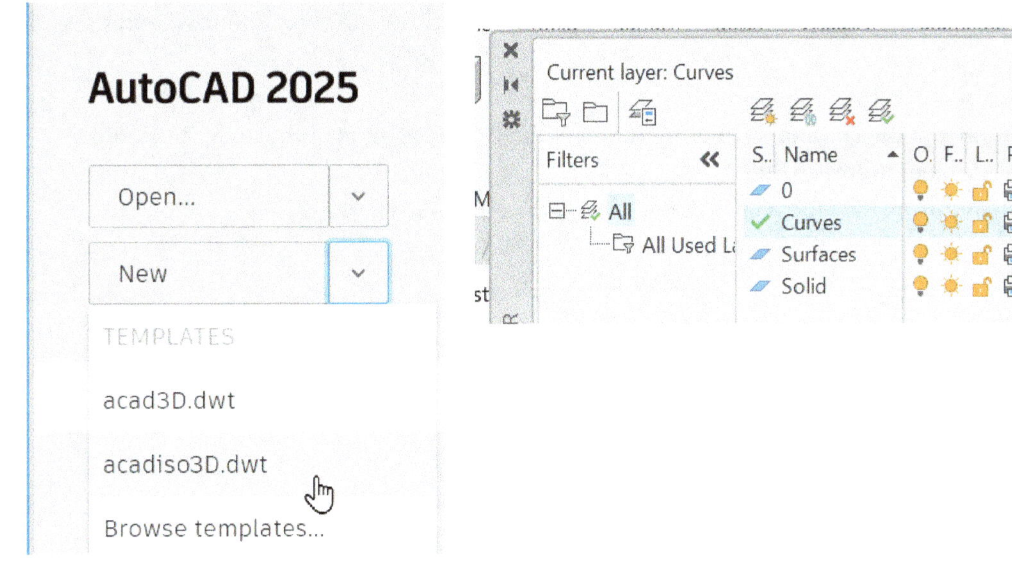

8. On the ribbon, click **Home** tab > **View** panel > **View Manager** drop-down > **Front**. The view orientation is changed to Front. Also, the X and Y axis of the UCS is set to Front view.
9. From the In-canvas controls, select **View Controls > Front**.
10. On the ribbon, click **Home > Draw > Polyline**. Next, create a polyline, as shown.

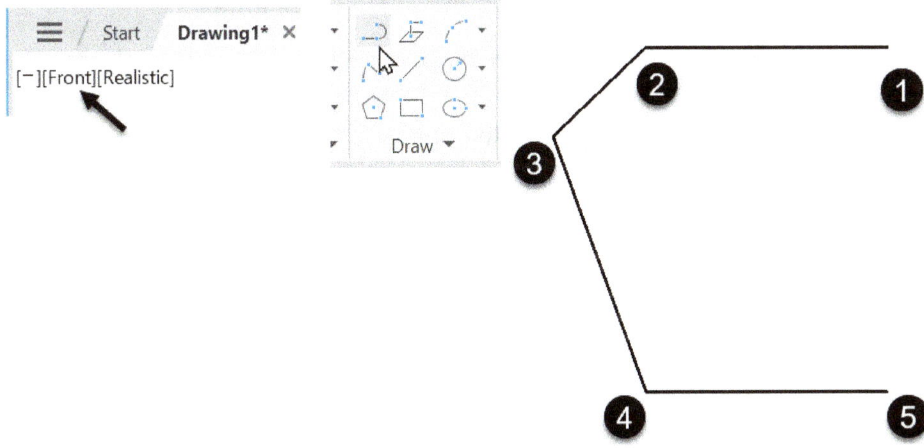

11. On the ribbon, click **Parametric > Geometric > Horizontal**. Select the lower horizontal line to constrain it horizontal. Likewise, select the upper horizontal line.

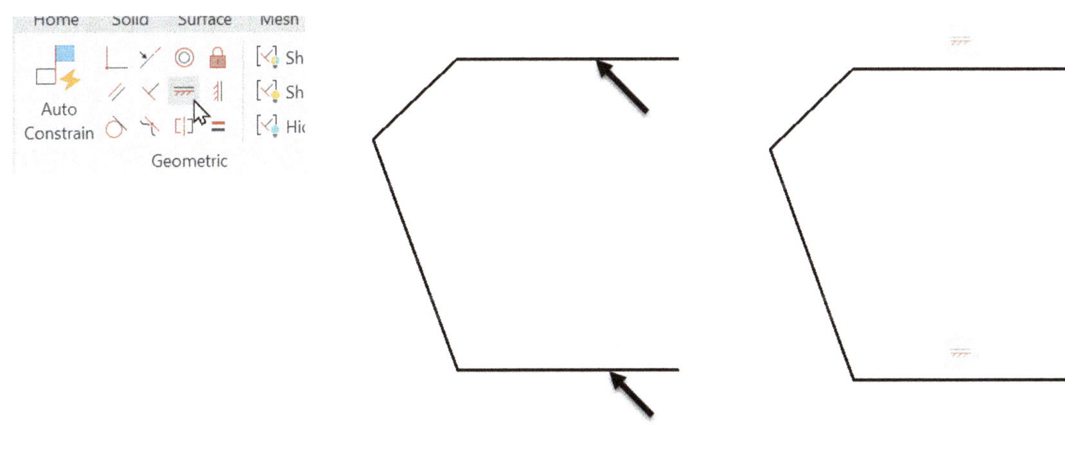

12. On the ribbon, click **Home > Modify > Scale**. Next, select the polyline from the graphics window, and press ENTER.
13. Select the lower left corner point as the base point.
14. Select the **Reference** option from the command line. Next, select the two endpoints of the lower horizontal line. This define the reference length for scaling.
15. Type 7 as the new length and press ENTER. The polyline is scaled to the new length.

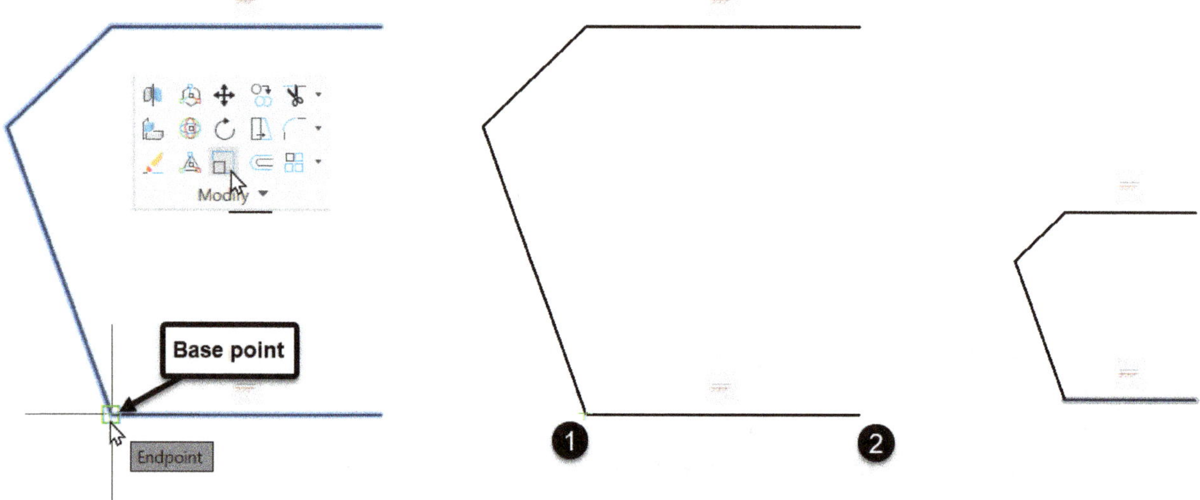

16. Expand the **Modify** panel and click the **Edit Polyline** command. Next, select the polyline from the graphic window.
17. Select **Spline** from the command line to convert the polyline into a spline. Press ENTER to exit the command.

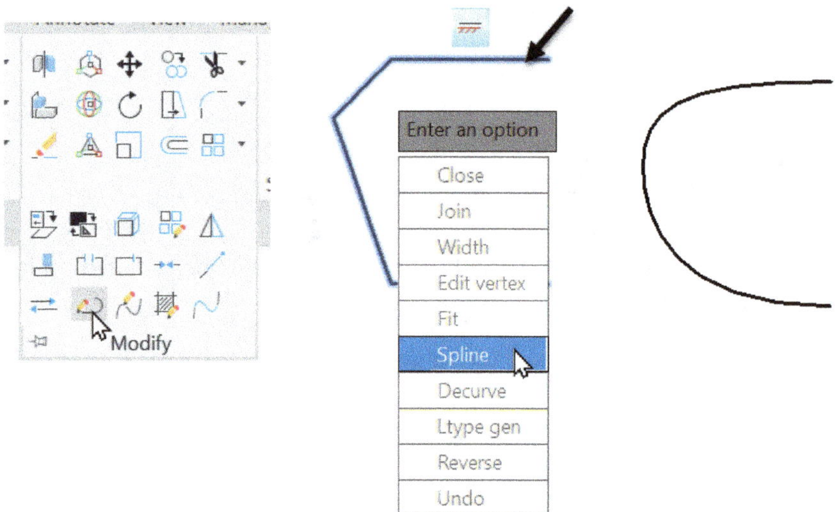

18. On the ribbon, click **Home > Layers > Layers** drop-down > **Surfaces**.
19. On the ribbon, click **Surface > Create > Revolve**. Next, select the spline and press ENTER.
20. Select the endpoints of the two splines to define the revolution axis, as shown.
21. Type 360 in the command line and press ENTER to revolve the spline by full 360 degrees.

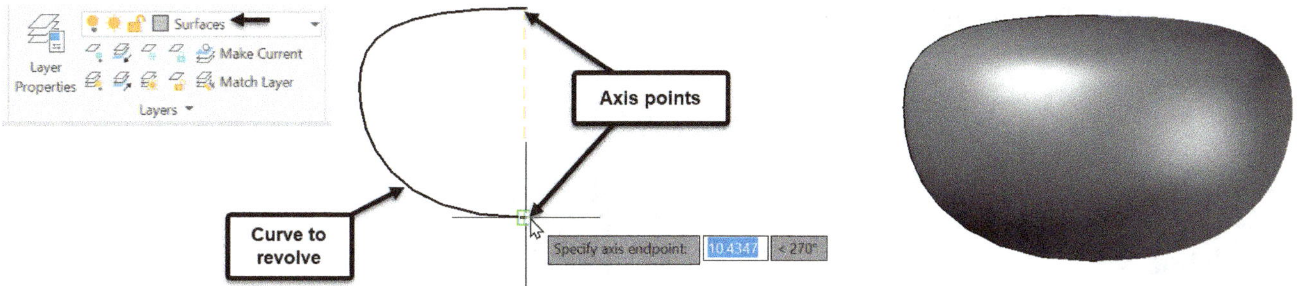

22. On the ribbon, click **Home > Layers > Layers** drop-down > **Curves**.
23. In the In-Canvas Controls, select **Visual Style Controls > Wireframe**.
24. On the ribbon, click **Home > Draw > Line** and select the lower endpoint of the spline to define the start point of the line.
25. Move the pointer toward right. Type **12** in the Length box and press the TAB key. Next, type 30 in the Angle box and press ENTER to create an inclined line.

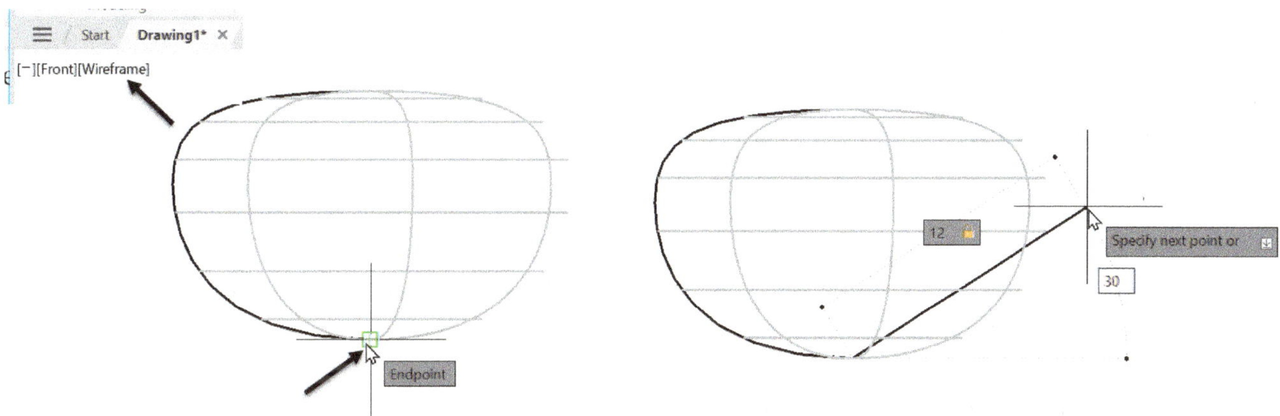

26. From the In-Canvas Controls, select **Visual Style Controls > Shades of Gray**.
27. On the ribbon, click **Surface > Edit > Trim**. Next, select the surface and press ENTER.
28. Select the inclined line and press ENTER to define the rimming tool.
29. Click in the lower portion of the surface to remove it. Press ENTER.

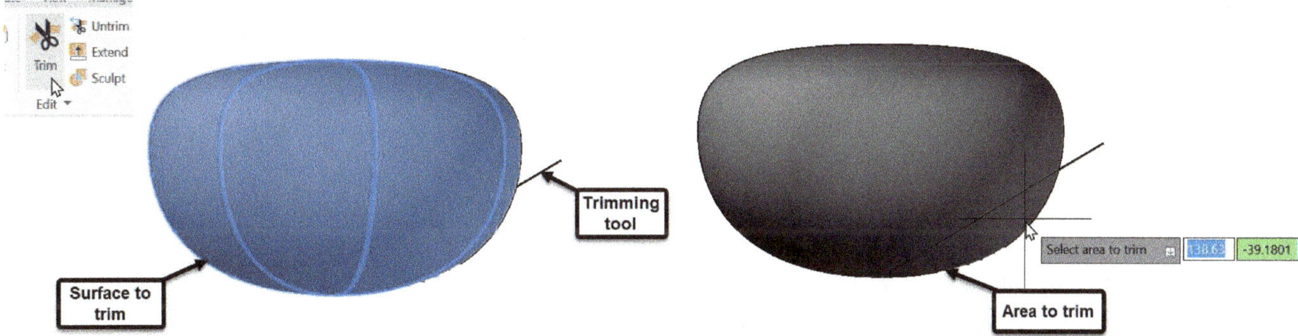

30. Activate the **Orthomode** icon on the Status bar.
31. On the ribbon, click **Home > Draw > Line**. Next, select the lower endpoint of the inclined line to specify the start point of the line.

32. Move the pointer horizontally toward right. Type **15** and press ENTER to create a horizontal line. Press ESC.
33. Select the horizontal line and click on the X-axis of the Move gizmo.
34. Move the pointer toward right, type 15 and press ENTER.

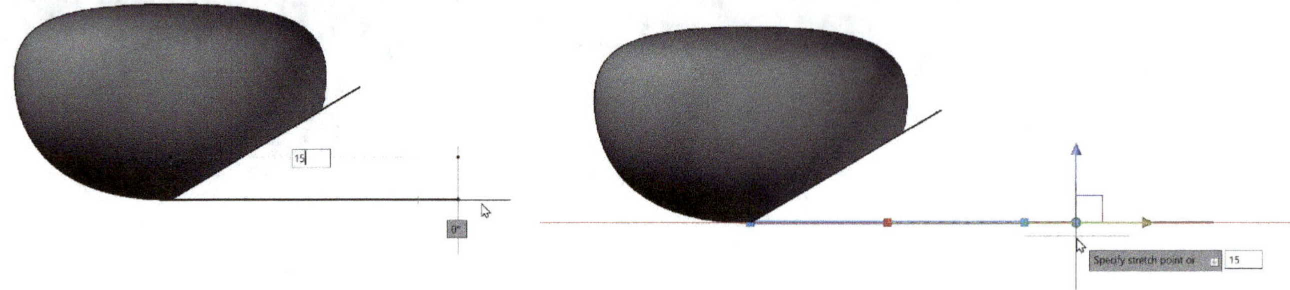

35. On the ribbon, click **Home > Modify > Offset**. Next, type **1.5** in the command line and press ENTER.
36. Select the horizontal line, move the pointer upward and click to create an offset line.

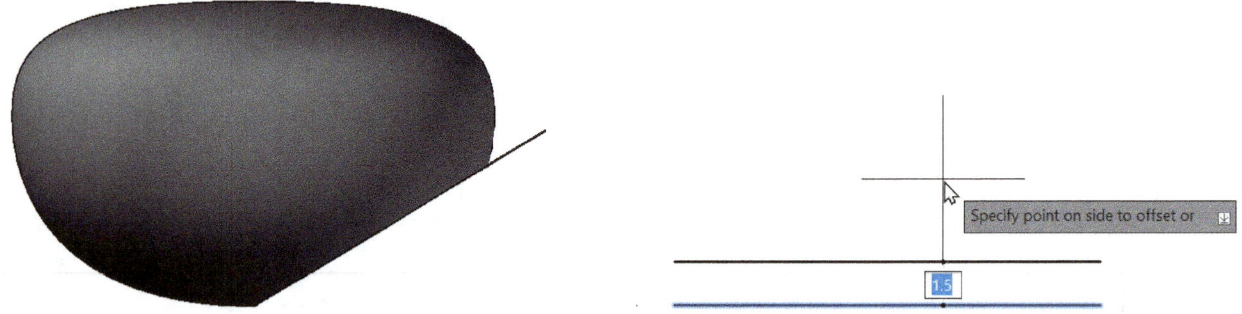

37. On the ribbon, click **Home > Layers > Layers** drop-down > **Surfaces**.
38. On the ribbon, click **Surface > Create > Revolve**. Next, select the lower horizontal line and press ENTER.
39. Select the **Object** option from the command line. Next, select the upper horizontal line to define the revolution axis.
40. Type 360 in the command line and press ENTER.

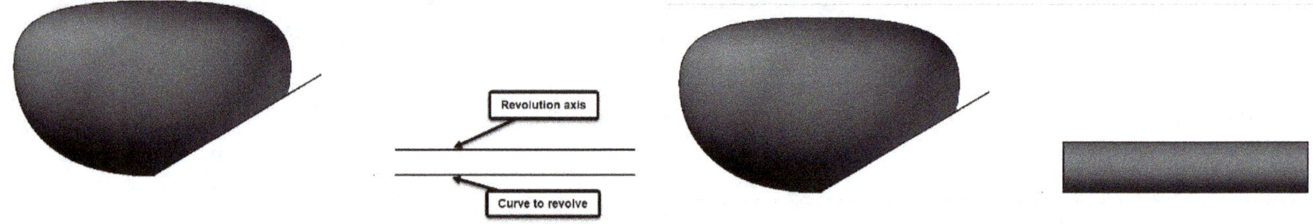

41. From the In-canvas controls, select **View Controls > SE Isometric**.
42. On the Navigation Bar, click the **Orbit** icon. Next, press and hold the left mouse button and drag the pointer until the open edges of the surface model are displayed, as shown.
43. On the ribbon, click **Surface > Create > Loft**. Next, select the **Join multiple edges** option from the command line.
44. Select the open edge of the revolved surface and press ENTER.
45. Select the **Join multiple edges** option from the command line.
46. Select the circular edge of the second revolved surface, and then press ENTER.
47. Press ENTER to display the preview of the lofted surface. Also, notice the grips on selected edges.
48. Click on the Continuity grip displayed on the first edge and select Tangent (G1).
49. Likewise, click the Continuity grip on the second edge and select Tangent (G1).

50. Press ENTER to create the lofted surface.

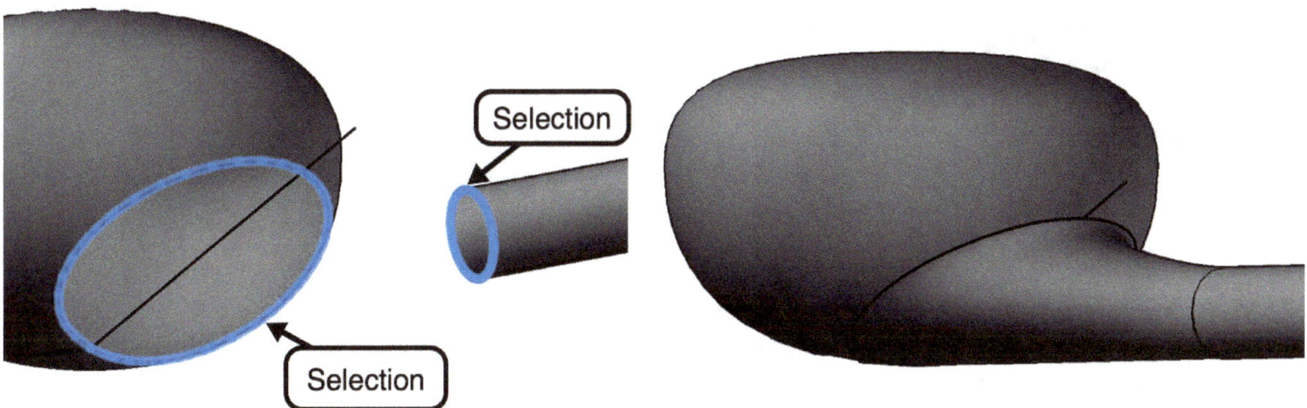

51. Click **Surface > Create > Offset** on the ribbon.
52. Proceed by selecting the two revolved surfaces that you've previously created. Confirm your selection by pressing the 'ENTER' key.
53. Verify that the arrows displayed on your selected surfaces are pointing inwards. Select the **Flip direction** option if the arrows are displayed in the outward direction.
54. Select the **Solid** option from the command line. Next, type **0.2** in the command line and press ENTER to thickness to the revolved surfaces.

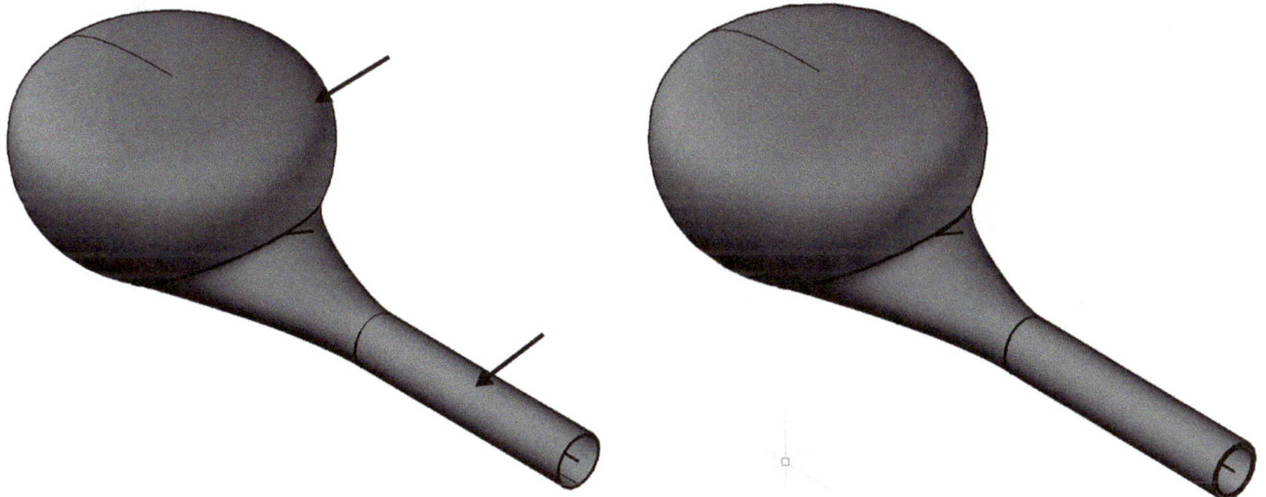

55. Click **Home > Modify > Thicken** on the ribbon. Next, select the lofted surface and press ENTER.
56. Type **-0.2** in the command line and press ENTER to thickness to the lofted surface.

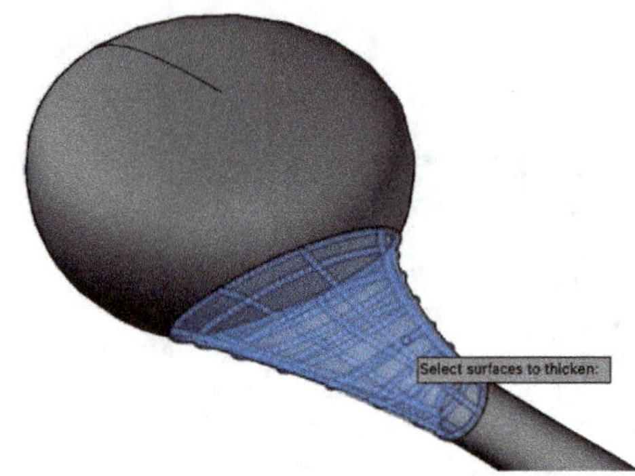

57. Type CYLINDER in the command line and press ENTER.
58. Click at an arbitrary point in the graphics window to define the center point of the cylinder.
59. Move the pointer outward, type 0.15, and then press ENTER.
60. Move the pointer upward, type 5 and press ENTER.

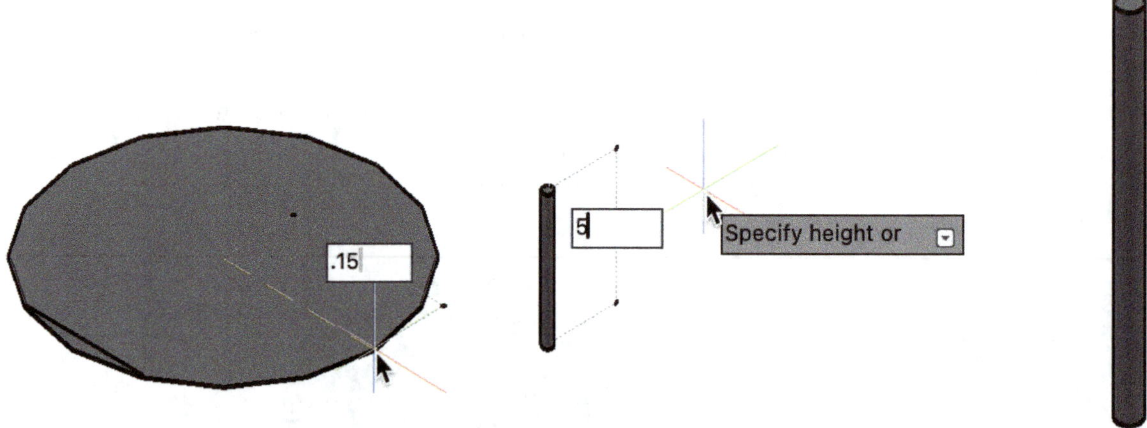

61. Turn ON the **3D Object Snap** icon on the status bar.
62. Select the cylinder from the graphics window. Type **M** in the command line and press ENTER.
63. Select the 3D center of the cylinder to define the base point.
64. Move the pointer near to the center of the revolved surface and select the 3D Vertex, as shown.

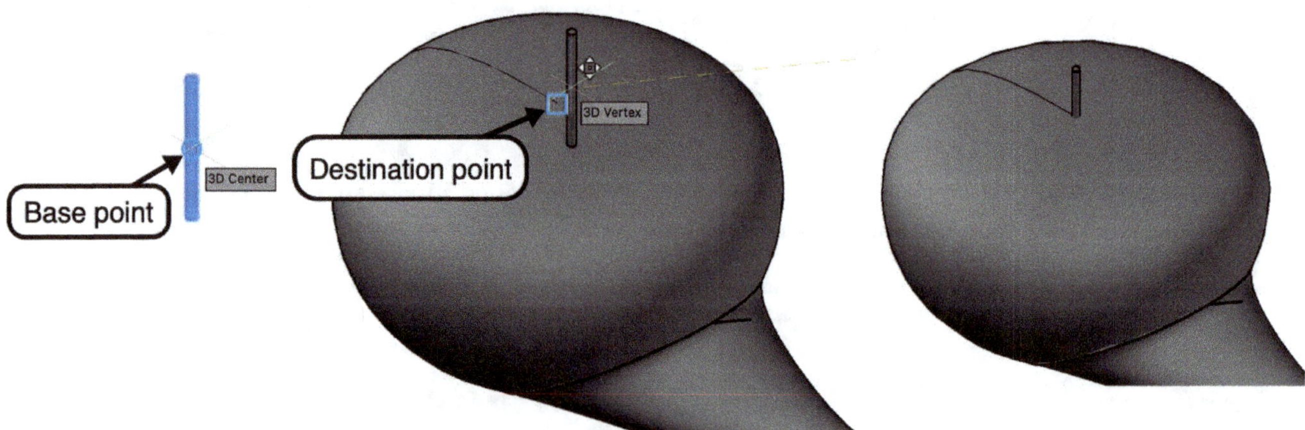

65. Select the cylinder and type ARRAY in the command line and press ENTER.
66. Select the RECTANGULAR option from the command line.

67. Select the Columns option from the command line. Next, type 1 and press ENTER to define the number of columns.

68. Press ENTER to accept the default spacing value between the columns.

69. Select the Rows option from the command line. Next, type **7** in the command line and press ENTER to define the number of rows.

70. Type 1 and press ENTER to define the spacing between the rows.

71. Press ENTER to create the rectangular array, as shown.

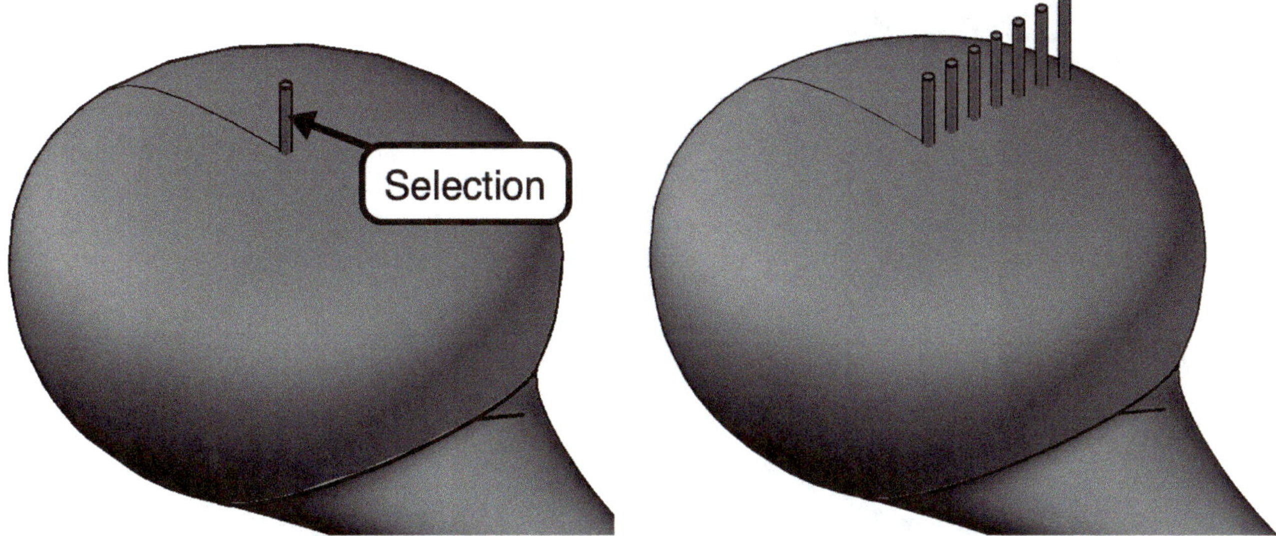

72. Select the six cylinders of the rectangular array. Next, type ARRAY in the command line and press ENTER.

73. Select the **POlar** option from the command line. After this, select the center point of the cylinder that has not been selected previously. This point will serve as you as the centerpoint of the polar array.

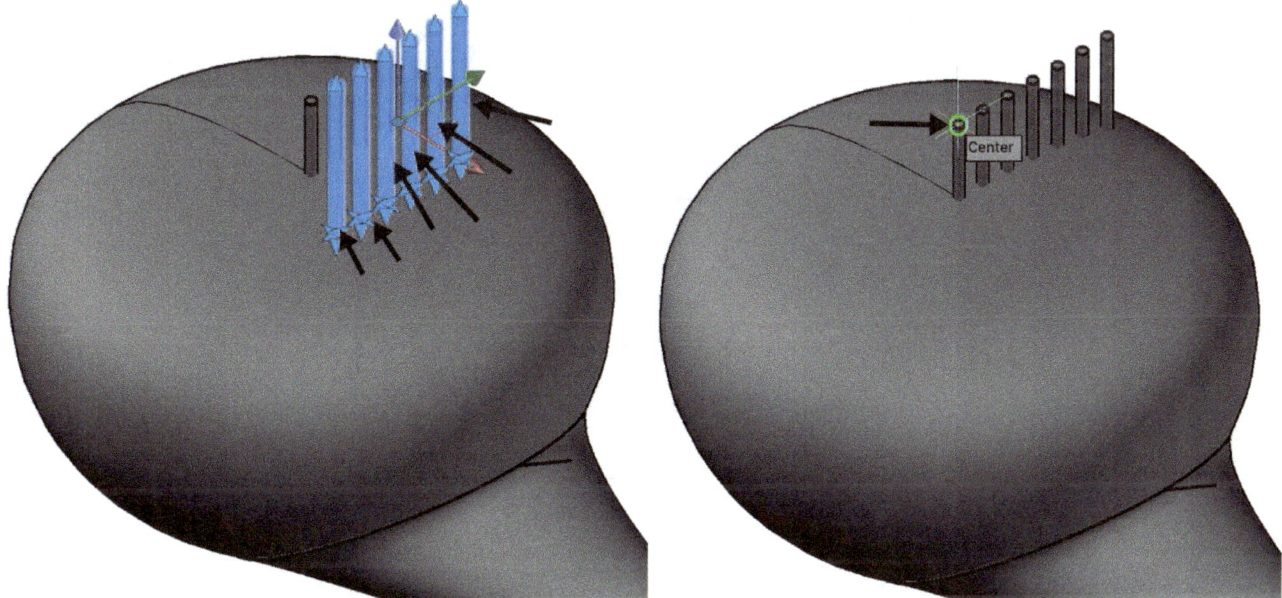

74. Select the **Items** option from the command line. Next, type **8** in the command line and press ENTER.

75. Press ENTER to create the polar array.

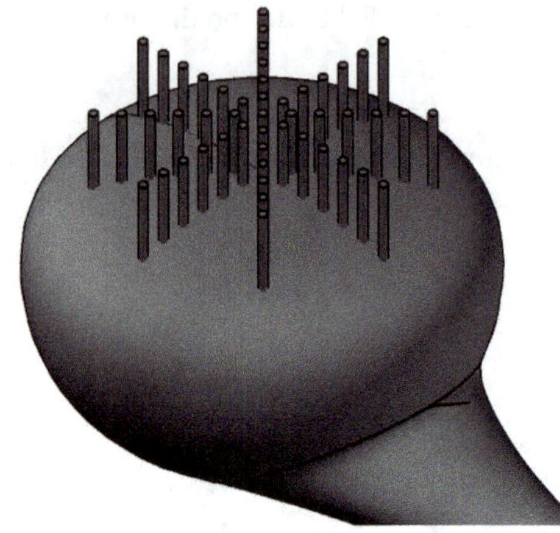

76. Type SUBTRACT in the command line and press ENTER. Next, select the large portion of the model and press ENTER.

77. Create a selection window across all the cylinders, and then press ENTER. The cylinders are subtracted from the model.

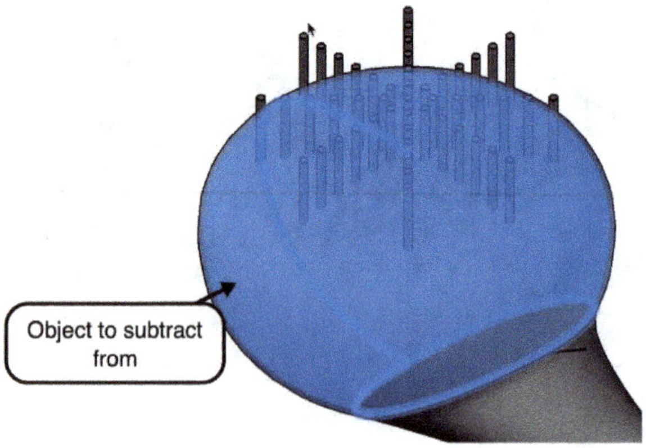

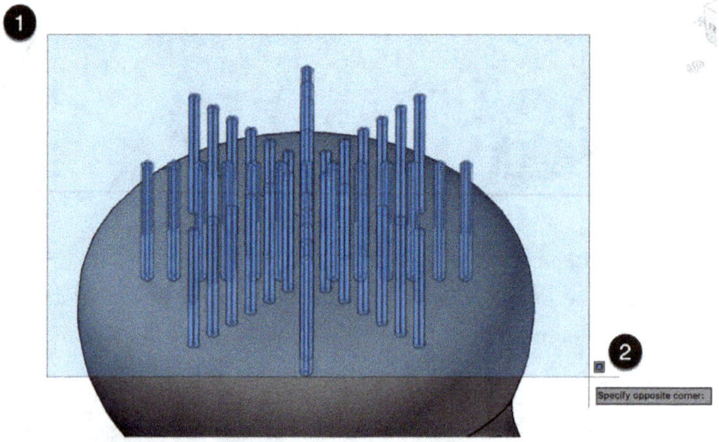

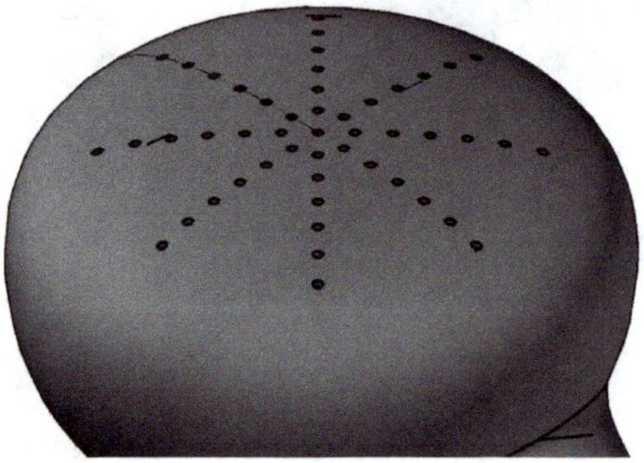

78. Save and close the drawing.

Questions

1. What is the use of the **Trim** command?
2. How many types of loft surfaces can be created in AutoCAD?
3. Why do we use the **Patch** command?

4. Which command can be used to bridge the gap between two surfaces?
5. List the extend type options that can be used to extend surfaces from an edge.